Java Programming on Linux

Nathan Meyers

Waite Group Press
A Division of Macmillan USA, Inc.
201 West 103rd St., Indianapolis, Indiana, 46290 USA

Java Programming on Linux

International Standard Book Number: 1-57169-166-9

Library of Congress Catalog Card Number: 99-65624

Printed in the United States of America

First Printing: December 1999

01 00 99 4 3 2 1

Trademarks

All terms mentioned in this book that are known to be trademarks or service marks have been appropriately capitalized. Waite Group Press cannot attest to the accuracy of this information. Use of a term in this book should not be regarded as affecting the validity of any trademark or service mark.

Warning and Disclaimer

Every effort has been made to make this book as complete and as accurate as possible, but no warranty or fitness is implied. The information provided is on an "as is" basis. The authors and the publisher shall have neither liability nor responsibility to any person or entity with respect to any loss or damages arising from the information contained in this book or from the use of the CD or programs accompanying it.

ASSOCIATE PUBLISHER
Michael Stephens

ACQUISITIONS EDITOR
Don Roche

DEVELOPMENT EDITOR
Robyn Thomas

MANAGING EDITOR
Charlotte Clapp

COPY EDITOR
Geneil Breeze

INDEXER
Joy Dean Lee

PROOFREADERS
Tony Reitz
Wendy Ott

TECHNICAL EDITORS
Luke Jones
Michael Jarvis
Juan Jose Sierralta P.

TEAM COORDINATOR
Pamalee Nelson

MEDIA DEVELOPER
Todd Pfeffer

INTERIOR DESIGN
Gary Adair

COVER DESIGN
Alan Clements

COPY WRITER
Eric Borgert

LAYOUT TECHNICIANS
Steve Geiselman
Brad Lenser

CONTENTS AT A GLANCE

TABLE OF CONTENTS

ABOUT THE AUTHOR

Nathan Meyers spent 20 years in the corporate software trenches, as a developer and architect for Hewlett-Packard Company, working in handheld calculators, UNIX workstations, and inkjet printers. His experience includes development of embedded systems, device driver implementation, creation of development tools, definition and implementation work on the X Window System and the Common Desktop Environment, development of 2D and 3D graphics applications, UNIX application performance tuning, design of evolutionary algorithms, and implementation of financial algorithms.

Nathan left HP in 1999 to pursue other opportunities in the worlds of Linux and Java. Besides books like this, he has published in the *Hewlett-Packard Journal*, The *X Resource Journal*, and the *Linux Journal*. He participates actively in the Java/Linux community and manages this book's Web site at `http://www.javalinux.net`—visit the site for information, updates, errata, or just to send email to the author.

DEDICATION

To Vicki.

ACKNOWLEDGMENTS

It takes a village to make a book, and this book has benefited from the talents of many important contributors.

First, I'd like to thank Margot Maley of Waterside Productions and Don Roche of Macmillan Computer Publishing, who worked together to bring this project into existence. Development editor Robyn Thomas and project editor Charlotte Clapp coordinated the complex logistics required to turn my words into a real book. Copy editor Geneil Breeze kept my use of the language honest, and technical editors Luke Jones, Michael Jarvis, and Juan Jose Sierralta P. checked my work on the technical side. To anyone else I've neglected to mention: My sincere gratitude and my apologies for the oversight.

Beyond the efforts that went into creating this book, I must also acknowledge the heroic efforts in the Java, Linux, and Open Source communities that have made this book both possible and of value. To the many brilliant developers behind the Blackdown organization, Transvirtual Technologies, Cygnus Solutions, IBM AlphaWorks, and many other organizations mentioned in the book: Thank you for making Java on Linux a great place to do software and a great place to do business.

TELL US WHAT YOU THINK!

As the reader of this book, *you* are our most important critic and commentator. We value your opinion and want to know what we're doing right, what we could do better, what areas you'd like to see us publish in, and any other words of wisdom you're willing to pass our way.

You can fax, email, or write me directly to let me know what you did or didn't like about this book—as well as what we can do to make our books stronger.

Please note that I cannot help you with technical problems related to the topic of this book, and that due to the high volume of mail I receive, I might not be able to reply to every message.

When you write, please be sure to include this book's title and author as well as your name and phone or fax number. I will carefully review your comments and share them with the author and editors who worked on the book.

Fax: 317-581-4770

E-mail: `mstephens@mcp.com`

Mail: Michael Stephens
Associate Publisher
Sams Publishing
201 West 103rd Street
Indianapolis, IN 46290 USA

LINUX AND JAVA: THE CHOICE OF A NEW MILLENNIUM

Welcome to Java. Welcome to Linux. Welcome to the five-year revolution.

Five years ago, as Microsoft Windows 95 swept the world, Linux and Java were tiny blips on the radar. In 1995, The term "Open Source" had not yet been coined, Linux was an underground movement, and Java was struggling to prove itself a working technology.

What a difference five years makes!

In the past few years of explosive Internet growth, both Linux and Java have assumed crucial roles in advancing network technologies and shaping the Web. Both have had to mature quickly, and, with the recent releases of the Linux 2.2 kernel and the Java 2 Platform, both demand to be taken seriously as technologies and as businesses.

Which brings us to this book.

Linux and Java go together like, well… cream and coffee. Linux offers a powerful, stable, efficient operating system; Java offers a powerful and portable applications platform of huge and growing popularity. You've probably already used the two together—if you've ever run Netscape Navigator on Linux. But there is much more to Java than applets and browsers. This book will help you take the next step: to the world of Java applications, Java development, and Java Web services.

Who Is This Book's Intended Audience?

If you need to use Java and Linux together, this book is for you. The book has a strong focus on development tools and techniques, but we also cover topics of use to nondevelopers (for example, Java installation and configuration) and administrators (for example, Java Web services).

What Do You Need to Know Prior to Reading This Book?

Some previous exposure to both Java and Linux will be helpful, although we do include introductions to both technologies. This book does not try to *teach* you Java or Linux (many other fine books already do so)—it focuses on how you can use the two together.

What Will You Learn from This Book?

This book will teach you how to install and use a Java environment under Linux, how to develop Java under Linux, and how to deploy your Java applications to Linux and other platforms.

What Software Will You Need?

You will need a Linux distribution and a Java Software Development Kit—both are available for free online. You can also buy reasonably priced Linux distributions on CD-ROM. This book will tell you how to get all the software you need.

How This Book Is Organized

This book is organized into 15 parts, first introducing the technologies and then covering installation, configuration, development, and deployment of Java on Linux.

The parts of the book are as follows:

- **Part I: A Brief Introduction to Java**—If you're new to Java, this part takes you on a brief tour of the language and the environment.
- **Part II: A Brief Introduction to Linux**—If you're new to Linux, this part gives you a brief introduction to the operating system and helps you get started setting up a Linux system.
- **Part III: Setting Up for Java Development and Deployment on Linux**—This part describes the pieces you need to enable Java deployment and development in your Linux environment.
- **Part IV: The Blackdown Port: A Sun Java SDK for Linux**—The Blackdown organization is the group responsible for porting Sun's Java software to Linux. This part of the book describes how to obtain and install Java runtime and development software from Blackdown.
- **Part V: Tools in the Blackdown JSDK**—The Java Software Development Kit (JSDK) from Blackdown includes all the pieces you need to develop, test, and run Java. Here we describe the tools and how to use them.
- **Part VI: Additional Java Runtime Environments**—The Sun software distributed by Blackdown is not the last word in running Java on Linux. This part describes alternative Java environments you can use under Linux.
- **Part VII: Additional Java Runtime Components**—This part of the book describes additional components to make your Java environment faster, better, and more capable.

- **Part VIII: Compilers and Debuggers**—You have many Java development tool choices beyond the SDK. Here we present some alternative compilers and debuggers you can use.
- **Part IX: IDEs, GUI Builders, and RAD Tools**—This part explores advanced development tools—integrated development environments, user interface builders, and rapid application development tools—available for use on Linux. One such tool, Inprise JBuilder, is bundled on the accompanying CD-ROM.
- **Part X: Miscellaneous Development Tools**—Here we explore some tools that can assist your Java development efforts under Linux.
- **Part XI: Java Application Distribution**—This part of the book helps you distribute your Java applications to the rest of the world, including users on other operating systems.
- **Part XII: Linux Platform Issues**—This part discusses issues specific to using Java on the Linux platform, such as accessing native platform capabilities and dealing with the X Window System.
- **Part XIII: Java Performance**—This part explores Java performance: why it's slow, why it's improving, and how you can tune your own applications for better performance.
- **Part XIV: Java and Linux on Servers**—Java and Linux both have important roles on three-tier applications servers and Web servers. This part of the book discusses using Linux and Java for server applications.
- **Part XV: Appendixes**—Here you'll find an index of programs provided in the book, some code listings, and some pointers to additional resources.

Visit Our Web Site

This book has its own Web site: `http://www.javalinux.net`. Please visit the site for the latest updates, errata, and downloads.

Conventions Used in This Book

This section describes the important typographic, terminology, and command conventions used in this book.

Typographic Conventions Used in This Book

The following typographic conventions are used in this book:

- Code lines, commands, statements, variables, and any text you type or see onscreen appears in a `mono` typeface. ***`Bold italic mono`*** typeface is often used to represent the user's input.

- Command syntax descriptions use the following notation to describe commands and arguments:
    - monospaced text—This represents the literal text of a command or option.
    - *<monospaced italics in angle-brackets>*—Angle-brackets and italic text represent placeholders in a command description. These placeholders are replaced by commands or options described in the text.
    - *[<optional arguments>]*—Brackets surround optional arguments. A vertical stroke may separate multiple choices for an optional argument.
    - {on¦off}—Curly braces surround a required multiple-choice argument, with choices separated by a vertical stroke.

  For example, a syntax description like this

```
java [-green¦-native] [<options>] <class>
```

  could result in the command

```
java -green -classpath . MyClass
```

- The ➥ icon is used before a line of code that is really a continuation of the preceding line. Sometimes a line of code is too long to fit as a single line on the page. If you see ➥ before a line of code, remember that it's part of the line immediately above it.
- Long listings of code or output are printed with line numbers to aid in reading. If a line is too wide to fit on the page, the remainder appears in the following line without a line number.
- The book also contains *Subtleties* sidebars that explore a topic in more detail. The information here may not be of immediate use but is helpful in better understanding the topic or solving difficult problems.

Naming Conventions Used in This Book

The naming of Sun Java releases has been a matter of some confusion over the years. This book adopts a convention consistent with Sun's most recent practices:

- JDK—A JDK is a Java technology release, such as JDK1.0, JDK1.1, and JDK1.2. (Its original meaning was "Java Development Kit," but common usage has broadened it to mean an entire technology release. This is discussed in more detail in Chapter 10, "Java Components for Linux," in the section on "A Glossary of Sun Java Terminology.")
- SDK—An SDK is a Software Development Kit. Every Java technology release is accompanied by an SDK that includes tools, such as compilers and debuggers, for Java development.
- JRE—A JRE is a Java Runtime Environment. This is a subset of the SDK targeted at deployment platforms. It contains everything needed to run Java programs but no development tools.

Command Shell Conventions in This Book

In UNIX and Linux environments, users have a choice of *command shells*—interactive command interpreters—to use for running commands in terminal windows.

This book will assume the use of `bash` (the Bourne-Again SHell), which is the most popular Linux command shell. Command input lines will be shown with this prompt:

```
bash$
```

So a user interaction with `bash` could look like this:

```
bash$ echo Hello World
Hello World
bash$
```

When an input line is too long in a Linux command shell, you can end it with the backslash character and continue it on the next line:

```
bash$ echo The quick brown fox jumps over the lazy \
dog
The quick brown fox jumps over the lazy dog
bash$
```

For most interactions discussed in this book, the choice of command shell has little effect on how commands are entered. But there are two important exceptions.

Setting Environment Variables

Different command shells use different commands for setting environment variables. When this book specifies setting of variables, it will use the `bash` notation:

```
bash$ FOO=bar
bash$ export FOO
```

or the shorter form:

```
bash$ export FOO=bar
```

or, occasionally, the form used to set the variable for the duration of a single command:

```
bash$ FOO=bar <command>. . .
```

For users who prefer the popular `csh` (C-shell) or `tcsh` (a `csh` clone), you will need to perform your own translation to the `csh`-style notation:

```
setenv FOO bar
```

Environment Initialization File

The name of the initialization file is another important command shell difference.

When you start a new login session running `bash`, it reads a file called `~/.bash_profile` (that's `.bash_profile` in your home directory) for any user-specific setup of your environment. This book sometimes instructs you to add commands to that file for setting environment variables.

If you are a `csh` or `tcsh` user, you will need to translate these instructions. The initialization file it reads is called `~/.login` (`.login` in your home directory)—this is where you will need to add the corresponding `setenv` commands.

PART I

A BRIEF INTRODUCTION TO JAVA

The first part of the book provides a brief introduction to Java. If you're a Linux user or developer coming to Java for the first time, you may find the Java concept a bit bewildering because Java is a lot of things: a language, an architecture, an applications platform, and more.

So we begin with a look at what Java really is, where and how it is used, what it offers to programmers, and what sort of applications capabilities it provides.

CHAPTER 1

WHAT IS JAVA?

This chapter gives you the 10-minute tour of Java. If you're already experienced with Java, you might want to skip ahead. On the other hand, if you're new here, you might find that Java is *not* exactly what you thought it was. It's not just a language, and it's not just for Web browsers.

So what exactly is Java? It's a language. It's a machine architecture. It's a loading model. It's a file format. It's an applications environment (several different applications environments, actually). It's a specification. And it's an implementation.

Java began life as a failed Sun research project called *Oak*, targeted at embedded operation in appliances. In 1995, Sun repackaged Oak as a portable "Internet programming language" and positioned it initially as a way to run programs in Web browsers. The result was something of a misfire: Web applets were not a huge success, and even today they occupy a largely specialized niche. But Java displayed usefulness in other areas, and interest in Java for different tasks—particularly Web services and enterprise connectivity—skyrocketed. Java has since settled into a number of important application areas (we explore more below), including, at long last, appliances!

The Many Faces of Java

Let's dissect Java in a bit more detail...

The Java Language

By the time Sun announced Java in 1995, C++ and object-oriented programming had been around for years. C++ had grown, in episodic spurts, from a preprocessor into a full-featured compiled language. It had become the language of choice for projects of all scales, and it had been through several stages of standardization—culminating in the acceptance of the ANSI C++ standard in 1998.

C++ had also, along the way, picked up considerable baggage. It had a substantial number of non-object-oriented artifacts, and it had become a difficult language to write compilers for. It was also difficult to achieve complete portability: even the excellent ANSI standardization did not completely shield developers from platform-specific language porting headaches.

One of Java's goals was to fix what was wrong with C++, with a special focus on the error-prone aspects of C++ development—those that tend to take up too much debugging time. In this it has certainly succeeded: Java developers (especially C++ converts) find the language well-suited for rapid prototyping and development. Java's remedies include:

- Strengthening the object orientation and eliminating non-object-oriented features (for example, macros, globals)
- Eliminating the error-prone direct manipulation of memory pointers and the confusion of referencing and dereferencing
- Getting the developer out of the messy memory management business
- Adding type safety
- Performing runtime checking for such common problems as illegal typecasting, bad array subscripts, and null object references
- Supporting multithreaded programming directly in the language
- Improving exception handling

A detailed language specification is available, both in printed form and from Sun's Web site (`http://java.sun.com`). Like most specs, it is better as a reference work than a learning tool. For actually learning the language, a good place to start would be *Java Unleashed* (Sams).

Chapter 2, "Moving from C++ to Java," uses some programming examples to take a closer look at the differences between Java and C++. Despite the differences, Java looks much like C++, and experience suggests that C++ programmers can pick it up quickly and easily. So although this book is not in the business of teaching the language, the introduction and the examples should be enough to get you well past the "Hello World" stage.

The Java Machine Architecture

The Java specification describes not only the high-level language but also the low-level machine and instruction set it runs on: a concurrent, abstract stack machine with an architecture and a small bytecode instruction set closely tied to the language (see Figure 1.1). This is roughly equivalent to dictating the CPU on which a language can be used, although a better analog is the P-code machine that was used in the development of UCSD Pascal some 20 years back.

FIGURE 1.1

Java defines a low-level architecture and instruction set closely aligned with the high-level language.

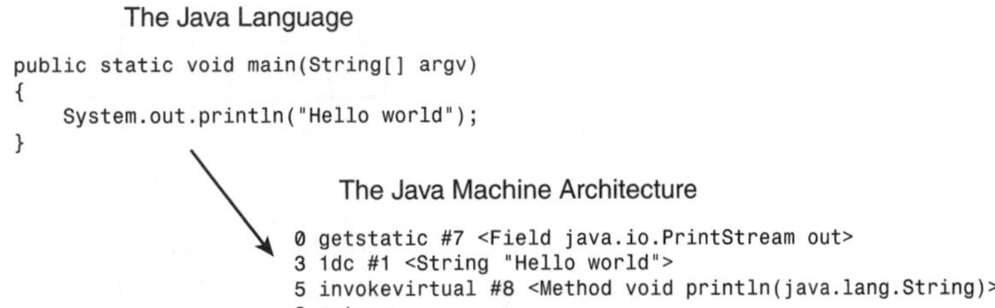
The Java Language
public static void main(String[] argv)
{
System.out.println("Hello world");
}
The Java Machine Architecture
0 getstatic #7 <Field java.io.PrintStream out>
3 ldc #1 <String "Hello world">
5 invokevirtual #8 <Method void println(java.lang.String)>
8 return

Implementation of the architecture—as, for example, a silicon Java chip or as a virtual machine—is left as an exercise for individual vendors. (This has turned out to be a challenge to the acceptance of Java, but virtual machines are now available for Linux and many other environments.)

In addition to describing an execution engine, the spec describes certain machine behaviors: startup, shutdown, and, most interestingly, loading.

The Java Loading Model

The Java loading model is, ultimately, what makes Java unique. Loading of Java modules (or *classes*, to be more correct) happens dynamically during program execution. This is a radical change for generations of programmers accustomed to the compile-link-load-run cycle for building and running programs and is resulting in new approaches to structuring application functionality.

The loading of Java classes consists of several steps (see Figure 1.2):

1. Reading the bits
2. Verifying that the bits describe a well-structured class containing well-structured Java code
3. Building a global class structure
4. Resolving references
5. Controlling access—allowing an application or environment to decide access rules for class loading (such as restriction to trusted sources)

Loading of classes happens as needed, at any time during program execution—either when a class is first referenced or when the application explicitly requests that a class be loaded. The class-loading and security mechanisms are themselves classes and can be modified by subclassing: Developers can define new sources of Java functionality not envisioned by Java's creators.

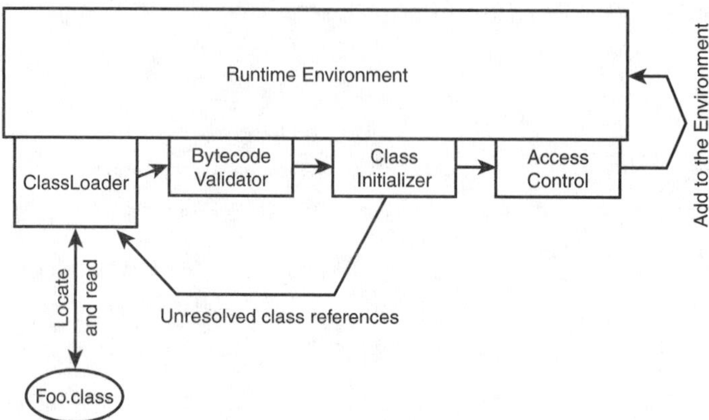

FIGURE 1.2
The Java class loader builds the environment during application execution.

The concept of runtime loading of functionality is certainly not new. We see it routinely in dynamically loaded libraries, object models (CORBA, COM, and so on), and the *plug-in* capability of many products. What is new is the full integration of class loading with the language and the environment: it's never before been this easy, flexible, or extensible. Allowing class loading from arbitrary sources (local disk, the Web, networked devices, a dynamic code generator, and so on) is a notable advance in object-oriented programming: it treats executable code objects with the same facility previously reserved for data objects.

The loading model, combined with the portability of the code itself, gives Java bragging rights as an "Internet programming language."

The Java Class File Format

Just as Java defines a portable instruction set, it defines a platform-neutral package for Java code: the class file. Class files are usually generated by a Java compiler (they are the Java analog of *.o* object files), after which they are ready to run (recall that linking happens at runtime). Class files are typically found sitting on file systems or bundled into archives (*zip* files, or the closely related Java archive *jar* files), where Java's default class-loading mechanism expects to find them with the filename suffix *.class*. By subclassing the class loader, as discussed previously, applications can introduce a class file from any source.

The Java Applications Environment

As any UNIX/Linux programmer knows, modern applications run in a rich environment provided by libraries (system, GUI, utility, and so on) and subsystems (X, printing, and so on). Java, although not an operating system (OS), is substantially in the OS business: It must provide a portable applications environment for everything from basic I/O services to string manipulation to GUIs to networking. Java has undergone three major releases, during which the applications environment has grown from minimal to substantial:

- JDK1.0—Sun's initial release, heavily hyped but not ready for prime time. A basic applications environment with a basic GUI component (*AWT*, the Abstract Windowing Toolkit) built on top of native platform GUI mechanisms.
- JDK1.1—A substantial improvement, introducing basic printing support, a better event model, the JavaBeans component model, I18N, reflection, remote method invocation, a security framework, and database connectivity. The latter three areas represent Java's move into distributed *enterprise* applications.
- JDK1.2 (officially The Java 2 Platform, version 1.2)—Many consider this the first ready-for-prime-time Java. It is huge but useful, introducing security enhancements, a robust 2D graphics imaging model, the JFC Swing GUI toolkit (a native Java look and feel), an accessibility API, drag-and-drop support, the collections classes, improved persistence support, reference objects, an audio API, CORBA support, and more.

The language and architecture have also evolved with each release (nested classes, for example, appeared in version 1.1), but the environment has changed most dramatically.

When we speak of JDK1.1 or JDK1.2, we are referring to a complete application environment—Java Virtual Machine (JVM) + class libraries—that is used for two distinct purposes:

- Running applications (Figure 1.3)—Applications are standalone programs with the same rights and responsibilities as programs in any other language. Like C++ programs, standalone Java programs begin with a call to `main()` and end, typically, with a call to `exit()`. A standalone program is usually run by invoking a JVM and specifying a class file to execute.

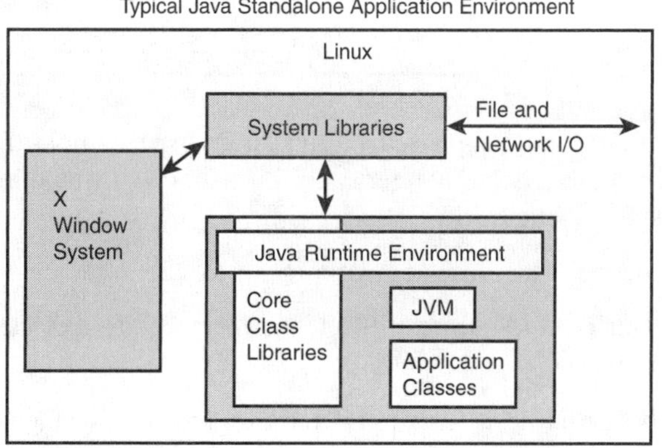

FIGURE 1.3
Java applications run in a platform-neutral environment within the host environment.

- Running applets (Figure 1.4)—Applets run in browsers, embedded in Web pages, typically under the control of a Java Runtime Environment (JRE) built into the browser. Applets differ in three major respects from applications:
  - The applet environment contains a restrictive security manager that prevents applets from affecting the world outside the browser (such as the local file system) and constrains the behavior of class loading and networking.
  - Graphics happens to windows controlled by the browser—typically embedded in a Web page, although browsers can launch top-level applet windows.
  - Applets have a different life cycle from applications, described in terms of when they are initially loaded, when they are started and stopped by the browser due to page visibility, and when they are finally unloaded from the browser. There is no `main()` in applets.

Applets are typically run when a browser reads a page containing the HTML tags to load and execute a Java class.

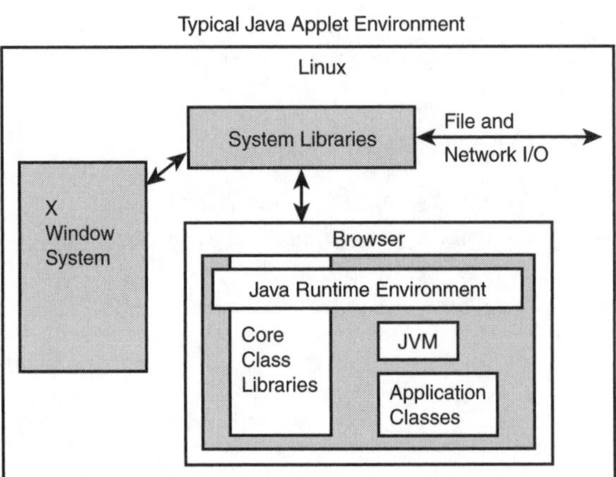

FIGURE 1.4
Java applets run in a platform-neutral environment provided by a browser.

Differences aside, both applets and applications expect a full JRE. So a browser supporting JDK1.2 (as of this writing, neither major browser does) would include the full, gigantic JDK1.2 environment—Swing toolkit and all.

Java does define other, simpler environments for use in more constrained applications:

- PersonalJava—A subset of JDK1.1 for personal devices such as Portable Digital Assistants.
- EmbeddedJava—A subset of JDK1.1 for use in embedded controllers, with extensions targeted at real-time environments. EmbeddedJava is a political hot potato at the moment: A number of vendors with deep experience in real-time systems were so dissatisfied with Sun's EmbeddedJava work that they formed the J-Consortium in early 1999 to work toward better, vendor-neutral real-time Java extensions.

- JavaCard—A Java environment for use in smart cards, "credit cards with brains," designed to support the application and transaction requirements of that market.
- JavaTV—A Java environment for use with television-enabled applications such as interactive programming and video-on-demand.
- JavaPhone—A set of API extensions, on top of PersonalJava or EmbeddedJava, for development of telephony applications.

In mid-1999, Sun announced the Java 2 Platform Micro Edition, a unification targeted at subsuming these technologies.

We examine the core JRE classes in more detail in Chapter 3, "A Look at the Java Core Classes."

The Java Specification and Implementation

In the preceding sections, we have repeatedly mentioned specifications: Java is, first and foremost, a *specification*. The complete specs for the language, the class file format, the virtual machine, and the runtime environment are available from Sun—in printed form from a bookstore, or in electronic form online (no charge; `http://java.sun.com`).

Given the Java specification, it is possible for anyone to create any part of Java—a compiler, a VM, an SDK—without any encumbrances to Sun. Later, you learn of some "cleanroom" Java pieces, built entirely from specs, available on Linux.

Sun has also created a *reference implementation* of everything in the spec: JVM, core libraries, and a development kit containing a full complement of tools. Sun ships two commercial implementations, for Solaris and Windows NT, that were created from the reference implementation. It also licenses the reference implementation to other vendors, which is the basis for commercial Java ports on such platforms as HP-UX, AIX, Ultrix, and others. The reference implementation is also the basis for the Blackdown SDK for Linux, which gets extensive coverage beginning in Chapter 13, "Blackdown: The Official Linux Port."

Use of the reference implementation comes at a price: The source is available for no charge, but any products built from it are encumbered by licensing obligations to Sun. The licensing terms are reasonably generous to anyone building a noncommercial implementation; all others pay fees, resulting in an important revenue stream for Sun.

Other Java Technologies

Sun has many other focused Java components, outside the core platform, in various stages of specification and implementation (see Chapter 4, "Additional Sun Java Class Library Specs," for more details). Among them:

- Java3D—Support for 3D imaging
- Java Media Framework—Multimedia support
- Java Servlets—Java on Web servers

- Java Cryptography Extensions—A framework for private- and public-key cryptography
- JavaHelp—A full-featured help system
- Jini—A framework for creating communities of "smart" devices, including automatic network configuration and resource discovery
- JavaSpeech—An API for speech recognition and synthesis
- Java 2 Enterprise Edition—A collection of technologies—directory, database, email, messaging, transaction, and so on—targeted at deployment in the enterprise environment

Where Is Java Used?

Some settings in which Java has found a home (beginning with the two traditional ones) are as follows:

- Standalone Java applications hosted by a JRE under many different operating systems: Linux, NT, MacOS, all important flavors of UNIX, IBM's mainframe OSs, and so on.
- Applet JRE environments provided by Netscape Navigator and Microsoft Internet Explorer Web browsers.
- Web servers, for programmatic generation of Web content.
- Application servers, integrating the activities of enterprise applications, databases, and Web activities.
- Java PCs—Sun's JavaOS is an operating system, intended for use in network computers and appliances, in which Java classes are the native application format.
- Inside Database Management Systems (DBMSs) such as Oracle and Sybase, supporting stored procedures for smart database queries.
- Television set-top boxes, running JavaTV.
- Smart cards—a complete Java Virtual Machine plus the card-holder's data can reside in a chip on a small plastic card.
- Embedded controllers in consumer and industrial devices: printers, cameras, robots, and so on.
- Jewelry—rings, wristwatches, money clips, and so on with built-in JVMs and a waterproof hardware interface. They are used for identification, e-commerce, and cryptography (yes, Java-based *secret decoder rings!*).

In later chapters, we explore how some of these environments are being deployed in Linux.

What Can't You Do in Java?

Java is, in many ways, a computer scientist's dream. It brings together many of the most interesting technologies of the past 20 years, from garbage collection to architecture-neutral code to on-the-fly optimization to runtime validation to OOP. Many of these technologies have not become mainstream because, in the real world, they're just too slow.

That is also Java's problem: it's slow. We examine performance issues (and what to do about them) in more detail later. The performance story undoubtedly will improve, but there is good reason to doubt that Java will ever challenge compiled native applications in terms of speed. Among the problems Java cannot handle today:

- Performance-critical problems—These still require native applications or, at the very least, native-code components in Java applications.
- Large problems—Problems with large memory or I/O requirements require the application to take an active role in managing memory or I/O—*application tuning* makes the difference between usable and unusable software in such demanding areas as simulations and DBMSs. Java is not a supportive environment for such problems.
- Platform-specific problems—Java takes great pains to achieve platform-independence, to the point of denying you many capabilities you take for granted in native languages or even in many platform-independent scripting languages. You cannot, without writing a native code component, detect or create a symbolic link, implement an X Window manager, read UNIX environment variables, identify the owner of a file, change tty settings, and so on. (We explore platform issues, including solutions to some of these problems, in Chapters 55, "JNI: Mixing Java and Native Code on Linux," and 56, "X Window System Tips and Tricks.")
- GUIs—Of course Java does GUIs—Swing is a first-rate toolkit. But GUI performance needs a great deal of attention if Java is to be a serious GUI platform. As of this writing, Java is enjoying much more success in non-GUI environments, such as servers, than in GUI environments such as applets.

If it seems, at this point in the chapter, that Java is everywhere...well, it has certainly fired the collective imagination of the computing and networking worlds. In reality, Java technology is a complex mix of software, bloatware, vaporware, and marketing; and it lives in a charged climate of intense industry politics between Sun Microsystems, its competitors, its partners, the courts, and the user and developer communities. Java is certainly not the answer to every problem, but it is (like Linux) a highly interesting place to work, play, and build the future of the Internet.

Summary

We have taken a high-level look at Java, exploring its role as a software technology, an architecture, and an Internet language. Before we delve into the world of Java on Linux, we take a few more chapters to explore topics of interest to Java newcomers: moving from C++ to Java programming, understanding the runtime environment, and Java extensions.

CHAPTER 2

MOVING FROM C++ TO JAVA

Continuing our whirlwind tour of Java, this chapter provides a brief look at the language differences between C++ and Java. We take an unusual approach: using small projects to point out important differences. This is an introduction, not a language course; if you want to really study and learn the language, a good place to start is *Java Unleashed* (Sams).

Project #1: Hello World

We begin with a slightly modified *Hello World* project in C++ (Listing 2.1), illustrating some important differences in I/O, array, and string manipulation.

LISTING 2.1 `helloworld.c`

```
#include <iostream.h>
#include <string.h>

//
// A modified "hello world": steps through argv and says hello to
// everything in argv. If an argument happens to be "world", we
// throw in a bang at the end.
//
int main(int argc, char *argv[])
{
    for (int i = 1; i < argc; i++)
    {
        cout << "Hello, " << argv[i];
        if (!strcmp(argv[i], "world")) cout << '!';
        cout << '\n';
    }
}
```

This version simply steps through the command-line arguments, outputting a **`Hello`** message for each argument. If the argument happens to be the word "world," a bang (!) is appended.

Listing 2.2 shows an equivalent program in Java:

LISTING 2.2 `HelloWorld.java`

```
package com.macmillan.nmeyers;

class HelloWorld
{
    public static void main(java.lang.String[] argv)
    {
        for (int i = 0; i < argv.length; i++)
        {
            java.lang.System.out.print("Hello, " + argv[i]);
            if (argv[i].equals("world"))
                java.lang.System.out.print('!');
            java.lang.System.out.print('\n');
        }
    }
}
```

Some differences to note between the examples:

- Java classes reside in a hierarchical namespace, in which classes are completely specified by a package name (analogous to a directory path) and a class name (analogous to a filename), with "." used as a separator. Two classes seen in the preceding example are **`java.lang.String`**, and **`java.lang.System`**. The "." is also used to separate variable names from member names (for example, member name **`equals()`** in

`HelloWorld.java`:8).[1] The `HelloWorld` class *also* resides in a package—`com.macmillan.nmeyers` (following standard naming guidelines for identifying the vendor). It's common and accepted practice for small, nonshipping projects to omit the package directive and reside in the *unnamed package*.

- There are no header files in Java. The Java compiler learns about class APIs directly from class files found at compile-time. (Countless C++ programming hours are lost to problems with header files.)
- Strings are first-class objects, unlike the C++ `char *`. They do not depend on null terminators and include such object operations as `String.equals()` (`HelloWorld.java`:10).
- Arrays, such as the String array passed to `main()`, know their own length (`HelloWorld.java`:7).
- Java does not allow globals—variables, constants, procedures, anything! Even the `main()` procedure is a *class method* (Java's equivalent of C++ *static methods*). The JVM isn't running a global procedure called `main()`; it's running a static class member called `com.macmillan.nmeyers.HelloWorld.main()`.
- The argument vector differs from C++: the command-line arguments begin with `argv[0]`, not `argv[1]`.

There is a minor fraud (for instructive purposes) in the preceding example: Java programmers do not usually specify the fully qualified class name; they use just the class basename. Listing 2.3 shows a more typical form of the source.

Listing 2.3 `HelloWorld.java` as a Java developer would really write it.

```
package com.macmillan.nmeyers;

class HelloWorld2
{
    public static void main(String[] argv)
    {
        for (int i = 0; i < argv.length; i++)
```

continued on next page

[1]Unfortunately, the language spec badly overloads the "." separator. The method `java.lang.System.out.print()`, for example, consists of:

- `java.lang`: Package Name
- `System:` Class name
- `out`: Class (static) variable; C++ would call this `System::out`
- `print()`: Method for `out`

As we shall see below, the separator also separates nested class names. Internally, Java uses three different separators, which the high-level language does not reflect.

continued from previous page

```
        {
            System.out.print("Hello, " + argv[i]);
            if (argv[i].equals("world"))
                System.out.print('!');
            System.out.print('\n');
        }
    }
}
```

Differences from the previous listing are shown in **bold**. For most classes (except those from the `java.lang` package and those in the class's own package), a Java `import` statement is needed to allow this shorthand.

Project #2: A Binary Tree

We take on a larger project here, involving some data structures. *Wordtree* is a simple project that counts the occurrences of distinctive words in its input and looks for specific words requested by the user. Specifically, it performs the following steps:

1. Reads text from `stdin`
2. Builds a simple, unbalanced binary tree of words from the input text, keeping a frequency count
3. Takes words from the command line and scans for their presence in the text, keeping a separate hit count
4. Traverses the tree, dumping the words and the counts

For example, reading `stdin` from the terminal:

```
bash$ wordtree quick fox foobar brown
the quick brown fox jumps over the lazy dog
^D
No such word: foobar
brown: 1, 1
dog: 1, 0
fox: 1, 1
jumps: 1, 0
lazy: 1, 0
over: 1, 0
quick: 1, 1
the: 2, 0
```

The output reports that the word "foobar," requested on the command line, does not appear in the text at all. The word "brown" appears once in the text and once in the command line. The word "the" appears twice in the text but not at all on the command line.

Wordtree in C++

The interesting classes in wordtree.C (Listing 2.4) are:

- `Node`—A node in our binary tree
- `Dictionary`—Container for our binary tree
- `ErrorMsg`—A small class used to throw an exception

LISTING 2.4 wordtree.C

```
#include <iostream.h>
#include <string.h>

// Node: Represent a node in our dictionary tree
class Node
{
public:
    char *mystring;
    int input_count;
    int other_count;
    Node *left, *right;
    // Constructor: Create a local copy of the word and zero the count
    Node(char *s)
    {
        mystring = new char[strlen(s) + 1];
        strcpy(mystring, s);
        input_count = 0;
        other_count = 0;
        left = right = NULL;
    }
    // Destructor: Delete local copy of the word
    ~Node()
    {
        delete[] mystring;
    }
    // Comparison operators
    operator<(Node &n)
    {
        return strcmp(mystring, n.mystring) < 0;
    }
    operator==(Node &n)
    {
        return !strcmp(mystring, n.mystring);
    }
    operator!=(Node &n)
    {
        return strcmp(mystring, n.mystring) != 0;
    }
    operator>(Node &n)
```

continued on next page

continued from previous page

```
    {
        return strcmp(mystring, n.mystring) > 0;
    }
    // Define a way to output this node
    friend ostream& operator<<(ostream &str, Node &n)
    {
        return str << n.mystring << ": " << n.input_count << ", "
                   << n.other_count;
    }
    // In-order recursive traversal code: arg is a function to be
    // executed for each node
    void traverse(void(*proc)(Node &))
    {
        if (left) left->traverse(proc);
        proc(*this);
        if (right) right->traverse(proc);
    }
    // Method to increment the count for a node matching the requested
    // key
    void count_word(Node &);
};

// Here is our main dictionary, including root of the tree
class Dictionary
{
    Node *root;
public:
    Dictionary(istream &);
    // Start an in-order traversal on the root
    void traverse(void(*proc)(Node &))
    {
        root->traverse(proc);
    }
    // Look for this word in the dictionary. If we find it, increment
    // its counter.
    void count_word(char *word)
    {
        // Create an automatic instance of node to use as key
        Node node(word);
        // Start searching at root
        root->count_word(node);
    }
};

// We'll use this class to throw an exception
class ErrorMsg
{
public:
    char *message;
    // Constructor: A message and a missing word to concatenate
    ErrorMsg(char *msg, char *word)
    {
```

```
        // Allocate enough space to hold the concatenated message plus
        // a space plus null
        message = new char[strlen(msg) + strlen(word) + 2];
        strcpy(message, msg);
        strcat(message, " ");
        strcat(message, word);
    }
    ~ErrorMsg()
    {
        delete[] message;
    }
    friend ostream& operator<<(ostream &str, ErrorMsg &msg)
    {
        return str << msg.message;
    }
};

// This is the function we'll use for node traversal
void print_a_word(Node &node)
{
    cout << node << '\n';
}

int main(int argc, char *argv[])
{
    Dictionary dictionary(cin);
    for (int i = 1; i < argc; i++)
    {
        try { dictionary.count_word(argv[i]); }
        catch (ErrorMsg &msg)
        {
            cerr << msg << '\n';
        }
    }
    dictionary.traverse(print_a_word);
}

Dictionary::Dictionary(istream &str)
{
    char word[1024];
    root = NULL;
    // Build a simple, unbalanced binary tree containing all words we
    // scan from str.
    while (!(str >> word).fail())
    {
        // If tree is empty, build root from first word
        Node *newnode;
        if (!root) newnode = root = new Node(word);
        else
        {
            // Build a local Node to use as a key
            Node key(word);
```

continued on next page

continued from previous page

```
            // Start search from root
            newnode = root;
            // Continue until we find matching node
            while (key != *newnode)
            {
                if (key < *newnode)
                {
                    if (!newnode->left) newnode->left = new Node(word);
                    newnode = newnode->left;
                }
                else
                {
                    if (!newnode->right) newnode->right = new Node(word);
                    newnode = newnode->right;
                }
            }
        }
        newnode->input_count++;
    }
}

void Node::count_word(Node &key)
{
    // Look for a matching node in the tree. If we find it, increment the
    // counter, else throw an exception.
    if (key == *this)
    {
        other_count++;
        return;
    }
    if (key < *this && left) left->count_word(key);
    else if (key > *this && right) right->count_word(key);
    else throw(ErrorMsg("No such word:", key.mystring));
}
```

The dictionary is constructed (`Dictionary::Dictionary(istream &)`) by parsing words out of `stdin` and building a tree full of `Node`s, using the words as the keys. Methods are provided (`Dictionary::count_word()`, `Node::count_word()`) to search the tree for a match from the command line, and to traverse the tree in order (`Dictionary::traverse()`, `Node::traverse()`) and execute a caller-supplied function for each node.

Wordtree in Java

This modest project illuminates a number of differences. The first difference is that Java compilers expect you to package every class (except nested classes) in its own source file with a matching name as shown in Listings 2.5–2.9:

LISTING 2.5 `Node.java`

```
public class Node
{
    public String mystring;
    public int inputCount = 0;
    public int otherCount = 0;
    public Node left = null;
    public Node right = null;
    public Node(String s)
    {
        mystring = s;
    }
    public int compareTo(Object n)
    {
        return mystring.compareTo(((Node)n).mystring);
    }
    public String toString()
    {
        return mystring + ": " + inputCount + ", " + otherCount;
    }
    public void traverse(TraverseFunc tf)
    {
        if (left != null) left.traverse(tf);
        tf.traverseFunc(this);
        if (right != null) right.traverse(tf);
    }
    public void countWord(Node key) throws NoSuchEntryException
    {
        int compare = key.compareTo(this);
        if (compare == 0)
        {
            otherCount++;
            return;
        }
        if (compare < 0 && left != null) left.countWord(key);
        else if (compare > 0 && right != null) right.countWord(key);
        else throw new NoSuchEntryException("No such word: " + key.mystring);
    }
}
```

LISTING 2.6 `Dictionary.java`

```
import java.io.*;
import java.util.*;

public class Dictionary
{
    public Node root = null;
```

continued on next page

continued from previous page

```
    // Constructor: Build a tree by parsing words from a reader
    public Dictionary(Reader r) throws IOException
    {
        // The reader classes don't know how to extract words from
        // input, so we'll build our own word extractor
        BufferedReader reader = new BufferedReader(r);
        String currentLine;
        // Read a line
        while ((currentLine = reader.readLine()) != null)
        {
            // Build a string tokenizer
            StringTokenizer tokenizer = new StringTokenizer(currentLine);
            while (tokenizer.hasMoreTokens())
            {
                String word = tokenizer.nextToken();
                Node newnode;
                if (root == null) newnode = root = new Node(word);
                else
                {
                    // Build a key
                    Node key = new Node(word);
                    // Start at root
                    newnode = root;
                    // Continue until we find a matching node
                    int compare;
                    while ((compare = key.compareTo(newnode)) != 0)
                    {
                        if (compare < 0)
                        {
                            if (newnode.left == null)
                                newnode.left = new Node(word);
                            newnode = newnode.left;
                        }
                        else
                        {
                            if (newnode.right == null)
                                newnode.right = new Node(word);
                            newnode = newnode.right;
                        }
                    }
                }
                newnode.inputCount++;
            }
        }
    }
    // Traverser
    public void traverse(TraverseFunc tf)
    {
        root.traverse(tf);
    }
    // Look for word and increment count
    public void countWord(String word) throws NoSuchEntryException
```

```
        {
            root.countWord(new Node(word));
        }
}
```

LISTING 2.7 NoSuchEntryException.java

```
public class NoSuchEntryException extends Exception
{
    public NoSuchEntryException(String str)
    {
        super(str);
    }
}
```

LISTING 2.8 TraverseFunc.java

```
public interface TraverseFunc
{
    void traverseFunc(Node n);
}
```

LISTING 2.9 WordTree.java

```
import java.io.*;

public class WordTree
{
    static public void main(String[] argv)
    {
        Dictionary dictionary = null;
        try { dictionary = new Dictionary(new InputStreamReader(System.in)); }
        catch (IOException e)
        {
            System.err.println(e);
            System.exit(1);
        }
        for (int i = 0; i < argv.length; i++)
        {
            try { dictionary.countWord(argv[i]); }
            catch (NoSuchEntryException e)
            {
                System.err.println(e.getMessage());
            }
        }
        dictionary.traverse(new PrintMeClass());
    }
```

continued on next page

continued from previous page

```
24        static public class PrintMeClass implements TraverseFunc
25        {
26            public void traverseFunc(Node n)
27            {
28                System.out.println(n);
29            }
30        }
31    }
```

Some differences evident in the project:

- Class declarations include all method code; the code cannot live elsewhere, as in the C++ implementation of the `Dictionary(istream&)` constructor.
- Scope declarations for class members appear with each member declaration. There are four possible scopes: `public`, `private`, `protected`, and `package`. The first three are similar to C++; the fourth limits access to other classes in the same package (and is the default if none is specified).
- We never work directly with pointers in Java, we use *object references*: these behave much like C++ *references* (pointers in disguise), but they are assignable like pointers. Compare `wordtree.C`:11 to `Node.java`:6–7. The latter is creating references, initially empty, that will be assigned later.
- The word `null` is a real keyword denoting an unassigned reference (`Node.java`:6–7). It is not a macro for zero, as with the C++ `NULL`. Java compilers (at least those based on Sun's code) do not even support macros, which are considered very non-object-oriented.
- Java does not allow operator or typecast overloading. We've replaced the overloaded comparison operators (`wordtree.C`:27–42) with a different comparison function (`Node.java`:12–15). We've replaced the C++ `ostream operator<<` (`wordtree.C`:44–48) with a function that generates a text representation (`Node.java`:16–19). All Java objects have a `toString()` method, which is responsible for creating a text representation for output.
- Typecasting is somewhat less common in Java than in C++, but it does occur. In `Node.java`:14, we downcast an argument of type `java.lang.Object` (the primal superclass of everything) to `Node`. Runtime checking is always performed for a typecast; an exception is thrown for an invalid coercion.
- We cannot use function pointers, as in `wordtree.C`'s handling of the traversal-time function (`wordtree.C`:51–56,126). Instead, we define an *interface* (a pure abstract class) called `TraverseFunc` that is required by the traversal code (`Node.java`:20–25), and implemented by a nested class (`WordTree.java`:24–30) for use in the traversal call (`WordTree.java`:22).
- Java's strong typing avoids cross-pollution between integers, booleans, and object reference values: a `null` reference != integer 0 != boolean `false`. Compare `wordtree.C`:53, which uses a pointer value as a boolean, to the corresponding line at `Node.java`:22, which uses a boolean expression. Similarly, integers cannot be used as boolean expressions.

- The import statements (`Dictionary.java`:1–2) allow us to use shorthand references to classes instead of fully qualified names: `BufferedReader` instead of `java.io.BufferedReader`, `StringTokenizer` instead of `java.util.StringTokenizer`. In this example, we use a wildcard notation (`import java.io.*`) to import entire packages; some developers prefer to individually import each class to be used (`import java.io.BufferedReader`, for example).
- Exceptions must be declared where they are thrown (`Node.java`:26). They must be caught upstream (`WordTree.java`:17–20) and declared by all methods between the throw and the catch. (`Dictionary.java`:58-61). The Java compiler does not let you forget to keep track of your exceptions: It would consider `Dictionary.countWord()` in error if it did not include the `throws` clause due to one of its callees.
- Java includes an Exception class, which is subclassed (`NoSuchEntryException.java`) and thrown when exceptions are needed.
- Relationship to a superclass is declared with an `extends` clause (`NoSuchEntryException.java`:1) and to a superinterface with an `implements` clause (`WordTree.java`:24). A class can have one superclass and many superinterfaces, which is the closest Java comes to multiple inheritance. Superclass initialization is handled with a `super()` call (`NoSuchEntryException.java`:5).
- Primitive types (`char`, `byte`, `int`, `float`, `short`, `long`, `double`, and `boolean`) are allocated much as in C++; objects are not. A class instance cannot be allocated automatically on the stack (`wordtree.C`:117) or as an array element; you must first create the object reference(s) and then allocate an instance(s) for it (`WordTree.java`:7–8).

  This restriction applies to array as well as to stack variables: If you want an array of object `FooBar`, you create an array of `FooBar` references and then assign an instance to each reference: "`FooBar fooBar = new FooBar[2]; fooBar[0] = new FooBar(); fooBar[1] = new FooBar();`."
- No `delete` or `delete[]` keywords anywhere! Garbage collection cleans up class objects after all references to them disappear. After `WordTree.main()` terminates, there are no remaining references to the `Dictionary` it allocated on line 8—so that instance can be garbage-collected. That instance contains, in turn, the tree's root node reference, which contains references to children, and so on. By the time the garbage collector has shaken out all unreferenced objects, the entire dictionary has been garbage-collected and returned to free memory.
- No destructors, even if we want them. Java has *finalizers*, which are called when (and if) the object is garbage-collected at some unspecified future time.

Project #3: Multithreading

One final example shows Java's multithreading support. Here is a simple multithreaded program to count to 20, outputting the numbers as we go. One thread is responsible for the even numbers, another for the odd numbers.

ThreadCount in C++

We see in the C++ program (Listing 2.10) a reliance on the POSIX `pthreads` interface, a library-supplied mechanism to create and manage threads. Classes of interest:

- `counter`—A class that encapsulates our counter, and the mutex and condition variable required to implement thread safety.
- `odd_counter`—A class encapsulating the odd counter, which increments the counter when it is odd. Most of the code is devoted to various `pthread` synchronization calls: locking the counter, waiting for a signal from the other thread that it has been changed, signaling a change to the other thread, unlocking the counter.

  The counter also includes a static function needed to start up the class. Because `pthread_create()` is a C function that expects a function pointer (not an object), the `startup()` function—which `pthread_create()` can handle—effectively encapsulates the object.
- `even_counter`—The other counter.

The main thread launches the other two threads, waits for them to finish, and then exits.

LISTING 2.10 `threadcount.C`

```
#include <pthread.h>
#include <iostream.h>

// threadcount: A multi-threaded program that counts to 20

// This is our main counter and its thread-safety components
class counter
{
public:
    pthread_cond_t condition;
    pthread_mutex_t mutex;
    int value;
    counter()
    {
        condition = (pthread_cond_t)PTHREAD_COND_INITIALIZER;
        mutex = (pthread_mutex_t)PTHREAD_MUTEX_INITIALIZER;
        value = 0;
    }
};

// This class encapsulates functionality to increment the counter
// when it is odd
class odd_counter
{
    counter &ctr;
    odd_counter(counter &c) : ctr(c)    {}
    void count()
    {
```

```
        // Lock the counter
        pthread_mutex_lock(&ctr.mutex);

        // Count to 20
        while (ctr.value < 20)
        {
            // If value is currently even, wait for a change
            while (!(ctr.value & 1))
                pthread_cond_wait(&ctr.condition, &ctr.mutex);
            // Change the value
            ctr.value++;
            // Signal the change
            pthread_cond_broadcast(&ctr.condition);
            // Print results
            cout << ctr.value << '\n';
        }
        pthread_mutex_unlock(&ctr.mutex);
    }
public:
    // A static function (suitable for passing to pthread_create) to
    // create and start up our counter
    static void *startup(void *c)
    {
        // Create an automatic instance of class and call count() method
        odd_counter(*(counter *)c).count();
        return 0;
    }
};

// This class encapsulates functionality to increment the counter
// when it is even
class even_counter
{
    counter &ctr;
    even_counter(counter &c) : ctr(c)   {}
    void count()
    {
        // Lock the counter
        pthread_mutex_lock(&ctr.mutex);

        // Count to 20
        while (ctr.value < 19)
        {
            // If value is currently odd, wait for a change
            while (ctr.value & 1)
                pthread_cond_wait(&ctr.condition, &ctr.mutex);
            // Change the value
            ctr.value++;
            // Signal the change
            pthread_cond_broadcast(&ctr.condition);
            // Print results
```

continued on next page

continued from previous page

```
                cout << ctr.value << '\n';
            }
            pthread_mutex_unlock(&ctr.mutex);
        }
public:
    // A static function (suitable for passing to pthread_create) to
    // create and start up our counter
    static void *startup(void *c)
    {
        // Create an automatic instance of class and call count() method
        even_counter(*(counter *)c).count();
        return 0;
    }
};

int main()
{
    // Our counter
    counter cnt;
    pthread_t thread1, thread2;
    // Start first thread with odd_counter, passing it our counter
    pthread_create(&thread1, NULL, odd_counter::startup, &cnt);
    // Start second thread with even_counter, passing it our counter
    pthread_create(&thread2, NULL, even_counter::startup, &cnt);
    // Hang around for threads to end
    pthread_join(thread1, NULL);
    pthread_join(thread2, NULL);
    // Done!
    exit(0);
}
```

ThreadCount in Java

Threading support is built in to the language, and all objects include basic plumbing to support synchronization. The source (Listings 2.11–2.14) is much simpler.

LISTING 2.11 `Counter.java`

```
class Counter
{
    public int value;
}
```

LISTING 2.12 `EvenCounter.java`

```
class EvenCounter implements Runnable
{
    Counter counter;
    EvenCounter(Counter c)
```

```
    {
        counter = c;
    }
    public void run()
    {
        synchronized(counter)
        {
            while (counter.value < 19)
            {
                while ((counter.value & 1) == 1)
                {
                    try { counter.wait(); }
                    catch (InterruptedException e)      {}
                }
                counter.value++;
                counter.notifyAll();
                System.out.println(counter.value);
            }
        }
    }
}
```

LISTING 2.13 OddCounter.java

```
class OddCounter implements Runnable
{
    Counter counter;
    OddCounter(Counter c)
    {
        counter = c;
    }
    public void run()
    {
        synchronized(counter)
        {
            while (counter.value < 20)
            {
                while ((counter.value & 1) == 0)
                {
                    try { counter.wait(); }
                    catch (InterruptedException e)      {}
                }
                counter.value++;
                counter.notifyAll();
                System.out.println(counter.value);
            }
        }
    }
}
```

LISTING 2.14 ThreadCount.java

```
1   // ThreadCount: A multi-threaded program that counts to 20
2
3   class ThreadCount
4   {
5       static void main(String[] argv)
6       {
7           Counter counter = new Counter();
8           (new Thread(new OddCounter(counter))).start();
9           (new Thread(new EvenCounter(counter))).start();
10      }
11  }
```

Some differences to note:

- No mutexes or condition variables in the `Counter` class. The necessary synchronization plumbing is built in to all objects—it's inherited from the `java.lang.Object` superclass. The synchronized clause (`EvenCounter.java`:10, `OddCounter.java`:10) provides locking of the `Counter` object during the code block. The `java.lang.Object.wait()` (`EvenCounter.java`:16, `OddCounter.java`:16) and `java.lang.Object.notifyAll()` (`EvenCounter.java`:20, `OddCounter.java`:20) methods handle the interthread synchronization.
- Recalling our earlier use of interfaces instead of function pointers, the `java.lang.Thread` constructor (invoked at `ThreadCount.java`:8-9) expects a class that implements the `Runnable` interface. This interface contains a single entry point: `run()`, the method to be run by the new thread.
- After threads are created, they are started with a call to the `java.lang.Thread.start()` method (`ThreadCount.java`:8-9).
- Notice that `ThreadCount.main()` does not wait for the threads to complete. Java programs terminate after the last thread has exited or when `java.lang.System.exit()` is called. GUI applications launch additional threads to handle the event loops, so they do not terminate until the app explicitly exits.

Moving On

There's more to Java than a handful of examples, of course, but these small projects should give a developer who is conversant in C++ a brief overview of the language. Like all examples in the book, this code is available on the CD-ROM for further play. We have avoided discussing how to compile or run Java because the exact details depend on your choice of tools: that will get extensive attention later.

Summary

Java bears many structural similarities to C++, with differences largely concentrated in areas that make development easier and less prone to error. This chapter has, through example, provided a glimpse into how Java's approaches to memory management, arrays, type safety, handling of pointers and references, exceptions, and multi-threading simplify the design of applications.

CHAPTER 3

A LOOK AT THE JAVA CORE CLASSES

A Brief Introduction to Java

The Java Runtime Environment—the Java Virtual Machine (JVM) and the collection of classes that define the facilities available to Java programs—is not an operating system. But it's getting close. To create the capable, platform-independent runtime environment found in JDK1.2, the class libraries have grown substantially.[1]

The numbers are a bit overwhelming: JDK1.1 has 22 packages containing 392 classes, implementing 3,671 methods. JDK1.2 has 59 packages containing 1,457 classes, implementing 14,618 methods. And these are only the *public* and *protected* classes; we're not including the classes and methods you can't reach from outside. (As of this writing, the Blackdown JDK1.2—ported from the Sun reference implementation—takes more than 20MB of disk space for the JVM, the compressed core class libraries, and the native support libraries.)

---

[1] One might convincingly argue that Java has become an OS, given the amount of OS-type functionality it now provides. Although some of this functionality is simply a platform-neutral wrapper around native capabilities, an increasing amount of capability (such as GUIs, security, and imaging) is provided by extensive support in the Java platform itself.

In this chapter, we take a high-level look at the packages and classes that make up the Java run-time environment. This chapter serves more as an introduction than a reference. A complete class and method reference is an invaluable aid, but it's too big to print. Class references and tutorials are available in bookstores, in pieces: buy one thick book to study the Java Foundation Classes, another for security, another for CORBA, and so on. For a comprehensive reference, the best place to start is the 80MB worth of JDK1.2 API HTML documentation available, free of charge, from Sun's Java site (visit `http://java.sun.com` and drill down through the Documentation link).

For each package, we will provide an overall package description, describe any particularly interesting classes, and delve into detail where appropriate. We will also list classes and interfaces in each of the packages.

Package `java.applet`

The `java.applet` package handles the basic requirements for applets—applications that run in Web browsers and in similar embedded contexts. All applets must be derived from class `Applet`.

The `Applet` class includes life cycle entry points for applet loading, startup, shutdown, and unloading; non-trivial applet classes must override some or all of these methods. (Unlike standalone applications, applets are not entered through a `main()` entry point.) The class also includes methods to facilitate interaction with the browser environment, such as playing audio, writing status messages, and interacting with other applets on the page.

Here is a trivial example of an applet with a single pushbutton:

```
import java.applet.*;
import java.awt.*;

public class TrivialApplet extends Applet
{
    public TrivialApplet()
    {
        add(new Button("Hello World!"));
    }
}
```

Some HTML code to display the applet:

```
<html>
<body>
<h1>Hello World Applet</h1>
<applet code="TrivialApplet.class"
        width="100"
        height="25">No Applet?</applet>
</body>
</html>
```

And the result, viewed in Netscape Navigator, is shown in Figure 3.1.

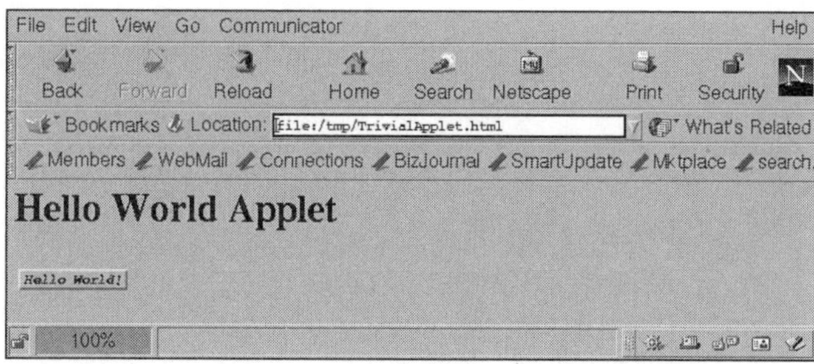

FIGURE 3.1
A trivial applet running in the Netscape browser.

Listing 3.1 shows all public classes and interfaces in the `java.applet` package.

LISTING 3.1 `java.applet` Classes and Interfaces List

```
public class java.applet.Applet extends java.awt.Panel
public interface java.applet.AppletContext extends java.lang.Object
public interface java.applet.AppletStub extends java.lang.Object
public interface java.applet.AudioClip extends java.lang.Object
```

Package `java.awt`

The `java.awt` package is the home of the Abstract Windowing Toolkit (AWT), the core Java graphic component. Among the AWT's functions are the following:

- A platform-independent interface to the native graphical rendering environment (The X Window System, Microsoft Windows, MacOS, OS/2, browser internal, and so on) for 2D rendering and keyboard/mouse input.
- A platform-independent GUI, built on top of native GUIs (Motif, Microsoft Windows, browser-provided widgets, and so on). In JDK1.2, this role is being subsumed by the new Swing toolkit. We discuss the reasons and the details later in the chapter in our examination of package `javax.swing`.
- A platform-independent event mechanism for handling window-system and GUI events such as window resizing, focus changes, button-pressing, and window visibility changes.
- A layout management framework to support GUI component layout.
- A mechanism for printing from Java applications.
- A 2D graphical rendering model and primitives for basic rendering operations such as drawing lines, rectangles, polygons, and such.

It is in the latter area—2D rendering model—that the AWT has changed most significantly between JDK1.1 and JDK1.2. JDK1.2 introduced a new model, `Graphics2D`, that incorporates techniques from computer graphics to improve graphical rendering capabilities.

Prior to `Graphics2D`, the Java 2D rendering model was the X Window System rendering model: limited color palette, bitmapped fonts, pixel-based coordinate system, and non-blended pixel rendering. The capabilities in `Graphics2D` do a much better job of mapping the real world—smooth objects and infinite color palettes—to the constrained world of bitmapped computer displays. You do not have to use the new capabilities; they are disabled by default, and they can exact a performance cost. But they are there if you need them.

The new capabilities will sound familiar to anyone familiar with the image processing aspects of 2D graphics: antialiasing, fractional font metrics, coordinate transformations, alpha blending, dithering, scalable fonts. `Graphics2D` brings these capabilities to all JDK1.2 environments—including those with display devices that do not support them. It achieves this magic, in most implementations, by performing its rendering entirely in JVM memory and blitting (copying pixel-for-pixel) the results to the display device. The result: graphics performance can suffer significantly if you use these capabilities.

Here is a modest example of what `Graphics2D`'s new rendering capabilities can do for you. Figures 3.2 and 3.3 show two waterfall charts of the default Java sans-serif font, at various sizes from 10 to 20 pixels in height (the program that generated this output, `WaterFall`, can be found in Appendix B, "Miscellaneous Program Listings"):

ABCDEFGHIJKLMNOPQRSTUVWXYZ
ABCDEFGHIJKLMNOPQRSTUVWXYZ
ABCDEFGHIJKLMNOPQRSTUVWXYZ
ABCDEFGHIJKLMNOPQRSTUVWXYZ
ABCDEFGHIJKLMNOPQRSTUVWXYZ
ABCDEFGHIJKLMNOPQRSTUVWXYZ
ABCDEFGHIJKLMNOPQRSTUVWXYZ
ABCDEFGHIJKLMNOPQRSTUVWXYZ
ABCDEFGHIJKLMNOPQRSTUVWXYZ
ABCDEFGHIJKLMNOPQRSTUVWXYZ
ABCDEFGHIJKLMNOPQRSTUVWXYZ

FIGURE 3.2
Waterfall with standard X-style rendering.

ABCDEFGHIJKLMNOPQRSTUVWXYZ
ABCDEFGHIJKLMNOPQRSTUVWXYZ
ABCDEFGHIJKLMNOPQRSTUVWXYZ
ABCDEFGHIJKLMNOPQRSTUVWXYZ
ABCDEFGHIJKLMNOPQRSTUVWXYZ
ABCDEFGHIJKLMNOPQRSTUVWXYZ
ABCDEFGHIJKLMNOPQRSTUVWXYZ
ABCDEFGHIJKLMNOPQRSTUVWXYZ
ABCDEFGHIJKLMNOPQRSTUVWXYZ
ABCDEFGHIJKLMNOPQRSTUVWXYZ
ABCDEFGHIJKLMNOPQRSTUVWXYZ

FIGURE 3.3
Waterfall with antialiasing and fractional font metrics.

The first example is typical of text rendering on bitmapped displays: jagged edges, inconsistent spacing, abrupt changes in the perceived stroke weight as the point size increases. The second example, using `Graphics2D` to transform the image from an idealized high-resolution space to a low-resolution bitmapped space, yields generally better output. (Unfortunately, the half-toning techniques required for printing this book tend to muddle the results on the printed page. The best way to compare is to run the `WaterFall` program, provided in the appendices and on the CD-ROM.)

Listing 3.2 shows all public classes and interfaces in the `java.awt` package.

LISTING 3.2 `java.awt` Classes and Interfaces List

```
public class java.awt.AWTError extends java.lang.Error
public abstract class java.awt.AWTEvent extends java.util.EventObject
public class java.awt.AWTEventMulticaster extends java.lang.Object
    implements java.awt.event.ActionListener
    implements java.awt.event.AdjustmentListener
    implements java.awt.event.ComponentListener
    implements java.awt.event.ContainerListener
    implements java.awt.event.FocusListener
    implements java.awt.event.InputMethodListener
    implements java.awt.event.ItemListener
    implements java.awt.event.KeyListener
    implements java.awt.event.MouseListener
    implements java.awt.event.MouseMotionListener
    implements java.awt.event.TextListener
    implements java.awt.event.WindowListener
public class java.awt.AWTException extends java.lang.Exception
public final class java.awt.AWTPermission extends
 java.security.BasicPermission (new in 1.2)
public interface java.awt.ActiveEvent extends
 java.lang.Object (new in 1.2)
public interface java.awt.Adjustable extends java.lang.Object
public final class java.awt.AlphaComposite extends
 java.lang.Object (new in 1.2)
    implements java.awt.Composite
public class java.awt.BasicStroke extends
 java.lang.Object (new in 1.2)
    implements java.awt.Stroke
public class java.awt.BorderLayout extends java.lang.Object
    implements java.awt.LayoutManager2
    implements java.io.Serializable
public class java.awt.Button extends java.awt.Component
public class java.awt.Canvas extends java.awt.Component
public class java.awt.CardLayout extends java.lang.Object
    implements java.awt.LayoutManager2
    implements java.io.Serializable
public class java.awt.Checkbox extends java.awt.Component
    implements java.awt.ItemSelectable
public class java.awt.CheckboxGroup extends java.lang.Object
    implements java.io.Serializable
```

continued on next page

continued from previous page

```
public class java.awt.CheckboxMenuItem extends java.awt.MenuItem
    implements java.awt.ItemSelectable
public class java.awt.Choice extends java.awt.Component
    implements java.awt.ItemSelectable
public class java.awt.Color extends java.lang.Object
    implements java.awt.Paint
    implements java.io.Serializable
public abstract class java.awt.Component extends java.lang.Object
    implements java.awt.MenuContainer
    implements java.awt.image.ImageObserver
    implements java.io.Serializable
public final class java.awt.ComponentOrientation extends
 java.lang.Object (new in 1.2)
    implements java.io.Serializable
public interface java.awt.Composite extends
 java.lang.Object (new in 1.2)
public interface java.awt.CompositeContext extends
 java.lang.Object (new in 1.2)
public class java.awt.Container extends java.awt.Component
public class java.awt.Cursor extends java.lang.Object
    implements java.io.Serializable
public class java.awt.Dialog extends java.awt.Window
public class java.awt.Dimension extends java.awt.geom.Dimension2D
    implements java.io.Serializable
public class java.awt.Event extends java.lang.Object
    implements java.io.Serializable
public class java.awt.EventQueue extends java.lang.Object
public class java.awt.FileDialog extends java.awt.Dialog
public class java.awt.FlowLayout extends java.lang.Object
    implements java.awt.LayoutManager
    implements java.io.Serializable
public class java.awt.Font extends java.lang.Object
    implements java.io.Serializable
public abstract class java.awt.FontMetrics extends java.lang.Object
    implements java.io.Serializable
public class java.awt.Frame extends java.awt.Window
    implements java.awt.MenuContainer
public class java.awt.GradientPaint extends
 java.lang.Object (new in 1.2)
    implements java.awt.Paint
public abstract class java.awt.Graphics extends java.lang.Object
public abstract class java.awt.Graphics2D extends
 java.awt.Graphics (new in 1.2)
public abstract class java.awt.GraphicsConfigTemplate extends
 java.lang.Object (new in 1.2)
    implements java.io.Serializable
public abstract class java.awt.GraphicsConfiguration extends
 java.lang.Object (new in 1.2)
public abstract class java.awt.GraphicsDevice extends
 java.lang.Object (new in 1.2)
public abstract class java.awt.GraphicsEnvironment
 extends java.lang.Object (new in 1.2)
```

```
public class java.awt.GridBagConstraints extends java.lang.Object
    implements java.io.Serializable
    implements java.lang.Cloneable
public class java.awt.GridBagLayout extends java.lang.Object
    implements java.awt.LayoutManager2
    implements java.io.Serializable
public class java.awt.GridLayout extends java.lang.Object
    implements java.awt.LayoutManager
    implements java.io.Serializable
public class java.awt.IllegalComponentStateException extends
 java.lang.IllegalStateException
public abstract class java.awt.Image extends java.lang.Object
public class java.awt.Insets extends java.lang.Object
    implements java.io.Serializable
    implements java.lang.Cloneable
public interface java.awt.ItemSelectable extends java.lang.Object
public class java.awt.Label extends java.awt.Component
public interface java.awt.LayoutManager extends java.lang.Object
public interface java.awt.LayoutManager2 extends java.lang.Object
    implements java.awt.LayoutManager
public class java.awt.List extends java.awt.Component
    implements java.awt.ItemSelectable
public class java.awt.MediaTracker extends java.lang.Object
    implements java.io.Serializable
public class java.awt.Menu extends java.awt.MenuItem
    implements java.awt.MenuContainer
public class java.awt.MenuBar extends java.awt.MenuComponent
    implements java.awt.MenuContainer
public abstract class java.awt.MenuComponent extends
 java.lang.Object
    implements java.io.Serializable
public interface java.awt.MenuContainer extends java.lang.Object
public class java.awt.MenuItem extends java.awt.MenuComponent
public class java.awt.MenuShortcut extends java.lang.Object
    implements java.io.Serializable
public interface java.awt.Paint extends
 java.lang.Object (new in 1.2)
    implements java.awt.Transparency
public interface java.awt.PaintContext extends
 java.lang.Object (new in 1.2)
public class java.awt.Panel extends java.awt.Container
public class java.awt.Point extends java.awt.geom.Point2D
    implements java.io.Serializable
public class java.awt.Polygon extends java.lang.Object
    implements java.awt.Shape
    implements java.io.Serializable
public class java.awt.PopupMenu extends java.awt.Menu
public interface java.awt.PrintGraphics extends java.lang.Object
public abstract class java.awt.PrintJob extends java.lang.Object
public class java.awt.Rectangle extends java.awt.geom.Rectangle2D
    implements java.awt.Shape
    implements java.io.Serializable
public class java.awt.RenderingHints extends
```

continued on next page

continued from previous page

```
 java.lang.Object (new in 1.2)
    implements java.lang.Cloneable
    implements java.util.Map
public abstract class java.awt.RenderingHints.Key extends
 java.lang.Object (new in 1.2)
public class java.awt.ScrollPane extends java.awt.Container
public class java.awt.Scrollbar extends java.awt.Component
    implements java.awt.Adjustable
public interface java.awt.Shape extends java.lang.Object
public interface java.awt.Stroke extends
 java.lang.Object (new in 1.2)
public final class java.awt.SystemColor extends java.awt.Color
    implements java.io.Serializable
public class java.awt.TextArea extends java.awt.TextComponent
public class java.awt.TextComponent extends java.awt.Component
public class java.awt.TextField extends java.awt.TextComponent
public class java.awt.TexturePaint extends
 java.lang.Object (new in 1.2)
    implements java.awt.Paint
public abstract class java.awt.Toolkit extends java.lang.Object
public interface java.awt.Transparency extends
 java.lang.Object (new in 1.2)
public class java.awt.Window extends java.awt.Container
```

Package `java.awt.color`

This package supports *color management* in Java—the use of device-independent color spaces such as *sRGB* instead of the device-dependent RGB commonly used in bitmapped graphics (the reason blue looks different on your display and your printer). These classes will eventually replace the functionality provided by the `java.awt.Color` class, but for now, this package is a work-in-progress.

Color management, which has long been a part of high-end graphic arts environments, is still not heavily used on mainstream systems. It offers much in the way of reliable and consistent color output, but it also presents the difficult and expensive problem of keeping your devices (monitors and printers) precisely calibrated. If you want to learn more about color management and sRGB, a paper published by the World Wide Web Consortium provides some detail: http://www.w3.org/Graphics/Color/sRGB.html.

Listing 3.3 shows all public classes and interfaces in the `java.awt.color` package.

LISTING 3.3 `java.awt.color` Classes and Interfaces List

```
public class java.awt.color.CMMException extends
 java.lang.RuntimeException (new in 1.2)
public abstract class java.awt.color.ColorSpace extends
 java.lang.Object (new in 1.2)
public class java.awt.color.ICC_ColorSpace extends
 java.awt.color.ColorSpace (new in 1.2)
```

```
public class java.awt.color.ICC_Profile extends
 java.lang.Object (new in 1.2)
public class java.awt.color.ICC_ProfileGray extends
 java.awt.color.ICC_Profile (new in 1.2)
public class java.awt.color.ICC_ProfileRGB extends
 java.awt.color.ICC_Profile (new in 1.2)
public class java.awt.color.ProfileDataException extends
 java.lang.RuntimeException (new in 1.2)
```

Package `java.awt.datatransfer`

This package provides a platform-independent interface for data transfer between applications using the Clipboard. In the X Window System (and in Microsoft Windows, for that matter), the Clipboard is used when you select the `cut` or `copy` menu item in one application and the `paste` menu item to transfer data to another application.

Like many Java features, this is a lowest-common-denominator approach to supporting native platform capabilities. It supports a data transfer mechanism found on many graphical platforms, while ignoring a unique (and popular) X mechanism called *Primary Selection*—which uses mouse buttons instead of `cut`, `copy`, and `paste` menu selections.

In Chapter 56, "X Window System Tips and Tricks," in the section "XClipboard: A JNI-Based Cut-and-Paste Tool" we present a tool to access *Primary Selection*.

Listing 3.4 shows all public classes and interfaces in the `java.awt.datatransfer` package.

LISTING 3.4 `java.awt.datatransfer` Classes and Interfaces List

```
public class java.awt.datatransfer.Clipboard extends
 java.lang.Object
public interface java.awt.datatransfer.ClipboardOwner extends
 java.lang.Object
public class java.awt.datatransfer.DataFlavor extends
 java.lang.Object
    implements java.io.Externalizable
    implements java.lang.Cloneable
public interface java.awt.datatransfer.FlavorMap extends
 java.lang.Object (new in 1.2)
public class java.awt.datatransfer.StringSelection extends
 java.lang.Object
    implements java.awt.datatransfer.ClipboardOwner
    implements java.awt.datatransfer.Transferable
public final class java.awt.datatransfer.SystemFlavorMap extends
 java.lang.Object (new in 1.2)
    implements java.awt.datatransfer.FlavorMap
public interface java.awt.datatransfer.Transferable extends
 java.lang.Object
public class java.awt.datatransfer.UnsupportedFlavorException
 extends java.lang.Exception
```

Package `java.awt.dnd`

This package, new in JDK1.2, provides platform-independent drag-and-drop (DnD) capabilities by integrating Java with native DnD mechanisms. It supports DnD among Java applications and between Java and non-Java applications.

Listing 3.5 shows all public classes and interfaces in the `java.awt.dnd` package.

LISTING 3.5 `java.awt.dnd` Classes and Interfaces List

```
public interface java.awt.dnd.Autoscroll extends
 java.lang.Object (new in 1.2)
public final class java.awt.dnd.DnDConstants extends
 java.lang.Object (new in 1.2)
public class java.awt.dnd.DragGestureEvent extends
 java.util.EventObject (new in 1.2)
public interface java.awt.dnd.DragGestureListener extends
 java.lang.Object (new in 1.2)
    implements java.util.EventListener
public abstract class java.awt.dnd.DragGestureRecognizer extends
 java.lang.Object (new in 1.2)
public class java.awt.dnd.DragSource extends
 java.lang.Object (new in 1.2)
public class java.awt.dnd.DragSourceContext extends
 java.lang.Object (new in 1.2)
    implements java.awt.dnd.DragSourceListener
public class java.awt.dnd.DragSourceDragEvent extends
 java.awt.dnd.DragSourceEvent (new in 1.2)
public class java.awt.dnd.DragSourceDropEvent extends
 java.awt.dnd.DragSourceEvent (new in 1.2)
public class java.awt.dnd.DragSourceEvent extends
 java.util.EventObject (new in 1.2)
public interface java.awt.dnd.DragSourceListener extends
 java.lang.Object (new in 1.2)
    implements java.util.EventListener
public class java.awt.dnd.DropTarget extends
 java.lang.Object (new in 1.2)
    implements java.awt.dnd.DropTargetListener
    implements java.io.Serializable
public class java.awt.dnd.DropTarget.DropTargetAutoScroller extends
 java.lang.
 Object (new in 1.2)
    implements java.awt.event.ActionListener
public class java.awt.dnd.DropTargetContext extends
 java.lang.Object (new in 1.2)
public class java.awt.dnd.DropTargetContext.TransferableProxy
 extends java.lang.
 Object (new in 1.2)
    implements java.awt.datatransfer.Transferable
public class java.awt.dnd.DropTargetDragEvent extends java.awt.dnd.
 DropTargetEvent (new in 1.2)
public class java.awt.dnd.DropTargetDropEvent extends java.awt.dnd.
```

```
 DropTargetEvent (new in 1.2)
public class java.awt.dnd.DropTargetEvent extends
 java.util.EventObject (new in 1.2)
public interface java.awt.dnd.DropTargetListener extends
 java.lang.Object (new in 1.2)
    implements java.util.EventListener
public class java.awt.dnd.InvalidDnDOperationException extends
 java.lang.
 IllegalStateException (new in 1.2)
public abstract class java.awt.dnd.MouseDragGestureRecognizer
 extends java.awt.dnd.
 DragGestureRecognizer (new in 1.2)
    implements java.awt.event.MouseListener
    implements java.awt.event.MouseMotionListener
```

Package `java.awt.event`

This package defines the classes and interfaces that support the Java event-handling mechanism. Event-handling is used to implement application behavior triggered by external events (such as pressing a button in the GUI), and is based on a broadcast/listener model: objects interested in receiving events register their interest with objects capable of sending events. When events occur, notification is broadcast to the interested listeners. (To those who have been around since the Java 1.0 days, this mechanism was substantially changed in 1.1.)

A quick demonstration is shown in Listing 3.6. We'll extend the `TrivialApplet` (presented in the "Package `java.applet`" section) by adding some mouse-press and mouse-release behavior. The applet will handle the event by sending "button pressed" and "button released" messages to the browser status line.

LISTING 3.6 Extending the `TrivialApplet` Behavior

```
import java.applet.*;
import java.awt.*;
import java.awt.event.*;

public class TrivialApplet2 extends Applet implements MouseListener
{
    public TrivialApplet2()
    {
        // Allocate and install our button
        Button button = new Button("Hello World!");
        add(button);
        // Register this class as a listener for mouse events. This
        // call expects a MouseListener as an argument
        button.addMouseListener(this);
    }
    // Implementation of the MouseListener interface. When
    // we implement an interface, we must implement all
    // methods... even those we don't care about.
    public void mouseClicked(MouseEvent e)      {}
```

continued on next page

continued from previous page

```
20        public void mouseEntered(MouseEvent e)       {}
21        public void mouseExited(MouseEvent e)        {}
22        public void mousePressed(MouseEvent e)
23        {
24            showStatus("Button pressed");
25        }
26        public void mouseReleased(MouseEvent e)
27        {
28            showStatus("Button released");
29        }
30    }
```

On line 14, we register the `TrivialApplet2` class as a listener. The class fulfills the basic requirement of listening for mouse events—it implements the `MouseListener` interface. Lines 22-29 implement the new actions.

The result, viewed in Netscape Navigator, is shown in Figure 3.4.

FIGURE 3.4
Trivial applet with a mouse listener added.

Listing 3.7 shows all public classes and interfaces in the `java.awt.event` package.

LISTING 3.7 `java.awt.event` Classes and Interfaces List

```
public interface java.awt.event.AWTEventListener extends
 java.lang.Object (new in 1.2)
    implements java.util.EventListener
public class java.awt.event.ActionEvent extends java.awt.AWTEvent
public interface java.awt.event.ActionListener extends
 java.lang.Object
    implements java.util.EventListener
public class java.awt.event.AdjustmentEvent extends
 java.awt.AWTEvent
public interface java.awt.event.AdjustmentListener extends
 java.lang.Object
    implements java.util.EventListener
public abstract class java.awt.event.ComponentAdapter extends
 java.lang.Object
    implements java.awt.event.ComponentListener
```

```
public class java.awt.event.ComponentEvent extends
 java.awt.AWTEvent
public interface java.awt.event.ComponentListener extends
 java.lang.Object
    implements java.util.EventListener
public abstract class java.awt.event.ContainerAdapter extends
 java.lang.Object
    implements java.awt.event.ContainerListener
public class java.awt.event.ContainerEvent extends
 java.awt.event.ComponentEvent
public interface java.awt.event.ContainerListener extends
 java.lang.Object
    implements java.util.EventListener
public abstract class java.awt.event.FocusAdapter extends
 java.lang.Object
    implements java.awt.event.FocusListener
public class java.awt.event.FocusEvent extends
 java.awt.event.ComponentEvent
public interface java.awt.event.FocusListener extends
 java.lang.Object
    implements java.util.EventListener
public abstract class java.awt.event.InputEvent extends
 java.awt.event.ComponentEvent
public class java.awt.event.InputMethodEvent extends
 java.awt.AWTEvent (new in 1.2)
public interface java.awt.event.InputMethodListener extends
 java.lang.Object (new in 1.2)
    implements java.util.EventListener
public class java.awt.event.InvocationEvent extends
 java.awt.AWTEvent (new in 1.2)
    implements java.awt.ActiveEvent
public class java.awt.event.ItemEvent extends java.awt.AWTEvent
public interface java.awt.event.ItemListener extends
 java.lang.Object
    implements java.util.EventListener
public abstract class java.awt.event.KeyAdapter extends
 java.lang.Object
    implements java.awt.event.KeyListener
public class java.awt.event.KeyEvent extends
 java.awt.event.InputEvent
public interface java.awt.event.KeyListener extends java.lang.Object
    implements java.util.EventListener
public abstract class java.awt.event.MouseAdapter extends
java.lang.Object
    implements java.awt.event.MouseListener
public class java.awt.event.MouseEvent extends
 java.awt.event.InputEvent
public interface java.awt.event.MouseListener extends
 java.lang.Object
    implements java.util.EventListener
public abstract class java.awt.event.MouseMotionAdapter extends
 java.lang.Object
    implements java.awt.event.MouseMotionListener
```

continued on next page

continued from previous page

```
public interface java.awt.event.MouseMotionListener extends
 java.lang.Object
    implements java.util.EventListener
public class java.awt.event.PaintEvent extends
 java.awt.event.ComponentEvent
public class java.awt.event.TextEvent extends java.awt.AWTEvent
public interface java.awt.event.TextListener extends
 java.lang.Object
    implements java.util.EventListener
public abstract class java.awt.event.WindowAdapter extends
 java.lang.Object
    implements java.awt.event.WindowListener
public class java.awt.event.WindowEvent extends
 java.awt.event.ComponentEvent
public interface java.awt.event.WindowListener extends
 java.lang.Object
    implements java.util.EventListener
```

Package `java.awt.font`

This package, new to JDK1.2, supports detailed manipulation and use of scalable typefaces. Most ordinary GUI and printing applications will not need these capabilities, but they are valuable for desktop publishing, graphic arts, and other applications with complex typographic requirements.

Listing 3.8 shows all public classes and interfaces in the `java.awt.font` package.

LISTING 3.8 `java.awt.font` Classes and Interfaces List

```
public class java.awt.font.FontRenderContext extends
 java.lang.Object (new in 1.2)
public final class java.awt.font.GlyphJustificationInfo extends java.lang.
 Object (new in 1.2)
public final class java.awt.font.GlyphMetrics extends
 java.lang.Object (new in 1.2)
public abstract class java.awt.font.GlyphVector extends
 java.lang.Object (new in 1.2)
    implements java.lang.Cloneable
public abstract class java.awt.font.GraphicAttribute extends
 java.lang.Object (new in 1.2)
public final class java.awt.font.ImageGraphicAttribute extends
 java.awt.font.
 GraphicAttribute (new in 1.2)
public final class java.awt.font.LineBreakMeasurer extends
 java.lang.Object (new in 1.2)
public abstract class java.awt.font.LineMetrics extends
 java.lang.Object (new in 1.2)
public interface java.awt.font.MultipleMaster extends
 java.lang.Object (new in 1.2)
public interface java.awt.font.OpenType extends
 java.lang.Object (new in 1.2)
```

```
public final class java.awt.font.ShapeGraphicAttribute extends
  java.awt.font.
 GraphicAttribute (new in 1.2)
public final class java.awt.font.TextAttribute extends
 java.text.AttributedCharacterIterator.
 Attribute (new in 1.2)
public final class java.awt.font.TextHitInfo extends
 java.lang.Object (new in 1.2)
public final class java.awt.font.TextLayout extends
 java.lang.Object (new in 1.2)
    implements java.lang.Cloneable
public class java.awt.font.TextLayout.CaretPolicy extends
 java.lang.Object (new in 1.2)
public final class java.awt.font.TextLine.TextLineMetrics extends
 java.lang.Object (new in 1.2)
public final class java.awt.font.TransformAttribute extends
 java.lang.Object (new in 1.2)
    implements java.io.Serializable
```

Package `java.awt.geom`

This package, new to JDK1.2, is associated with the new `Graphics2D` capabilities. The classes here support drawing, manipulation, and transformation of objects representing two-dimensional geometric primitives—arcs, lines, points, rectangles, ellipses, parametric curves—in a floating point coordinate space.

Listing 3.9 shows all public classes and interfaces in the `java.awt.geom` package.

LISTING 3.9 `java.awt.geom` Classes and Interfaces List

```
public class java.awt.geom.AffineTransform extends
 java.lang.Object (new in 1.2)
    implements java.io.Serializable
    implements java.lang.Cloneable
public abstract class java.awt.geom.Arc2D extends
 java.awt.geom.RectangularShape (new in 1.2)
public class java.awt.geom.Arc2D.Double extends
 java.awt.geom.Arc2D (new in 1.2)
public class java.awt.geom.Arc2D.Float extends
 java.awt.geom.Arc2D (new in 1.2)
public class java.awt.geom.Area extends
 java.lang.Object (new in 1.2)
    implements java.awt.Shape
    implements java.lang.Cloneable
public abstract class java.awt.geom.CubicCurve2D extends
java.lang.Object (new in 1.2)
    implements java.awt.Shape
    implements java.lang.Cloneable
public class java.awt.geom.CubicCurve2D.Double extends
 java.awt.geom.CubicCurve2D (new in 1.2)
public class java.awt.geom.CubicCurve2D.Float extends
```

continued on next page

continued from previous page

```
 java.awt.geom.CubicCurve2D (new in 1.2)
public abstract class java.awt.geom.Dimension2D extends
 java.lang.Object (new in 1.2)
    implements java.lang.Cloneable
public abstract class java.awt.geom.Ellipse2D extends
 java.awt.geom.RectangularShape (new in 1.2)
public class java.awt.geom.Ellipse2D.Double extends
 java.awt.geom.Ellipse2D (new in 1.2)
public class java.awt.geom.Ellipse2D.Float extends
 java.awt.geom.Ellipse2D (new in 1.2)
public class java.awt.geom.FlatteningPathIterator extends
java.lang.Object (new in 1.2)
    implements java.awt.geom.PathIterator
public final class java.awt.geom.GeneralPath extends
 java.lang.Object (new in 1.2)
    implements java.awt.Shape
    implements java.lang.Cloneable
public class java.awt.geom.IllegalPathStateException extends java.lang.
 RuntimeException (new in 1.2)
public abstract class java.awt.geom.Line2D extends
 java.lang.Object (new in 1.2)
    implements java.awt.Shape
    implements java.lang.Cloneable
public class java.awt.geom.Line2D.Double extends
 java.awt.geom.Line2D (new in 1.2)
public class java.awt.geom.Line2D.Float extends
 java.awt.geom.Line2D (new in 1.2)
public class java.awt.geom.NoninvertibleTransformException extends java.lang.
 Exception (new in 1.2)
public interface java.awt.geom.PathIterator extends
 java.lang.Object (new in 1.2)
public abstract class java.awt.geom.Point2D extends
 java.lang.Object (new in 1.2)
    implements java.lang.Cloneable
public class java.awt.geom.Point2D.Double extends
 java.awt.geom.Point2D (new in 1.2)
public class java.awt.geom.Point2D.Float extends
 java.awt.geom.Point2D (new in 1.2)
public abstract class java.awt.geom.QuadCurve2D extends
 java.lang.Object (new in 1.2)
    implements java.awt.Shape
    implements java.lang.Cloneable
public class java.awt.geom.QuadCurve2D.Double extends
 java.awt.geom.QuadCurve2D (new in 1.2)
public class java.awt.geom.QuadCurve2D.Float extends
 java.awt.geom.QuadCurve2D (new in 1.2)
public abstract class java.awt.geom.Rectangle2D extends java.awt.geom.
 RectangularShape (new in 1.2)
public class java.awt.geom.Rectangle2D.Double extends
 java.awt.geom.Rectangle2D (new in 1.2)
public class java.awt.geom.Rectangle2D.Float extends
 java.awt.geom.Rectangle2D (new in 1.2)
public abstract class java.awt.geom.RectangularShape extends
```

```
java.lang.Object (new in 1.2)
    implements java.awt.Shape
    implements java.lang.Cloneable
public abstract class java.awt.geom.RoundRectangle2D extends java.awt.geom.
 RectangularShape (new in 1.2)
public class java.awt.geom.RoundRectangle2D.Double extends java.awt.geom.
 RoundRectangle2D (new in 1.2)
public class java.awt.geom.RoundRectangle2D.Float extends java.awt.geom.
 RoundRectangle2D (new in 1.2)
```

Package `java.awt.im`

This package, new to JDK1.2, supports *input methods* that allow large alphabets (such as ideographic representations of the Japanese, Chinese, and Korean languages) to be entered on small keyboards. A common example is the use of the phonetic Japanese *Katakana* alphabet to spell out and enter glyphs from the ideographic *Kanji* alphabet.

Listing 3.10 shows all public classes and interfaces in the `java.awt.im` package.

LISTING 3.10 `java.awt.im` Classes and Interfaces List

```
public class java.awt.im.InputContext extends java.lang.Object (new in 1.2)
public class java.awt.im.InputMethodHighlight extends
 java.lang.Object (new in 1.2)
public interface java.awt.im.InputMethodRequests extends
 java.lang.Object (new in 1.2)
public final class java.awt.im.InputSubset extends
 java.lang.Character.Subset (new in 1.2)
```

Package `java.awt.image`

This package, which has grown substantially in JDK1.2, supports manipulation of bitmapped images. The newer capabilities are not of interest to most GUI programs but are of considerable utility to image processing applications.

As a demonstration of image manipulation, the SlideShow utility in Appendix B, "Miscellaneous Program Listings," loads and displays images from `.gif` and `.jpg` image files, optionally rescaling and/or sharpening them for display. The small excerpt in Listing 3.11 shows the use of `java.awt.image` capabilities to handle the transformations.

LISTING 3.11 Excerpt of SlideShow.java, Showing the Use of `java.awt.image` Transformations

```
        // If we want to rescale, set up the filter
        if (rescale.isSelected())
        {
            // Find our current image size
            Dimension dim = getSlideDimension();
            if (dim == null) return;
            double xscale = (double)width / (double)dim.width;
```

continued on next page

continued from previous page

```
            double yscale = (double)height / (double)dim.height;
            double xyscale = Math.min(xscale, yscale);
            // Set hints for maximum quality
            RenderingHints hints =
                new RenderingHints(
                    RenderingHints.KEY_ANTIALIASING,
                    RenderingHints.VALUE_ANTIALIAS_ON);
            hints.add(
                new RenderingHints(
                    RenderingHints.KEY_COLOR_RENDERING,
                    RenderingHints.VALUE_COLOR_RENDER_QUALITY));
            ImageFilter rescaleFilter =
                new BufferedImageFilter(
                    new AffineTransformOp(
                        AffineTransform.getScaleInstance(xyscale, xyscale),
                        hints));
            transformedSlide = Toolkit.getDefaultToolkit().createImage(
                        new FilteredImageSource(
                            transformedSlide.getSource(), rescaleFilter));
        }
        // If we want to sharpen, set up the filter
        if (sharpen.isSelected())
        {
            float ctr = 2, offc = -.125f;
            ImageFilter sharpenFilter =
                new BufferedImageFilter(
                    new ConvolveOp(
                        new Kernel(3, 3, new float[]
                                       { offc, offc, offc,
                                         offc, ctr , offc,
                                         offc, offc, offc })));
            transformedSlide = Toolkit.getDefaultToolkit().createImage(
                        new FilteredImageSource(
                            transformedSlide.getSource(), sharpenFilter));
        }
```

Listing 3.12 shows all public classes and interfaces in the `java.awt.image` package.

LISTING 3.12 `java.awt.image` Classes and Interfaces List

```
public class java.awt.image.AffineTransformOp extends
 java.lang.Object (new in 1.2)
    implements java.awt.image.BufferedImageOp
    implements java.awt.image.RasterOp
public class java.awt.image.AreaAveragingScaleFilter extends
java.awt.image.ReplicateScaleFilter
public class java.awt.image.BandCombineOp extends java.lang.Object (new in 1.2)
    implements java.awt.image.RasterOp
public final class java.awt.image.BandedSampleModel extends java.awt.image.
 ComponentSampleModel (new in 1.2)
public class java.awt.image.BufferedImage extends java.awt.Image (new in 1.2)
    implements java.awt.image.WritableRenderedImage
public class java.awt.image.BufferedImageFilter extends
```

```
java.awt.image.ImageFilter (new in 1.2)
    implements java.lang.Cloneable
public interface java.awt.image.BufferedImageOp extends
java.lang.Object (new in 1.2)
public class java.awt.image.ByteLookupTable extends
 java.awt.image.LookupTable (new in 1.2)
public class java.awt.image.ColorConvertOp extends
 java.lang.Object (new in 1.2)
    implements java.awt.image.BufferedImageOp
    implements java.awt.image.RasterOp
public abstract class java.awt.image.ColorModel extends java.lang.Object
    implements java.awt.Transparency
public class java.awt.image.ComponentColorModel extends
java.awt.image.ColorModel (new in 1.2)
public class java.awt.image.ComponentSampleModel extends
 java.awt.image.SampleModel (new in 1.2)
public class java.awt.image.ConvolveOp extends java.lang.Object (new in 1.2)
    implements java.awt.image.BufferedImageOp
    implements java.awt.image.RasterOp
public class java.awt.image.CropImageFilter extends java.awt.image.ImageFilter
public abstract class java.awt.image.DataBuffer extends
java.lang.Object (new in 1.2)
public final class java.awt.image.DataBufferByte extends
 java.awt.image.DataBuffer (new in 1.2)
public final class java.awt.image.DataBufferInt extends
 java.awt.image.DataBuffer (new in 1.2)
public final class java.awt.image.DataBufferShort extends
 java.awt.image.DataBuffer (new in 1.2)
public final class java.awt.image.DataBufferUShort extends
 java.awt.image.DataBuffer (new in 1.2)
public class java.awt.image.DirectColorModel extends
 java.awt.image.PackedColorModel
public class java.awt.image.FilteredImageSource extends java.lang.Object
    implements java.awt.image.ImageProducer
public interface java.awt.image.ImageConsumer extends java.lang.Object
public class java.awt.image.ImageFilter extends java.lang.Object
    implements java.awt.image.ImageConsumer
    implements java.lang.Cloneable
public interface java.awt.image.ImageObserver extends java.lang.Object
public interface java.awt.image.ImageProducer extends java.lang.Object
public class java.awt.image.ImagingOpException extends
java.lang.RuntimeException (new in 1.2)
public class java.awt.image.IndexColorModel extends java.awt.image.ColorModel
public class java.awt.image.Kernel extends java.lang.Object (new in 1.2)
    implements java.lang.Cloneable
public class java.awt.image.LookupOp extends java.lang.Object (new in 1.2)
    implements java.awt.image.BufferedImageOp
    implements java.awt.image.RasterOp
public abstract class java.awt.image.LookupTable extends
 java.lang.Object (new in 1.2)
public class java.awt.image.MemoryImageSource extends java.lang.Object
    implements java.awt.image.ImageProducer
public class java.awt.image.MultiPixelPackedSampleModel extends java.awt.image.
```

continued on next page

continued from previous page

```
 SampleModel (new in 1.2)
public abstract class java.awt.image.PackedColorModel extends java.awt.image.
 ColorModel (new in 1.2)
public class java.awt.image.PixelGrabber extends java.lang.Object
    implements java.awt.image.ImageConsumer
public class java.awt.image.PixelInterleavedSampleModel extends
 java.awt.image.
 ComponentSampleModel (new in 1.2)
public abstract class java.awt.image.RGBImageFilter extends
 java.awt.image.ImageFilter
public class java.awt.image.Raster extends java.lang.Object (new in 1.2)
public class java.awt.image.RasterFormatException extends java.lang.
 RuntimeException (new in 1.2)
public interface java.awt.image.RasterOp extends java.lang.Object (new in 1.2)
public interface java.awt.image.RenderedImage extends
java.lang.Object (new in 1.2)
public class java.awt.image.ReplicateScaleFilter extends
java.awt.image.ImageFilter
public class java.awt.image.RescaleOp extends java.lang.Object (new in 1.2)
    implements java.awt.image.BufferedImageOp
    implements java.awt.image.RasterOp
public abstract class java.awt.image.SampleModel extends
java.lang.Object (new in 1.2)
public class java.awt.image.ShortLookupTable extends
 java.awt.image.LookupTable (new in 1.2)
public class java.awt.image.SinglePixelPackedSampleModel extends java.awt.image.
 SampleModel (new in 1.2)
public interface java.awt.image.TileObserver extends
 java.lang.Object (new in 1.2)
public class java.awt.image.WritableRaster extends
java.awt.image.Raster (new in 1.2)
public interface java.awt.image.WritableRenderedImage extends
 java.lang.Object (new in 1.2)
    implements java.awt.image.RenderedImage
```

Package `java.awt.image.renderable`

This package, new to JDK1.2, supports *rendering-independent images*, images managed in a resolution-independent manner.

Listing 3.13 shows all public classes and interfaces in the `java.awt.image.renderable` package.

LISTING 3.13 `java.awt.image.renderable` Classes and Interfaces List

```
public interface java.awt.image.renderable.ContextualRenderedImageFactory
 extends java.lang.Object (new in 1.2)
    implements java.awt.image.renderable.RenderedImageFactory
public class java.awt.image.renderable.ParameterBlock extends
 java.lang.Object (new in 1.2)
    implements java.io.Serializable
```

```
    implements java.lang.Cloneable
public class java.awt.image.renderable.RenderContext extends
 java.lang.Object (new in 1.2)
    implements java.lang.Cloneable
public interface java.awt.image.renderable.RenderableImage extends java.lang.
 Object (new in 1.2)
public class java.awt.image.renderable.RenderableImageOp extends
 java.lang.Object (new in 1.2)
    implements java.awt.image.renderable.RenderableImage
public class java.awt.image.renderable.RenderableImageProducer extends
 java.lang.Object (new in 1.2)
    implements java.awt.image.ImageProducer
    implements java.lang.Runnable
public interface java.awt.image.renderable.RenderedImageFactory extends
 java.lang.Object (new in 1.2)
```

Package `java.awt.print`

Good printing support has been a latecomer to Java. JDK1.1 began to introduce a printing model, and this package, new to JDK1.2, upgrades the model. The classes provided here allow you to manage print jobs, page formats, paper, and books.

When you print from a Java/Linux application, the AWT generates a PostScript™ file and sends it to the print spooling subsystem, where it will print properly if you send it to a PostScript-capable printer. To learn more about printing from Linux, including how to print PostScript if you do not have such a printer, see the "Printing HOWTO" published on the Linux help page at `http://www.linux.org/help/howto.html`.

Listing 3.14 shows all public classes and interfaces in the `java.awt.print` package.

LISTING 3.14 `java.awt.print` Classes and Interfaces List

```
public class java.awt.print.Book extends java.lang.Object (new in 1.2)
    implements java.awt.print.Pageable
public class java.awt.print.PageFormat extends java.lang.Object (new in 1.2)
    implements java.lang.Cloneable
public interface java.awt.print.Pageable extends java.lang.Object (new in 1.2)
public class java.awt.print.Paper extends java.lang.Object (new in 1.2)
    implements java.lang.Cloneable
public interface java.awt.print.Printable extends java.lang.Object (new in 1.2)
public class java.awt.print.PrinterAbortException extends java.awt.print.
 PrinterException (new in 1.2)
public class java.awt.print.PrinterException extends
 java.lang.Exception (new in 1.2)
public interface java.awt.print.PrinterGraphics extends
 java.lang.Object (new in 1.2)
public class java.awt.print.PrinterIOException extends java.awt.print.
 PrinterException (new in 1.2)
public abstract class java.awt.print.PrinterJob extends
 java.lang.Object (new in 1.2)
```

Package java.beans

JavaBeans is the name for the Java component architecture. Beans are modular, reusable pieces of Java functionality that describe themselves (their inputs, outputs, and behavior) so that they can easily be dropped into and manipulated by other applications. Beans are easy to write—many core platform classes *are* beans—and are most frequently built by following some simple stylistic rules when building classes.

This package provides a collection of premium Bean functionality. Some Beans need these classes to enable advanced configuration capabilities; many do not.

Listing 3.15 shows all public classes and interfaces in the `java.beans` package.

LISTING 3.15 java.beans Classes and Interfaces List

```
public interface java.beans.AppletInitializer extends
 java.lang.Object (new in 1.2)
public class java.beans.BeanDescriptor extends java.beans.FeatureDescriptor
public interface java.beans.BeanInfo extends java.lang.Object
public class java.beans.Beans extends java.lang.Object
public interface java.beans.Customizer extends java.lang.Object
public interface java.beans.DesignMode extends java.lang.Object (new in 1.2)
public class java.beans.EventSetDescriptor extends java.beans.FeatureDescriptor
public class java.beans.FeatureDescriptor extends java.lang.Object
public class java.beans.IndexedPropertyDescriptor extends
 java.beans.PropertyDescriptor
public class java.beans.IntrospectionException extends java.lang.Exception
public class java.beans.Introspector extends java.lang.Object
public class java.beans.MethodDescriptor extends java.beans.FeatureDescriptor
public class java.beans.ParameterDescriptor extends
java.beans.FeatureDescriptor
public class java.beans.PropertyChangeEvent extends java.util.EventObject
public interface java.beans.PropertyChangeListener extends java.lang.Object
    implements java.util.EventListener
public class java.beans.PropertyChangeSupport extends java.lang.Object
    implements java.io.Serializable
public class java.beans.PropertyDescriptor extends java.beans.FeatureDescriptor
public interface java.beans.PropertyEditor extends java.lang.Object
public class java.beans.PropertyEditorManager extends java.lang.Object
public class java.beans.PropertyEditorSupport extends java.lang.Object
    implements java.beans.PropertyEditor
public class java.beans.PropertyVetoException extends java.lang.Exception
public class java.beans.SimpleBeanInfo extends java.lang.Object
    implements java.beans.BeanInfo
public interface java.beans.VetoableChangeListener extends java.lang.Object
    implements java.util.EventListener
public class java.beans.VetoableChangeSupport extends java.lang.Object
    implements java.io.Serializable
public interface java.beans.Visibility extends java.lang.Object
```

Package `java.beans.beancontext`

This package, new to JDK1.2, supports *Bean Contexts*, hierarchical containers for JavaBeans. The JDK1.1 JavaBeans model allows containers (tools or applications that use Beans) to discover the capabilities and services provided by a Bean. JDK1.2 Bean Contexts add an inverse capability—they allow Beans to discover the capabilities of the environment in which they are being used.

Listing 3.16 shows all public classes and interfaces in the `java.beans.beancontext` package.

LISTING 3.16 `java.beans.beancontext` Classes and Interfaces List

```
public interface java.beans.beancontext.BeanContext extends
 java.lang.Object (new in 1.2)
    implements java.beans.DesignMode
    implements java.beans.Visibility
    implements java.beans.beancontext.BeanContextChild
    implements java.util.Collection
public interface java.beans.beancontext.BeanContextChild extends
 java.lang.Object (new in 1.2)
public interface java.beans.beancontext.BeanContextChildComponentProxy extends
 java.lang.Object (new in 1.2)
public class java.beans.beancontext.BeanContextChildSupport extends
 java.lang.Object (new in 1.2)
    implements java.beans.beancontext.BeanContextChild
    implements java.beans.beancontext.BeanContextServicesListener
    implements java.io.Serializable
public interface java.beans.beancontext.BeanContextContainerProxy extends
 java.lang.Object (new in 1.2)
public abstract class java.beans.beancontext.BeanContextEvent extends
 java.util.EventObject (new in 1.2)
public class java.beans.beancontext.BeanContextMembershipEvent extends
 java.beans.beancontext.
 BeanContextEvent (new in 1.2)
public interface java.beans.beancontext.BeanContextMembershipListener extends
 java.lang.Object (new in 1.2)
    implements java.util.EventListener
public interface java.beans.beancontext.BeanContextProxy extends
 java.lang.Object (new in 1.2)
public class java.beans.beancontext.BeanContextServiceAvailableEvent extends
 java.beans.beancontext.BeanContextEvent (new in 1.2)
public interface java.beans.beancontext.BeanContextServiceProvider extends
 java.lang.Object (new in 1.2)
public interface java.beans.beancontext.BeanContextServiceProviderBeanInfo
 extends java.lang.Object (new in 1.2)
    implements java.beans.BeanInfo
public class java.beans.beancontext.BeanContextServiceRevokedEvent extends
 java.beans.beancontext.BeanContextEvent (new in 1.2)
public interface java.beans.beancontext.BeanContextServiceRevokedListener
 extends java.lang.Object (new in 1.2)
    implements java.util.EventListener
```

continued on next page

continued from previous page

```
public interface java.beans.beancontext.BeanContextServices extends
 java.lang.Object (new in 1.2)
    implements java.beans.beancontext.BeanContext
    implements java.beans.beancontext.BeanContextServicesListener
public interface java.beans.beancontext.BeanContextServicesListener extends
 java.lang.Object (new in 1.2)
    implements java.beans.beancontext.BeanContextServiceRevokedListener
public class java.beans.beancontext.BeanContextServicesSupport extends
 java.beans.beancontext.
 BeanContextSupport (new in 1.2)
    implements java.beans.beancontext.BeanContextServices
public class java.beans.beancontext.BeanContextServicesSupport.
 BCSSProxyServiceProvider extends java.lang.Object (new in 1.2)
    implements java.beans.beancontext.BeanContextServiceProvider
    implements java.beans.beancontext.BeanContextServiceRevokedListener
public class java.beans.beancontext.BeanContextServicesSupport.
 BCSSServiceProvider extends java.lang.Object (new in 1.2)
    implements java.io.Serializable
public class java.beans.beancontext.BeanContextSupport extends
 java.beans.beancontext.
 BeanContextChildSupport (new in 1.2)
    implements java.beans.PropertyChangeListener
    implements java.beans.VetoableChangeListener
    implements java.beans.beancontext.BeanContext
    implements java.io.Serializable
public final class java.beans.beancontext.BeanContextSupport.BCSIterator
 extends java.lang.Object (new in 1.2)
    implements java.util.Iterator
```

Package `java.io`

An important core package, `java.io`, provides basic file Input/Output (I/O) support. Classes are provided to support byte-oriented I/O, character-oriented I/O, line-oriented I/O, buffering, filtering, I/O to arrays instead of files, and I/O of Java primitive types and serialized Java classes.

One important data and I/O capability introduced in JDK1.1 was support of Internationalization (I18N) by representing multibyte *characters* as distinct entities from *bytes*. This is reflected in the existence of the distinct `byte` and `char` data types, and different `java.io` classes to support the two types. Classes descended from `java.io.InputStream` and `java.io.OutputStream` handle bytes, while those descended from `java.io.Reader` and `java.io.Writer` handle characters.

Each of the `java.io` capabilities comes in its own class—one class provides character-oriented I/O, another provides buffering, and so on. You can achieve combinations of these capabilities by stringing the classes together. For example, an object to provide buffered, line-oriented (including tracking of line numbers) reading of multibyte characters from a file can be created with the following code:

```
LineNumberReader reader =  new LineNumberReader(new FileReader("filename"));
```

Listing 3.17 shows all public classes and interfaces in the `java.io` package.

LISTING 3.17 java.io Classes and Interfaces List

```
public class java.io.BufferedInputStream extends java.io.FilterInputStream
public class java.io.BufferedOutputStream extends java.io.FilterOutputStream
public class java.io.BufferedReader extends java.io.Reader
public class java.io.BufferedWriter extends java.io.Writer
public class java.io.ByteArrayInputStream extends java.io.InputStream
public class java.io.ByteArrayOutputStream extends java.io.OutputStream
public class java.io.CharArrayReader extends java.io.Reader
public class java.io.CharArrayWriter extends java.io.Writer
public class java.io.CharConversionException extends java.io.IOException
public interface java.io.DataInput extends java.lang.Object
public class java.io.DataInputStream extends java.io.FilterInputStream
    implements java.io.DataInput
public interface java.io.DataOutput extends java.lang.Object
public class java.io.DataOutputStream extends java.io.FilterOutputStream
    implements java.io.DataOutput
public class java.io.EOFException extends java.io.IOException
public interface java.io.Externalizable extends java.lang.Object
    implements java.io.Serializable
public class java.io.File extends java.lang.Object
    implements java.io.Serializable
    implements java.lang.Comparable
public final class java.io.FileDescriptor extends java.lang.Object
public interface java.io.FileFilter extends java.lang.Object (new in 1.2)
public class java.io.FileInputStream extends java.io.InputStream
public class java.io.FileNotFoundException extends java.io.IOException
public class java.io.FileOutputStream extends java.io.OutputStream
public final class java.io.FilePermission extends
 java.security.Permission (new in 1.2)
    implements java.io.Serializable
public class java.io.FileReader extends java.io.InputStreamReader
public class java.io.FileWriter extends java.io.OutputStreamWriter
public interface java.io.FilenameFilter extends java.lang.Object
public class java.io.FilterInputStream extends java.io.InputStream
public class java.io.FilterOutputStream extends java.io.OutputStream
public abstract class java.io.FilterReader extends java.io.Reader
public abstract class java.io.FilterWriter extends java.io.Writer
public class java.io.IOException extends java.lang.Exception
public abstract class java.io.InputStream extends java.lang.Object
public class java.io.InputStreamReader extends java.io.Reader
public class java.io.InterruptedIOException extends java.io.IOException
public class java.io.InvalidClassException extends java.io.
 ObjectStreamException
public class java.io.InvalidObjectException extends java.io.
 ObjectStreamException
public class java.io.LineNumberInputStream extends java.io.FilterInputStream
 (deprecated in 1.1)
public class java.io.LineNumberReader extends java.io.BufferedReader
public class java.io.NotActiveException extends java.io.ObjectStreamException
public class java.io.NotSerializableException extends java.io.
 ObjectStreamException
public interface java.io.ObjectInput extends java.lang.Object
```

continued on next page

continued from previous page

```
    implements java.io.DataInput
public class java.io.ObjectInputStream extends java.io.InputStream
    implements java.io.ObjectInput
    implements java.io.ObjectStreamConstants
public abstract class java.io.ObjectInputStream.GetField extends
 java.lang.Object (new in 1.2)
public interface java.io.ObjectInputValidation extends java.lang.Object
public interface java.io.ObjectOutput extends java.lang.Object
    implements java.io.DataOutput
public class java.io.ObjectOutputStream extends java.io.OutputStream
    implements java.io.ObjectOutput
    implements java.io.ObjectStreamConstants
public abstract class java.io.ObjectOutputStream.PutField extends
 java.lang.Object (new in 1.2)
public class java.io.ObjectStreamClass extends java.lang.Object
    implements java.io.Serializable
public interface java.io.ObjectStreamConstants extends java.lang.Object
public abstract class java.io.ObjectStreamException extends java.io.IOException
public class java.io.ObjectStreamField extends java.lang.Object
    implements java.lang.Comparable
public class java.io.OptionalDataException extends java.io.
 ObjectStreamException
public abstract class java.io.OutputStream extends java.lang.Object
public class java.io.OutputStreamWriter extends java.io.Writer
public class java.io.PipedInputStream extends java.io.InputStream
public class java.io.PipedOutputStream extends java.io.OutputStream
public class java.io.PipedReader extends java.io.Reader
public class java.io.PipedWriter extends java.io.Writer
public class java.io.PrintStream extends java.io.FilterOutputStream
public class java.io.PrintWriter extends java.io.Writer
public class java.io.PushbackInputStream extends java.io.FilterInputStream
public class java.io.PushbackReader extends java.io.FilterReader
public class java.io.RandomAccessFile extends java.lang.Object
    implements java.io.DataInput
    implements java.io.DataOutput
public abstract class java.io.Reader extends java.lang.Object
public class java.io.SequenceInputStream extends java.io.InputStream
public interface java.io.Serializable extends java.lang.Object
public final class java.io.SerializablePermission extends java.security.
 BasicPermission (new in 1.2)
public class java.io.StreamCorruptedException extends java.io.
 ObjectStreamException
public class java.io.StreamTokenizer extends java.lang.Object
public class java.io.StringBufferInputStream extends java.io.InputStream
 (deprecated in 1.1)
public class java.io.StringReader extends java.io.Reader
public class java.io.StringWriter extends java.io.Writer
public class java.io.SyncFailedException extends java.io.IOException
public class java.io.UTFDataFormatException extends java.io.IOException
public class java.io.UnsupportedEncodingException extends java.io.IOException
public class java.io.WriteAbortedException extends java.io.
 ObjectStreamException
public abstract class java.io.Writer extends java.lang.Object
```

Package java.lang

This package contains core classes fundamental to the design of the Java language and runtime environment. Among the classes included here are:

- Errors and exceptions that can be generated by the Java Virtual Machine (as distinguished from those generated by class code). For example, the JVM generates `java.lang.ClassFormatError` if it tries to read an invalid Java class file.
- Core language types such as `Class`, `ClassLoader`, `Thread`, and `Runtime`.
- Wrappers around primitive data types, allowing them to be manipulated as classes.

Listing 3.18 shows all public classes and interfaces in the `java.lang` package.

LISTING 3.18 java.lang Classes and Interfaces List

```
public class java.lang.AbstractMethodError extends java.lang.
 IncompatibleClassChangeError
public class java.lang.ArithmeticException extends java.lang.RuntimeException
public class java.lang.ArrayIndexOutOfBoundsException extends java.lang.
 IndexOutOfBoundsException
public class java.lang.ArrayStoreException extends java.lang.RuntimeException
public final class java.lang.Boolean extends java.lang.Object
    implements java.io.Serializable
public final class java.lang.Byte extends java.lang.Number
    implements java.lang.Comparable
public final class java.lang.Character extends java.lang.Object
    implements java.io.Serializable
    implements java.lang.Comparable
public class java.lang.Character.Subset extends java.lang.Object (new in 1.2)
public final class java.lang.Character.UnicodeBlock extends
 java.lang.Character.Subset (new in 1.2)
public final class java.lang.Class extends java.lang.Object
    implements java.io.Serializable
public class java.lang.ClassCastException extends java.lang.RuntimeException
public class java.lang.ClassCircularityError extends java.lang.LinkageError
public class java.lang.ClassFormatError extends java.lang.LinkageError
public abstract class java.lang.ClassLoader extends java.lang.Object
public class java.lang.ClassNotFoundException extends java.lang.Exception
public class java.lang.CloneNotSupportedException extends java.lang.Exception
public interface java.lang.Comparable extends java.lang.Object (new in 1.2)
public final class java.lang.Compiler extends java.lang.Object
public final class java.lang.Double extends java.lang.Number
    implements java.lang.Comparable
public class java.lang.Error extends java.lang.Throwable
public class java.lang.Exception extends java.lang.Throwable
public class java.lang.ExceptionInInitializerError extends
 java.lang.LinkageError
public final class java.lang.Float extends java.lang.Number
    implements java.lang.Comparable
public class java.lang.IllegalAccessError extends java.lang.
```

continued on next page

continued from previous page

```
 IncompatibleClassChangeError
public class java.lang.IllegalAccessException extends java.lang.Exception
public class java.lang.IllegalArgumentException extends
 java.lang.RuntimeException
public class java.lang.IllegalMonitorStateException extends
 java.lang.RuntimeException
public class java.lang.IllegalStateException extends java.lang.RuntimeException
public class java.lang.IllegalThreadStateException extends java.lang.
 IllegalArgumentException
public class java.lang.IncompatibleClassChangeError extends
 java.lang.LinkageError
public class java.lang.IndexOutOfBoundsException extends java.lang.
 RuntimeException
public class java.lang.InheritableThreadLocal extends java.lang.ThreadLocal
 (new in 1.2)
public class java.lang.InstantiationError extends java.lang.
 IncompatibleClassChangeError
public class java.lang.InstantiationException extends java.lang.Exception
public final class java.lang.Integer extends java.lang.Number
    implements java.lang.Comparable
public class java.lang.InternalError extends java.lang.VirtualMachineError
public class java.lang.InterruptedException extends java.lang.Exception
public class java.lang.LinkageError extends java.lang.Error
public final class java.lang.Long extends java.lang.Number
    implements java.lang.Comparable
public final class java.lang.Math extends java.lang.Object
public class java.lang.NegativeArraySizeException extends java.lang.
 RuntimeException
public class java.lang.NoClassDefFoundError extends java.lang.LinkageError
public class java.lang.NoSuchFieldError extends java.lang.
 IncompatibleClassChangeError
public class java.lang.NoSuchFieldException extends java.lang.Exception
public class java.lang.NoSuchMethodError extends java.lang.
 IncompatibleClassChangeError
public class java.lang.NoSuchMethodException extends java.lang.Exception
public class java.lang.NullPointerException extends java.lang.RuntimeException
public abstract class java.lang.Number extends java.lang.Object
    implements java.io.Serializable
public class java.lang.NumberFormatException extends java.lang.
 IllegalArgumentException
public class java.lang.Object extends (none)
public class java.lang.OutOfMemoryError extends java.lang.VirtualMachineError
public class java.lang.Package extends java.lang.Object (new in 1.2)
public abstract class java.lang.Process extends java.lang.Object
public interface java.lang.Runnable extends java.lang.Object
public class java.lang.Runtime extends java.lang.Object
public class java.lang.RuntimeException extends java.lang.Exception
public final class java.lang.RuntimePermission extends java.security.
 BasicPermission (new in 1.2)
public class java.lang.SecurityException extends java.lang.RuntimeException
public class java.lang.SecurityManager extends java.lang.Object
public final class java.lang.Short extends java.lang.Number
    implements java.lang.Comparable
```

```
public class java.lang.StackOverflowError extends java.lang.VirtualMachineError
public final class java.lang.String extends java.lang.Object
    implements java.io.Serializable
    implements java.lang.Comparable
public final class java.lang.StringBuffer extends java.lang.Object
    implements java.io.Serializable
public class java.lang.StringIndexOutOfBoundsException extends java.lang.
 IndexOutOfBoundsException
public final class java.lang.System extends java.lang.Object
public class java.lang.Thread extends java.lang.Object
    implements java.lang.Runnable
public class java.lang.ThreadDeath extends java.lang.Error
public class java.lang.ThreadGroup extends java.lang.Object
public class java.lang.ThreadLocal extends java.lang.Object (new in 1.2)
public class java.lang.Throwable extends java.lang.Object
    implements java.io.Serializable
public class java.lang.UnknownError extends java.lang.VirtualMachineError
public class java.lang.UnsatisfiedLinkError extends java.lang.LinkageError
public class java.lang.UnsupportedClassVersionError extends java.lang.
 ClassFormatError (new in 1.2)
public class java.lang.UnsupportedOperationException extends java.lang.
 RuntimeException (new in 1.2)
public class java.lang.VerifyError extends java.lang.LinkageError
public abstract class java.lang.VirtualMachineError extends java.lang.Error
public final class java.lang.Void extends java.lang.Object
```

Package `java.lang.ref`

This package, new to JDK1.2, introduces the limited capability for an application to interact with the garbage collector. The `java.lang.ref` classes provide three new types of object references: *soft*, *weak*, and *phantom*.

Ordinary object references in Java (`Foo foo = new Foo()`) are *hard references*; the objects will not be garbage-collected until all such references disappear (for example, when `foo` goes out of scope).

The behavior of hard references is not always desirable—it is sometimes useful to create a reference that does not prevent its data from being garbage-collected. For example, you may need to construct a table of objects currently being used by an application; when the object is no longer referenced *outside the table*, it can be garbage-collected.

These classes give you such a capability. JDK1.2 also includes some utility classes that use the capability. For example, the `java.util.WeakHashMap` class uses `java.lang.ref.WeakReference` to implement an associative map that automatically removes entries no longer referenced anywhere outside the map.

Listing 3.19 shows all public classes and interfaces in the `java.lang.ref` package.

LISTING 3.19 `java.lang.ref` Classes and Interfaces List

```
public class java.lang.ref.PhantomReference extends java.lang.ref.Reference
 (new in 1.2)
public abstract class java.lang.ref.Reference extends java.lang.Object
 (new in 1.2)
public class java.lang.ref.ReferenceQueue extends java.lang.Object (new in 1.2)
public class java.lang.ref.SoftReference extends java.lang.ref.Reference
 (new in 1.2)
public class java.lang.ref.WeakReference extends java.lang.ref.Reference
 (new in 1.2)
```

Package `java.lang.reflect`

This package allows applications to *look at* classes—to learn the details of what fields, methods, constructors, and interfaces a class provides. Java uses this *reflection* mechanism with JavaBeans to ascertain what capabilities a Bean supports. In Chapter 47, "DumpClass: A Tool for Querying Class Structure," we present a utility that uses these classes to provide a dump of useful API information about any class.

Listing 3.20 shows all public classes and interfaces in the `java.lang.reflect` package.

LISTING 3.20 `java.lang.reflect` Classes and Interfaces List

```
public class java.lang.reflect.AccessibleObject extends java.lang.Object
 (new in 1.2)
public final class java.lang.reflect.Array extends java.lang.Object
public final class java.lang.reflect.Constructor extends java.lang.reflect.
 AccessibleObject
    implements java.lang.reflect.Member
public final class java.lang.reflect.Field extends java.lang.reflect.
 AccessibleObject
    implements java.lang.reflect.Member
public class java.lang.reflect.InvocationTargetException extends
 java.lang.Exception
public interface java.lang.reflect.Member extends java.lang.Object
public final class java.lang.reflect.Method extends java.lang.reflect.
 AccessibleObject
    implements java.lang.reflect.Member
public class java.lang.reflect.Modifier extends java.lang.Object
public final class java.lang.reflect.ReflectPermission extends java.security.
 BasicPermission (new in 1.2)
```

Package `java.math`

This package provides arbitrary-precision floating point and integer arithmetic.

Listing 3.21 shows all public classes and interfaces in the `java.math` package.

LISTING 3.21 `java.math` Classes and Interfaces List

```
public class java.math.BigDecimal extends java.lang.Number
    implements java.lang.Comparable
public class java.math.BigInteger extends java.lang.Number
    implements java.lang.Comparable
```

Package `java.net`

The `java.net` package is home to Java's core network functionality. Java is a highly Web-friendly programming environment, with support for easy manipulation of URLs and extensible classes for interpretation and handling of their contents.

Listing 3.22 shows all public classes and interfaces in the `java.net` package.

LISTING 3.22 `java.net` Classes and Interfaces List

```
public abstract class java.net.Authenticator extends java.lang.Object
 (new in 1.2)
public class java.net.BindException extends java.net.SocketException
public class java.net.ConnectException extends java.net.SocketException
public abstract class java.net.ContentHandler extends java.lang.Object
public interface java.net.ContentHandlerFactory extends java.lang.Object
public final class java.net.DatagramPacket extends java.lang.Object
public class java.net.DatagramSocket extends java.lang.Object
public abstract class java.net.DatagramSocketImpl extends java.lang.Object
    implements java.net.SocketOptions
public interface java.net.FileNameMap extends java.lang.Object
public abstract class java.net.HttpURLConnection extends java.net.URLConnection
public final class java.net.InetAddress extends java.lang.Object
    implements java.io.Serializable
public abstract class java.net.JarURLConnection extends java.net.URLConnection
 (new in 1.2)
public class java.net.MalformedURLException extends java.io.IOException
public class java.net.MulticastSocket extends java.net.DatagramSocket
public final class java.net.NetPermission extends java.security.
 BasicPermission (new in 1.2)
public class java.net.NoRouteToHostException extends java.net.SocketException
public final class java.net.PasswordAuthentication extends java.lang.Object
 (new in 1.2)
public class java.net.ProtocolException extends java.io.IOException
public class java.net.ServerSocket extends java.lang.Object
public class java.net.Socket extends java.lang.Object
public class java.net.SocketException extends java.io.IOException
public abstract class java.net.SocketImpl extends java.lang.Object
    implements java.net.SocketOptions
public interface java.net.SocketImplFactory extends java.lang.Object
public interface java.net.SocketOptions extends java.lang.Object
public final class java.net.SocketPermission extends java.security.Permission
(new in 1.2)
```

continued on next page

continued from previous page

```
    implements java.io.Serializable
public final class java.net.URL extends java.lang.Object
    implements java.io.Serializable
public class java.net.URLClassLoader extends java.security.SecureClassLoader
 (new in 1.2)
public abstract class java.net.URLConnection extends java.lang.Object
public class java.net.URLDecoder extends java.lang.Object (new in 1.2)
public class java.net.URLEncoder extends java.lang.Object
public abstract class java.net.URLStreamHandler extends java.lang.Object
public interface java.net.URLStreamHandlerFactory extends java.lang.Object
public class java.net.UnknownHostException extends java.io.IOException
public class java.net.UnknownServiceException extends java.io.IOException
```

Package `java.rmi`

This package supports *Remote Method Invocation*, the object-flavored successor to Sun's RPC (*Remote Procedure Call*) mechanism. RMI allows an object to invoke a method on another object over the network, just as the older RPC allows procedure invocation over the network.

RMI's competitors are the widely adopted CORBA and DCOM network component models. And although CORBA and DCOM are platform-neutral, RMI is closely tied to Java's architecture. Its main advantages are as follows:

- CORBA and DCOM require that arguments and return values for method invocations be translated to a platform-neutral representation; no such translation is required for RMI. (Of course, Java objects already enjoy, by definition, a platform-neutral representation.)
- Java objects can be passed as parameters and return values. If a participant in an RMI transaction encounters an unknown object type, it can request information about the class.
- RMI supports distributed garbage collection over the network.

If you need a Java-specific network component model, use RMI. For a platform-neutral model, JDK1.2 offers extensive support for CORBA in the `org.omg.CORBA` packages and subpackages.

Listing 3.23 shows all public classes and interfaces in the `java.rmi` package.

LISTING 3.23 `java.rmi` Classes and Interfaces List

```
public class java.rmi.AccessException extends java.rmi.RemoteException
public class java.rmi.AlreadyBoundException extends java.lang.Exception
public class java.rmi.ConnectException extends java.rmi.RemoteException
public class java.rmi.ConnectIOException extends java.rmi.RemoteException
public class java.rmi.MarshalException extends java.rmi.RemoteException
public final class java.rmi.MarshalledObject extends java.lang.Object
 (new in 1.2)
    implements java.io.Serializable
public final class java.rmi.Naming extends java.lang.Object
public class java.rmi.NoSuchObjectException extends java.rmi.RemoteException
public class java.rmi.NotBoundException extends java.lang.Exception
```

```
public class java.rmi.RMISecurityException extends java.lang.
 SecurityException (deprecated in 1.2)
public class java.rmi.RMISecurityManager extends java.lang.SecurityManager
public class java.rmi.RemoteException extends java.io.IOException
public class java.rmi.ServerError extends java.rmi.RemoteException
public class java.rmi.ServerException extends java.rmi.RemoteException
public class java.rmi.ServerRuntimeException extends java.rmi.
 RemoteException (deprecated in 1.2)
public class java.rmi.StubNotFoundException extends java.rmi.RemoteException
public class java.rmi.UnexpectedException extends java.rmi.RemoteException
public class java.rmi.UnknownHostException extends java.rmi.RemoteException
public class java.rmi.UnmarshalException extends java.rmi.RemoteException
```

Package `java.rmi.activation`

This package, part of RMI, supports the use of persistent remote components. This new JDK1.2 capability allows Java applications to create remote objects that can be executed as they are needed without having to run all the time (as in JDK1.1).

Listing 3.24 shows all public classes and interfaces in the `java.rmi.activation` package.

LISTING 3.24 `java.rmi.activation` Classes and Interfaces List

```
public abstract class java.rmi.activation.Activatable extends java.rmi.server.
 RemoteServer (new in 1.2)
public class java.rmi.activation.ActivateFailedException extends java.rmi.
 RemoteException (new in 1.2)
public final class java.rmi.activation.ActivationDesc extends java.lang.Object
 (new in 1.2)
    implements java.io.Serializable
public class java.rmi.activation.ActivationException extends java.lang.Exception
(new in 1.2)
public abstract class java.rmi.activation.ActivationGroup extends java.rmi.server.
 UnicastRemoteObject (new in 1.2)
    implements java.rmi.activation.ActivationInstantiator
public final class java.rmi.activation.ActivationGroupDesc extends java.lang.
 Object (new in 1.2)
    implements java.io.Serializable
public class java.rmi.activation.ActivationGroupDesc.CommandEnvironment extends
 java.lang.Object (new in 1.2)
    implements java.io.Serializable
public class java.rmi.activation.ActivationGroupID extends java.lang.Object
 (new in 1.2)
    implements java.io.Serializable
public class java.rmi.activation.ActivationID extends java.lang.Object
 (new in 1.2)
    implements java.io.Serializable
public interface java.rmi.activation.ActivationInstantiator extends java.lang.
 Object (new in 1.2)
    implements java.rmi.Remote
public interface java.rmi.activation.ActivationMonitor extends java.lang.
 Object (new in 1.2)
```

continued on next page

continued from previous page

```
    implements java.rmi.Remote
public interface java.rmi.activation.ActivationSystem extends java.lang.
 Object (new in 1.2)
    implements java.rmi.Remote
public interface java.rmi.activation.Activator extends java.lang.Object
 (new in 1.2)
    implements java.rmi.Remote
public class java.rmi.activation.UnknownGroupException extends java.rmi.
 activation.
 ActivationException (new in 1.2)
public class java.rmi.activation.UnknownObjectException extends java.rmi.
 activation.ActivationException (new in 1.2)
```

Package `java.rmi.dgc`

This package, part of RMI, supports distributed garbage collection. It supports the capability of RMI servers to track the use of objects by remote clients, and to garbage-collect those that are no longer in use.

Listing 3.25 shows all public classes and interfaces in the `java.rmi.dgc` package.

LISTING 3.25 `java.rmi.dgc` Classes and Interfaces List

```
public interface java.rmi.dgc.DGC extends java.lang.Object
    implements java.rmi.Remote
public final class java.rmi.dgc.Lease extends java.lang.Object
    implements java.io.Serializable
public final class java.rmi.dgc.VMID extends java.lang.Object
    implements java.io.Serializable
```

Package `java.rmi.registry`

This package, part of RMI, supports access to the *registry* - the mechanism through which networked components register their presence and are discovered by clients.

Listing 3.26 shows all public classes and interfaces in the `java.rmi.registry` package.

LISTING 3.26 `java.rmi.registry` Classes and Interfaces List

```
public final class java.rmi.registry.LocateRegistry extends java.lang.Object
public interface java.rmi.registry.Registry extends java.lang.Object
    implements java.rmi.Remote
public interface java.rmi.registry.RegistryHandler extends java.lang.Object
 (deprecated in 1.2)
```

Package `java.rmi.server`

This package, part of RMI, provides the classes needed to support a networked RMI server—they provide the basic plumbing connecting RMI clients to RMI servers.

Listing 3.27 shows all public classes and interfaces in the `java.rmi.server` package.

LISTING 3.27 `java.rmi.server` Classes and Interfaces List

```
public class java.rmi.server.ExportException extends java.rmi.RemoteException
public interface java.rmi.server.LoaderHandler extends java.lang.Object
 (deprecated in 1.2)
public class java.rmi.server.LogStream extends java.io.PrintStream
 (deprecated in 1.2)
public final class java.rmi.server.ObjID extends java.lang.Object
    implements java.io.Serializable
public class java.rmi.server.Operation extends java.lang.Object
 (deprecated in 1.2)
public class java.rmi.server.RMIClassLoader extends java.lang.Object
public interface java.rmi.server.RMIClientSocketFactory extends java.lang.
 Object (new in 1.2)
public interface java.rmi.server.RMIFailureHandler extends java.lang.Object
public interface java.rmi.server.RMIServerSocketFactory extends java.lang.
 Object (new in 1.2)
public abstract class java.rmi.server.RMISocketFactory extends java.lang.Object
    implements java.rmi.server.RMIClientSocketFactory
    implements java.rmi.server.RMIServerSocketFactory
public interface java.rmi.server.RemoteCall extends java.lang.Object
 (deprecated in 1.2)
public abstract class java.rmi.server.RemoteObject extends java.lang.Object
    implements java.io.Serializable
    implements java.rmi.Remote
public interface java.rmi.server.RemoteRef extends java.lang.Object
    implements java.io.Externalizable
public abstract class java.rmi.server.RemoteServer extends java.rmi.server.
 RemoteObject
public abstract class java.rmi.server.RemoteStub extends java.rmi.server.
 RemoteObject
public class java.rmi.server.ServerCloneException extends java.lang.
 CloneNotSupportedException
public class java.rmi.server.ServerNotActiveException extends java.lang.
 Exception
public interface java.rmi.server.ServerRef extends java.lang.Object
    implements java.rmi.server.RemoteRef
public interface java.rmi.server.Skeleton extends java.lang.Object
 (deprecated in 1.2)
public class java.rmi.server.SkeletonMismatchException extends java.rmi.
 RemoteException (deprecated in 1.2)
public class java.rmi.server.SkeletonNotFoundException extends java.rmi.
 RemoteException (deprecated in 1.2)
public class java.rmi.server.SocketSecurityException extends java.rmi.server.
 ExportException
public final class java.rmi.server.UID extends java.lang.Object
    implements java.io.Serializable
public class java.rmi.server.UnicastRemoteObject extends java.rmi.server.
 RemoteServer
public interface java.rmi.server.Unreferenced extends java.lang.Object
```

Package java.security

This package, which has grown significantly in JDK1.2, is the main interface to the Java security framework.

Security is a fundamental design component of the Java platform and has undergone large changes with each Java release. The changes for JDK1.2 included introduction of a fine-grained access control mechanism, in which policies can be defined to precisely control the privileges granted to applications and applets: read and/or write access to files or directories, permissions to use some or all available networking capabilities, and so on.

By default, Java applications on Linux run with capabilities equivalent to those of the user running the application: If you can use a certain feature or write a certain file from C++, you can do it from Java. The mechanisms provided by `java.security` allow for finer control of those permissions: Users can be granted or denied specific permissions based on systemwide configuration, per-user configuration, and the degree of trust assigned to the application being run.

Java cannot, of course, override Linux security mechanisms to give users extra capabilities—nothing in `java.security` can grant `root` user privileges to an ordinary user. But by supporting detailed security constraints on applications, `java.security` provides a new and useful level of protection when running untrusted applications.

Java's security mechanism also handles cryptographic operations, certification of trusted sources, and class loading.

Listing 3.28 shows all public classes and interfaces in the `java.security` package.

LISTING 3.28 `java.security` Classes and Interfaces List

```
public final class java.security.AccessControlContext extends java.lang.Object
 new in 1.2)
public class java.security.AccessControlException extends java.lang.
 SecurityException (new in 1.2)
public final class java.security.AccessController extends java.lang.Object
 (new in 1.2)
public class java.security.AlgorithmParameterGenerator extends java.lang.Object
(new in 1.2)
public abstract class java.security.AlgorithmParameterGeneratorSpi extends
 java.lang.Object (new in 1.2)
public class java.security.AlgorithmParameters extends java.lang.Object
 (new in 1.2)
public abstract class java.security.AlgorithmParametersSpi extends java.lang.
 Object (new in 1.2)
public final class java.security.AllPermission extends java.security.Permission
(new in 1.2)
public abstract class java.security.BasicPermission extends java.security.
Permission (new in 1.2)
    implements java.io.Serializable
public interface java.security.Certificate extends java.lang.Object
 (deprecated in 1.2)
```

```
public class java.security.CodeSource extends java.lang.Object (new in 1.2)
    implements java.io.Serializable
public class java.security.DigestException extends java.security.
 GeneralSecurityException
public class java.security.DigestInputStream extends java.io.FilterInputStream
public class java.security.DigestOutputStream extends java.io.
 FilterOutputStream
public class java.security.GeneralSecurityException extends java.lang.
 Exception (new in 1.2)
public interface java.security.Guard extends java.lang.Object (new in 1.2)
public class java.security.GuardedObject extends java.lang.Object (new in 1.2)
    implements java.io.Serializable
public abstract class java.security.Identity extends java.lang.Object
(deprecated in 1.2)
    implements java.io.Serializable
    implements java.security.Principal
public abstract class java.security.IdentityScope extends java.security.Identity
 (deprecated in 1.2)
public class java.security.InvalidAlgorithmParameterException extends
 java.security.GeneralSecurityException (new in 1.2)
public class java.security.InvalidKeyException extends java.security.KeyException
public class java.security.InvalidParameterException extends java.lang.
 IllegalArgumentException
public interface java.security.Key extends java.lang.Object
    implements java.io.Serializable
public class java.security.KeyException extends java.security.
 GeneralSecurityException
public class java.security.KeyFactory extends java.lang.Object (new in 1.2)
public abstract class java.security.KeyFactorySpi extends java.lang.Object
 (new in 1.2)
public class java.security.KeyManagementException extends java.security.
 KeyException
public final class java.security.KeyPair extends java.lang.Object
    implements java.io.Serializable
public abstract class java.security.KeyPairGenerator extends java.security.
 KeyPairGeneratorSpi
public abstract class java.security.KeyPairGeneratorSpi extends java.lang.
 Object (new in 1.2)
public class java.security.KeyStore extends java.lang.Object (new in 1.2)
public class java.security.KeyStoreException extends java.security.
 GeneralSecurityException (new in 1.2)
public abstract class java.security.KeyStoreSpi extends java.lang.Object
 (new in 1.2)
public abstract class java.security.MessageDigest extends java.security.
 MessageDigestSpi
public abstract class java.security.MessageDigestSpi extends java.lang.Object
 (new in 1.2)
public class java.security.NoSuchAlgorithmException extends java.security.
 GeneralSecurityException
public class java.security.NoSuchProviderException extends java.security.
 GeneralSecurityException
public abstract class java.security.Permission extends java.lang.Object
(new in 1.2)
```

continued on next page

continued from previous page

```
        implements java.io.Serializable
        implements java.security.Guard
    public abstract class java.security.PermissionCollection extends java.lang.Object
     (new in 1.2)
        implements java.io.Serializable
    public final class java.security.Permissions extends java.security.
     PermissionCollection (new in 1.2)
        implements java.io.Serializable
    public abstract class java.security.Policy extends java.lang.Object
    (new in 1.2)
    public interface java.security.Principal extends java.lang.Object
    public interface java.security.PrivateKey extends java.lang.Object
        implements java.security.Key
    public interface java.security.PrivilegedAction extends java.lang.Object
     (new in 1.2)
    public class java.security.PrivilegedActionException extends java.lang.
     Exception (new in 1.2)
    public interface java.security.PrivilegedExceptionAction extends java.lang.
     Object (new in 1.2)
    public class java.security.ProtectionDomain extends java.lang.Object (new in 1.2)
    public abstract class java.security.Provider extends java.util.Properties
    public class java.security.ProviderException extends java.lang.RuntimeException
    public interface java.security.PublicKey extends java.lang.Object
        implements java.security.Key
    public class java.security.SecureClassLoader extends java.lang.ClassLoader
    (new in 1.2)
    public class java.security.SecureRandom extends java.util.Random
    public abstract class java.security.SecureRandomSpi extends java.lang.Object
     (new in 1.2)
        implements java.io.Serializable
    public final class java.security.Security extends java.lang.Object
    public final class java.security.SecurityPermission extends java.security.
     BasicPermission (new in 1.2)
    public abstract class java.security.Signature extends java.security.
     SignatureSpi
    public class java.security.SignatureException extends java.security.
     GeneralSecurityException
    public abstract class java.security.SignatureSpi extends java.lang.Object
     (new in 1.2)
    public final class java.security.SignedObject extends java.lang.Object
     (new in 1.2)
        implements java.io.Serializable
    public abstract class java.security.Signer extends java.security.Identity
     (deprecated in 1.2)
    public class java.security.UnrecoverableKeyException extends java.security.
     GeneralSecurityException (new in 1.2)
    public final class java.security.UnresolvedPermission extends java.security.
     Permission (new in 1.2)
        implements java.io.Serializable
```

Package java.security.acl

This package, an obsolete part of `java.security`, is superceded by classes in the JDK1.2 `java.security`.

Listing 3.29 shows all public classes and interfaces in the `java.security.acl` package.

LISTING 3.29 `java.security.acl` Classes and Interfaces List

```
public interface java.security.acl.Acl extends java.lang.Object
    implements java.security.acl.Owner
public interface java.security.acl.AclEntry extends java.lang.Object
    implements java.lang.Cloneable
public class java.security.acl.AclNotFoundException extends java.lang.Exception
public interface java.security.acl.Group extends java.lang.Object
    implements java.security.Principal
public class java.security.acl.LastOwnerException extends java.lang.Exception
public class java.security.acl.NotOwnerException extends java.lang.Exception
public interface java.security.acl.Owner extends java.lang.Object
public interface java.security.acl.Permission extends java.lang.Object
```

Package java.security.cert

This package, part of `java.security`, supports *certificates*—encrypted documents from a trusted source that guarantee the validity of a public encryption/decryption key. This is the technology that underlies, among other things, the *Secure Sockets Layer* (SSL) encryption used in Web browsers.

Listing 3.30 shows all public classes and interfaces in the `java.security.cert` package.

LISTING 3.30 `java.security.cert` Classes and Interfaces List

```
public abstract class java.security.cert.CRL extends java.lang.Object
 (new in 1.2)
public class java.security.cert.CRLException extends java.security.
 GeneralSecurityException (new in 1.2)
public abstract class java.security.cert.Certificate extends java.lang.Object
 (new in 1.2)
public class java.security.cert.CertificateEncodingException extends
 java.security.cert.CertificateException (new in 1.2)
public class java.security.cert.CertificateException extends java.security.
 GeneralSecurityException (new in 1.2)
public class java.security.cert.CertificateExpiredException extends
 java.security.cert.CertificateException (new in 1.2)
public class java.security.cert.CertificateFactory extends java.lang.Object
 (new in 1.2)
public abstract class java.security.cert.CertificateFactorySpi extends
 java.lang.Object (new in 1.2)
public class java.security.cert.CertificateNotYetValidException extends
```

continued on next page

continued from previous page

```
 java.security.cert.CertificateException (new in 1.2)
public class java.security.cert.CertificateParsingException extends
 java.security.cert.CertificateException (new in 1.2)
public abstract class java.security.cert.X509CRL extends java.security.cert.CRL
 (new in 1.2)
    implements java.security.cert.X509Extension
public abstract class java.security.cert.X509CRLEntry extends java.lang.Object
 (new in 1.2)
    implements java.security.cert.X509Extension
public abstract class java.security.cert.X509Certificate extends java.security.
 cert.Certificate (new in 1.2)
    implements java.security.cert.X509Extension
public interface java.security.cert.X509Extension extends java.lang.Object
 (new in 1.2)
```

Package `java.security.interfaces`

This package, part of `java.security`, defines interfaces needed for generation of RSA and DSA-type cryptographic keys.

Listing 3.31 shows all public classes and interfaces in the `java.security.interfaces` package.

LISTING 3.31 `java.security.interfaces` Classes and Interfaces List

```
public interface java.security.interfaces.DSAKey extends java.lang.Object
public interface java.security.interfaces.DSAKeyPairGenerator extends
 java.lang.Object
public interface java.security.interfaces.DSAParams extends java.lang.Object
public interface java.security.interfaces.DSAPrivateKey extends
 java.lang.Object
    implements java.security.PrivateKey
    implements java.security.interfaces.DSAKey
public interface java.security.interfaces.DSAPublicKey extends java.lang.Object
    implements java.security.PublicKey
    implements java.security.interfaces.DSAKey
public interface java.security.interfaces.RSAPrivateCrtKey extends
 java.lang.Object (new in 1.2)
    implements java.security.interfaces.RSAPrivateKey
public interface java.security.interfaces.RSAPrivateKey extends
 java.lang.Object (new in 1.2)
    implements java.security.PrivateKey
public interface java.security.interfaces.RSAPublicKey extends
 java.lang.Object (new in 1.2)
    implements java.security.PublicKey
Package java.security.spec
```

Package `java.security.spec`

This package, part of `java.security`, is new to JDK1.2 and supports key specifications and algorithm parameters for encryption specifications.

Listing 3.32 shows all public classes and interfaces in the `java.security.spec` package.

LISTING 3.32 `java.security.spec` Classes and Interfaces List

```
public class java.security.spec.DSAParameterSpec extends java.lang.Object
 (new in 1.2)
    implements java.security.interfaces.DSAParams
    implements java.security.spec.AlgorithmParameterSpec
public class java.security.spec.DSAPrivateKeySpec extends java.lang.Object
 (new in 1.2)
    implements java.security.spec.KeySpec
public class java.security.spec.DSAPublicKeySpec extends java.lang.Object
 (new in 1.2)
    implements java.security.spec.KeySpec
public abstract class java.security.spec.EncodedKeySpec extends java.lang.
 Object (new in 1.2)
    implements java.security.spec.KeySpec
public class java.security.spec.InvalidKeySpecException extends java.security.
 GeneralSecurityException (new in 1.2)
public class java.security.spec.InvalidParameterSpecException extends
 java.security.GeneralSecurityException (new in 1.2)
public class java.security.spec.PKCS8EncodedKeySpec extends java.security.spec.
 EncodedKeySpec (new in 1.2)
public class java.security.spec.RSAPrivateCrtKeySpec extends java.security.
 spec.RSAPrivateKeySpec (new in 1.2)
public class java.security.spec.RSAPrivateKeySpec extends java.lang.Object
 (new in 1.2)
    implements java.security.spec.KeySpec
public class java.security.spec.RSAPublicKeySpec extends java.lang.Object
(new in 1.2)
    implements java.security.spec.KeySpec
public class java.security.spec.X509EncodedKeySpec extends java.security.spec.
 EncodedKeySpec (new in 1.2)
```

Package `java.sql`

This package provides the JDBC interface for Java access to databases. It includes the necessary classes for constructing and executing SQL (Structured Query Language) queries against a DBMS.

To use a particular database, you must obtain a JDBC *driver* for that database—such drivers are available for almost all DBMSes available on Linux. In Chapter 67, "Java, Linux, and Three-Tiered Architectures," we will explore a simple database query application using the free MySQL database.

Listing 3.33 shows all public classes and interfaces in the `java.sql` package.

LISTING 3.33 `java.sql` Classes and Interfaces List

```
public interface java.sql.Array extends java.lang.Object (new in 1.2)
public class java.sql.BatchUpdateException extends java.sql.SQLException
 (new in 1.2)
public interface java.sql.Blob extends java.lang.Object (new in 1.2)
public interface java.sql.CallableStatement extends java.lang.Object
    implements java.sql.PreparedStatement
public interface java.sql.Clob extends java.lang.Object (new in 1.2)
public interface java.sql.Connection extends java.lang.Object
public class java.sql.DataTruncation extends java.sql.SQLWarning
public interface java.sql.DatabaseMetaData extends java.lang.Object
public class java.sql.Date extends java.util.Date
public interface java.sql.Driver extends java.lang.Object
public class java.sql.DriverManager extends java.lang.Object
public class java.sql.DriverPropertyInfo extends java.lang.Object
public interface java.sql.PreparedStatement extends java.lang.Object
    implements java.sql.Statement
public interface java.sql.Ref extends java.lang.Object (new in 1.2)
public interface java.sql.ResultSet extends java.lang.Object
public interface java.sql.ResultSetMetaData extends java.lang.Object
public interface java.sql.SQLData extends java.lang.Object (new in 1.2)
public class java.sql.SQLException extends java.lang.Exception
public interface java.sql.SQLInput extends java.lang.Object (new in 1.2)
public interface java.sql.SQLOutput extends java.lang.Object (new in 1.2)
public class java.sql.SQLWarning extends java.sql.SQLException
public interface java.sql.Statement extends java.lang.Object
public interface java.sql.Struct extends java.lang.Object (new in 1.2)
public class java.sql.Time extends java.util.Date
public class java.sql.Timestamp extends java.util.Date
public class java.sql.Types extends java.lang.Object
```

Package `java.text`

The `java.text` package handles localized representation of dates, text, numbers, and messages. By delegating the problems of character iteration, number and date formatting and parsing, and text collation to classes that are loaded at runtime, this package allows you to write locale-independent code and let the Java handle much of the localization work.

Listing 3.34 shows all public classes and interfaces in the `java.text` package.

LISTING 3.34 `java.text` Classes and Interfaces List

```
public class java.text.Annotation extends java.lang.Object (new in 1.2)
public interface java.text.AttributedCharacterIterator extends java.lang.Object
 (new in 1.2)
    implements java.text.CharacterIterator
public class java.text.AttributedCharacterIterator.Attribute extends
 java.lang.Object (new in 1.2)
    implements java.io.Serializable
public class java.text.AttributedString extends java.lang.Object (new in 1.2)
public abstract class java.text.BreakIterator extends java.lang.Object
    implements java.lang.Cloneable
```

```
public interface java.text.CharacterIterator extends java.lang.Object
    implements java.lang.Cloneable
public class java.text.ChoiceFormat extends java.text.NumberFormat
public final class java.text.CollationElementIterator extends java.lang.Object
public final class java.text.CollationKey extends java.lang.Object
    implements java.lang.Comparable
public abstract class java.text.Collator extends java.lang.Object
    implements java.lang.Cloneable
    implements java.util.Comparator
public abstract class java.text.DateFormat extends java.text.Format
public class java.text.DateFormatSymbols extends java.lang.Object
    implements java.io.Serializable
    implements java.lang.Cloneable
public class java.text.DecimalFormat extends java.text.NumberFormat
public final class java.text.DecimalFormatSymbols extends java.lang.Object
    implements java.io.Serializable
    implements java.lang.Cloneable
public class java.text.FieldPosition extends java.lang.Object
public abstract class java.text.Format extends java.lang.Object
    implements java.io.Serializable
    implements java.lang.Cloneable
public class java.text.MessageFormat extends java.text.Format
public abstract class java.text.NumberFormat extends java.text.Format
public class java.text.ParseException extends java.lang.Exception
public class java.text.ParsePosition extends java.lang.Object
public class java.text.RuleBasedCollator extends java.text.Collator
public class java.text.SimpleDateFormat extends java.text.DateFormat
public final class java.text.StringCharacterIterator extends java.lang.Object
    implements java.text.CharacterIterator
```

Package `java.util`

The `java.util` package is an assortment of extremely useful classes, including

- `java.util.Date`—Representation of time and date.
- `java.util.Calendar`—Localized formatting, parsing, and interpretation of date and time fields. A subclass of `Calendar` is provided for the Gregorian calendar, and future support is intended for various lunar and national calendars.
- `java.util.Bitset`—Arbitrary-length bit arrays.
- Properties and resources—Management of persistent properties and locale-specific resources (such as localized messages).
- `java.util.StringTokenizer`—A simple tokenizer for extracting words from strings.
- `java.util.Random`—Random number generation.
- The Collections Classes—Classes for lists, arrays, balanced trees, sets, and hashmaps—so you never have to reinvent those particular wheels.

Listing 3.35 shows all public classes and interfaces in the `java.util` package.

LISTING 3.35 java.util Classes and Interfaces List

```
public abstract class java.util.AbstractCollection extends java.lang.Object
 (new in 1.2)
    implements java.util.Collection
public abstract class java.util.AbstractList extends java.util.
 AbstractCollection (new in 1.2)
    implements java.util.List
public abstract class java.util.AbstractMap extends java.lang.Object
 (new in 1.2)
    implements java.util.Map
public abstract class java.util.AbstractSequentialList extends java.util.
 AbstractList (new in 1.2)
public abstract class java.util.AbstractSet extends java.util.
 AbstractCollection (new in 1.2)
    implements java.util.Set
public class java.util.ArrayList extends java.util.AbstractList (new in 1.2)
    implements java.io.Serializable
    implements java.lang.Cloneable
    implements java.util.List
public class java.util.Arrays extends java.lang.Object (new in 1.2)
public class java.util.BitSet extends java.lang.Object
    implements java.io.Serializable
    implements java.lang.Cloneable
public abstract class java.util.Calendar extends java.lang.Object
    implements java.io.Serializable
    implements java.lang.Cloneable
public interface java.util.Collection extends java.lang.Object (new in 1.2)
public class java.util.Collections extends java.lang.Object (new in 1.2)
public interface java.util.Comparator extends java.lang.Object (new in 1.2)
public class java.util.ConcurrentModificationException extends java.lang.
 RuntimeException (new in 1.2)
public class java.util.Date extends java.lang.Object
    implements java.io.Serializable
    implements java.lang.Cloneable
    implements java.lang.Comparable
public abstract class java.util.Dictionary extends java.lang.Object
public class java.util.EmptyStackException extends java.lang.RuntimeException
public interface java.util.Enumeration extends java.lang.Object
public class java.util.EventObject extends java.lang.Object
    implements java.io.Serializable
public class java.util.GregorianCalendar extends java.util.Calendar
public class java.util.HashMap extends java.util.AbstractMap (new in 1.2)
    implements java.io.Serializable
    implements java.lang.Cloneable
    implements java.util.Map
public class java.util.HashSet extends java.util.AbstractSet (new in 1.2)
    implements java.io.Serializable
    implements java.lang.Cloneable
    implements java.util.Set
public class java.util.Hashtable extends java.util.Dictionary
    implements java.io.Serializable
    implements java.lang.Cloneable
    implements java.util.Map
public interface java.util.Iterator extends java.lang.Object (new in 1.2)
public class java.util.LinkedList extends java.util.AbstractSequentialList
```

```
 (new in 1.2)
    implements java.io.Serializable
    implements java.lang.Cloneable
    implements java.util.List
public interface java.util.List extends java.lang.Object (new in 1.2)
    implements java.util.Collection
public interface java.util.ListIterator extends java.lang.Object (new in 1.2)
    implements java.util.Iterator
public abstract class java.util.ListResourceBundle extends java.util.
 ResourceBundle
public final class java.util.Locale extends java.lang.Object
    implements java.io.Serializable
    implements java.lang.Cloneable
public interface java.util.Map extends java.lang.Object (new in 1.2)
public interface java.util.Map.Entry extends java.lang.Object (new in 1.2)
public class java.util.MissingResourceException extends java.lang.
 RuntimeException
public class java.util.NoSuchElementException extends java.lang.
 RuntimeException
public class java.util.Observable extends java.lang.Object
public interface java.util.Observer extends java.lang.Object
public class java.util.Properties extends java.util.Hashtable
public final class java.util.PropertyPermission extends java.security.
 BasicPermission (new in 1.2)
public class java.util.PropertyResourceBundle extends java.util.ResourceBundle
public class java.util.Random extends java.lang.Object
    implements java.io.Serializable
public abstract class java.util.ResourceBundle extends java.lang.Object
public interface java.util.Set extends java.lang.Object (new in 1.2)
    implements java.util.Collection
public class java.util.SimpleTimeZone extends java.util.TimeZone
public interface java.util.SortedMap extends java.lang.Object (new in 1.2)
    implements java.util.Map
public interface java.util.SortedSet extends java.lang.Object (new in 1.2)
    implements java.util.Set
public class java.util.Stack extends java.util.Vector
public class java.util.StringTokenizer extends java.lang.Object
    implements java.util.Enumeration
public abstract class java.util.TimeZone extends java.lang.Object
    implements java.io.Serializable
    implements java.lang.Cloneable
public class java.util.TooManyListenersException extends java.lang.Exception
public class java.util.TreeMap extends java.util.AbstractMap (new in 1.2)
    implements java.io.Serializable
    implements java.lang.Cloneable
    implements java.util.SortedMap
public class java.util.TreeSet extends java.util.AbstractSet (new in 1.2)
    implements java.io.Serializable
    implements java.lang.Cloneable
    implements java.util.SortedSet
public class java.util.Vector extends java.util.AbstractList
    implements java.io.Serializable
    implements java.lang.Cloneable
    implements java.util.List
public class java.util.WeakHashMap extends java.util.AbstractMap (new in 1.2)
    implements java.util.Map
```

Package `java.util.jar`

This package, new to JDK1.2, supports the *Java ARchive* (jar) format—the primary format for packaging Java class libraries and resources. A jar archive is identical to a *zip* archive (discussed later in the chapter), with the optional addition of a *manifest* file containing meta-information about the archive contents.

Listing 3.36 shows all public classes and interfaces in the `java.util.jar` package.

LISTING 3.36 `java.util.jar` Classes and Interfaces List

```
public class java.util.jar.Attributes extends java.lang.Object (new in 1.2)
    implements java.lang.Cloneable
    implements java.util.Map
public class java.util.jar.Attributes.Name extends java.lang.Object
 (new in 1.2)
public class java.util.jar.JarEntry extends java.util.zip.ZipEntry (new in 1.2)
public class java.util.jar.JarException extends java.util.zip.ZipException
 (new in 1.2)
public class java.util.jar.JarFile extends java.util.zip.ZipFile (new in 1.2)
public class java.util.jar.JarInputStream extends java.util.zip.ZipInputStream
 (new in 1.2)
public class java.util.jar.JarOutputStream extends java.util.zip.
 ZipOutputStream (new in 1.2)
public class java.util.jar.Manifest extends java.lang.Object (new in 1.2)
    implements java.lang.Cloneable
```

Package `java.util.zip`

This package supports the *zip* file format (the same one that has been in use since MS-DOS days), a standard compressed archive format used for packaging Java classes and resources. Because Java can load classes and resources directly from zip and jar archives, it is possible to ship entire complex applications packed into a single archive file.

This package also supports reading and writing of the *gzip* file format—the application of zip's compression algorithm to a single file instead of an archive.

Listing 3.37 shows all public classes and interfaces in the `java.util.zip` package.

LISTING 3.37 `java.util.zip` Classes and Interfaces List

```
public class java.util.zip.Adler32 extends java.lang.Object
    implements java.util.zip.Checksum
public class java.util.zip.CRC32 extends java.lang.Object
    implements java.util.zip.Checksum
public class java.util.zip.CheckedInputStream extends java.io.FilterInputStream
public class java.util.zip.CheckedOutputStream extends java.io.
 FilterOutputStream
public interface java.util.zip.Checksum extends java.lang.Object
```

```
public class java.util.zip.DataFormatException extends java.lang.Exception
public class java.util.zip.Deflater extends java.lang.Object
public class java.util.zip.DeflaterOutputStream extends java.io.
 FilterOutputStream
public class java.util.zip.GZIPInputStream extends java.util.zip.
 InflaterInputStream
public class java.util.zip.GZIPOutputStream extends java.util.zip.
 DeflaterOutputStream
public class java.util.zip.Inflater extends java.lang.Object
public class java.util.zip.InflaterInputStream extends java.io.
 FilterInputStream
public class java.util.zip.ZipEntry extends java.lang.Object
    implements java.lang.Cloneable
    implements java.util.zip.ZipConstants
public class java.util.zip.ZipException extends java.io.IOException
public class java.util.zip.ZipFile extends java.lang.Object
    implements java.util.zip.ZipConstants
public class java.util.zip.ZipInputStream extends java.util.zip.
 InflaterInputStream
    implements java.util.zip.ZipConstants
public class java.util.zip.ZipOutputStream extends java.util.zip.

DeflaterOutputStream
    implements java.util.zip.ZipConstants
```

Package `javax.accessibility`

This package, new in JDK1.2, supports assistive user interface technologies. This package is a *contract*: user interface (UI) components that fulfill the contract are compatible with screen readers, screen magnifiers, and other technologies intended to assist disabled users. Specifically, by implementing these interfaces, components are contracting to provide enough information about themselves to support any sort of assistive technology.

Note

This package started out as a Java extension that was later incorporated into Java's core functionality. As with all such packages, its name begins with "`javax`." Why were the packages not renamed with a "`java`" prefix when they were moved into the core? As Sun learned during the development of the Swing toolkit, developers take strong objection to the renaming of packages they depend on—so the "`javax`" name is a permanent feature.

The `javax.accessibility` classes are broken up into pieces supporting specific types of UI functionality. All UI components offering accessibility must implement `javax.accessibility.Accessible`. In addition, they must implement classes specific to their functionality: `javax.accessibility.AccessibleComponent` if they are visible onscreen, `javax.accessibility.AccessibleText` if they present textual information, and so on.

Listing 3.38 shows all public classes and interfaces in the `javax.accessibility` package.

LISTING 3.38 javax.accessibility Classes and Interfaces List

```
public interface javax.accessibility.Accessible extends java.lang.Object
 (new in 1.2)
public interface javax.accessibility.AccessibleAction extends java.lang.Object
 (new in 1.2)
public abstract class javax.accessibility.AccessibleBundle extends java.lang.
 Object (new in 1.2)
public interface javax.accessibility.AccessibleComponent extends java.lang.
 Object (new in 1.2)
public abstract class javax.accessibility.AccessibleContext extends java.lang.
 Object (new in 1.2)
public abstract class javax.accessibility.AccessibleHyperlink extends java.lang.
 Object (new in 1.2)
    implements javax.accessibility.AccessibleAction
public interface javax.accessibility.AccessibleHypertext extends java.lang.
 Object (new in 1.2)
    implements javax.accessibility.AccessibleText
public class javax.accessibility.AccessibleResourceBundle extends java.util.
 ListResourceBundle (new in 1.2)
public class javax.accessibility.AccessibleRole extends javax.accessibility.
 AccessibleBundle (new in 1.2)
public interface javax.accessibility.AccessibleSelection extends java.lang.
 Object (new in 1.2)
public class javax.accessibility.AccessibleState extends javax.accessibility.
 AccessibleBundle (new in 1.2)
public class javax.accessibility.AccessibleStateSet extends java.lang.Object
(new in 1.2)
public interface javax.accessibility.AccessibleText extends java.lang.Object
 (new in 1.2)
public interface javax.accessibility.AccessibleValue extends java.lang.Object
 (new in 1.2)
```

Package javax.swing

The Swing toolkit, provided by the javax.swing package, is one of the most significant (and largest) changes between JDK1.1 and JDK1.2.

Swing is a GUI toolkit, intended to replace the GUI components provided in the AWT. The change is important; Java has enjoyed limited success as a GUI platform due to the AWT's shortcomings, and Swing is Sun's serious attempt to improve the story.

And what an attempt! In its entirety, Swing comprises over 1,200 classes, making it arguably the world's largest and most complex GUI toolkit. For most applications, fortunately, developers need to deal with a few dozen of these classes. Many books have been written on Swing—a good place to start is *JFC Unleashed* (Sams), which explores Swing and its related components in detail.

So, what problem are these 1,200+ classes trying to solve?

When Java started out in the GUI business, the AWT was positioned as the bridge to native window system functionality. It provided a basic set of GUI components—menu, scrollbar, text editor, check box, list, drop-down list, canvas, pushbutton, and label—with which Java applications could build complete interfaces. Each component was implemented with a corresponding *peer* component in the native window system (standard GUI components in Microsoft Windows and MacOS; any GUI toolkit, usually Motif, in UNIX environments; other, possibly proprietary, implementations on PersonalJava and other platforms). Two things went wrong with the scenario:

- By choosing a *lowest common denominator* set of GUI components, the AWT was a weak toolkit, giving Java applications many fewer GUI components than were available to native applications. This shortcoming was exacerbated when Microsoft filled the gap with the Application Foundation Classes (AFC), which include a highly capable, Windows-only Java GUI toolkit.
- It has turned out to be exceedingly difficult to build GUI applications that look good in all possible Java environments.

We'll illustrate the latter point with a modest example. Listing 3.39 is a simple AWT app, written to function both as an applet (it's derived from `java.applet.Applet`) and an application (it contains a `main()` that builds a top-level `java.awt.Frame` to enclose the GUI). The app is a collection of five AWT components thrown together in an ugly arrangement.

LISTING 3.39 Simple AWT app `GuiMess`

```
import java.awt.*;
import java.awt.event.*;
import java.applet.*;

public class GuiMess extends Applet
{
    // Constructor: Fill up with a passel of GUI components.
    public GuiMess()
    {
        // We'll use the BorderLayout manager
        setLayout(new BorderLayout());
        // Start adding things... an option menu
        Choice choice = new Choice();
        add(choice, BorderLayout.NORTH);
        choice.add("Choice 1");
        choice.add("Choice 2");
        choice.add("Choice 3");
        choice.add("Choice 4");
        choice.add("Choice 5");
        // A checkbox
        add(new Checkbox("Checkbox"), BorderLayout.WEST);
        // A scrolled text area
        TextArea text = new TextArea();
        text.setText("The quick brown fox jumps over the lazy dog.");
        add(text, BorderLayout.CENTER);
```

continued on next page

continued from previous page

```
        // A button
        add(new Button("Button"), BorderLayout.EAST);
        // And a list
        List list = new List();
        list.add("Item 1");
        list.add("Item 2");
        list.add("Item 3");
        list.add("Item 4");
        list.add("Item 5");
        add(list, BorderLayout.SOUTH);
    }
    public static void main(String[] argv)
    {
        Frame frame = new Frame();
        GuiMess guiMess = new GuiMess();
        frame.add(guiMess);
        frame.pack();
        frame.setVisible(true);
        frame.addWindowListener(new WindowAdapter() {
            public void windowClosing(WindowEvent ev)
            {
                System.exit(0);
            }
        });
    }
}
```

Figure 3.5 shows the applet under Microsoft Windows with the two major browsers.

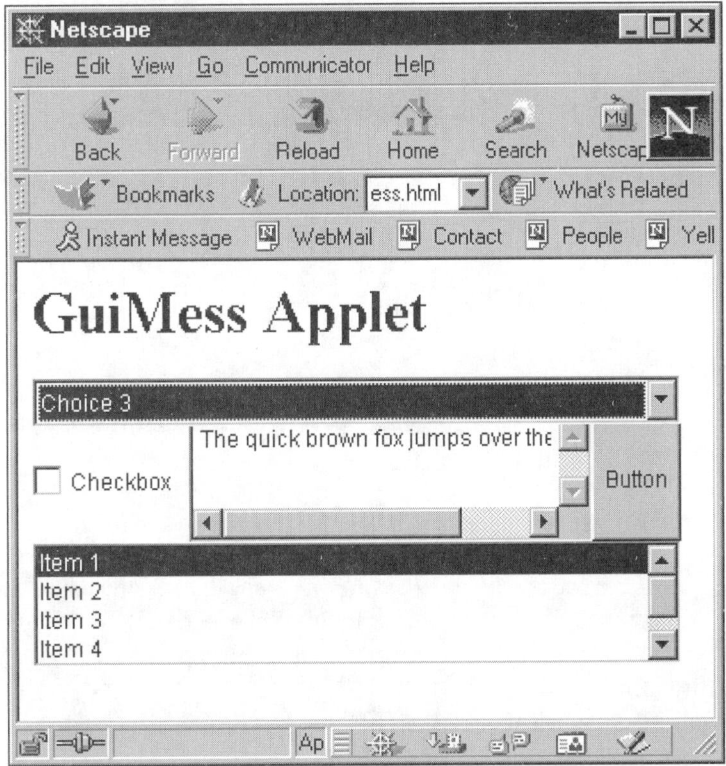

FIGURE 3.5
GuiMess applet viewed in Windows NT under MSIE and Netscape Navigator.

Both instances shown in Figure 3.5 are running in browsers that use the native Windows GUIs to implement the AWT, and look and feel similar. Figure 3.6 shows some views of the same app under Linux.

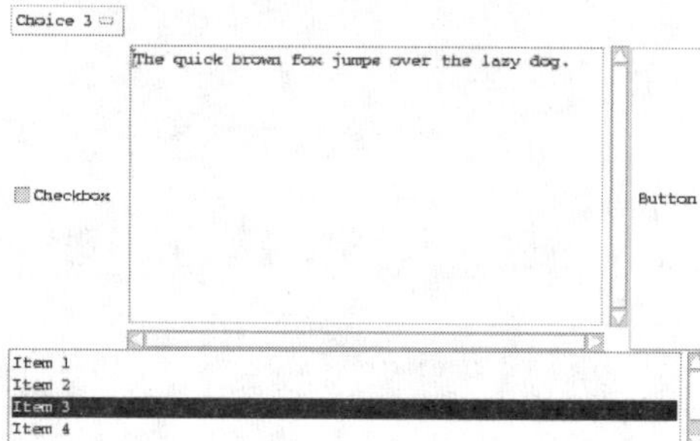

FIGURE 3.6
GuiMess running under Linux as a Netscape Navigator applet and as a standalone program.

Both instantiations shown in Figure 3.6 use the Motif toolkit to implement the AWT. The look is very different, particularly in the drop-down Choice menu, and it's unlikely that a GUI designer happy with the Windows version will be happy with what shows up under Linux. Figure 3.7 gives us one final point of comparison.

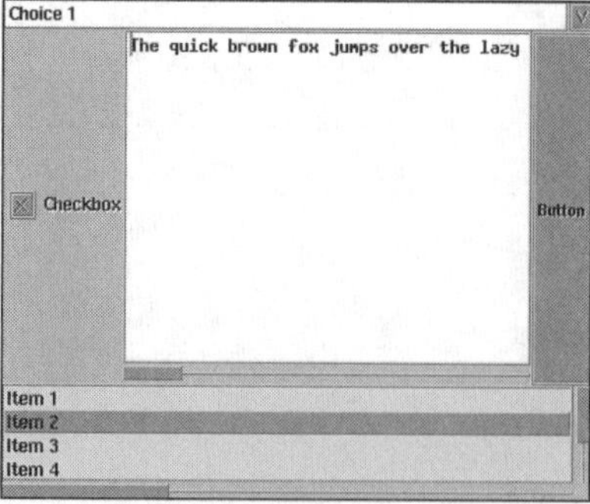

FIGURE 3.7
Running the standalone GuiMess application on Linux under Kaffe.

The free Kaffe implementation of Java (see Chapter 26, "Kaffe: A Cleanroom Java Environment,") provides its own, non-Motif version of the AWT: it's handsome, and again different from the others, but it's a real AWT that meets the Sun specification. Some ambitious individuals in the Java/Linux community have also proposed (and may be implementing) AWTs based on such popular toolkits as Gtk+, Qt, and Tk.

The point of this exploration is to note the differences that even a simple Java AWT-based GUI must endure. For complex GUI layouts, the story gets worse: the Web is full of applets that are carefully tuned to look good under Microsoft Windows but are virtually unusable elsewhere—unreadable labels, text fields too small to type in, and so on.

Enter Swing, the all-Java GUI and Sun's answer to the AWT problems. Swing is a core component of JDK1.2 but is also available for use as an add-on for JDK1.1 (see "Java Foundation Classes" in Chapter 11, "Choosing an Environment: 1.1 or 1.2?"). Before any further discussion of Swing, let's rewrite our application to use Swing (see Listing 3.40).

LISTING 3.40 `GuiSwing`, a Swing-Base Rewrite of `GuiMess`

```
import java.awt.BorderLayout;
import java.awt.event.*;
import javax.swing.*;

public class GuiSwing extends JApplet
{
    // Constructor: Fill up with a passel of GUI components.
    public GuiSwing()
    {
        // We'll use the BorderLayout manager
        getContentPane().setLayout(new BorderLayout());
        // Start adding things... an option menu
        JComboBox choice = new JComboBox();
        // We don't want user editing of the input
        choice.setEditable(false);
        getContentPane().add(choice, BorderLayout.NORTH);
        choice.addItem("Choice 1");
        choice.addItem("Choice 2");
        choice.addItem("Choice 3");
        choice.addItem("Choice 4");
        choice.addItem("Choice 5");
        // A checkbox
        getContentPane().add(new JCheckBox("Checkbox"),
         BorderLayout.WEST);
        // A scrolled text area. Unlike AWT, the Swing text area needs
        // a scrollpane supplied externally.
        JTextArea text = new JTextArea();
        text.setText("The quick brown fox jumps over the lazy dog.");
        text.setRows(4);
        getContentPane().add(new JScrollPane(text), BorderLayout.
         CENTER);
        // A button
```

continued on next page

continued from previous page

```
        getContentPane().add(new JButton("Button"), BorderLayout.EAST);
        // And a list Unlike AWT, the Swing list component area needs a
        // scrollpane supplied externally.
        DefaultListModel listModel = new DefaultListModel();
        listModel.addElement("Item 1");
        listModel.addElement("Item 2");
        listModel.addElement("Item 3");
        listModel.addElement("Item 4");
        listModel.addElement("Item 5");
        JList list = new JList(listModel);
        list.setVisibleRowCount(4);
        getContentPane().add(new JScrollPane(list),
         BorderLayout.SOUTH);
    }
    public static void main(String[] argv)
    {
        JFrame frame = new JFrame();
        GuiSwing guiSwing = new GuiSwing();
        frame.getContentPane().add(guiSwing);
        frame.pack();
        frame.setVisible(true);
        frame.addWindowListener(new WindowAdapter() {
            public void windowClosing(WindowEvent ev)
            {
                System.exit(0);
            }
        });
    }
}
```

The rewrite is not terribly difficult; Swing components more than subsume the GUI capabilities of the AWT, and the interfaces are different but not radically so. Figure 3.8 shows the resulting application, run under the Blackdown JDK:

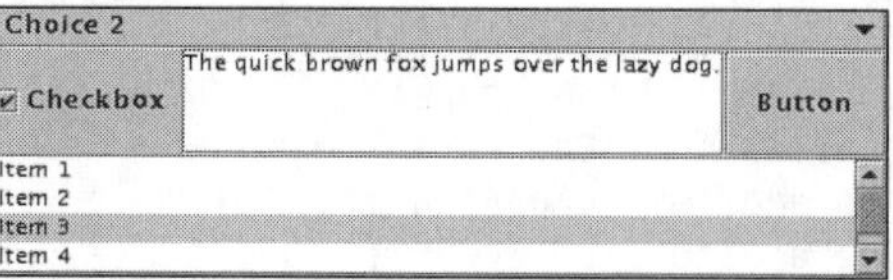

FIGURE 3.8
GuiSwing application running under Linux Blackdown JDK.

By including Swing in the JDK1.2, Sun has designed a distinct Java platform look-and-feel that reliably works everywhere. Briefly, here is what Swing brings to the party:

- A GUI toolkit implemented entirely in Java, usable with any JVM.
- A rich collection of capable low-level widgets (buttons, scrollbars, sliders, and such) and higher-level GUI abstractions (file browser, tree viewer, table viewer, application desktop).
- A *lightweight* implementation that creates and manages the GUI components entirely within the application, rather than creating multiple GUI components in the native window system. (Despite the *lightweight* moniker, this approach imposes some heavy performance costs that we explore in more detail later.)

- A model/view paradigm that separates the viewing and data-modeling of complex GUI components.
- A *Pluggable Look and Feel* that allows the GUI to assume a native Java look (which Sun calls the *Metal* look and feel) or to assume other personalities.

Note

The Swing Pluggable Look and Feel offers substantial control over appearance and behavior. In addition to Metal, the available personalities are clones of some familiar faces: Motif, Microsoft Windows, and MacOS. These alternate personalities can be enabled either with system resource settings or by making explicit calls from the code. My personal editorial opinion, which seems to be widely held, is that Metal provides an excellent and distinctive Java look—without the need to masquerade as any other toolkit.

- Automatic support of double-buffering, which results in smooth, no-flicker graphical rendering.

Swing is a first-rate toolkit and the future of Java GUIs. Its major downside is performance. We explore some reasons and remedies in Chapters 58, "A Heavy Look at Lightweight Toolkits," and 59, "An Approach to Improving Graphical Rendering Performance."

Listing 3.41 shows all public classes and interfaces in the `javax.swing` package.

LISTING 3.41 `javax.swing` Classes and Interfaces List

```
public abstract class javax.swing.AbstractAction extends java.lang.Object (
 new in 1.2)
    implements java.io.Serializable
    implements java.lang.Cloneable
    implements javax.swing.Action
public abstract class javax.swing.AbstractButton extends javax.swing.JComponent
 (new in 1.2)
    implements java.awt.ItemSelectable
    implements javax.swing.SwingConstants
public abstract class javax.swing.AbstractButton.AccessibleAbstractButton
 extends javax.swing.JComponent.AccessibleJComponent (new in 1.2)
    implements javax.accessibility.AccessibleAction
    implements javax.accessibility.AccessibleValue
public class javax.swing.AbstractButton.ButtonChangeListener extends java.lang.
 Object (new in 1.2)
    implements java.io.Serializable
    implements javax.swing.event.ChangeListener
public abstract class javax.swing.AbstractListModel extends java.lang.Object
 (new in 1.2)
    implements java.io.Serializable
    implements javax.swing.ListModel
public interface javax.swing.Action extends java.lang.Object (new in 1.2)
    implements java.awt.event.ActionListener
```

continued on next page

continued from previous page

```
public class javax.swing.BorderFactory extends java.lang.Object (new in 1.2)
public interface javax.swing.BoundedRangeModel extends java.lang.Object
 (new in 1.2)
public class javax.swing.Box extends java.awt.Container (new in 1.2)
    implements javax.accessibility.Accessible
public class javax.swing.Box.AccessibleBox extends javax.accessibility.
 AccessibleContext (new in 1.2)
    implements java.io.Serializable
    implements javax.accessibility.AccessibleComponent
public class javax.swing.Box.Filler extends java.awt.Component (new in 1.2)
    implements javax.accessibility.Accessible
public class javax.swing.Box.Filler.AccessibleBoxFiller extends
 javax.accessibility.
 AccessibleContext (new in 1.2)
    implements java.io.Serializable
    implements javax.accessibility.AccessibleComponent
public class javax.swing.BoxLayout extends java.lang.Object (new in 1.2)
    implements java.awt.LayoutManager2
    implements java.io.Serializable
public class javax.swing.ButtonGroup extends java.lang.Object (new in 1.2)
    implements java.io.Serializable
public interface javax.swing.ButtonModel extends java.lang.Object (new in 1.2)
    implements java.awt.ItemSelectable
public interface javax.swing.CellEditor extends java.lang.Object (new in 1.2)
public class javax.swing.CellRendererPane extends java.awt.Container
 (new in 1.2)
    implements javax.accessibility.Accessible
public class javax.swing.CellRendererPane.AccessibleCellRendererPane extends
 javax.accessibility.AccessibleContext (new in 1.2)
    implements java.io.Serializable
    implements javax.accessibility.AccessibleComponent
public interface javax.swing.ComboBoxEditor extends java.lang.Object
 (new in 1.2)
public interface javax.swing.ComboBoxModel extends java.lang.Object
 (new in 1.2)
    implements javax.swing.ListModel
public class javax.swing.DebugGraphics extends java.awt.Graphics (new in 1.2)
public class javax.swing.DefaultBoundedRangeModel extends java.lang.Object
 (new in 1.2)
    implements java.io.Serializable
    implements javax.swing.BoundedRangeModel
public class javax.swing.DefaultButtonModel extends java.lang.Object
 (new in 1.2)
    implements java.io.Serializable
    implements javax.swing.ButtonModel
public class javax.swing.DefaultCellEditor extends java.lang.Object
 (new in 1.2)
    implements java.io.Serializable
    implements javax.swing.table.TableCellEditor
    implements javax.swing.tree.TreeCellEditor
public class javax.swing.DefaultCellEditor.EditorDelegate extends java.lang.
 Object (new in 1.2)
    implements java.awt.event.ActionListener
```

```
    implements java.awt.event.ItemListener
    implements java.io.Serializable
public class javax.swing.DefaultComboBoxModel extends javax.swing.
 AbstractListModel (new in 1.2)
    implements java.io.Serializable
    implements javax.swing.MutableComboBoxModel
public class javax.swing.DefaultDesktopManager extends java.lang.Object
 (new in 1.2)
    implements java.io.Serializable
    implements javax.swing.DesktopManager
public class javax.swing.DefaultFocusManager extends javax.swing.FocusManager
 (new in 1.2)
public class javax.swing.DefaultListCellRenderer extends javax.swing.JLabel
 (new in 1.2)
    implements java.io.Serializable
    implements javax.swing.ListCellRenderer
public class javax.swing.DefaultListCellRenderer.UIResource extends javax.
 swing.DefaultListCellRenderer (new in 1.2)
    implements javax.swing.plaf.UIResource
public class javax.swing.DefaultListModel extends javax.swing.AbstractListModel
 (new in 1.2)
public class javax.swing.DefaultListSelectionModel extends java.lang.Object
 (new in 1.2)
    implements java.io.Serializable
    implements java.lang.Cloneable
    implements javax.swing.ListSelectionModel
public class javax.swing.DefaultSingleSelectionModel extends java.lang.Object
 (new in 1.2)
    implements java.io.Serializable
    implements javax.swing.SingleSelectionModel
public interface javax.swing.DesktopManager extends java.lang.Object
 (new in 1.2)
public abstract class javax.swing.FocusManager extends java.lang.Object
 (new in 1.2)
public class javax.swing.GrayFilter extends java.awt.image.RGBImageFilter
 (new in 1.2)
public interface javax.swing.Icon extends java.lang.Object (new in 1.2)
public class javax.swing.ImageIcon extends java.lang.Object (new in 1.2)
    implements java.io.Serializable
    implements javax.swing.Icon
public class javax.swing.JApplet extends java.applet.Applet (new in 1.2)
    implements javax.accessibility.Accessible
    implements javax.swing.RootPaneContainer
public class javax.swing.JApplet.AccessibleJApplet extends javax.
 accessibility.AccessibleContext (new in 1.2)
    implements java.io.Serializable
    implements javax.accessibility.AccessibleComponent
public class javax.swing.JButton extends javax.swing.AbstractButton
 (new in 1.2)
    implements javax.accessibility.Accessible
public class javax.swing.JButton.AccessibleJButton extends javax.swing.
 AbstractButton.AccessibleAbstractButton (new in 1.2)
public class javax.swing.JCheckBox extends javax.swing.JToggleButton
```

continued on next page

continued from previous page

(***new in 1.2***)
    implements javax.accessibility.Accessible
public class **javax.swing.JCheckBox.AccessibleJCheckBox** extends javax.swing.
JToggleButton.AccessibleJToggleButton (***new in 1.2***)
public class **javax.swing.JCheckBoxMenuItem** extends javax.swing.JMenuItem
(***new in 1.2***)
    implements javax.accessibility.Accessible
    implements javax.swing.SwingConstants
public class **javax.swing.JCheckBoxMenuItem.AccessibleJCheckBoxMenuItem** extends
javax.swing.JMenuItem.AccessibleJMenuItem (***new in 1.2***)
public class **javax.swing.JColorChooser** extends javax.swing.JComponent
(***new in 1.2***)
    implements javax.accessibility.Accessible
public class **javax.swing.JColorChooser.AccessibleJColorChooser** extends
javax.swing.JComponent.AccessibleJComponent (***new in 1.2***)
public class **javax.swing.JComboBox** extends javax.swing.JComponent (***new in 1.2***)
    implements java.awt.ItemSelectable
    implements java.awt.event.ActionListener
    implements javax.accessibility.Accessible
    implements javax.swing.event.ListDataListener
public class **javax.swing.JComboBox.AccessibleJComboBox** extends javax.swing.
JComponent.AccessibleJComponent (***new in 1.2***)
    implements javax.accessibility.AccessibleAction
public interface **javax.swing.JComboBox.KeySelectionManager** extends java.lang.
Object (***new in 1.2***)
public abstract class **javax.swing.JComponent** extends java.awt.Container
(***new in 1.2***)
    implements java.io.Serializable
public abstract class **javax.swing.JComponent.AccessibleJComponent** extends
javax.accessibility.
AccessibleContext (***new in 1.2***)
    implements java.io.Serializable
    implements javax.accessibility.AccessibleComponent
public class **javax.swing.JComponent.AccessibleJComponent.**
AccessibleContainerHandler extends java.lang.Object (***new in 1.2***)
    implements java.awt.event.ContainerListener
public class **javax.swing.JDesktopPane** extends javax.swing.JLayeredPane
(***new in 1.2***)
    implements javax.accessibility.Accessible
public class **javax.swing.JDesktopPane.AccessibleJDesktopPane** extends javax.
swing.JComponent.AccessibleJComponent (***new in 1.2***)
public class **javax.swing.JDialog** extends java.awt.Dialog (***new in 1.2***)
    implements javax.accessibility.Accessible
    implements javax.swing.RootPaneContainer
    implements javax.swing.WindowConstants
public class **javax.swing.JDialog.AccessibleJDialog** extends javax.accessibility.
AccessibleContext (***new in 1.2***)
    implements java.io.Serializable
    implements javax.accessibility.AccessibleComponent
public class **javax.swing.JEditorPane** extends javax.swing.text.JTextComponent
(***new in 1.2***)
public class **javax.swing.JEditorPane.AccessibleJEditorPane** extends
javax.swing.text.JTextComponent.AccessibleJTextComponent (***new in 1.2***)

```
public class javax.swing.JEditorPane.AccessibleJEditorPaneHTML extends
 javax.swing.JEditorPane.AccessibleJEditorPane (new in 1.2)
public class javax.swing.JEditorPane.JEditorPaneAccessibleHypertextSupport
 extends javax.swing.JEditorPane.AccessibleJEditorPane (new in 1.2)
    implements javax.accessibility.AccessibleHypertext
public class javax.swing.JEditorPane.JEditorPaneAccessibleHypertextSupport.
 HTMLLink extends javax.accessibility.AccessibleHyperlink (new in 1.2)
public class javax.swing.JFileChooser extends javax.swing.JComponent
 (new in 1.2)
    implements javax.accessibility.Accessible
public class javax.swing.JFileChooser.AccessibleJFileChooser extends
 javax.swing.JComponent.AccessibleJComponent (new in 1.2)
public class javax.swing.JFrame extends java.awt.Frame (new in 1.2)
    implements javax.accessibility.Accessible
    implements javax.swing.RootPaneContainer
    implements javax.swing.WindowConstants
public class javax.swing.JFrame.AccessibleJFrame extends javax.accessibility.
 AccessibleContext (new in 1.2)
    implements java.io.Serializable
    implements javax.accessibility.AccessibleComponent
public class javax.swing.JInternalFrame extends javax.swing.JComponent
 (new in 1.2)
    implements javax.accessibility.Accessible
    implements javax.swing.RootPaneContainer
    implements javax.swing.WindowConstants
public class javax.swing.JInternalFrame.AccessibleJInternalFrame extends
 javax.swing.JComponent.AccessibleJComponent (new in 1.2)
    implements javax.accessibility.AccessibleValue
public class javax.swing.JInternalFrame.JDesktopIcon extends javax.swing.
 JComponent (new in 1.2)
    implements javax.accessibility.Accessible
public class javax.swing.JInternalFrame.JDesktopIcon.AccessibleJDesktopIcon
 extends javax.swing.JComponent.AccessibleJComponent (new in 1.2)
    implements javax.accessibility.AccessibleValue
public class javax.swing.JLabel extends javax.swing.JComponent (new in 1.2)
    implements javax.accessibility.Accessible
    implements javax.swing.SwingConstants
public class javax.swing.JLabel.AccessibleJLabel extends javax.swing.
 JComponent.AccessibleJComponent (new in 1.2)
public class javax.swing.JLayeredPane extends javax.swing.JComponent
 (new in 1.2)
    implements javax.accessibility.Accessible
public class javax.swing.JLayeredPane.AccessibleJLayeredPane extends javax.
 swing.JComponent.AccessibleJComponent (new in 1.2)
public class javax.swing.JList extends javax.swing.JComponent (new in 1.2)
    implements javax.accessibility.Accessible
    implements javax.swing.Scrollable
public class javax.swing.JList.AccessibleJList extends javax.swing.JComponent.
 AccessibleJComponent (new in 1.2)
    implements java.beans.PropertyChangeListener
    implements javax.accessibility.AccessibleSelection
    implements javax.swing.event.ListDataListener
    implements javax.swing.event.ListSelectionListener
```

continued on next page

continued from previous page

```
public class javax.swing.JList.AccessibleJList.AccessibleJListChild extends
 javax.accessibility.AccessibleContext (new in 1.2)
    implements javax.accessibility.Accessible
    implements javax.accessibility.AccessibleComponent
public class javax.swing.JMenu extends javax.swing.JMenuItem (new in 1.2)
    implements javax.accessibility.Accessible
    implements javax.swing.MenuElement
public class javax.swing.JMenu.AccessibleJMenu extends javax.swing.JMenuItem.
 AccessibleJMenuItem (new in 1.2)
    implements javax.accessibility.AccessibleSelection
public class javax.swing.JMenu.WinListener extends java.awt.event.WindowAdapter
 (new in 1.2)
    implements java.io.Serializable
public class javax.swing.JMenuBar extends javax.swing.JComponent (new in 1.2)
    implements javax.accessibility.Accessible
    implements javax.swing.MenuElement
public class javax.swing.JMenuBar.AccessibleJMenuBar extends javax.swing.
 JComponent.AccessibleJComponent (new in 1.2)
    implements javax.accessibility.AccessibleSelection
public class javax.swing.JMenuItem extends javax.swing.AbstractButton
 (new in 1.2)
    implements javax.accessibility.Accessible
    implements javax.swing.MenuElement
public class javax.swing.JMenuItem.AccessibleJMenuItem extends javax.swing.
 AbstractButton.AccessibleAbstractButton (new in 1.2)
    implements javax.swing.event.ChangeListener
public class javax.swing.JOptionPane extends javax.swing.JComponent
 (new in 1.2)
    implements javax.accessibility.Accessible
public class javax.swing.JOptionPane.AccessibleJOptionPane extends javax.swing.
 JComponent.AccessibleJComponent (new in 1.2)
public class javax.swing.JPanel extends javax.swing.JComponent (new in 1.2)
    implements javax.accessibility.Accessible
public class javax.swing.JPanel.AccessibleJPanel extends javax.swing.
 JComponent.AccessibleJComponent (new in 1.2)
public class javax.swing.JPasswordField extends javax.swing.JTextField
 (new in 1.2)
public class javax.swing.JPasswordField.AccessibleJPasswordField extends
 javax.swing.JTextField.AccessibleJTextField (new in 1.2)
public class javax.swing.JPopupMenu extends javax.swing.JComponent (new in 1.2)
    implements javax.accessibility.Accessible
    implements javax.swing.MenuElement
public class javax.swing.JPopupMenu.AccessibleJPopupMenu extends javax.swing.
 JComponent.AccessibleJComponent (new in 1.2)
public class javax.swing.JPopupMenu.Separator extends javax.swing.JSeparator
 (new in 1.2)
public class javax.swing.JProgressBar extends javax.swing.JComponent
 (new in 1.2)
    implements javax.accessibility.Accessible
    implements javax.swing.SwingConstants
public class javax.swing.JProgressBar.AccessibleJProgressBar extends javax.
 swing.JComponent.AccessibleJComponent (new in 1.2)
    implements javax.accessibility.AccessibleValue
```

public class **javax.swing.JRadioButton** extends javax.swing.JToggleButton (***new in 1.2***)
    implements javax.accessibility.Accessible
public class **javax.swing.JRadioButton.AccessibleJRadioButton** extends javax.swing.JToggleButton.AccessibleJToggleButton (***new in 1.2***)
public class **javax.swing.JRadioButtonMenuItem** extends javax.swing.JMenuItem (***new in 1.2***)
    implements javax.accessibility.Accessible
public class **javax.swing.JRadioButtonMenuItem.AccessibleJRadioButtonMenuItem** extends javax.swing.JMenuItem.AccessibleJMenuItem (***new in 1.2***)
public class **javax.swing.JRootPane** extends javax.swing.JComponent (***new in 1.2***)
    implements javax.accessibility.Accessible
public class **javax.swing.JRootPane.AccessibleJRootPane** extends javax.swing.JComponent.AccessibleJComponent (***new in 1.2***)
public class **javax.swing.JRootPane.RootLayout** extends java.lang.Object (***new in 1.2***)
    implements java.awt.LayoutManager2
    implements java.io.Serializable
public class **javax.swing.JScrollBar** extends javax.swing.JComponent (***new in 1.2***)
    implements java.awt.Adjustable
    implements javax.accessibility.Accessible
public class **javax.swing.JScrollBar.AccessibleJScrollBar** extends javax.swing.JComponent.AccessibleJComponent (***new in 1.2***)
    implements javax.accessibility.AccessibleValue
public class **javax.swing.JScrollPane** extends javax.swing.JComponent (***new in 1.2***)
    implements javax.accessibility.Accessible
    implements javax.swing.ScrollPaneConstants
public class **javax.swing.JScrollPane.AccessibleJScrollPane** extends javax.swing.JComponent.AccessibleJComponent (***new in 1.2***)
    implements javax.swing.event.ChangeListener
public class **javax.swing.JScrollPane.ScrollBar** extends javax.swing.JScrollBar (***new in 1.2***)
    implements javax.swing.plaf.UIResource
public class **javax.swing.JSeparator** extends javax.swing.JComponent (***new in 1.2***)
    implements javax.accessibility.Accessible
    implements javax.swing.SwingConstants
public class **javax.swing.JSeparator.AccessibleJSeparator** extends javax.swing.JComponent.AccessibleJComponent (***new in 1.2***)
public class **javax.swing.JSlider** extends javax.swing.JComponent (***new in 1.2***)
    implements javax.accessibility.Accessible
    implements javax.swing.SwingConstants
public class **javax.swing.JSlider.AccessibleJSlider** extends javax.swing.JComponent.AccessibleJComponent (***new in 1.2***)
    implements javax.accessibility.AccessibleValue
public class **javax.swing.JSplitPane** extends javax.swing.JComponent (***new in 1.2***)
    implements javax.accessibility.Accessible
public class **javax.swing.JSplitPane.AccessibleJSplitPane** extends javax.swing.JComponent.AccessibleJComponent (***new in 1.2***)
    implements javax.accessibility.AccessibleValue
public class **javax.swing.JTabbedPane** extends javax.swing.JComponent

continued on next page

continued from previous page

(***new in 1.2***)
    implements java.io.Serializable
    implements javax.accessibility.Accessible
    implements javax.swing.SwingConstants
public class **javax.swing.JTabbedPane.AccessibleJTabbedPane** extends javax.swing.JComponent.AccessibleJComponent (***new in 1.2***)
    implements javax.accessibility.AccessibleSelection
    implements javax.swing.event.ChangeListener
public class **javax.swing.JTabbedPane.ModelListener** extends java.lang.Object (***new in 1.2***)
    implements java.io.Serializable
    implements javax.swing.event.ChangeListener
public class **javax.swing.JTable** extends javax.swing.JComponent (***new in 1.2***)
    implements javax.accessibility.Accessible
    implements javax.swing.Scrollable
    implements javax.swing.event.CellEditorListener
    implements javax.swing.event.ListSelectionListener
    implements javax.swing.event.TableColumnModelListener
    implements javax.swing.event.TableModelListener
public class **javax.swing.JTable.AccessibleJTable** extends javax.swing.JComponent.AccessibleJComponent (***new in 1.2***)
    implements java.beans.PropertyChangeListener
    implements javax.accessibility.AccessibleSelection
    implements javax.swing.event.CellEditorListener
    implements javax.swing.event.ListSelectionListener
    implements javax.swing.event.TableColumnModelListener
    implements javax.swing.event.TableModelListener
public class **javax.swing.JTable.AccessibleJTable.AccessibleJTableCell** extends javax.accessibility.AccessibleContext (***new in 1.2***)
    implements javax.accessibility.Accessible
    implements javax.accessibility.AccessibleComponent
public class **javax.swing.JTextArea** extends javax.swing.text.JTextComponent (***new in 1.2***)
public class **javax.swing.JTextArea.AccessibleJTextArea** extends javax.swing.text.JTextComponent.AccessibleJTextComponent (***new in 1.2***)
public class **javax.swing.JTextField** extends javax.swing.text.JTextComponent (***new in 1.2***)
    implements javax.swing.SwingConstants
public class **javax.swing.JTextField.AccessibleJTextField** extends javax.swing.text.JTextComponent.AccessibleJTextComponent (***new in 1.2***)
public class **javax.swing.JTextPane** extends javax.swing.JEditorPane (***new in 1.2***)
public class **javax.swing.JToggleButton** extends javax.swing.AbstractButton (***new in 1.2***)
    implements javax.accessibility.Accessible
public class **javax.swing.JToggleButton.AccessibleJToggleButton** extends javax.swing.AbstractButton.AccessibleAbstractButton (***new in 1.2***)
    implements java.awt.event.ItemListener
public class **javax.swing.JToggleButton.ToggleButtonModel** extends javax.swing.DefaultButtonModel (***new in 1.2***)
public class **javax.swing.JToolBar** extends javax.swing.JComponent (***new in 1.2***)
    implements javax.accessibility.Accessible
    implements javax.swing.SwingConstants
public class **javax.swing.JToolBar.AccessibleJToolBar** extends javax.swing.

JComponent.ccessibleJComponent (***new in 1.2***)
public class **javax.swing.JToolBar.Separator** extends javax.swing.JSeparator (***new in 1.2***)
  implements javax.accessibility.Accessible
public class **javax.swing.JToolTip** extends javax.swing.JComponent (***new in 1.2***)
  implements javax.accessibility.Accessible
public class **javax.swing.JToolTip.AccessibleJToolTip** extends javax.swing. JComponent.AccessibleJComponent (***new in 1.2***)
public class **javax.swing.JTree** extends javax.swing.JComponent (***new in 1.2***)
  implements javax.accessibility.Accessible
  implements javax.swing.Scrollable
public class **javax.swing.JTree.AccessibleJTree** extends javax.swing.JComponent. AccessibleJComponent (***new in 1.2***)
  implements javax.accessibility.AccessibleSelection
  implements javax.swing.event.TreeExpansionListener
  implements javax.swing.event.TreeModelListener
  implements javax.swing.event.TreeSelectionListener
public class **javax.swing.JTree.AccessibleJTree.AccessibleJTreeNode** extends javax.accessibility.AccessibleContext (***new in 1.2***)
  implements javax.accessibility.Accessible
  implements javax.accessibility.AccessibleAction
  implements javax.accessibility.AccessibleComponent
  implements javax.accessibility.AccessibleSelection
public class **javax.swing.JTree.DynamicUtilTreeNode** extends javax.swing.tree. DefaultMutableTreeNode (***new in 1.2***)
public class **javax.swing.JTree.EmptySelectionModel** extends javax.swing.tree. DefaultTreeSelectionModel (***new in 1.2***)
public class **javax.swing.JTree.TreeModelHandler** extends java.lang.Object (***new in 1.2***)
  implements javax.swing.event.TreeModelListener
public class **javax.swing.JTree.TreeSelectionRedirector** extends java.lang.Object (***new in 1.2***)
  implements java.io.Serializable
  implements javax.swing.event.TreeSelectionListener
public class **javax.swing.JViewport** extends javax.swing.JComponent (***new in 1.2***)
  implements javax.accessibility.Accessible
public class **javax.swing.JViewport.AccessibleJViewport** extends javax.swing. JComponent.AccessibleJComponent (***new in 1.2***)
public class **javax.swing.JViewport.ViewListener** extends java.awt.event. ComponentAdapter (***new in 1.2***)
  implements java.io.Serializable
public class **javax.swing.JWindow** extends java.awt.Window (***new in 1.2***)
  implements javax.accessibility.Accessible
  implements javax.swing.RootPaneContainer
public class **javax.swing.JWindow.AccessibleJWindow** extends javax.accessibility. AccessibleContext (***new in 1.2***)
  implements java.io.Serializable
  implements javax.accessibility.AccessibleComponent
public class **javax.swing.KeyStroke** extends java.lang.Object (***new in 1.2***)
  implements java.io.Serializable
public interface **javax.swing.ListCellRenderer** extends java.lang.Object (***new in 1.2***)
public interface **javax.swing.ListModel** extends java.lang.Object (***new in 1.2***)
public interface **javax.swing.ListSelectionModel** extends java.lang.Object

continued on next page

continued from previous page

```
 (new in 1.2)
public abstract class javax.swing.LookAndFeel extends java.lang.Object
 (new in 1.2)
public interface javax.swing.MenuElement extends java.lang.Object (new in 1.2)
public class javax.swing.MenuSelectionManager extends java.lang.Object
 (new in 1.2)
public interface javax.swing.MutableComboBoxModel extends java.lang.Object
 (new in 1.2)
    implements javax.swing.ComboBoxModel
public class javax.swing.OverlayLayout extends java.lang.Object (new in 1.2)
    implements java.awt.LayoutManager2
    implements java.io.Serializable
public class javax.swing.ProgressMonitor extends java.lang.Object (new in 1.2)
public class javax.swing.ProgressMonitorInputStream extends
java.io.FilterInputStream
 (new in 1.2)
public interface javax.swing.Renderer extends java.lang.Object (new in 1.2)
public class javax.swing.RepaintManager extends java.lang.Object (new in 1.2)
public interface javax.swing.RootPaneContainer extends java.lang.Object
 (new in 1.2)
public interface javax.swing.ScrollPaneConstants extends java.lang.Object
 (new in 1.2)
public class javax.swing.ScrollPaneLayout extends java.lang.Object
 (new in 1.2)
    implements java.awt.LayoutManager
    implements java.io.Serializable
    implements javax.swing.ScrollPaneConstants
public class javax.swing.ScrollPaneLayout.UIResource extends javax.swing.
 ScrollPaneLayout (new in 1.2)
    implements javax.swing.plaf.UIResource
public interface javax.swing.Scrollable extends java.lang.Object (new in 1.2)
public interface javax.swing.SingleSelectionModel extends java.lang.Object
 (new in 1.2)
public class javax.swing.SizeRequirements extends java.lang.Object
 (new in 1.2)
    implements java.io.Serializable
public interface javax.swing.SwingConstants extends java.lang.Object
 (new in 1.2)
public class javax.swing.SwingUtilities extends java.lang.Object (new in 1.2)
    implements javax.swing.SwingConstants
public class javax.swing.Timer extends java.lang.Object (new in 1.2)
    implements java.io.Serializable
public class javax.swing.ToolTipManager extends java.awt.event.MouseAdapter
 (new in 1.2)
    implements java.awt.event.MouseMotionListener
public class javax.swing.ToolTipManager.insideTimerAction extends java.lang.
 Object (new in 1.2)
    implements java.awt.event.ActionListener
public class javax.swing.ToolTipManager.outsideTimerAction extends java.lang.
 Object (new in 1.2)
    implements java.awt.event.ActionListener
public class javax.swing.ToolTipManager.stillInsideTimerAction extends
 java.lang.Object (new in 1.2)
```

```
    implements java.awt.event.ActionListener
public class javax.swing.UIDefaults extends java.util.Hashtable (new in 1.2)
public interface javax.swing.UIDefaults.ActiveValue extends java.lang.Object
 (new in 1.2)
public interface javax.swing.UIDefaults.LazyValue extends java.lang.Object
 (new in 1.2)
public class javax.swing.UIManager extends java.lang.Object (new in 1.2)
    implements java.io.Serializable
public class javax.swing.UIManager.LookAndFeelInfo extends java.lang.Object
 (new in 1.2)
public class javax.swing.UnsupportedLookAndFeelException extends java.lang.
 Exception (new in 1.2)
public class javax.swing.ViewportLayout extends java.lang.Object (new in 1.2)
    implements java.awt.LayoutManager
    implements java.io.Serializable
public interface javax.swing.WindowConstants extends java.lang.Object
 (new in 1.2)
```

Package `javax.swing.border`

This package is part of Swing and provides a collection of stylish borders with which to surround your GUI components. We will use some of these borders in a performance analyzer project in Chapter 60, "PerfAnal: A Free Performance Analysis Tool."

Listing 3.42 shows all public classes and interfaces in the `javax.swing.border` package.

LISTING 3.42 `javax.swing.border` Classes and Interfaces List

```
public abstract class javax.swing.border.AbstractBorder extends java.lang.
 Object (new in 1.2)
    implements java.io.Serializable
    implements javax.swing.border.Border
public class javax.swing.border.BevelBorder extends javax.swing.border.
 AbstractBorder (new in 1.2)
public interface javax.swing.border.Border extends java.lang.Object
 (new in 1.2)
public class javax.swing.border.CompoundBorder extends javax.swing.border.
 AbstractBorder (new in 1.2)
public class javax.swing.border.EmptyBorder extends javax.swing.border.
 AbstractBorder (new in 1.2)
    implements java.io.Serializable
public class javax.swing.border.EtchedBorder extends javax.swing.border.
 AbstractBorder (new in 1.2)
public class javax.swing.border.LineBorder extends javax.swing.border.
 AbstractBorder (new in 1.2)
public class javax.swing.border.MatteBorder extends javax.swing.border.
 EmptyBorder (new in 1.2)
public class javax.swing.border.SoftBevelBorder extends javax.swing.border.
 BevelBorder (new in 1.2)
public class javax.swing.border.TitledBorder extends javax.swing.border.
 AbstractBorder (new in 1.2)
```

Package javax.swing.colorchooser

This package is part of Swing. It solves the age-old problem of implementing a GUI-based color selection dialog without relying on the highly variable (often nonexistent) support provided by various operating systems.Listing 3.43 shows all public classes and interfaces in the javax.swing.colorchooser package.

LISTING 3.43 javax.swing.colorchooser Classes and Interfaces List

```
public abstract class javax.swing.colorchooser.AbstractColorChooserPanel
 extends javax.swing.JPanel (new in 1.2)
public class javax.swing.colorchooser.ColorChooserComponentFactory extends
 java.lang.Object (new in 1.2)
public interface javax.swing.colorchooser.ColorSelectionModel extends
 java.lang.Object (new in 1.2)
public class javax.swing.colorchooser.DefaultColorSelectionModel extends
 java.lang.Object (new in 1.2)
    implements java.io.Serializable
    implements javax.swing.colorchooser.ColorSelectionModel
```

Package javax.swing.event

This package is part of Swing. It describes the rich universe of events and event listeners added to Java by the Swing toolkit.

Listing 3.44 shows all public classes and interfaces in the javax.swing.event package.

LISTING 3.44 javax.swing.event Classes and Interfaces List

```
public class javax.swing.event.AncestorEvent extends java.awt.AWTEvent
 (new in 1.2)
public interface javax.swing.event.AncestorListener extends java.lang.Object
 (new in 1.2)
    implements java.util.EventListener
public abstract class javax.swing.event.CaretEvent extends java.util.EventObject
 (new in 1.2)
public interface javax.swing.event.CaretListener extends java.lang.Object
 (new in 1.2)
    implements java.util.EventListener
public interface javax.swing.event.CellEditorListener extends java.lang.Object
 (new in 1.2)
    implements java.util.EventListener
public class javax.swing.event.ChangeEvent extends java.util.EventObject
 (new in 1.2)
public interface javax.swing.event.ChangeListener extends java.lang.Object
 (new in 1.2)
    implements java.util.EventListener
public interface javax.swing.event.DocumentEvent extends java.lang.Object
 (new in 1.2)
public interface javax.swing.event.DocumentEvent.ElementChange extends
```

```
 java.lang.Object (new in 1.2)
public final class javax.swing.event.DocumentEvent.EventType extends
 java.lang.Object (new in 1.2)
public interface javax.swing.event.DocumentListener extends java.lang.Object
 (new in 1.2)
    implements java.util.EventListener
public class javax.swing.event.EventListenerList extends java.lang.Object
 (new in 1.2)
    implements java.io.Serializable
public class javax.swing.event.HyperlinkEvent extends java.util.EventObject
 (new in 1.2)
public final class javax.swing.event.HyperlinkEvent.EventType extends
 java.lang.Object (new in 1.2)
public interface javax.swing.event.HyperlinkListener extends java.lang.Object
 (new in 1.2)
    implements java.util.EventListener
public abstract class javax.swing.event.InternalFrameAdapter extends java.lang.
 Object (new in 1.2)
    implements javax.swing.event.InternalFrameListener
public class javax.swing.event.InternalFrameEvent extends java.awt.AWTEvent
 (new in 1.2)
public interface javax.swing.event.InternalFrameListener extends java.lang.Object
 (new in 1.2)
    implements java.util.EventListener
public class javax.swing.event.ListDataEvent extends java.util.EventObject
 (new in 1.2)
public interface javax.swing.event.ListDataListener extends java.lang.Object
 (new in 1.2)
    implements java.util.EventListener
public class javax.swing.event.ListSelectionEvent extends java.util.EventObject
 (new in 1.2)
public interface javax.swing.event.ListSelectionListener extends java.lang.
 Object (new in 1.2)
    implements java.util.EventListener
public class javax.swing.event.MenuDragMouseEvent extends java.awt.event.
 MouseEvent (new in 1.2)
public interface javax.swing.event.MenuDragMouseListener extends java.lang.Object
 (new in 1.2)
    implements java.util.EventListener
public class javax.swing.event.MenuEvent extends java.util.EventObject
 (new in 1.2)
public class javax.swing.event.MenuKeyEvent extends java.awt.event.KeyEvent
 (new in 1.2)
public interface javax.swing.event.MenuKeyListener extends java.lang.Object
 (new in 1.2)
    implements java.util.EventListener
public interface javax.swing.event.MenuListener extends java.lang.Object
 (new in 1.2)
    implements java.util.EventListener
public abstract class javax.swing.event.MouseInputAdapter extends java.lang.
 Object (new in 1.2)
    implements javax.swing.event.MouseInputListener
public class javax.swing.event.PopupMenuEvent extends java.util.EventObject
```

continued on next page

continued from previous page

```
    (new in 1.2)
public interface javax.swing.event.PopupMenuListener extends java.lang.Object
 (new in 1.2)
    implements java.util.EventListener
public final class javax.swing.event.SwingPropertyChangeSupport extends
 java.beans.PropertyChangeSupport (new in 1.2)
public class javax.swing.event.TableColumnModelEvent extends java.util.
 EventObject (new in 1.2)
public interface javax.swing.event.TableColumnModelListener extends java.lang.
 Object (new in 1.2)
    implements java.util.EventListener
public class javax.swing.event.TableModelEvent extends java.util.EventObject
 (new in 1.2)
public interface javax.swing.event.TableModelListener extends java.lang.Object
 (new in 1.2)
    implements java.util.EventListener
public class javax.swing.event.TreeExpansionEvent extends java.util.EventObject
 (new in 1.2)
public interface javax.swing.event.TreeExpansionListener extends java.lang.
 Object (new in 1.2)
    implements java.util.EventListener
public class javax.swing.event.TreeModelEvent extends java.util.EventObject
 (new in 1.2)
public interface javax.swing.event.TreeModelListener extends java.lang.Object
 (new in 1.2)
    implements java.util.EventListener
public class javax.swing.event.TreeSelectionEvent extends java.util.EventObject
 (new in 1.2)
public interface javax.swing.event.TreeSelectionListener extends java.lang.
 Object (new in 1.2)
    implements java.util.EventListener
public interface javax.swing.event.TreeWillExpandListener extends java.lang.
 Object (new in 1.2)
    implements java.util.EventListener
public class javax.swing.event.UndoableEditEvent extends java.util.EventObject
 (new in 1.2)
public interface javax.swing.event.UndoableEditListener extends java.lang.
 Object (new in 1.2)
    implements java.util.EventListener
```

Package `javax.swing.filechooser`

This package is part of Swing and describes the extensible utility classes used in the implementation of the Swing file chooser dialog. The `FileSystemView` class is intended, at some future date, to allow the file chooser to discern platform-specific details about files (such as ownership, permissions, and mode bits in the UNIX/Linux world).

Listing 3.45 shows all public classes and interfaces in the `javax.swing.filechooser` package.

LISTING 3.45 `javax.swing.filechooser` Classes and Interfaces List

```
public abstract class javax.swing.filechooser.FileFilter extends
 java.lang.Object (new in 1.2)
public abstract class javax.swing.filechooser.FileSystemView extends
 java.lang.Object (new in 1.2)
public abstract class javax.swing.filechooser.FileView extends
 java.lang.Object (new in 1.2)
```

Package `javax.swing.plaf`

This hefty package and its collection of subpackages is part of Swing and describes the framework for the *Pluggable Look and Feel* capability of the Swing GUI components. Each of the pluggable personalities performs its magic by extending the `javax.swing.plaf` classes.

Listing 3.46 shows all public classes and interfaces in the `javax.swing.plaf` package.

LISTING 3.46 `javax.swing.plaf` Classes and Interfaces List

```
public class javax.swing.plaf.BorderUIResource extends java.lang.Object
 (new in 1.2)
    implements java.io.Serializable
    implements javax.swing.border.Border
    implements javax.swing.plaf.UIResource
public class javax.swing.plaf.BorderUIResource.BevelBorderUIResource extends
 javax.swing.border.BevelBorder (new in 1.2)
    implements javax.swing.plaf.UIResource
public class javax.swing.plaf.BorderUIResource.CompoundBorderUIResource
 extends javax.swing.border.CompoundBorder (new in 1.2)
    implements javax.swing.plaf.UIResource
public class javax.swing.plaf.BorderUIResource.EmptyBorderUIResource extends
 javax.swing.border.
 EmptyBorder (new in 1.2)
    implements javax.swing.plaf.UIResource
public class javax.swing.plaf.BorderUIResource.EtchedBorderUIResource extends
 javax.swing.border.EtchedBorder (new in 1.2)
    implements javax.swing.plaf.UIResource
public class javax.swing.plaf.BorderUIResource.LineBorderUIResource extends
 javax.swing.border.LineBorder (new in 1.2)
    implements javax.swing.plaf.UIResource
public class javax.swing.plaf.BorderUIResource.MatteBorderUIResource extends
 javax.swing.border.MatteBorder (new in 1.2)
    implements javax.swing.plaf.UIResource
public class javax.swing.plaf.BorderUIResource.TitledBorderUIResource extends
 javax.swing.border.TitledBorder (new in 1.2)
    implements javax.swing.plaf.UIResource
public abstract class javax.swing.plaf.ButtonUI extends javax.swing.plaf.
 ComponentUI (new in 1.2)
public abstract class javax.swing.plaf.ColorChooserUI extends javax.swing.plaf.
 ComponentUI (new in 1.2)
public class javax.swing.plaf.ColorUIResource extends java.awt.Color
 (new in 1.2)
```

continued on next page

continued from previous page

```
    implements javax.swing.plaf.UIResource
public abstract class javax.swing.plaf.ComboBoxUI extends javax.swing.plaf.
 ComponentUI (new in 1.2)
public abstract class javax.swing.plaf.ComponentUI extends java.lang.Object
 new in 1.2)
public abstract class javax.swing.plaf.DesktopIconUI extends javax.swing.plaf.
 ComponentUI (new in 1.2)
public abstract class javax.swing.plaf.DesktopPaneUI extends javax.swing.plaf.
 ComponentUI (new in 1.2)
public class javax.swing.plaf.DimensionUIResource extends java.awt.Dimension
 (new in 1.2)
    implements javax.swing.plaf.UIResource
public abstract class javax.swing.plaf.FileChooserUI extends javax.swing.plaf.
 ComponentUI (new in 1.2)
public class javax.swing.plaf.FontUIResource extends java.awt.Font (new in 1.2)
    implements javax.swing.plaf.UIResource
public class javax.swing.plaf.IconUIResource extends java.lang.Object
 (new in 1.2)
    implements java.io.Serializable
    implements javax.swing.Icon
    implements javax.swing.plaf.UIResource
public class javax.swing.plaf.InsetsUIResource extends java.awt.Insets
 (new in 1.2)
    implements javax.swing.plaf.UIResource
public abstract class javax.swing.plaf.InternalFrameUI extends javax.swing.
 plaf.ComponentUI (new in 1.2)
public abstract class javax.swing.plaf.LabelUI extends javax.swing.plaf.
 ComponentUI (new in 1.2)
public abstract class javax.swing.plaf.ListUI extends javax.swing.plaf.
 ComponentUI (new in 1.2)
public abstract class javax.swing.plaf.MenuBarUI extends javax.swing.plaf.
 ComponentUI (new in 1.2)
public abstract class javax.swing.plaf.MenuItemUI extends javax.swing.plaf.
 ButtonUI (new in 1.2)
public abstract class javax.swing.plaf.OptionPaneUI extends javax.swing.plaf.
 ComponentUI (new in 1.2)
public abstract class javax.swing.plaf.PanelUI extends javax.swing.plaf.
 ComponentUI (new in 1.2)
public abstract class javax.swing.plaf.PopupMenuUI extends javax.swing.plaf.
 ComponentUI (new in 1.2)
public abstract class javax.swing.plaf.ProgressBarUI extends javax.swing.plaf.
 ComponentUI (new in 1.2)
public abstract class javax.swing.plaf.ScrollBarUI extends javax.swing.plaf.
 ComponentUI (new in 1.2)
public abstract class javax.swing.plaf.ScrollPaneUI extends javax.swing.plaf.
 ComponentUI (new in 1.2)
public abstract class javax.swing.plaf.SeparatorUI extends javax.swing.plaf.
 ComponentUI (new in 1.2)
public abstract class javax.swing.plaf.SliderUI extends javax.swing.plaf.
 ComponentUI (new in 1.2)
public abstract class javax.swing.plaf.SplitPaneUI extends javax.swing.plaf.
 ComponentUI (new in 1.2)
public abstract class javax.swing.plaf.TabbedPaneUI extends javax.swing.plaf.
```

```
 ComponentUI (new in 1.2)
public abstract class javax.swing.plaf.TableHeaderUI extends javax.swing.plaf.
 ComponentUI (new in 1.2)
public abstract class javax.swing.plaf.TableUI extends javax.swing.plaf.
 ComponentUI (new in 1.2)
public abstract class javax.swing.plaf.TextUI extends javax.swing.plaf.
 ComponentUI (new in 1.2)
public abstract class javax.swing.plaf.ToolBarUI extends javax.swing.plaf.
 ComponentUI (new in 1.2)
public abstract class javax.swing.plaf.ToolTipUI extends javax.swing.plaf.
 ComponentUI (new in 1.2)
public abstract class javax.swing.plaf.TreeUI extends javax.swing.plaf.
 ComponentUI (new in 1.2)
public abstract class javax.swing.plaf.ViewportUI extends javax.swing.plaf.
 ComponentUI (new in 1.2)
```

Package `javax.swing.plaf.basic`

This package is part of Swing and provides the basic look and feel of Swing GUI components. Many of these components are used or extended by the pluggable personalities.

Listing 3.47 shows all public classes and interfaces in the `javax.swing.plaf.basic` package.

LISTING 3.47 `javax.swing.plaf.basic` Classes and Interfaces List

```
public class javax.swing.plaf.basic.BasicArrowButton extends javax.swing.
 JButton (new in 1.2)
    implements javax.swing.SwingConstants
public class javax.swing.plaf.basic.BasicBorders extends java.lang.Object
(new in 1.2)
public class javax.swing.plaf.basic.BasicBorders.ButtonBorder extends
 javax.swing.border.AbstractBorder (new in 1.2)
    implements javax.swing.plaf.UIResource
public class javax.swing.plaf.basic.BasicBorders.FieldBorder extends
 javax.swing.border.AbstractBorder (new in 1.2)
    implements javax.swing.plaf.UIResource
public class javax.swing.plaf.basic.BasicBorders.MarginBorder extends
 javax.swing.border.AbstractBorder (new in 1.2)
    implements javax.swing.plaf.UIResource
public class javax.swing.plaf.basic.BasicBorders.MenuBarBorder extends
 javax.swing.border.AbstractBorder (new in 1.2)
    implements javax.swing.plaf.UIResource
public class javax.swing.plaf.basic.BasicBorders.RadioButtonBorder extends
 javax.swing.plaf.basic.BasicBorders.ButtonBorder (new in 1.2)
public class javax.swing.plaf.basic.BasicBorders.SplitPaneBorder extends
 java.lang.Object (new in 1.2)
    implements javax.swing.border.Border
    implements javax.swing.plaf.UIResource
public class javax.swing.plaf.basic.BasicBorders.ToggleButtonBorder extends
 javax.swing.plaf.basic.BasicBorders.ButtonBorder (new in 1.2)
public class javax.swing.plaf.basic.BasicButtonListener extends java.lang.
 Object (new in 1.2)
```

continued on next page

continued from previous page

```
    implements java.awt.event.FocusListener
    implements java.awt.event.MouseListener
    implements java.awt.event.MouseMotionListener
    implements java.beans.PropertyChangeListener
    implements javax.swing.event.ChangeListener
public class javax.swing.plaf.basic.BasicButtonUI extends javax.swing.plaf.
 ButtonUI (new in 1.2)
public class javax.swing.plaf.basic.BasicCheckBoxMenuItemUI extends javax.
 swing.plaf.basic.BasicMenuItemUI (new in 1.2)
public class javax.swing.plaf.basic.BasicCheckBoxUI extends javax.swing.
 plaf.basic.BasicRadioButtonUI (new in 1.2)
public class javax.swing.plaf.basic.BasicColorChooserUI extends javax.
 swing.plaf.ColorChooserUI (new in 1.2)
public class javax.swing.plaf.basic.BasicColorChooserUI.PropertyHandler extends
 java.lang.Object (new in 1.2)
    implements java.beans.PropertyChangeListener
public class javax.swing.plaf.basic.BasicComboBoxEditor extends java.lang.
 Object (new in 1.2)
    implements java.awt.event.FocusListener
    implements javax.swing.ComboBoxEditor
public class javax.swing.plaf.basic.BasicComboBoxEditor.UIResource extends
 javax.swing.plaf.basic.BasicComboBoxEditor (new in 1.2)
    implements javax.swing.plaf.UIResource
public class javax.swing.plaf.basic.BasicComboBoxRenderer extends javax.swing.
 JLabel (new in 1.2)
    implements java.io.Serializable
    implements javax.swing.ListCellRenderer
public class javax.swing.plaf.basic.BasicComboBoxRenderer.UIResource extends
 javax.swing.plaf.basic.BasicComboBoxRenderer (new in 1.2)
    implements javax.swing.plaf.UIResource
public class javax.swing.plaf.basic.BasicComboBoxUI extends javax.swing.plaf.
 ComboBoxUI (new in 1.2)
public class javax.swing.plaf.basic.BasicComboBoxUI.ComboBoxLayoutManager
 extends java.lang.Object (new in 1.2)
    implements java.awt.LayoutManager
public class javax.swing.plaf.basic.BasicComboBoxUI.FocusHandler extends
 java.lang.Object (new in 1.2)
    implements java.awt.event.FocusListener
public class javax.swing.plaf.basic.BasicComboBoxUI.ItemHandler extends
 java.lang.Object (new in 1.2)
    implements java.awt.event.ItemListener
public class javax.swing.plaf.basic.BasicComboBoxUI.KeyHandler extends
 java.awt.event.KeyAdapter (new in 1.2)
public class javax.swing.plaf.basic.BasicComboBoxUI.ListDataHandler extends
 java.lang.Object (new in 1.2)
    implements javax.swing.event.ListDataListener
public class javax.swing.plaf.basic.BasicComboBoxUI.PropertyChangeHandler
 extends java.lang.Object (new in 1.2)
    implements java.beans.PropertyChangeListener
public class javax.swing.plaf.basic.BasicComboPopup extends javax.swing.
 JPopupMenu (new in 1.2)
    implements javax.swing.plaf.basic.ComboPopup
public class javax.swing.plaf.basic.BasicComboPopup.InvocationKeyHandler
```

```
 extends java.awt.event.KeyAdapter (new in 1.2)
public class javax.swing.plaf.basic.BasicComboPopup.InvocationMouseHandler
 extends java.awt.event.MouseAdapter (new in 1.2)
public class javax.swing.plaf.basic.BasicComboPopup.
 InvocationMouseMotionHandler extends java.awt.event.MouseMotionAdapter
 (new in 1.2)
public class javax.swing.plaf.basic.BasicComboPopup.ItemHandler extends
 java.lang.Object (new in 1.2)
    implements java.awt.event.ItemListener
public class javax.swing.plaf.basic.BasicComboPopup.ListDataHandler extends
 java.lang.Object (new in 1.2)
    implements javax.swing.event.ListDataListener
public class javax.swing.plaf.basic.BasicComboPopup.ListMouseHandler extends
 java.awt.event.MouseAdapter (new in 1.2)
public class javax.swing.plaf.basic.BasicComboPopup.ListMouseMotionHandler
 extends java.awt.event.MouseMotionAdapter (new in 1.2)
public class javax.swing.plaf.basic.BasicComboPopup.ListSelectionHandler
 extends java.lang.Object (new in 1.2)
    implements javax.swing.event.ListSelectionListener
public class javax.swing.plaf.basic.BasicComboPopup.PropertyChangeHandler
 extends java.lang.Object (new in 1.2)
    implements java.beans.PropertyChangeListener
public class javax.swing.plaf.basic.BasicDesktopIconUI extends javax.swing.
 plaf.DesktopIconUI (new in 1.2)
public class javax.swing.plaf.basic.BasicDesktopIconUI.MouseInputHandler
 extends javax.swing.event.MouseInputAdapter (new in 1.2)
public class javax.swing.plaf.basic.BasicDesktopPaneUI extends javax.swing.
 plaf.DesktopPaneUI (new in 1.2)
public class javax.swing.plaf.basic.BasicDesktopPaneUI.CloseAction extends
 javax.swing.AbstractAction (new in 1.2)
public class javax.swing.plaf.basic.BasicDesktopPaneUI.MaximizeAction extends
 javax.swing.AbstractAction (new in 1.2)
public class javax.swing.plaf.basic.BasicDesktopPaneUI.MinimizeAction extends
 javax.swing.AbstractAction (new in 1.2)
public class javax.swing.plaf.basic.BasicDesktopPaneUI.NavigateAction extends
 javax.swing.AbstractAction (new in 1.2)
public class javax.swing.plaf.basic.BasicDirectoryModel extends javax.swing.
 AbstractListModel (new in 1.2)
    implements java.beans.PropertyChangeListener
public class javax.swing.plaf.basic.BasicEditorPaneUI extends javax.swing.
 plaf.basic.BasicTextUI (new in 1.2)
public class javax.swing.plaf.basic.BasicFileChooserUI extends javax.swing.
 plaf.FileChooserUI (new in 1.2)
public class javax.swing.plaf.basic.BasicFileChooserUI.AcceptAllFileFilter
 extends javax.swing.filechooser.FileFilter (new in 1.2)
public class javax.swing.plaf.basic.BasicFileChooserUI.ApproveSelectionAction
 extends javax.swing.AbstractAction (new in 1.2)
public class javax.swing.plaf.basic.BasicFileChooserUI.BasicFileView extends
 javax.swing.filechooser.FileView (new in 1.2)
public class javax.swing.plaf.basic.BasicFileChooserUI.CancelSelectionAction
 extends javax.swing.AbstractAction (new in 1.2)
public class javax.swing.plaf.basic.BasicFileChooserUI.
 ChangeToParentDirectoryAction extends javax.swing.AbstractAction (new in 1.2)
```

continued on next page

continued from previous page

public class **javax.swing.plaf.basic.BasicFileChooserUI.DoubleClickListener** extends java.awt.event.MouseAdapter (***new in 1.2***)
public class **javax.swing.plaf.basic.BasicFileChooserUI.GoHomeAction** extends javax.swing.AbstractAction (***new in 1.2***)
public class **javax.swing.plaf.basic.BasicFileChooserUI.NewFolderAction** extends javax.swing.AbstractAction (***new in 1.2***)
public class **javax.swing.plaf.basic.BasicFileChooserUI.SelectionListener** extends java.lang.Object (***new in 1.2***)
    implements javax.swing.event.ListSelectionListener
public class **javax.swing.plaf.basic.BasicFileChooserUI.UpdateAction** extends javax.swing.AbstractAction (***new in 1.2***)
public class **javax.swing.plaf.basic.BasicGraphicsUtils** extends java.lang.Object (***new in 1.2***)
public class **javax.swing.plaf.basic.BasicIconFactory** extends java.lang.Object (***new in 1.2***)
    implements java.io.Serializable
public class **javax.swing.plaf.basic.BasicInternalFrameTitlePane** extends javax.swing.JComponent (***new in 1.2***)
public class **javax.swing.plaf.basic.BasicInternalFrameTitlePane.CloseAction** extends javax.swing.AbstractAction (***new in 1.2***)
public class **javax.swing.plaf.basic.BasicInternalFrameTitlePane.IconifyAction** extends javax.swing.AbstractAction (***new in 1.2***)
public class **javax.swing.plaf.basic.BasicInternalFrameTitlePane.MaximizeAction** extends javax.swing.AbstractAction (***new in 1.2***)
public class **javax.swing.plaf.basic.BasicInternalFrameTitlePane.MoveAction** extends javax.swing.AbstractAction (***new in 1.2***)
public class **javax.swing.plaf.basic.BasicInternalFrameTitlePane.PropertyChangeHandler** extends java.lang.Object (***new in 1.2***)
    implements java.beans.PropertyChangeListener
public class **javax.swing.plaf.basic.BasicInternalFrameTitlePane.RestoreAction** extends javax.swing.AbstractAction (***new in 1.2***)
public class **javax.swing.plaf.basic.BasicInternalFrameTitlePane.SizeAction** extends javax.swing.AbstractAction (***new in 1.2***)
public class **javax.swing.plaf.basic.BasicInternalFrameTitlePane.SystemMenuBar** extends javax.swing.JMenuBar (***new in 1.2***)
public class **javax.swing.plaf.basic.BasicInternalFrameTitlePane.TitlePaneLayout** extends java.lang.Object (***new in 1.2***)
    implements java.awt.LayoutManager
public class **javax.swing.plaf.basic.BasicInternalFrameUI** extends javax.swing.plaf.InternalFrameUI (***new in 1.2***)
public class **javax.swing.plaf.basic.BasicInternalFrameUI.BasicInternalFrameListener** extends java.lang.Object (***new in 1.2***)
    implements javax.swing.event.InternalFrameListener
public class **javax.swing.plaf.basic.BasicInternalFrameUI.BorderListener** extends javax.swing.event.MouseInputAdapter (***new in 1.2***)
    implements javax.swing.SwingConstants
public class **javax.swing.plaf.basic.BasicInternalFrameUI.ComponentHandler** extends java.lang.Object (***new in 1.2***)
    implements java.awt.event.ComponentListener
public class **javax.swing.plaf.basic.BasicInternalFrameUI.GlassPaneDispatcher** extends java.lang.Object (***new in 1.2***)
    implements javax.swing.event.MouseInputListener
public class **javax.swing.plaf.basic.BasicInternalFrameUI.InternalFrameLayout**

extends java.lang.Object (***new in 1.2***)
implements java.awt.LayoutManager
public class **javax.swing.plaf.basic.BasicLabelUI** extends javax.swing.plaf.LabelUI (***new in 1.2***)
implements java.beans.PropertyChangeListener
public class **javax.swing.plaf.basic.BasicListUI** extends javax.swing.plaf.ListUI (***new in 1.2***)
public class **javax.swing.plaf.basic.BasicListUI.FocusHandler** extends java.lang.Object (***new in 1.2***)
implements java.awt.event.FocusListener
public class **javax.swing.plaf.basic.BasicListUI.ListDataHandler** extends java.lang.Object (***new in 1.2***)
implements javax.swing.event.ListDataListener
public class **javax.swing.plaf.basic.BasicListUI.ListSelectionHandler** extends java.lang.Object (***new in 1.2***)
implements javax.swing.event.ListSelectionListener
public class **javax.swing.plaf.basic.BasicListUI.MouseInputHandler** extends java.lang.Object (***new in 1.2***)
implements javax.swing.event.MouseInputListener
public class **javax.swing.plaf.basic.BasicListUI.PropertyChangeHandler** extends java.lang.Object (***new in 1.2***)
implements java.beans.PropertyChangeListener
public abstract class **javax.swing.plaf.basic.BasicLookAndFeel** extends javax.swing.LookAndFeel (***new in 1.2***)
implements java.io.Serializable
public class **javax.swing.plaf.basic.BasicMenuBarUI** extends javax.swing.plaf.MenuBarUI (***new in 1.2***)
public class **javax.swing.plaf.basic.BasicMenuItemUI** extends javax.swing.plaf.MenuItemUI (***new in 1.2***)
public class **javax.swing.plaf.basic.BasicMenuItemUI.MouseInputHandler** extends java.lang.Object (***new in 1.2***)
implements javax.swing.event.MouseInputListener
public class **javax.swing.plaf.basic.BasicMenuUI** extends javax.swing.plaf.basic.BasicMenuItemUI (***new in 1.2***)
public class **javax.swing.plaf.basic.BasicMenuUI.ChangeHandler** extends java.lang.Object (***new in 1.2***)
implements javax.swing.event.ChangeListener
public class **javax.swing.plaf.basic.BasicOptionPaneUI** extends javax.swing.plaf.OptionPaneUI (***new in 1.2***)
public class **javax.swing.plaf.basic.BasicOptionPaneUI.ButtonActionListener** extends java.lang.Object (***new in 1.2***)
implements java.awt.event.ActionListener
public class **javax.swing.plaf.basic.BasicOptionPaneUI.ButtonAreaLayout** extends java.lang.Object (***new in 1.2***)
implements java.awt.LayoutManager
public class **javax.swing.plaf.basic.BasicOptionPaneUI.PropertyChangeHandler** extends java.lang.Object (***new in 1.2***)
implements java.beans.PropertyChangeListener
public class **javax.swing.plaf.basic.BasicPanelUI** extends javax.swing.plaf.PanelUI (***new in 1.2***)
public class **javax.swing.plaf.basic.BasicPasswordFieldUI** extends javax.swing.plaf.basic.BasicTextFieldUI (***new in 1.2***)
public class **javax.swing.plaf.basic.BasicPopupMenuSeparatorUI** extends

continued on next page

continued from previous page

javax.swing.plaf.basic.BasicSeparatorUI (***new in 1.2***)
public class **javax.swing.plaf.basic.BasicPopupMenuUI** extends javax.swing.plaf.PopupMenuUI (***new in 1.2***)
public class **javax.swing.plaf.basic.BasicProgressBarUI** extends javax.swing.plaf.ProgressBarUI (***new in 1.2***)
public class **javax.swing.plaf.basic.BasicProgressBarUI.ChangeHandler** extends java.lang.Object (***new in 1.2***)
implements javax.swing.event.ChangeListener
public class **javax.swing.plaf.basic.BasicRadioButtonMenuItemUI** extends javax.swing.plaf.basic.BasicMenuItemUI (***new in 1.2***)
public class **javax.swing.plaf.basic.BasicRadioButtonUI** extends javax.swing.plaf.basic.BasicToggleButtonUI (***new in 1.2***)
public class **javax.swing.plaf.basic.BasicScrollBarUI** extends javax.swing.plaf.ScrollBarUI (***new in 1.2***)
implements java.awt.LayoutManager
implements javax.swing.SwingConstants
public class **javax.swing.plaf.basic.BasicScrollBarUI.ArrowButtonListener** extends java.awt.event.MouseAdapter (***new in 1.2***)
public class **javax.swing.plaf.basic.BasicScrollBarUI.ModelListener** extends java.lang.Object (***new in 1.2***)
implements javax.swing.event.ChangeListener
public class **javax.swing.plaf.basic.BasicScrollBarUI.PropertyChangeHandler** extends java.lang.Object (***new in 1.2***)
implements java.beans.PropertyChangeListener
public class **javax.swing.plaf.basic.BasicScrollBarUI.ScrollListener** extends java.lang.Object (***new in 1.2***)
implements java.awt.event.ActionListener
public class **javax.swing.plaf.basic.BasicScrollBarUI.TrackListener** extends java.awt.event.MouseAdapter (***new in 1.2***)
implements java.awt.event.MouseMotionListener
public class **javax.swing.plaf.basic.BasicScrollPaneUI** extends javax.swing.plaf.ScrollPaneUI (***new in 1.2***)
implements javax.swing.ScrollPaneConstants
public class **javax.swing.plaf.basic.BasicScrollPaneUI.HSBChangeListener** extends java.lang.Object (***new in 1.2***)
implements javax.swing.event.ChangeListener
public class **javax.swing.plaf.basic.BasicScrollPaneUI.PropertyChangeHandler** extends java.lang.Object (***new in 1.2***)
implements java.beans.PropertyChangeListener
public class **javax.swing.plaf.basic.BasicScrollPaneUI.VSBChangeListener** extends java.lang.Object (***new in 1.2***)
implements javax.swing.event.ChangeListener
public class **javax.swing.plaf.basic.BasicScrollPaneUI.ViewportChangeHandler** extends java.lang.Object (***new in 1.2***)
implements javax.swing.event.ChangeListener
public class **javax.swing.plaf.basic.BasicSeparatorUI** extends javax.swing.plaf.SeparatorUI (***new in 1.2***)
public class **javax.swing.plaf.basic.BasicSliderUI** extends javax.swing.plaf.SliderUI (***new in 1.2***)
public class **javax.swing.plaf.basic.BasicSliderUI.ActionScroller** extends javax.swing.AbstractAction (***new in 1.2***)
public class **javax.swing.plaf.basic.BasicSliderUI.ChangeHandler** extends java.lang.Object (***new in 1.2***)

implements javax.swing.event.ChangeListener
public class **javax.swing.plaf.basic.BasicSliderUI.ComponentHandler** extends java.awt.event.ComponentAdapter (***new in 1.2***)
public class **javax.swing.plaf.basic.BasicSliderUI.FocusHandler** extends java.lang.Object (***new in 1.2***)
implements java.awt.event.FocusListener
public class **javax.swing.plaf.basic.BasicSliderUI.PropertyChangeHandler** extends java.lang.Object (***new in 1.2***)
implements java.beans.PropertyChangeListener
public class **javax.swing.plaf.basic.BasicSliderUI.ScrollListener** extends java.lang.Object (***new in 1.2***)
implements java.awt.event.ActionListener
public class **javax.swing.plaf.basic.BasicSliderUI.TrackListener** extends javax.swing.event.MouseInputAdapter (***new in 1.2***)
public class **javax.swing.plaf.basic.BasicSplitPaneDivider** extends java.awt.Container (***new in 1.2***)
implements java.beans.PropertyChangeListener
public class **javax.swing.plaf.basic.BasicSplitPaneDivider.DividerLayout** extends java.lang.Object (***new in 1.2***)
implements java.awt.LayoutManager
public class **javax.swing.plaf.basic.BasicSplitPaneDivider.DragController** extends java.lang.Object (***new in 1.2***)
public class **javax.swing.plaf.basic.BasicSplitPaneDivider.MouseHandler** extends java.awt.event.MouseAdapter (***new in 1.2***)
implements java.awt.event.MouseMotionListener
public class **javax.swing.plaf.basic.BasicSplitPaneDivider.VerticalDragController** extends javax.swing.plaf.basic.BasicSplitPaneDivider.DragController (***new in 1.2***)
public class **javax.swing.plaf.basic.BasicSplitPaneUI** extends javax.swing.plaf.SplitPaneUI (***new in 1.2***)
public class **javax.swing.plaf.basic.BasicSplitPaneUI.BasicHorizontalLayoutManager** extends java.lang.Object (***new in 1.2***)
implements java.awt.LayoutManager2
public class **javax.swing.plaf.basic.BasicSplitPaneUI.BasicVerticalLayoutManager** extends javax.swing.plaf.basic.BasicSplitPaneUI.BasicHorizontalLayoutManager (***new in 1.2***)
public class **javax.swing.plaf.basic.BasicSplitPaneUI.FocusHandler** extends java.awt.event.FocusAdapter (***new in 1.2***)
public class **javax.swing.plaf.basic.BasicSplitPaneUI.KeyboardDownRightHandler** extends java.lang.Object (***new in 1.2***)
implements java.awt.event.ActionListener
public class **javax.swing.plaf.basic.BasicSplitPaneUI.KeyboardEndHandler** extends java.lang.Object (***new in 1.2***)
implements java.awt.event.ActionListener
public class **javax.swing.plaf.basic.BasicSplitPaneUI.KeyboardHomeHandler** extends java.lang.Object (***new in 1.2***)
implements java.awt.event.ActionListener
public class **javax.swing.plaf.basic.BasicSplitPaneUI.KeyboardResizeToggleHandler** extends java.lang.Object (***new in 1.2***)
implements java.awt.event.ActionListener
public class **javax.swing.plaf.basic.BasicSplitPaneUI.KeyboardUpLeftHandler** extends java.lang.Object (***new in 1.2***)

continued on next page

continued from previous page

```
    implements java.awt.event.ActionListener
public class javax.swing.plaf.basic.BasicSplitPaneUI.PropertyHandler extends
 java.lang.Object (new in 1.2)
    implements java.beans.PropertyChangeListener
public class javax.swing.plaf.basic.BasicTabbedPaneUI extends javax.swing.plaf.
 TabbedPaneUI (new in 1.2)
    implements javax.swing.SwingConstants
public class javax.swing.plaf.basic.BasicTabbedPaneUI.FocusHandler extends
 java.awt.event.FocusAdapter (new in 1.2)
public class javax.swing.plaf.basic.BasicTabbedPaneUI.MouseHandler extends
 java.awt.event.MouseAdapter (new in 1.2)
public class javax.swing.plaf.basic.BasicTabbedPaneUI.PropertyChangeHandler
 extends java.lang.Object (new in 1.2)
    implements java.beans.PropertyChangeListener
public class javax.swing.plaf.basic.BasicTabbedPaneUI.TabSelectionHandler
 extends java.lang.Object (new in 1.2)
    implements javax.swing.event.ChangeListener
public class javax.swing.plaf.basic.BasicTabbedPaneUI.TabbedPaneLayout
 extends java.lang.Object (new in 1.2)
    implements java.awt.LayoutManager
public class javax.swing.plaf.basic.BasicTableHeaderUI extends javax.swing.
 plaf.TableHeaderUI (new in 1.2)
public class javax.swing.plaf.basic.BasicTableHeaderUI.MouseInputHandler
 extends java.lang.Object (new in 1.2)
    implements javax.swing.event.MouseInputListener
public class javax.swing.plaf.basic.BasicTableUI extends javax.swing.plaf.
 TableUI (new in 1.2)
public class javax.swing.plaf.basic.BasicTableUI.FocusHandler extends
 java.lang.Object (new in 1.2)
    implements java.awt.event.FocusListener
public class javax.swing.plaf.basic.BasicTableUI.KeyHandler extends java.lang.
 Object (new in 1.2)
    implements java.awt.event.KeyListener
public class javax.swing.plaf.basic.BasicTableUI.MouseInputHandler extends
 java.lang.Object (new in 1.2)
    implements javax.swing.event.MouseInputListener
public class javax.swing.plaf.basic.BasicTextAreaUI extends javax.swing.plaf.
 basic.BasicTextUI (new in 1.2)
public class javax.swing.plaf.basic.BasicTextFieldUI extends javax.swing.plaf.
 basic.BasicTextUI (new in 1.2)
public class javax.swing.plaf.basic.BasicTextPaneUI extends javax.swing.plaf.
 basic.BasicEditorPaneUI (new in 1.2)
public abstract class javax.swing.plaf.basic.BasicTextUI extends javax.swing.
 plaf.TextUI (new in 1.2)
    implements javax.swing.text.ViewFactory
public class javax.swing.plaf.basic.BasicTextUI.BasicCaret extends javax.
 swing.text.DefaultCaret (new in 1.2)
    implements javax.swing.plaf.UIResource
public class javax.swing.plaf.basic.BasicTextUI.BasicHighlighter extends javax.
 swing.text.DefaultHighlighter (new in 1.2)
    implements javax.swing.plaf.UIResource
public class javax.swing.plaf.basic.BasicToggleButtonUI extends javax.swing.
 plaf.basic.BasicButtonUI (new in 1.2)
```

public class **javax.swing.plaf.basic.BasicToolBarSeparatorUI** extends javax.swing.plaf.basic.BasicSeparatorUI (***new in 1.2***)
public class **javax.swing.plaf.basic.BasicToolBarUI** extends javax.swing.plaf.ToolBarUI (***new in 1.2***)
    implements javax.swing.SwingConstants
public class **javax.swing.plaf.basic.BasicToolBarUI.DockingListener** extends java.lang.Object (***new in 1.2***)
    implements javax.swing.event.MouseInputListener
public class **javax.swing.plaf.basic.BasicToolBarUI.DragWindow** extends java.awt.Window (***new in 1.2***)
public class **javax.swing.plaf.basic.BasicToolBarUI.FrameListener** extends java.awt.event.WindowAdapter (***new in 1.2***)
public class **javax.swing.plaf.basic.BasicToolBarUI.PropertyListener** extends java.lang.Object (***new in 1.2***)
    implements java.beans.PropertyChangeListener
public class **javax.swing.plaf.basic.BasicToolBarUI.ToolBarContListener** extends java.lang.Object (***new in 1.2***)
    implements java.awt.event.ContainerListener
public class **javax.swing.plaf.basic.BasicToolBarUI.ToolBarFocusListener** extends java.lang.Object (***new in 1.2***)
    implements java.awt.event.FocusListener
public class **javax.swing.plaf.basic.BasicToolTipUI** extends javax.swing.plaf.ToolTipUI (***new in 1.2***)
public class **javax.swing.plaf.basic.BasicTreeUI** extends javax.swing.plaf.TreeUI (***new in 1.2***)
public class **javax.swing.plaf.basic.BasicTreeUI.CellEditorHandler** extends java.lang.Object (***new in 1.2***)
    implements javax.swing.event.CellEditorListener
public class **javax.swing.plaf.basic.BasicTreeUI.ComponentHandler** extends java.awt.event.ComponentAdapter (***new in 1.2***)
    implements java.awt.event.ActionListener
public class **javax.swing.plaf.basic.BasicTreeUI.FocusHandler** extends java.lang.Object (***new in 1.2***)
    implements java.awt.event.FocusListener
public class **javax.swing.plaf.basic.BasicTreeUI.KeyHandler** extends java.awt.event.KeyAdapter (***new in 1.2***)
public class **javax.swing.plaf.basic.BasicTreeUI.MouseHandler** extends java.awt.event.MouseAdapter (***new in 1.2***)
public class **javax.swing.plaf.basic.BasicTreeUI.MouseInputHandler** extends java.lang.Object (***new in 1.2***)
    implements javax.swing.event.MouseInputListener
public class **javax.swing.plaf.basic.BasicTreeUI.NodeDimensionsHandler** extends javax.swing.tree.AbstractLayoutCache.NodeDimensions (***new in 1.2***)
public class **javax.swing.plaf.basic.BasicTreeUI.PropertyChangeHandler** extends java.lang.Object (***new in 1.2***)
    implements java.beans.PropertyChangeListener
public class **javax.swing.plaf.basic.BasicTreeUI.SelectionModelPropertyChangeHandler** extends java.lang.Object (***new in 1.2***)
    implements java.beans.PropertyChangeListener
public class **javax.swing.plaf.basic.BasicTreeUI.TreeCancelEditingAction** extends javax.swing.AbstractAction (***new in 1.2***)
public class **javax.swing.plaf.basic.BasicTreeUI.TreeExpansionHandler** extends java.lang.Object (***new in 1.2***)

continued on next page

continued from previous page

```
    implements javax.swing.event.TreeExpansionListener
public class javax.swing.plaf.basic.BasicTreeUI.TreeHomeAction extends
 javax.swing.AbstractAction (new in 1.2)
public class javax.swing.plaf.basic.BasicTreeUI.TreeIncrementAction extends
 javax.swing.AbstractAction (new in 1.2)
public class javax.swing.plaf.basic.BasicTreeUI.TreeModelHandler extends
 java.lang.Object (new in 1.2)
    implements javax.swing.event.TreeModelListener
public class javax.swing.plaf.basic.BasicTreeUI.TreePageAction extends
 javax.swing.AbstractAction (new in 1.2)
public class javax.swing.plaf.basic.BasicTreeUI.TreeSelectionHandler extends
 java.lang.Object (new in 1.2)
    implements javax.swing.event.TreeSelectionListener
public class javax.swing.plaf.basic.BasicTreeUI.TreeToggleAction extends
 javax.swing.AbstractAction (new in 1.2)
public class javax.swing.plaf.basic.BasicTreeUI.TreeTraverseAction extends
 javax.swing.AbstractAction (new in 1.2)
public class javax.swing.plaf.basic.BasicViewportUI extends javax.swing.plaf.
 ViewportUI (new in 1.2)
public interface javax.swing.plaf.basic.ComboPopup extends java.lang.Object
 (new in 1.2)
public class javax.swing.plaf.basic.DefaultMenuLayout extends javax.swing.
 BoxLayout (new in 1.2)
    implements javax.swing.plaf.UIResource
```

Package `javax.swing.plaf.metal`

This package is part of Swing and provides the look and feel behavior for Swing's default Metal personality.

Listing 3.48 shows all public classes and interfaces in the `javax.swing.plaf.metal` package.

LISTING 3.48 `javax.swing.plaf.metal` Classes and Interfaces List

```
public class javax.swing.plaf.metal.DefaultMetalTheme extends javax.swing.
 plaf.metal.
 MetalTheme (new in 1.2)
public class javax.swing.plaf.metal.MetalBorders extends java.lang.Object
 (new in 1.2)
public class javax.swing.plaf.metal.MetalBorders.ButtonBorder extends javax.
 swing.border.AbstractBorder (new in 1.2)
    implements javax.swing.plaf.UIResource
public class javax.swing.plaf.metal.MetalBorders.Flush3DBorder extends
 javax.swing.border.AbstractBorder (new in 1.2)
    implements javax.swing.plaf.UIResource
public class javax.swing.plaf.metal.MetalBorders.InternalFrameBorder extends
 javax.swing.border.AbstractBorder (new in 1.2)
    implements javax.swing.plaf.UIResource
public class javax.swing.plaf.metal.MetalBorders.MenuBarBorder extends
 javax.swing.border.AbstractBorder (new in 1.2)
    implements javax.swing.plaf.UIResource
public class javax.swing.plaf.metal.MetalBorders.MenuItemBorder extends
```

javax.swing.border.AbstractBorder (***new in 1.2***)
implements javax.swing.plaf.UIResource

public class **javax.swing.plaf.metal.MetalBorders.PopupMenuBorder** extends javax.swing.border.AbstractBorder (***new in 1.2***)
implements javax.swing.plaf.UIResource

public class **javax.swing.plaf.metal.MetalBorders.RolloverButtonBorder** extends javax.swing.plaf.metal.MetalBorders.ButtonBorder (***new in 1.2***)

public class **javax.swing.plaf.metal.MetalBorders.ScrollPaneBorder** extends javax.swing.border.AbstractBorder (***new in 1.2***)
implements javax.swing.plaf.UIResource

public class **javax.swing.plaf.metal.MetalBorders.TextFieldBorder** extends javax.swing.plaf.metal.MetalBorders.Flush3DBorder (***new in 1.2***)

public class **javax.swing.plaf.metal.MetalBorders.ToolBarBorder** extends javax.swing.border.AbstractBorder (***new in 1.2***)
implements javax.swing.SwingConstants
implements javax.swing.plaf.UIResource

public class **javax.swing.plaf.metal.MetalButtonUI** extends javax.swing.plaf.basic.BasicButtonUI (***new in 1.2***)

public class **javax.swing.plaf.metal.MetalCheckBoxIcon** extends java.lang.Object (***new in 1.2***)
implements java.io.Serializable
implements javax.swing.Icon
implements javax.swing.plaf.UIResource

public class **javax.swing.plaf.metal.MetalCheckBoxUI** extends javax.swing.plaf.metal.MetalRadioButtonUI (***new in 1.2***)

public class **javax.swing.plaf.metal.MetalComboBoxButton** extends javax.swing.JButton (***new in 1.2***)

public class **javax.swing.plaf.metal.MetalComboBoxEditor** extends javax.swing.plaf.basic.BasicComboBoxEditor (***new in 1.2***)

public class **javax.swing.plaf.metal.MetalComboBoxEditor.UIResource** extends javax.swing.plaf.metal.MetalComboBoxEditor (***new in 1.2***)
implements javax.swing.plaf.UIResource

public class **javax.swing.plaf.metal.MetalComboBoxIcon** extends java.lang.Object ***new in 1.2***)
implements java.io.Serializable
implements javax.swing.Icon

public class **javax.swing.plaf.metal.MetalComboBoxUI** extends javax.swing.plaf.basic.BasicComboBoxUI (***new in 1.2***)

public class **javax.swing.plaf.metal.MetalComboBoxUI.MetalComboBoxLayoutManager** extends javax.swing.plaf.basic.BasicComboBoxUI.ComboBoxLayoutManager (***new in 1.2***)

public class **javax.swing.plaf.metal.MetalComboBoxUI.MetalComboPopup** extends javax.swing.plaf.basic.BasicComboPopup (***new in 1.2***)

public class **javax.swing.plaf.metal.MetalComboBoxUI.MetalPropertyChangeListener** extends javax.swing.plaf.basic.BasicComboBoxUI.PropertyChangeHandler (***new in 1.2***)

public class **javax.swing.plaf.metal.MetalDesktopIconUI** extends javax.swing.plaf.basic.BasicDesktopIconUI (***new in 1.2***)

public class **javax.swing.plaf.metal.MetalFileChooserUI** extends javax.swing.plaf.basic.BasicFileChooserUI (***new in 1.2***)

public class **javax.swing.plaf.metal.MetalFileChooserUI.DirectoryComboBoxAction** extends javax.swing.AbstractAction (***new in 1.2***)

public class **javax.swing.plaf.metal.MetalFileChooserUI.DirectoryComboBoxModel**

continued on next page

continued from previous page

extends javax.swing.AbstractListModel (***new in 1.2***)
implements javax.swing.ComboBoxModel
public class **javax.swing.plaf.metal.MetalFileChooserUI.FileRenderer** extends javax.swing.DefaultListCellRenderer (***new in 1.2***)
public class **javax.swing.plaf.metal.MetalFileChooserUI.FilterComboBoxModel** extends javax.swing.AbstractListModel (***new in 1.2***)
implements java.beans.PropertyChangeListener
implements javax.swing.ComboBoxModel
public class **javax.swing.plaf.metal.MetalFileChooserUI.FilterComboBoxRenderer** extends javax.swing.DefaultListCellRenderer (***new in 1.2***)
public class **javax.swing.plaf.metal.MetalFileChooserUI.SingleClickListener** extends java.awt.event.MouseAdapter (***new in 1.2***)
public class **javax.swing.plaf.metal.MetalIconFactory** extends java.lang.Object (***new in 1.2***)
implements java.io.Serializable
public class **javax.swing.plaf.metal.MetalIconFactory.FileIcon16** extends java.lang.Object (***new in 1.2***)
implements java.io.Serializable
implements javax.swing.Icon
public class **javax.swing.plaf.metal.MetalIconFactory.FolderIcon16** extends java.lang.Object (***new in 1.2***)
implements java.io.Serializable
implements javax.swing.Icon
public class **javax.swing.plaf.metal.MetalIconFactory.TreeControlIcon** extends java.lang.Object (***new in 1.2***)
implements java.io.Serializable
implements javax.swing.Icon
public class **javax.swing.plaf.metal.MetalIconFactory.TreeFolderIcon** extends javax.swing.plaf.metal.MetalIconFactory.FolderIcon16 (***new in 1.2***)
public class **javax.swing.plaf.metal.MetalIconFactory.TreeLeafIcon** extends javax.swing.plaf.metal.MetalIconFactory.FileIcon16 (***new in 1.2***)
public class **javax.swing.plaf.metal.MetalInternalFrameUI** extends javax.swing.plaf.basic.BasicInternalFrameUI (***new in 1.2***)
public class **javax.swing.plaf.metal.MetalLabelUI** extends javax.swing.plaf.basic.BasicLabelUI (***new in 1.2***)
public class **javax.swing.plaf.metal.MetalLookAndFeel** extends javax.swing.plaf.basic.BasicLookAndFeel (***new in 1.2***)
public class **javax.swing.plaf.metal.MetalPopupMenuSeparatorUI** extends javax.swing.plaf.metal.MetalSeparatorUI (***new in 1.2***)
public class **javax.swing.plaf.metal.MetalProgressBarUI** extends javax.swing.plaf.basic.BasicProgressBarUI (***new in 1.2***)
public class **javax.swing.plaf.metal.MetalRadioButtonUI** extends javax.swing.plaf.basic.BasicRadioButtonUI (***new in 1.2***)
public class **javax.swing.plaf.metal.MetalScrollBarUI** extends javax.swing.plaf.basic.BasicScrollBarUI (***new in 1.2***)
public class **javax.swing.plaf.metal.MetalScrollButton** extends javax.swing.plaf.basic.BasicArrowButton (***new in 1.2***)
public class **javax.swing.plaf.metal.MetalScrollPaneUI** extends javax.swing.plaf.basic.BasicScrollPaneUI (***new in 1.2***)
public class **javax.swing.plaf.metal.MetalSeparatorUI** extends javax.swing.plaf.basic.BasicSeparatorUI (***new in 1.2***)
public class **javax.swing.plaf.metal.MetalSliderUI** extends javax.swing.plaf.basic.BasicSliderUI (***new in 1.2***)

```
public class javax.swing.plaf.metal.MetalSliderUI.MetalPropertyListener extends
 javax.swing.plaf.basic.BasicSliderUI.PropertyChangeHandler (new in 1.2)
public class javax.swing.plaf.metal.MetalSplitPaneUI extends javax.swing.plaf.
 basic.BasicSplitPaneUI (new in 1.2)
public class javax.swing.plaf.metal.MetalTabbedPaneUI extends javax.swing.plaf.
 basic.BasicTabbedPaneUI (new in 1.2)
public class javax.swing.plaf.metal.MetalTabbedPaneUI.TabbedPaneLayout extends
 javax.swing.plaf.basic.BasicTabbedPaneUI.TabbedPaneLayout (new in 1.2)
public class javax.swing.plaf.metal.MetalTextFieldUI extends javax.swing.plaf.
 basic.BasicTextFieldUI (new in 1.2)
public abstract class javax.swing.plaf.metal.MetalTheme extends java.lang.
 Object (new in 1.2)
public class javax.swing.plaf.metal.MetalToggleButtonUI extends javax.swing.
 plaf.basic.BasicToggleButtonUI (new in 1.2)
public class javax.swing.plaf.metal.MetalToolBarUI extends javax.swing.
 plaf.basic.BasicToolBarUI (new in 1.2)
public class javax.swing.plaf.metal.MetalToolBarUI.MetalContainerListener
 extends java.lang.Object (new in 1.2)
    implements java.awt.event.ContainerListener
public class javax.swing.plaf.metal.MetalToolBarUI.MetalDockingListener extends
 javax.swing.plaf.basic.BasicToolBarUI.DockingListener (new in 1.2)
public class javax.swing.plaf.metal.MetalToolBarUI.MetalRolloverListener
 extends java.lang.Object (new in 1.2)
    implements java.beans.PropertyChangeListener
public class javax.swing.plaf.metal.MetalToolTipUI extends javax.swing.plaf.
 basic.BasicToolTipUI (new in 1.2)
public class javax.swing.plaf.metal.MetalTreeUI extends javax.swing.plaf.basic.
 BasicTreeUI (new in 1.2)
```

Package javax.swing.plaf.multi

This package is part of Swing and provides the hooks to extend Swing's built-in pluggable personalities.

Listing 3.49 shows all public classes and interfaces in the `javax.swing.plaf.multi` package.

LISTING 3.49 javax.swing.plaf.multi Classes and Interfaces List

```
public class javax.swing.plaf.multi.MultiButtonUI extends javax.swing.
 plaf.ButtonUI (new in 1.2)
public class javax.swing.plaf.multi.MultiColorChooserUI extends javax.
 swing.plaf.ColorChooserUI (new in 1.2)
public class javax.swing.plaf.multi.MultiComboBoxUI extends javax.swing.plaf.
 ComboBoxUI (new in 1.2)
public class javax.swing.plaf.multi.MultiDesktopIconUI extends javax.swing.
 plaf.DesktopIconUI (new in 1.2)
public class javax.swing.plaf.multi.MultiDesktopPaneUI extends javax.swing.
 plaf.DesktopPaneUI (new in 1.2)
public class javax.swing.plaf.multi.MultiFileChooserUI extends javax.swing.
 plaf.FileChooserUI (new in 1.2)
public class javax.swing.plaf.multi.MultiInternalFrameUI extends javax.swing.
 plaf.InternalFrameUI (new in 1.2)
```

public class **javax.swing.plaf.multi.MultiLabelUI** extends javax.swing.plaf.LabelUI (*new in 1.2*)
public class **javax.swing.plaf.multi.MultiListUI** extends javax.swing.plaf.ListUI (*new in 1.2*)
public class **javax.swing.plaf.multi.MultiLookAndFeel** extends javax.swing.LookAndFeel (*new in 1.2*)
public class **javax.swing.plaf.multi.MultiMenuBarUI** extends javax.swing.plaf.MenuBarUI (*new in 1.2*)
public class **javax.swing.plaf.multi.MultiMenuItemUI** extends javax.swing.plaf.MenuItemUI (*new in 1.2*)
public class **javax.swing.plaf.multi.MultiOptionPaneUI** extends javax.swing.plaf.OptionPaneUI (*new in 1.2*)
public class **javax.swing.plaf.multi.MultiPanelUI** extends javax.swing.plaf.PanelUI (*new in 1.2*)
public class **javax.swing.plaf.multi.MultiPopupMenuUI** extends javax.swing.plaf.PopupMenuUI (*new in 1.2*)
public class **javax.swing.plaf.multi.MultiProgressBarUI** extends javax.swing.plaf.ProgressBarUI (*new in 1.2*)
public class **javax.swing.plaf.multi.MultiScrollBarUI** extends javax.swing.plaf.ScrollBarUI (*new in 1.2*)
public class **javax.swing.plaf.multi.MultiScrollPaneUI** extends javax.swing.plaf.ScrollPaneUI (*new in 1.2*)
public class **javax.swing.plaf.multi.MultiSeparatorUI** extends javax.swing.plaf.SeparatorUI (*new in 1.2*)
public class **javax.swing.plaf.multi.MultiSliderUI** extends javax.swing.plaf.SliderUI (*new in 1.2*)
public class **javax.swing.plaf.multi.MultiSplitPaneUI** extends javax.swing.plaf.SplitPaneUI (*new in 1.2*)
public class **javax.swing.plaf.multi.MultiTabbedPaneUI** extends javax.swing.plaf.TabbedPaneUI (*new in 1.2*)
public class **javax.swing.plaf.multi.MultiTableHeaderUI** extends javax.swing.plaf.TableHeaderUI (*new in 1.2*)
public class **javax.swing.plaf.multi.MultiTableUI** extends javax.swing.plaf.TableUI (*new in 1.2*)
public class **javax.swing.plaf.multi.MultiTextUI** extends javax.swing.plaf.TextUI (*new in 1.2*)
public class **javax.swing.plaf.multi.MultiToolBarUI** extends javax.swing.plaf.ToolBarUI (*new in 1.2*)
public class **javax.swing.plaf.multi.MultiToolTipUI** extends javax.swing.plaf.ToolTipUI (*new in 1.2*)
public class **javax.swing.plaf.multi.MultiTreeUI** extends javax.swing.plaf.TreeUI (*new in 1.2*)
public class **javax.swing.plaf.multi.MultiViewportUI** extends javax.swing.plaf.ViewportUI (*new in 1.2*)

Package `javax.swing.table`

This package, part of Swing, provides classes and interfaces for dealing with the table-viewing GUI. These classes can be used to customize appearance and semantics of the viewer.

Listing 3.50 shows all public classes and interfaces in the `javax.swing.table` package.

LISTING 3.50 `javax.swing.table` Classes and Interfaces List

```
public abstract class javax.swing.table.AbstractTableModel extends java.
 lang.Object (new in 1.2)
    implements java.io.Serializable
    implements javax.swing.table.TableModel
public class javax.swing.table.DefaultTableCellRenderer extends javax.swing.
 JLabel (new in 1.2)
    implements java.io.Serializable
    implements javax.swing.table.TableCellRenderer
public class javax.swing.table.DefaultTableCellRenderer.UIResource extends
 javax.swing.table.DefaultTableCellRenderer (new in 1.2)
    implements javax.swing.plaf.UIResource
public class javax.swing.table.DefaultTableColumnModel extends java.lang.
 Object (new in 1.2)
    implements java.beans.PropertyChangeListener
    implements java.io.Serializable
    implements javax.swing.event.ListSelectionListener
    implements javax.swing.table.TableColumnModel
public class javax.swing.table.DefaultTableModel extends javax.swing.table.
 AbstractTableModel (new in 1.2)
    implements java.io.Serializable
public class javax.swing.table.JTableHeader extends javax.swing.JComponent
 (new in 1.2)
    implements javax.accessibility.Accessible
    implements javax.swing.event.TableColumnModelListener
public class javax.swing.table.JTableHeader.AccessibleJTableHeader extends
 javax.swing.JComponent.AccessibleJComponent (new in 1.2)
public interface javax.swing.table.TableCellEditor extends java.lang.Object
 (new in 1.2)
    implements javax.swing.CellEditor
public interface javax.swing.table.TableCellRenderer extends java.lang.Object
 (new in 1.2)
public class javax.swing.table.TableColumn extends java.lang.Object
 (new in 1.2)
    implements java.io.Serializable
public interface javax.swing.table.TableColumnModel extends java.lang.Object
 (new in 1.2)
public interface javax.swing.table.TableModel extends java.lang.Object

 (new in 1.2)
```

Package `javax.swing.text`

This package, part of Swing, provides classes and interfaces associated with the single- and multiline text editing components. These classes can customize appearance and semantics of the text editors.

One interesting and useful class is the `StyledEditorKit`, which describes a skeleton text-editing framework that can be extended to build editors for styled documents. Subpackages are provided (shown later in this chapter) that specialize this class for HTML and Rich Text Format (RTF) documents.

Listing 3.51 shows all public classes and interfaces in the `javax.swing.text` package.

LISTING 3.51 `javax.swing.text` Classes and Interfaces List

```
public abstract class javax.swing.text.AbstractDocument extends java.lang.
 Object (new in 1.2)
    implements java.io.Serializable
    implements javax.swing.text.Document
public abstract class javax.swing.text.AbstractDocument.AbstractElement
 extends java.lang.Object (new in 1.2)
    implements java.io.Serializable
    implements javax.swing.text.Element
    implements javax.swing.text.MutableAttributeSet
    implements javax.swing.tree.TreeNode
public interface javax.swing.text.AbstractDocument.AttributeContext extends
 java.lang.Object (new in 1.2)
public class javax.swing.text.AbstractDocument.BranchElement extends
 javax.swing.text.AbstractDocument.AbstractElement (new in 1.2)
public interface javax.swing.text.AbstractDocument.Content extends
 java.lang.Object (new in 1.2)
public class javax.swing.text.AbstractDocument.DefaultDocumentEvent
 extends javax.swing.undo.CompoundEdit (new in 1.2)
    implements javax.swing.event.DocumentEvent
public class javax.swing.text.AbstractDocument.ElementEdit extends
 javax.swing.undo.AbstractUndoableEdit (new in 1.2)
    implements javax.swing.event.DocumentEvent.ElementChange
public class javax.swing.text.AbstractDocument.LeafElement extends javax.
 swing.text.AbstractDocument.AbstractElement (new in 1.2)
public abstract class javax.swing.text.AbstractWriter extends java.lang.Object
 (new in 1.2)
public interface javax.swing.text.AttributeSet extends java.lang.Object
 (new in 1.2)
public class javax.swing.text.BadLocationException extends java.lang.Exception
 (new in 1.2)
public class javax.swing.text.BoxView extends javax.swing.text.CompositeView
 (new in 1.2)
public interface javax.swing.text.Caret extends java.lang.Object (new in 1.2)
public class javax.swing.text.ChangedCharSetException extends java.io.
 IOException (new in 1.2)
public class javax.swing.text.ComponentView extends javax.swing.text.View
 (new in 1.2)
public abstract class javax.swing.text.CompositeView extends javax.swing.text.
 View (new in 1.2)
public class javax.swing.text.DefaultCaret extends java.awt.Rectangle
 (new in 1.2)
    implements java.awt.event.FocusListener
    implements java.awt.event.MouseListener
    implements java.awt.event.MouseMotionListener
    implements javax.swing.text.Caret
public class javax.swing.text.DefaultEditorKit extends javax.swing.text.
 EditorKit (new in 1.2)
public class javax.swing.text.DefaultEditorKit.BeepAction extends javax.swing.
```

```
 text.TextAction (new in 1.2)
public class javax.swing.text.DefaultEditorKit.CopyAction extends javax.swing.
 text.TextAction (new in 1.2)
public class javax.swing.text.DefaultEditorKit.CutAction extends javax.swing.
 text.TextAction (new in 1.2)
public class javax.swing.text.DefaultEditorKit.DefaultKeyTypedAction extends
 javax.swing.text.TextAction (new in 1.2)
public class javax.swing.text.DefaultEditorKit.InsertBreakAction extends
 javax.swing.text.TextAction (new in 1.2)
public class javax.swing.text.DefaultEditorKit.InsertContentAction extends
 javax.swing.text.TextAction (new in 1.2)
public class javax.swing.text.DefaultEditorKit.InsertTabAction extends javax.
 swing.text.TextAction (new in 1.2)
public class javax.swing.text.DefaultEditorKit.PasteAction extends javax.
 swing.text.TextAction (new in 1.2)
public class javax.swing.text.DefaultHighlighter extends javax.swing.text.
 LayeredHighlighter (new in 1.2)
public class javax.swing.text.DefaultHighlighter.DefaultHighlightPainter extends
 javax.swing.text.LayeredHighlighter.LayerPainter (new in 1.2)
public class javax.swing.text.DefaultStyledDocument extends javax.swing.text.
 AbstractDocument (new in 1.2)
    implements javax.swing.text.StyledDocument
public class javax.swing.text.DefaultStyledDocument.AttributeUndoableEdit
 extends javax.swing.undo.AbstractUndoableEdit (new in 1.2)
public class javax.swing.text.DefaultStyledDocument.ElementBuffer extends
 java.lang.Object (new in 1.2)
    implements java.io.Serializable
public class javax.swing.text.DefaultStyledDocument.ElementSpec extends
 java.lang.Object (new in 1.2)
public class javax.swing.text.DefaultStyledDocument.SectionElement extends
 javax.swing.text.AbstractDocument.BranchElement (new in 1.2)
public abstract class javax.swing.text.DefaultTextUI extends javax.swing.plaf.
 basic.BasicTextUI (new in 1.2) (deprecated in 1.2)
public interface javax.swing.text.Document extends java.lang.Object
 (new in 1.2)
public abstract class javax.swing.text.EditorKit extends java.lang.Object
 (new in 1.2)
    implements java.io.Serializable
    implements java.lang.Cloneable
public interface javax.swing.text.Element extends java.lang.Object
 (new in 1.2)
public class javax.swing.text.ElementIterator extends java.lang.Object
 (new in 1.2)
    implements java.lang.Cloneable
public class javax.swing.text.FieldView extends javax.swing.text.PlainView
 (new in 1.2)
public class javax.swing.text.GapContent extends javax.swing.text.GapVector
 (new in 1.2)
    implements java.io.Serializable
    implements javax.swing.text.AbstractDocument.Content
public interface javax.swing.text.Highlighter extends java.lang.Object
 (new in 1.2)
public interface javax.swing.text.Highlighter.Highlight extends java.lang.
```

continued on next page

continued from previous page

Object (***new in 1.2***)
public interface **javax.swing.text.Highlighter.HighlightPainter** extends java.lang.Object (***new in 1.2***)
public class **javax.swing.text.IconView** extends javax.swing.text.View (***new in 1.2***)
public abstract class **javax.swing.text.JTextComponent** extends javax.swing.JComponent (***new in 1.2***)
    implements javax.accessibility.Accessible
    implements javax.swing.Scrollable
public class **javax.swing.text.JTextComponent.AccessibleJTextComponent** extends javax.swing.JComponent.AccessibleJComponent (***new in 1.2***)   implements javax.accessibility.AccessibleText
    implements javax.swing.event.CaretListener
    implements javax.swing.event.DocumentListener
public class **javax.swing.text.JTextComponent.KeyBinding** extends java.lang.Object (***new in 1.2***)
public interface **javax.swing.text.Keymap** extends java.lang.Object (***new in 1.2***)
public class **javax.swing.text.LabelView** extends javax.swing.text.View (***new in 1.2***)
public abstract class **javax.swing.text.LayeredHighlighter** extends java.lang.Object (***new in 1.2***)
    implements javax.swing.text.Highlighter
public abstract class **javax.swing.text.LayeredHighlighter.LayerPainter** extends java.lang.Object (***new in 1.2***)
    implements javax.swing.text.Highlighter.HighlightPainter
public interface **javax.swing.text.MutableAttributeSet** extends java.lang.Object (***new in 1.2***)
    implements javax.swing.text.AttributeSet
public class **javax.swing.text.ParagraphView** extends javax.swing.text.BoxView (***new in 1.2***)
    implements javax.swing.text.TabExpander
public class **javax.swing.text.PasswordView** extends javax.swing.text.FieldView (***new in 1.2***)
public class **javax.swing.text.PlainDocument** extends javax.swing.text.AbstractDocument (***new in 1.2***)
public class **javax.swing.text.PlainView** extends javax.swing.text.View (***new in 1.2***)
    implements javax.swing.text.TabExpander
public interface **javax.swing.text.Position** extends java.lang.Object (***new in 1.2***)
public final class **javax.swing.text.Position.Bias** extends java.lang.Object (***new in 1.2***)
public class **javax.swing.text.Segment** extends java.lang.Object (***new in 1.2***)
public class **javax.swing.text.SimpleAttributeSet** extends java.lang.Object (***new in 1.2***)
    implements java.io.Serializable
    implements java.lang.Cloneable
    implements javax.swing.text.MutableAttributeSet
public final class **javax.swing.text.StringContent** extends java.lang.Object (***new in 1.2***)
    implements java.io.Serializable
    implements javax.swing.text.AbstractDocument.Content
public interface **javax.swing.text.Style** extends java.lang.Object (***new in 1.2***)

```
    implements javax.swing.text.MutableAttributeSet
public class javax.swing.text.StyleConstants extends java.lang.Object
 (new in 1.2)
public class javax.swing.text.StyleConstants.CharacterConstants extends javax.
 swing.text.StyleConstants (new in 1.2)
    implements javax.swing.text.AttributeSet.CharacterAttribute
public class javax.swing.text.StyleConstants.ColorConstants extends javax.
 swing.text.StyleConstants (new in 1.2)
    implements javax.swing.text.AttributeSet.CharacterAttribute
    implements javax.swing.text.AttributeSet.ColorAttribute
public class javax.swing.text.StyleConstants.FontConstants extends javax.swing.
 text.StyleConstants (new in 1.2)
    implements javax.swing.text.AttributeSet.CharacterAttribute
    implements javax.swing.text.AttributeSet.FontAttribute
public class javax.swing.text.StyleConstants.ParagraphConstants extends javax.
 swing.text.StyleConstants (new in 1.2)
    implements javax.swing.text.AttributeSet.ParagraphAttribute
public class javax.swing.text.StyleContext extends java.lang.Object
 (new in 1.2)
    implements java.io.Serializable
    implements javax.swing.text.AbstractDocument.AttributeContext
public class javax.swing.text.StyleContext.NamedStyle extends java.lang.Object
 (new in 1.2)
    implements java.io.Serializable
    implements javax.swing.text.Style
public class javax.swing.text.StyleContext.SmallAttributeSet extends java.lang.
 Object (new in 1.2)
    implements javax.swing.text.AttributeSet
public interface javax.swing.text.StyledDocument extends java.lang.Object
 (new in 1.2)
    implements javax.swing.text.Document
public class javax.swing.text.StyledEditorKit extends javax.swing.text.
 DefaultEditorKit (new in 1.2)
public class javax.swing.text.StyledEditorKit.AlignmentAction extends
javax.swing.text.StyledEditorKit.StyledTextAction (new in 1.2)
public class javax.swing.text.StyledEditorKit.BoldAction extends javax.swing.
 text.StyledEditorKit.StyledTextAction (new in 1.2)
public class javax.swing.text.StyledEditorKit.FontFamilyAction extends
 javax.swing.text.StyledEditorKit.StyledTextAction (new in 1.2)
public class javax.swing.text.StyledEditorKit.FontSizeAction extends
 javax.swing.text.StyledEditorKit.StyledTextAction (new in 1.2)
public class javax.swing.text.StyledEditorKit.ForegroundAction extends
 javax.swing.text.StyledEditorKit.StyledTextAction (new in 1.2)
public class javax.swing.text.StyledEditorKit.ItalicAction extends javax.swing.
text.StyledEditorKit.StyledTextAction (new in 1.2)
public abstract class javax.swing.text.StyledEditorKit.StyledTextAction extends
 javax.swing.text.
 TextAction (new in 1.2)
public class javax.swing.text.StyledEditorKit.UnderlineAction extends
 javax.swing.text.StyledEditorKit.StyledTextAction (new in 1.2)
public interface javax.swing.text.TabExpander extends java.lang.Object
 (new in 1.2)
public class javax.swing.text.TabSet extends java.lang.Object (new in 1.2)
```

continued on next page

continued from previous page

```
        implements java.io.Serializable
    public class javax.swing.text.TabStop extends java.lang.Object (new in 1.2)
        implements java.io.Serializable
    public interface javax.swing.text.TabableView extends java.lang.Object
     (new in 1.2)
    public abstract class javax.swing.text.TableView extends javax.swing.text.
     BoxView (new in 1.2)
    public class javax.swing.text.TableView.TableCell extends javax.swing.text.
     BoxView (new in 1.2)
        implements javax.swing.text.TableView.GridCell
    public class javax.swing.text.TableView.TableRow extends javax.swing.text.
     BoxView (new in 1.2)
    public abstract class javax.swing.text.TextAction extends javax.swing.
     AbstractAction (new in 1.2)
    public class javax.swing.text.Utilities extends java.lang.Object (new in 1.2)
    public abstract class javax.swing.text.View extends java.lang.Object
     (new in 1.2)
        implements javax.swing.SwingConstants
    public interface javax.swing.text.ViewFactory extends java.lang.Object
     (new in 1.2)
    public class javax.swing.text.WrappedPlainView extends javax.swing.text.BoxView
    (new in 1.2)
        implements javax.swing.text.TabExpander
```

Package `javax.swing.text.html`

This package and its subpackage, part of Swing, specialize the `javax.swing.StyledEditorKit` class to support HTML editing. Sun describes the `StyledEditorKit` capabilities as "the set of things needed by a text component to be a reasonably functioning editor."

Using these classes will not give you a free world-class HTML browser or editor—it lacks, among other things, any menus or buttons to *access* the editing functionality. But they do provide a basic HTML (version 3.2) editor and viewer that can be customized to meet an application's browsing or editing requirements.

Listing 3.52 shows all public classes and interfaces in the `javax.swing.text.html` package.

LISTING 3.52 `javax.swing.text.html` Classes and Interfaces List

```
    public class javax.swing.text.html.BlockView extends javax.swing.text.BoxView
     (new in 1.2)
    public class javax.swing.text.html.CSS extends java.lang.Object (new in 1.2)
    public final class javax.swing.text.html.CSS.Attribute extends java.lang.
     Object (new in 1.2)
    public class javax.swing.text.html.FormView extends javax.swing.text.
    ComponentView (new in 1.2)
        implements java.awt.event.ActionListener
    public class javax.swing.text.html.FormView.MouseEventListener extends
     java.awt.event.
     MouseAdapter (new in 1.2)
    public class javax.swing.text.html.HTML extends java.lang.Object (new in 1.2)
    public final class javax.swing.text.html.HTML.Attribute extends java.lang.
```

```
Object (new in 1.2)
public class javax.swing.text.html.HTML.Tag extends java.lang.Object
 (new in 1.2)
public class javax.swing.text.html.HTML.UnknownTag extends javax.swing.text.
 html.HTML.
 Tag (new in 1.2)
    implements java.io.Serializable
public class javax.swing.text.html.HTMLDocument extends javax.swing.text.
 DefaultStyledDocument (new in 1.2)
public class javax.swing.text.html.HTMLDocument.BlockElement extends
javax.swing.text.
 AbstractDocument.BranchElement (new in 1.2)
public class javax.swing.text.html.HTMLDocument.HTMLReader extends javax.swing.
 text.html.HTMLEditorKit.ParserCallback (new in 1.2)
public class javax.swing.text.html.HTMLDocument.HTMLReader.BlockAction extends
 javax.swing.text.html.HTMLDocument.HTMLReader.TagAction (new in 1.2)
public class javax.swing.text.html.HTMLDocument.HTMLReader.CharacterAction
 extends javax.swing.text.html.HTMLDocument.HTMLReader.TagAction (new in 1.2)
public class javax.swing.text.html.HTMLDocument.HTMLReader.FormAction extends
 javax.swing.text.html.HTMLDocument.HTMLReader.SpecialAction (new in 1.2)
public class javax.swing.text.html.HTMLDocument.HTMLReader.HiddenAction extends
 javax.swing.text.html.HTMLDocument.HTMLReader.TagAction (new in 1.2)
public class javax.swing.text.html.HTMLDocument.HTMLReader.IsindexAction extends
 javax.swing.text.html.HTMLDocument.HTMLReader.TagAction (new in 1.2)
public class javax.swing.text.html.HTMLDocument.HTMLReader.ParagraphAction extends
 javax.swing.text.html.HTMLDocument.HTMLReader.BlockAction (new in 1.2)
public class javax.swing.text.html.HTMLDocument.HTMLReader.PreAction extends
 javax.swing.text.html.HTMLDocument.HTMLReader.BlockAction (new in 1.2)
public class javax.swing.text.html.HTMLDocument.HTMLReader.SpecialAction
 extends javax.swing.text.html.HTMLDocument.HTMLReader.TagAction (new in 1.2)
public class javax.swing.text.html.HTMLDocument.HTMLReader.TagAction extends
 java.lang.
 Object (new in 1.2)
public abstract class javax.swing.text.html.HTMLDocument.Iterator extends
 java.lang.
 Object (new in 1.2)
public class javax.swing.text.html.HTMLDocument.RunElement extends javax.
 swing.text.
 AbstractDocument.LeafElement (new in 1.2)
public class javax.swing.text.html.HTMLEditorKit extends javax.swing.text.
 StyledEditorKit (new in 1.2)
public class javax.swing.text.html.HTMLEditorKit.HTMLFactory extends java.lang.
 Object (new in 1.2)
    implements javax.swing.text.ViewFactory
public abstract class javax.swing.text.html.HTMLEditorKit.HTMLTextAction
 extends javax.swing.text.StyledEditorKit.StyledTextAction (new in 1.2)
public class javax.swing.text.html.HTMLEditorKit.InsertHTMLTextAction extends
 javax.swing.text.html.HTMLEditorKit.HTMLTextAction (new in 1.2)
public class javax.swing.text.html.HTMLEditorKit.LinkController extends java.
 awt.event.
 MouseAdapter (new in 1.2)
    implements java.io.Serializable
public abstract class javax.swing.text.html.HTMLEditorKit.Parser extends java.
```

continued on next page

continued from previous page

```
 lang.Object (new in 1.2)
public class javax.swing.text.html.HTMLEditorKit.ParserCallback extends java.
 lang.Object (new in 1.2)
public class javax.swing.text.html.HTMLFrameHyperlinkEvent extends javax.swing.
 event.HyperlinkEvent (new in 1.2)
public class javax.swing.text.html.HTMLWriter extends javax.swing.text.
 AbstractWriter (new in 1.2)
public class javax.swing.text.html.InlineView extends javax.swing.text.
 LabelView (new in 1.2)
public class javax.swing.text.html.ListView extends javax.swing.text.html.
 BlockView (new in 1.2)
public class javax.swing.text.html.MinimalHTMLWriter extends javax.swing.text.
 AbstractWriter (new in 1.2)
public class javax.swing.text.html.ObjectView extends javax.swing.text.
 ComponentView (new in 1.2)
public class javax.swing.text.html.Option extends java.lang.Object (new in 1.2)
public class javax.swing.text.html.ParagraphView extends javax.swing.text.
 ParagraphView (new in 1.2)
public class javax.swing.text.html.StyleSheet extends javax.swing.text.
 StyleContext (new in 1.2)
public class javax.swing.text.html.StyleSheet.BoxPainter extends java.lang.
 Object (new in 1.2)
    implements java.io.Serializable
public class javax.swing.text.html.StyleSheet.ListPainter extends java.lang.
 Object (new in 1.2)
    implements java.io.Serializable
```

Package `javax.swing.text.html.parser`

This package, part of Swing, provides supporting classes for HTML document parsing.

Listing 3.53 shows all public classes and interfaces in the `javax.swing.text.html.parser` package.

LISTING 3.53 `javax.swing.text.html.parser` Classes and Interfaces List

```
public final class javax.swing.text.html.parser.AttributeList extends java.
 lang.Object (new in 1.2)
    implements java.io.Serializable
    implements javax.swing.text.html.parser.DTDConstants
public final class javax.swing.text.html.parser.ContentModel extends java.
 lang.Object (new in 1.2)
    implements java.io.Serializable
public class javax.swing.text.html.parser.DTD extends java.lang.Object
 (new in 1.2)
    implements javax.swing.text.html.parser.DTDConstants
public interface javax.swing.text.html.parser.DTDConstants extends java.
 lang.Object (new in 1.2)
public class javax.swing.text.html.parser.DocumentParser extends javax.swing.
```

```
  text.html.parser.
  Parser (new in 1.2)
public final class javax.swing.text.html.parser.Element extends java.lang.
  Object (new in 1.2)
    implements java.io.Serializable
    implements javax.swing.text.html.parser.DTDConstants
public final class javax.swing.text.html.parser.Entity extends java.lang.
  Object (new in 1.2)
    implements javax.swing.text.html.parser.DTDConstants
public class javax.swing.text.html.parser.Parser extends java.lang.Object
  (new in 1.2)
    implements javax.swing.text.html.parser.DTDConstants
public class javax.swing.text.html.parser.ParserDelegator extends javax.swing.
  text.html.
  HTMLEditorKit.Parser (new in 1.2)
public class javax.swing.text.html.parser.TagElement extends java.lang.Object
  (new in 1.2)
```

Package `javax.swing.text.rtf`

This package, part of Swing, provides an editor kit for building a *Rich Text Format* (RTF) editor. RTF is commonly used as a lowest-common-denominator–styled document format among Microsoft Windows applications.

As with the HTML editor discussed previously, do not expect this class to give you a world-class editing tool. The functionality provided is basic, and must be customized to meet the RTF viewing and editing needs of the application.

Listing 3.54 shows all public classes and interfaces in the `javax.swing.text.rtf` package.

LISTING 3.54 `javax.swing.text.rtf` Classes and Interfaces List

```
public class javax.swing.text.rtf.RTFEditorKit extends javax.swing.text.
  StyledEditorKit (new in 1.2)
```

Package `javax.swing.tree`

This package, part of Swing, provides classes for modeling the data behind the `javax.swing.JTree` tree viewer GUI (discussed previously in the section "Package javax.swing"). By separating the modeling from the viewing of the data, Swing allows you to model the data with structures that best fit the data, instead of force-fitting the data into data structures provided by the GUI.

In Chapter 60, "`PerfAnal`: A Free Performance Analysis Tool," we will explore a performance analysis tool that uses `javax.swing.JTree` and the classes in this package to view and navigate performance data collected from Java applications.

Listing 3.55 shows all public classes and interfaces in the `javax.swing.tree` package.

LISTING 3.55 `javax.swing.tree` Classes and Interfaces List

```
public abstract class javax.swing.tree.AbstractLayoutCache extends java.lang.
 Object (new in 1.2)
    implements javax.swing.tree.RowMapper
public abstract class javax.swing.tree.AbstractLayoutCache.NodeDimensions
 extends java.lang.
 Object (new in 1.2)
public class javax.swing.tree.DefaultMutableTreeNode extends java.lang.
 Object (new in 1.2)
    implements java.io.Serializable
    implements java.lang.Cloneable
    implements javax.swing.tree.MutableTreeNode
public class javax.swing.tree.DefaultTreeCellEditor extends java.lang.Object
 (new in 1.2)
    implements java.awt.event.ActionListener
    implements javax.swing.event.TreeSelectionListener
    implements javax.swing.tree.TreeCellEditor
public class javax.swing.tree.DefaultTreeCellEditor.DefaultTextField extends
 javax.swing.JTextField (new in 1.2)
public class javax.swing.tree.DefaultTreeCellEditor.EditorContainer extends
 java.awt.Container (new in 1.2)
public class javax.swing.tree.DefaultTreeCellRenderer extends javax.swing.
 JLabel (new in 1.2)
    implements javax.swing.tree.TreeCellRenderer
public class javax.swing.tree.DefaultTreeModel extends java.lang.Object
 (new in 1.2)
    implements java.io.Serializable
    implements javax.swing.tree.TreeModel
public class javax.swing.tree.DefaultTreeSelectionModel extends java.lang.
 Object (new in 1.2)
    implements java.io.Serializable
    implements java.lang.Cloneable
    implements javax.swing.tree.TreeSelectionModel
public class javax.swing.tree.ExpandVetoException extends java.lang.Exception
 (new in 1.2)
public class javax.swing.tree.FixedHeightLayoutCache extends javax.swing.tree.
 AbstractLayoutCache (new in 1.2)
public interface javax.swing.tree.MutableTreeNode extends java.lang.Object
 (new in 1.2)
    implements javax.swing.tree.TreeNode
public interface javax.swing.tree.RowMapper extends java.lang.Object
 (new in 1.2)
public interface javax.swing.tree.TreeCellEditor extends java.lang.Object
 (new in 1.2)
    implements javax.swing.CellEditor
public interface javax.swing.tree.TreeCellRenderer extends java.lang.Object
 (new in 1.2)
public interface javax.swing.tree.TreeModel extends java.lang.Object
 (new in 1.2)
```

```
public interface javax.swing.tree.TreeNode extends java.lang.Object
 (new in 1.2)
public class javax.swing.tree.TreePath extends java.lang.Object
 (new in 1.2)
    implements java.io.Serializable
public interface javax.swing.tree.TreeSelectionModel extends java.lang.Object
 (new in 1.2)
public class javax.swing.tree.VariableHeightLayoutCache extends javax.swing.
 tree.AbstractLayoutCache (new in 1.2)
```

Package javax.swing.undo

This package, part of Swing, provides classes to support creation of an Undo/Redo stack for arbitrary editing components.

Listing 3.56 shows all public classes and interfaces in the javax.swing.undo package.

LISTING 3.56 javax.swing.undo Classes and Interfaces List

```
public class javax.swing.undo.AbstractUndoableEdit extends java.lang.
 Object (new in 1.2)
    implements java.io.Serializable
    implements javax.swing.undo.UndoableEdit
public class javax.swing.undo.CannotRedoException extends java.lang.
 RuntimeException (new in 1.2)
public class javax.swing.undo.CannotUndoException extends java.lang.
 RuntimeException (new in 1.2)
public class javax.swing.undo.CompoundEdit extends javax.swing.undo.
 AbstractUndoableEdit (new in 1.2)
public class javax.swing.undo.StateEdit extends javax.swing.undo.
 AbstractUndoableEdit (new in 1.2)
public interface javax.swing.undo.StateEditable extends java.lang.Object
 (new in 1.2)
public class javax.swing.undo.UndoManager extends javax.swing.undo.
 CompoundEdit (new in 1.2)
    implements javax.swing.event.UndoableEditListener
public interface javax.swing.undo.UndoableEdit extends java.lang.Object
 (new in 1.2)
public class javax.swing.undo.UndoableEditSupport extends java.lang.Object
 (new in 1.2)
```

Package org.omg.CORBA

This package and its subpackages, new in JDK1.2, support the *Common Object Request Broker Architecture* (CORBA)—a standard from the *Open Management Group* (OMG)from the *Open Management Group* (OMG) for interoperability among networked applications. The high-level functionality provided by CORBA is similar to that from RMI (discussed previously), but CORBA is a widely adopted, platform-neutral mechanism that does not offer some of the Java-specific features of RMI.

Detailed specifications and information about CORBA are available from the OMG Web site at `http://www.omg.org/`.

Listing 3.57 shows all public classes and interfaces in the `org.omg.CORBA` package.

LISTING 3.57 `org.omg.CORBA` Classes and Interfaces List

```
public interface org.omg.CORBA.ARG_IN extends java.lang.Object (new in 1.2)
public interface org.omg.CORBA.ARG_INOUT extends java.lang.Object (new in 1.2)
public interface org.omg.CORBA.ARG_OUT extends java.lang.Object (new in 1.2)
public abstract class org.omg.CORBA.Any extends java.lang.Object (new in 1.2)
    implements org.omg.CORBA.portable.IDLEntity
public final class org.omg.CORBA.AnyHolder extends java.lang.Object (new in 1.2)
    implements org.omg.CORBA.portable.Streamable
public final class org.omg.CORBA.BAD_CONTEXT extends org.omg.CORBA.
 SystemException (new in 1.2)
public final class org.omg.CORBA.BAD_INV_ORDER extends org.omg.CORBA.
 SystemException (new in 1.2)
public final class org.omg.CORBA.BAD_OPERATION extends org.omg.CORBA.
 SystemException (new in 1.2)
public final class org.omg.CORBA.BAD_PARAM extends org.omg.CORBA.
 SystemException (new in 1.2)
public interface org.omg.CORBA.BAD_POLICY extends java.lang.Object (new in 1.2)
public interface org.omg.CORBA.BAD_POLICY_TYPE extends java.lang.Object
 (new in 1.2)
public interface org.omg.CORBA.BAD_POLICY_VALUE extends java.lang.Object
 (new in 1.2)
public final class org.omg.CORBA.BAD_TYPECODE extends org.omg.CORBA.
 SystemException (new in 1.2)
public final class org.omg.CORBA.BooleanHolder extends java.lang.Object
 (new in 1.2)
    implements org.omg.CORBA.portable.Streamable
public final class org.omg.CORBA.Bounds extends org.omg.CORBA.UserException
 (new in 1.2)
public final class org.omg.CORBA.ByteHolder extends java.lang.Object
 (new in 1.2)
    implements org.omg.CORBA.portable.Streamable
public final class org.omg.CORBA.COMM_FAILURE extends org.omg.CORBA.
 SystemException (new in 1.2)
public interface org.omg.CORBA.CTX_RESTRICT_SCOPE extends java.lang.Object
 (new in 1.2)
public final class org.omg.CORBA.CharHolder extends java.lang.Object
 (new in 1.2)
    implements org.omg.CORBA.portable.Streamable
public class org.omg.CORBA.CompletionStatus extends java.lang.Object
 (new in 1.2)
    implements org.omg.CORBA.portable.IDLEntity
public abstract class org.omg.CORBA.Context extends java.lang.Object
 (new in 1.2)
public abstract class org.omg.CORBA.ContextList extends java.lang.Object
 (new in 1.2)
public final class org.omg.CORBA.DATA_CONVERSION extends org.omg.CORBA.
```

```
 SystemException (new in 1.2)
public class org.omg.CORBA.DefinitionKind extends java.lang.Object
 (new in 1.2)
    implements org.omg.CORBA.portable.IDLEntity
public interface org.omg.CORBA.DomainManager extends java.lang.Object
 (new in 1.2)
    implements org.omg.CORBA.Object
public final class org.omg.CORBA.DoubleHolder extends java.lang.Object
 (new in 1.2)
    implements org.omg.CORBA.portable.Streamable
public interface org.omg.CORBA.DynAny extends java.lang.Object (new in 1.2)
    implements org.omg.CORBA.Object
public interface org.omg.CORBA.DynArray extends java.lang.Object (new in 1.2)
    implements org.omg.CORBA.DynAny
    implements org.omg.CORBA.Object
public interface org.omg.CORBA.DynEnum extends java.lang.Object (new in 1.2)
    implements org.omg.CORBA.DynAny
    implements org.omg.CORBA.Object
public interface org.omg.CORBA.DynFixed extends java.lang.Object (new in 1.2)
    implements org.omg.CORBA.DynAny
    implements org.omg.CORBA.Object
public interface org.omg.CORBA.DynSequence extends java.lang.Object
 (new in 1.2)
    implements org.omg.CORBA.DynAny
    implements org.omg.CORBA.Object
public interface org.omg.CORBA.DynStruct extends java.lang.Object (new in 1.2)
    implements org.omg.CORBA.DynAny
    implements org.omg.CORBA.Object
public interface org.omg.CORBA.DynUnion extends java.lang.Object (new in 1.2)
    implements org.omg.CORBA.DynAny
    implements org.omg.CORBA.Object
public interface org.omg.CORBA.DynValue extends java.lang.Object (new in 1.2)
    implements org.omg.CORBA.DynAny
    implements org.omg.CORBA.Object
public abstract class org.omg.CORBA.DynamicImplementation extends org.omg.
 CORBA.portable.ObjectImpl (new in 1.2)
public abstract class org.omg.CORBA.Environment extends java.lang.Object
 (new in 1.2)
public abstract class org.omg.CORBA.ExceptionList extends java.lang.Object
 (new in 1.2)
public final class org.omg.CORBA.FREE_MEM extends org.omg.CORBA.
 SystemException (new in 1.2)
public final class org.omg.CORBA.FixedHolder extends java.lang.Object
 (new in 1.2)
    implements org.omg.CORBA.portable.Streamable
public final class org.omg.CORBA.FloatHolder extends java.lang.Object
 (new in 1.2)
    implements org.omg.CORBA.portable.Streamable
public interface org.omg.CORBA.IDLType extends java.lang.Object (new in 1.2)
    implements org.omg.CORBA.IRObject
    implements org.omg.CORBA.Object
    implements org.omg.CORBA.portable.IDLEntity
public final class org.omg.CORBA.IMP_LIMIT extends org.omg.CORBA.
```

continued on next page

continued from previous page

```
 SystemException (new in 1.2)
public final class org.omg.CORBA.INITIALIZE extends org.omg.CORBA.
 SystemException (new in 1.2)
public final class org.omg.CORBA.INTERNAL extends org.omg.CORBA.
 SystemException (new in 1.2)
public final class org.omg.CORBA.INTF_REPOS extends org.omg.CORBA.
 SystemException (new in 1.2)
public final class org.omg.CORBA.INVALID_TRANSACTION extends org.omg.CORBA.
 SystemException (new in 1.2)
public final class org.omg.CORBA.INV_FLAG extends org.omg.CORBA.
 SystemException (new in 1.2)
public final class org.omg.CORBA.INV_IDENT extends org.omg.CORBA.
 SystemException (new in 1.2)
public final class org.omg.CORBA.INV_OBJREF extends org.omg.CORBA.
 SystemException (new in 1.2)
public class org.omg.CORBA.INV_POLICY extends org.omg.CORBA.SystemException
 (new in 1.2)
public interface org.omg.CORBA.IRObject extends java.lang.Object (new in 1.2)
    implements org.omg.CORBA.Object
    implements org.omg.CORBA.portable.IDLEntity
public final class org.omg.CORBA.IntHolder extends java.lang.Object
 (new in 1.2)
    implements org.omg.CORBA.portable.Streamable
public final class org.omg.CORBA.LongHolder extends java.lang.Object
 (new in 1.2)
    implements org.omg.CORBA.portable.Streamable
public final class org.omg.CORBA.MARSHAL extends org.omg.CORBA.SystemException
 (new in 1.2)
public final class org.omg.CORBA.NO_IMPLEMENT extends org.omg.CORBA.
 SystemException (new in 1.2)
public final class org.omg.CORBA.NO_MEMORY extends org.omg.CORBA.
 SystemException (new in 1.2)
public final class org.omg.CORBA.NO_PERMISSION extends org.omg.CORBA.
 SystemException (new in 1.2)
public final class org.omg.CORBA.NO_RESOURCES extends org.omg.CORBA.
 SystemException (new in 1.2)
public final class org.omg.CORBA.NO_RESPONSE extends org.omg.CORBA.
 SystemException (new in 1.2)
public abstract class org.omg.CORBA.NVList extends java.lang.Object
 (new in 1.2)
public final class org.omg.CORBA.NameValuePair extends java.lang.Object
 (new in 1.2)
    implements org.omg.CORBA.portable.IDLEntity
public abstract class org.omg.CORBA.NamedValue extends java.lang.Object
 (new in 1.2)
public final class org.omg.CORBA.OBJECT_NOT_EXIST extends org.omg.CORBA.
 SystemException (new in 1.2)
public final class org.omg.CORBA.OBJ_ADAPTER extends org.omg.CORBA.SystemException
(new in 1.2)
public abstract class org.omg.CORBA.ORB extends java.lang.Object (new in 1.2)
public interface org.omg.CORBA.Object extends java.lang.Object (new in 1.2)
public final class org.omg.CORBA.ObjectHolder extends java.lang.Object
 (new in 1.2)
```

```
    implements org.omg.CORBA.portable.Streamable
public final class org.omg.CORBA.PERSIST_STORE extends org.omg.CORBA.
 SystemException (new in 1.2)
public interface org.omg.CORBA.PRIVATE_MEMBER extends java.lang.Object
 (new in 1.2)
public interface org.omg.CORBA.PUBLIC_MEMBER extends java.lang.Object
 (new in 1.2)
public interface org.omg.CORBA.Policy extends java.lang.Object (new in 1.2)
    implements org.omg.CORBA.Object
public final class org.omg.CORBA.PolicyError extends org.omg.CORBA.
 UserException (new in 1.2)
public abstract class org.omg.CORBA.Principal extends java.lang.
 Object (new in 1.2) (deprecated in 1.2)
public final class org.omg.CORBA.PrincipalHolder extends java.lang.
 Object (new in 1.2) (deprecated in 1.2)
    implements org.omg.CORBA.portable.Streamable
public abstract class org.omg.CORBA.Request extends java.lang.Object
 (new in 1.2)
public abstract class org.omg.CORBA.ServerRequest extends java.lang.Object
 (new in 1.2)
public final class org.omg.CORBA.ServiceDetail extends java.lang.Object
 (new in 1.2)
    implements org.omg.CORBA.portable.IDLEntity
public class org.omg.CORBA.ServiceDetailHelper extends java.lang.Object
 (new in 1.2)
public final class org.omg.CORBA.ServiceInformation extends java.lang.Object
 (new in 1.2)
    implements org.omg.CORBA.portable.IDLEntity
public class org.omg.CORBA.ServiceInformationHelper extends java.lang.Object
 (new in 1.2)
public final class org.omg.CORBA.ServiceInformationHolder extends java.lang.
 Object (new in 1.2)
    implements org.omg.CORBA.portable.Streamable
public class org.omg.CORBA.SetOverrideType extends java.lang.Object
 (new in 1.2)
    implements org.omg.CORBA.portable.IDLEntity
public final class org.omg.CORBA.ShortHolder extends java.lang.Object
 (new in 1.2)
    implements org.omg.CORBA.portable.Streamable
public final class org.omg.CORBA.StringHolder extends java.lang.Object
 (new in 1.2)
    implements org.omg.CORBA.portable.Streamable
public final class org.omg.CORBA.StructMember extends java.lang.Object
 (new in 1.2)
    implements org.omg.CORBA.portable.IDLEntity
public abstract class org.omg.CORBA.SystemException extends java.lang.
 RuntimeException (new in 1.2)
public class org.omg.CORBA.TCKind extends java.lang.Object (new in 1.2)
public final class org.omg.CORBA.TRANSACTION_REQUIRED extends org.omg.CORBA.
 SystemException (new in 1.2)
public final class org.omg.CORBA.TRANSACTION_ROLLEDBACK extends org.omg.CORBA.
 SystemException (new in 1.2)
public final class org.omg.CORBA.TRANSIENT extends org.omg.CORBA.
```

continued on next page

continued from previous page

```
 SystemException (new in 1.2)
public abstract class org.omg.CORBA.TypeCode extends java.lang.Object
 (new in 1.2)
   implements org.omg.CORBA.portable.IDLEntity
public final class org.omg.CORBA.TypeCodeHolder extends java.lang.Object
 (new in 1.2)
   implements org.omg.CORBA.portable.Streamable
public final class org.omg.CORBA.UNKNOWN extends org.omg.CORBA.SystemException
 (new in 1.2)
public interface org.omg.CORBA.UNSUPPORTED_POLICY extends java.lang.Object
 (new in 1.2)
public interface org.omg.CORBA.UNSUPPORTED_POLICY_VALUE extends java.lang.
 Object (new in 1.2)
public final class org.omg.CORBA.UnionMember extends java.lang.Object
 (new in 1.2)
   implements org.omg.CORBA.portable.IDLEntity
public final class org.omg.CORBA.UnknownUserException extends org.omg.CORBA.
 UserException (new in 1.2)
public abstract class org.omg.CORBA.UserException extends java.lang.Exception
 (new in 1.2)
   implements org.omg.CORBA.portable.IDLEntity
public interface org.omg.CORBA.VM_ABSTRACT extends java.lang.Object
 (new in 1.2)
public interface org.omg.CORBA.VM_CUSTOM extends java.lang.Object (new in 1.2)
public interface org.omg.CORBA.VM_NONE extends java.lang.Object (new in 1.2)
public interface org.omg.CORBA.VM_TRUNCATABLE extends java.lang.Object
 (new in 1.2)
public final class org.omg.CORBA.ValueMember extends java.lang.Object
 (new in 1.2)
   implements org.omg.CORBA.portable.IDLEntity
public class org.omg.CORBA.WrongTransaction extends org.omg.CORBA.
 UserException (new in 1.2)e
```

Package `org.omg.CORBA.DynAnyPackage`

This package, part of CORBA, defines some exceptions thrown by the `org.omg.CORBA.DynAny` interface.

Listing 3.58 shows all public classes and interfaces in the `org.omg.CORBA.DynAny` package.

LISTING 3.58 `org.omg.CORBA.DynAny` Package Classes and Interfaces List

```
public final class org.omg.CORBA.DynAnyPackage.Invalid extends org.omg.CORBA.
 UserException (new in 1.2)
public final class org.omg.CORBA.DynAnyPackage.InvalidSeq extends org.omg.
 CORBA.UserException (new in 1.2)
public final class org.omg.CORBA.DynAnyPackage.InvalidValue extends org.omg.
 CORBA.UserException (new in 1.2)
public final class org.omg.CORBA.DynAnyPackage.TypeMismatch extends org.omg.
 CORBA.UserException (new in 1.2)
```

Package `org.omg.CORBA.ORBPackage`

This package, part of CORBA, defines some exceptions thrown by CORBA methods.

Listing 3.59 shows all public classes and interfaces in the `org.omg.CORBA.ORBPackage` package.

LISTING 3.59 `org.omg.CORBA.ORBPackage` Classes and Interfaces List

```
public final class org.omg.CORBA.ORBPackage.InconsistentTypeCode extends
 org.omg.CORBA.UserException (new in 1.2)
public class org.omg.CORBA.ORBPackage.InvalidName extends org.omg.CORBA.
 UserException (new in 1.2)
```

Package `org.omg.CORBA.TypeCodePackage`

This package, part of CORBA, defines some exceptions thrown by CORBA methods.

Listing 3.60 shows all public classes and interfaces in the `org.omg.CORBA.TypeCodePackage` package.

LISTING 3.60 `org.omg.CORBA.TypeCodePackage` Classes and Interfaces List

```
public final class org.omg.CORBA.TypeCodePackage.BadKind extends org.omg.CORBA.
 UserException (new in 1.2)
public final class org.omg.CORBA.TypeCodePackage.Bounds extends org.omg.CORBA.
 UserException (new in 1.2)
```

Package `org.omg.CORBA.portable`

This package, part of CORBA, provides a portability layer that allows code to be used with Object Request Brokers (ORBs) from different vendors.

Listing 3.61 shows all public classes and interfaces in the `org.omg.CORBA.portable` package.

LISTING 3.61 `org.omg.CORBA.portable` Classes and Interfaces List

```
public class org.omg.CORBA.portable.ApplicationException extends java.lang.
 Exception (new in 1.2)
public abstract class org.omg.CORBA.portable.Delegate extends java.lang.Object
 (new in 1.2)
public abstract class org.omg.CORBA.portable.InputStream extends java.io.
 InputStream (new in 1.2)
public interface org.omg.CORBA.portable.InvokeHandler extends java.lang.Object
 (new in 1.2)
public abstract class org.omg.CORBA.portable.ObjectImpl extends java.lang.
 Object (new in 1.2)
    implements org.omg.CORBA.Object
public abstract class org.omg.CORBA.portable.OutputStream extends java.io.
```

continued on next page

continued from previous page

```
 OutputStream (new in 1.2)
public final class org.omg.CORBA.portable.RemarshalException extends java.lang.
 Exception (new in 1.2)
public interface org.omg.CORBA.portable.ResponseHandler extends java.lang.
 Object (new in 1.2)
public class org.omg.CORBA.portable.ServantObject extends java.lang.Object
 (new in 1.2)
public interface org.omg.CORBA.portable.Streamable extends java.lang.Object
 (new in 1.2)
```

Package org.omg.CosNaming

This package, part of CORBA, provides an API to name services.

Listing 3.62 shows all public classes and interfaces in the `org.omg.CORBA.CosNaming` package.

LISTING 3.62 `org.omg.CosNaming` Classes and Interfaces List

```
public final class org.omg.CosNaming.Binding extends java.lang.Object
 (new in 1.2)
    implements org.omg.CORBA.portable.IDLEntity
public class org.omg.CosNaming.BindingHelper extends java.lang.Object
 (new in 1.2)
public final class org.omg.CosNaming.BindingHolder extends java.lang.Object
 (new in 1.2)
    implements org.omg.CORBA.portable.Streamable
public interface org.omg.CosNaming.BindingIterator extends java.lang.Object
 (new in 1.2)
    implements org.omg.CORBA.Object
    implements org.omg.CORBA.portable.IDLEntity
public class org.omg.CosNaming.BindingIteratorHelper extends java.lang.Object
 (new in 1.2)
public final class org.omg.CosNaming.BindingIteratorHolder extends java.lang.
 Object (new in 1.2)
    implements org.omg.CORBA.portable.Streamable
public class org.omg.CosNaming.BindingListHelper extends java.lang.Object
(new in 1.2)
public final class org.omg.CosNaming.BindingListHolder extends java.lang.Object
 (new in 1.2)
    implements org.omg.CORBA.portable.Streamable
public final class org.omg.CosNaming.BindingType extends java.lang.Object
(new in 1.2)
    implements org.omg.CORBA.portable.IDLEntity
public class org.omg.CosNaming.BindingTypeHelper extends java.lang.Object
 (new in 1.2)
public final class org.omg.CosNaming.BindingTypeHolder extends java.lang.Object
 (new in 1.2)
    implements org.omg.CORBA.portable.Streamable
public class org.omg.CosNaming.IstringHelper extends java.lang.Object
 (new in 1.2)
public final class org.omg.CosNaming.NameComponent extends java.lang.Object
```

```
(new in 1.2)
   implements org.omg.CORBA.portable.IDLEntity
public class org.omg.CosNaming.NameComponentHelper extends java.lang.Object
 (new in 1.2)
public final class org.omg.CosNaming.NameComponentHolder extends java.lang.
 Object (new in 1.2)
   implements org.omg.CORBA.portable.Streamable
public class org.omg.CosNaming.NameHelper extends java.lang.Object (new in 1.2)
public final class org.omg.CosNaming.NameHolder extends java.lang.Object
 (new in 1.2)
   implements org.omg.CORBA.portable.Streamable
public interface org.omg.CosNaming.NamingContext extends java.lang.Object
 (new in 1.2)
   implements org.omg.CORBA.Object
   implements org.omg.CORBA.portable.IDLEntity
public class org.omg.CosNaming.NamingContextHelper extends java.lang.Object
 (new in 1.2)
public final class org.omg.CosNaming.NamingContextHolder extends java.lang.
 Object (new in 1.2)
   implements org.omg.CORBA.portable.Streamable
public abstract class org.omg.CosNaming._BindingIteratorImplBase extends org.
 omg.CORBA.
 DynamicImplementation (new in 1.2)
   implements org.omg.CosNaming.BindingIterator
public class org.omg.CosNaming._BindingIteratorStub extends org.omg.CORBA.
 portable.ObjectImpl (new in 1.2)
   implements org.omg.CosNaming.BindingIterator
public abstract class org.omg.CosNaming._NamingContextImplBase extends org.omg.
 CORBA.
 DynamicImplementation (new in 1.2)
   implements org.omg.CosNaming.NamingContext
public class org.omg.CosNaming._NamingContextStub extends org.omg.CORBA.
 portable.
 ObjectImpl (new in 1.2)
   implements org.omg.CosNaming.NamingContext
```

Package `org.omg.CosNaming.NamingContextPackage`

This package, part of CORBA, describes exceptions thrown by classes in package `org.omg.CosNaming`.

Listing 3.63 shows all public classes and interfaces in the `org.omg.CORBA.CosNaming.NamingContextPackage` package.

LISTING 3.63 `org.omg.CosNaming.NamingContextPackage` Classes and Interfaces List

```
public final class org.omg.CosNaming.NamingContextPackage.AlreadyBound extends
 org.omg.CORBA.
 UserException (new in 1.2)
   implements org.omg.CORBA.portable.IDLEntity
public class org.omg.CosNaming.NamingContextPackage.AlreadyBoundHelper extends
 java.lang.Object (new in 1.2)
```

continued on next page

continued from previous page

```
public final class org.omg.CosNaming.NamingContextPackage.AlreadyBoundHolder
 extends java.lang.Object (new in 1.2)
    implements org.omg.CORBA.portable.Streamable
public final class org.omg.CosNaming.NamingContextPackage.CannotProceed extends
 org.omg.CORBA.UserException (new in 1.2)
    implements org.omg.CORBA.portable.IDLEntity
public class org.omg.CosNaming.NamingContextPackage.CannotProceedHelper extends
 java.lang.Object (new in 1.2)
public final class org.omg.CosNaming.NamingContextPackage.CannotProceedHolder
 extends java.lang.Object (new in 1.2)
    implements org.omg.CORBA.portable.Streamable
public final class org.omg.CosNaming.NamingContextPackage.InvalidName extends
 org.omg.CORBA.UserException (new in 1.2)
    implements org.omg.CORBA.portable.IDLEntity
public class org.omg.CosNaming.NamingContextPackage.InvalidNameHelper extends
 java.lang.Object (new in 1.2)
public final class org.omg.CosNaming.NamingContextPackage.InvalidNameHolder
 extends java.lang.Object (new in 1.2)
    implements org.omg.CORBA.portable.Streamable
public final class org.omg.CosNaming.NamingContextPackage.NotEmpty extends
 org.omg.CORBA.UserException (new in 1.2)
    implements org.omg.CORBA.portable.IDLEntity
public class org.omg.CosNaming.NamingContextPackage.NotEmptyHelper extends
 java.lang.Object (new in 1.2)
public final class org.omg.CosNaming.NamingContextPackage.NotEmptyHolder
 extends java.lang.Object (new in 1.2)
    implements org.omg.CORBA.portable.Streamable
public final class org.omg.CosNaming.NamingContextPackage.NotFound extends
 org.omg.CORBA.UserException (new in 1.2)
    implements org.omg.CORBA.portable.IDLEntity
public class org.omg.CosNaming.NamingContextPackage.NotFoundHelper extends
 java.lang.Object (new in 1.2)
public final class org.omg.CosNaming.NamingContextPackage.NotFoundHolder
 extends java.lang.Object (new in 1.2)
    implements org.omg.CORBA.portable.Streamable
public final class org.omg.CosNaming.NamingContextPackage.NotFoundReason
 extends java.lang.Object (new in 1.2)
    implements org.omg.CORBA.portable.IDLEntity
public class org.omg.CosNaming.NamingContextPackage.NotFoundReasonHelper
 extends java.lang.Object (new in 1.2)
public final class org.omg.CosNaming.NamingContextPackage.NotFoundReasonHolder
 extends java.lang.Object (new in 1.2)
    implements org.omg.CORBA.portable.Streamable
```

Summary

This chapter has presented a high-level view of the JDK1.2 class libraries. The details of using the libraries are not specific to Linux, and can fill (and have filled) many books. To explore the libraries in more detail, two good references are *Java 1.2 Class Libraries Unleashed* and *JFC Unleashed* (Sams).

CHAPTER 4

ADDITIONAL SUN JAVA CLASS LIBRARY SPECS

Additional class libraries available from Sun, either as specs or as implemented class libraries, fall into two categories:

- Standard Extensions—Class libraries targeted at interesting markets. A standard extension must have a full specification, a reference implementation, and a test suite.
- Enterprise Technologies—Class libraries focused on server-side requirements. This is an umbrella category covering numerous technologies in various degrees of implementation: some of them are already core components, some are already standard extensions, and the remainder lack all the necessary pieces to be considered either.

Some of these pieces depend on JDK1.2, and availability is highly variable. For standard extensions implemented entirely in Java, working versions are available today from Sun. Extensions described as "Pure Java" or "100% Pure Java" have passed a specific conformance test suite (see section 10.1), but any extension implemented in Java should work on Linux.

For extensions that require some non-Java, native OS support, availability depends on a porting effort (such as one by the Blackdown Linux porting team) or a cleanroom implementation by an outside developer.

The bottom line: If you want to depend on these technologies, make sure that they are available for the development and deployment platforms you care about. In many cases, you can ship copies of these libraries for deployment, either free or after obtaining licenses from Sun. Details are provided on the Sun Web pages devoted to the particular technologies.

Standard Extensions

Here's the current list. All of these are available from Sun for download, from its main Java Web site at `http://java.sun.com`.

JavaBeans Activation Framework (JAF)

The JAF is a pure-Java library that supports deployment of JavaBeans components to handle arbitrary data types. For example, if you have written a Bean that knows how to display a new, previously unsupported graphics file format, the JAF handles the mapping between the requirement ("display a file of this type in this browser window") and the Bean with the capability.

As a pure-Java component, the JAF works with Linux and any other Java-compliant platform.

Java Naming and Directory Interface (JNDI)

The JNDI is a Java API to standard enterprise naming and directory services, such as Lightweight Directory Access Protocol (LDAP), Novell Directory Services (NDS), Internet Domain Name System (DNS), Network Information System (NIS), and others. JNDI provides a uniform interface to these services, freeing the developer from dealing with a plethora of different APIs for different services. A Service Provider Interface allows new services to be added.

JNDI is implemented in Java and works with Linux and any other Java-compliant platform. Sun announced in summer of 1999 that JNDI will become a core component of JDK1.3.

JavaMail

The JavaMail API provides classes to support an email system and includes service providers for the popular Internet Message Access Protocol (IMAP) and Simple Mail Transport Protocol (SMTP) protocols, with an optional Post Office Protocol (POP3) provider also available. Sun is relying on other vendors to supply service providers for other protocols (MAPI, NNTP, Lotus Notes, and so on). JavaMail depends on the JNDI extension (discussed previously).

JavaMail is implemented in Java and works with Linux and any other Java-compliant platform.

InfoBus

InfoBus is a support API for JavaBeans components. It facilitates communications among Beans by creating an *information bus* abstraction for handling exchange of data.

As a pure-Java component, InfoBus works with Linux and any other Java-compliant platform.

Java3D

Java3D is a 3D rendering API for support of modeling, gaming, and other 3D applications.

Java3D depends on underlying platform graphics capabilities and is not available in a Java-only version. Sun provides versions for Solaris and Windows (based on the OpenGL graphics API) and is testing a version for Windows based on the DirectX graphics API.

We discuss a Linux version of Java3D in Chapter 34, "Java 3D Extension."

Java Media Framework (JMF)

The JMF creates a framework for multimedia playback, capture, and manipulation. The version 1.0 API supports only playback; version 2.0 (currently in early access) adds capture, support for plug-in CODECs, broadcast, and manipulation.

Versions of the JMF implemented entirely in Java are available, as are higher-performing platform-specific versions for Solaris and Windows.

Java Servlet API

One of the most important and successful Java technologies, ***servlets*** are Java programs that run on Web servers. They are the Java analog of ***CGI scripts***, which run in response to browser requests for particular URLs.

Web server-side programs are a hot and contentious area in the Web development world, and there is no shortage of debate over the relative merits of Java servlets, Perl, and other comparable technologies. The true answer to this debate is: use the technology that does the job for you.

Sun provides a pure-Java implementation of a development kit for servlets. The actual environment in which servlets run must, of course, be provided by Web servers themselves. Many free and commercial Web servers, such as Sun's own Web server product, support servlets. In Chapter 65, "Java on the Web: Java Servlets and Apache JServ," we set up a Web server with servlet support, built entirely from free components.

Java Cryptography Extension (JCE)

The JCE creates a framework for support of public- and private-key cryptography algorithms. The implementation includes service providers for some common encryption algorithms (DES, Blowfish, Diffie-Hellman) and an interface that allows adding other service providers.

Sun's implementation of JCE is completely in Java and works with Linux and any other Java-compliant platform. Due to export restrictions, it is only available for download to sites in the USA and Canada. However, cleanroom implementations of the JCE are available from vendors outside the USA.

JavaHelp

JavaHelp is a pure-Java help system—Sun's answer to the horribly uneven support for help systems among various computing platforms. JavaHelp supports authoring and display of HTML-based help on a wide variety of Java-compliant platforms.

As a pure-Java component, JavaHelp works with Linux and any other Java-compliant platform.

Java Communications API (JavaComm)

JavaComm provides an API for access to serial and parallel ports on your system. Such support is platform-specific, and Sun ships versions for Windows and Solaris. Chapter 37, "KJC: Kopi Java Compiler," describes a partial implementation available for Linux.

Java Management API (JMX) (specification only)

JMX (currently in early access) is a framework for management of networked services and resources, through such protocols as SNMP (Simplified Network Management Protocol). Using JMX, you can develop management tools and agents to assist in running networks. It is currently in specification form and no implementation is available.

Java Advanced Imaging (JAI)

The JAI API supports advanced, high-performance imaging capabilities beyond what is provided in the core image classes. It is targeted at advanced markets such as medical imaging, seismological imaging, and document processing.

JAI is available in a Java implementation usable on any Java-compliant platform. Versions will also appear that take advantage of native platform computation and imaging capabilities.

Enterprise Technologies

The following sections provide a brief rundown of Java's Enterprise Technologies. Those that are not part of the core classes or the standard extensions just described are slated to become standard extensions in the near future.

Enterprise JavaBeans (EJB)

Not to be confused with the JavaBean component model, EJB is a specification for deployment of reusable business logic components.

Confused? The similarity of names is unfortunate. Like JavaBeans, EJB is about reusable components. The similarity ends there: JavaBeans are arbitrary self-describing components usable in a wide variety of contexts, whereas EJB is a highly constrained environment for delivery of services. In short, the difference between JavaBeans and Enterprise JavaBeans is that they have nothing to do with each other.

What is an EJBean? It's a class that models a piece of ***business logic***—the role of a teller in a banking transaction, an accounting rule in an order processing system, and so on.

What do you do with an EJBean? You place it in a container in an EJB application server (see Figure 4.1).

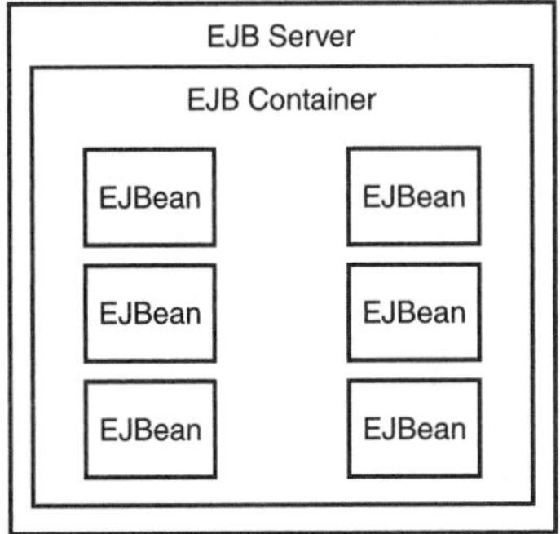

FIGURE 4.1
Enterprise JavaBeans deployed in an enterprise application server.

The structure ***around*** the EJBean handles the many minutiae of enterprise applications—security, database connectivity, network access, persistence, threading, RMI, and so on—while the EJBean concentrates on providing basic logic. The application server is then configured to support processes within the enterprise—for example, a Web-based product ordering system (see Figure 4.2).

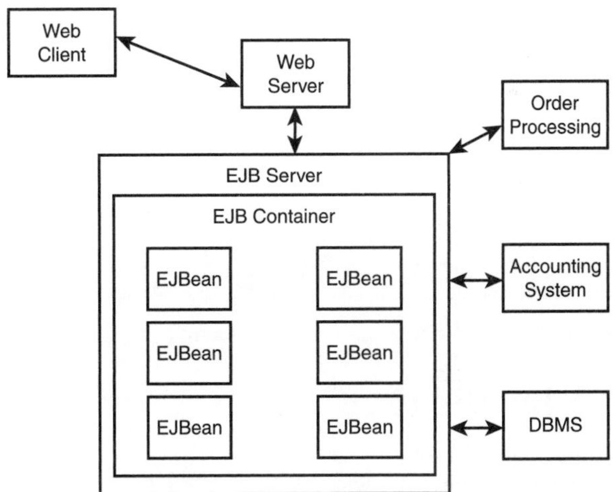

FIGURE 4.2
A Web-based product ordering system built around EJB.

From within the EJB server, EJBeans are deployed as needed in the business processes. For instance, an applet running on the Web client may need to execute a piece of business logic to check product inventory. It might invoke that logic in a server-resident EJBean method through an RMI call (see Figure 4.3).

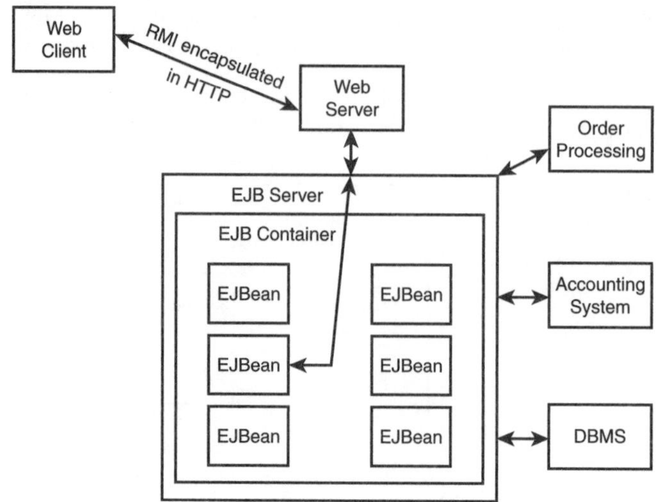

FIGURE 4.3
Using EJB to provide business logic for a client-side requirement.

This is an example of a ***session bean***: a service performed on behalf of a client. EJB also defines ***entity beans***: persistent objects that represent data, such as cached database entries.

These diagrams (Figures 4.1, 4.2, and 4.3) are, of course, simplifications. These are big problems, and EJB is a big, hairy spec still in early adoption (and in competition with other technologies). These pictures provide only a quick snapshot of the capabilities.

The EJB spec solidified in early 1999, and Sun does not yet ship any reference implementations for EJB servers or containers. That should change with shipment of Java 2 Enterprise Edition (scheduled for late 1999). However, EJB is already supported by a number of commercial vendors of application servers and is showing promise as an important enterprise application integration be technology.

JavaServer Pages (JSP)

A companion be technology to Java Servlets, JSP supports embedding of Java source code in Web pages. The best-known competing technology is Microsoft's Active Server Pages (ASP), but similar technologies also exist for embedding of Perl and other languages.

A reference implementation is available in Sun's JavaServer Web Development Kit (JSWDK), available for download from `http://java.sun.com`.

Java Servlet

Already a standard extension (discussed previously), servlets are like CGI scripts: an entire URL is implemented programmatically. Contrast that with JSP, in which small pieces of Java source code are embedded in otherwise static HTML.

Java Naming and Directory Interface

Already a standard extension (previously mentioned).

Java IDL

Interface Definition Language (IDL) is the portable specification language used to describe data passed among CORBA-compliant distributed applications. ***Java IDL*** is Sun's term for the combination of JDK1.2 (which supports parts of the CORBA specification) and the idl2java compiler, separately available from Sun, that generates the necessary stubs and skeletons Java needs to interface with CORBA.

The idl2java compiler is a native program, distributed for Solaris and Windows by Sun and not yet available for Linux. If you need to compile IDL into Java for use with the JDK1.2 CORBA classes, you will need to do so on an Windows or Solaris platform.

Java Database Connectivity (JDBC)

The JDBC API is part of the core Java class libraries.

Java Message Service (JMS)

JMS is a Java API for the relatively new area of ***enterprise messaging***—infrastructures to support secure, reliable message-passing among applications. It is currently in specification form, with no implementation available.

Java Transaction API (JTA)

JTA is a Java API to support interaction with distributed transaction systems. It is currently in specification form, with no implementation available.

Java Transaction Service (JTS)

JTS supports implementation of servers for distributed transaction systems. It is currently in specification form, with no implementation available.

JavaMail

The JavaMail API is already a standard extension (previously mentioned).

RMI/IIOP

RMI/IIOP is an integration mechanism that supports encapsulating Java RMI calls in the Internet Inter-Orb Protocol (IIOP) used in CORBA environments. In summer of 1999, Sun announced its upcoming availability with JDK1.3.

Summary

This chapter has described extension and enterprise APIs for Java, which are targeted at supporting Java application development in specific environments. This is an area that is rapidly changing, as APIs undergo revision, release, acceptance, and, in some cases, incorporation into the core Java specification.

PART II

A BRIEF INTRODUCTION TO LINUX

We took a few chapters to introduce Java; now we take a few chapters to introduce Linux.

The past ten years have witnessed a remarkable explosion in personal computing. The success of Microsoft, Intel, and the PC industry in penetrating the home and the office has put huge amounts of computing power into the hands of normal human beings who don't know a bit from a byte and who have no idea what an operating system is. They know, simply, that their computer tends to work most of the time.

Against this background, the emergence of a new PC-based operating system as an important force in the world is one of history's most unlikely events. This part of the book examines what Linux is, where it comes from, how it is being used, and how you can obtain it for your own use.

CHAPTER 5

WHAT IS LINUX?

This chapter gives you the 10-minute tour of Linux. If you are already an experienced Linux user, you might want to skip ahead. Our purpose, for the benefit of Java developers new to Linux, is to give some basic background and help get you started.

We begin with a look at UNIX, including a bit of history to help understand how UNIX and Linux got to be what they are today. For readers unfamiliar with some of these details, they will be relevant to understanding the platform-specific issues faced by Java on the Linux platform.

For readers interested in deep coverage of Linux, we recommend *Linux Unleashed* (Sams).

What Is UNIX?

The UNIX operating system has been around since 1969 and is the longest-running and most spectacularly successful experiment in the history of computer science. It originated in the halls of Bell Labs, at the hands of two researchers: Ken Thompson and Dennis Ritchie. Over the years, UNIX has served as a primary development and test bed for innovations in computer architecture, operating systems design, memory management, file systems, database management systems, languages and compilers, I/O architectures, multitasking and multiprocessing, and computer networking. UNIX is closely associated with the development and evolution of the protocols that make up the Internet, and UNIX-based servers make up a large part of the infrastructure of the Internet.

UNIX spent its infancy behind the walls of Bell Labs' parent corporation, AT&T, where it was used internally throughout the company. It began to spread beyond the confines of Bell Labs in the mid-1970s, infiltrating computer science departments at several universities. As AT&T began to commercialize UNIX, several universities started their own research programs based on UNIX, and innovation proliferated. The most influential university activity took place at UC Berkeley, and, with help from government research grants, Berkeley became the home of a public-sector UNIX development stream. During much of the 1980s, the AT&T and BSD (Berkeley System Distribution) streams continued in parallel, both competing with and influencing each other.

As UNIX was increasingly commercialized in the 1980s, the differences between AT&T and BSD UNIX resulted in competitive tensions among UNIX vendors and headaches for independent software vendors and customers. These problems have been blamed for preventing widespread consumer and business acceptance of UNIX—and the huge success of the Intel/Microsoft architecture certainly underscores that point. But UNIX continues to survive and thrive because it solves problems that other OSs do not. And the standardization efforts of the past several years have helped to reduce the difficulties of supporting the UNIX platform (that the vendors have not eliminated those difficulties entirely is another reason for the ascent of Linux).

The commercial implementations of UNIX sold most widely today include Hewlett-Packard Company's HP-UX, Sun Microsystems' Solaris, Compaq/DEC's Ultrix, IBM's AIX, and SGI's IRIX.

The Structure of UNIX

More than any other operating system, UNIX is made up of many small parts and—to recycle an old cliché—greatly exceeds the sum of its parts. The OS is constructed in layers, with core operations performed by a privileged kernel and everything else happening in isolated concurrent activity streams called *processes*—the system creates concurrence by dividing the CPU and other resources among the processes and switching between processes tens or hundreds of times a second.

The isolation among processes, and the isolation enforced between processes and the kernel, is a major reason behind UNIX's stability—the relatively high immunity to interference between programs, and the general inability of user programs to damage the system.

Figure 5.1 gives a general idea of the structure of UNIX.

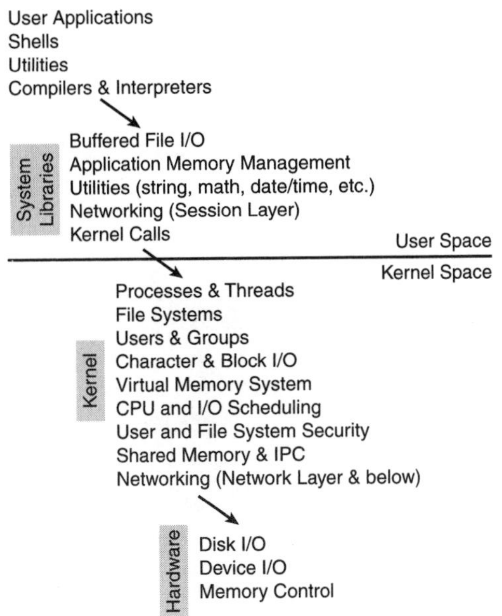

FIGURE 5.1
UNIX's layered structure supports multitasking and enforces protective isolation among processes as well as between processes and the kernel.

The system was designed by software developers for software developers, which resulted in a rich environment for software development—a distinction that UNIX still enjoys today. It also resulted in a rich collection of tools and utilities that make it easy for software developers to work on UNIX and to easily build complex tools out of simple tools. That such utilities, completely nongraphical and blessed with such obscure names as sed, awk, grep, vi, troff, cpio, and so on, never fired the imagination of the general public is another reason UNIX did not penetrate the consumer and business market. (We will explore important tools for use in development work in Chapter 9, "Setting Up a Linux Development Environment.")

And there is something else missing from the picture....

UNIX and GUIs

Until the late 1980s, the UNIX world was largely text-oriented. UNIX applications, tools, and utilities tended not to rely on graphics of any form. Applications that needed graphics, 2D or 3D, had to code to the proprietary graphical interfaces provided by each of the UNIX vendors and create their own GUIs: not a friendly environment for innovation.

This began to change with the advent of the X Window System, which arose from research at MIT's Laboratory for Computer Science. The X Window System serves 2D graphical applications with a networked client/server model, in which applications rendering graphics are *clients*, and workstations providing those rendering capabilities are *servers*. Figure 5.2 shows an X application in its simplest form.

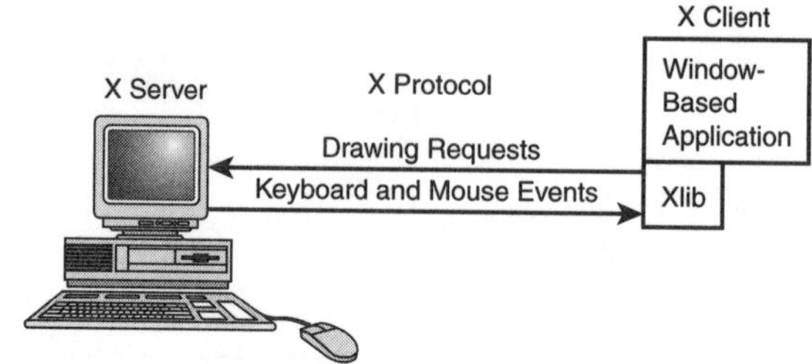

FIGURE 5.2
Basic X-based application architecture.

The X Window System defines a standard set of services to be provided by an X display server, and a standard network protocol through which applications can create and control windows, render text and graphics, and interact with the user. Because the X protocol is network-transparent, applications need not reside on the same system as the X server. Users with inexpensive workstations can run compute-intensive graphical applications on large servers while enjoying full graphical I/O from their desks.

This vendor-neutral approach to distributed graphics gained the support of all UNIX vendors, who formed the MIT X Consortium to further the evolution of X. But something is still missing from the picture....

The X Window System is not a GUI. It is, by design and intention, everything needed to create a GUI—basic windows, rendering, images, and so on—but it lacks the higher-level abstractions that make up a graphical user interface: pushbuttons, text editors, scrollbars, and the like. Design of GUIs, and of window managers (the "traffic cops" responsible for controlling how various applications share the screen space in the X server), was left as an exercise for the UNIX vendors.

The UNIX vendors rose to the challenge, competing fiercely for several years and, finally, converging on a GUI toolkit, *Motif*, and a Desktop (window manager + extras), the *Common Desktop Environment* (CDE). So a more complete picture of a typical X application environment looks like Figure 5.3.

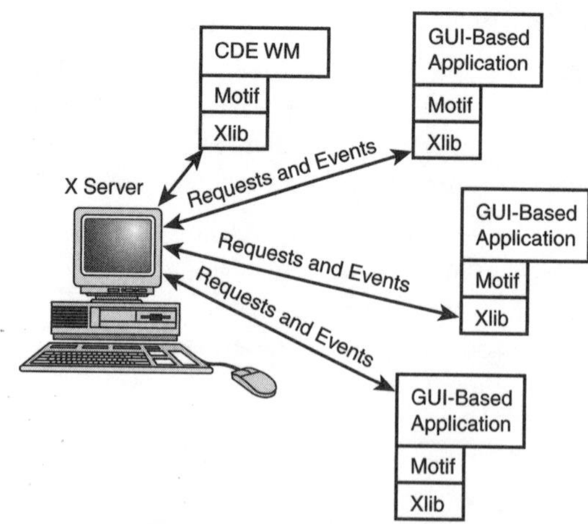

FIGURE 5.3
X Window System GUI and application environment architecture.

Each GUI-based application interacts with the X server, and the CDE window manager controls the behavior of the desktop (window geometry and borders, icons, overall look and feel). Applications also interact with each other, and with the window manager, using inter-client protocols. And because all interactions take place over network-transparent protocols, all these components—applications, window manager, and the X server—can be running on different systems.

As complex as this appears, most of the interaction details shown in the diagram are handled by the toolkits. Writing GUI applications for X is not difficult.

Subtleties

The relationship among the X Window System, GUI toolkits, and the window manager is strange and new if you're coming from the non-UNIX world. They are all separate components in UNIX and Linux:

- The X Window System server runs the display, keyboard, and mouse. It is responsible for basic graphics rendering.
- GUI toolkits are separate components, bound with individual applications. Motif is the most commercial toolkit but (despite the suggestion of the previous diagram) not the only one. So, for example, the logic to implement a button or text box resides with the GUI toolkit, not with the X server—different applications using different toolkits routinely coexist under X.
- The window manager, a component of the desktop, handles controlling how applications share the space on the X display. It is just another application, albeit one with special privileges to control layout and visibility of other applications. CDE is the most commercial, but not the only, desktop, and recent development work within the open source community has led to exciting alternatives to CDE (more in Chapter 7, "Configuring Your Linux Desktop").

To illustrate, Figure 5.4 shows a typical screen dump from my X display. I am running a desktop called KDE, which is responsible for the background color, the icons, the buttons at the bottom, the placement of my application windows, and the decorations around the application windows.

The topmost application is a terminal emulator, kvt, which uses the Qt GUI toolkit. Below that is an instance of Netscape, which uses Motif. And below that is a remote-dialup script that uses the Tk GUI toolkit. When we start running Java applications with the Swing interface, we will find yet another GUI sharing the desktop.

Because the desktop controls the look and feel (and your personal satisfaction) for the system, we will explore the topic of configuring your desktop in Chapter 7, "Configuring Your Linux Desktop."

A Brief Comment on UNIX/X Versus Microsoft Windows

Although the differences between the UNIX and Microsoft architectures are well beyond the scope of this book, a brief observation will be helpful in illuminating the platform-specific issues later in the book.

In the Microsoft architecture, the GUI, the window system, and the desktop are all integral to the kernel, and applications must run locally (even sharing some address space with the kernel). By contrast, the various X components are independent, non-kernel processes, and UNIX enforces a significant amount of isolation between processes and the kernel.

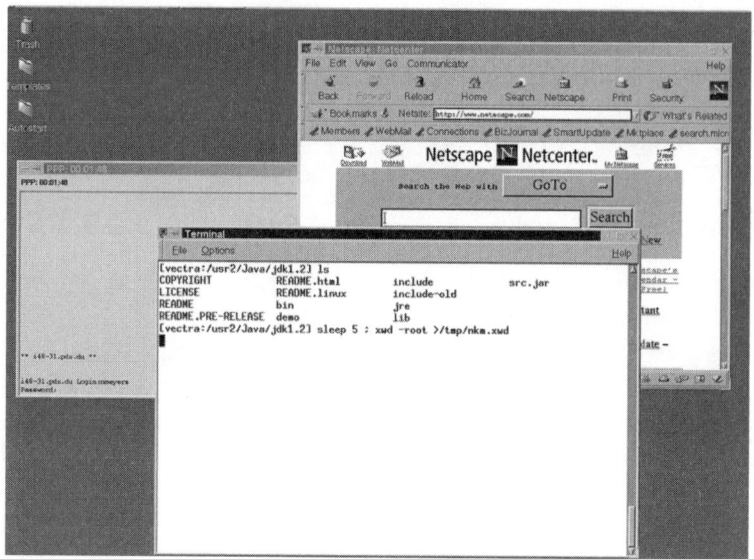

FIGURE 5.4
A dump of the author's desktop, showing a Linux desktop (KDE) and three different applications running with three different toolkits.

The close integration of Microsoft Windows has important advantages (GUI performance, consistency of interfaces) *and* major disadvantages (huge and complex operating system, lack of flexibility, fragility, lack of portability). As you will see when examining platform-specific performance issues, the distributed nature of the X Window System creates Java performance challenges unique to UNIX and Linux platforms. The good news: tuning Java application performance on one platform often benefits performance on all platforms.

What Is Linux?

Having briefly explored 30 years of computer science history, we can begin to answer the question: What is Linux? A little more history....

UNIX has grown up in a mixed academic/commercial environment, and its history is full of talented innovators who find the pursuit of computer science at least as interesting as making money, if not more so. Like all scientists, computer scientists like to work in packs and tend to prefer collaboration over working behind locked doors.

The growth of the computer industry naturally led to tensions between making science and making money. The problem is not unique to computer science: we see it in physics (the electronics industry), biology (the bioengineering and pharmaceutical industries), and elsewhere.

What is unique to computer science is that the scientists fought back. Linux is but one example, and two names stand out as particularly crucial in the development of that example: Richard Stallman and Linus Torvalds.

Richard Stallman: The Apostle of Free Software

Richard Stallman, formerly of MIT, founded the GNU project in 1984 (`http://www.gnu.org`). GNU (a recursive acronym for "GNU is Not UNIX") set out to write a completely free replacement for UNIX. His reasons, which he has described in passionate writings, stem from a personal conviction that the commercialization of UNIX was seriously stifling innovation in the field, and from deep convictions about the ethics of intellectual property law.

In founding GNU, Stallman set out to create a new category of software: *free* software, where *free* denoted something much broader than a zero-dollar price tag. Free software, in the GNU lexicon, means software that the user is free to run, free to modify, free to share, and free to improve. This notion has gained much currency in the past two years, with the emergence of the Open Source software movement.

Recalling our earlier illustration, a UNIX system consists of a kernel, system libraries, and many tools and utilities. As of this writing, the GNU kernel (called the *Hurd*—an obscure acronym) is not finished, but everything else is. The GNU project has built an extensive collection of free versions of many UNIX utilities and libraries. And, most significantly, GNU developed a compiler and core library for the C programming language—a critical piece of technology for OS development.

Linus Torvalds: Kernel Hacker

Linus Torvalds, a Finnish computer science student, was a user of the Minix operating system (a small, academic UNIX-like OS) when he decided he could write a better one himself. He set to the task and, in 1991, published version 0.02 of the Linux kernel for the Intel 80386 CPU. It wasn't much to look at, but it fired the imagination of kernel hackers throughout the Internet world, and a movement was born.

Linus and his cadre of like-minded hackers continued their collaborative work (Linux is truly a product of the Internet), and, in 1994, Linus published version 1.0 of the Linux kernel. It was not the world's first UNIX for the 80386 architecture—Xenix was available in the commercial market—but it was free, and it worked well on this widely available CPU. Suddenly, millions of old and new affordable computers had a potential future as UNIX platforms. Current market research suggests that Linux now runs on as many platforms as do all other UNIXes combined.

Of course, an operating system is more than a kernel. With the availability of the Linux kernel, a new opportunity opened up for Richard Stallman's unfinished work.

Linux Kernel + GNU = Linux OS

With some simple addition, Kernel + GNU, you have a fully functional UNIX-like OS. We say *UNIX-like*, not UNIX, because GNU and Linux are original works: not a single line is licensed from the holders of the UNIX franchise. But the functionality is all in place, and the Linux community tracks the evolving standards and keeps Linux current.

Because of GNU's central role in the Linux environment, you will also hear Linux called "GNU/Linux," "The GNU System on Linux," or some similar name. These are all alternative names for the same thing, and this book opts for the common convention: we'll use "Linux" to describe the OS.

There is, of course, more to the Linux OS than the kernel and the GNU components. The XFree86 project contributes the important X Window System, many utilities were derived from the Berkeley UNIX effort, and a wide variety of tools and drivers come from individual and corporate contributors. The job of assembling all these pieces into a product has created a new type of business: Linux distributions.

We will talk about these businesses, with increasingly well-known names such as Red Hat and Caldera, in the Chapter 6, "How to Obtain and Install Linux."

Linux Platforms

Linux started out life on the Intel *x*86 architecture but, thanks to its portable design and implementation, has found a home on more computing platforms than any other OS. Table 5.1 lists the platforms on which Linux is or will be available as of this writing:

TABLE 5.1 Linux Platforms

Vendor	Computer	CPU
(many)	PC	Intel x86
(several)	Workstations/Servers	PowerPC
Compaq	Workstations/Servers	Alpha
HP	Workstations/Servers	PA-RISC
(several)	Workstations/Servers	Intel ia64
SGI	Workstations/Servers	MIPS
Sun	Workstations/Servers	Sparc
Corel, etc.	Appliances/etc.	StrongARM

Many of the preceding ports came into being through independent volunteer efforts, but the past year has seen a major embrace of Linux by all major UNIX vendors. The port to ia64, for example, is being spearheaded by HP and is targeted for availability when the first ia64 platforms ship in mid-2000.

Linux is used in a huge range of environments, from small embedded systems to clustered supercomputers. It's a popular choice for *x*86-based PCs that have fallen behind the growing demands of supporting Microsoft operating systems. And Linux enjoys a dominant role in the running of the Internet, from Web servers to firewalls to routers. The degree of Linux's success is astonishing: no novelist could have invented it. As truth, it is utterly stranger than fiction.

Summary

This chapter has provided a high-level architectural view of Linux and of the environment—OS, graphical display, and GUI—in which Linux applications run. As Linux continues to gain acceptance, its role in the Internet, and consequently in the world of Java, will become increasingly visible and important.

CHAPTER 6

HOW TO OBTAIN AND INSTALL LINUX

This chapter is for Java users and developers who are new to Linux; it is targeted at helping you run Linux for the first time. We discuss Linux distributions—what they are, how to get them, and how to install them.

Linux is very different from other PC operating systems. Unlike Microsoft Windows or IBM OS/2, it is not a monolithic offering from a large OS vendor. Linux is a collection of many pieces—a kernel, drivers, libraries, utilities, compilers, windowing system, desktop, toys and games, and so on—that come from hundreds of different sources. This is good news for Linux users: the abundance of choice allows you to build systems targeted to specific needs, such as software development, Internet firewalls, Web servers, X terminals, and network routers, to name a few.

The choices you face in building a Linux system *could* be overwhelming, but they are not. An entirely new business, the packaging of Linux distributions, has grown up around the problem of shipping and installing systems. A Linux distribution is a collection of the pieces you need to build a system, plus an automatic installation program to do the heavy lifting.

The three basic steps to installing a distribution are

1. Choose and obtain a distribution.
2. Boot up the distribution from floppy or CD-ROM.
3. Follow the instructions on your screen.

We discuss the first topic here, with a look at the most popular distributions. Because the landscape is ever-changing, it's a good idea to check on the latest available distributions: A good source of information on current distributions is `http://www.linux.org/dist`.

The full, gory details of installing Linux are beyond the scope of this book, but we illustrate with a few screen shots to give you a general idea of what you will experience.

Choosing a Distribution

Four major commercial distributions, plus several smaller commercial, derivative, and non-commercial distributions are available for Linux. The commercial distribution vendors add value, and derive much of their income, from packaging and selling the media and books that make up the distributions. Their distributions include all the free components you need for Linux in addition to value-added installation and configuration software and some commercial software from various sources.

The commercial distributions are usually sold in two forms: a reasonably priced bundle of media and books available through computer stores and mail order, and free versions available on the Web (and bundled with almost every Linux book sold). The free versions come without bundled commercial software or support. My recommendation, if you choose a commercial distribution, is that your first Linux purchase be a commercial bundle; the printed materials and the free support can greatly speed you through the early learning curve.

The non-commercial distributions, and the free versions of the commercial distributions, are also commonly available from a number of CD-ROM distributors, such as CheapBytes (`http://www.cheapbytes.com`), Linux System Labs (`http://www.lsl.com`), and others.

Let's look at the distribution vendors, beginning with the big four.

Red Hat Software

Red Hat Software (`http://www.redhat.com`) is emerging as a big name in distribution vendors, with the highest commercial and investor recognition of any Linux business. It has long been a popular distribution in the home market and is moving seriously into the corporate market. Services include a Linux portal (its home page), a growing knowledge base of Linux advice, a research & development lab focused on solving Linux usability problems, and commercial support services.

I am a Red Hat user, so the examples in this book will tend to be Red Hat-centric. But don't let my example prejudice you; there are other excellent distributions.

Caldera

Caldera (`http://www.caldera.com`) is more focused on the business market and on back-room servers than is Red Hat. The company started out as a Novell startup and boasts a strong competence (and a commercial product suite) in hosting Novell networks on Linux boxes. Caldera also bundles a professional office suite, Star Office. Services include a knowledge base, professional support, and education.

SuSE

SuSE (`http://www.suse.com`), based in Germany, is Europe's largest distribution vendor. It is now pushing aggressively into the North American market and is business-focused with a strong competence in databases. Its products and services include enhanced X Window System display servers, professional office bundles, installation support, and a support database.

TurboLinux

TurboLinux (`http://www.turbolinux.com`) is a Japan-based distribution focused on high-performance clusters and on back-room servers for Internet and Web services. TurboLinux also boasts a strong competency in Asian language support, and is the leading distribution in Asia.

Mandrake

Mandrake (`http://www.linuxmandrake.com`) is a noncommercial derivative of Red Hat. Its focus is on making distributions easy to install—particularly the thorny problems of installing and configuring the desktop and detecting hardware devices. A Mandrake distribution is a free Red Hat distribution plus a friendlier install process, for which Mandrake has received good reviews in the trade press.

Debian

Debian (`http://www.debian.org`) is a noncommercial distribution published by Software In The Public Interest, Inc. The distribution has a reputation as being difficult to install, easy to maintain, and of high quality.

Slackware

Slackware (`http://www.slackware.com`) is published by Walnut Creek CD-ROM, a company that specializes in selling collections of shareware and freeware.

Walking Through an Installation

Let's do a brief walkthrough of a Red Hat 6.0 installation to give you an idea of what is involved in the process. Our intent is to provide a brief overview; the Red Hat Linux Installation Guide provides much more detail.

The packaged product comes with a bootable CD-ROM and some boot floppies. If you have a free version without the boot floppies, the CD-ROM includes some floppy disk images and a DOS executable, `RAWRITE.EXE`, which you can use to create the floppies from a DOS or Windows machine. (You probably don't need the floppies; most modern PCs can boot from CD-ROM. But if you do, just use `RAWRITE` to create the floppy, as in the example in Figure 6.1 with the Red Hat CD-ROM in the D: drive. After creating the floppy, you can exit DOS/Windows and begin the installation process.

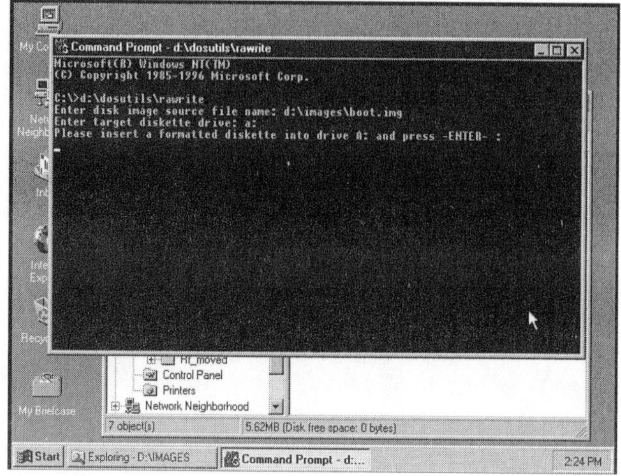

FIGURE 6.1
Running the `RAWRITE.EXE` utility to create Linux boot disks from a Microsoft Windows environment.

Reboot your machine with the boot CD-ROM or floppy in place. After booting, you see the initial Red Hat installation screen (see Figure 6.2).

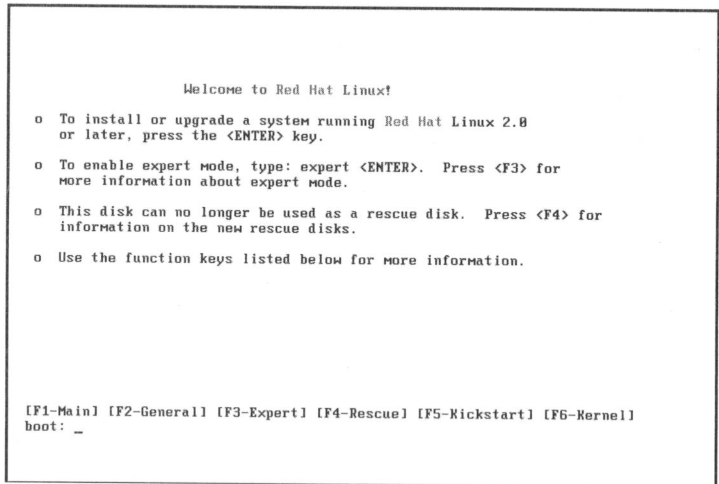

FIGURE 6.2
Initial Red Hat installation startup screen.

After you press Enter, the system loads a small installation kernel and welcomes you to the start of the installation process (see Figure 6.3).

You navigate through this process using the Tab key and the spacebar; there is no mouse capability yet. You need to answer a few screens of questions about language, keyboard, and installation media, and then answer a crucial question (see Figure 6.4).

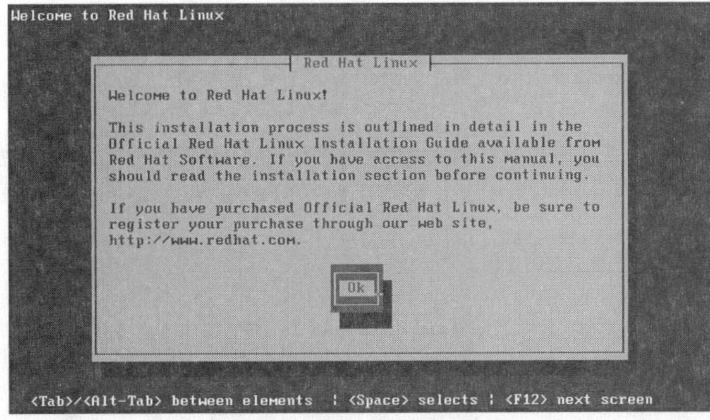

FIGURE 6.3
Start of the Red Hat installation process.

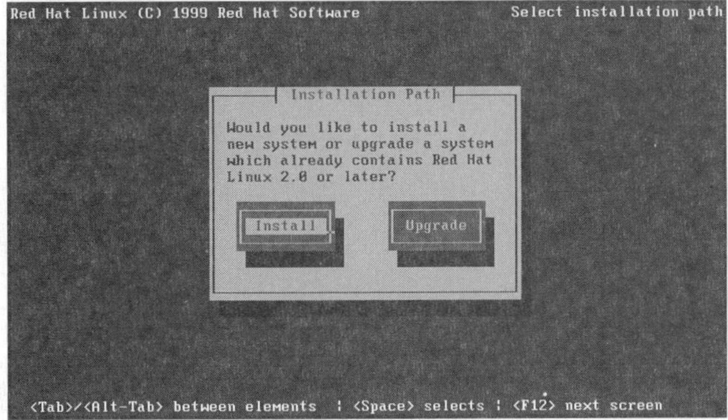

FIGURE 6.4
The first important question in Red Hat installation.

Because this is a new installation, select Install to continue. Next, choose an installation type (see Figure 6.5).

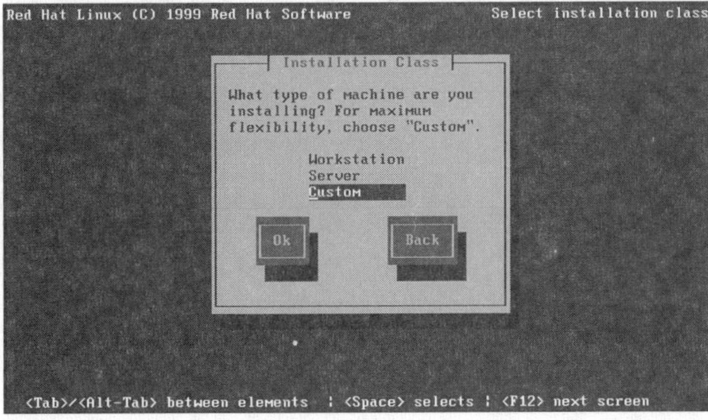

FIGURE 6.5
You can choose certain default configurations, or choose Custom to exercise full control over system setup.

You make your choice, and after a few more screens of questions, it is time to partition your disk drive. Red Hat allows you to choose between the traditional Linux fdisk program and the friendlier Disk Druid. Choose the latter, and see its interface (see Figure 6.6).

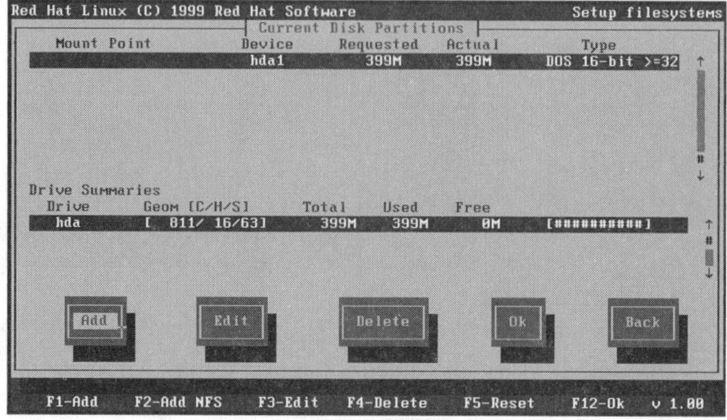

FIGURE 6.6
Disk Druid shows your disk partitions. At the moment, your only partition is an MS Windows partition that fills the entire drive.

This is bad news: your entire drive is occupied by a DOS/Windows partition. Red Hat installation does not provide a way to shrink the partition. Some commercial (such as PartitionMagic) and free products allow you to resize existing DOS disks outside this installation process. But because you do not want to keep this Windows installation, delete the partition. Then use the Add function to create three new partitions for Linux (see Figure 6.7).

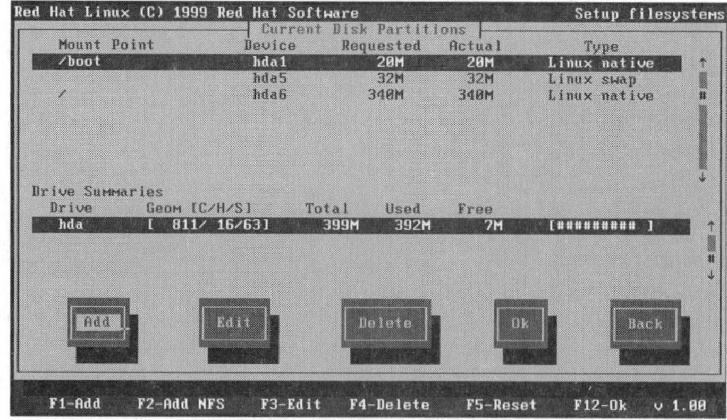

FIGURE 6.7
New drive configuration, after deleting the Windows partition and creating three new partitions.

You have designated a small partition at the beginning of the drive to hold the boot files, a large partition for the main file system, and a 32MB swap partition. (Because of some decades-old architectural decisions in PC design, *x*86 machines cannot boot from disk locations with high cylinder addresses. This drive is not large enough to have such a problem, but the 10GB disk in your other PC *is* large enough.)

After a series of screens to check and format the disk partitions, you now must choose which components to install (see Figure 6.8).

FIGURE 6.8
Red Hat installation allows you to choose the components you need for your environment.

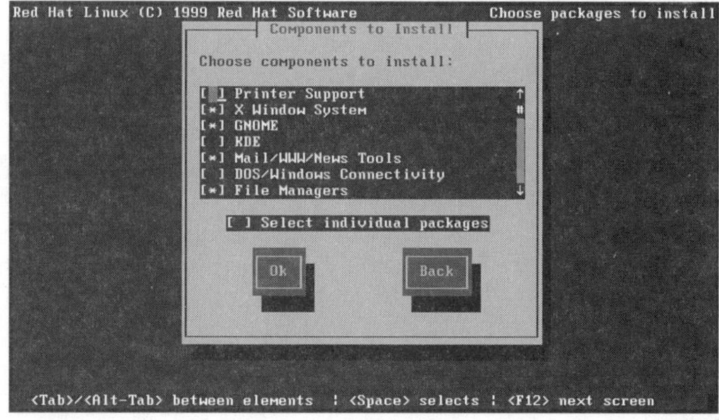

Here is where you customize your system: choose development components if you want a development system, database or Web servers for back-room duty, X Window System for a graphical workstation, and so on. If you make some wrong choices, components can easily be added or removed later. You will not find Java here; you will learn in later chapters how to obtain Java components for Linux.

After you have selected the pieces you want, you click Ok and stand by while the disks are formatted and the system is installed.

You then see a series of configuration screens for setting up the mouse, networking, time zone, system services, printers, passwords, boot disk (it's a good idea to create a boot floppy), boot loader, and X Server. After completing the installation steps, the system reboots and starts up a new, fully functional Linux system.

If you find after installation that you need additional software from the CD-ROM, you can install it using the *Red Hat Package Manager* (RPM) utility. In Chapter 9, "Setting Up a Linux Development Environment," we discuss what components you need to set up a development environment on Linux.

Your Turn

This chapter gave you a brief look at obtaining and installing Linux. Despite the practical difficulties of building an OS that can deal with today's huge selection of hardware (and the weak level of Linux support from most hardware vendors), the Linux community and distribution vendors have done an outstanding job of creating an OS that is easy to install and administer.

A few simple guidelines as you build your own Linux system:

- Many software products (including the Java SDK for Linux) list the distributions with which they are known to work. It is a good idea to consult that when choosing a distribution.

- Avoid strange, off-market peripherals on your PC. Standard peripherals are more likely to be supported.
- Plan ahead how you want to allocate your hard drive between Linux and other operating systems.
- You have a great deal of choice in choosing the look and feel of your graphical desktop. We will explore that in more detail in the next chapter, Chapter 7, "Configuring Your Linux Desktop."
- Help is available from distribution vendors, Linux-oriented Web sites (`http://www.linux.org`, among others), local user groups, and user communities for various software products. Competing claims notwithstanding, Linux is the best-supported OS in the industry.

You will find, after an initial learning curve, that your Linux box is easier to run, more powerful, and more reliable and stable than any other *x*86-based operating system.

Summary

This chapter has looked at the major Linux distributions and provided a glimpse of the steps required to install a Linux system. This is a dynamic area, with distribution vendors continually improving the quality, robustness, ease-of-use, and ease of administration of their products.

CHAPTER 7

CONFIGURING YOUR LINUX DESKTOP

The desktop is the overall look and feel of the X windowing environment. You'll spend a lot of time staring at the desktop, and it can be bewildering if you're moving from other windowing environments, such as Windows, OS/2, or Macintosh, to Linux. Your installation process will probably choose a desktop for you; if you don't like the choice, you can change it.

As we discussed in Chapter 5, "What Is Linux?," the graphical I/O system is not built into the Linux kernel. It consists of separate components: an X server, GUI toolkits used by programs (not our immediate concern in this chapter), and the desktop. The desktop gives the graphical environment its personality, and its functions usually include

- Window management—Controlling the size, placement, and visibility of windows; drawing and placing icons; drawing borders around windows; implementing the button functionality in the window borders (iconify, maximize, close, and so on); customizing behavior around application requirements.
- Integration—Providing a networked facility for discovery and launch of services, and communication between services.
- Paging—Supporting easy navigation between applications.
- Workspaces—Managing multiple virtual desktops.
- Front panel—A sort of "dashboard" that displays system status and handles launching of common applications.

- File management—A GUI and drag-and-drop interface for navigating and manipulating the file system, and launching applications from the file system and the desktop.
- Session management—Saving and restoring X Window System clients and settings between sessions.
- Utilities—Common utilities, such as a text editor, mail reader, calculator, datebook, media player, backup tool, and help system.
- Tchotchkes and Gewgaws—Many desktops include some games, screen savers, and other such diversions.
- Configuration—Tools for easy configuration of desktop look and behavior.

The *Common Desktop Environment* (CDE) adopted by the commercial UNIX vendors does all these things, but because of its cost and licensing terms, it has not been widely embraced by the Linux community. The result has been a proliferation of window managers and desktops, some original and some highly derivative. Choosing a comfortable desktop can make your time spent on Linux pleasant. Conversely, choosing a bad desktop can make you a Linux-hater. The objective of this chapter is to help you over this hurdle.

In these examples, I refer heavily to my particular distribution, Red Hat 6.0. (This is a matter of convenient illustration, not an endorsement. There are simply too many different distributions to describe them all.) Your results may vary, and you probably will need to refer to documentation with your distribution.

Starting the X Window System

The two customary ways of starting up the X Window System are

- Launch it from a console shell with the `xinit` command.
- Log in through an X Display Manager.

Many distributions give you this option at installation time. For example, when the Red Hat installer asks whether you want to run the X server automatically, answering yes results in running an X Display Manager, as shown in Figure 7.1. Choosing automatic X startup is generally the right choice. It starts up a full desktop instead of the minimal X environment usually launched by `xinit`.

The next few sections look at the most popular and easily available desktops. The first two are state-of-the-art, representing current GUI development activity in the Linux community. The third is older, more stable, and not as original, but it borrows some familiar looks from some well-known desktops on other platforms.

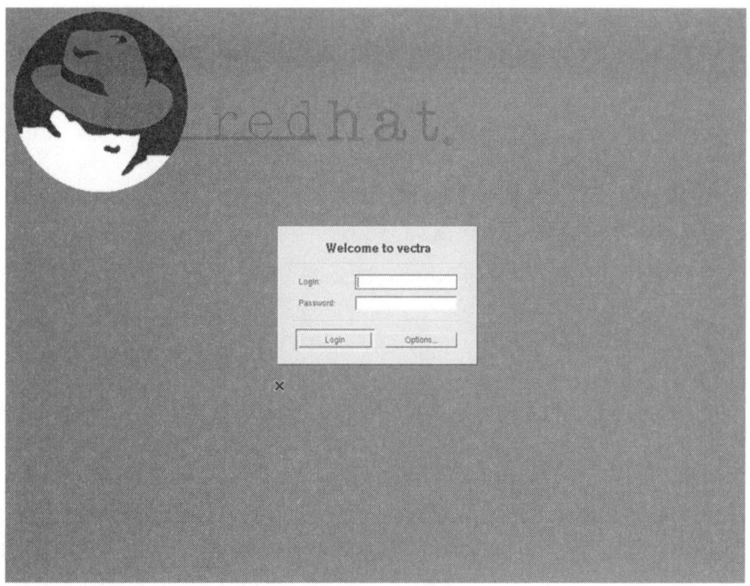

FIGURE 7.1
Red Hat 6.0 Gnome Display Manager login screen.

The K Desktop Environment (KDE)

The K Desktop Environment is an open source desktop with considerable acceptance in the Linux community. It is full-featured and mature, with all the desktop capabilities mentioned previously (see Figure 7.2).

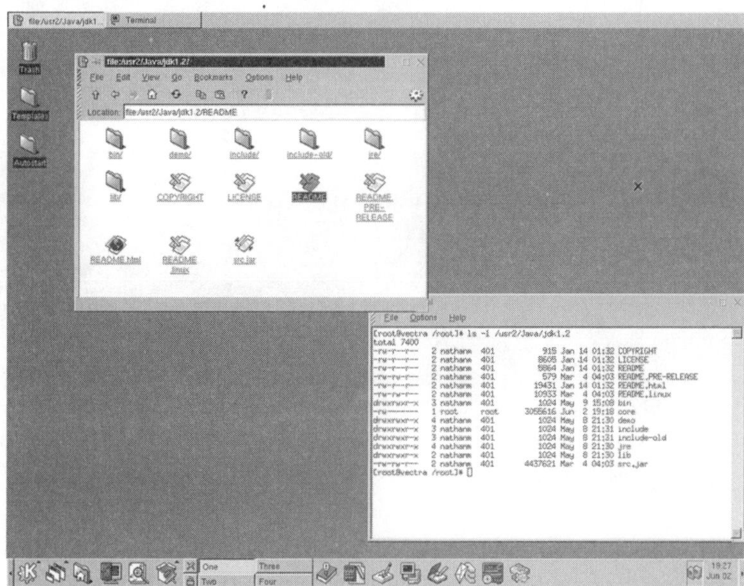

FIGURE 7.2
The K Desktop Environment.

Configuration menus allow you to add your own applications and install new *actions*—programs to be run when files are launched from the file manager or the desktop.

KDE is available from `http://www.kde.org` and depends on the qt GUI library, available from `http://www.troll.no`. Both are shipped with Red Hat 6.0 and available as Red Hat packages (`kdebase`, a collection of other `kde*` packages, and `qt`) on the installation media. (We discuss the Red Hat Package Manager (`RPM`) and other packaging tools in Chapter 8, "Installing Additional Linux Software.")

This is the current desktop to beat, although it is feeling some competitive heat from the Enlightenment Desktop.

The Gnome Enlightenment Desktop

The Enlightenment Desktop is an open source product of research at Red Hat Software (The Gnome Desktop) and a loose consortium of independent developers (The Enlightenment Window Manager). It's an attractive and powerful desktop (see Figure 7.3).

FIGURE 7.3
The Gnome Enlightenment Desktop.

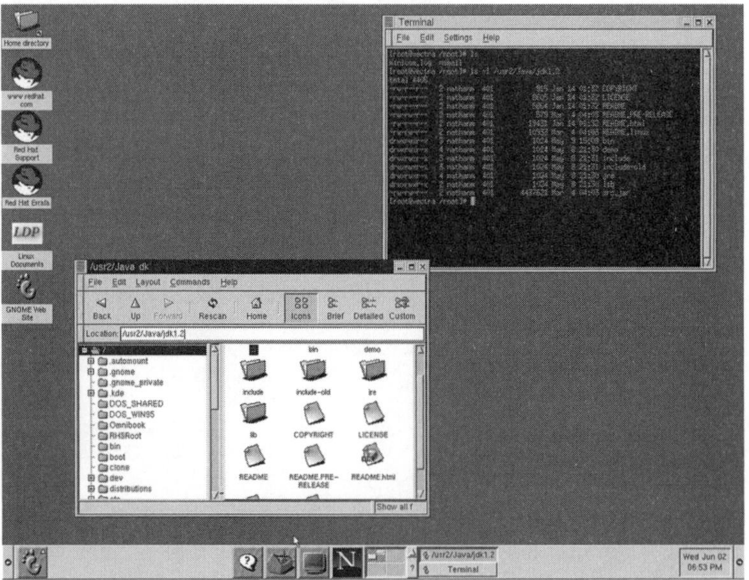

Enlightenment also features the full complement of desktop functionality described earlier in the chapter. Using configuration menus, it is easy to add your own applications and define new actions.

Enlightenment is currently Red Hat's favored desktop and the default installed by the 6.0 distribution. It is less mature than KDE, and my own experience suggests that it's still rough around the edges—but that will undoubtedly improve.

Enlightenment is available from `http://www.enlightenment.org`. It relies on the Gnome product, available from `http://www.gnome.org`. Both are shipped with Red Hat 6.0 and available as Red Hat packages (`enlightenment`, `gnome-core`, and a collection of additional `gnome-*` packages) from the installation media.

AnotherLevel

AnotherLevel is a combination of an older desktop (`fvwm2`) and some predefined configurations that give `fvwm2` a look approximating some familiar desktops—Windows 95 (see Figure 7.4), Motif Window Manager (see Figure 7.5), and NextStep(see Figure 7.6).

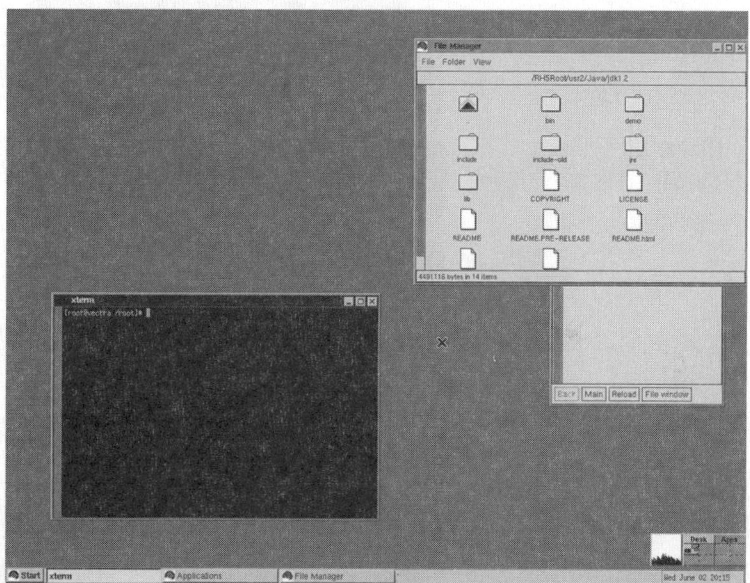

FIGURE 7.4
AnotherLevel's Windows 95 personality.

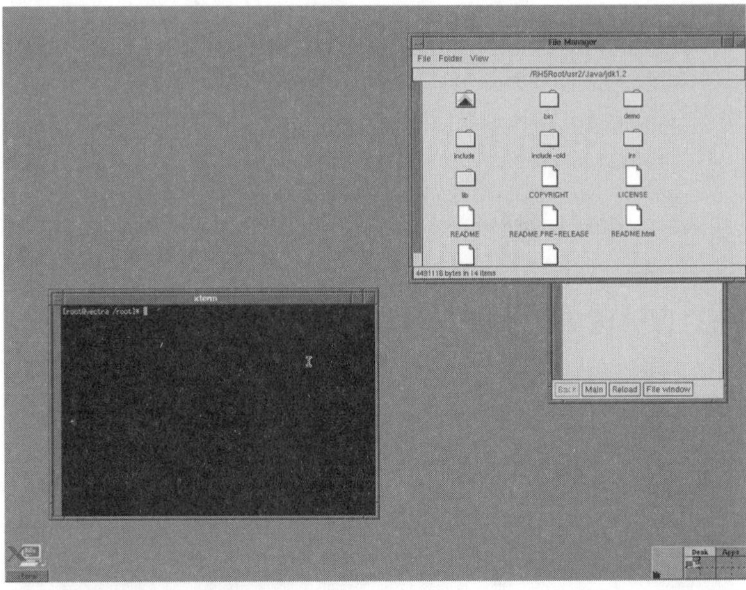

FIGURE 7.5
AnotherLevel's Motif Window Manager personality.

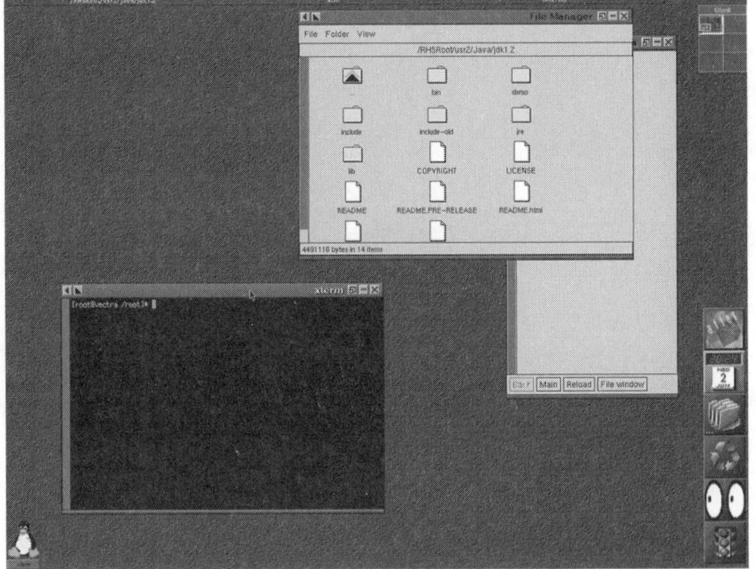

FIGURE 7.6
AnotherLevel's NextStep personality.

To change the look while running AnotherLevel, left-click on the root menu and look for the Quit button. This leads you to a `Switch to` button. Use this button to select which AnotherLevel desktop you want to run.

These desktops are usable, but, unlike KDE and Enlightenment, they are collections of tired old components thrown together into a desktop and decorated to look familiar. They have the advantage of being smaller and faster than the newer desktops, but they are not full desktops—lacking, for example, drag-and-drop interoperability, MIME file type recognition, and any sort of networked integration mechanism.

AnotherLevel is available at free software repositories such as `http://sunsite.unc.edu` and is shipped on most installation media. On Red Hat media, you need the packages for `fvwm` and `AnotherLevel`.

Selecting a Desktop

Installing the desktop product—from the Red Hat packages or other distributions—is the first step to turning on your selected desktop. The second step is to tell the system which one you want to use.

This is another topic that varies by distribution; you will need to refer to your particular documentation. The Gnome Display Manager in Red Hat 6.0 gives you the option to choose your desktop at login time (see Figure 7.7).

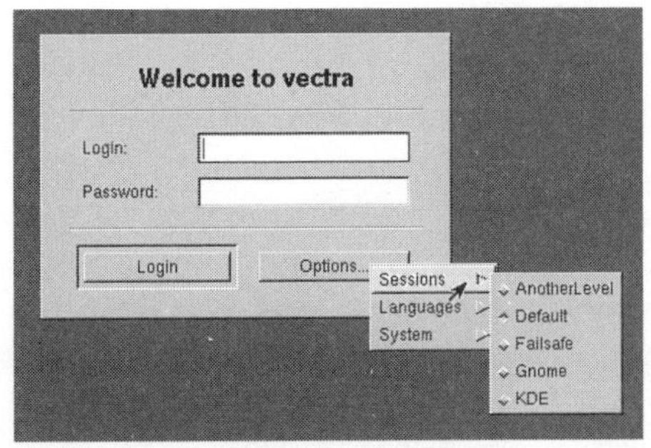

FIGURE 7.7
Red Hat 6.0 Gnome Display Manager login screen lets you select your desktop.

After you have logged in, you have the option of setting a default desktop (again, this is Gnome-specific behavior). Run the `/usr/bin/switchdesk` utility and choose your desktop through the interface (see Figure 7.8). Under Red Hat, you need to install the packages for `switchdesk` and `switchdesk-gnome` to use this utility.

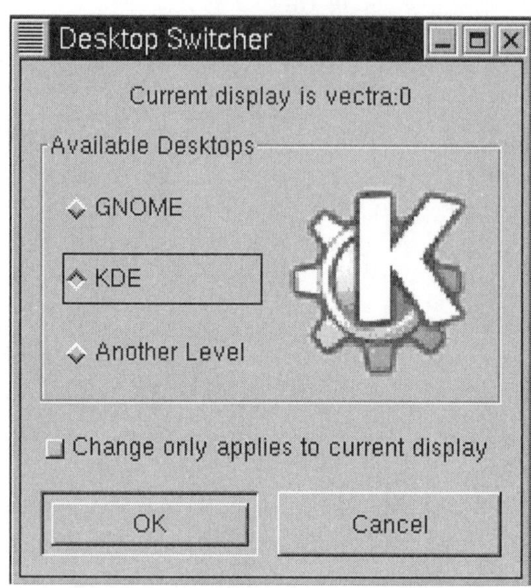

FIGURE 7.8
The `switchdesk` utility lets you set your default desktop.

Your default desktop, when you next log in, will be your new selection.

Summary

The Linux environment offers a plethora of choices for configuring the graphical desktop. This chapter has presented a brief tour of the available desktops and includes pointers intended to start you toward choosing the best one for your needs.

CHAPTER 8

INSTALLING ADDITIONAL LINUX SOFTWARE

Installing a new Linux system gives you a PC full of software, but it doesn't give you everything you need. For your Java development, you'll need to install Java tools, of course, along with other development tools, utilities, and extensions. Later chapters discuss a variety of components you need for Java development on Linux —but where do you get them and how do you install them?

Your first source of software is your Linux distribution media. Many standard tools and utilities are provided on the distribution media in package management format.

Package Management

Most Linux distributions use a package management tool for distributing and installing software. If you are a user of Red Hat, Caldera, SuSE, Debian, or many other distributions, your installation distribution media will include dozens or hundreds of packages ready for installation. Many other packages are published on the Web in standard package management formats.

Package management tools handle important details of installing software: clean installation, update, upgrade, and uninstallation; identifying and enforcing dependencies between packages; protecting and respecting customizations you make to installed packages. Surprisingly, package management is a relatively recent concept in the UNIX world (Microsoft Windows environments have some similar, if more fragile, approaches), and much of the innovation in package management is occurring in the Linux community.

rpm

The *Red Hat Package Manager* (*rpm*) is the most commonly used and is the standard package management tool for Red Hat, Caldera, and SuSE distributions (among others). Although it originated with Red Hat Software, *rpm* has taken on a life independent of that vendor, has its own development and support community (`http://www.rpm.org`), and has been ported to many UNIX platforms.

The RPM terminology may be a bit confusing, so here is what to look for in any discussion of Red Hat packages:

- The program for installing and managing packages is called *rpm*.
- The term RPM describes the package format itself, and is also used as shorthand for packages—for example, "obtain the RPM for the COBOL compiler."

RPM packages are shipped in files suffixed `.rpm`; your distribution media (for Red Hat, Caldera, and so on) is full of `.rpm` files, and installing one is a simple matter of running (as root):

```
bash$ rpm -i <rpmfile>
```

You might occasionally need to build an RPM from a source RPM (<*something*>`.src.rpm`)—for example, if an available RPM is not compatible with your installed version of the C library. On Red Hat systems, performing the following step

```
bash$ rpm –rebuild <rpm_source_file>
```

builds a binary (installable) RPM and places it in the `/usr/src/redhat/RPMS` hierarchy. From there, it is installed with the `-i` option, as shown previously. For other distributions, see the *rpm* documentation for details on building from source.

Other *rpm* options allow package query, update, and uninstallation. For developers, there are options to support package creation and management. An extensive man page (use the command `man rpm`) documents *rpm*'s options and capabilities.

The *rpm* tool is command-line oriented, but a GUI interface called *xrpm* is available from many repositories.

dpkg

The Debian packager (*dpkg*) is the package manager used on Debian systems; files suffixed `.deb` are *dpkg* packages. It also offers a menu-driven interface, *dselect*.

Because RPM is the more popular package format, *rpm* can be used on Debian systems. However, Debian recommends instead the use of a tool called *alien*—a package converter available from Debian and elsewhere—to convert `.rpm` packages to `.deb`.

Other Package Management Technologies

Other technologies for general-purpose package management are in use or in development: GNU Stow, CMU Depot, Bell Labs NSBD. However, you are not likely to run into these technologies without taking some trouble to look for them.

Beyond general-purpose package management, individual products may have their own package management technologies: Perl is an example. These technologies do not interfere with the general-purpose package management, and in fact Perl and other such products are available in standard package management formats.

Non-Package Software Distributions

Not all software products are distributed in package form. Many are distributed in tarfiles or zipfiles, sometimes in source form, and require you to do some work to install them. Examples include the Blackdown Java port for Linux and standard Java extensions published by Sun. (For products under active development, RPMs are sometimes available but are not always current.)

The following sections discuss some formats you are likely to encounter.

Compressed Tarball Binary Distribution

These are archives in the hierarchical UNIX tar format, compressed with *gzip* or *bzip2* (see the section "Compressing and Archiving: tar, gzip, bzip2, zip, unzip " in Chapter 9, "Setting Up a Linux Development Environment"). Typical file suffixes are `.tar.gz`, `.tgz`, `.tar.bz2`, and `tar.Z`. It is a common, but not universal, practice that the contents of the archive are stored with relative filenames under a subdirectory whose name echoes the archive name. For example, an archive called `foo-1.2.tar.gz` contains all of its contents in a subdirectory called `foo-1.2`.

To install a compressed tarball, choose an installation location, use *cd* to move to that directory, and unpack the archive. For example:

```
bash$ mkdir -p /usr/local/foo
bash$ cd /usr/local/foo
bash$ gzip -d <~/foo-1.2.tar.gz ¦ tar xvf -
... a bunch of output shows product unpacking into the foo-1.2 subdirectory ...
```

For archives packed in `.bz2` format, simply use *bzip2* instead of *gzip* as shown in the preceding example.

Archives packed in the old UNIX `.Z` compression format (some of Sun's distributions use it) can be unpacked with *gzip* as shown in the preceding example.

The Blackdown Linux distribution is among the many products shipped as compressed tarballs, with more recent Blackdown releases using the `.bz2` compression format exclusively.

Compressed Tarball Source Distribution

This is a common format for products distributed in source form. The tarball includes full sources plus enough intelligence (ideally) to build the product on Linux or any other UNIX environment. The four steps to installing the products are as follows:

1. Unpack it somewhere.

   Wherever you unpack is a temporary location for purposes of building—it's not your final installation directory. Example:

   ```
   bash$ mkdir -p /tmp/foo
   bash$ cd /tmp/foo
   bash$ gzip -d <~/foo-1.2.src.tar.gz | tar xvf -
   ```

2. Configure it.

   There should be a `README` file somewhere with instructions on building. Most projects use the GNU *autoconf* technology, which automatically configures for correct building on Linux and many other operating systems. For such projects, configuring the product usually looks like this:

   ```
   bash$ ./configure
   <... a lot of output ...>
   ```

   A list of configuration options, including how to specify installation directories, is available by asking for help:

   ```
   bash$ ./configure -help
   ```

3. Build it.

   After configuration, building the project is usually done with a single *make* command:

   ```
   bash$ make
   <... a lot of output ...>
   ```

4. Install it.

   The `README` or `INSTALL` file has instructions, which for many projects consists of

   ```
   bash$ make install
   ```

The product will be installed in some predefined directories (determined by whomever made the distribution). You can usually override the destination directories with options specified during the `./configure` step (shown previously).

This method of software distribution is widely used. The downside is that there is no package management. Some distributions include a "`make uninstall`" capability to support removal, but this sort of distribution is susceptible to many of the problems solved by package management: inability to cleanly upgrade or uninstall, possibility of stepping on other software, difficulty of assembling a consistent set of components that interoperate properly. (Don't panic! Problems are rare, but you need to be aware of the possibility.)

Zip Binary and Source Distributions

The other widely used format for software distribution is zipfiles, although this is more generally true in the Microsoft Windows world than in UNIX/Linux. The procedures described earlier for compressed tarballs apply just as well to zipfiles; the difference is in the use of the *unzip* utility instead of *tar*, *gzip*, and *bzip2*.

Unpacking zipfiles is easy:

```
bash$ unzip -v foo-1.2.zip
```

Beyond that, instructions are identical to those for tarballs (given previously).

Sun distributes many of its standard Java extensions (see Chapter 4, "Additional Sun Java Class Library Specs") in zipfile format.

Linux Software Repositories

There is no central global source for Linux software, but there are several large repositories that serve as software depots and as mirrors for product distribution sites. The following sections discuss two to get you started.

Sunsite

The Sunsite repository at the University of North Carolina (`http://sunsite.unc.edu/pub`) is a major distribution site for GNU projects, other open-source projects, Linux technology, and Linux distributions.

Red Hat users can find distributions, official RPMs, and contributed RPMs under `http://sunsite.unc.edu/pub/linux/distributions/redhat/`. Similar resources are available for other distributions.

Rpmfind

The rpmfind site, `http://rpmfind.net/linux/RPM/`, is a huge catalog of available RPM packages. Not all the packages are stored at rpmfind—much of the information here is pointers to other download sites—but it is a reliable way to find almost any RPM package published anywhere.

Summary

This chapter has surveyed the common methods and formats with which software is distributed for Linux. In understanding how to use software published in these formats, you can install and use any of the thousands of tools and products available for Linux.

PART III

SETTING UP FOR JAVA DEVELOPMENT AND DEPLOYMENT ON LINUX

Linux excels as a development environment, in the tradition of the UNIX systems on which it is based. This part of the book examines the pieces you need to support development on Linux: the compilers, utilities, and methods you need to do the work.

We also examine the deployment question—how to select a deployment environment for your Java applications—and take a look at the open source world in which many of the development tools were themselves developed.

CHAPTER 9

SETTING UP A LINUX DEVELOPMENT ENVIRONMENT

The UNIX/Linux platform has from its inception been a rich environment for software development. This chapter looks at some of the basic Linux tools you need (or might want) to support your own development efforts. As in earlier chapters, this chapter includes some Red Hat-centric advice on where to find these tools.

All these tools (except for the simple GUI-based text editors) are extensively documented. Depending on your needs and your learning curve, the following documentation tools are at your disposal:

- Online manual pages (commonly called *man pages*) are published and installed for most tools on a Linux system. You can use the Linux `man` command to view the pages on a terminal. For example

  ```
  bash$ man gcc
  ```

  displays the documentation for the GNU C compiler.

- The help systems that come with the K Desktop Environment and Gnome Enlightenment show you relevant documentation.

- Many fine books have been published on these tools and are as close as your nearest technical bookstore.

In the final section of this chapter, we set up a small Java project to demonstrate the use of these tools.

Command Shell

You are running a command shell—an interactive command interpreter—as soon as you log in or run a terminal emulator on the desktop. The most popular Linux shell is `bash`, but you have several choices. Here is a brief survey of the options.

bash

GNU `bash` is the *Bourne Again Shell*, based on the Bourne shell long used under UNIX. If you have Linux, you have `bash`; it is installed as a core component with all distributions.

bash Command-Line Editing

`bash` gives you command-line editing—the ability to reuse and edit previous commands. Its `behavior` is, by default, modeled after the `emacs` text editor. Editing can be as simple as using the arrow, Backspace, Insert, and Delete keys. Or you can use the `emacs` control- and metacharacter commands to move through the command stack and perform more advanced editing. See the `bash` man page for more detail:

```
bash$ man bash
```

If you prefer editing modeled after the popular AT&T `vi` editor, you can turn it on with a `set` command:

```
bash$ set -o vi
```

You can make `vi`-style editing the default behavior by adding the `set -o vi` command to the `~/.bashrc` file. With `vi`-style editing, you use the Esc key to switch modes and `vi`'s various single-letter commands to edit commands and navigate the command stack.

bash Configuration Files

Two configuration files are important to configuring and customizing `bash` behavior (UNIX/Linux shells interpret the ~ character as designating your home directory):

- `~/.bashrc` is run by the shell whenever you start up a new instance of bash. It is typically used to set modes and macros.
- `~/.bash_profile` is run by the shell whenever a login shell is started. If that file is absent, `~/.profile` is used instead. Entries in this file are typically used to configure your environment and set environment variables.

bash Environment Variables

Environment variables are set in `bash` with an = assignment, with no spaces before or after the operator:

```
bash$ FOO=bar
```

Environment variables must be exported to be visible to processes launched by the shell:

```
bash$ export FOO
```

These two steps can be combined:

```
bash$ export FOO=bar
```

Many examples in this book assume you are using `bash`, and we will commonly use this one-line assign/export command to illustrate the use of an environment variable.

Finally, a temporary environment variable can be specified for the duration of a single command, by combining the assignment and the command invocation on the same line:

```
bash$ FOO=bar /usr/local/bin/foobar
```

This style of assignment is occasionally used in the book to illustrate the use of an environment variable.

tcsh

`tcsh` is modeled after the UNIX C Shell, an interactive shell that uses commands and behaviors modeled after the C programming language. If you prefer to use this shell, install `tcsh` on your system (it is available as an RPM on Red Hat distributions) and use the `chsh` command to change your login shell:

```
bash$ chsh -s /bin/tcsh
password: <type your password here>
```

Two configuration files are important to configuring and customizing tcsh behavior:

- `~/.tcshrc` is run by the shell whenever you start up a new instance of `tcsh`. If that file is absent, `~/.cshrc` is invoked instead.
- `~/.login` is run by the shell whenever a login shell is started.

Other Shells

Other shells, available for Linux but less popular, include

- `ash`—A simple Bourne-like shell
- `ksh`—A public-domain version of the Korn (Bourne-like) shell

Text Editor

You'll need a text editor, of course. You can choose from the traditional powerhouse editors, `vi` or `emacs`, or some simpler GUI and non-GUI editors.

Whichever editor you choose, it's a good idea to set an `EDITOR` environment variable so that other programs can know what your favorite editor is. If you use a Bourne-type shell, add

```
export EDITOR=<your favorite editor name>
```

to your `~/.bash_profile` file. If you use a C-shell, add

```
setenv EDITOR <your favorite editor name>
```

to your `~/.login` file.

vi—Visual Editor

The vi editor is a longtime UNIX staple whose lineage dates back to AT&T's stewardship of UNIX. It's a powerful, full-featured, page-oriented editor widely used in the UNIX world. The most popular version for Linux is vim, a highly enhanced *vi* available from virtually all Linux distributions. On the Red Hat 6.0 distribution, installing the RPMs for vim-common and vim-enhanced will give you vim.

vim normally runs in a terminal window; you can use the graphical version, gvim, to run it in its own GUI window. On Red Hat, this requires loading the additional RPM for vim-X11.

An interesting enhanced vim capability is *syntax coloring* to aid in editing Java and other languages. It's best used with the GUI version, gvim, and is enabled by typing

```
:syntax on
```

while in the editor, or adding the command syntax on to the .exrc file in your home directory.

emacs

The emacs editor, one of the first GNU project publications, is one of the most popular and powerful page-oriented editors in the UNIX world. It is sufficiently different from the other major editor, vi, that it's difficult to be conversant in both at the same time. UNIX users tend to be strong partisans of either vi or emacs, but not both.

For historical reasons, emacs comes in two major flavors: *GNU Emacs* and *XEmacs*, which branched several years ago from common source. There are numerous differences, in features and philosophy, between the two—most notably that XEmacs is better integrated with the X Window System. But both have similar capabilities, and choosing one over the other is largely a matter of personal taste.

GNU Emacs is available from all Linux distributions, and from the GNU project (http://www.gnu.org). Under Red Hat 6.0, installing the RPMs for emacs and emacs-X11 will give you GNU Emacs.

XEmacs is also widely available. Although not as frequently included in core Linux distributions as GNU Emacs, it can easily be found in source, binary, and RPM forms at all major Linux software repositories.

The true power of emacs, beyond editing text, is its configurability. It includes a built-in interpreter for the LISP programming language, which has been used to customize emacs into a stunning variety of useful configurations. Among the many customization packages available for emacs are a mail reader, an outline editor, and an automated psychotherapist. In Chapter 44, "The Emacs JDE," we will examine a complete Java integrated development environment (including *syntax coloring*) built from emacs.

Often imitated but never duplicated, emacs has inspired some smaller, simpler clones. Editors such as joe and jed, available with many Linux distributions, provide some emacs-like functionality in smaller packages.

kedit

`kedit` isEnvironment a simple GUI-based editor, shipped with the K Desktop and available through a button on the main panel (see Figure 9.1).

FIGURE 9.1
KDE button to launch a simple GUI-based text editor.

The capabilities are simple and intuitive. This is certainly not a powerful programmer's editor, and not a good long-term choice for a developer, but it's an easy way to start editing text for UNIX/Linux newcomers. A screen shot is shown in Figure 9.2.

FIGURE 9.2
The kedit editor, bundled with KDE.

File Edit Options Help

```
public class HelloWorld
{
    public static void main(String[] argv)
    {
        System.out.println("Hello world");
    }
}
```

INS Line: 5 Col: 29

gEdit

The Gnome/Enlightenment desktop includes its own text editor, `gEdit`. It can be launched from the application menus on the root window (see Figure 9.3).

Like `kedit` (discussed earlier), `gEdit` presents a simple, intuitive editor for text-editing (see Figure 9.4). Also like `kedit`, `gEdit` is a good starter editor but not a good long-term choice for developers.

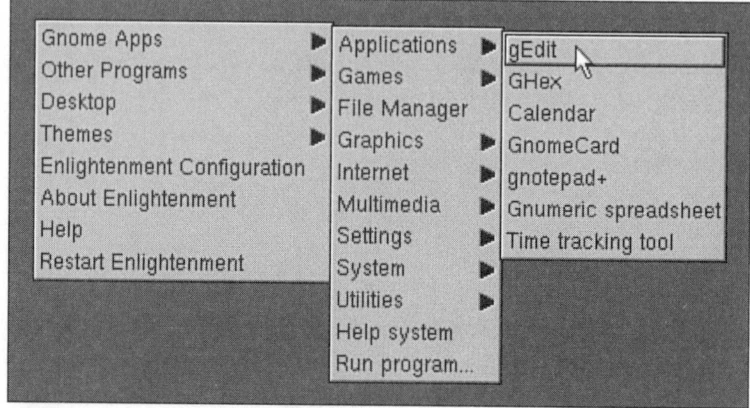

FIGURE 9.3
Launching `gEdit` from the Gnome/Enlightenment root window.

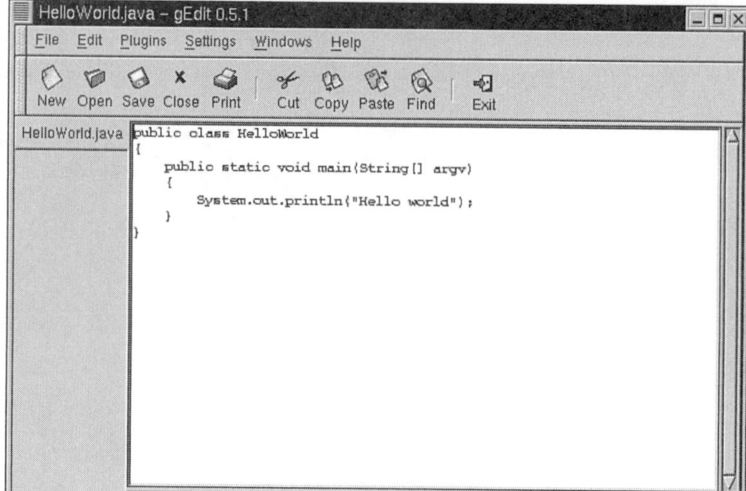

FIGURE 9.4
The gEdit editor, bundled with Gnome/Enlightenment.

Build Management Tool: `make`

`make`, another longtime standard UNIX tool, is used to maintain programs under development by keeping object files current with source files. GNU Make, the standard `make` in the Linux world, is available from all Linux distributions. On Red Hat distributions, load the RPM for `make`.

Version Management Tool: `cvs`

`cvs`, the *Concurrent Versions System*, is a revision control system—an invaluable tool for tracking and maintaining source code. In a nutshell, `cvs` maintains a repository that keeps copies of all versions of your source files.

A cvs Local Repository

A local cvs repository serves two important functions in a development project:

- Acts as a central code store, where a developer (or collaborating developers) can keep master copies of the source, including experimental branches that can later be merged into the main source trunk. cvs includes facilities to allow several developers to work on the same code without stepping on each other's toes.
- Acts as an archive, allowing you to recover all past versions of source. The revisions are stored in a compact form, keeping the repository from exploding in size.

A sample project (see "Creating a Sample Project" later in the chapter) illustrates basic repository setup and use.

cvs Remote Repository Servers

cvs supports client/server architectures, with the repository living on a server and clients able to interact (check out, check in, manage, and so on) remotely. Several of the open source projects discussed in later chapters use such repositories, through which they allow read-only access to the larger community.

If you need to check out source from a remote cvs repository, the steps are as follows:

1. Obtain the repository name (CVSROOT), module name(s), and password for the project.
2. Log in to the remote repository:

```
bash$ cvs -d '<repository name>' login
CVS password: <password>
```

3. Check out the source, using compression to improve network throughput:

```
bash$ cvs -z3 -d '<repository name>' co <module name(s)>
<...output describing checkout activities...>
```

After the checked-out tree has been created, you no longer need the -d option: The name of the repository is stored within the tree and automatically used for future cvs activity.

Obtaining cvs

cvs, and the underlying rcs (*Revision Control System*) tool it depends on, are available on most Linux distributions and from free software repositories such as http://www.sunsite.edu. On Red Hat releases, install the RPMs for cvs and rcs.

cvs is a command-line utility, and our later examples will use the command-line interface. A GUI-based front-end is available, called tkCVS, from http://www.cyclic.com/tkcvs/.

Compression and Archiving: `tar`, `gzip`, `bzip2`, `zip`, `unzip`

Four compression and archiving utilities are heavily used in the Linux and Java development worlds. As mentioned in the discussion on adding Linux software (see Chapter 8, "Installing Additional Linux Software"), all these tools may be necessary for obtaining and installing components you need for development work.

Tape ARchiver: `tar`

The `tar` utility creates archives in a standard format, commonly used for distribution of software packages. Virtually all Linux distributions install GNU `tar` as part of system setup.

Compressor: `gzip`

`gzip` is a data compressor based on the Lempel-Ziv compression algorithm. It is the most commonly used compression format for distribution of UNIX- and Linux-related software. Most Linux distributions install `gzip` during system setup.

In addition to its role in software distribution, `gzip` is typically used to compress the Linux kernel image used at Linux boot time.

Compressor: `bzip2`

`bzip2` is a newer compressor than `gzip`, using a different compression algorithm and often achieving significantly better compression than `gzip`. Many of the new distributions of Java for Linux are only available in `bzip2` format.

Most Linux distributions do not install `bzip2` by default, but it is usually available as part of the distribution. On Red Hat systems, install the RPM for `bzip2`.

Archiver/Compressor: `zip` and `unzip`

`zip` is a compressed archive format that has been in use since the MS-DOS days. It serves two important roles in Java development:

- It is a standard Java archive format; Java can run classes directly out of a ZIP format. The *Java ARchive* (JAR) format is closely related to ZIP.
- ZIP is a common software distribution format, and you may need the `zip` utility to unpack software.

`zip` and `unzip` are available with virtually all Linux distributions. On Red Hat systems, install the RPMs for `zip` and `unzip`.

The GNU C Compiler: gcc

The GNU C compiler is the standard compiler in the open source world. Beyond its crucial role in free systems such as Linux, FreeBSD, and the GNU Hurd, this compiler enjoys considerable use on commercial operating systems such as HP-UX, Solaris, AIX, NT, and others.

Older versions of this compiler were packaged as `gcc` (GNU C Compiler), later releases came from the `egcs` (Experimental GNU Compiler Suite) branch project, and a reunification in spring of 1999 brought the two projects back together as `gcc` (now meaning GNU Compiler Collection). The maintainer of `gcc` for the open source community is Cygnus Solutions (`http://egcs.cygnus.com`).

The compiler consists of core technology for code generation and optimization, some related support libraries, and a number of front ends for different languages, including C, C++, and, most recently, Java (see Chapter 31, "`gcj`: A Compiled Java Solution").

`gcc` is available with all Linux distributions. On Red Hat 6.0 systems, install the RPMs for `egcs` and `egcs-c++`. You will also need the RPM for `binutils`, which supplies the GNU linker and other utilities to support development. (The compiler package name will undoubtedly change as the reunified `gcc` compiler is adopted.)

Creating a Sample Project

We'll build a simple project, assuming use of the standard Java Software Development Kit components from the Blackdown Java SDK (see Chapter 11, "Choosing an Environment: 1.1 or 1.2?").

Creating the Project

We begin by creating a new directory, immediately below our home directory, for our `HelloWorld` project:

```
bash$ mkdir ~/helloworld
bash$ cd ~/helloworld
```

Using your favorite editor, create a `HelloWorld.java, as shown in Listing` 9.1 (as always, the line numbers are for illustration; not part of the source).

LISTING 9.1 HelloWorld.java

```
public class HelloWorld
{
    public static void main(String[] argv)
    {
        System.out.println("Hello world");
    }
}
```

And create a `Makefile` (Listing 9.2) that knows how to build our project.

LISTING 9.2 Makefile

```
1   .PHONY: all clean
2
3   all:    HelloWorld.class
4
5   HelloWorld.class:       HelloWorld.java
6           javac HelloWorld.java
7
8   clean:
9           rm -f *.class
```

The most important part of the `Makefile` is lines 5-6. Line 5 describes the target file we are building (`HelloWorld.class`), and the sources it depends on (`HelloWorld.java`); line 6 gives the command to build the target from the source by running the Java compiler, `javac`.

There are two other rules in the Makefile:

- Line 3 describes a target called `all`, which is our shorthand for "the entire project." The entire project has dependencies, at the moment, on one class file, `HelloWorld.class`.
- Lines 8-9 describe a target called `clean`, which is our shorthand for "clean up the directory." The `clean` target has no dependencies (nothing after the "`:`"), and executes one command, shown on line 9.

The one other entry in the `Makefile`, line 1, informs `make` that two of the targets are "phony" targets. We will never build a file called "all" or a file called "clean": these are just rules we need to use in the course of development.

We're ready to build the project. We tell `make` to build the entire project:

```
bash$ make all
javac HelloWorld.java
bash$
```

The `make` process echoes its actions (`javac HelloWorld.java`) and completes. We run the program:

```
bash$ java HelloWorld
Hello world
bash$
```

Finally, we clean up the directory, removing everything that isn't source:

```
bash$ make clean
rm -f *.class
bash$
```

Creating the cvs Repository

Now that we have a project, we create a `cvs` source repository. First, create a new directory somewhere to hold the repository:

```
bash$ mkdir ~/helloworld.cvsroot
bash$
```

And initialize the repository from within our project directory:

```
bash$ cvs -d ~/helloworld.cvsroot init
bash$ cvs -d ~/helloworld.cvsroot co .
cvs checkout: Updating .
? HelloWorld.java
? Makefile
cvs checkout: Updating CVSROOT
U CVSROOT/checkoutlist
U CVSROOT/commitinfo
U CVSROOT/cvswrappers
U CVSROOT/editinfo
U CVSROOT/loginfo
U CVSROOT/modules
U CVSROOT/notify
U CVSROOT/rcsinfo
U CVSROOT/taginfo
bash$
```

To update our current project from the repository:

```
bash$ cvs update
cvs update: Updating .
? HelloWorld.java
? Makefile
cvs update: Updating CVSROOT
bash$
```

The lines with the "?" tell us that there are two files the repository doesn't know about: our two source files, which have not yet been checked in. We check them in— a two-step process of adding them and then committing the changes:

```
bash$ cvs add HelloWorld.java Makefile
cvs add: scheduling file `HelloWorld.java' for addition
cvs add: scheduling file `Makefile' for addition
cvs add: use 'cvs commit' to add these files permanently
bash$ cvs commit -m'First checkin'
cvs commit: Examining .
cvs commit: Examining CVSROOT
cvs commit: Committing .
RCS file: /home/nathanm/helloworld.cvsroot/./HelloWorld.java,v
done
Checking in HelloWorld.java;
/home/nathanm/helloworld.cvsroot/./HelloWorld.java,v  <—  HelloWorld.java
initial revision: 1.1
done
RCS file: /home/nathanm/helloworld.cvsroot/./Makefile,v
done
Checking in Makefile;
/home/nathanm/helloworld.cvsroot/./Makefile,v  <—  Makefile
initial revision: 1.1
done
bash$
```

(We specified a message, `First Checkin` in the `cvs commit` command. Had we not done this, `cvs` would have started up a text editor and solicited a message.)

Growing the Project

We now have a working project. Let's grow the project by creating a new class (Listing 9.3) responsible for the "Hello World" message.

LISTING 9.3 WorldMessage.java

```
import java.io.*;

public class WorldMessage
{
    PrintWriter pw;
    WorldMessage(PrintWriter writer)
    {
        pw = writer;
    }
    public void print()
    {
        pw.println("Hello world");
    }
}
```

and modifying our main class (Listing 9.4) to use the new class.

LISTING 9.4 HelloWorld.java, Modified to Use the New WorldMessage Class

```
import java.io.*;

public class HelloWorld
{
    public static void main(String[] argv)
    {
        PrintWriter pw = new PrintWriter(System.out);
        WorldMessage msg = new WorldMessage(pw);
        msg.print();
        pw.close();
    }
}
```

Finally, we update the Makefile (Listing 9.5) to reflect our new classes and dependencies.

LISTING 9.5 Makefile, Updated with the New Class

```
.PHONY: all clean

all:    HelloWorld.class WorldMessage.class

HelloWorld.class:       HelloWorld.java WorldMessage.class
        javac HelloWorld.java

WorldMessage.class:     WorldMessage.java
```

```
                javac WorldMessage.java

clean:
                rm -f *.class
```

Notice that `HelloWorld.class` has gained a new dependency: the `WorldMessage.class` from which it gets an important class definition. Because of this dependency, `make` will automatically determine that it needs to build `WorldMessage.class` before it builds `HelloWorld.class` (`make` uses a file's last modification time to ascertain when a target must be rebuilt because it is older than its dependency):

```
bash$ make
javac WorldMessage.java
javac HelloWorld.java
bash$
```

Why didn't we say `make all`? Because `all` is the first rule, thus the default rule, in the `Makefile`.

We're ready to run:

```
bash$ java HelloWorld
Hello world
bash$
```

Updating the cvs Repository

First we clean up our nonsource files:

```
bash$ make clean
rm -f *.class
bash$
```

Then update our project from the repository:

```
bash$ cvs update
cvs update: Updating .
M HelloWorld.java
M Makefile
? WorldMessage.java
cvs update: Updating CVSROOT
bash$
```

The `cvs` messages tell us that two of our files have been modified, and that `WorldMessage.java` is unknown. We add it to the repository and commit the changes:

```
bash$ cvs add WorldMessage.java
cvs add: scheduling file `WorldMessage.java' for addition
bash$ cvs commit -m'Split out the printing functionality'
cvs commit: Examining .
cvs commit: Examining CVSROOT
cvs commit: Committing .
Checking in HelloWorld.java;
/home/nathanm/helloworld.cvsroot/./HelloWorld.java,v  <—  HelloWorld.java
new revision: 1.2; previous revision: 1.1
```

```
done
Checking in Makefile;
/home/nathanm/helloworld.cvsroot/./Makefile,v  <--  Makefile
new revision: 1.2; previous revision: 1.1
done
RCS file: /home/nathanm/helloworld.cvsroot/./WorldMessage.java,v
done
Checking in WorldMessage.java;
/home/nathanm/helloworld.cvsroot/./WorldMessage.java,v  <--  WorldMessage.java
initial revision: 1.1
done
bash$
```

We see from the messages that `cvs` is committing the latest modifications to the repository and adding the new `WorldMessage.java` source.

`cvs` supports projects that span directory hierarchies; we can easily add and manage subdirectories as needed to grow the project.

Subtleties

We've glossed over some important details, which will get more attention later:

- The structure of the directories becomes a bit more complex when your class files are placed in packages, as they should be for real projects. This is discussed in Chapter 14, "Configuring the Linux JSDK/JRE Environment," in the section "Classes Loaded from File Systems."
- Our use of `make` in these examples is naïve: dependency among application modules is a tricky issue in Java. Unlike C++ and many other languages, the correspondence between source files and class files is not simple (particularly when nested and anonymous classes are used), and it is possible and reasonable to have circular dependencies among class files. These are difficult problems for `make` to handle.
- Java compilers are beginning to address this problem (see the `-depend` option for the Sun and Jikes compilers in Chapters 19, "The Java Compiler: `javac`," and 36, "The Jikes Compiler"). There are also `make`-compatible, compiler-independent ad hoc solutions to the problem: I'll share my own in Chapter 48, "`JMakeDepend`: A Project Build Management Utility."

To GUI or Not to GUI?

We have concentrated on command-line utilities in this chapter—a common practice in the UNIX world. There are, in fact, many fine GUIs available to help with most aspects of the development process. Later in the book (see Part IX, "IDEs, GUI Builders, and RAD Tools"), we will explore some integrated development environments (IDEs) that combine many of the build steps—editing, compiling, running—into a single GUI.

One pleasantly surprising aspect of UNIX development is the number of good GUI tools that have been built by gluing together traditional components (perhaps we should call them *GLUIs*) with powerful scripting languages such as Perl and Tcl/Tk/Wish. The `tkCVS` tool mentioned earlier in the chapter, for example, uses a handful of Wish (*WIndowing SHell*) scripts to build a capable GUI around cvs's cryptic commands. Figure 9.5 is a screen dump of the tkCVS interface as it appeared for our sample project, before we added the last set of changes to the repository. It uses a familiar *file browser* paradigm while providing a reasonable set of buttons (with pop-up tooltips) and menus to access cvs's full capabilities.

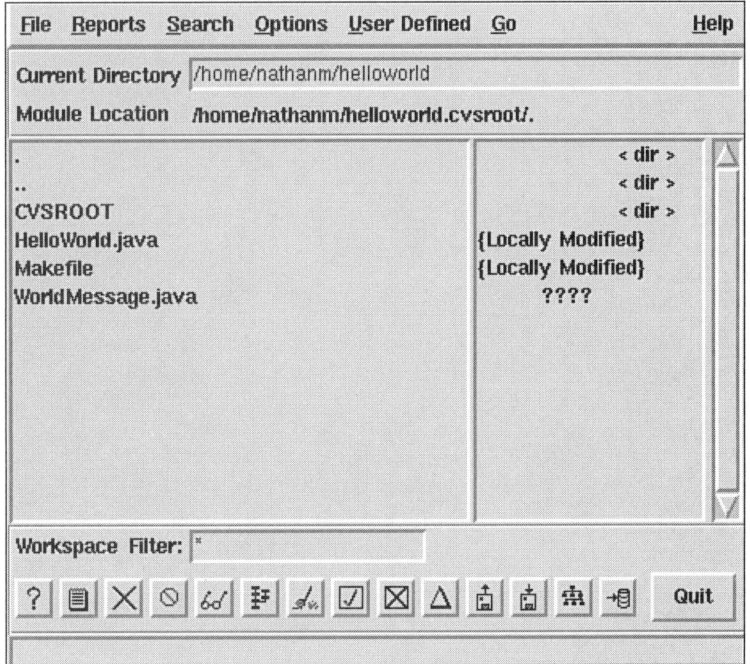

FIGURE 9.5
The tkCVS GUI.

Summary

This chapter has presented an overview of the tools and techniques for setting up a development environment on Linux. The tools discussed here will put you in the native language development business and start you down the road toward Java development. In Chapter 10, "Java Components for Linux," we examine the parts and pieces you need to add Java language support to your system.

CHAPTER 10

JAVA COMPONENTS FOR LINUX

Java development and deployment involves several components that, if you're coming from a non-Java background, may seem strange and unfamiliar. The terrain is very much in evolution: Java applications can be built in many different ways, and run-time environments can be purchased whole or assembled from spare parts.

This chapter summarizes the types of tools used with Java on Linux and surveys the spare parts. This will serve as background for the next several parts of the book, in which we discuss where to find these tools and how to use them.

A Glossary of Sun Java Terminology

When Java tools and environments are described, they invariably use the terminology that Sun associates with its releases. This is a sufficiently confusing area for which we will provide not one, but two glossaries. Keep in mind that Java has been released in three versions: 1.0, 1.1, and 1.2.

First, the glossary of traditional Java terminology:

- 100% Pure Java—A trademarked term indicating that an API is implemented entirely in Java and has been certified to have no platform-specific dependencies. Although it is impossible to guarantee absolute portability across Java platforms, this certification (provided as a fee-based service by Sun for vendor products) increases confidence in a Java-based product's portability. Among Sun's own Standard Extensions, many of them are implemented entirely in Java, but only some carry this certification.

- Class path—This describes where Java's built-in class loader looks for classes and can include class files and archives located on local media and on the Web. We discuss how Java finds classes in more detail in Chapter 14, "Configuring the Linux SDK/JRE Environment," in the section "How Java Finds Classes."
- Core class libraries—These are the required class libraries specified for a particular release of Java; if you don't have all of these libraries, you don't have a full runtime environment. Class libraries are occasionally developed externally to the core and later added—JFC Swing was developed and distributed as an extension for JDK1.1 and included in the core for JDK1.2.

  Many of the core class libraries include platform-native code, which is shipped in native shared libraries as part of the runtime environment. Platform-native code is used to implement such platform-specific features as graphical rendering (for the `java.awt` package) and native file I/O (for the `java.io` package).
- JDK—The *Java Development Kit* is Sun's reference software development kit. The same term is also commonly used as a synonym for a Java platform release—for example, by browsers and apps claiming to be "JDK1.1-compliant." (This confusing use is now standard practice, so we will follow it and instead use the term *SDK* to denote the software development kit. With the release of the Java 2 Platform, Sun is encouraging the use of a new term, *J2SDK*, for the software development kit.)

  The SDK includes the JRE (discussed next) and development tools: compiler, debugger, documentation generator, and so on. Beginning in Chapter 17, "The Java Application Launchers: java, jre, and oldjava," we will examine the components that make up the SDK for Linux.
- JRE—The *Java Runtime Environment* is the JVM (discussed next) and the core class libraries that define a complete environment in which Java applications run. JREs are available as standalone application environments (which you get from the Blackdown Linux port of the Sun code), and are also bundled with Web browsers. For the new version of this term, see *J2RE* in the next glossary.
- JVM—The *Java Virtual Machine* is the core of a runtime environment—a program that knows how to interpret Java classes.
- Standard extension—A standard extension is a Java enhancement specified by Sun—not as part of the core functionality but as functionality considered useful and desirable. An example is the Java3D specification for 3D graphical rendering. All standard extensions have, by definition, a full API specification, a reference implementation, and a test suite.

Figure 10.1 shows a schematic of the pieces.

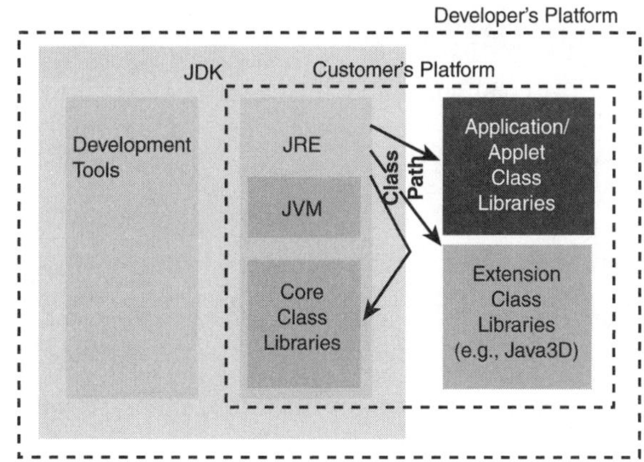

FIGURE 10.1
The Java Software Development Kit, used by developers, and the Java Runtime Environment, used in deployment environments.

And now the glossary of new terms:

- Java 2 Platform— A *Java platform* is an abstraction: a specification of an environment in which Java applications and applets run. When Sun introduced version 1.2 of Java, it chose (for marketing purposes) to relaunch it as the Java 2 Platform (there was no prior Java 1 platform).

  This designation is not to be confused, although it often is, with the *versioning scheme* used to identify releases: 1.0, 1.1, and 1.2 (to date). The current release of Java is officially called The Java 2 Platform Version 1.2, and the next version will be The Java 2 Platform Version 1.3.

- Java Foundation Classes—A marketing term describing a subset of the core class libraries—AWT, Swing, pluggable look and feel, accessibility, Java2D, and drag-and-drop.

- J2RE—The Java 2 Runtime Environment, Standard Edition. This is the new name for the JRE associated with the Java 2 Platform. The latest release is officially called the Java 2 Runtime Environment Version 1.2.

- J2SDK—The Java 2 Software Development Kit, Standard Edition. This is the new name for the SDK associated with the Java 2 Platform. The latest release is officially called the Java 2 Software Development Kit Version 1.2.

- J2SE—The Java 2 Platform Standard Edition. This is the official name of the Java 2 Platform for client platforms such as browsers and desktop machines.

Why Standard Edition? Because there are two other editions:

- The Java 2 Enterprise Edition (J2EE) is slated for release in late 1999. J2EE consists of the J2SE plus a number of server-oriented standard extensions (Enterprise Java Beans, Servlets, Java Server Pages, and more).

- The Java 2 Micro Edition, announced in mid-1999, is targeted at constrained environments such as personal and embedded applications.

Undoubtedly, more acronyms are in the works.

Java Development and Runtime Components

As you shop for Java components, you'll find the items detailed in the following sections.

Java Compilers

Java compilers generate Java class files (suffixed `.class`) from Java source files (suffixed `.java`). The Sun SDK includes a Java compiler, `javac`, which is itself a Java application.

Because the class file and language specifications are public and easily available, anyone can write a compiler. Some worthwhile variants that have appeared are as follows:

- Java compilers implemented as native applications, of which the best example is Jikes (see Chapter 36, "The Jikes Compiler").
- Java compilers that implement a superset of the Java language, such as the Generic Java Compiler (see Chapter 38, "Generic Java Compilers").
- Compilers that compile from other high-level languages into Java bytecodes. This is not a wildly popular activity—the Java instruction set is not particularly well suited to other languages—but is home to some worthwhile academic and commercial efforts. Such compilers exist for Scheme, Eiffel, SmallTalk, C++, Cobol, and numerous other languages.

Java Native Compilers

These are compilers that get you from Java (`.java` and/or `.class` files) into native code for your Linux (or some other) environment. The obvious reason is speed, and the obvious tradeoff is portability. Sun does not supply any such compilers, but we will explore one in Chapter 31, "gcj: A Compiled Java Solution."

Core Class Libraries

Sun supplies a complete set of core class libraries in its reference implementation, so any Sun-licensed port will include them. But the specs are public, and anyone who doesn't like Sun's implementation or its licensing terms is free to write his own. This is how Java ends up running on such small-market platforms such as the Amiga and Next.

Variants you will find are as follows:

- Cleanroom implementations (without any licensed code from Sun) of core class libraries bundled with a cleanroom JVM (see Chapter 26, "Kaffe: A Cleanroom Java Environment").
- Cleanroom implementations of core class libraries independent of a JVM (see Chapter 28, "GNU Classpath: Cleanroom Core Class Libraries").

These alternative implementations offer you the opportunity to mix-and-match components in a Java development or runtime environment.

JVM

Like the core class libraries (discussed previously), the JVM is supplied by Sun but can also be created from specifications. Variants you will find are as follows:

- Cleanroom implementations of JVMs bundled with class libraries (see Chapter 26, Kaffe: A Cleanroom Java Environment).
- Cleanroom implementations of JVMs without any class libraries (Japhar, Chapter 27, "Japhar: A Cleanroom JVM").

JIT Compilers

Java is an interpreted language, which is bad news for performance. Just-in-time (JIT) compilers add runtime optimization to Java by compiling pieces of the application into fast native code as the app is running. This is a crucially important area, as Java seeks to solve its well-known performance problems.

JITs are available from Sun (one is bundled with JDK1.2) and from outside developers (see Chapter 33, "Just-In-Time Compilers"). There is extensive commercial JIT activity for the Microsoft Windows platform, and Linux will undoubtedly receive more attention in this area.

Much of the recent activity in this area has been focused on new JVM designs that subsume the work of JITs (see Chapter 30, "Sun HotSpot Performance Engine" and Chapter 29, "Mozilla ElectricalFire: A New JVM").

The major downside to JITs and similar technologies is that they show more value on long-lived server applications than in client applications and applets.

Debuggers

Sun ships a basic, non-GUI debugger with the SDK, and other choices are available (see Chapter 39, "The Jikes Debugger"). JDK1.2 introduced a new debugging interface, which is intended to improve the quantity and quality of available debuggers.

Profilers

Performance analysis tools have been a weak presence in the Java world, but the story is improving. Sun introduced a new profiling interface in JDK1.2, and we will explore an analysis application based on the interface in Chapter 60, "Perfanal: A Free Performance Analysis Tool."

Applet Viewers

Applet viewers provide the functionality to test-drive applets outside Web browsers, which is especially useful for developing applets relying on runtime environments that are not yet supported in browsers. An applet viewer is bundled with Sun's SDK.

Documentation Generators

Java code is certainly not self-documenting, but Sun has defined a relatively low-pain methodology for generating documentation by extracting class information and comments from Java source files. One such tool, `javadoc`, is bundled with Sun's SDK, and alternatives are available (see Chapter 38, "Generic Java Compilers," in the section "PizzaDoc").

Decompilers

Java, as an interpreted language, is eminently decompilable and suitable for reverse engineering. Although Sun does not provide any decompilers, the market is well served by commercial and free products (see Chapter 46, "Jad: A Java Decompiler").

Obfuscators

For developers who do not want to have their code reverse-engineered, *obfuscators* are the answer to decompilers. Free and commercial offerings are available. Obfuscators do their job by scrambling class and member names before you ship a product and creating scrambled code that works correctly but is difficult to decompile.

The battle between decompilers and obfuscators is an escalating arms race. The best advice for developers who *must* protect their super-secret algorithms is to run the code on a trusted server and not let it near any client machines. (This advice applies just as readily to compiled code as to Java.)

Optimizers

Optimization can make Java code faster and smaller. Some optimization capability is provided by compilers, but the best offerings today seem to be optimization post-processors. Free and commercial products are available (see Chapter 53, "DashO: Optimizing Applications for Delivery").

Optimizer and obfuscator capabilities are often shipped in the same product for synergistic reasons. Optimized code is often more difficult to decompile, and a standard obfuscation technique—replacing long descriptive variable names with short obscure names—is also a useful size-reducing optimization.

Integrated Development Environment, GUI Builders, and RAD Tools

Integrated Development Environments combine certain common development activities—editing, compiling, running, debugging—into a single GUI application.

GUI builders are interactive GUI-based tools that allow you to lay out your desired GUI and then automatically generate code to implement the GUI.

Rapid Application Development (RAD) tools combine the two, and more (although the industry definition of RAD is a bit slippery and not universally agreed on). RAD tools concentrate on shortening the time-consuming steps of development. That typically means IDE, GUI-building, automatic code generation, and interpreters or incremental compilers for test-driving small changes.

In later parts of the book, we will discuss these terms in more detail and examine some tools that fall into these categories.

Summary

This chapter has provided an overview of the components that make up Java runtime and development environments. While the choices available in the Java world can be staggering, an understanding of the necessary components will help you collect the pieces you need for your development and deployment needs.

CHAPTER 11

CHOOSING AN ENVIRONMENT: 1.1 OR 1.2?

With the release of JDK1.2, Java became a much better place to create applications. Over time, JDK1.2 will penetrate many operating systems and browsers and generally be supported in the user community. But developers must face the inevitable question: In which environment should today's applications be developed?

If you are developing for your own use, simply choose what works best for you. If customers are involved—employers, contracting organizations, server administrators, intranet or Internet surfers, PC or workstation users—you need to decide on a delivery platform they can use. This chapter examines that issue.

Client, Server, or Other?

The first question to ask: For what environment are you developing Java applications? Every application environment has a unique user community, version stream, and requirements.

Client-Side Java

This chapter focuses on the question of client-side Java: deployment of applications to be run, or applets to be browsed, on machines deployed on an intranet or the Internet. In this market, you must consider the question of whether (and how) your consumers are ready for JDK1.2.

Constrained Java Environments

If you are developing for one of the constrained Java environments—PersonalJava, EmbeddedJava, JavaCard, JavaTV, or JavaPhone—then market acceptance and penetration of JDK1.2 is not particularly relevant to you. These environments have their own version streams, converging toward the Java 2 Platform Micro Edition announced by Sun in mid-1999.

Server-Side Java

If you are developing for the server side, the choice of environment is probably relevant to you. Some of JDK1.2's capabilities—graphics and GUI improvements—are of little or no interest. But others, such as CORBA support and security enhancements, could be critical to your enterprise applications.

Fortunately, servers tend to be a more controlled environment than clients: You can specify a target Java environment in which your application is to be deployed—subject, of course, to availability and the willingness of server administrators to install and support the environment.

JDK1.2 is available for Linux and other server platforms, and support should improve steadily through 1999. As an example of its use, we will configure a JDK1.2-compliant Web server with a servlet environment in Chapter 65, "Java on the Web: Java Servlets and Apache JServ."

JDK1.1: Now Widely Supported

A cautionary tale: JDK1.1 was introduced to the world in 1996. It took Netscape more than three years to achieve full compliance in its browser.

Clearly, the world cannot absorb Sun technology as quickly as Sun can push it out the door, and it may not yet be time to bet your business on JDK1.2. The story for Java 1.1 is more encouraging, as the following sections explain.

Supported Applet Environments

Modern releases of the two major browsers, Netscape Navigator and Microsoft Internet Explorer, support substantially all of Java 1.1, and it is becoming increasingly difficult to write a 1.1 applet that will not run on current browsers. Many subtle details are behind this generalization—areas of incomplete support, browser point releases, bugs, the Microsoft/Sun legal imbroglio—but 1.1 browser support is, in general, excellent.

You should, of course, always test your 1.1 applets with the available browsers, especially if you have dependencies that may cause trouble (JNI or RMI, for example). Be aware that, if you deploy to Microsoft Windows environments, Netscape uses a built-in JRE, whereas Microsoft Internet Explorer uses the JRE bundled with Windows—so results can vary by browser.

If you do not want to rely on native Microsoft or Netscape Java capabilities, the Java Plug-in technology from Sun, discussed in Chapter 50, "Deploying Applets with Java Plug-in," provides an alternative way to guarantee a fully 1.1-conformant applet environment on certain platforms. (A 1.2-version of the same technology is discussed later in the chapter.)

Good information about browser Java support, and how to "sniff" browsers to ascertain Java capabilities, can be found at developer sites for Netscape (`http://developer.netscape.com`) and Microsoft (`http://msdn.microsoft.com`).

Supported Application Environments

Support for standalone Java applications depends on the availability of a JRE for the target platform. Again, the story here is good for Java 1.1. All major platforms have good 1.1 ports available: JREs for many UNIX and mainframe platforms are available from the platform vendors. JREs for NT are available from Microsoft[1], Sun, and IBM. And, of course, Linux JREs are available from the Blackdown organization and IBM (as we will explore in detail in later chapters). In addition to JREs based on Sun sources, the free JVM/library components discussed in Chapters 26 "Kaffe: A Cleanroom Java Environment," 27 "Japhar: A Cleanroom JVM," and 28 "GNU Classpath: Cleanroom Core Class Libraries," are or will be available for many major and minor computing platforms.

That said, there is still an important challenge: ensuring that customers have the JRE installed. This is not so much a technical problem as a marketing/packaging/shipment problem: How do you make users install software needed to run your Java application? Fortunately, most or all major vendors allow you to freely redistribute the JRE. If you want to ship a Java application with a JRE for HP-UX, Solaris, NT, or whatever, you can do it. Just be sure to read, understand, and adhere to the redistribution terms imposed by the JRE distributors. We will explore that issue in Chapter 49, "Distributing Java Applications and JREs Installation."

JDK1.2: Supported Where and When?

JDK1.2 was introduced in late 1998. The best early support could be found on Solaris, Windows, and Linux.

The Linux port has enjoyed some support from Sun and has benefited from a cutting-edge volunteer porting effort by the Blackdown team. To those doing early JDK1.2 development work, Linux has turned out to be one of the best platforms for the job. The port is a huge undertaking—the native portion of the JDK grew enormously for the 1.2 release—but it seems reasonable to expect that most vendors will have a JDK1.2 story by the end of 1999.

---

[1]Is the Microsoft JRE fully compliant with the Java spec? This issue is at the core of the current Sun/Microsoft legal battles. Sun's complaints about Microsoft have centered on two major concerns:

- The Microsoft JRE does not fully support the Sun spec.
- Microsoft's development tools create "Java" code dependent on features available only on Microsoft platforms.

That said, this book will steer clear of the controversy and leave it to the courts. If you are developing Java applications on Linux, the issue of Microsoft's development tools obviously does not affect you. As far as deploying your Linux-developed applications and applets for Windows environments, your main concerns are

- Does your JDK1.1 app work under the Microsoft JRE, with adequate performance and reliability?
- Will Microsoft ever support JDK1.2?

The JDK1.2 story for browsers is not so clear. It is not known when Netscape Navigator or Microsoft Internet Explorer will support that environment. Given the importance of GUIs for applets, and the GUI advances offered by Swing, the question is of crucial importance. The next two sections discuss some interim and future possible answers to this problem.

Option 1: The Java Plug-In

An ideal solution to the browser support problem is to decouple the browser from its built-in JRE and allow the browser to leverage any convenient JRE (see Figure 11.1).

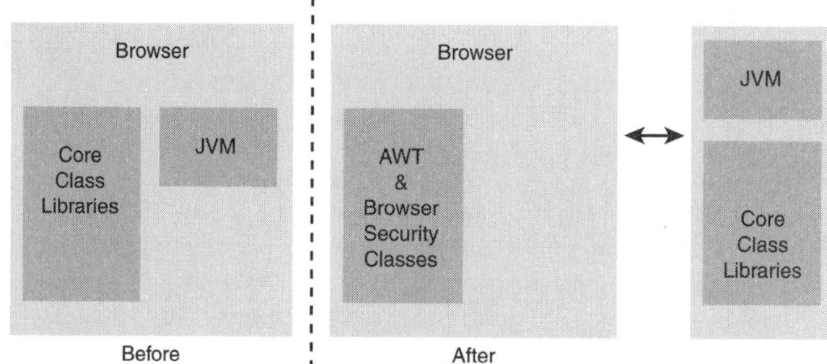

FIGURE 11.1
Browser environments are traditionally closely tied to a bundled or platform JRE. Present and future developments will separate the components.

Sun has done exactly this, with a mechanism called the Java Plug-in. The Java Plug-in uses the standard browser plug-in mechanisms to introduce a new JRE disguised as a plug-in. Running JDK1.2 applets then becomes a matter of activating that plug-in—much like browsing a multimedia file or Adobe PDF document.

The Java Plug-in is not a perfect solution: It is currently only supported on a few platforms, and the HTML tag for the applet must be modified to use the plug-in JRE. We'll discuss use and deployment of the Java Plug-in in Chapter 50, "Deploying Applets with Java Plug-In," as part of the overall discussion of applet and application deployment.

Option 2: Netscape Open Java Interface

Netscape is pursuing another approach to the same architectural idea: the *Open Java Interface* (OJI). Starting with its Communicator 5.0 product, Netscape will support an API through which any JRE can be integrated with the browser. In the long term, this should allow Netscape to exit the difficult business of porting the Sun JRE and instead rely on resident platform JREs.

The OJI will require some modest effort from JRE vendors: some glue code must be written to connect a JRE to Netscape. But OJI will offer two significant advantages:

- Any JRE, including those from the open-source community, can be used.
- Unlike the Java Plug-in (see Chapter 50), OJI does not require any changes to HTML code.

As of this writing, OJI is not yet available. But it clearly offers good promise as the solution for timely deployment of JDK1.2 and future releases.

JDK1.2 Features Available for JDK1.1

You can get some JDK1.2 benefits without moving to that environment by loading some supplemental classes available from Sun. These packages are JDK1.2 features that were released as JDK1.1 extensions and are discussed in the following sections.

Java Foundation Classes (JFC)

Portions of JFC are available for JDK1.1. These are implemented in Java—fully usable on Linux and elsewhere. To download, visit the Java site (`http://java.sun.com`) and go to the product page for the Java Foundation Classes to obtain the following components:

- JFC Swing Toolkit - including the pluggable look and feel.
- Accessibility API

The components have the same package name, `javax.swing`, as in JDK1.2. (Some earlier prereleases used different package names—`com.sun.java.swing` and `java.awt.swing`—an unfortunate source of confusion.)

Java Collections Classes

The 1.1 versions of these useful classes are distributed in conjunction with the InfoBus standard extension. Visit the Java site (`http://java.sun.com`) and go to the InfoBus product page for information on how to download these classes.

Unfortunately, these classes are in a different package (`com.sun.java.util.collections`) than their counterparts in JDK1.2 (`java.util and java.lang`). This was necessary because some environments—notably many browsers—refuse for security reasons to load classes called `java.util.*` or `java.lang.*` from outside their core library archives. So JDK1.1 code written to use these classes must be changed to work with JDK1.2.

JDK1.1 Apps Broken by JDK1.2

JDK1.2 is a proper superset of JDK1.1 but can, in some cases, break older applications. In most cases, these incompatibilities are the result of better enforcement of existing rules about class file format, argument values, security privileges, and so on.

The one area in which applications can become seriously broken, requiring some rewriting, is security. The security mechanism changed substantially between JDK1.1 and JDK1.2, and applications that implement their own security code are in danger of failure under JDK1.2. One visible example is HotJava, Sun's Java implementation of a Web browser. As of mid-1999, it was not yet usable with JDK1.2.

A short-term workaround is provided in the Sun JSDK, in the form of an application launcher that uses the old security mechanism—see the section on `oldjava` in Chapter 17, "The Java Application Launchers: java, jre, and oldjava."

For more complete information about incompatibilities, Sun publishes a compatibility document (`http://java.sun.com/products/jdk/1.2/compatibility.html`).

Summary

In choosing a deployment environment for your applications and applets, you need to balance the benefits of the new environments with a realistic view of their availability in the world. This chapter has presented a snapshot of the ever-changing landscape. The best advice when betting on new Java technology is this: proceed with caution.

CHAPTER 12

SOFTWARE LICENSING

Open Source Software (OSS) has become one of the best-known computing terms at the end of the 20th century—so much so that it has achieved the dubious status of buzzword: a term freely thrown around by people who only vaguely understand what it means.

If you work in the Linux world, and in some cases if you work in the Java world, you are dealing with OSS. This chapter takes a brief look at the meaning of OSS and at the various licenses. Our purpose is to introduce the licenses you are likely to encounter, *not* to give legal advice. If you choose to create software derived from an OSS-licensed product, you *must* understand and honor the terms of the license before you deploy your projects.

What Is OSS?

OSS is an elaboration of the concept of *free software*. Free software is nothing new: It has been a hallmark of UNIX development from the beginning and has found particularly passionate voices in the work of Richard Stallman (the GNU Project) and Eric Raymond (author of the influential essay "The Cathedral and the Bazaar," `http://www.tuxedo.org/~esr/writings/cathedral-bazaar/`). The basic idea behind free software is that you—the user or developer—are free to do useful work with the software beyond any artificial constraints imposed by the author or publisher of the software.

Common Open Source Licenses

An inherent part of free software is access to the source, giving you the freedom to fix it, improve it, or derive new software from it. But source access is not a sufficient condition for OSS, which must also be freely redistributable and must have licensing terms that do not unreasonably constrain your use of the source. The following sections look at licenses that are considered by the Open Source Initiative (`http://www.opensource.org`) to be compliant with its criteria for OSS.

The GNU General Public License (GPL)

The GPL is the best known, and probably most commonly used, OSS license. Informally known as the "copyleft," the text of the license begins with a statement of its ethos:

> The licenses for most software are designed to take away your freedom to share and change it. By contrast, the GNU General Public License is intended to guarantee your freedom to share and change free software—to make sure the software is free for all its users. This General Public License applies to most of the Free Software Foundation's software and to any other program whose authors commit to using it. (Some other Free Software Foundation software is covered by the GNU Library General Public License instead.) You can apply it to your programs, too.
>
> When we speak of free software, we are referring to freedom, not price. Our General Public Licenses are designed to make sure that you have the freedom to distribute copies of free software (and charge for this service if you wish), that you receive source code or can get it if you want it, that you can change the software or use pieces of it in new free programs; and that you know you can do these things.

After the preamble, the license spells out specific terms for copying, distributing, and modifying the licensed code. In a nutshell, the terms of the GPL are as follows:

- You may freely copy and redistribute GPL-licensed software.
- You may charge for distributing and maintaining GPL-licensed software but not for the software itself.
- Source code for GPL-licensed software must be made freely available, either published with any distribution of binaries, or available on request.
- Any derived work created from GPL-licensed source is also covered by the GPL.

The GPL has fueled much of the growth of Linux and the GNU utilities available for Linux, but it has turned out to be unpalatable in the commercial community. The requirement that any work derived from GPL-licensed source also be subject to the GPL has scared off businesses unwilling to give away their products or their sources—hence the popularity of the licenses listed in subsequent sections.

The GPL also includes a disclaimer of warranty, as do all other OSS licenses.

The GNU Library General Public License (LGPL)

The GNU *Library General Public License* (recently redubbed the *Lesser General Public License*) addresses one of the main objections to the GPL: that derived works must also be covered by the license. Free software published under the LGPL can be used to create products not covered by the LGPL.

The LGPL is especially important for OSS libraries. It allows you to link against an open source library (such as the indispensable GNU C library) without considering the resulting executable to be a derived work subject to GPL.

The Berkeley Software Distribution (BSD) License

The BSD License, derived from the BSD UNIX development stream, is a short, simple license that allows redistribution and reuse of software, and creation of derived works for free or commercial purpose. The main requirements it imposes are as follows:

- Preserve the integrity of the copyright notices when redistributing.
- Give credit where credit is due: If you derive a work from BSD-licensed software, you must mention this fact in advertising and promotional materials.

The X Window System License

A short and liberal license from MIT, this is little more than a warranty disclaimer. It grants unrestricted rights to modify, distribute, publish, sell, and reuse the software.

The Artistic License

This is a license through which (quoting the preamble) "the Copyright Holder maintains some semblance of artistic control over the development of the package" while enabling the customary modification and redistribution rights of open source. It was developed by Perl creator Larry Wall and strives to protect the integrity of the original public work while allowing the technology to be freely deployed in other products. For example, you cannot sell a proprietary Perl, but you can privately embed Perl (without publicly exposing its interfaces) in your own proprietary product.

Mozilla Public License (MPL)

The *MPL*, from the Netscape Mozilla project, is the first open source license to come from a major corporation, which is reflected in its precise and detailed legal language. The license spells out exactly how the code may be extended or incorporated into new products, and the ways in which derived works are or are not required to be open source. In a nutshell, sources derived from Mozilla's source must be open, whereas sources that interact with Mozilla only through APIs are not so constrained.

The license is a difficult read for non-attorneys, but it is also refreshingly to the point and free of philosophical declarations.

Q Public License (QPL)

The *QPL* is from Troll Tech, developers of the popular Qt GUI toolkit. The toolkit exists in two forms:

- A free version, covered by the open source QPL, that lets you use Qt in UNIX-type environments but prohibits you from distributing modifications or deriving commercial products.
- A commercial (non-QPL) version, with a licensing fee, that allows commercial exploitation. As the copyright holder, Troll Tech is free to distribute under multiple licenses. This is one example of the approaches some vendors are exploring to build businesses on OSS.

Sun Community Source License (SCSL)—Not Open Source

One license you will encounter in the Java world is the *SCSL*—the license under which Sun makes the Java reference implementation (and other products') source code available. No charge is associated with the SCSL: You can see the source for free. But it is *not* an open source license and should be used with caution.

The SCSL entitles you to obtain source, either for research and development, porting efforts, or creating derived works. It does not allow you to redistribute the source, and it requires that you negotiate a license with Sun for distribution of ports or derived works. Licensing of the Java sources is an important income stream for them.

An area of particular sensitivity in the open source community is the effect of "contamination" by the SCSL. Free Java projects such as Kaffe (see Chapter 26, "Kaffe: A Cleanroom Java Environment") and Japhar (see Chapter 27, "Japhar: A Cleanroom JVM") do not allow developers who have obtained an SCSL to contribute code to avoid contamination by people who have seen the encumbered Sun source.

That said, if you have a need to perform research or create products based on Sun's sources, visit its site (`http://java.sun.com`) and go to the product pages for the relevant source releases. In the course of obtaining the sources, you will go through the necessary steps to sign a Sun Community Source License.

Licensing Your Own Software

How should you license your own software?

That decision is usually up to you, but not always. If you are creating derived works based on another source (open source or otherwise), be sure to understand the licensing terms. You cannot, for example, derive a proprietary commercial product from GPL-licensed software.

Beyond such concerns, should you publish your own software under open source terms?

The basic business arguments in favor of OSS licensing are the following:

- Quality—Case study OSS efforts from the past 20 years have produced the astonishing collection of high-quality software from which the Internet is built, from low-level protocol stacks to Web servers.
- Business—Successful businesses can be built on top of OSS, including consulting, integration, distribution, service, and customization.
- Collaboration—The efforts of an involved user/developer community lead to better products, better quality, and new markets. It allows you to devote fewer of your own resources to development and QA. (This argument works if—a very big *if*—your product attracts an interested developer community.)
- Long-term value—The market value of a piece of software, proprietary or not, follows a rapid decay curve; keeping software proprietary buys you little protection in today's market.

(There is also a political/ethical argument that software should not be sold, patented, or otherwise protected like a commodity. This argument is controversial and far from universally accepted. Notice that *most* licenses do not prevent you from being in the business of selling and protecting software. But it is an important and vocal current of thought in the open-source world.)

We live in interesting times for OSS. Many innovative OSS business models are being explored by commercial enterprises; it is still too soon to know which of these models will work. Several major platform vendors have jumped on the Open Source train: SGI is releasing its XFS networked files system to the OSS community, and Hewlett-Packard Company has cosponsored (with O'Reilly & Associates) *SourceXChange*, a Web-based matchmaking service for OSS developers and companies seeking to do OSS development.

Is OSS for you? A good place to research the question is the Open Source Initiative (`http://www.opensource.org`). You can review the various licenses in their entirety and study the arguments in more detail than provided here.

Summary

This chapter has explored the common licenses you will encounter when working in the Linux and Java worlds. If you are in the business of selling or distributing software, you should understand the licensing terms of all software you depend on—and especially of all software from which you derive new works.

PART IV

THE BLACKDOWN PORT: A SUN JAVA SDK FOR LINUX

The center of gravity for much of the Java activity on Linux is the Blackdown port—a volunteer effort to port the Sun Java Software Development Kit to Linux. In this part, we focus on Blackdown: what it is, how to get it, and how to configure it and how to address problems encountered in the Linux enviroment.

CHAPTER 13

BLACKDOWN: THE OFFICIAL LINUX PORT

The Java implementation found on most systems is a port of the Sun Java Development Kit. Vendors such as HP, IBM, SGI, and Microsoft license the source, port the code, and pay fees to Sun for the right to distribute the SDK and the JRE.

The Blackdown port, under the auspices of the volunteer Blackdown organization, is the same thing—except that nobody is getting paid. The team is entirely volunteer, and the project is licensed from Sun under a no-cost noncommercial license agreement.

The history of SDK ports on Linux began with Randy Chapman's port of SDK1.0 and followed with Steve Byrne's leadership in porting SDK1.1. Karl Asha created the Blackdown site and the mailing lists. These three and numerous others have contributed engineering to create the Blackdown port, which enjoys the distinction (on Intel x86-based Linux boxes) of being among the leading-edge ports on the market. Ports also exist for Linux on Sparc, Alpha, and PowerPC platforms, although releases on these platforms usually lag behind the x86-based releases.

The Blackdown Web site is `http://www.blackdown.org` and features downloads of current SDKs and JREs, downloads of other Linux Java extensions, news, documentation, useful links, a FAQ, a bug-reporting and tracking system, and a lively mailing list whose participants include several engineers from Sun. (See Chapter 16, "Participating in the Blackdown Community" for more detail.)

The Blackdown site also posts *diffs*: lists of changes required to port the Sun source to Linux. The diffs, consisting of files published in a format generated by the GNU `diff` utility, can be applied as patches to Sun's SDK source to produce the Blackdown SDK source. So for developers who want to maintain their own sources, the diffs plus the Sun sources (available for free through the Sun Community License) will get you there.

Contents of the Blackdown SDK and JRE

As discussed in Chapter 10, "Java Components for Linux," in the section "A Glossary of Sun Java Terminology," the SDK is a full development environment, whereas the JRE is a subset that provides application runtime support. The SDK is provided under restrictive terms that prohibit you from redistributing it, whereas the JRE's more liberal terms allow you to redistribute it with your application. In other words: you can count on finding JRE components, *but not SDK components*, in a deployment environment.

Each distribution includes a `LICENSE` file detailing the exact terms.

Table 13.1 lists the major components comprising the SDK and JRE.

TABLE 13.1 Blackdown SDK and JRE Components

Component	SDK1.2	JRE1.2	SDK1.1	JRE1.1	More info
`appletviewer`	X		X		**Chapter 18**
`extcheck`	X				**Chapter 24**
`jar`	X		X		**Chapter 21**
`jarsigner`	X				**Chapter 24**
`java`	X	X	X		**Chapter 17**
`java_g`			X		**Chapter 17**
`javac`	X		X		**Chapter 19**
`javac_g`			X		**Chapter 19**
`javadoc`	X		X		**Chapter 23**
`javah`	X		X		**Chapter 22**
`javah_g`			X		**Chapter 22**
`javakey`			X	X	**Chapter 24**

Component	SDK1.2	JRE1.2	SDK1.1	JRE1.1	More info
`javap`	X		X		**Chapter 24**
`jdb`	X		X		**Chapter 20**
`jre`			X	X	**Chapter 17**
`jre_g`			X		**Chapter 17**
`keytool`	X	X			**Chapter 24**
`native2ascii`	X		X		**Chapter 24**
`oldjava`	X				**Chapter 17**
`policytool`	X	X			**Chapter 24**
`rmic`	X		X		**Chapter 24**
`rmid`	X	X			**Chapter 24**
`rmiregistry`	X	X	X	X	**Chapter 24**
`serialver`	X		X		**Chapter 24**
`tnameserv`	X	X			**Chapter 24**
Core class libraries	X	X	X	X	**Chapter 3**
Core config files	X	X	X	X	
Sun JIT compiler	X	X			**Chapter 14**
Scalable fonts	X	X			**Chapter 14**
JNI Headers	X		X		**Chapter 55**
Demos	X				

We will describe these components in detail in subsequent chapters.

Obtaining Blackdown Releases

The Blackdown project maintains several mirrors for distribution of the releases. If you visit the main site (`http://www.blackdown.org`), navigate to the download page, and select a mirror, you will find a directory hierarchy containing all the current and past releases from the project. The diagram in Figure 13.1 shows a small excerpt of the hierarchy, identifying the directories containing (as of this writing) the latest releases for various platforms. (Not shown are many other directories containing earlier releases.)

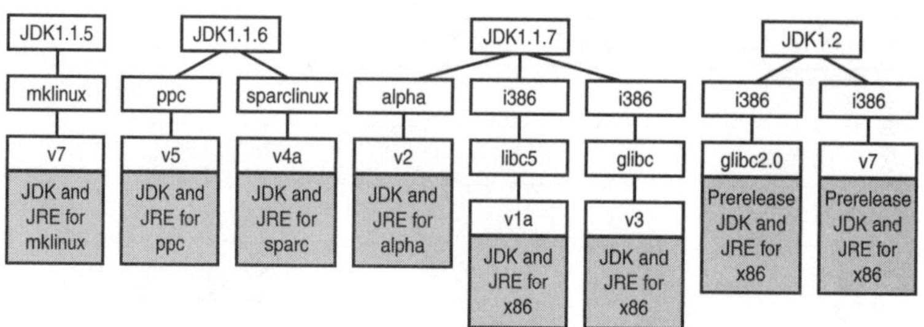

FIGURE 13.1
A snapshot of the latest Blackdown Java releases for Linux.

This chart will quickly go out of date, but it gives an overall idea of the tree's organization and the status of the various ports. Several different versioning schemes are in evidence here: minor Java releases (1.1.5, 1.1.6, 1.1.7), major Java releases (1.1 versus 1.2), versions of Blackdown releases (v5, v7, and so on), and versions of glibc (2.0, 2.1).

Within each directory containing SDKs and JREs are tar archives with the actual bits, compressed either with `gzip` (.gz) or the better `bzip2` (.bz2). (See Chapter 9, "Setting Up a Linux Development Environment," in the section "Compression and Archiving: `tar`, `gzip`, `bzip2`, `zip`, `unzip`" for details on archiving and compression utilities.)

Unpacking the archives is straightforward:

1. Decide where to install the product; create and cd to that directory. Example:

```
bash$ mkdir -p /usr/local/Java
bash$ cd /usr/local/Java
```

2. Uncompress and untar the file. Example:

```
bash$ gzip -d </tmp/jre_1.1.7-v3-glibc-x86.tar.gz ¦ tar xvf -
```

or

```
bash$ bzip2 -d </tmp/jre_1.1.7-v3-glibc-x86.tar.bz2 ¦ tar xvf -
```

Supported Linux Versions for the Blackdown SDK and JRE

Given the wide variety of Linux environments—many distributions, many versions of many libraries, many configurations, many platforms—building and distributing a product for Linux is a daunting task. The Blackdown port tries to avoid dependence on any one distribution or system configuration and instead ships several versions of its distributions to meet the needs of the user and development communities.

All the versions described in this chapter can be picked up from the Blackdown site or its mirrors.

JDK Versions for x86 Linux

Most Linux machines in the world run on the Intel x86 CPU architecture, and most of the Java/Linux development work has been for such machines. As of this writing, there are four *current* Blackdown JDK versions for x86 (and many older ones available at the download sites).

The following subsections discuss the four versions, but we begin with an important introduction to the reasons for version proliferation.

An Important Note About libc

The four current i386 Blackdown JDK distributions are differentiated by Java version (1.1 versus 1.2) *and* by dependencies on the C library. C library dependency is a confusing matter, and is the most common reason for failure to run the Blackdown JDK out of the box. This section discusses the Linux GNU C library, its recent history, how to identify your library version, and the importance of obtaining a Blackdown JDK that is compatible with the library.

The C library, libc, is a vital core component of any Linux or UNIX system. It provides core functionality for virtually every program that runs on the system—including the Java runtime. The shared version of this library, **/lib/libc.so.*<something>***, and its related components are used whenever a program is run, and the entire system is rife with dependencies on this library.

The Linux C library has gone through three important phases in recent history:

- libc5—This is the "old" C library. It was created by applying extensive, Linux-specific modifications to the C library distributed (for many operating systems) by the GNU project. Many older applications depend on this library, but support is starting to disappear; over time, progressively fewer products are maintaining libc5 compatibility. Many Linux distributions have moved to the newer libraries (discussed next) but continue to ship libc5 to support older applications.
- glibc2.0—The GNU project substantially rewrote its C library, incorporating changes for Linux compatibility. This new version 2 (in GNU's versioning stream) was adopted as version 6 (in Linux's numbering stream). Linux distributions with glibc support began to appear in 1998.
- glibc2.1—The glibc2.0 release was considered experimental, although it was stable and long-lived enough to be widely adopted (including by the Red Hat 5.x release stream). Revision 2.1 appeared in 1999, and a number of distributions have moved to this version.

When a Linux application is built, it becomes dependent on the library version it was linked against. libc5 programs require the libc5 library to run and glibc components require the glibc library to run.

For many Linux applications, that distinction is the whole story—they need libc5 or they need glibc. But for *some* programs there is an additional sensitivity to the glibc version: a program linked against glibc2.0 will not run on a system with glibc2.1, and vice versa. The Blackdown JDK1.2 port is such a program—you must obtain a version that matches your system.

Identifying Your System

What kind of C library does your system have? To answer, look for files named **/lib/libc.so.*<something>***:

- If you have a **libc.so.5** but not a **libc.so.6**, then you have a libc5 system.
- If you have a **libc.so.6**, and it is a symbolic link to **libc-2.0*<something>***, you have a glibc2.0 system.

- If you have a `libc.so.6`, and it is a symbolic link to `libc-2.1<something>`, you have a glibc2.1 system.

To install a Blackdown Java distribution, you must select one appropriate to your system.

Updating Your System

What if you want to move from libc5 to glibc—for example, to use JDK1.2—or move from glibc2.0 to glibc2.1?

Installation of the C library is a tricky affair. It involves not just `libc.so` but also a runtime linker (`ld-linux.so`) and dozens of other libraries with dependencies on libc. It is possible, if you install glibc incorrectly, to render your system inoperative.

The best way to move to the desired library is to install or upgrade your system to a Linux distribution *based on that library*—for example, Red Hat 5.x (glibc2.0) or 6.x (glibc2.1). If that is not an option, visit the Linux Online support center (`http://www.linux.org/help/howto.html`) and consult the Glibc2 HOWTO for detailed instructions.

JDK1.1 for libc5 x86 Systems

You should obtain this version if you want to run JDK1.1 on a glibc-based system. To run properly, you will need version 5.44 or greater of libc and a reasonably current version of `ld.so`.

The current (as of this writing) SDK1.1/JRE1.1 release is 1.1.7; unless you have a compelling reason to get an earlier release, get the latest. You will need to get the release from the `libc5` directory.

JDK1.1 for glibc x86 Systems

You should obtain this version if you want to run JDK1.1 on a glibc-based system.

The current (as of this writing) release is 1.1.7; unless you have a compelling reason to get an earlier release, get the latest. You will need to get the release from the `glibc` directory.

JDK1.2 for glibc2.0 x86 Systems

As of JDK1.2, the Blackdown releases no longer support libc5. But they have a similar library split—for the two versions of glibc. Unlike JDK1.1, JDK1.2 is unable to support both glibc revisions with a single release. If you are running a glibc2.0 system, you need to download a version of the SDK or JRE from the glibc2.0 directory.

JDK1.2 for glibc2.1 x86 Systems

If you are running a glibc2.1 system, you need to download a version of the SDK or JRE from the glibc2.1 directory.

JDK1.1 for Compaq Alpha Linux

The most recent release for the Alpha is 1.1.7. There are two versions, for 21064 and 21164 CPUs.

JDK1.1 for Sun Sparc Linux

The most recent release for Sparc Linux is 1.1.6.

JDK1.1 for PPC Linux

The most recent release for PowerPC Linux (Apple, IBM, and other PPC platforms) is 1.1.6.

JDK1.1 for MkLinux

The most recent release for MkLinux (mach-based Linux on PowerMac) is 1.1.5.

JDK1.1 for ARM

The most recent release for versions of Linux running on the ARM processor is is 1.1.8.

Basic Environment Setup

After you have installed the SDK, a few changes to your environment will put you in the Java business.

Setting the Environment for JDK1.1

Table 13.2 shows the three environment variables you need to set for your SDK1.1 or JRE1.1 environment.

TABLE 13.2 SDK1.1/JRE1.1 Environment Variables

Variable	Purpose	Example
`JAVA_HOME`	Specifies Java installation directory. This is optional; if not set, JDK1.1 infers a value by examining the path to the Java executables.	`JAVA_HOME=/usr/local/Java/jdk117_v3`
`PATH`	The standard UNIX/Linux variable for locating executables. Java's `bin/`directory should appear before any other directories that may contain executables of the same name (such as other installed Java environments!).	`PATH=$JAVA_HOME/bin:$PATH`
`CLASSPATH`	Tells Java where to find all classes at runtime. This is optional; if not set, JDK1.1 assumes the default example value to the right.	`CLASSPATH=$JAVA_HOME/lib/rt.jar:\$JAVA_HOME/lib/i18n.jar:\$JAVA_HOME/lib/classes.zip:.`

Recall that the format for setting variables under the bash shell requires setting and exporting the variable, as in this example:

```
bash$ export JAVA_HOME=/usr/local/Java/jdk117_v3
```

With the environment set up, you can try a quick test of the system. Write a program in file Hello.java:

```
public class Hello
{
    public static void main(String[] argv)
    {
        System.out.println("Hello World");
    }
}
```

Compile and run:

```
bash$ javac Hello.java
bash$ java Hello
Hello World
bash$
```

If your system is configured correctly, you should see the traditional Hello World output. Otherwise, the error you are most likely to see is one of these:

- command not found—You neglected to include the Java installation bin/ directory in your $PATH.
- Can't find class Hello—You neglected to include the current directory "." in the class path.

Chapter 14, "Configuring the Linux JSDK/JRE Environment," will cover some additional Java environment configuration options. If you encounter problems beyond the obvious two listed here, Chapter 15, "Troubleshooting the Blackdown JSDK/JRE Installation," can help you diagnose the difficulty.

Setting the Environment for JDK1.2

For JDK1.2, you set the same variables as for JDK1.1, but with different values (see Table 13.3):

TABLE 13.3 SDK1.2/JRE1.2 Environment Variables

Variable	Purpose	Example
JAVA_HOME	This variable is never used by JRE1.2 or SDK1.2. Its value is inferred from the location of the Java executable. But it is sometimes used by other Java applications. If set, it should point to the Java installation directory.	JAVA_HOME=/usr/local/Java/jdk1.2

Variable	Purpose	Example
PATH	The standard UNIX/Linux variable for locating executables. Java's `bin` directory should appear before any other directories that may contain executables of the same name (such as other installed Java environments!).	`PATH=$JAVA_HOME/bin:$PATH`
CLASSPATH	Tells Java where to find all *user* classes at runtime. We'll explain the 1.1/1.2 `CLASSPATH` differences in Chapter 14 in the section "How a Class Path Is Constructed for Applications."	`CLASSPATH=.`

Recall that the format for setting variables under the `bash` shell requires setting and exporting the variable, as in this example:

```
bash$ export JAVA_HOME=/usr/local/Java/jdk1.2
```

At this point, you may want to try the `Hello World` test described at the end of the previous section, "Setting the Environment for JDK1.1." If your system is not configured correctly, the error you are most likely to see is one of these:

- `command not found`—You neglected to include the Java installation `bin/` directory in your `$PATH`.
- `Can't find class Hello`—You neglected to include the current directory "`.`" in the class path.

Chapter 14 will cover some additional Java environment configuration options. If you encounter problems beyond the obvious two listed here, Chapter 15 can help you diagnose the difficulty.

Setting the `JDK_HOME` Environment Variable

Past practice has sometimes relied on another environment variable, `JDK_HOME`, in some startup scripts for Java programs. There is no need to set this variable, but if you do, it should have the same value as `$JAVA_HOME` to avoid breaking some applications.

Summary

This chapter introduced the Blackdown port of the Sun JDK for Linux. The discussion will continue in the next two chapters, with detailed exploration of JDK configuration and troubleshooting.

CHAPTER 14

CONFIGURING THE LINUX SDK/JRE ENVIRONMENT

We discussed a basic Java configuration in Chapter 13, "Blackdown: The Official Linux Port," in which setting or modifying a few environment variables—`JAVA_HOME`, `CLASSPATH`, and `PATH`—gets you started running Java. This chapter explores configuration of your environment in more depth, beginning with an important discussion of how Java finds classes.

This discussion is relevant to both SDK (your development environment) and JRE (the end-user's deployment environment). Where there are differences between JDK1.1 and JDK1.2, we will point them out.

The SDK documentation bundles, mentioned several times throughout the chapter, are not part of the Blackdown distributions. They can be obtained from the Java site (`http://java.sun.com`) by visiting the relevant SDK product page and downloading the SDK documentation.

How Java Finds Classes

The built-in Java class loader can load classes from two types of sources: file systems and archive files. A *class path*—a list of places to look, like the UNIX `PATH` variable—tells the class loader where to find the relevant file system directories and archive files.

The class path is a more complicated affair than we've portrayed so far. We'll delve into it in the next section; for now, think of it as an abstraction—a collection of locations to search for classes.

Classes Loaded from File Systems

Java classes can live in file systems, as individual files with the `.class` suffix. Location is a confusing matter, so we'll create a class file with an example:

Consider a simple project, in which I am doing development work in a directory called `/foo`. My source file, `Hello.java`, looks like this:

```
package bar.baz;

public class Hello
{
    public static void main(String[] argv)
    {
        System.out.println("Hello World");
    }
}
```

I have a subdirectory called `classes/`, into which I place my compiled classes when I build:

```
bash$ javac -d classes Hello.java
```

After compilation, my class can be found at location `/foo/classes/bar/baz/Hello.class`. Notice that the compiler placed the class in a hierarchical directory tree that reflects the full *package+class* name of my class, `bar.baz.Hello`. So the full file system path to my class file consists of two separate components: The path to the root of the class (`/foo/classes/`), and the relative path from the root to the actual class file (`bar/baz/Hello.class`).

For the Java class loader to find this class, it needs to know the location of the *root* of the class: the class path must include an entry for `/foo/classes`. The class loader derives the relative path to `Hello.class` from the name of the class itself.

The tricky but crucial requirement is this: The class file *must* be located on a path, *relative* to an entry in the class path, that matches its full package+class name. You can think of those "`.`" separators in the full package+class name as representing file system "`/`" separators—in fact, Java uses "`/`" internally for precisely that purpose.

Example

Here is an example, using a JDK1.2-style invocation, of how to load and run the class:

```
bash$ java -cp /foo/classes bar.baz.nmeyers.Hello
Hello World
bash$
```

And an example of what does not work:

```
bash$ java -cp /foo/classes/bar/baz Hello
Exception in thread "main" java.lang.NoClassDefFoundError: Hello (wrong
name: bar/baz/Hello)
   at java.lang.ClassLoader.defineClass0(Native Method)
   at java.lang.ClassLoader.defineClass(Compiled Code)
   at java.security.SecureClassLoader.defineClass(Compiled Code)
   at java.net.URLClassLoader.defineClass(Compiled Code)
```

```
    at java.net.URLClassLoader.access$1(Compiled Code)
    at java.net.URLClassLoader$1.run(Compiled Code)
    at java.security.AccessController.doPrivileged(Native Method)
    at java.net.URLClassLoader.findClass(Compiled Code)
    at java.lang.ClassLoader.loadClass(Compiled Code)
    at sun.misc.Launcher$AppClassLoader.loadClass(Compiled Code)
    at java.lang.ClassLoader.loadClass(Compiled Code)
    bash$
```

The class loader found the `Hello.class` file, as expected, but threw an exception because the class name requested (`Hello`) did not match the class name encoded in the file (`bar.baz.Hello`).

Classes Loaded from Archive Files

The built-in Java class loader supports two hierarchical archive formats:

- ZIP files—This is the familiar compressed archive that has been in use since MS-DOS days.
- Jar files—The *Java ARchive* format is identical to ZIP, with the optional addition of a file containing metadata about the classes in the archive.

As with file systems, the class resides in a `.class` file in the archive. As with the previous example, the full path to the class file consists of two components: the path to the root (now the archive is the root), and the relative path to the class file (a path within the archive). Using the previous example, we create such an archive and place it in the `/tmp` directory:

```
bash$ jar cvf /tmp/project.jar -C classes .
added manifest
adding: com/ (in=0) (out=0) (stored 0%)
adding: com/macmillan/ (in=0) (out=0) (stored 0%)
adding: com/macmillan/nmeyers/ (in=0) (out=0) (stored 0%)
adding: com/macmillan/nmeyers/Hello.class (in=437) (out=300) (deflated 31%)
bash$
```

Here, we use the SDK1.2 `jar` tool to create an archive, `/tmp/project.jar`, from everything in and below the root directory of the classes. The `jar` tool creates a default manifest and copies the file system hierarchy into the compressed archive. (The SDK1.1 `jar` has no `-C` option; you would need to `cd` to the classes directory to generate this jar file.)

To run from the archive, again using the JDK1.2-style invocation:

```
bash$ java -cp /tmp/project.jar com.macmillan.nmeyers.Hello
Hello World
bash$
```

Subtleties

Some subtleties embedded in these examples:

- We used an application-launch command line (`java`) as an example, but this discussion applies to all class references. All references are stored internally as full *package+class* references and subject to the same class-loading logic that is used for launching applications.
- Notice that we asked the `java` launcher to run `Hello`, not `Hello.class`. If you're new to Java, one of your first mistakes will be to try to run class files. Don't. With the `java` application launcher, you request a class name and let the class loader resolve it to a `.class` file somewhere.

How a Class Path Is Constructed for Applications

Construction of the class path became more complicated (but more robust) with JDK1.2, so we will split the discussion between JDK1.1 and JDK1.2. Note that this discussion is specific to the Sun implementation (other Java implementations may do it differently) running in UNIX/Linux environments (Windows systems, for example, use a different path separator).

JDK1.1 Class Path Construction

JDK1.1 defines a single class path—a colon-separated list of directories and archive files. The value of this class path depends on the presence of certain environment variables, as shown in Table 14.1.

TABLE 14.1 JDK1.1 Class Path Variables

Environment Variables	Class Path (newlines inserted for readability)
`CLASSPATH` defined	`$CLASSPATH`

`CLASSPATH` undefined
`JAVA_HOME` defined
	`.:`
	`$JAVA_HOME/classes:`
	`$JAVA_HOME/lib/classes.jar:`
	`$JAVA_HOME/lib/rt.jar:`
	`$JAVA_HOME/lib/i18n.jar:`
	`$JAVA_HOME/lib/classes.zip`

`CLASSPATH` undefined `JAVA_HOME` undefined	(same as above, where a value of `$JAVA_HOME` is inferred from the path to the `java` launcher executable)

These settings apply when launching an app, when compiling, and when launching other SDK tools. One exception is the appletviewer tool: it does not include "`.`" in the default class path.

The value of the class path can be changed by command-line options (shown in Table 14.2) to the application launcher.

TABLE 14.2 JDK1.1 Command-Line Options to Alter Class Paths

Command	Class Path
`java -classpath` *<newclasspath>*	*<newclasspath>*
`jre -classpath_`*<newclasspath>*	*<newclasspath>*
`jre -cp` *<newclasspath>*	*<newclasspath>*`:` *<current class path>*

Note that the `java` application launcher is shipped only with SDK1.1, whereas the `jre` launcher is shipped with SDK1.1 and JRE1.1: `jre` is intended for use in deployment environments.

Some of the other SDK tools, such as the Java compiler, also support a `-classpath` argument. For those that do not, you can change the class path by modifying the `CLASSPATH` environment variable.

JDK1.2 Class Path Construction

The JDK1.1 class path structure has caused countless headaches in development and deployment environments. The use of a single path for finding core classes, extensions, and user classes is confusing and easily misused.

For JDK1.2, Sun defined three mechanisms for locating classes—one for core classes needed to boot the environment, one for standard extensions, and one for user classes. It is also possible, with this new mechanism, to assign different degrees of trust and privilege to classes from the different sources. When the class loader needs to resolve a class name, it searches the three in order: core, extension, user.

Boot Class Path: Finding the Core Classes

The boot class path supplies the core Java classes—the huge collection of classes that comprise the Java 2 Platform. Defining `$JAVA_HOME` to mean the installation directory[1] of the SDK or JRE, Table 14.3 shows the default boot class path value.

[1] This is a notational convenience. JDK1.2 ignores the environment variable and always infers the value of `JAVA_HOME` from the path to the Java executables.

TABLE 14.3 Default Boot Class Paths

Installation	Default Boot Class Path

JRE1.2	`$JAVA_HOME/lib/rt.jar:`
	`$JAVA_HOME/lib/i18n.jar:`
	`$JAVA_HOME/classes`

SDK1.2	`$JAVA_HOME/jre/lib/rt.jar:`
	`$JAVA_HOME/jre/lib/i18n.jar:`
	`$JAVA_HOME/jre/classes`

One normally leaves the boot class path alone, but it can be changed with a nonstandard option to the `java` application launcher (see Chapter 17, "The Java Application Launchers: java, jre and oldjava," Section "Non-standard SDK1.2/JRE1.2 Options").

Extensions Class Path

Extensions are installed in a special directory within a JDK1.2 installation tree, as shown in table 14.4.

TABLE 14.4 JDK1.2 Extension Installation Directories

Installation	Extension Installation Directory
JRE1.2	`$JAVA_HOME/lib/ext`
SDK1.2	`$JAVA_HOME/jre/lib/ext`

The extensions must be packaged in jar files in that directory, and the choice of directory cannot be overridden.

User Class Path

The `CLASSPATH` environment variable functions as before, but now exclusively for your application classes. If `CLASSPATH` is not defined, the class path defaults to the current directory. It can be overridden with command-line options on the `java` application launcher, as shown in table 14.5 (there is no longer a `jre` application launcher).

TABLE 14.5 JDK1.2 Command-Line Options to Alter Class Paths

Command	Class Path
`java -classpath` *<newclasspath>*	*<newclasspath>*
`java -cp` *<newclasspath>*	*<newclasspath>*
`java -jar` *<jarfile>*	*<jarfile>*

The user class path is used by almost all JDK1.2 tools, with one exception. The SDK1.2 `appletviewer` application ignores the user class path entirely to better emulate browser deployment environments.

For Further Reading

The construction of class paths is explored in some detail in Sun's SDK1.2 documentation bundle. Table 14.6 identifies the files of interest.

TABLE 14.6 JDK1.2 Class Path Documentation

Document	Contents
`docs/tooldocs/findingclasses.html`	Information on how classes are located
`docs/guide/extensions/extensions.html`	Description of the Java Extensions Framework, including some subtleties on how extension class libraries can add other extension class libraries to the class path

How a Class Path Is Constructed for Applets

Although this topic is not highly relevant to setting up a Linux development platform, we'll give it brief mention.

The principles for applet class paths are no different than for applications: browsers such as Netscape have a class path that includes the core browser classes and centrally installed plug-ins, and any plug-ins installed under your home directory.

The interesting magic occurs when a browser encounters one of the HTML tags that start an applet (`<APPLET>`, `<OBJECT>`, or `<EMBED>`). These tags and their associated parameters (`code`, `codebase`, `object`) effectively modify the class path in the browser's JRE to include the networked source for the applet classes. Depending on the choice of tag parameters, the `<APPLET>` tag specifies either

- A `codebase` and an `object`—comparable to specifying a class path and a class with the `java` application launcher, or
- A specific `.class` file to be loaded—unlike launching applications

Adding Standard Extensions and Application Classes

Our discussion of class path construction has already touched on this topic, but we'll provide some specific instructions here.

What do we mean when we speak of standard extensions and application classes? What is the difference between the two? Not very much:

- A standard extension is a class library with expected wide usage among applications, published in the form of a Java ARchive (jar) file. Examples include the Java Cryptography Extension and the Java Naming and Directory Interface.
- An application is a collection of classes, published by you or someone else, probably in the form of a jar file.

While standard extensions and applications may be packaged similarly, the two cases are handled differently.

Adding Standard Extensions and Application Classes Under JDK1.1

The JDK1.1 class path model does not distinguish between standard extensions and any other collection of classes, although *you* may want to. A sensible approach is

- When installing a standard extension, select a place to install it and add the associated jar file(s) to your `CLASSPATH` environment variable.
- When installing a Java app, select a place to install it. To run the app, use the `jre -cp` command-line option to specify where its class file(s) can be found.

As you install more standard extensions on your system, your `CLASSPATH` will grow to reflect this—it serves as sort of a running history of what is installed on your system. You typically set your `CLASSPATH` in your `~/.bash_profile` file, so a system with the collections classes, Swing 1.1, Java Activation Framework, and JavaMail installed may include a `~/.bash_profile` entry looking something like this:

```
export CLASSPATH=/usr/local/Java/jdk117_v3/lib/rt.jar:\
/usr/local/Java/jdk117_v3/lib/i18n.jar:\
/usr/local/Java/jdk117_v3/lib/classes.zip:\
/usr/local/Java/1.1collections/lib/collections.jar:\
/usr/local/Java/swing-1.1/swingall.jar:\
/usr/local/Java/jaf-1.0.1/activation.jar:\
/usr/local/Java/javamail-1.1.2/mail.jar:\
.
```

Adding Standard Extensions and Application Classes Under JDK1.2

As the previous case shows, using the CLASSPATH variable to maintain a running history of where you have installed everything is ugly and troublesome. Under the JDK1.2 model, standard extensions are placed in a single location and need not clutter up the CLASSPATH. You need only install your standard extension jar files in this directory indicated in table 14.7.

TABLE 14.7 Standard Extension Installation Directories

Installation	Extension Installation Directory
JRE1.2	`$JAVA_HOME/lib/ext`
SDK1.2	`$JAVA_HOME/jre/lib/ext`

Alternatively, you can install the extension elsewhere and place symbolic links to the jar files in the `ext` directory.

Application classes are installed, as in JDK1.1, in some suitable location, and the CLASSPATH variable or the `java` launcher runtime options can be used to locate the classes.

Adding, Changing, and Configuring Fonts

Font support has changed significantly between JDK1.1 and JDK1.2. Whereas JDK1.1 relied exclusively on platform-native fonts provided by the underlying windowing system, JDK1.2 includes scalable font rasterizers that directly support common scalable font formats. In essence, JDK1.2 owns typeface glyph generation, just as it owns a GUI. This frees Java from the many weaknesses of X font support, albeit at a significant cost in performance.

In both JDK1.1 and JDK1.2, font names are described in a platform-neutral format consisting of a typeface name, a style, and a point size. For example, `foobar-bold-10` describes a 10-point bold font from the `foobar` family. Both environments also provide some standard *logical* names, `Serif`, `SansSerif`, `Monospaced`, `Dialog`, and `DialogInput`, to describe fonts used by the GUI; a 12-point version of the font used for dialogs would be called `Dialog-plain-12`. (For historical reasons, some environments provide logical fonts named `Helvetica`, `TimesRoman`, and `Courier`, although applications are officially discouraged from relying on those names.)

The mapping between the platform-neutral names and resident fonts occurs in the JRE's `lib/` subdirectory. We'll describe here how to use the font-related configuration files, options, and environment settings.

Configuring Fonts in JDK1.1

The font configuration files can be found in the `lib/` subdirectory of SDK1.1 and JRE1.1 installations. The relevant file is `font.properties`, and its many variants for locales (`font.properties.ja` for Japan, `font.properties.ru` for Russia, and so on).

The job of the `font.properties` files is to stitch together various X Window System fonts to support the two-byte *Unicode* set used by Java. Unicode supports all the characters in the world, whereas the individual X fonts do not. The `font.properties` files assign some property values that handle the mapping from X to Unicode. For example, this excerpt:

```
# Serif font definition
#
serif.plain.0=-adobe-times-medium-r-normal--*-%d-*-*-p-*-iso8859-1
serif.1=-itc-zapfdingbats-medium-r-normal--*-%d-*-*-p-*-adobe-fontspecific
serif.2=-adobe-symbol-medium-r-normal--*-%d-*-*-p-*-adobe-fontspecific

serif.italic.0=-adobe-times-medium-i-normal--*-%d-*-*-p-*-iso8859-1

serif.bold.0=-adobe-times-bold-r-normal--*-%d-*-*-p-*-iso8859-1

serif.bolditalic.0=-adobe-times-bold-i-normal--*-%d-*-*-p-*-iso8859-1
```

is mapping several different X fonts into the Java font designated `serif`. A common Adobe Times font (found in most X Window System installations) is mapped to Unicode characters 0x0000-0x00ff, a Zapf Dingbat font is mapped to the appropriate Unicode character range, as is a commonly found Adobe symbol font. Notice that four different treatments of the Times font—regular, italic, bold, and bold italic—are mapped into serif.0, whereas a single treatment of the other fonts is used for serif.1 and serif.2.

How is the mapping performed from these fonts into the Unicode character set? The answer lies in some property definitions further down in `font.properties`:

```
# Static FontCharset info.
#
# This information is used by the font which is not indexed by Unicode.
# Such fonts can use their own subclass of FontCharset.
#
fontcharset.serif.0=sun.io.CharToByteISO8859_1
fontcharset.serif.1=sun.awt.motif.CharToByteX11Dingbats
fontcharset.serif.2=sun.awt.CharToByteSymbol
```

Platform-specific classes (subclasses of `sun.io.CharToByteConverter`) shipped as part of the runtime environment provide the actual mappings into the Unicode character set.

Using a small Java program called `ShowFonts11` (see Appendix B, "Miscellaneous Program Listings"), let's take a look at the default fonts available in JDK1.1 (see Figure 14.1).

FIGURE 14.1
The standard logical fonts in JDK1.1.

Dialog-plain-16	**Dialog-bold-16**
Dialog-italic-16	***Dialog-bolditalic-16***
SansSerif-plain-16	**SansSerif-bold-16**
SansSerif-italic-16	***SansSerif-bolditalic-16***
Serif-plain-16	**Serif-bold-16**
Serif-italic-16	***Serif-bolditalic-16***
Monospaced-plain-16	**Monospaced-bold-16**
Monospaced-italic-16	***Monospaced-bolditalic-16***
DialogInput-plain-16	**DialogInput-bold-16**
DialogInput-italic-16	**DialogInput-bolditalic-16**

Subtleties

There are some assumptions buried in the `font.properties` font definition mappings:

- The platform-specific mappings assume a particular set of characters in the X fonts: that the iso8859-1 font indeed contains the expected characters, that the dingbats font contains the customary little pictures, and that the symbol font contains the expected assortment of Greek letters and mathematical symbols—all at the proper locations. If these assumptions are incorrect, Java will display some characters incorrectly or not at all.
- The font names on the right-hand side are expected to be the usual X Window System font names, with several fields wild-carded and with the familiar C/C++ "`%d`" integer format descriptor in the point size field. When Java needs to use a font in a particular size, it generates a font name containing the appropriate point size and requests the font from the X server.

Knowing your way around this file, you can now make changes or additions, as discussed in the following sections.

Changing JDK1.1 Font Assignments

We can edit the assignments to change the choice of X11 font. For example, we can replace the `SansSerif-plain` definition in `font.properties`

```
sansserif.plain.0=-adobe-helvetica-medium-r-normal--*-%d-*-*-p-*-iso8859-1
```

with another X font (admittedly a poor choice)

```
sansserif.plain.0=-schumacher-clean-medium-r-normal--*-%d-*-*-p-*-iso8859-1
```

resulting in this (unfortunate) change (see Figure 14.2).

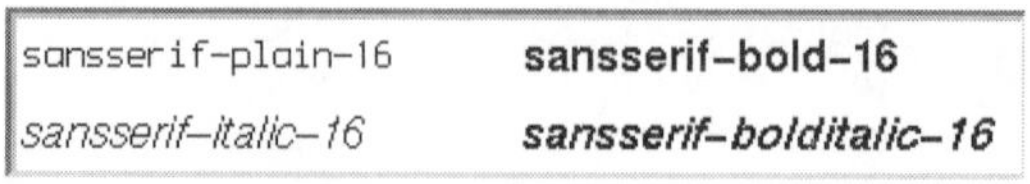

FIGURE 14.2
Modifying a standard font assignment.

sansserif-plain-16	**sansserif-bold-16**
sansserif-italic-16	***sansserif-bolditalic-16***

A complete list of available X11 fonts can be obtained by running the Linux `xlsfonts` utility.

Adding New JDK1.1 Fonts

We can also add an entirely new set of fonts:

```
# Add Bitstream Charter fonts
charter.plain.0=-bitstream-charter-medium-r-normal—*-%d-*-*-p-*-iso8859-1
charter.italic.0=-bitstream-charter-medium-i-normal—*-%d-*-*-p-*-iso8859-1
charter.bold.0=-bitstream-charter-bold-r-normal—*-%d-*-*-p-*-iso8859-1
charter.bolditalic.0=-bitstream-charter-bold-i-normal—*-%d-*-*-p-*-iso8859-1
# Add character mapping for Charter
fontcharset.charter.0=sun.io.CharToByteISO8859_1
```

resulting in this new font (see Figure 14.3).

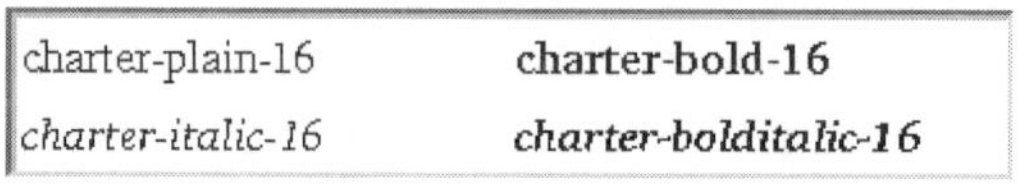

FIGURE 14.3
Adding a new font to JDK1.1.

charter-plain-16	**charter-bold-16**
charter-italic-16	***charter-bolditalic-16***

An unfortunate "feature" of Sun's Abstract Windowing Toolkit (AWT) implementation (but not all implementations) is that the `Toolkit.getFontList()` call—the only available JDK1.1 method for listing fonts—reports only the standard logical names. Our new Charter font will not appear in the listing but is available for use by the `java.awt.Font` constructors and factories.

Adding Font Aliases

The `font.properties` file also supports an alias naming mechanism:

```
alias.foobar=serif
```

with the predictable result (see Figure 14.4).

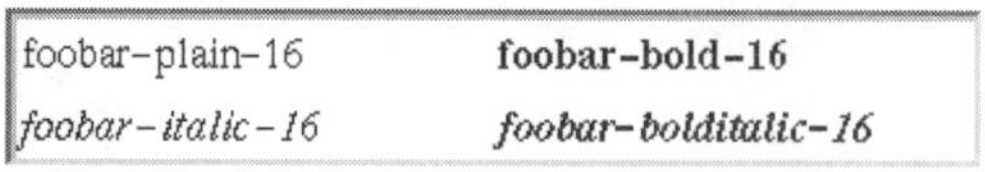

FIGURE 14.4
A new font name created with an alias.

foobar-plain-16	**foobar-bold-16**
foobar-italic-16	***foobar-bolditalic-16***

As with new fonts, aliased font names might not show up in a `ToolKit.getFontList()` listing.

Adding Fonts Not Installed in X

JDK1.1 obtains all of its fonts from the X server. To add a font not currently installed in the X Window System, first install the font in X and then add it to `font.properties` as described previously.

Configuring Fonts in JDK1.2

JDK1.2 supports scalable fonts as the primary method of glyph generation. Although it is still capable of obtaining fonts from the X server, its preferred approach is to work directly with scalable fonts in the form of TrueType, PostScript Type1, or F3 font files. By manipulating scalable font outlines, JDK1.2 can integrate font rendering with the full capabilities of `java.awt.Graphics2D`, which includes antialiasing, arbitrary affine transformations, and fractional font metrics (see Chapter 3, "A Look at the Java Core Classes," in the section "Package java.awt" for a demo).

In the following discussion, we will refer to a scalable font file, such as a TrueType `.ttf` or a Type1 `.pfb`, as a *scalable font program* (SFP).

To a first approximation, configuring JDK1.2 fonts looks much like configuring JDK1.1 fonts. The interesting difference is in how the fonts are found and *what* fonts are found. We begin with a discussion of the similarities, followed by a detailed look at the new ways in which JDK1.2 finds its fonts. A word of caution: while the JDK1.2 font mechanism gives Java impressive new text rendering capabilities, the details are complex and of interest only if you need the new capabilities.

Similarities to JDK1.1

Like JDK1.1, JDK1.2 uses a `font.properties` file. The contents look similar in both environments, and the previous discussion about defining the logical fonts and mapping them to Unicode still applies. We can see some minor differences in the choice of fonts in this excerpt:

```
# Serif font definition
#
serif.0=-b&h-lucidabright-medium-r-normal—*-%d-*-*-p-*-iso8859-1
serif.1=—zapf dingbats-medium-r-normal—*-%d-*-*-p-*-adobe-fontspecific
serif.2=—symbol-medium-r-normal—*-%d-*-*-p-*-adobe-fontspecific
```

but the character mappings appear identical:

```
fontcharset.serif.0=sun.io.CharToByteISO8859_1
fontcharset.serif.1=sun.awt.motif.CharToByteX11Dingbats
fontcharset.serif.2=sun.awt.CharToByteSymbol
```

and the advice on editing this file is unchanged from JDK1.1. One minor difference (as of this writing): the Blackdown distribution does not currently ship with `font.properties` files for other locales.

The crucial difference in JDK1.2 is in how those X font names are resolved. The following three sections explore the gritty details of where JDK1.2 fonts come from and how you can control this behavior.

Where and How JDK1.2 Gets Fonts

JDK1.2 is designed to render scalable fonts and it uses SFPs where it can find them. Where it cannot, it uses scalable fonts from the X server.

Where does it find SFPs? By default, in the following directories (the defaults may change in different locales):

`$JAVA_HOME/lib/fonts` (in a JRE1.2 installation), or

`$JAVA_HOME/jre/lib/fonts` (in a SDK1.2 installation)

`/usr/X11R6/lib/X11/fonts/Type1`

`/usr/X11R6/lib/X11/fonts/TrueType`

The JRE and SDK are bundled with a dozen Lucida SFPs, and the standard five logical fonts (`serif`, `sans serif`, and so on) are defined in terms of those fonts. In addition, the AWT looks for SFPs in two directories where X customarily places scalable fonts (this default path is compiled into `libfontmanager.so` in the Blackdown distribution). In all these cases, Java makes direct use of the SFPs in these directories—it is not getting the fonts through the X server.

After finding the SFPs, the AWT finds all scalable fonts available from the X server—those whose names contain the string `0-0-0-0`. (To see such a list, run `xlfd -fn '*0-0-0-0*'`.) All these fonts are made available for use by the application.

Figure 14.5 shows a view of our font architecture.

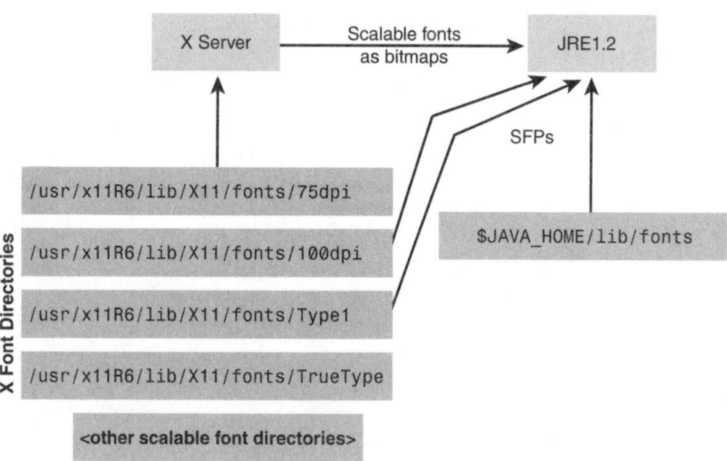

FIGURE 14.5
JDK1.2 obtains scalable fonts directly from scalable font programs and from the X server.

The `ShowFonts12` program (see Appendix B, "Miscellaneous Program Listings") is a JDK1.2 utility that displays all available Java fonts, rendering the samples with antialiasing and fractional font metrics. Let's examine a screen dump (see Figure 14.6).

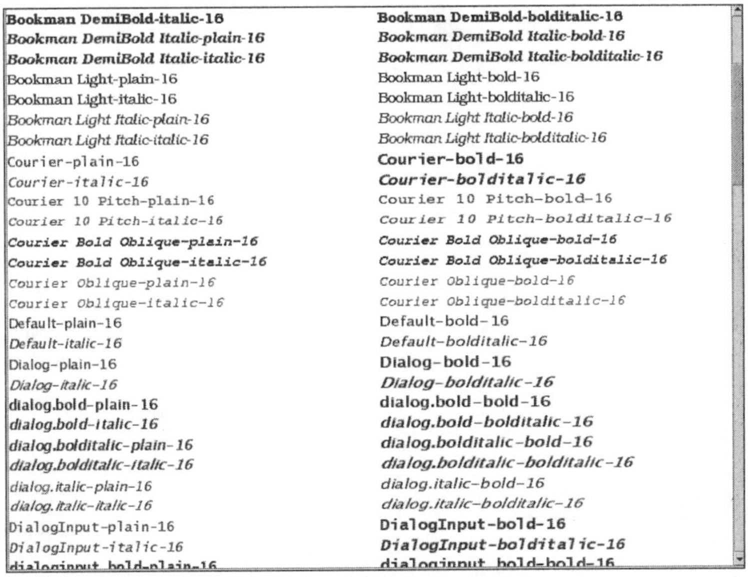

FIGURE 14.6
ShowFonts12 screen dump showing some of the available JDK1.2 fonts.

Bookman DemiBold-italic-16	Bookman DemiBold-bolditalic-16
Bookman DemiBold Italic-plain-16	Bookman DemiBold Italic-bold-16
Bookman DemiBold Italic-italic-16	Bookman DemiBold Italic-bolditalic-16
Bookman Light-plain-16	Bookman Light-bold-16
Bookman Light-italic-16	Bookman Light-bolditalic-16
Bookman Light Italic-plain-16	Bookman Light Italic-bold-16
Bookman Light Italic-italic-16	Bookman Light Italic-bolditalic-16
Courier-plain-16	Courier-bold-16
Courier-italic-16	Courier-bolditalic-16
Courier 10 Pitch-plain-16	Courier 10 Pitch-bold-16
Courier 10 Pitch-italic-16	Courier 10 Pitch-bolditalic-16
Courier Bold Oblique-plain-16	Courier Bold Oblique-bold-16
Courier Bold Oblique-italic-16	Courier Bold Oblique-bolditalic-16
Courier Oblique-plain-16	Courier Oblique-bold-16
Courier Oblique-italic-16	Courier Oblique-bolditalic-16
Default-plain-16	Default-bold-16
Default-italic-16	Default-bolditalic-16
Dialog-plain-16	Dialog-bold-16
Dialog-italic-16	Dialog-bolditalic-16
dialog.bold-plain-16	dialog.bold-bold-16
dialog.bold-italic-16	dialog.bold-bolditalic-16
dialog.bolditalic-plain-16	dialog.bolditalic-bold-16
dialog.bolditalic-italic-16	dialog.bolditalic-bolditalic-16
dialog.italic-plain-16	dialog.italic-bold-16
dialog.italic-italic-16	dialog.italic-bolditalic-16
DialogInput-plain-16	DialogInput-bold-16
DialogInput-italic-16	DialogInput-bolditalic-16
dialoginput.bold-plain-16	dialoginput.bold-bold-16

This is a portion of the universe of available fonts: you can see some of the standard logical fonts (dialog) as well as dozens of fonts picked up from elsewhere. Figure 14.7 takes a closer look at a detail from this dump.

FIGURE 14.7
Some typefaces are rendered with antialiasing; some are not.

Bookman I
Bookman I
Courier-
Courier-

You can see that some of the fonts are rendered with antialiasing, and some without. The Courier font comes from `/usr/X11R6/lib/X11/fonts/Type1`; it's an SFP used directly by the AWT. The Bookman font came from the X server: it cannot be antialiased (or transformed, or subjected to any of `java.awt.Graphics2D`'s other new capabilities). Of course, the situation would change if the AWT knew where it could find the actual SFP. The next section explores that topic.

Setting the JDK1.2 Font Path

The environment variable `JAVA_FONTS` can be used to override the JDK1.2 font path. If set, this variable overrides the entire path: SFPs will be found only in directories specified in this variable. So a reasonable setting on our sample system would copy the default path and append new directories:

```
export JAVA_FONTS=/usr/local/Java/jdk1.2/jre/lib/fonts:\
/usr/X11R6/lib/X11/fonts/Type1:\
/usr/X11R6/lib/X11/fonts/TrueType:\
/usr/share/fonts/default/Type1
```

The new entry at the end specifies a font directory that holds some other SFPs, including Bookman, published by URW. (The next section discusses the URW fonts in more detail.)

Running `ShowFonts12` again shows some differences (see Figure 14.8).

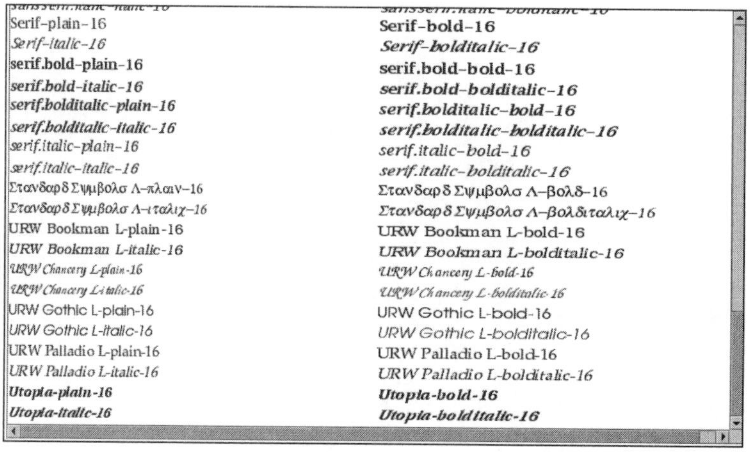

FIGURE 14.8 ShowFonts12 results, with some new fonts added to the `JAVA_FONTS` path.

The Bookman font appears, now under the name URW Bookman, and with antialiasing (see Figure 14.9).

FIGURE 14.9 New—an antialiased Bookman font.

We'll discuss the reason for the name change in the following Subtleties discussion.

Subtleties

We have glossed over some tricky subtleties about JDK1.2 font usage in this discussion. These will not affect most installations, but they can sometimes lead to unexpected behavior.

- JDK1.2's use of SFPs depends on file system access: the AWT needs to read the file. If you are running Java remotely from the X display host, the directories containing the SFPs used by Java (and pointed to by `JAVA_FONTS`) must be resident on a file system visible to that remote host.

  That restriction does not apply for fonts obtained from the X server—it is X's job to read those font files.

- When JDK1.2 uses SFPs, it relies on the `fonts.dir` file resident in the directory containing the SFP. Although that file was originally intended for use by the X server, the AWT uses it to map from the X-style names (in `font.properties`) to the SFP filenames. This name is also a filter: After JDK1.2 finds the SFP corresponding to that name, it ignores a font from the X server with the same name.

- The character mappings in `font.properties` (the `fontcharset.*` assignments) might not be used when JDK1.2 uses SFPs. Some SFPs already have Unicode mappings.

- Notice that `font.properties` has a reduced role in defining new fonts in JDK1.2. Whereas all new JDK1.1 fonts had to be defined in this file, JDK1.2 discovers available fonts in its font path and in the X server. However, you must call `GraphicsEnvironment.getAvailableFontFamilyNames()` before you can use these fonts: Even if you know the name of the font you want, the JDK may not find it until this call has been made.

- In generating its platform-neutral names, JDK1.2 must map what it knows about the fonts into the platform-neutral namespace. When handling a font from the X server, it constructs this platform-neutral name with information available from X; when handling an SFP, it constructs this name with data read from the SFP. The results can be drastically different, as the treatment of the Bookman font showed previously.

- You cannot assume that an SFP has all characters you need. If some are missing, then Java will render those characters incorrectly or not at all. The Lucida fonts bundled with Java are more complete than many other available SFPs.

- The interline spacing of fonts is a potentially confusing matter. In any application displaying text, interline spacing is determined from two font-specific statistics: the ***ascent*** and the ***descent***. The standard logical fonts are odd beasts, constructed from three different components—a base font plus a dingbat font plus a symbol font. For purposes of computing interline spacing, Java chooses the maximum ascent and descent of the fonts: A font you never see could end up affecting the spacing of a font you do see.

Case Study: Configuring JDK1.2 to Use URW Fonts

URW, a German design company and font foundry (`http://www.urwpp.de/home_e.htm`), donated some high-quality scalable fonts to the GhostScript community under GPL licensing terms. A number of Blackdown users have chosen to use these fonts for JDK1.2, both because of dissatisfaction with the bundled Lucida fonts and because most Linux systems do not have a scalable Zapf Dingbat font (or any Zapf Dingbat font) installed, resulting in this annoying message when starting a Java application:

```
Font specified in font.properties not found [—zapf dingbats-medium-r-normal—*-%d-
*-*-p-*-adobe-fontspecific]
```

The URW fonts are available from many sources, including as a Red Hat RPM (`urw-fonts`). The collection consists of 35 PostScript Type1 scalable fonts, plus supporting files and the important `fonts.dir` file. You can adopt these fonts for your own use by setting an appropriate font path, for example (based on where the Red Hat RPM installs the fonts):

```
export JAVA_FONTS=/usr/share/fonts/default/Type1:\
/usr/X11R6/lib/X11/fonts/Type1:\
/usr/X11R6/lib/X11/fonts/TrueType
```

and by changing entries in the `font.properties` file. The excerpts in Listing 14.1 describe a usable set of Java fonts.

LISTING 14.1 An Excerpt from the `font.properties` File Mapping the Free URW Fonts to Java's Logical Font Names

```
# Serif font definition
#
serif.0=-urw-Times-medium-r-normal—*-%d-*-*-p-*-iso8859-1
serif.1=-urw-Zapf Dingbats-medium-r-normal—*-%d-*-*-p-*-adobe-fontspecific
serif.2=-urw-Symbol-medium-r-normal—*-%d-*-*-p-*-adobe-fontspecific

serif.italic.0=-urw-Times-medium-i-normal—*-%d-*-*-p-*-iso8859-1
serif.italic.1=-urw-Zapf Dingbats-medium-r-normal—*-%d-*-*-p-*-adobe-fontspecific
serif.italic.2=-urw-Symbol-medium-r-normal—*-%d-*-*-p-*-adobe-fontspecific

serif.bold.0=-urw-Times-bold-r-normal—*-%d-*-*-p-*-iso8859-1
serif.bold.1=-urw-Zapf Dingbats-medium-r-normal—*-%d-*-*-p-*-adobe-fontspecific
serif.bold.2=-urw-Symbol-medium-r-normal—*-%d-*-*-p-*-adobe-fontspecific

serif.bolditalic.0=-urw-Times-bold-i-normal—*-%d-*-*-p-*-iso8859-1
serif.bolditalic.1=-urw-Zapf Dingbats-medium-r-normal—*-%d-*-*-p-*-adobe-
fontspecific
serif.bolditalic.2=-urw-Symbol-medium-r-normal—*-%d-*-*-p-*-adobe-fontspecific

# SansSerif font definition
#
sansserif.0=-urw-Helvetica-medium-r-normal—*-%d-*-*-p-*-iso8859-1
sansserif.1=-urw-Zapf Dingbats-medium-r-normal—*-%d-*-*-p-*-adobe-fontspecific
sansserif.2=-urw-Symbol-medium-r-normal—*-%d-*-*-p-*-adobe-fontspecific
```

```
sansserif.italic.0=-urw-Helvetica-medium-o-normal—*-%d-*-*-p-*-iso8859-1
sansserif.italic.1=-urw-Zapf Dingbats-medium-r-normal—*-%d-*-*-p-*-adobe-
fontspecific
sansserif.italic.2=-urw-Symbol-medium-r-normal—*-%d-*-*-p-*-adobe-fontspecific

sansserif.bold.0=-urw-Helvetica-bold-r-normal—*-%d-*-*-p-*-iso8859-1
sansserif.bold.1=-urw-Zapf Dingbats-medium-r-normal—*-%d-*-*-p-*-adobe-
fontspecific
sansserif.bold.2=-urw-Symbol-medium-r-normal—*-%d-*-*-p-*-adobe-fontspecific

sansserif.bolditalic.0=-urw-Helvetica-bold-o-normal—*-%d-*-*-p-*-iso8859-1
sansserif.bolditalic.1=-urw-Zapf Dingbats-medium-r-normal—*-%d-*-*-p-*-adobe-
fontspecific
sansserif.bolditalic.2=-urw-Symbol-medium-r-normal—*-%d-*-*-p-*-adobe-fontspecific

# Monospaced font definition
#
monospaced.0=-urw-Courier-medium-r-normal—*-%d-*-*-p-*-iso8859-1
monospaced.1=-urw-Zapf Dingbats-medium-r-normal—*-%d-*-*-p-*-adobe-fontspecific
monospaced.2=-urw-Symbol-medium-r-normal—*-%d-*-*-p-*-adobe-fontspecific

monospaced.italic.0=-urw-Courier-medium-o-normal—*-%d-*-*-p-*-iso8859-1
monospaced.italic.1=-urw-Zapf Dingbats-medium-r-normal—*-%d-*-*-p-*-adobe-
fontspecific
monospaced.italic.2=-urw-Symbol-medium-r-normal—*-%d-*-*-p-*-adobe-fontspecific

monospaced.bold.0=-urw-Courier-bold-r-normal—*-%d-*-*-p-*-iso8859-1
monospaced.bold.1=-urw-Zapf Dingbats-medium-r-normal—*-%d-*-*-p-*-adobe-
fontspecific
monospaced.bold.2=-urw-Symbol-medium-r-normal—*-%d-*-*-p-*-adobe-fontspecific

monospaced.bolditalic.0=-urw-Courier-bold-o-normal—*-%d-*-*-p-*-iso8859-1
monospaced.bolditalic.1=-urw-Zapf Dingbats-medium-r-normal—*-%d-*-*-p-*-adobe-
fontspecific
monospaced.bolditalic.2=-urw-Symbol-medium-r-normal—*-%d-*-*-p-*-adobe-
fontspecific

# Dialog font definition
#
dialog.0=-urw-Avantgarde-book-r-normal—*-%d-*-*-p-*-iso8859-1
dialog.1=-urw-Zapf Dingbats-medium-r-normal—*-%d-*-*-p-*-adobe-fontspecific
dialog.2=-urw-Symbol-medium-r-normal—*-%d-*-*-p-*-adobe-fontspecific

dialog.italic.0=-urw-Avantgarde-book-o-normal—*-%d-*-*-p-*-iso8859-1
dialog.italic.1=-urw-Zapf Dingbats-medium-r-normal—*-%d-*-*-p-*-adobe-fontspecific
dialog.italic.2=-urw-Symbol-medium-r-normal—*-%d-*-*-p-*-adobe-fontspecific

dialog.bold.0=-urw-Avantgarde-demibold-r-normal—*-%d-*-*-p-*-iso8859-1
dialog.bold.1=-urw-Zapf Dingbats-medium-r-normal—*-%d-*-*-p-*-adobe-fontspecific
dialog.bold.2=-urw-Symbol-medium-r-normal—*-%d-*-*-p-*-adobe-fontspecific
```

continued on next page

continued from previous page

```
dialog.bolditalic.0=-urw-Avantgarde-demibold-o-normal—*-%d-*-*-p-*-iso8859-1
dialog.bolditalic.1=-urw-Zapf Dingbats-medium-r-normal—*-%d-*-*-p-*-adobe-
fontspecific
dialog.bolditalic.2=-urw-Symbol-medium-r-normal—*-%d-*-*-p-*-adobe-fontspecific

# DialogInput font definition
#
dialoginput.0=-urw-Courier-medium-r-normal—*-%d-*-*-p-*-iso8859-1
dialoginput.1=-urw-Zapf Dingbats-medium-r-normal—*-%d-*-*-p-*-adobe-fontspecific
dialoginput.2=-urw-Symbol-medium-r-normal—*-%d-*-*-p-*-adobe-fontspecific

dialoginput.italic.0=-urw-Courier-medium-o-normal—*-%d-*-*-p-*-iso8859-1
dialoginput.italic.1=-urw-Zapf Dingbats-medium-r-normal—*-%d-*-*-p-*-adobe-
fontspecific
dialoginput.italic.2=-urw-Symbol-medium-r-normal—*-%d-*-*-p-*-adobe-fontspecific

dialoginput.bold.0=-urw-Courier-bold-r-normal—*-%d-*-*-p-*-iso8859-1
dialoginput.bold.1=-urw-Zapf Dingbats-medium-r-normal—*-%d-*-*-p-*-adobe-
fontspecific
dialoginput.bold.2=-urw-Symbol-medium-r-normal—*-%d-*-*-p-*-adobe-fontspecific

dialoginput.bolditalic.0=-urw-Courier-bold-o-normal—*-%d-*-*-p-*-iso8859-1
dialoginput.bolditalic.1=-urw-Zapf Dingbats-medium-r-normal—*-%d-*-*-p-*-adobe-
fontspecific
dialoginput.bolditalic.2=-urw-Symbol-medium-r-normal—*-%d-*-*-p-*-adobe-
fontspecific
```

A full version of this file can be found on the CD-ROM.

Figure 14.10 shows the result of these particular assignments to the URW fonts.

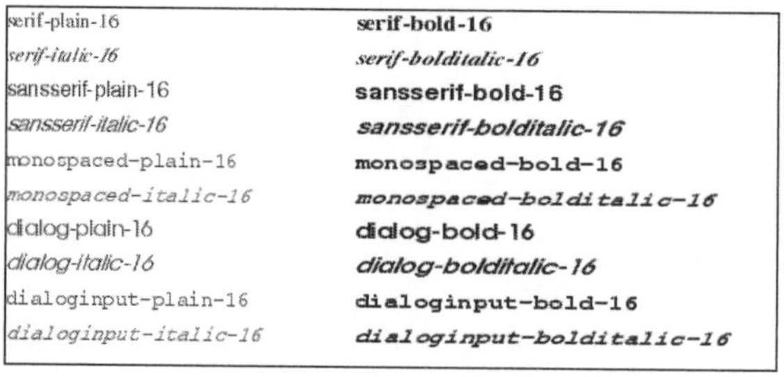

FIGURE 14.10
The standard logical fonts, mapped to the URW scalable fonts.

serif-plain-16	**serif-bold-16**
serif-italic-16	***serif-bolditalic-16***
sansserif-plain-16	**sansserif-bold-16**
sansserif-italic-16	***sansserif-bolditalic-16***
monospaced-plain-16	**monospaced-bold-16**
monospaced-italic-16	***monospaced-bolditalic-16***
dialog-plain-16	**dialog-bold-16**
dialog-italic-16	***dialog-bolditalic-16***
dialoginput-plain-16	**dialoginput-bold-16**
dialoginput-italic-16	***dialoginput-bolditalic-16***

For Further Reading

The SDK1.2 documentation bundle includes a writeup on the use of `font.properties` files in `docs/guide/internat/fontprop.html`.

Adding JIT Compilers

Just-in-time (JIT) compilers can noticeably improve Java performance. JDK1.2 comes with a default JIT compiler from Sun (JDK1.1 does not). Although they do not achieve the Holy Grail of native-level performance (and never will), JITs are an important Java performance tool.

The notion behind JIT is that Java code is compiled, on-the-fly, into native code for speedier execution. The compilation happens in a background thread during process execution, causing short-term application slowdown for the promise of longer-term speedup. Anyone is free to write a JIT: The JVM/JIT interface is well documented by Sun, and several are available (see Chapter 33, "Just-In-Time Compilers"). JITs have shown their greatest value in long-lived server processes, and, over time, they may lose favor to newer JVM designs that subsume JIT behavior (see Chapter 29, "Mozilla ElectricalFire: A New JVM," and 30, "Sun HotSpot Performance Engine").

JIT compilers are shipped as Linux-shared libraries and referenced from Java by a short form of the library name: extract the part of the name between the `lib` and `.so`, so a JIT called *tya* is shipped in library `libtya.so`. (This is the JDK's standard way of referencing all native shared libraries on Linux.)

Installing an Alternative JIT

There are two steps to installing a JIT. Table 14.8 describes the steps, and their variants for different JDK installations.

TABLE 14.8 Steps to Installing a JIT

Step	SDK1.1/ JRE1.1	JRE1.2	SDK1.2
Install the JIT where Java can find it	Install the JIT shared library in a standard shared library location (such as `/usr/lib`) ***or*** Set `LD_LIBRARY_PATH` environment variable to point to directory containing the JIT.	Install the JIT shared library in directory `lib/i386` of the JRE installation.	Install the JIT shared library in directory `jre/lib/i386` of the SDK installation.

continued on next page

continued from previous page

Step	SDK1.1/ JRE1.1	JRE1.2	SDK1.2
Tell Java to use the JIT	set JAVA_COMPILER=<*jit name*> run java or jre		
or			
run java or jre with the -Djava.compiler=<*jit name*> option			

Examples:

```
bash$ export JAVA_COMPILER=tya
bash$ java ...

bash$ java -Djava.compiler=tya ...
```

Disabling a JIT

By default, JDK1.1 runs without a JIT, and JDK1.2 runs with the default Sun JIT, `sunwjit`. To disable JIT, use one of the preceding techniques to specify an empty string:

Environment Variable	`bash$ export JAVA_COMPILER=` `bash$ java ...`
Command line	`bash$ java -Djava.compiler= ...`

Why would you ever want to disable a JIT? Two reasons:

- JITs sometimes cause bugs.
- If you get a Java stack dump, the results are more meaningful with the JIT disabled. Stack dump with JIT:

  ```
  java.lang.Exception: Stack trace
          at java.lang.Thread.dumpStack(Compiled Code)
          at Hello.main(Compiled Code)
  ```

  Stack dump without JIT:

  ```
  java.lang.Exception: Stack trace
          at java.lang.Thread.dumpStack(Thread.java:983)
          at Hello.main(Hello.java:11)
  ```

Accommodating Multiple Java Installations

It is possible to have multiple Java installations on one host—perhaps an SDK1.1 and SDK1.2, or a Sun SDK and Kaffe (see Chapter 26, "Kaffe: A Cleanroom Java Environment"). To ensure they do not interfere with each other, you must follow one simple guideline: ensure that the PATH, CLASSPATH, JAVA_HOME, and any dynamic-loader-related environment variables are all consistent with one of the installations.

Table 14.9 shows some example situations and appropriate environment settings[2].

TABLE 14.9 Example Java Environment Settings

Installation	Environment Settings
SDK1.2 in /usr/local/Java/jdk1.2	JAVA_HOME unset CLASSPATH=. PATH=/usr/local/Java/jdk1.2/bin:<...other paths...>
JRE1.1 in /usr/local/Java/jre1.1	JAVA_HOME=/usr/local/Java/jre1.1 CLASSPATH=/usr/local/Java/jre1.1/lib/rt.jar:/usr/local/Java/jre1.1/lib/i18n.jar:/usr/local/Java/jre1.1/lib/classes.zip:. PATH=/usr/local/Java/jre1.1/bin:<*...other paths...*>
Kaffe in /usr/local/Java/kaffe	JAVA_HOME unset CLASSPATH=/usr/local/Java/kaffe/share/kaffe/Klasses.jar:. PATH=/usr/local/Java/kaffe/bin:<*...other paths...*>

If you use any environment variables that affect dynamic loading (LD_LIBRARY_PATH or LD_PRELOAD, see the later section "Environment Variables Affecting the SDK/JRE"), they should not reference directories or libraries associated with a different Java installation.

Configuring JDK Security Settings

JRE and SDK installations include files that are used to configure the Java security mechanism. The relevant files can be found at the locations shown in Table 14.10.

---

[2]Not all Java implementations care about all these variables. Kaffe does not use JAVA_HOME, for example. And most environments do something reasonable if CLASSPATH is not defined. But if these variables are defined, it is important to define them consistently for the Java installation being used.

TABLE 14.10 Security Files

Installation	Security Files
SDK1.1/JRE1.1	`$JAVA_HOME/lib/security/java.security`
JRE1.2	`$JAVA_HOME/lib/security/*` (multiple files)
SDK1.2	`$JAVA_HOME/jre/lib/security/*` (multiple files)

These files can be used to install Java security providers and, in SDK1.2/JRE1.2, set detailed and fine-grained security policies. SDK1.2/JRE1.2 provides a GUI-based tool for administration of the `security/java.policy` file (see Chapter 24, "Miscellaneous SDK Development Tools," in the section "JDK1.2 GUI-Based Policy Administration Tool: policytool").

There is nothing Linux-specific about the contents of these files. Details on security configuration can be found in `docs/guide/security/index.html` of either the SDK1.1 or SDK1.2 documentation bundle.

Using Green Versus Native Threads

The Blackdown release supports the use of Sun's multithreading emulation (green threads) and native Linux threads. Default behavior is to use green threads in JDK1.1 and native threads in JDK1.2. You can explicitly choose the threading implementation with an environment variable or command-line option, as shown in Table 14.11.

TABLE 14.11 Settings to Choose a Runtime Threading Model.

Method	Example

Environment variable	`export THREADS_FLAG=green`
	or
	`export THREADS_FLAG=native`

Command-line option	`java -green ...`
	or
	`java -native ...`
	***Must* be the *first* command-line option.**

We will discuss green and native threads in more detail in Chapter 54, "Java, Linux, and Threads".

Environment Variables Affecting the SDK/JRE

We've discussed a few environment variables that affect the behavior of the Blackdown SDK/JRE. Table 14.12 provides a more comprehensive collection.

TABLE 14.12 Environment Variables Affecting SDK/JRE Behavior

Variable	SDK1.1/JRE1.1 Function	SDK1.2/JRE1.2 Function
CLASSPATH	Colon-separated list of directories and archives containing core, extensions, and user classes. See JDK1.1 Class Path Construction."	Colon-separated list of directories and archives containing user classes. See "JDK1.2 Class Path Construction."
DEBUG_PROG	Specifies the name of a native debugger to use on the java executable. The java launch script runs the java executable under the debugger - typically for purposes of debugging the java executable or native code in the application.	Specifies the name of a native debugger to use on the java executable. The java launch script runs the java executable under the debugger - typically for purposes of debugging the java executable or native code in the application.
DISPLAY	Specifies the X Window System display to which Java sends graphical/GUI I/O (normally set when you are running under X; the meaning of this variable is explained in the man page for the X Window System: run `man X`). If unset, Java runs a GUI-less executable	Specifies the X Window System display to which Java sends graphical/GUI I/O. Unlike in JDK1.1, there is no special behavior if this variable is not set. JDK1.2 automatically avoids any dependencies on X libraries or the X server if the AWT is not used.

continued on next page

continued from previous page

Variable	SDK1.1/JRE1.1 Function	SDK1.2/JRE1.2 Function
	with no dependencies on the native AWT library or any X libraries—suitable for use on servers. This requires that the application have no use of the AWT. (See also NS_JAVA, below.)	
`DO_NOT_CHECK_MEM`	**Only active when running with green threads.** If set, disables some AWT memory-bug checking: a risky performance enhancement.	**Only active when running with green threads.** If set, disables some AWT memory-bug checking: a risky performance enhancement.
`DO_NOT_FREE`	**Only active when running with green threads.** If set, disables all freeing of heap memory.	**Only active when running with green threads.** If set, disables all freeing of heap memory.
`DYN_JAVA`	If set, runs a version of the java executable with a dynamically—instead of statically—linked Motif library. Requires that your system have an installation of Motif library (or the lesstif clone from `http://www.lesstif.org`).	
`JAVA_COMPILER`	Specifies a JIT compiler—see "Adding JIT Compilers." If unset, JVM defaults to no JIT compilation.	Specifies a JIT compiler —see "Adding JIT Compilers" If unset, JVM defaults to using the Sun `sunwjit` JIT compiler.

Variable	SDK1.1/JRE1.1 Function	SDK1.2/JRE1.2 Function
`JAVA_FONTS`		Specifies a font path for SFPs. See "Setting the JDK1.2 Font Path." If unset, a default font path is used.
`JAVA_HOME`	Location of the top of the SDK/JRE installation. If set, this is used by the JDK to find class and native shared libraries.	
`JDK_NO_KERNEL_FIX`	**Only active when running with green threads.** If set, disables a workaround for a kernel `accept()` bug.	**Only active when running with green threads.** If set, disables a workaround for a kernel `accept()` bug.
`LD_LIBRARY_PATH`	A standard Linux environment variable for the *dynamic loader*: a colon-separated list specifying non-standard directories for loading of dynamic libraries, including JNI and JIT libraries.	A standard Linux environment variable for the *dynamic loader*: a colon-separated list specifying nonstandard directories for loading of dynamic libraries, including JNI libraries. This flag does not affect loading of JIT libraries in JDK1.2 (see "Adding JIT Compilers" about installing JITs).
`LD_PRELOAD`	A standard Linux environment variable for the *dynamic loader*: a colon-separated list of shared libraries (`.so` files) to be loaded before execution begins. Typically used to:	A standard Linux environment variable for the *dynamic loader*: a colon-separated list of shared libraries (`.so` files) to be loaded before execution begins. Typically used to:

continued on next page

continued from previous page

Variable	SDK1.1/JRE1.1 Function	SDK1.2/JRE1.2 Function
	Override an application's default choice for a shared library, or Override certain symbols provided by other shared libraries. (Example: Chapter 56, "X Window System Tips and Tricks."	Override an application's default choice for a shared library, or Override certain symbols provided by other shared libraries. (Example: section "Xwinwrap:). Controlling Colormap and Visual Usage.")
`NS_JAVA`	If set, runs a GUI-less version of the Java executable with no dependencies on the native AWT library or any X libraries—suitable for use on servers. This requires that the application have no use of the AWT.	(Not needed in JDK1.2 - the JDK automatically avoids any dependencies on X libraries or the X server if the AWT is not used.)
`THREADS_FLAG`	If set to `green`, forces use of green threads. If set to `native`, forces use of native threads. See "Green Versus Native Threads."	If set to `green`, forces use of green threads. If set to `native`, forces use of native threads. See "Green Versus Native Threads."

Summary

This chapter has explored the details of how to configure the Blackdown port of the Sun JDK on Linux. With this background, you should be able to understand and handle many configuration issues that can arise in a Linux deployment environment. But if problems arise beyond the areas discussed in this chapter, see Chapter 15 to learn more about Blackdown troubleshooting.

CHAPTER 15

TROUBLESHOOTING THE BLACKDOWN SDK/JRE INSTALLATION

A Yourf Blackdown installation will work perfectly the first time, and you will never have cause for complaint.

In the event that this prophecy is inaccurate, this chapter addresses some of the problems Java/Linux users have encountered and what to do about them.

Before you dive into detailed troubleshooting, the first questions to ask when you encounter Java failures are do you have a capable system (kernel 2.0 or 2.2, *at least* 32MB of virtual memory) and have you loaded the proper version of the JDK for your system. (See Chapter 13, "Blackdown: The Official Linux Port," in the section "Supported Linux Versions for the Blackdown SDK and JRE.")

To check your kernel version, use the command:

```
uname -r
```

A value of 2.0 or 2.2 (followed by subordinate version numbers) indicates kernel version 2.0 or 2.2.

To check your memory, use this command to report your memory size in KB:

```
free
```

Total virtual memory is the sum of total memory and total swap. Even 32MB may feel pinched—see the "System Memory Limits" section, later in this chapter, for a discussion on increasing your virtual memory.

After eliminating these obvious causes, take a look at the common problems and the sections in this chapter where they are discussed listed in Table 15.1.

Table 15.1 Common Java/Linux Problems

Problem or Message	Relevant Section
`Warning: Cannot allocate colormap entry for default background.`	Insufficient Colors to Allocate
`Font specified in font.properties not found[—zapf dingbats-medium-r-normal—*-%d-*-*-p-*-adobe-fontspecific]`	JDK1.2 Missing Dingbat Fonts
Loading failures in core JDK shared native libraries: `error in loading shared libraries: ... : undefined symbol` `error in loading shared libraries: ... : cannot open shared object file: No such file or directory`	Trouble Loading JDK Core Shared Libraries
Failure to find classes: `java.lang.NoClassDefFoundError` or similar problem reported during compilation or execution of Java applications.	Java Failures to Find Classes: Compilation and Execution
`Exception in thread "main" java.lang. UnsatisfiedLinkError: ... libawt.so: ... cannot open shared object file: No such file or directory`	AWT Dependence on X Libraries
`Warning: JIT compiler ... not found. Will use interpreter.`	Cannot Find JIT Compiler
Failure to run with your display depth or visual: `Raster IntegerInterleavedRaster: ... incompatible with ColorModel ...` `Display type and depth not supported`	Limited Support of X Visuals

Problem or Message	Relevant Section
`Error: can't find libjava.so`	Java Startup Script Directory Dependencies
Java uses *a lot* of processes	Java Use of the Linux Process Table
Java insists on an X display or the X libraries even though the application does not open any windows.	AWT Dependencies on X Availability
The application mysteriously freezes or dies	Unexplained Application Flakiness
Java runs out of memory: `Exception in thread ... java.lang.OutOfMemoryError **Out of memory, exiting**`	Increasing Java Memory Limits
`Exception in thread ... java.lang.UnsatisfiedLinkError:` ... (cannot load JNI libraries)	Finding JNI Libraries
Cannot find include files when building native-interface libraries.	Finding JNI Include Files
Order of activities/output is different between green threads and native threads, or between Linux and other platforms.	Implementation-Dependent Threading Behavior

Insufficient Colors to Allocate

This message

```
Warning: Cannot allocate colormap entry for default background.
```

often appears on systems with 8-bit-deep X displays when you start up a Java Abstract Windowing Toolkit (AWT) application. It means that the X colormap is crowded by applications requiring many colors—the most common offender is Netscape Navigator.

The solution is not to run the offending applications, or to run them with an option to install their own colormap. Not all applications have such an option, but Netscape does:

```
netscape -install ...
```

There's a side effect: you see flashing "technicolor" displays whenever you give the focus to an application with its own installed colormap. But this solution ensures that everyone gets enough colors.

Java does not offer an option to install its own colormap—see Chapter 56, "X Window System Tips and Tricks" section "Xwinwrap: Controlling Colormap and Visual Usage" for a workaround to this oversight.

JDK1.2 Missing Dingbat Fonts

The AWT builds insufficient colors to allocate collection of default ***logical fonts*** from fonts it finds on the system, as discussed in Chapter 14, "Configuring the Linux SDK/JRE Environment" in the section "Adding, Changing, and Configuring Fonts." Its assumptions about available fonts are sometimes wrong, and in the case of the Zapf Dingbats font, are almost always wrong for Linux systems. This message

```
Font specified in font.properties not found [—zapf dingbats-medium-r
-normal—*-%d-*-*-p-*-adobe-fontspecific]
```

indicates that the Zapf Dingbats font, a collection of small icons, cannot be found.

The solution is to install a scalable Zapf Dingbat font somewhere that Java can find it, either in the X server or in a directory readable by the AWT. The section "Case Study: Configuring JDK1.2 to Use URW Fonts" in Chapter 14 provides a case study in installing a full new set of fonts to replace the default assignments. It will solve this problem, but it is also more work than you absolutely need to do. Here is the quick two-step solution:

1. Obtain and install the URW fonts described in the section "Case Study: Configuring JDK1.2 to Use URW Fonts" of Chapter 14.
2. Either add the new font directory to the X server font path

   ```
   bash$ xset fp+ /usr/share/fonts/default/Type1
   ```

   or modify Java's font path to find the new directory:

   ```
   bash$ export JAVA_FONTS=$JAVA_HOME/jre/lib/fonts:\
   /usr/X11R6/lib/X11/fonts/Type1:\
   /usr/X11R6/lib/X11/fonts/TrueType:\
   /usr/share/fonts/default/Type1
   ```

(These sample instructions assume where the bundled JDK fonts are located and where the URW fonts are installed. Your mileage may vary.)

To make these settings stick

- If you change the X server font path, your desktop should save the change when you log out and restore it in future sessions.
- If you set `JAVA_FONTS`, place the `export` command in your `~/.bash_profile`, to be run whenever you log in to a shell.

As discussed in "Adding, Changing, and Configuring Fonts in JDK1.2" in Chapter 14, you will get better-looking results with the `JAVA_FONTS` alternative.

Trouble Loading JDK Core Shared Libraries

The succession of changes to Linux's core C library, *libc*, has created occasional incompatibilities between applications and libraries. To allow for this, the Blackdown team builds multiple versions of its releases to support the variety of Linux *libc* configurations.

If your Java startup fails with an error message about loading a shared library and the message refers to one of the Java libraries (`libjava.so`, `libhpi.so`, `libjvm.so`, or some of the others bundled with the JRE and SDK), you have probably installed the wrong JDK for your system.

This problem may also manifest itself as an inexplicable failure in one of the JDK scripts: `No such file or directory`.

See the discussion in Chapter 13, "Blackdown; The Official Linux Port" in the section titled "Supported Linux Versions for the Blackdown SDK and JRE" on how to identify your version of libc and choose the right version of the JDK1.1 or JDK1.2 Blackdown port.

Java Failures to Find Classes: Compilation and Execution

Java needs a class path to locate classes to be loaded at execution time, or resolved at compilation time. JDK1.1 uses a single class path for finding all classes (see Chapter 14 in the section "JDK1.1 Class Path Construction"), whereas JDK1.2 uses a multitiered approach (see Chapter 14 in the section "JDK1.2 Class Path Construction").

In both environments, the rules that apply during execution also apply when you compile Java sources with *javac*: the `CLASSPATH` variable or the `-classpath` option must identify the source of all classes (SDK1.1) or all user classes (SDK1.2). If you cannot find a class at execution or compilation time, your class path is missing something.

Many other compilers, such as Jikes (see Chapter 36, "The Jikes Compiler") and gjc (see Chapter 38, "Generic Java Compilers," in the section "GJ: The Generic Java Compiler"), do not use the JDK1.2 model for locating classes. Although they run under JDK1.2 and fully support JDK1.2 compilation, these compilers must be told where to find all classes, either with the `CLASSPATH` variable or the `-classpath` option. If the compiler cannot find a class at compilation time, your class path is missing something.

AWT Dependence on X Libraries

The AWT has dependencies on certain shared libraries from the X Window System; `libICE.so.6`, `libSM.so.6`, `libX11.so.6`, `libXext.so.6`, `libXp.so.6`, `libXpm.so.4`, and `libXt.so.6`. If Java reports a failure to load one of these shared libraries required by `libawt.so`, you need to obtain current XFree86 libraries. For Red Hat users, the relevant RPM is `XFree86-libs`.

The AWT also might have a dependence on the Motif library `libXm.so.2`. In JDK1.1, this dependence is controllable with the `DYN_JAVA` environment variable (see Chapter 14 in the section "Environment Variables Affecting the SDK/JRE"). Other Java implementations, such as the Linux JDK from IBM, can also have this dependence. In this case, you need to obtain a Motif or Motif-compatible library. A commercial Motif library is available from Metro Link Incorporated (`http://www.metrolink.com/`); a free Motif clone, LessTif, is available from the LessTif home page, `http://www.lesstif.org/`. RPM distributions of LessTif are available from RPM repositories.

Cannot Find JIT Compiler

See the discussion in the section titled "Adding JIT Compilers" in Chapter 14 on how to install a Just-in-Time (JIT) compiler where the Java Virtual Machine can find it (the requirements are different between JDK1.1 and JDK1.2).

Another (remote) possibility: some of the Blackdown JDK1.2 prereleases contained incorrect permissions settings for the bundled JIT. If you cannot load the default JDK1.2 *sunwjit* compiler, check the permissions on the libsunwjit.so file in the libraries directory of the JRE1.2 or SDK1.2 tree. If the file is not readable or executable, do the following in the directory containing the file:

```
chmod 0755 sunwjit.so
```

Limited Support of X Visuals

Java was developed in an X Window System environment (Solaris) that does not support the wide range of X display depths and visuals found in the Linux world. Although the AWT works well with common 8-bit pseudo-color display, it is not uncommon to see a message like

```
Raster IntegerInterleavedRaster: ... incompatible with ColorModel ...
```

when running on 16-, 24-, or 32-bit/pixel displays dissimilar to any found in the Solaris world.

The interim solution, until the AWT is improved to handle a wider choice of displays, is to run your X server in a mode Java can support. See the Chapter 56 section "Experimenting with X Server Settings" for a discussion of setting X server depth and visual modes.

Java Startup Script Directory Dependencies

The startup script that launches java, javac, and other SDK/JRESDK applications employs some shell programming tricks to figure out where it is installed and where to find its libraries. The message

```
Error: can't find libjava.so
```

indicates that the logic has failed. The most likely cause is that you are launching Java through a symbolic link from somewhere outside the installation. Unfortunately, this breaks the logic in the script. You need to delete the offending link and reference the Java installation directly. You can do this by including the installation bin directory in `$PATH`

```
bash$ PATH=/usr/local/Java/jdk1.2/bin:$PATH
bash$ java ...
```

or by fully specifying the path to the executable:

```
bash$ /usr/local/Java/jdk1.2/java ...
```

This error might also occur if you try to run Java executables while you are in the installation bin directory.

Java Use of the Linux Process Table

If you run Java with native threads, you may notice a process list like this when running `ps avx`:

```
  PID TTY      STAT   TIME  MAJFL    TRS   DRS   RSS %MEM COMMAND
23250 ttyp2    S      0:07   3573      9 30066 12996 10.1 java
23274 ttyp2    S      0:00      0      9 30066 12996 10.1 java
23275 ttyp2    S      0:00      0      9 30066 12996 10.1 java
23276 ttyp2    S      0:00      0      9 30066 12996 10.1 java
23277 ttyp2    S      0:00      0      9 30066 12996 10.1 java
23278 ttyp2    S      0:01     52      9 30066 12996 10.1 java
23279 ttyp2    S      0:00      0      9 30066 12996 10.1 java
23280 ttyp2    S      0:00      5      9 30066 12996 10.1 java
23281 ttyp2    S      0:00      0      9 30066 12996 10.1 java
```

The result is nine (nine!) Java processes, each taking 30MB of virtual memory! But the output is deceptive: it really shows nine execution threads sharing the same 30MB of memory.

In Linux, threads are given slots in the process table: every thread has its own process ID (PID). Unfortunately, there is no information in the `ps` output to indicate this relationship between the PIDs—only the common memory size hints at the relationship.

We discuss this further when we examine platform-specific threading issues in Chapter 54, "Java, Linux, and Threads."

AWT Dependencies on X Availability

If you are running the JDK in a server environment, without a GUI or any graphical I/O, you may still encounter some dependencies on X libraries or the presence of an X server.

Dependence on X Libraries

If your application does not use the AWT at all, you have no need of X libraries. In JDK1.1, you can run a version of the application launcher without any X library dependence by setting the `NS_JAVA` environment variable:

```
bash$ export NS_JAVA=1
bash# java ...
```

JDK1.2 does not require such a step: it automatically avoids any dependencies on any X libraries unless the application uses the AWT.

GUI-Less AWT Dependence on X

If you use the AWT *without* any GUI or graphical I/O—for example, to generate bitmapped images—you will find that Java still insists on using X libraries and connecting to an X server.

You can work around this dependence by using a special display-less X server called *Xvfb*. We discuss the details in the Chapter 56 section "Server-Side AWT: Using AWT/X Without a Display Device," as part of the exploration of X server tips and tricks.

Unexplained Application Flakiness

If an application unexpectedly dies, freezes, or is generally flaky, and the problem is unique to Linux, two good suspects are threading and JIT. The following sections discuss the details.

Threads

Thread behavior on Linux has been a challenge to the Blackdown port, and caused a significant delay in the JDK1.2 release. When in doubt, run with green threads (`java -green` ...) and see if the problem goes away.

If it does, you may have encountered a bug in the JDK—but it's also very likely you have encountered a bug in the application. See the section "Implementation-Dependent Threading Behavior" later in this chapter.

JIT

Just-in-Time (JIT) compilation is always a good suspect in flaky behavior, and there are known problems with the Sun JIT that are unique to Linux. Running without JIT compilation (section "Disabling a JIT" of Chapter 14) is a good way to determine if it is implicated. You can also try using one of the alternate JIT compilers (see Chapter 33, "Just-In-Time Compilers") for comparison.

The Sun JIT that shipped with Blackdown JDK1.2 is beyond the control of the Blackdown team: Sun provides it in binary form (evidently due to licensing issues with outside sources). Problems with that JIT should be reported to Blackdown (Chapter 16, "Participating in the Blackdown Community" in the section "Reporting Bugs") with an easy-to-reproduce case; from there, they can be passed on to Sun.

Increasing Java Memory Limits

Java applications can be heavy consumers of memory. The following sections discuss some memory walls you may encounter.

Java Heap Limit

The message

```
Exception in thread ... java.lang.OutOfMemoryError
```

indicates that the heap has hit its maximum size. To increase this limit, use the `-mx` (JDK1.1) or `-Xmx` (JDK1.2) options described in Chapter 17, "The Java Application Launchers: *java*, *jre*, and *oldjava*." If you are running appletviewer, you can pass these options through to the application launcher by prefixing them with the `-J` option (see Chapter 18, "The Java Applet Viewer: *appletviewer*").

System Memory Limits

The message

```
**Out of memory, exiting**
```

indicates that your Linux system is out of memory. If this happens immediately, on application startup, you can try reducing Java's initial and maximum memory limits with the `-mx` and `-ms` (JDK1.1) or `-Xmx` and `-Xms` (JDK1.2) options described in Chapter 17.

But if your application really needs the memory it's requesting, playing with *java* memory settings will not solve the problem: you need to find additional system memory. Beyond the obvious step of killing any other memory-intensive processes, the long-term solution is to increase available memory on your system. The following sections discuss your options.

Using All Available Physical Memory

Verify that Linux has found all physical memory on the system, by running the free utility. Versions of Linux prior to 2.0.36 need help discovering physical memory beyond 64MB. You can use the `mem=` boot-time directive to specify your memory size.

When Linux presents the Linux Loader (LILO) prompt during boot, you can specify memory size as part of startup. For example:

```
LILO: linux mem=128m
```

If you can successfully boot and find the new memory available, you should make this standard boot behavior by modifying `/etc/lilo.conf` and running `/sbin/lilo`.

Information on configuring LILO can be found on the `lilo` and `lilo.conf` man pages (run `man lilo` or man `lilo.conf`), and in the LILO Mini-Howto available from `http://www.linux.org/help/minihowto.html`. Note that it is *always* a good idea, when experimenting with LILO settings, to try those settings with a non-default boot image before adding the settings to the default boot image.

Adding Physical Memory

Experience suggests that even simple Java applications can eat a lot of memory. You may find that adding physical memory is the only reasonable solution for achieving respectable performance. If you add physical memory beyond 64MB on a pre-2.0.36 Linux system, read the previous section on "Using All Available Memory."

Adding Swap Space

You can increase your system's virtual memory by adding swap space. Swap can be added with physical disk partitions or with dedicated space from an existing file system. The relevant Linux commands are `fdisk` (create disk partitions), `mkswap` (initialize a swap area for use), and `swapon` (add swap to the system).

Finding JNI Libraries

When you use a class with a dependence on native libraries, Java needs to know where to find the libraries. Native shared libraries either need to be placed in the JDK installation itself (for example, in the `jre/lib/i386 subdirectory` of an SDK1.2 installation), or have their directories referenced in the `LD_LIBRARY_PATH` environment variable or the system property `java.library.path`. Shared native libraries cannot be found through the class path.

Example:

If you depend on a native library shipped in directory /foo:

```
bash$ export LD_LIBRARY_PATH=/foo
```

will allow you to find it at runtime. The path can consist of multiple directories, separated by the colon (`:`) character. To add a new directory to an existing path:

```
bash$ LD_LIBRARY_PATH=$LD_LIBRARY_PATH:foo
```

Example:

You can use the Java system property `java.library.path` for the same purpose:

```
bash$ java -Djava.library.path=/foo ...
```

Finding JNI Include Files

As the Java native-interface model has evolved into the current JNI, old models have begun losing support. JDK1.2 still supports some older models, but gently discourages you from using them by making them more difficult to compile. If you are trying to build a native-interface module under SDK1.2 and encounter a missing include file (`cannot find oobj.h`, or whatever), you will probably find it under the SDK's `include-old/` subdirectory. Add that directory to your compiler include path.

Implementation-Dependent Threading Behavior

The Java threading model leaves many aspects of multi-threaded behavior unspecified, including:

- Whether thread scheduling is preemptive, or when thread-switching may occur
- How time slices are allocated for threads
- How different thread priorities are supported

This flexibility allows for Java support on many platforms, but it has also caused trouble for developers who do not practice good discipline in their multithreaded programming. Applications that run smoothly on one platform may find themselves facing deadlocks, race conditions, or other unexpected behaviors on other platforms. Applications that work well with green threads may fail with native threads, or vice versa.

Multithreaded programming is challenging; our trivial example in the section "Project #3: Multi-Threading" of Chapter 2, "Moving from C++ to Java," devoted roughly half its code to thread synchronization. Two areas of particular danger are the Swing toolkit and the collections classes. For performance reasons (synchronization is expensive), neither is thread-safe: your application must synchronize multithreaded access to these classes.

Assistance is available: For the container classes, you can use the thread-safe wrappers provided by many of the classes. For Swing, it is recommended that you use `SwingUtilities.invokeLater()` or `SwingUtilities.invokeAndWait()` to schedule GUI activities for execution in the AWT event thread.

While it is impossible to draw up a definitive list, here are some hints that you may have thread synchronization bugs in an application:

- The application has deadlocks or race conditions that are unique to a platform, or to a threading model.
- Threads that run on one platform do not get any time on another platform or different threading model.
- The order of activities or outputs varies in unexpected ways between different platforms or different threading models.
- Adding or removing calls to `Thread.yield()` fixes or breaks the application. Performing explicit yields can be important if a compute-intensive thread is hogging the CPU, but you should be wary of "fixing" broken applications with them.

Chapter 54, "Java, Linux, and Threads," discusses the specifics of Java threading behavior on Linux.

Summary

This chapter has discussed some of the common problems found when using the Blackdown JDK on Linux. The information is unavoidably incomplete—new problems will pop up as the JDK and Linux continue to evolve. To find the latest help for current problems, consider using the available resources provided by the Blackdown project:

- The Java/Linux FAQ from the Blackdown site (`http://www.blackdown.org`) contains up-to-the-minute troubleshooting hints that cover problems observed with the latest releases and on specific Linux distributions.
- The Blackdown mailing list frequently discusses specific problems users encounter with the JDK. Start by searching the archives and, if you need help, ask. See the section "Blackdown Mailing Lists" in Chapter 16 for more information on the mailing list.

CHAPTER 16

PARTICIPATING IN THE BLACKDOWN COMMUNITY

The Blackdown organization and Web site were created in 1995 and serve as the focal point for Blackdown activities—notably the Linux/i386 port of the Sun JDK. Members of the Blackdown community are also interested in the JDK on other Linux platforms, other Java implementations for Linux, and tools and toys available for Java work in Linux.

The Blackdown Web Site

Information available at the Blackdown Web site (`http://www.blackdown.org`) includes

- Status on Linux JDK porting efforts, including ports from outside the Blackdown project (Alpha, PowerPC, and Sparc)
- Locations of mirrors for downloads of Linux ports—both JDK ports and ports of platform-specific standard extensions (such as Java3D)
- An extensive FAQ
- Links to information about products from Sun, third-party Java products, and Java tools available for Linux
- Mailing lists (See the following section "Blackdown Mailing Lists.")
- A bug-tracking system (See the later section "Reporting Bugs.")

Blackdown Mailing Lists

Blackdown operates two mailings lists: one for general discussion and a digest version of the same.

To subscribe to the general discussion list, send an email message to `java-linux-request@java.blackdown.org` with the word `subscribe` in the subject line. To unsubscribe, send a message to the same address with the word `unsubscribe` in the subject line. To participate, send your contributions to `java-linux@java.blackdown.org`.

An archive of past discussion is maintained on the Web, at `http://www.mail-archive.com/java-linux@java.blackdown.org/`. The archive includes search capabilities.

As with any civilized mailing list, it is wise to practice basic etiquette. Reasoned discussion is welcome; flaming is not. Check the archives before asking a question that has already been discussed to death. Accord the other participants some basic respect—remember that everyone here is on the same side. Most importantly for maintaining the high quality of discussion: stick to the topic. The topic is Java on Linux, not beginning Java programming, beginning Linux, nor industry politics.

If you prefer to receive only a digest of the discussion, send your subscribe/unsubscribe messages to `java-linux-digest-request@java.blackdown.org`.

Reporting Bugs

Blackdown uses the Web-based Jitterbug bug-tracking system to report and track defects.

If you have a bug to report in the Blackdown JDK port, first take the following three steps:

1. Visit the page of known Blackdown bugs to see whether the bug is already known. The Blackdown site provides a "bug reporting" link to this page.
2. If you have access to another Java platform, try to reproduce the bug there. If the bug is not specific to Linux/i386, it is not a Blackdown bug.
3. Look for the bug in the Javasoft Bug Parade (see Appendix C, "Important Resources," the section on "Javasoft Bug Parade,") to see whether it is a known bug.

If you have a legitimate Blackdown bug, visit the bug-reporting page at `http://www.blackdown.org/cgi-bin/jdk`. The Jitterbug system is reasonably straightforward and self-explanatory. The main screen includes options for submitting new bugs, searching the database for existing bugs, and browsing the various categories (done, incoming, pending, and so on) of bug reports. Again, it is a good idea to search for relevant existing bugs before submitting your own report.

If you do submit a bug report, be brief and specific. Include a small Java program that reproduces the bug. Vague, general reports ("Swing doesn't work") are not likely to get attention.

Summary

The Blackdown organization serves as the focus of Java porting activity on Linux. Tune in to Blackdown to get the latest ports, the latest news on Java/Linux activities, and the combined wisdom of other users of Java on Linux.

PART V

TOOLS IN THE BLACKDOWN SDK

The Blackdown port ships with the full complement of Sun SDK tools[md]everything found in the Solaris or Windows SDKs can be found here. This part provides a brief guide to the important development tools in both SDK1.1 and SDK1.2, describes their use, explains the differences between the two environments, and offers usage and implementation details specific to the Linux versions.

CHAPTER 17

THE JAVA APPLICATION LAUNCHERS: `java`, `jre`, AND `oldjava`

The Java application launchers are the application entry points into Java: they start up the JVM, point it at the class libraries it needs, and tell it which class to load. After loading the main class, the JVM calls the class's `main()` procedure to start the program. End users do not have to know about application launchers. A deployed application can hide launch details in a shell script (UNIX/Linux), batch file (Microsoft Windows), or iconic action.

In the JDK1.1 environment, Sun provided two versions of the launcher: `java` and `jre`. The first was shipped only with the SDK and targeted at developers. The second, lacking the developer-oriented options, was targeted at deployment environments.

In JDK1.2, Sun combined the two into a single `java` launcher. It's a better solution but with an unfortunate side effect: It breaks all older application-launch scripts—the only launcher shipped on JDK1.1 deployment platforms (`jre`) is not present on JDK1.2 deployment platforms.

SDK1.2 introduced another launcher, `oldjava`. For older applications broken by the drastic JDK1.2 changes in class path construction and security mechanisms, the `oldjava` launcher emulates the pre-1.2 mechanisms.

java Launcher

The **java** command launches a Java application by starting a JVM and loading the application classes.

Synopsis:

```
java [-green ¦ -native] [<options>] <classname> [<arguments>]
java [-green ¦ -native] [<options>] -jar <jarfile> [<arguments>]
```

(Second form is SDK1.2/JRE1.2 only.)

Platform: SDK1.2, JRE1.2, SDK1.1

Note that the launcher requires a class name, not a filename. It is the class loader's job to resolve this class name to a **.class** file resident on a file system or in an archive.

Options:

Options from 1.1 and 1.2 are listed together, with indications of which options (or which names for options) are unique to one of the platforms.

- -checksource (SDK1.1 only) and -cs (SDK1.1 only)—Before loading a class, check whether its source is newer than the class file. If yes, then recompile the class before loading.
- -classpath <path> and -cp <*path*> (SDK1.2/JRE1.2)—Set the class path used for finding all classes (SDK1.1) or all user classes (SDK1.2/JRE1.2). In both environments, this option overrides the default class path or any class path defined by **$CLASSPATH**.
- -D<*propertyName*>=<*newValue*>—Assign a value to a Java property. Some standard property names, such as **java.compiler**, affect JDK behavior. Other properties are simply used to pass values into the program. Java applications do not have access to read or set UNIX/Linux environment variables; this mechanism serves as a platform-neutral replacement.
- -green—Force the JVM to use the Sun "green" thread emulation package, which is a user-space emulation of kernel threading. If specified, this *must* be the first option on the command line.
- -help—Print a help message.
- -jar <*jarfile*> (SDK1.2/JRE1.2 only)—Specify a jar archive to execute. The launcher depends on information in the archive's manifest to identify the main class. This option completely defines the user class path; all class path elements defined by **$CLASSPATH** or -classpath are ignored.
- -ms*n* (SDK1.1) and -Xms*n* (SDK1.2/JRE1.2)—Specify the starting size of the memory heap. The value *n* is a number specified in bytes, kbytes (suffixed with k), or mbytes (suffixed with m).
- -mx*n* (SDK1.1) and -Xmx*n* (SDK1.2/JRE1.2)—Specify the maximum size of the memory heap. The value *n* is a number specified in bytes, kbytes (suffixed with k), or mbytes

(suffixed with `m`). If the JVM must grow beyond this size, it will throw an exception. This value must be greater than or equal to the starting size specified by `-ms`*n* or `-Xms`*n*.

- `-native`—Force the JVM to use the "native" platform thread API, which is the POSIX *Pthread* interface. This generally[1] means that kernel threads will be used. If specified, this *must* be the first option on the command line.

  As part of our discussion of platform-specific issues, we'll explore threads in more detail in Chapter 54, "Java, Linux, and Threads."

- `-noasyncgc` (SDK1.1 only)—Disable the asynchronous garbage collection thread. Garbage collection will only occur when the application requests it or runs out of memory.
- `-noclassgc` (SDK1.1) and `-Xnoclassgc` (SDK1.2/JRE1.2)—Disable garbage collection of unused space associated with classes (as opposed to space associated with class instances).
- `-noverify` (SDK1.1)—Disable verification of classes.
- `-oss`*n* (SDK1.1 only)—Specify the maximum stack size for Java code in bytes, kbytes (suffixed with `k`), or mbytes (suffixed with `m`).
- `-ss`*n* (SDK1.1 only)—Specify the maximum stack size for native code in bytes, kbytes (suffixed with `k`), or mbytes (suffixed with `m`).
- `-v` (SDK1.1), `-verbose`, `-verbosegc` (SDK1.1), `-verbose:class` (SDK1.2/JRE1.2), `-verbose:gc` (SDK1.2/JRE1.2), `-verbose:jni` (SDK1.2/JRE1.2)—These options enable the JVM's verbose mode, selectively or nonselectively reporting on class-loading, garbage collection, and use of JNI methods and interfaces.
- `-verify` (SDK1.1)—Enable verification of all classes. Only code executed is verified, not all code in the class. Contrast with `-noverify` and `-verifyremote`.
- `-verifyremote` (SDK1.1)—Verify all code loaded through a class loader. This is the default verification behavior. Contrast with `-noverify` and `-verify`.
- `-version`—Print the SDK/JRE version number.

Nonstandard SDK1.2/JRE1.2 Options:

These are SDK1.2/JRE1.2 options specific to the current JVM behavior; their future support and their support in other JVMs (such as HotSpot) is not guaranteed. All nonstandard options begin with `-X`. As the previous options list shows, certain SDK1.1 options became nonstandard options in SDK1.2/JRE1.2.

- `-X`—List available nonstandard options.
- `-Xbootclasspath:<new classpath>`—Override the boot class path, from which Java loads its core classes.
- `-Xcheck:jni`—Perform additional checks for JNI functions.

1Native threading sometimes implies kernel-space threading, but not always. For more detail, see the discussion of threading APIs (Chapter 54, "Java, Linux, and Threads," section "Lightweight Process Implementation Details").

- `-Xdebug`—Run the JVM with the debugger enabled. A "password" is printed out that can be used by a Java debugger to attach to the running JVM.
- `-Xnoclassgc`—Disable garbage collection of unused space associated with classes. This is the JDK1.2 version of the `-noclassgc` option.
- `-Xms`*n*—Specify the starting size of the memory heap in bytes, kbytes (suffixed with `k`), or mbytes (suffixed with `m`). This is the JDK1.2 version of the `-ms`*n* option.
- `-Xmx`*n*—Specify the maximum size of the memory heap in bytes, kbytes (suffixed with `k`), or mbytes (suffixed with `m`). This is the JDK1.2 version of the `-mx`*n* option.
- `-Xrs`—Reduce the use of operating system signals.
- `-Xrunhprof:<commands>`—SDK1.2/JRE1.2 supports a new profiling interface, accessed through a native C/C++ API. The *Java Virtual Machine Profiling Interface* (JVMPI) is intended for use by tools vendors to develop performance analysis tools for Java. SDK1.2/JRE1.2 ships with a sample JVMPI application, *hprof*, that gathers and saves profiling data to a file. Use `-Xrunhprof:help` to print out a list of legal commands.

  In Chapter 60, "PerfAnal: A Free Performance Analysis Tool," we will describe profiling in more detail and introduce a useful GUI-based tool for analyzing data collected by the hprof profiler.

`java_g` Launcher

The SDK offers a debuggable, non-optimized version of the `java` launcher, `java_g`. This version fills an important role in SDK1.1, where it is needed to perform debugging and profiling.

An SDK1.2 version of `java_g` is available, primarily to support debugging of the JVM itself. But you are unlikely to need it for your own development work: Application debugging and profiling are supported by the regular SDK1.2 `java` launcher.

Synopsis:

```
java_g  [-green | -native] [<options>] <classname> [<arguments>]
```

Platform: SDK1.1

The `java_g` launcher supports all options supported by the `java` launcher, plus some additional options to support debugging and profiling.

New Options:

- `-debug`—Run the JVM with the debugger enabled. A "password" is printed out that can be used by a Java debugger to attach to the running JVM.
- `-prof`—Collect and save profile data into file `./java.prof`. Note that this capability is limited compared to the profiling capabilities in JDK1.2.
- `-prof:<file>`—Collect and save profile data into the specified file.
- `-t`—Print a trace of Java instructions executed.

jre Launcher

This component, the only launcher shipped with JRE1.1, is the deployment-side counterpart to the java launcher used by developers. It was discontinued in SDK1.2/JRE1.2, in favor of using a single launcher in both development and deployment environments.

Synopsis:

jre [-green ¦ -native] [<*options*>] <*classname*> [<*arguments*>]

Platform: SDK1.1/JRE1.1

The options supported by jre substantially overlap those supported by the java launcher, with a few differences that orient it toward deployment use instead of development.

Options:

- -classpath <*path*>—Set the class path for finding all classes. Equivalent to the SDK1.1 java -classpath option.
- -cp <*path*>—Prepend the specified path to the existing class path.
- -D<*propertyName*>=<*newValue*>—Identical option to java launcher (above).
- -green—Run with "green" threads, as in the java launcher.
- -help—Print a usage message, as in the java launcher.
- -ms*n*—Specify initial memory heap size, as in the SDK1.1 java launcher.
- -mx*n*—Specify maximum memory heap size, as in the SDK1.1 java launcher.
- -native—Run with "native" threads, as in the java launcher.
- -noasyncgc—Disable asynchronous garbage collection, as in the SDK1.1 java launcher.
- -noclassgc—Disable class garbage collection, as in the SDK1.1 java launcher.
- -nojit—Disable just-in-time compilation.
- -noverify—Disable class verification, as in the SDK1.1 java launcher.
- -oss*n*—Specify the maximum stack space for Java code, as in the SDK1.1 java launcher.
- -ss*n*—Specify the maximum stack space for native code, as in the SDK1.1 java launcher.
- -v and -verbose—Verbosely report class loading, garbage collection, and JNI activity, as in the SDK1.1 java launcher.
- -verbosegc—Verbosely report garbage collection activity, as in the SDK1.1 java launcher.
- -verify—Verify executed code, as in the SDK1.1 java launcher.
- -verifyremote—Verify all loaded classes, as in the SDK1.1 java launcher.

`jre_g` Launcher

The `jre_g` launcher is a non-optimized version of the `jre` launcher. It appears to exist for purposes of debugging the launcher itself, and offers no options for application debugging or profiling.

Synopsis:

```
jre_g [-green | -native] [<options>] <classname> [<arguments>]
```

Platform: SDK1.1

Options are the same as for `jre`, discussed in the previous section.

`oldjava` Launcher

JDK1.2 introduced disruptive changes in class loading and security that break some older applications. The `oldjava` launcher is a temporary expedient to work around the problem. It supports execution of older applications by taking the following steps:

- It emulates the old class path model. A single class path (the boot class path) is used for core, extension, and user classes. It also disables the new extensions mechanism, in which extensions are automatically found in a central directory.
- It emulates the old security model. User classes have the same privileges as core classes.

Using `oldjava` to run older applications does not guarantee success, but it improves the chances. Some older applications include, in their launch scripts, intricate (and obsolete) dependencies on the layout of the SDK or JRE installation tree. Obviously, `oldjava` cannot do anything about such dependencies.

Synopsis:

```
oldjava [-green | -native] [<options>] <classname> [<arguments>]
```

Platform: SDK1.2

The options for `oldjava` are more or less compatible with JRE1.2/SDK1.2 `java` options, with a few changes.

Options Changes:

- `-classpath` *<path>* and `-cp` *<path>*—Override the boot class path, which is used for finding all classes, not just core classes.
- The `-jar` option is disabled in `oldjava`.

Subtleties

There is one additional confusing subtlety. The `CLASSPATH` environment variable specifies a user class path to be searched after the boot class path. It defaults to the current directory if not set. This behavior is unaffected by the `-classpath` and `-cp` options, which change only the boot class path; this is the only case for any Java launcher in which the `-classpath` option does not cause `$CLASSPATH` to be ignored.

For Further Reading

The SDK1.1 and SDK1.2 documentation bundles include launcher documentation on the following pages:

`java`	`docs/tooldocs/solaris/java.html`
`jre` (SDK1.1 bundle only)	`docs/tooldocs/solaris/jre.html`

Summary

This chapter has explored the Java application launchers used to run Java programs in a Linux environment. The launchers perform the first essential step of application execution: starting up a virtual machine and loading the application classes. The next chapter examines an important variant—a launcher you can use to run applets.

CHAPTER 18

THE JAVA APPLET VIEWER: appletviewer

The Java applet viewer is a development tool that allows you to test-drive applets before they are deployed for use in browsers. By creating an applet test bed with the current SDK environment, `appletviewer` lets you test applets in ways not possible with browsers: with a newer JDK, for example, or running under a debugger. Until browsers widely support JDK1.2, `appletviewer` is the only way to run JDK1.2 applets on many platforms.

Running appletviewer

The `appletviewer` invocation starts the viewer, reads the Web page specified by the URL, and loads and runs the applet referenced in the page.

Synopsis:

```
appletviewer [-green | -native] [<options>] <URL>
```

Platform: SDK1.2 SDK1.1

Options:

- `-debug`—Runs `appletviewer` under the `jdb` debugger. Note the difference from the `-debug` option for application launchers described in Chapter 17, "The Java Application Launchers: `java`, `jre`, and `oldjava`," which starts the app but doesn't start a debugger.

- -encoding <*encoding*_name>—Specifies the character encoding used in the HTML file referenced by the URL.
- -green—Forces the JVM to use the Sun "green" thread emulation package, which is a user-space emulation of kernel threading. If specified, this ***must*** be the first option on the command line.
- -J<*java_option*>—Specifies options to be passed to the JVM. These options are passed, with the -J stripped off, to the **java** executable that is actually running the applet—see the option definitions in Chapter 17 in the section "**java** Launcher."
- -native—Forces the JVM to use the "native" platform thread API. If specified, this must be the first option on the command line.

appletviewer: A Simple Browser

The appletviewer tool functions as a simple browser, reading an HTML file and handling the applet-related tags. After loading the applet class referenced by the tags, it calls the applet startup methods init() and start() to begin execution. The tool creates a restricted execution environment comparable to the "sandbox" environment in a browser but with some additional GUI controls that allow you to modify security settings.

The purpose of appletviewer is to test applets, not Web pages or interaction with Web browsers. It has limited HTML parsing capability and no HTML display capability. The HTML should be small and simple—just enough to specify the applet. The following sections discuss the relevant tags and give some examples.

Specifying an Applet with the <applet> Tag

The traditional HTML tag for applets is <applet>. To illustrate, we write a simple test applet and the supporting HTML.

Our Swing-based applet displays a single pushbutton that, when pressed or released, sends a message to the browser status line. The button label and the text of the messages are specified as applet parameters in the HTML. Here is the code:

```
import java.awt.event.*;
import javax.swing.*;

//
// Simple applet to display a pushbutton and a status message associated
// with button press and release (more precisely: associated with mouse
// click activity on the button).
//
public class ButtonStatus extends JApplet
{
    JButton button;
    public ButtonStatus()
    {
```

```
            button = new JButton();
            getContentPane().add(button);
        }
        public void init()
        {
            button.setText(getParameter("ButtonText"));
            button.addMouseListener(new MouseAdapter() {
                public void mousePressed(MouseEvent e)
                {
                    showStatus(getParameter("ButtonDownMsg"));
                };
                public void mouseReleased(MouseEvent e)
                {
                    showStatus(getParameter("ButtonUpMsg"));
                };
            });
        }
    }
```

Here is the HTML:

```
<html>
<body>
<h1>Hello World Applet</h1>
<applet code="ButtonStatus.class"
        ButtonText="Press Me"
        ButtonDownMsg="Button is Down"
        ButtonUpMsg="Button is Up"
        width="200"
        height="100">No Applet?</applet>
</body>
</html>
```

Figure 18.1 shows the result.

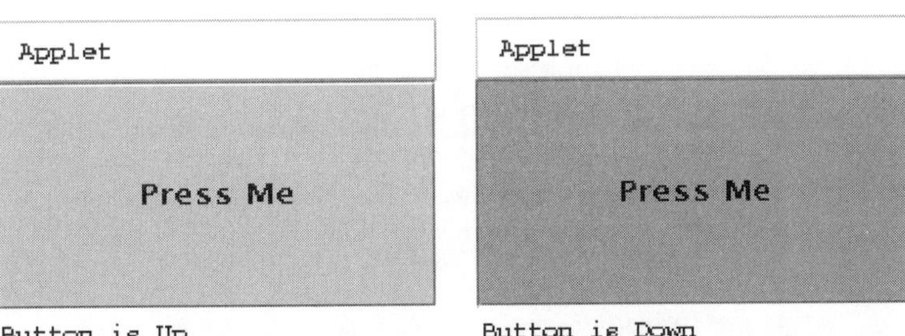

FIGURE 18.1
ButtonStatus applet with button released (left) and pressed (right).

Specifying an Applet for Netscape with the <embed> Tag (SDK1.2 Only)

The `<embed>` tag is a Netscape extension, added in Netscape 4.*x*, to support embedded objects of arbitrary types—including applets exercising the Java Plug-in. Here is our HTML, rewritten to use this Netscape-specific tag and run the Java Plug-in:

```
<html>
<body>
<h1>Hello World Applet</h1>
<EMBED type="application/x-java-applet;version=1.2"
code = "ButtonStatus.class"
WIDTH = "200"
HEIGHT = "100"
ButtonText="Press Me"
ButtonDownMsg="Button is Down"
ButtonUpMsg="Button is Up"
pluginspage="http://java.sun.com/products/plugin/1.2/plugin-install.html">
<NOEMBED>
No Applet?
</NOEMBED></EMBED>
</body>
</html>
```

The SDK1.2 version of `appletviewer` understands the `<embed>` tag as an applet tag, although it ignores certain attributes (`src`, `type`, `pluginspage`) that are important to proper operation of the applet in Netscape.

Specifying an Applet for MSIE with the `<object>` Tag (SDK1.2 Only)

The `<object>` tag is an HTML 4.0 extension that, in Microsoft Internet Explorer (4.*x* and later), supports the Java Plug-in. Here is our HTML, rewritten to use the `<object>` tag and run the Java Plug-in:

```
<html>
<body>
<h1>Hello World Applet</h1>
<OBJECT classid="clsid:8AD9C840-044E-11D1-B3E9-00805F499D93"
WIDTH = "200"
HEIGHT = "100"
codebase="http://java.sun.com/products/plugin/1.2/jinstall-12-
➥win32.cab#Version=1,2,0,0">
<PARAM NAME = CODE VALUE = "ButtonStatus.class" >
<PARAM NAME="type" VALUE="application/x-java-applet;version=1.2">
<PARAM NAME="ButtonText" VALUE="Press Me">
<PARAM NAME="ButtonDownMsg" VALUE="Button is Down">
<PARAM NAME="ButtonUpMsg" VALUE="Button is Up">
No Applet?
</OBJECT>

</body>
</html>
```

The SDK1.2 version of `appletviewer` understands the `<object>` tag as an applet tag, although it ignores certain parameters (`classid`, `type`, `codebase`) that are important to proper operation of the applet in MSIE.

For Further Reading

The SDK1.1 and SDK1.2 documentation bundles include relevant documentation on the following pages:

appletviewer	docs/tooldocs/solaris/appletviewer.html
HTML tags (SDK1.2 only)	docs/tooldocs/solaris/appletviewertags.html

The discussion of the Java Plug-in in Chapter 50, "Deploying Applets with Java Plug-in," will discuss `<embed>` and `<object>` in more detail and will also explain how to publish JDK1.2 applets targeted to work on all browsers.

Summary

The **appletviewer** tool lets you test-drive applets in ways that are not possible from existing Web browsers—you can test with the latest JVMs, modify security settings, and perform debugging. Although its lack of browser capabilities makes it unsuitable for fully testing applet-enabled Web pages, **appletviewer** is the best way to test applets with current Java execution environments.

CHAPTER 19

THE JAVA COMPILER: JAVAC

This is the primary development tool for users of the SDK. The Java compiler compiles `.java` source files to `.class` bytecode objects—the executables understood by the Java Virtual Machine.

Running javac

The `javac` invocation compiles the specified Java source files. The compiler is itself a Java application, so the invocation results in launching a JVM to run the Java compiler classes.

Synopsis:

```
javac [-green ¦ -native] [<options>] <source files>
javac [-green ¦ -native] [<options>] [<source files>] [@<files>] (SDK1.2 only)
```

The SDK1.2 version offers a convenience for projects with a long list of source files: The `@` option allows the compiler to read a list of source files from a file instead of a crowded command line.

Platform: SDK1.2 SDK1.1

Options:

- `-classpath` *<classpath>*—Set the class path to be searched during compilation. If this option is not specified, `$CLASSPATH` is used.

Compile-time handling of the class path is similar to runtime handling: The SDK1.1 class path must include the core classes, whereas SDK1.2 handles the core classes separately (see the definition of `-bootclasspath`, later in this chapter).

Note that this option controls where the compiler looks for classes. It does not control where the JVM *running* the compiler looks for classes. If necessary, that can be done with the `-J` option (discussed later).

- `-d` *`<directory>`*—Specify a directory into which the `.class` files are to go. The compiler places classes into a hierarchical subtree of this directory based on the full *package+class* name. See the discussion in Chapter 14, "Configuring the Linux SDK/JRE Environment," in the section "Classes Loaded from File Systems" for more detail.

  If this option is not specified, `.class` files are placed in the current directory. If the classes are part of a package, you will not be able to run them from this directory (also discussed in Chapter 14 in the section "Classes Loaded from File Systems").

- `-deprecation`—Generate fatal errors when using deprecated classes. If this option is not specified, use of deprecated classes generates a compile-time warning.
- `-encoding` *`<encoding>`*—Specify the character encoding for the source files. If unspecified, `javac` uses the default encoding for the current locale.
- `-g`—Save full debugging information into the `.class` files. If not specified, default behavior is to save some information—source filename and line numbers but no info on local variables.
- `-g:none` (SDK1.2 only)—Prevent *any* debugging information from being saved into the `.class` files.
- `-g:`*`<list of keywords>`* (SDK1.2 only)—Selectively save debugging information into the `.class` file. The *`<list of keywords>`* is a comma-separated list containing any or all of the words `source`, `lines`, or `vars`.
- `-green`—Force the JVM to use the Sun "green" thread emulation package, which is a user-space emulation of kernel threading. If specified, this must be the first option on the command line.
- `-J`*`<option>`*—Specify options to be passed to the `java` application launcher that is running the compiler. Options are passed, with the `-J` stripped, to the `java` command line.
- `-native`—Force the JVM to use the "native" platform thread API. If specified, this must be the first option on the command line.
- `-nowarn`—Disable warning messages.
- `-O`—Optimize code for better runtime performance—usually at the cost of code size and debuggability. The SDK1.1 documentation warns of risks in the use of this option; SDK1.2 has removed some of the riskier behavior.

  There is some consensus in the user community that the best optimization is performed by postprocessors that operate on the entire project after compilation. We will examine such a product in Chapter 53, "DashO: Optimizing Applications for Delivery."

- `-sourcepath` *<sourcepath>* (SDK1.2 only)—Specify a colon-separated path to be searched for source files. Path components can include directories and compressed ZIP and JAR archives.
- `-verbose`—Print verbose messages on which class files are being compiled and which classes are being loaded by the JVM.

SDK1.2 Cross-Compilation Options:

SDK1.2 supplies these options to support cross-compilation—the generation of classes compatible with earlier Java platforms:

- `-bootclasspath` *<bootclasspath>*—Change the search path the compiler uses to resolve references to core classes. Using this option, you can point the boot class path at JDK1.1 core libraries to compile for that platform.
- `-extdirs` *<directories>*—Use these extension directories— directories containing Java extension JAR archives—instead of the standard location for SDK1.2/JRE1.2 extensions.
- `-target` *<version>*—Specify a target JVM—`1.1` or `1.2`. If `1.1` is specified (the default), `javac` generates code that will run on JDK1.1 and JDK1.2 virtual machines. If `1.2` is specified, the generated code will not run on a JDK1.1 virtual machine.

SDK1.2 Nonstandard Options:

- `-X`—Print a list of available nonstandard options.
- `-Xdepend`—Perform a dependency analysis. This replaces the SDK1.1 java `-checksource` runtime option with a more sensible compile time option. It causes `javac` to search all reachable classes for source files that are newer than their corresponding objects, and to recompile the offending classes. This results in reasonable, but not completely robust, decisions on which files need to be recompiled.

  Unfortunately, this option substantially slows compilation. We will explore an alternate approach to this problem in Chapter 48, "JMakeDepend: A Project Build Management Utility."
- `-Xstdout`—Send messages to `stdout` (`System.out`) instead of the default `stderr` (`System.err`).
- `-Xverbosepath`— Generate verbose information describing where source and class files are found.

Subtleties

- The classes that make up the Java compiler itself live in different places in the two environments. In SDK1.1, they live in the `classes.zip` file that also holds the core classes. In SDK1.2, they are shipped in a separate `tools.jar`. Developers who rely on some of those classes to build their own tools need to add the new jarfile in SDK1.2.

- The `-d` and `-classpath` options are completely independent. Although `-d` specifies where classes are to be written, it does not affect where classes are searched. This can cause surprises.

  Consider a project with two classes, `Foo` and `Bar`, compiled into directory `baz` (`javac -d baz ...`), in which class `Foo` contains references to class `Bar`. If you need to change and recompile only `Foo.java`, you must specify `-d baz` *and* you must also include `baz` in the class path. This will tell the compiler where to place `Foo.class` and where to resolve the reference to class `Bar`.

  (Had you recompiled both files at once, the modification to the class path would have been unnecessary. We will discuss some of the intricacies of dependency analysis in our `JMakeDepend` project in Chapter 48, "JMakeDepend: A Project Build Management Utility.")

javac_g Compiler

This version of the compiler is a normal part only of SDK1.1. A version is available for SDK1.2, but you are unlikely ever to need it.

Synopsis:

```
javac_g [-green | -native] [<options>] <source files>
```

Platform: SDK1.1

This is a nonoptimized version of the compiler used for debugging the compiler itself.

For Further Reading

The SDK1.1 and SDK1.2 documentation bundles include relevant documentation on the following pages:

```
javac docs/tooldocs/solaris/javac.html
```

Summary

This chapter has presented `javac`, the compiler bundled with the Sun SDK. This tool is not your only choice of compiler; later chapters will offer looks at alternative free compilers, integrated development environments, fast compilers, and compilers supporting language extensions.

CHAPTER 20

THE JAVA DEBUGGER: JDB

The SDK includes an interactive, non-GUI debugger, `jdb`. Like the well-known `gdb` and `dbx` UNIX debuggers, `jdb` offers a text-based command interface allowing you to control execution and examine application contexts and data structures.

Running jdb

You can debug both applications and applets with `jdb`. You also have the option of launching an application/applet from `jdb` or attaching to an existing, running instance.

Synopsis:

```
jdb [-green | -native] [<options>] [<class>] [<arguments>]
jdb [-green | -native] -host <hostname> -password <password>
appletviewer [-green | -native] -debug [<options>] <URL>
```

The first form of this command is for launching and debugging applications. Invocation is identical to launching an application with the `java` application launcher options(see Chapter 17, "The Java Application Launchers: java, jre, and oldjava"), a class name, and arguments to be passed to `main()`. (According to Sun documentation, all `java` launcher options can be used here—experience suggests otherwise.)

If no *<class>* is specified, the debugger is started without a class loaded—one can be loaded later with a debugger command.

Example

To debug an application that is normally launched with

```
bash$ java com.foo.bar arg1 arg2
```

launch a debugger with

```
bash$ jdb com.foo.bar arg1 arg2
```

The second form of the command debugs an application that is already running. The original application must have been launched with the `-debug` option; the *<password>* is the ***Agent password*** returned at application invocation.

Example

If you use `jdb` to attach to an already running application, you must follow certain practices when launching that application.

Under SDK1.1, you must launch the application with `java_g`:

```
bash$ java_g -debug com.foo.bar arg1 arg2
Agent password=5k53pk
```

Under SDK1.2, you must include the SDK's `tools.jar` in the class path when launching, and you must disable just-in-time compilation:

```
bash$ java -debug -Djava.compiler= -classpath $JAVA_HOME/lib/
[ic:ccc]tools.jar:. com.foo.bar arg1 arg2
Agent password=5k53pk
```

Now you are ready to debug:

```
bash$ jdb -host localhost -password 5k53pk
```

The third form of the command is for debugging applets. See `appletviewer` (Chapter 18, "The Java Applet Viewer: appletviewer") for a list of options.

Platform: SDK1.2 SDK1.1

Options:

- `-classpath`—Passed to debuggee JVM for use as its class path.
- `-dbgtrace`—Print out information for debugging the debugger.
- `-D`*<propertyName>*`=`*<newValue>*—Passed to debuggee JVM to set property values for the target application.
- `-green`—Force the JVM to use the Sun "green" thread emulation package, which is a user-space emulation of kernel threading. If specified, this *must* be the first option on the command line. Note that this affects the operation of the debugger executable but not of the JVM running the application being debugged. Use the `THREADS_FLAG` environment variable to affect that JVM.
- `-help`—Print out a usage message.

- `-host` *<hostname>*—Host on which existing process to be debugged is running.
- `-native`—Force the JVM to use the "native" platform thread API. If specified, this *must* be the first option on the command line.
- `-password` *<password>*—Agent password for existing process to be debugged.
- `-version`—Print out version of `jdb`.
- `-X`*<non-standard java option>* (SDK1.2 only)—Passed to debuggee JVM.

jdb Commands

Commands used in the debugger text-based UI are as follows:

Thread Management

- `threads [`*<threadgroup>*`]`—List all the current threads in a thread group. If no argument is specified, the default thread group (as set by `threadgroup`, discussed later in this list) is used. A *<threadgroup>* of `system` results in showing all threads.

  For each thread, the list shows the name of the thread, the name of the thread class (`java.lang.Thread` or a derived class), and the current status of the thread. For commands (discussed next) requiring a *<thread id>*, the ordinal numbers (`1`, `2`, `3`, …) shown in this command's output are used.
- `thread` *<thread id>*—Set the default thread to be used for thread-specific commands, such as stack navigation.
- `suspend [`*<thread ids>*`]`—Suspend one or more threads. The optional *<thread ids>* argument is a list (separated by spaces) of one or more thread IDs. If none is specified, all nonsystem threads are suspended. Some debugger operations, such as listing local variables, can only be performed on suspended threads.
- `resume [`*<thread ids>*`]`—Resume (unsuspend) one or more threads. The optional *<thread ids>* argument is a list (separated by spaces) of one or more thread numbers. If none is specified, all threads are resumed.
- `where [`*<thread id>*`]¦[all]`—Print a stack dump for the specified *<thread id>*, for all threads, or (if no argument is specified) for the default thread.
- `wherei [`*<thread id>*`]¦[all]`—Print a stack dump, plus PC information, for the specified *<thread id>*, for all threads, or (if no argument is specified) for the default thread.
- `threadgroups`—List all thread groups.
- `threadgroup` *<name>*—Set the default thread group for the various thread operations. The *<name>* is taken from the `threadgroups` list, discussed in the preceding item.

Viewing Data

- `print` *<id(s)>*—Print one or more items, where an item can be a local, instance, or class variable, or a class name. When printing a class variable, it is apparently necessary to qualify it with the class name (for example, `classname.varname`). All items are printed in their `toString()` format.
- `dump` *<id(s)>*—Print one or more items, as in the preceding command, but in a detailed format.
- `locals`—Print the names and values of all local variables.
- `classes`—List all known classes and interfaces.
- `methods` *<class id>*—List all methods for a specified class.

Breakpoints and Stack Navigation

- `stop in` *<class id>*`.`*<method>* and `stop in` *<class id>*`.`*<method>*`[(`*<argument_type>*`,...)]` (SDK1.2 only)—Set a breakpoint in a named method. The SDK1.2 version allows you to optionally qualify the method name with full signature (argument types) information.
- `stop at` *<class id>*`:`*<line>*—Set a breakpoint at a specified line number in the *<class id>* source.
- `up [`*n*`]`—Move specified number of frames up a thread's stack. If the optional argument is not specified, it defaults to 1.
- `down [`*n*`]`—Move specified number of frames down a thread's stack. If the optional argument is not specified, it defaults to 1.
- `clear` *<class id>*`.`*<method>*`[(`*<argument_type>*`,...)]` (SDK1.2 only)—Clear a breakpoint in a method.
- `clear` *<class id>*`:`*<line>*—Clear a breakpoint at a specified line number in the *<class id>* source.
- `step`—Execute the current line.
- `step up`—Execute the remainder of the current procedure until return to the caller.
- `stepi`—Execute the current bytecode instruction.
- `next`—Execute the current line, stepping over method calls.
- `cont`—Continue (currently stopped) execution.

Exceptions

- `catch` *<class id>*—Break when a specified exception occurs.
- `ignore` *<class id>*—Ignore the specified exception.

Source

- list [*<line number>*¦*<method>*]—List source code at the specified line number, for the specified method, or (if neither specified) around the current location in source.
- use [*<source file path>*]—Set the current path for finding source files. If no argument is specified, prints the current path.

Resources

- memory—Show the current memory usage: free and total memory.
- gc—Force garbage collection to occur and reclaim unreferenced objects.

Debugger Control

- load *<classname>*—Load a specified class for debugging.
- run [*<class>* [*<args>*]]—Run the specified class with the specified arguments for main(). If no argument is specified, run the class and arguments specified in the jdb startup command line.
- !!—Repeat the last jdb command executed.
- help, ?—List jdb commands.
- exit, quit—End the debugging session.

Future Directions

The jdb debugger is built on top of an old interface called the *Java Debugger API*, which interacts with a running JVM over a network connection. Sun describes jdb as a "proof-of-concept" for that API, whose architecture is shown in Figure 20.1.

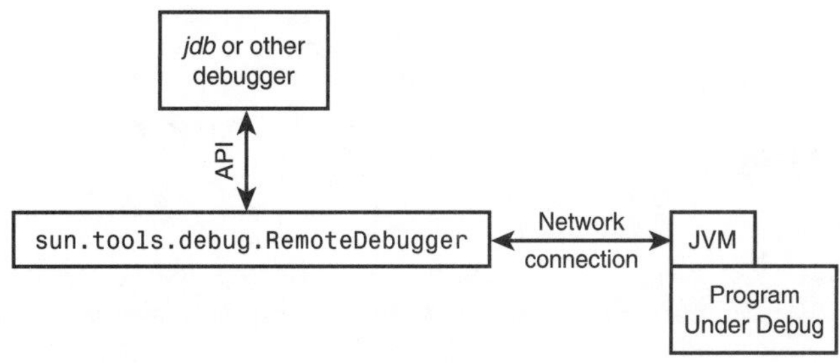

FIGURE 20.1
Java Debugger API.

SDK1.2 introduced a new multitiered debugging approach, the *Java Platform Debugging Architecture*, consisting of a low-level native-code interface, a network protocol, and a debugging API (see Figure 20.2).

FIGURE 20.2
Java Platform Debugging Architecture.

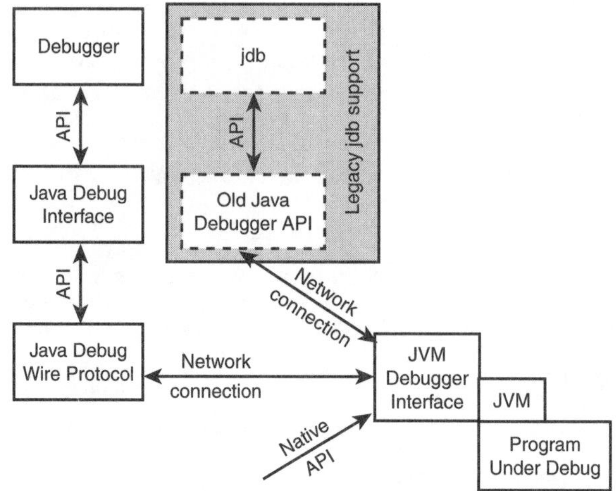

The new architecture was not fully implemented in time for SDK1.2 and is scheduled for a later release, which will probably include another "proof-of-concept" debugger. Sun's longer-term intent is to enable third-party tool developers to build better debuggers. The Java Debug Interface is intended to be the primary API for debuggers, but implementers are free to use the other interfaces, including the low-level JVMDI native interface for possible implementation of in-process debugging.

For Further Reading

The SDK1.1 and SDK1.2 documentation bundles include relevant documentation on the following pages:

```
jdb  docs/tooldocs/solaris/jdb.html
```

Summary

This chapter has explored `jdb`, a text-based debugger supplied with the SDK. Although `jdb` does the job, it is not the last or best word in Java debuggers. We will explore some alternatives—different debuggers, as well as GUI wrappers for `jdb`, in Chapter 39, "The Jikes Debugger," and Chapter 40, "DDD: The Data Display Debugger."

CHAPTER 21

THE JAVA ARCHIVER: jar

The `jar` tool manages *Java ARchive* files—compressed hierarchical archives modeled after the ZIP file format. Jar files contain class and resource files for an application or extension and can include a manifest containing metadata and digital signatures.

Applications can be run, and extensions loaded, from jar files referenced in the class path and (in JDK1.2) referenced by the `java -jar` option or installed in the standard extensions directory. Jar files are also the standard way to package multiple-class applets for deployment on the Web.

Running jar

The `jar` command line offers options similar to those for the UNIX Tape ARchiver (`tar`) utility, with modes to support creation, update, listing, and extraction of archives.

Synopsis:

```
jar [-green | -native] c [vfm0M] [<jarfile>] [<manifest>] [-C <dir>] <files>
jar [-green | -native] u [vfm0M] [<jarfile>] [<manifest>] [-C <dir>] <files>
jar [-green | -native] t [vf0] [<jarfile>] [<files>]
jar [-green | -native] x [vf0] [<jarfile>] [<files>]
```

Platform: SDK1.2, SDK1.1

The first form of the jar invocation creates a new archive file, whereas the second form updates an existing archive. The specified <*files*> are placed in the archive; if a directory is specified, it and its contents are recursively added. The use and position of the <*jarfile*> and <*manifest*> arguments are related to the use of the options, see the following list of options.

The third form of the jar invocation lists the contents of an archive, and the fourth form extracts the contents from an archive. If any <*files*> are specified, they are listed or extracted. Otherwise, *all* files in the archive are listed or extracted. The files are extracted into a hierarchical directory structure reflecting that of the archive.

Options:

- 0—(zero) Disable compression of the archive entries. If not specified, archive entries are compressed using ZIP-style compression.
- -C (SDK1.2 only)— Change directory to the specified <*dir*> before processing the <*files*>. For example, if the root of your project class hierarchy is the classes/ subdirectory, build an archive with the command:

  ```
  jar cvf /tmp/myproject.jar -C classes .
  ```

  (Recalling the discussion in the "Classes Loaded from Archive Files" section of Chapter 14, "Configuring the Linux JSDK/JRE Environment," the archive must be created relative to the root of the class hierarchy. The SDK1.1 jar, lacking the -C option, requires you to change directory (cd) to the classes/ directory before creating the archive.)
- f—Specify a jar file on which to operate. If none is specified, input operations (t, x) operate on stdin, output operations (c) on stdout, and input/output operations (u) read a jar file from stdin and write a jar file to stdout.

  A <*jarfile*> parameter is supplied to jar if and only if this option has been specified. If the m option is also specified, the order of the <*jarfile*> and <*manifest*> parameters must match the order in which the f and m options were specified.
- -green—Force the JVM running jar to use the Sun "green" thread emulation package, which is a user-space emulation of kernel threading. If specified, this must be the first option on the command line.
- m—Specify a manifest file to be placed into the archive. If this option is not specified, jar creates a default manifest file.

  A <*manifest*> parameter is supplied to jar if and only if this option has been specified. If the f option is also specified, the order of the <*jarfile*> and <*manifest*> parameters must match the order in which the f and m options were specified.
- M—Do not include a manifest file in the archive.
- -native—Force the JVM running jar to use the "native" platform thread API. If specified, this must be the first option on the command line.
- v—Run jar in verbose mode.

For Further Reading

The SDK1.1 and SDK1.2 documentation bundles include relevant documentation on the following pages:

jar	docs/tooldocs/solaris/jar.html
Jar Guide	docs/guide/jar/jarGuide.html
Manifest and Signature Specification	docs/guide/jar/manifest.html

Summary

This chapter has presented the Java ARchiver, `jar`. The Java archive format, in defining a compressed, self-contained, self-describing repository, lets you easily package entire applications and applets for distribution and for deployment on Web servers.

CHAPTER 22

THE JAVA NATIVE CODE HEADER AND STUB FILE GENERATOR: `javah`

The `javah` utility is one of the primary tools for Java Native Interface (JNI) development. It generates the C and C++ header files you need to support native code that can be called from Java.

Running `javah`

Given one or more Java classes containing declarations for `native` methods, the `javah` invocation generates header files for use by the native source files.

Synopsis:

```
javah [-green ¦ -native] [<options>] <classes>
```

Java has historically supported two different approaches for integrating native code with Java code—the Native Method Interface (NMI) and the Java Native Interface (JNI). You can use `javah` to support either, but you should be aware that the newer JNI is the path to long-term supportability while NMI is headed toward obsolescence.

We will explore the details of interfacing with native code in Chapter 55, " JNI: Mixing Java and Native Code on Linux."

Platform: SDK1.2, SDK1.1

Options:

- `-bootclasspath` *<path>* (SDK1.2 only)—Set the class path for core classes looked up by `javah`.
- `-classpath` *<path>*—Set the class path for all classes (SDK1.1) or user classes (SDK1.2) looked up by `javah`.
- `-d` *<dir>*—Place output files in the specified directory. If this option is not specified, `javah` places its output files in the current directory. Do not combine with the `-o` option.
- `-force` (SDK1.2 only)—Force output files to always be written. If this option is not specified, `javah` will not rewrite output files that it believes to be current with respect to the classes from which they were generated. (The default behavior is evidently intended to avoid triggering unnecessary rebuilds of the native code.)
- `-green`—Force the JVM to use the Sun "green" thread emulation package, which is a user-space emulation of kernel threading. If specified, this must be the first option on the command line.
- `-help`—Print out a list of command-line options.
- `-jni`—Generate headers for the JNI interface. This is the default behavior of SDK1.2. If this option is not specified for SDK1.1, `javah` generates NMI headers.
- `-native`—Force the JVM to use the "native" platform thread API. If specified, this must be the first option on the command line.
- `-o` *<file>*—Specify an output file. Normally, output is placed in one or more files whose names are derived from the class names. If this option is specified, all output is concatenated into a single file. Do not combine with the `-d` option.
- `-old` (SDK1.2 only)—Generate header files for the old NMI interface. This is the default behavior of SDK1.1. If this option is not specified for SDK1.2, `javah` generates JNI headers.
- `-stubs`—Generate C/C++ program stubs. This is only relevant for the NMI interface. If this option is used under SDK1.2, you must also specify the `-old` option.
- `-td` *<dir>* (SDK1.1 only)—Specify a directory (overriding the default `/tmp`) for `javah` to place its temporary files.
- `-trace` (SDK1.1 only)—Add tracing information to the stubs file.
- `-v` (SDK1.1) and `-verbose` (SDK1.2)—Generate verbose output.
- `-version`—Print `javah` version information.

javah_g

Platform: SDK1.1

This is a non-optimized version of **javah**, suitable for running under a debugger. Invocation and use is identical to **javah**.

For Further Reading

The SDK1.1 and SDK1.2 documentation bundles include relevant documentation on the following page:

javah	docs/tooldocs/solaris/javah.html

Summary

This chapter has presented **javah**, the header file generator for support of interfacing between Java and native code. In Chapter 55, "JNI: Mixing Java and Native Code on Linux," we will further explore the interface, discuss specific requirements for Linux, and present an example of its use.

CHAPTER 23

THE JAVA DOCUMENTATION GENERATOR: javadoc

The javadoc tool generates HTML documentation from Java source files. It is the tool used by Sun to generate the extensive class reference in the SDK documentation bundles.

Running javadoc

The javadoc invocation can be applied to individual source files or, most conveniently, to entire packages.

Synopsis:

```
javadoc [-green | -native] [<options>] [<packages>] [<sources>] [@<files>] (SDK1.2)
javadoc [-green | -native] [<options>] [<packages>] [<sources>] (SDK1.1)
```

The javadoc tool is Sun's answer to the perennial problem of documenting your interfaces. It reads Java source files and generates many files of API documentation. It's almost magic—free documentation!—except that it does require some developer help to generate useful documents. It looks for comments, in a stylized format, to explain the API being documented. We'll describe and illustrate with an example later in the chapter.

The capabilities of javadoc grew substantially between SDK1.1 and SDK1.2. The SDK1.1 version was a self-contained utility. SDK1.2, on the other hand, is built on top of *doclets*, an extensible architecture for document formatting. The *standard doclet* shipped with the SDK1.2 javadoc supports HTML generation; other doclets could potentially support Windows help files or XML output.

The optional SDK1.2 @<*files*> argument allows you to read command-line options from a file instead of a (possibly very long) javadoc command line.

Platform: SDK1.2, SDK1.1

Options:

- -1.1 (SDK1.2 only)—Emulate SDK1.1 behavior. SDK1.2 javadoc output has changed substantially from SDK1.1. If you need to generate the old format, this option swaps in a doclet class that produces 1.1-style output.
- -author—Include @author paragraphs from the source code comments. (This option is built in to SDK1.1, and provided by the standard doclet in SDK1.2.)
- -bootclasspath <*pathlist*> (SDK1.2 only)—Override the class path used by the JVM for loading boot classes.
- -classpath <*pathlist*>—Specify class path for loading all classes (SDK1.1) or user classes (SDK1.2).

  This path is also searched for the source files if a -sourcepath option (discussed later in this list) is not specified.
- -d <*directory*>—Specify a directory in which to place the javadoc output. Defaults to the current directory. (This option is built in to SDK1.1, and provided by the standard doclet in SDK1.2.)
- -doclet <*class*> (SDK1.2 only)—Specify a doclet class to use instead of the standard doclet. This allows you to generate output in some format other than HTML. If you use a different doclet class, built-in javadoc options will still be supported, but options provided by the standard doclet (such as -d) may no longer be supported or even be meaningful.
- -docletpath <*path*> (SDK1.2 only)—Specify a class path for finding doclet class files.
- -docencoding <*name*>—Specify the encoding to be used for javadoc output. (This option is built in to SDK1.1, and provided by the standard doclet in SDK1.2.)
- -encoding <*name*>—Specify the encoding used in the source files.
- -extdirs <*dirlist*> (SDK1.2 only)—Specify an alternate location for the JDK1.2 extensions directory.
- -green—Force the JVM to use the Sun "green" thread emulation package, which is a user-space emulation of kernel threading. If specified, this must be the first option on the command line.
- -help—Print a list of options.
- -J<*flag*>—Specify an option to be passed to the JVM running javadoc. This option is passed, with the -J stripped, to the java application launcher that runs javadoc.
- -locale <*name*> (SDK1.2 only)—Specify the locale to be targeted for javadoc output.
- -native—Force the JVM to use the "native" platform thread API. If specified, this must be the first option on the command line.

- `-nodeprecated`—Do not include `@deprecated` information from the source code comments. (This option is built in to SDK1.1, and provided by the standard doclet in SDK1.2.)
- `-noindex`—Do not generate a class index. (This option is built in to SDK1.1, and provided by the standard doclet in SDK1.2.)
- `-notree`—Do not generate a class hierarchy list. (This option is built in to SDK1.1, and provided by the standard doclet in SDK1.2.)
- `-overview` *<file>* (SDK1.2 only)—Specify an externally authored file to be added to the `javadoc` overview page.
- `-package`—Generate documentation on public, protected, and package-accessible classes and members.
- `-private`—Generate documentation on all classes and members.
- `-protected`—Generate documentation on public and protected classes and members. This is the default behavior.
- `-public`—Generate documentation only on public classes and members.
- `-sourcepath` *<pathlist>*—Specify a path to search for source files. If not specified, defaults to the class path.

Note

Source files must reside in a hierarchy that reflects the package name whether or not you use the `-sourcepath` option. For purposes of generating documentation, `javadoc` finds source files the same way the Java class loader finds class files (see Chapter 14, "Configuring the Linux JSDK/JRE Environment," in the section "Classes Loaded from File Systems").

- `-verbose` (SDK1.2 only)—Generate verbose output to the terminal.
- `-version`—Include `@version` information from the source code comments. (This option is built-in to SDK1.1, and provided by the standard doclet in SDK1.2.)

Options for the Standard doclet

These options, usable on the SDK1.2 `javadoc` command line, are specific to the standard doclet used to generate the default output format. Some of these reflect options that were built in to the SDK1.1 `javadoc` and migrated to the standard doclet in SDK1.2.

- `-author`—Include `@author` paragraphs from the source code comments.
- `-bottom` *<html-code>*—Specify HTML to be included at the bottom of each generated page.

Note

With the `-bottom` and other options (`-doctitle`, `-footer`, and `-header`) that specify HTML on the command line, the *`<html-code>`* may contain spaces and characters such as <, >, and &, that are interpreted by `bash` or other command shells. You can protect this argument from the shell by enclosing it in single quotes. For example:

```
javadoc -bottom '<B>My Footer</B>'
```

Everything between the single quotes is passed to `javadoc` without interpretation by the shell, except for the single-quote character itself and the backslash. You can pass a single quote within the argument by preceding it with a backslash:

```
javadoc -bottom '<B>A Single-Quote \' Here</B>'
```

And you can pass a backslash by preceding it with another backslash:

```
javadoc -bottom '<B>A Backslash \\ Here</B>'
```

- `-d` *`<directory>`*—Specify a directory in which to place the `javadoc` output. Defaults to the current directory.
- `-docencoding` *<name>*—Specify the encoding to be used for `javadoc` output.
- `-doctitle` *`<html-code>`*—Specify HTML to be included at the top of the overview summary file.
- `-footer` *`<html-code>`*—Specify HTML to be included at the bottom of each generated page, to the right of the lower navigation bar.
- `-group` *<name>* *<p1>*:*<p2>*—In a `javadoc` project documenting more than one package, this option specifies groupings of packages under broad categories. The information is used in laying out the overview page.
- `-header` *`<html-code>`*—Specify HTML to be included at the top of each generated page.
- `-helpfile` *`<file>`*—Specify an externally authored help file to be linked to the "HELP" buttons on the top and bottom navigation bars in the generated pages.
- `-link` *`<url>`*—Specify an existing set of `javadoc` documentation for purposes of cross-referencing. If the documentation you are currently generating contains references to classes described in the existing *`<url>`*, `javadoc` will include HTML links to the existing documentation wherever those references occur.

  For example, if this option references a URL containing `javadoc` output for the core classes, then any reference to core classes/members in the generated pages will be linked to the appropriate location in the existing core class documentation.
- `-linkoffline` *`<url>`* *`<packageListUrl>`*—Specify an existing *offline* set of `javadoc` documentation for purposes of cross-referencing. This is a variant of the `-link` option. Normally, the `-link` option causes the standard doclet to examine a *package-list* file, found at the target *`<url>`*, listing the packages described in the documentation. The standard doclet uses the information in that list to derive the correct links into that

documentation. If the list is unavailable (perhaps missing, or you do not have current access to *<url>*), you can provide your own and reference it with the *<packageListUrl>* argument to the **-linkoffline** option.

- **-nodeprecated**—Do not include **@deprecated** information from the source code comments.
- **-nodeprecatedlist**—Do not generate documentation for deprecated classes.
- **-nohelp**—Do not include the HELP link in the top and bottom navigation bars on the generated pages.
- **-noindex**—Do not generate a class index.
- **-nonavbar**—Do not generate top and bottom navigation bars in the generated pages.
- **-notree**—Do not generate a class hierarchy list.
- **-splitindex**—Split the class index file into multiple files—one for entries starting with "A," one for "B," and so on. This is a useful option for large libraries: if not specified, the index occupies a single (possibly very large) page.
- **-stylesheetfile** *<path>*—Specify a cascading style sheet (**.css**) file to be associated with the documentation. If none is specified, **javadoc** generates a default.
- **-use**—Generate "use" pages that describe each class's and package's customer. In other words: who uses this class?
- **-version**—Include **@version** information from the source code comments.
- **-windowtitle** *<text>*—Specifies the window title for the documentation—the title that will appear on the window title bar while the documentation is being browsed. If not specified, defaults to the **-doctitle** value.

javadoc Source

The source material for **javadoc** is provided by stylized comments in Java source code. These comments, delimited by the sequence **/**** and ***/**, are placed immediately before the item (class, interface, or member) being described. This information will end up in an HTML document, and should follow the authoring conventions for well-formed HTML. As with any HTML document, it should use HTML escapes for any magic characters appearing in the text (for example, **<** for the < character). The **javadoc** comments for a class, interface, or field, begin with a single-line description in HTML. This is followed by a detailed multiline description in HTML. This is followed by *tags* that provide specific, detailed information about the API being documented—inputs, outputs, exceptions, cross-references, and so on. When **javadoc** generates its output, it organizes the tags into relevant sections of the document.

The next section of this chapter provides an example of the use of **javadoc** tags, and an illustration of how they appear in the output documentation. Here are the tags currently supported by **javadoc**:

- @author *<name>*—Identify the author of this part of javadoc documentation.
- @deprecated *<text>*—Identify a class member as deprecated and not intended for current use. The *<text>*, which can include an explanation or a pointer to another class or member, is included in a bold, italicized message with the API description.
- @exception *<class> <description>*—Describe an exception class thrown by this method. The *<description>* text appears in the javadoc output as an explanation of the exception.
- {@link *<target> <text>*} (SDK1.2 only)—Insert an inline link into the documentation, containing *<text>* as the linked text. The *<target>* can either be a URL or a reference to another package, class, or class member. The @link tag can appear anywhere in javadoc source (see Note).

Note

If the *<target>* field in a {@link} or @see tag is a reference to another package, class, or class member, it takes the general form *<package>.<class>#<member>*, with one or more fields specified. Possible forms of the *<target>* field include:

- *<package>* (for example, java.lang)
- *<class>* (for example, Object)
- *<package>.<class>* (for example, java.lang.Object)
- #*<member>* (for example, #toString())
- *<package>.<class>#<member>* (for example, java.lang.Object#toString())

The details of turning this reference into a link and a URL are automatically handled by javadoc.

- @param *<param-name> <description>*—Describe a parameter passed to this method.
- @return *<description>*—Describe the return value of this method.
- @see "*<quoted string>*"—Describe a related piece of information, which will appear in the "see also" section of the javadoc output. According to Sun, this form of @see is broken in JDK1.2 and should not be used (see Note).
- @see *<markup>*—Describe a related piece of information. The *<markup>* field is HTML markup describing a link (see Note). For example:

```
@see <a href="http://foo/bar">Foo Bar</a>
```

- @see *<target>* [*<label>*]—Describe a related piece of information (see Note). The *<target>* field is a reference to a package, class, or class member, of the form *<package>.<class>#<member>*.
- @since *<text>*—Describe when this component was added to the API. Example: @since JDK1.1 .
- @serial [*<field description>*] (SDK1.2 only)—Document a default serializable field, and include an optional description of the field. This tag allows javadoc to generate a specification for the serial representation of a class.

- `@serialField` *`<fieldname>`* *`<fieldtype>`* *`<field description>`* (SDK1.2 only)—Document an `ObjectStreamField` component.
- `@serialData` *`<data description>`* (SDK1.2 only)—Document data written by `writeObject()` when an object is serialized.
- `@throws` *`<class>`* *`<description>`* (SDK1.2 only)—Describe an exception thrown by this method. The *`<description>`* text appears in the `javadoc` output as an explanation of the exception. This tag is as synonym for `@exception`.
- `@version` *`<text>`*—Add a "version" subheading to generated documentation.

Example

Listings 23.1 and 23.2 contain a modest example to illustrate basic operation. Our two-class "Hello World" project is full of comments for `javadoc`.

LISTING 23.1 `Hello.java` Source

```
package com.bogus;
import java.io.*;

/**
 * This class is responsible for generating the important "Hello"
 * message, as well as for instantiating and exercising another
 * class that generates the "World" message.
 *
 * @author Nathan Meyers
 * @see com.bogus.World
 */
public class Hello
{
    /**
     * The output writer.
     */
    protected PrintWriter pwriter;
    /**
     * The instance of the World class we will exercise.
     */
    protected World world;
    /**
     * Construct a Hello object capable of outputting to the specified
     * PrintWriter.
     *
     * @param pw The PrintWriter to write to.
     */
    public Hello(PrintWriter pw)
    {
    pwriter = pw;
    world = new World(pw);
```

continued on next page

continued from previous page

```
        }
        /**
         * Say the magic word.
         *
         * @return Nothing!
         */
        public void print()
        {
        pwriter.print("Hello ");
            world.print();
        }
        /**
         * The main() method for the application.
         */
        public static void main(String[] argv)
        {
        PrintWriter pw = new PrintWriter(new OutputStreamWriter(System.out));
            (new Hello(pw)).print();
        pw.close();
        }
}
```

LISTING 23.2 `World.java` Source

```
package com.bogus;
import java.io.*;

/**
 * This class generates the much-beloved "World" message.
 */
public class World
{
        /**
         * The output writer.
         */
        protected PrintWriter pwriter;
        /**
         * Simple World constructor.
         *
         * @param pw The PrintWriter to write to.
         */
        public World(PrintWriter pw)
        {
        pwriter = pw;
        }
        /**
         * Say the magic word.
         */
        public void print()
        {
        pwriter.println("World");
        }
}
```

To build our documentation, we place these files into a class hierarchy reflecting the package name, build a destination directory, and invoke the SDK1.2 `javadoc` on the package name:

```
bash$ mkdir -p com/bogus
bash$ cp *.java com/bogus
bash$ mkdir /tmp/javadoc
bash$ javadoc -sourcepath . -d /tmp/javadoc com.bogus
```

The result is a documentation tree (see Figure 23.1).

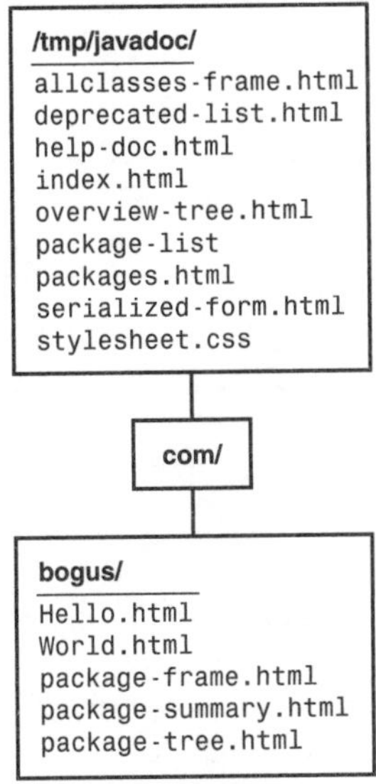

FIGURE 23.1
`javadoc` documentation tree.

Figure 23.2 shows the browser entry to the documentation.

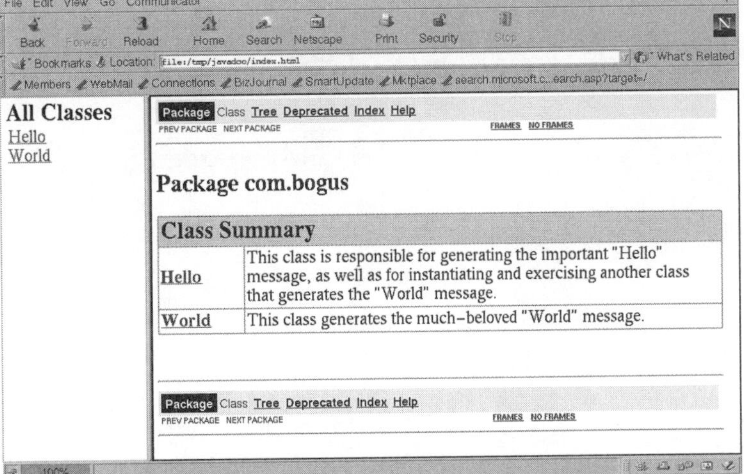

FIGURE 23.2
Main documentation page for our package.

For Further Reading

The SDK1.1 and SDK1.2 documentation bundles include detailed `javadoc` documentation on the following pages:

`javadoc`	`docs/tooldocs/solaris/javadoc.html`
`javadoc` enhancements (SDK1.2 only)	`docs/tooldocs/javadoc/index.html`
An overview of doclets (SDK1.2 only)	`docs/tooldocs/javadoc/overview.html`
The standard doclet (SDK1.2 only)	`docs/tooldocs/javadoc/standard-doclet.html`
How to write Doc comments for `javadoc`	Javadoc product page at `http://java.sun.com`.

Summary

This chapter has presented `javadoc`, Sun's standard tool for generating Java API documentation. By defining a standard format for adding documentation to code, the `javadoc` approach simplifies the generation of API documents and allows advanced tools (such as integrated development environments and rapid application development tools) to add automated documentation support.

CHAPTER 24

MISCELLANEOUS SDK DEVELOPMENT TOOLS

Having covered the important day-to-day tools, this chapter briefly mentions some others to be found in the Blackdown SDK.

Java Class File Disassembler: `javap`

The `javap` tool dumps information on classes and, optionally, generates a disassembled bytecode listing of class contents.

Usage

The `javap` invocation operates on one or more classes found in the class path.

Synopsis:

```
javap [-green ¦ -native] [<options>] <classes>
```

This tool is useful for dumping detailed information about class contents. It provides both the ability to dump class structures and to disassemble method bytecodes.

While `javap` can be invaluable for certain tasks (we make good use of it in chapter 38, "Generic Java Compilers," in the section "Retrofitting"), it suffers two noticeable shortcomings:

- It provides no information about inherited class members. In Chapter 47, "DumpClass: A Tool for Querying Class Structure," we present an alternative tool that addresses this problem.
- It tends to crash when disassembling bytecodes. Many alternative decompilation tools are available to do the job, including one discussed in Chapter 46, "Jad: A Java Decompiler."

Platform: SDK1.2, SDK1.1

Options:

- `-b`—Enforce backward compatibility with older versions.
- `-bootclasspath` *<pathlist>* (SDK1.2 only)—Specify the class path to be searched for root classes.
- `-c`—Generate a disassembly listing.
- `-classpath` *<pathlist>*—Specify the class path for all (SDK1.1) or user (SDK1.2) classes.
- `-extdirs` *<dirs>* (SDK1.2 only)—Specify an alternate location for the JDK1.2 extensions directory.
- `-green`—Force the JVM to use the Sun "green" thread emulation package, which is a user-space emulation of kernel threading. If specified, this must be the first option on the command line.
- `-help` (SDK1.2 only)—Print a list of options.
- `-J`*<flag>*—Specify an option to be passed to the JVM running `javap`. This option is passed, with the `-J` stripped, to the `java` application launcher that runs `javap`.
- `-l`—Dump tables of line number and local variable information.
- `-native`—Force the JVM to use the "native" platform thread API. If specified, this must be the first option on the command line.
- `-package`—List public, protected, and package-accessible classes and methods.
- `-private`—List all classes and methods.
- `-protected`—List public and protected classes and methods.
- `-public`—List public classes and methods.
- `-s`—Print type signatures (in internal Java format) for class members.
- `-verbose`—Print information on stack size and local variables for methods.

- `-verify` (SDK1.1 only)—Run the bytecode verifier on classes. (In SDK1.2, use "`java -verify`", as discussed in Chapter 17, "The Java Application Launchers: `java`, `jre` and `oldjava`").
- `-version` (SDK1.1 only)—Print `javap` version information.

For Further Reading

The SDK1.1 and SDK1.2 documentation bundles include `javap` documentation on the following page:

javap	docs/tooldocs/solaris/javap.html

Java Standard Extension Checker: `extcheck`

The `extcheck` utility checks an extension jar file for conflicts with any existing installed extensions—a worthwhile sanity check before installing a new extension.

Usage

The `extcheck` invocation checks the Java archive specified on the command line. Because the check is based on metadata stored in the archive's manifest, `extcheck` will fail for jar files not containing this metadata.

Synopsis:

```
extcheck [-green ¦ -native] [-verbose] <jarfile>
```

Platform: SDK1.2

For Further Reading

The SDK1.2 documentation bundle includes `extcheck` documentation on the following page:

extcheck	docs/tooldocs/solaris/extcheck.html

Source Code Character Set Converter: `native2ascii`

The `native2ascii` utility supports translation between the character sets used locally and the standard universal Unicode character set used by Java to encode textual information. *Unicode* is a superset of the old American Standard Code for Information Interchange (ASCII)—hence the name.

Usage

The **native2ascii** invocation allows you to convert from locale-specific native encoding to Unicode, or to perform a reverse conversion from Unicode to native.

Synopsis:

```
native2ascii [-green ¦ -native] [-reverse] [-encoding <encoding>] [<inputfile>
[<outputfile>]]
```

Platform: SDK1.2, SDK1.1

For Further Reading

The SDK1.1 and SDK1.2 documentation bundles include **native2ascii** documentation on the following page:

```
native2ascii            docs/tooldocs/solaris/native2ascii.html
```

Class Serial Version Number Generator: serialver

The **serialver** utility supports *serialization*—the ability to represent a complete object as a sequence of bytes for storage, retrieval, and transmission. Serialized objects are sensitive to class structure; any changes to a class can break compatibility between the class definition and a serialized instance of the class.

The use of serial version IDs avoids compatibility disasters by associating a unique number—based on class name and structure—with serialized objects. If class structure changes, its serial version ID also changes and incompatibilities with older serialized objects are easily detected.

Usage

The **serialver** invocation takes a class name and generates a line of Java source code—a definition of the **serialVersionUID** variable that you can include in the class source. Note that you can only use **serialver** on classes that implement the **java.io.Serializable** interface.

Synopsis:

```
serialver [-green ¦ -native] -show¦<class>
```

Although normally a batch tool, **serialver** supports an option, **-show**, that runs a GUI for interactive use.

Platform: SDK1.2, SDK1.1

For Further Reading

The SDK1.1 and SDK1.2 documentation bundles include **`serialver`** documentation on the following page:

`serialver    docs/tooldocs/solaris/serialver.html`

CORBA Support: `tnameserv`

JDK1.2 introduced core Java support of the Common Object Request Broker Architecture (CORBA) for use of distributed services. That support consists of classes for creation of CORBA clients and servers (the `org.omg.CORBA.*` packages and classes) and the utility described here.

One of the core services in a CORBA environment is ***name services***, used for locating objects in the CORBA space. SDK1.2 provides a sample implementation of a simple COS (*Common Object Services*) name server.

Usage

The **`tnameserv`** invocation starts up the COS server. Once running, the server handles requests for registration and location of services.

Synopsis:

```
tnameserv [-green ¦ -native] [-ORBInitialPort <port>]
```

The server listens at TCP port 900, unless overridden with the **`-ORBInitialPort`** option.

Platform: SDK1.2

Where's the IDL Compiler?

An important component of CORBA developer support is an Interface Description Language (IDL) compiler, for mapping generic CORBA interface descriptions to the language interfaces used in a particular CORBA implementation. Sun's version of such a tool, **`idl2java`**, is a native-code product that is not currently available for Linux. There do not appear to be any substitutes available; IDL compilers are closely coupled to their accompanying CORBA implementations, so IDL compilers from other vendors will not work.

Until a Linux-usable version of **`idl2java`** is available, you can either avoid the use of Sun's JDK1.2 CORBA implementation (many fine free and commercial third-party ORBs are available) or use a Microsoft Windows or Solaris version of the compiler.

For Further Reading

The SDK1.2 documentation bundle includes **`tnameserv`** documentation on the following page:

`tnameserv    docs/guide/idl/jidlNaming.html`

RMI Support: `rmic`, `rmid`, `rmiregistry`

The Remote Method Invocation (RMI) is Sun's network protocol for support of distributed objects. The general idea is similar to CORBA—objects can invoke other objects' methods and pass data, in an architecture-neutral format, over the network. But the RMI specification is much simpler than CORBA and is designed for the specific needs of Java.

The Java core classes include the necessary components for implementing RMI client and server objects. The tools described here, variously supplied with the SDK and JRE, provide development-side support and deployment-side network infrastructure for implementing an RMI-enabled application.

RMI Stubs/Skeleton Generator: `rmic`

Objects designed to provide RMI-based services must implement the `java.rmi.Remote` interface, an empty interface whose only purpose is to advertise that a class is intended for RMI use.

For such classes, the `rmic` utility generates *stub* and *skeleton* classes that provide client-side and server-side (respectively) methods for requesting and providing services. For every class requested in the `rmic` invocation, two new `.class` files containing the stub and skeleton methods are generated.

Synopsis:

`rmic [-green | -native] [<options>] <classes>`

Platform: SDK1.2, SDK1.1

Options:

- `-classpath <path>`—Specify the class path to search for all classes (SDK1.1) or user classes (SDK1.2).
- `-d <directory>`—Specify a destination directory for the generated classes and sources. The output files will be placed into a file hierarchy representing the package hierarchy of the classes they describe. If this option is not specified, all generated files will be placed in the current directory.
- `-depend`—Perform some dependency analysis, causing recompiles for classes that are out-of-date relative to other classes.
- `-g`—Include debugging information in the generated class files.
- `-green`—Force the JVM to use the Sun "green" thread emulation package, which is a user-space emulation of kernel threading. If specified, this must be the first option on the command line.
- `-J<flag>`—Specify an option to be passed to the JVM running `rmic`. This option is passed, with the `-J` stripped, to the `java` application launcher that runs `rmic`.

- `-keep` and `-keepgenerated`—Keep the generated intermediate `.java` source files. If not specified, only the `.class` files are generated. Source files are placed into the same location as their corresponding `.class` files.
- `-native`—Force the JVM to use the "native" platform thread API. If specified, this must be the first option on the command line.
- `-nowarn`—Disable compiler warnings.
- `-v1.1` (SDK1.2 only)—Create stubs and skeletons that conform to the JDK1.1 stub protocol.
- `-v1.2` (SDK1.2 only)—Create stubs and skeletons that conform to the JDK1.2 stub protocol.
- `-vcompat` (SDK1.2 only)—Create stubs and skeletons that support both JDK1.1 and JDK1.2 stub protocols.
- `-verbose`—Generate verbose output.

RMI Activation System Daemon: `rmid`

JDK1.2 added a new capability: automatic RMI object activation. The RMI Daemon (`rmid`) provides the necessary infrastructural support by handling requests for activation.

Synopsis:

```
rmid [-green | -native] [-port <num>] [-log <dir>] [-stop] [-C<option>]
```

Platform: SDK1.2, JRE1.2

Options:

- `-C<option>`—Specify a command-line option to be passed (with the `-C` stripped) to processes spawned by `rmid`.
- `-green`—Force the JVM to use the Sun "green" thread emulation package, which is a user-space emulation of kernel threading. If specified, this must be the first option on the command line.
- `-log <dir>`—Specify a directory in which `rmid` will keep its logs. If this option is not specified, the default is the current directory in which `rmid` was started.
- `-native`—Force the JVM to use the "native" platform thread API. If specified, this must be the first option on the command line.
- `-port <port#>`—Specify a listening port, overriding the default TCP port 1098.
- `-stop`—Stop the daemon listening at the default or specified (`-port`) port number.

RMI Activation System Daemon: `rmiregistry`

RMI environments require a registry service to support server registration and client location of services. The `rmiregistry` utility provides such a service.

Synopsis:

```
rmiregistry [<port>]
```

If a port is not specified, `rmiregistry` listens at TCP port 1099.

Platform: SDK1.2, JRE1.2, SDK1.1, JRE1.2

For Further Reading

The SDK1.1 and SDK1.2 documentation bundles include documentation on RMI and its tools on the following pages:

`rmic`	`docs/tooldocs/solaris/rmic.html`
`rmid` (SDK1.2 only)	`docs/tooldocs/solaris/rmid.html`
`rmiregistry`	`docs/tooldocs/solaris/rmiregistry.html`
RMI information	`docs/guide/rmi/index.html`

Security Administration Tools: `jarsigner`, `javakey`, `keytool`, `policytool`

These tools, in various incarnations in SDK1.1 and SDK1.2, support the Java security mechanisms for distribution of signed, trusted applications. The application signatures created and managed by these tools interact with the permissions granted in a JDK deployment environment (see Chapter 14, "Configuring the Linux SDK/JRE Environment," in the section "Security Settings").

Note that these tools do not support signing of applets or extensions for Web browsers from Netscape and Microsoft. These are browser-specific issues, and are addressed by tools and techniques supplied by Netscape (`http://developer.netscape.com:80/docs/manuals/signedobj/`) and Microsoft (`http://www.microsoft.com/Java/security/default.htm`).

Jar Digital Signature Tool: `jarsigner`

The `jarsigner` utility administers digital signatures in a jar file. Combined with `keytool`, which is discussed later, it comprises the main toolset for managing signatures and signing applications under JDK1.2.

Synopsis:

```
jarsigner [-green ¦ -native] [<options>] <jarfile> <alias>
jarsigner [-green ¦ -native] -verify [<options>] <jarfile>
```

Platform: SDK1.2

Options:

- `-certs`—Increase verbosity of `-verify -verbose` operation by including information on each certificate stored.
- `-green`—Force the JVM to use the Sun "green" thread emulation package, which is a user-space emulation of kernel threading. If specified, this must be the first option on the command line.
- `-internalsf`—Store an internal copy of the signature file.
- `-keypass` *<password>*—Specify a password for private key protection.
- `-keystore` *<url>*—Specify location of the keystore. Defaults to user's personal keystore in `~/.keystore`.
- `-native`—Force the JVM to use the "native" platform thread API. If specified, this must be the first option on the command line.
- `-sectionsonly`—Do not include a header in the jar file's `.SF` signature file. Defaults to the alias name if not specified.
- `-sigfile` *<file>*—Specify a base name for the jar file's signature files.
- `-signedjar` *<file>*—Specify a new name for the signed version of the jar file. If not specified, overwrites the original jar file.
- `-storepass` *<password>*—Set a signature for access to the keystore.
- `-storetype` *<type>*—Specify the type of keystore.
- `-verbose`—Generate verbose output.
- `-verify`—Verify the signatures in the jarfile.

JDK1.1 Key Administration Tool: `javakey`

The `javakey` utility manages keys and digital signatures in archive files under JDK1.1. Its functionality is superceded in JDK1.2 by `jarsigner` and `keytool`. The underlying security mechanism is replaced with an entirely new mechanism in JDK1.2.

Synopsis:

```
javakey [-green¦-native] -c <identity> [true¦false]
javakey [-green¦-native] -cs <signer> [true¦false]
javakey [-green¦-native] -dc <certfile>
javakey [-green¦-native] -ec <idOrSigner> <certnum> <certoutfile>
javakey [-green¦-native] -ek <idOrSigner> <pubfile> [<privfile>]
```

```
javakey [-green¦-native] -g <signer> <algorithm> <keysize> [<pubfile>] [<privfile>]
javakey [-green¦-native] -gc <directivefile>
javakey [-green¦-native] -gk <signer> <algorithm> <keysize> [<pubfile>]
➥[<privfile>]
javakey [-green¦-native] -gs <directivefile> <jarfile>
javakey [-green¦-native] -ic <idOrSigner> <certsrcfile>
javakey [-green¦-native] -ii <idOrSigner>
javakey [-green¦-native] -ik <identity> <keysrcfile>
javakey [-green¦-native] -ikp <signer> <pubfile> <privfile>
javakey [-green¦-native] -l
javakey [-green¦-native] -ld
javakey [-green¦-native] -li <idOrSigner>
javakey [-green¦-native] -r <idOrSigner>
javakey [-green¦-native] -t <idOrSigner> [true¦false]
```

Platform: SDK1.1, JRE1.1

JDK1.2 Key Administration Tool: `keytool`

The `keytool` utility manages a repository of keys and digital signatures.

Synopsis:

```
keytool [-green¦-native] -certreq [<options>]
keytool [-green¦-native] -delete -alias <alias> [<options>]
keytool [-green¦-native] -export [<options>]
keytool [-green¦-native] -genkey [<options>]
keytool [-green¦-native] -help
keytool [-green¦-native] -identitydb [<options>]
keytool [-green¦-native] -import [<options>]
keytool [-green¦-native] -keyclone -dest <dest_alias> [<options>]
keytool [-green¦-native] -keypasswd [<options>]
keytool [-green¦-native] -list [<options>]
keytool [-green¦-native] -printcert [<options>]
keytool [-green¦-native] -selfcert [<options>]
keytool [-green¦-native] -storepasswd [<options>]
```

Platform: SDK1.2, JRE1.2

Options:

- `-alias` *<alias>*—Specify alias for this keystore entry (`certreq`, `export`, `genkey`, `import`, `keyclone`, `keypasswd`, `list`, `selfcert`).
- `-dname` *<dname>*—Specify the distinguished name (`genkey`, `selfcert`).
- `-file` *<cert_file>*—Specify certificate (`.cer`) file (`export`, `import`, `printcert`).
- `-file` *<csr_file>*—Specify certificate signing request (`.csr`) file (`certreq`).
- `-file` *<idb_file>*—Specify JDK1.1 Identity Database (`.idb`) file (`identitydb`).
- `-green`—Force the JVM to use the Sun "green" thread emulation package, which is a user-space emulation of kernel threading. If specified, this must be the first option on the command line.

- `-keyalg` *<keyalg>*—Specify the name of the key algorithm (`genkey`).
- `-keypass` *<keypass>*—Specify password to protect the private key (`certreq`, `dest`, `genkey`, `import`, `selfcert`).
- `-keypass` *<old_keypass>*—Specify the private key password to be changed (`keypasswd`).
- `-keysize` *<keysize>*—Specify the size (in bits) of the key to generate (`genkey`).
- `-keystore` *<keystore>*—Specify the location of the keystore (defaults to `~/.keystore`) (`alias`, `certreq`, `dest`, `export`, `genkey`, `identitydb`, `import`, `keypasswd`, `list`, `selfcert`, `storepasswd`).
- `-native`—Force the JVM to use the "native" platform thread API. If specified, this must be the first option on the command line.
- `-new` *<new_keypass>*—Specify the new private key password (`dest`, `keypasswd`).
- `-new` *<new_storepass>*—Specify the new keystore password (`storepasswd`).
- `-noprompt`—Do not interact with the user (`import`).
- `-rfc`—Output the certificate in the text format described by the RFC1421 standard (`export`, `list`).
- `-sigalg` *<sigalg>*—Specify the algorithm to be used for the signature (`certreq`, `genkey`, `selfcert`).
- `-storepass` *<storepass>*—Specify the password for the keystore (`alias`, `certreq`, `dest`, `export`, `genkey`, `identitydb`, `import`, `keypasswd`, `list`, `selfcert`, `storepasswd`).
- `-storetype` *<storetype>*—Specify the type of the keystore (`alias`, `certreq`, `dest`, `export`, `genkey`, `identitydb`, `import`, `keypasswd`, `list`, `selfcert`, `storepasswd`).
- `-trustcacerts`—Add the certificates in the central JDK1.2 certificate store to the chain of trust (`import`).
- `-v`—Run with verbose output.
- `-validity` *<valDays>*—Specify a validity period (in days) for the certificate. (`genkey`, `selfcert`).

JDK1.2 GUI-Based Policy Administration Tool: `policytool`

This tool provides a GUI for manipulation of the JDK1.2 java.policy security file (see the "Security Settings" section in Chapter 14) and individual user policy files.

Synopsis:

```
policytool [-green ¦ -native] [-file <file>]
```

Platform: SDK1.2, JRE1.2

For Further Reading

The SDK1.1 documentation bundle includes documentation on JDK1.1 security administration and its tools on following pages:

`javakey`	`docs/tooldocs/solaris/javakey.html`
Java security	`docs/guide/security/index.html`

The SDK1.2 documentation bundle includes documentation on JDK1.2 security administration and its tools on following pages:

`jarsigner`	`docs/tooldocs/solaris/jarsigner.html`
`keytool`	`docs/tooldocs/solaris/keytool.html`
`policytool`	`docs/tooldocs/solaris/policytool.html`
Java security	`docs/guide/security/index.html`

Summary

This chapter has provided a quick reference to SDK tools that, while perhaps not as heavily used as those described in earlier chapters, play important roles in the development and deployment of Java applications.

PART VI

ADDITIONAL JAVA RUNTIME ENVIRONMENTS

Thus far, we have focused on the basic component that puts Linux in the Java business: the Sun JDK.

Despite the vast quantity of available Sun Java software, the true story of Java's acceptance can be seen in the wealth of Java activity beyond Sun's walls (and sometimes beyond its reach), from cleanroom JVMs to development systems to language extensions.

In this part, we examine alternative runtime environments—solutions that do not depend on the Blackdown JDK or, in some cases, on any Sun-supplied software. Some of these are available and usable today (Kaffe, IBM SDK); others are promising projects—not yet ready for prime time but offering the promise of vendor-neutral Java (Japhar, GNU Classpath). We'll also take a look at some promising new JVM approaches (ElectricalFire, HotSpot) and some native-compiled Java solutions (`gcj`, TowerJ).

CHAPTER 25

THE IBM JDK PORT

The IBM JDK port for Linux is a port of the Sun Java SDK to the Linux platform. As of this writing, IBM's offering consists only of an SDK1.1, but will undoubtedly grow to include JRE1.1, SDK1.2 and JRE1.2 offerings.

Platforms: SDK1.1

IBM is one of Java's most vocal boosters and may hold the distinction of shipping the most JDK ports of any major vendor. It supports Java on OS/2, OS/390, AS/400, AIX, VM/ESA, and Microsoft Windows. In mid-1999, IBM added Linux to the mix, releasing its own Linux JDK to the world.

The IBM Linux JDK is (as of this writing), released through the IBM AlphaWorks site—http://alphaworks.ibm.com. To find it, navigate from the home page to the AlphaWorks *technology* page and look for Java offerings. The product is shipped as a compressed binary tarball, and installation and configuration is similar to that for the Blackdown JDK.

The major differences between the IBM and Blackdown JDKs are as follows:

- Based on current observation, Blackdown will tend to have technology available sooner than IBM. (It is unclear whether this pattern, established with early releases, will continue.)
- Blackdown supports a larger variety of Linux configurations; the IBM release targets only the Linux 2.2 kernel with glibc 2.1.

- The IBM release ships for native threads only; Blackdown supports native and green threads.
- The IBM release incorporates proprietary IBM technology for garbage collection, JIT, and possibly other areas. These should introduce performance gains over the vanilla Sun code in the Blackdown port, and early results have been promising.
- The structure of the product trees are virtually identical, except that the IBM JDK uses directories named `linux/` for native components, whereas the Blackdown JDK uses directories named for the target platform architecture (`i386/`, for example).

System Requirements

The IBM JDK requires Linux kernel 2.2, glibc version 2.1 (see Chapter 13, "Blackdown: The Official Linux Port," in the section "An Important Note About `libc`") and support of the X Window System. A static version of the Motif toolkit is linked into the product, so there is no dependence on a shared Motif library.

If an application does not use the AWT, the IBM JVM will run without any dependencies on the AWT libraries or shared X11 libraries—meaning, as with the Blackdown port, that it is usable for non-graphics applications in server environments without the X Window System.

The AlphaWorks Linux JDK Web Site

All software distributed by IBM's AlphaWorks site includes its own FAQ, discussion area, description of system requirements, and download links.The Web-based discussion forum is the center of the IBM/Linux/JDK community. This is the place to ask questions, help other users, and make your voice heard.

Summary

This chapter has discussed the IBM port of the Sun JDK to Linux. Just as IBM has found helping Linux to be in its commercial interests, other vendors will certainly follow suit and we can expect more good proprietary technologies to find their way to Linux. It is anyone's guess what this means in the long term—which vendors will help Java succeed on Linux, and what role the Blackdown organization will play. But the trend bodes well for Java's success on the Linux platform.

CHAPTER 26

KAFFE: A CLEANROOM JAVA ENVIRONMENT

Kaffe is a cleanroom implementation of the Java runtime environment.

Platform: Almost JRE1.1

The Open Source revolution has created a plethora of brave new business models hardly imagined when Java first appeared. Transvirtual Technologies, Inc., (`http://www.transvirtual.com`) is one such example: a company that makes its living by both selling and giving away its work.

Transvirtual's technology is Kaffe, a cleanroom implementation of Java, developed entirely from specs without any licensed Sun code. The company earns its income by licensing and porting its technology for use in embedded environments: handhelds, smart cards, appliances, and the like. It also gives away its technology, under GPL terms, in the form of JDK implementations for desktop computers.

Kaffe enjoys the distinction of support on the largest number of desktop CPUs (i386, Sparc, Alpha, Motorola 68K, PowerPC, MIPS, PA-RISC, and StrongARM) and operating systems (including Linux, FreeBSD, HP-UX, Solaris, OSF/1, AmigaOS, AIX, Irix, and more) of any Java implementation.

Transvirtual's product line consists of Kaffe Custom Edition (the commercial product) and Kaffe Desktop Edition (the GPL product). Kaffe is nominally a PersonalJava environment—it claims full compliance with current PersonalJava specs—but it also implements substantial portions of JDK1.1 and a few parts of JDK1.2 in its JVM and core libraries.

Transvirtual grabbed some headlines with a mid-1999 announcement about one capability exceeding that of the Sun JDK. In collaboration with Microsoft, it has enhanced Kaffe with multiplatform versions of Microsoft's Java extensions. With Kaffe, you can run Microsoft's extended Java code (which, technically and legally speaking, is not considered to be Java) on many platforms.

Obtaining and Installing Kaffe

Kaffe is freely available from Transvirtual's Web site (`http://www.transvirtual.com`), from the Kaffe Web site (`http://www.kaffe.org`), and from many software repositories. It is also distributed, in RPM form, with Red Hat and other Linux distributions.

The source distribution from the Kaffe Web site is built with GNU's `autoconf` technology, and is easily unpacked and built on Linux (see Chapter 8, "Installing Additional Linux Software," in the section "Compressed Tarball Source Distribution"). RPMs and Debian packages are also available for both source and binaries; installation is straightforward.

The one caution to note is that the Kaffe distributions are configured to install their components (including executables named `java`, `javac`, `javadoc`, and so on) in standard locations, such as `/usr/bin` and `/usr/lib`, or `/usr/local/bin` and `/usr/local/lib`. If you are also using another Java environment on your system, ***be sure*** to set up your environment to consistently use one Java at a time (see Chapter 14, "Configuring the Linux JSDK/JRE Environment," in the section "Accommodating Multiple Java Installations"). This includes ensuring that the proper executables are found first in the `$PATH`. Running Sun's JVM with Kaffe's core classes, or vice versa, creates some remarkably strange and confusing problems.

Contents of the Kaffe Distribution

Here are the installation locations for the Red Hat Kaffe RPM. If you build instead from the Kaffe source distribution, the default target is `/usr/local/*`, which you can override with configuration options.

- Core executables in `/usr/bin`: `appletviewer`, `install-jar`, `jar`, `java`, `javac`, `javadoc`, `javakey`, `javap`, `jdb`, `kaffe`, `kaffeh`, `kfc native2ascii`, `report-kaffe-bug`, `rmic`, `rmiregistry`, `serialver`.
- Documentation, including FAQs, developer information, and licensing terms, in `/usr/doc/kaffe-`*<ver>*`/`, where *<ver>* is the current version number.
- C/C++ header files for use with JNI in `/usr/include/kaffe/`.
- Shared libraries for all native components, including AWT, I/O, math, and networking, in `/usr/lib/kaffe/`.
- A `kaffe` man page in `/usr/man/man1/`.
- Kaffe core class files in `/usr/share/kaffe/`.

The entire installation, as of this writing, takes a tidy 4MB.

System Requirements and Dependencies

Kaffe requires a Linux 2.*x* system. If you run AWT applications, you will need X Window System library support on the system. The AWT is implemented without any dependence on Motif or any other GUI libraries.

Dependence on libc version is determined entirely by the system on which Kaffe is built. If you build Kaffe from a source distribution, then you will have a version appropriate for your system. If you obtain an RPM, the `rpm` tool should prevent you from installing a version you cannot run.

Comparisons to the Sun JDK

The Java specifications cover the language, class format, core libraries and extensions, and JVM—in essence, the environment in which Java applications run. They do not cover implementation details, configuration, development environment, or tools. We will do some brief comparisons here and in the next several sections.

Kaffe Performance

Kaffe is slick and compact. Overall performance is very good, and startup performance is considerably faster than that of the Sun JDK.

Kaffe Tools

Kaffe is primarily a runtime environment, not a development kit. It does supply a few tools (described later in the chapter, in the section "Kaffe Tools"), as well as scripts to launch the customary Sun SDK tools from Sun's SDK class libraries if they are available.

Does Kaffe Swing?

Yes! Put the JFC Swing 1.1 class library in your class path or install it as an extension jar file, and you have full use of Swing GUI components.

Configuring Kaffe

Almost none of the Sun-related configuration information (see Chapter 14) is relevant to configuring Kaffe. The following sections explain how Kaffe does it.

Specifying the Class Path

Kaffe uses an enhanced JDK1.1 model for finding classes—a single class path for everything (see the section "JDK1.1 Class Path Construction" in Chapter 14 for a discussion of Sun's JDK1.1 model). The class path is specified for application execution in one of two ways:

- Fully specified with a `-classpath` option to the application launcher
- Specified by `$CLASSPATH`, to which Kaffe automatically appends its core class library (`Klasses.jar`), its extension class libraries, and, if found, `classes.zip`. (Kaffe does not ship a `classes.zip`—you can add Sun's SDK1.1 `classes.zip` here by copying or linking it into Kaffe's `share/kaffe/` directory.)

Kaffe has one JDK1.2-style class path enhancement: a `-jar` option that launches an application from a jar file.

No Configuration Properties Files

Kaffe does not rely on any configuration properties files such as `font.properties`. Configuration is performed by a `java.awt.Defaults` class bundled in the core classes. You can override the defaults by building your own `java.awt.Defaults` class and placing it before the core libraries in the class path.

If you need to build your own `java.awt.Defaults` class, the easiest approach is to copy and modify the source from the Kaffe distribution. The rationale for specifying defaults with a class instead of a file is speed, robustness, and avoiding the need for additional file system access at startup.

Configuring Security

Kaffe does not yet have a security manager to configure.

Kaffe Fonts

The standard logical font names—`Default`, `Monospaced`, `SansSerif`, `Serif`, `Dialog`, `DialogInput`, `ZapfDingbats`—are mapped to X Window System fonts in the `java.awt.Defaults` class (discussed in the earlier section, "No Configuration Properties Files"). All GUI components have reasonable default fonts, and any of those fonts can be obtained through the normal `java.awt.Font` constructors or factories (the names are *case-sensitive*).

In addition, Kaffe can open other X Window System fonts by family name. For example, if you have a Helvetica font installed in X, requesting a `helvetica-plain-12` in Java will give you a 12-point Helvetica font.

Kaffe also lets you open a font using the platform-specific X font name. These names are usable with the `java.awt.Font` constructor (see the following example), but not with methods that use the platform-neutral font name format (such as `Font.decode()`).

Example:

```
Font font = new Font("-adobe-utopia-bold-r-normal-0-200-75-75-p-0-
➥iso8859-1", Font.PLAIN, 0);
```

The second and third arguments, specifying style and size, are ignored—that information is already present in the X-style XLFD name. The most interesting fields are

- Family name (2nd field): `utopia`
- Weight (3rd field): `bold`
- Slant (4th field): `r` (`r`=roman, `i`=italic, `o`=oblique)
- Pointsize*10 (7th field): `200` (that is, 20 points)
- Horizontal and vertical display resolution (8th and 9th fields): `75` (specified in dpi)

A list of X fonts is available from the Linux `xlsfonts` utility. To use any of the fonts reported by `xlsfonts`, substitute your desired pointsize*10 and display resolution into the 7th through 9th fields. A pointsize of 0 defaults to 12 points; a display resolution of 0 defaults to your actual display resolution.

Adding JIT Compilers

Kaffe has JIT built in. External JIT compilers are not supported.

Environment Variables

Table 26.1 lists some variables that are meaningful in Kaffe.

TABLE 26.1 Environment Variables Affecting Kaffe Execution

Variable	Function
`CLASSPATH`	Class path for non-core components. Kaffe automatically appends entries for core components. If not specified, defaults to the current directory.
`KAFFE_DEBUG`	Used for debugging Kaffe. If set to `GDB`, runs Kaffe under the GNU debugger. If set to `GNU emacs` or `Xemacs`, runs Kaffe under the GNU debugger in an Emacs window.
`KAFFEHOME`	Optional. If set, should point to where Kaffe's core classes are installed (`/usr/share/kaffe` in the case of the Red Hat RPM).
`KAFFELIBRARYPATH`	Optional. If set, should point to where Kaffe's native shared libraries are installed (`/usr/lib/kaffe` in the case of the Red Hat RPM).

The `kafferc` File

Kaffe can optionally perform system- or user-specific initialization at startup. If a `share/kaffe/.kafferc` file exists in the Kaffe distribution directories and/or a `.kafferc` file exists in the user's home directory, Kaffe will source these files into its startup shell before launching the application.

Kaffe Tools

Kaffe includes enough tools to put you into the development and runtime business, but does not include a clone of everything found in the Sun SDK. The following sections discuss the tools included with Kaffe, as well as how you can use Sun's tools with Kaffe.

Kaffe's `java` Application Launcher

Application launch is similar to launching under JDK1.1, although several launcher options are not yet supported.

Synopsis:

```
java [<options>] <class>
```

A few interesting Kaffe-specific options (or Kaffe-specific behaviors) are

- `-classpath`—Specify the complete path for finding all classes: core, extension, user (*like* JDK1.1). If this option is not used, `$CLASSPATH` is honored and Kaffe automatically appends its core and extension classes (*unlike* JDK1.1, which does not automatically append classes).
- `-help`—Print a usage message, including information on which options are not yet supported.
- `-jar`—Run the application from a jar file.
- `-verbosejit`—Print verbose output on the activities of the built-in JIT compiler.

Kaffe's `appletviewer` Applet Tester

Like the Sun SDK, Kaffe includes a facility to test-drive applets under its own virtual machine.

Synopsis:

```
appletviewer <HTMLfile>
```

The invocation is different from Sun's SDK: The applet viewer will not load a URL, only a file.

Kaffe's `javac` Java Compiler

Kaffe bundles a Java compiler with its distribution- the Kopi compiler described in chapter 37, "The Kopi Java Compiler." Kaffe also includes a `javac` script that launches the Kopi compiler with the familiar `javac` command.

Synopsis:

```
_javac_[<options>]_<source_files>_
```

Kaffe's `kaffeh` JNI Stub Generator

Kaffe's `kaffeh` tool is the Kaffe-flavored version of Sun's `javah`. Like `javah`, `kaffeh` requires the `-jni` option to generate JNI-compatible header files; otherwise, it generates header files for the pre-JNI nonportable interface. `kaffeh` does not offer an option to generate a stub `.c` file.

Kaffe's `install-jar` Utility

This tool supports management of installed extensions.

Synopsis:

```
install-jar <jarfile>
```

The invocation runs a simple shell script that installs a jar file into Kaffe's `share/kaffe/` directory.

Running Non-Kaffe Tools

Kaffe does not ship its own versions of `jar`, `javadoc`, `javakey`, `javap`, `jdb`, `native2ascii`, `rmic`, `rmiregistry`, or `serialver`. It supplies scripts that launch them, under the Kaffe JVM, from Sun's SDK1.1 `classes.zip`. To use these tools, you must have that archive in the class path, or a copy of that archive (or symlink to it) in Kaffe's `share/kaffe/` subdirectory.

The Kaffe Site

Kaffe has its own development community, mailing list, `cvs` source tree (you can check out the current, up-to-the-second source), and JitterBug bug-tracking database—all found at the Kaffe Web site (`http://www.kaffe.org`). Developers who have not been tainted by conflicting licenses (such as the Sun Community License, discussed in Chapter 12, "Software Licensing," in the section "Sun Community Source License (SCSL)—Not Open Source") are welcome to contribute to ongoing Kaffe development.

Summary

This chapter has discussed Kaffe, a fully functional and widely available cleanroom implementation of the Java runtime. While creating Sun JDK ports on Linux and many other platforms has been slow and tortuous, Kaffe has demonstrated notable success in building working software and a working business with an open-source cleanroom implementation of the Java specifications.

CHAPTER 27

JAPHAR: A CLEANROOM JVM

Japhar is a free, open source Java Virtual Machine.

Platforms: <JRE1.1

A product of The Hungry Programmers (`http://www.hungry.com`), Japhar is a cleanroom JVM covered by the GNU LGPL. As of this writing, it is still in early development and nowhere near ready for production use.

Japhar's most direct competitor is Kaffe, discussed in Chapter 26, "Kaffe: A Cleanroom Java Environment." Here is a quick checklist of differences between the two:

- Kaffe works; Japhar is still in very early development.
- Kaffe is a full runtime environment; Japhar is only a JVM and requires separate core Java libraries. These separate libraries can come from the Sun JDK or elsewhere (see Chapter 28, "GNU Classpath: Cleanroom Core Class Libraries").
- Kaffe is associated with a commercial organization, which publishes an open source version under GPL licensing terms—you can obtain more favorable terms by buying a license. Japhar is noncommercial and released under LGPL, which offers you more latitude than GPL in how it can be deployed (see Chapter 12, "Software Licensing," in the section "The GNU LGPL").
- Kaffe does JIT compilation; Japhar currently does not.

- Japhar currently uses native threads; Kaffe does not.
- Kaffe's capabilities and rate of growth are determined largely by the business needs of its publisher, whereas Japhar focuses relentlessly on tracking the latest specs as quickly as possible.
- Kaffe has garbage collection; Japhar currently does not.

Obtaining and Installing Japhar

Japhar is distributed in source form from the project site, `http://www.japhar.org`. A link on the main page takes you to information on obtaining the code. You can grab the source in one of two ways:

- Download a compressed archive, unpack, and build—it uses GNU `autoconf` technology (see Chapter 8, "Installing Additional Linux Software," in the section "Compressed Tarball Source Distribution") for easy building.
- Check out current source from the project `cvs` tree. You need `cvs` (see Chapter 9, "Setting Up a Linux Development Environment," in the section "`cvs`") to access the project cvs repository. Use the techniques described in Chapter 9 in the section "`cvs` Remote Repository Servers" to obtain Japhar source. The necessary repository name, module name, and password are supplied on the Japhar site.

To build Japhar, you need a Linux 2.*x* development environment that includes development support—libraries and header files—for X and Motif. (For Motif, you can substitute the Hungry Programmers' Lesstif product, available from `http://www.lesstif.org` and also in package form from many repositories and Linux distributions.)

To build Japhar, you may also need a willingness to hack. Japhar is characteristic of many young projects: The build process is not entirely robust, is occasionally broken by recent changes, and has not been tested on a wide variety of configurations. You may need to hack source or Makefiles to succeed in building. The best source of information and help is the Japhar mailing list—see details on the Japhar home page.

After unpacking the archive or installing from `cvs`, you build Japhar with the customary `configure/make` sequence. The `configure` script has several options to determine what local facilities—X, Motif, an existing JDK—it should expect to find. Assuming that you have Motif and an existing JDK, the steps to building Japhar should look something like this:

```
bash$ ./configure —with-jdk=$(JAVA_HOME)
<...lots of output...>
bash$ make
<...lots of output...>
bash$ make install
<...lots of output...>
```

These steps will configure, build, and install Japhar in some standard `/usr/local/*` locations (you can override the default target locations by specifying the `-prefix=` option to the `configure` script).

The result of the `—with-jdk` option is to copy several components from the Sun JDK—core class libraries, configuration files, and so on—into Japhar's installation directories. It is recommended that you use JDK1.1. The option can also be used with JDK1.2, but Japhar's limited (to date) JDK1.2 support makes success less likely.

Contents of Japhar

A Japhar installation includes five subdirectories:

- `bin/`—This contains Japhar executables, including scripts to launch standard JDK applications from the JDK core class archives (see "Non-Japhar Tools," later in this chapter).
- `include/`—This contains header files to support native interfaces, including JNI and the Japhar Foreign Function Interface (FFI).
- `info/`—This contains documents formatted for the Linux `info` documentation system.
- `lib/`—This contains all of Japhar's native libraries. Included are the native components of AWT and other class libraries that require native components.
- `share/`—This contains all of Japhar's core and extension classes. When Japhar is configured with the `—with-jdk` option, core class libraries from the resident JDK are copied into this directory.

Configuring Japhar

Most Japhar configuration occurs when the build-time `configure` script is run: use `./configure —help` to see all the options.

The configuration controls you can exercise at runtime are

- The class path. This is specified in the usual way, through `$CLASSPATH` or a command-line option (`—classpath`). Japhar automatically *appends* any `.jar` and `.zip` archives found in its `share/` subdirectory to the class path. Japhar does not, however, include the share directory *itself* in the class path. If you have some classes (not contained in archives) rooted in that directory, you must add that directory to the specified class path.
- Various properties files in the `lib` subdirectory, copied from the Sun JDK at installation.

Available Japhar Tools

Japhar is a runtime tool—you will not find compilers or many other development tools in the distribution. This section describes what *is* included in a Japhar installation.

The japhar Application Launcher

The application launcher is called japhar, not java as in some other JVMs. It employs the double-dash command-line option format common with GNU applications.

Synopsis:

```
japhar [<options>] <class> [<args>]
```

Options:

- —classpath=<*classpath*>—Specify the search path for user classes. Note the use of — and =, unlike most other Java implementations. If this option is not specified, $CLASSPATH is used. In either case, Japhar automatically adds all .jar and .zip files found in its share/ subdirectory to the class path.
- —help—Print a usage message.
- —verbose:{gc|jni|class|method}—Turn on verbosity for garbage collection, JNI, class, and/or method activities. You can specify multiple items, separated by commas.
- —version—Print the Japhar version number.

The japharh Native Stub Generator

The japharh tool serves a function similar to javah: generating header and/or stub files—with an additional option to dump class information.

Synopsis:

```
japharh [<options>] <classes>
```

Options:

- -classpath=<*classpath*>—Specify the class path for user classes.
- -d=<*path*>—Specify a destination directory.
- -dump [-ascii]—Dump a disassembled version of the class file contents as unformatted text.
- -dump -html—Dump a disassembled version of the class file contents in HTML format.
- -header—Generate native headers for the classes requested on the command line. This is the default behavior if no options are specified.
- -help—Print a help message.
- -stubs—Generate native stubs files for the classes requested on the command line.
- -version—Print version information.

The `japhar-config` Tool

This tool generates information useful for native code that needs to interact with Japhar. The information it returns, such as compiler flags, link flags, and installation locations, can be used when compiling or linking native code intended to work with Japhar.

Synopsis:

`japhar-config` *<sub-command>*

Sub-commands (specify exactly *one* of the following):

- `–version`—Print version information.
- `–help`—Print a usage message.
- `–help` *<sub-command>*—Print more detailed information on a particular sub-command.
- `link`—Print link-line options to properly link the correct libraries.
- `link-jvmdi`—Print link-line options to properly link against the Japhar JVMDI implementation.
- `compile`—Print compile-line options for building native applications against Japhar.
- `info [`*<var>*`]`—Print a description of the various directories comprising the Japhar installation. Possible values for *<var>* are `includedir`, `mandir`, `infodir`, `libdir`, `localstatedir`, `sysconfdir`, `datadir`, `libexecdir`, `sbindir`, `bindir`, `prefix`, and `exec_prefix`. If *<var>* is specified (example: `japhar-config info bindir`), only that directory is described; otherwise, information is printed on all directories.
- `–prefix`—A backward-compatible synonym for the `info prefix` sub-command.
- `–exec-prefix`—A backward-compatible synonym for the `info exec-prefix` sub-command.
- `–libs`—A backward-compatible synonym for the `link` sub-command.
- `–cflags`—A backward-compatible synonym for the `compile` sub-command.

Non-Japhar Tools

Japhar does not ship its own versions of `appletviewer`, `extcheck`, `jar`, `jarsigner`, `javac`, `javadoc`, `javah`, `javakey`, `javap`, `jdb`, `keytool`, `native2ascii`, `policytool`, `rmic`, `rmid`, `rmiregistry`, `serialver`, or `tnameserv`. It supplies scripts of the same name that launch those tools, running under the Japhar JVM, from Sun's JDK1.1 `classes.zip` archive.

Japhar JDK Compatibility

Japhar is targeting JDK1.2 compatibility and, as an interim target, JDK 1.1 compatibility. It has not fully achieved either, but, as of this writing, its 1.1 compatibility is reasonably good and reporting a fairly high success rate in compatibility tests.

Summary

This chapter has examined Japhar, an open source clone of the Java Virtual Machine. Taken together, Japhar and the GNU ClassPath project (discussed in the next chapter) will comprise a full Java clone whose liberal licensing terms will let you deploy Java capabilities anywhere without encumbrance.

CHAPTER 28

GNU CLASSPATH: CLEANROOM CORE CLASS LIBRARIES

GNU Classpath is a cleanroom implementation of the JDK core classes.

Platform: <JDK1.1

The GNU *Classpath* project is, for the Java world, what the C library is for the C/C++ world: an attempt to create a freely available set of indispensable core classes for application use. It is initially targeted at the Japhar JVM (see Chapter 27, "Japhar: A Cleanroom JVM"). The combination of the two comprises a free, LGPL-licensed Java environment that you can modify, adapt, and redistribute without owing Sun any licensing fees.

GNU Classpath is a young project—as of this writing, the current release was 0.00. Trying to use Classpath is not, at present, for the faint of heart.

Obtaining and Installing Classpath

Classpath is distributed in source form from the project Web site, `http://www.classpath.org`. You can grab the source in one of two ways:

- Download a compressed tarball of the most recent release. It uses GNU `autoconf` technology (see Chapter 8, "Installing Additional Linux Software," in the section "Compressed Tarball Source Distribution") for easy building.

- Check out the current source from the project cvs tree. You need cvs (see Chapter 9, "Setting Up a Linux Development Environment," in the section "cvs") to access the project cvs repository. Use the techniques described in Chapter 9 in the section "cvs Remote Repository Servers" to obtain Classpath source. The Classpath home page contains the details on accessing the repository.

To build Classpath, you need a basic Linux 2.*x* C/C++ development environment. There are no dependencies on X or Motif development environments.

A word of caution: To build Classpath, you may also need a willingness to hack. Classpath is characteristic of many young projects: The build process is not particularly robust, is occasionally broken by recent changes, and has not been tested on a wide variety of configurations. Even when you succeed in building, the library may on any given day be nonfunctional, broken on certain Linux releases, or somehow incompatible with current Japhar versions. The best source of information and help is the Classpath mailing list—see details on the Classpath home page.

After unpacking the tarball or installing from cvs, you build Classpath with the customary configure/make sequence. The default behavior is to build binaries for use with Japhar and not to rebuild the .class files (which are included in the distribution). The configure script expects to find Japhar's bin directory in $PATH. It runs japhar-config (see the section "The japhar-config Tool" in Chapter 27) to collect information on Japhar's installed location:

```
bash$ ./configure
<...lots of output...>
bash$ make
<...lots of output...>
bash$ make install
<...lots of output...>
```

The make install step places Classpath directly into the Japhar installation. Native shared libraries are placed in Japhar's lib subdirectory, and the class library is installed under Japhar's shared subdirectory. The classes are not installed in a .zip or .jar archive but in a hierarchical tree on the file system.

Running Japhar/Classpath

After Classpath installs itself into the Japhar installation, you need to ensure that Japhar's shared directory is in the class path:

```
bash$ export CLASSPATH=/usr/local/japhar/shared:.
bash$ japhar ...
```

Because Japhar ***appends*** its installed .zip and .jar archives to the class path (see Chapter 27, in the section "Configuring Japhar"), it will find and use the Classpath classes before it finds the (possibly) installed Sun JDK class Classpathlibraries.

Classpath JDK Compatibility

The project's stated goal at present is for Classpath 1.0 to fully support JDK1.1 and largely support JDK1.2. Links on the Classpath home page point to information about the current state of compatibility.

Support for Other JVMs

Classpath is planning to support other JVMs but does not currently do so.

Summary

This chapter has discussed the GNU Classpath project. Although still in an early state, Classpath offers the promise of core Java class libraries whose open-source licensing terms will enable Java solutions on many more platforms than will ever be supported by Sun JDK ports.

CHAPTER 29

MOZILLA ELECTRICALFIRE: A NEW JVM

ElectricalFire is a cleanroom Java Virtual Machine from Netscape's Mozilla organization.

Platform: <1.1

One casualty of the shifting business sands under Netscape Corporation is ElectricalFire (EF), a canceled commercial product turned open source. EF started out as a commercial JVM, intended for mid-1998 release, and was canceled in early 1998 when Netscape made a strategic move away from Java. A year later, it was turned into an open source project under the auspices of Mozilla.org—the same organization developing new browser engines for Netscape Navigator and Communicator (`http://www.mozilla.org`).

EF is a cleanroom JVM, like Kaffe and Japhar, but it takes a novel approach to Java bytecode compilation. It *never* interprets Java bytecodes; it *always* compiles to native instructions before running a piece of code. EF does not even contain a bytecode interpreter. One rationale behind this design is the elimination of any behavior that differs between interpreted and compiled code. (Such differences may stem from interpreter bugs, JIT compiler bugs, or even application bugs that lead to race conditions or other speed/execution-order sensitivities. EF reduces the number of potential failure paths.)

The EF compiler is just-in-time: classes are compiled as they are needed. It currently offers a fairly complete x86 back-end code generator and partial implementations of code generators for PowerPC, PA-RISC, and Sparc architectures.

Looking beyond JIT compilation, EF is exploring the potential role of batch compilation, either during or before application startup. The primary advantages to be gained are to eliminate the performance "choppiness" caused by bursts of JIT activity, and to take advantage of global information that can lead to better optimization.

Current project status is, in the words of the Web site (http://www.mozilla.org/projects/ef/), "just starting to get interesting." The JVM passes many of the Java Compatibility Kit tests, meaning that it runs Java code pretty well, but it is still far from supporting the many Java classes that require native platform integration (AWT, among many others). The project team is hoping to be able to leverage GNU Classpath (see Chapter 28, "GNU Classpath: Cleanroom Core Class Libraries") to create a complete Java platform.

You can run EF today, using the Sun JDK1.2 libraries. Although capabilities are limited, it is possible to get past the important "Hello World" checkpoint.

Obtaining and Building ElectricalFire

The only way to get EF today is by checkout from a networked cvs tree (see Chapter 9, "Setting Up a Linux Development Environment," in the section "cvs Remote Repository Servers"). The Web site includes download and build instructions, available by following a link from the home page.

To build and use EF, you need a JDK1.2 installation (just the core classes), Perl, and a C/C++ Linux development environment. You need to check out two sections from the Mozilla cvs source tree: nsprpub (the Netscape Portable Runtime) and ef (the ElectricalFire source).

Instructions for using the Mozilla cvs repository are posted at http://www.mozilla.org/cvs.html. Note that you do *not* need to check out everything—just projects mozilla/nsprpub and mozilla/ef.

Building the Utility Libraries

We'll use $TOP to refer to the top of the checked-out cvs tree.

To build the nsprpub libraries, cd to the $TOP/mozilla/nsprpub directory and make. When you're finished, some shared libraries will have been placed into the $TOP/mozilla/dist/<*arch*>/lib directory, where <*arch*> is some name reflecting your current OS and architecture (for my current setup, <*arch*> is Linux2.2.5_x86_PTH_DBG.OBJ).

Building ElectricalFire

To prepare to build EF:

1. Set CLASSPATH to point to your JDK1.2 class libraries:

```
bash$ export CLASSPATH=/usr/local/Java/jdk1.2/jre/lib/rt.jar
```

2. Set LD_LIBRARY_PATH and LD_RUN_PATH to point to the directory containing the nsprpub libraries:

```
bash$ export LD_LIBRARY_PATH=$TOP/mozilla/dist/Linux2.2.5_x86_PTH_DBG.OBJ/lib
bash$ export LD_RUN_PATH=$TOP/mozilla/dist/Linux2.2.5_x86_PTH_DBG.OBJ/lib
```

($LD_RUN_PATH is used by the linker to locate libraries at link time.)

3. cd to the $TOP/mozilla/ef directory.

You're now ready to build ElectricalFire with make. Experience suggests that you may need to hack some Makefiles or source to successfully complete the build.

Running ElectricalFire

The build steps just described result in an executable, sajava, in the $TOP/mozilla/ef/dist/*<arch>*/bin directory, and some shared libraries in $TOP/mozilla/ef/dist/*<arch>*/lib. The executable, short for "StandAlone Java," is the application launcher—the replacement for java.

To run sajava, you need to tweak your environment a bit more:

1. Add the EF shared libraries to your LD_LIBRARY_PATH:

```
bash$ LD_LIBRARY_PATH=$LD_LIBRARY_PATH:\
$TOP/mozilla/ef/dist/Linux2.2.5_x86_PTH_DBG.OBJ/lib
```

2. Add the EF bin directory to your PATH:

```
bash$ PATH=$PATH:$TOP/mozilla/ef/dist/Linux2.2.5_x86_PTH_DBG.OBJ/bin
```

Now you're ready to run. EF uses the JDK1.1 model for CLASSPATH (see Chapter 14, "Configuring the Linux JSDK/JRE Environment," in the section "JDK1.1 Class Path Construction"). You need to include all core and user class path components: the JDK1.2 rt.jar archive and any directories from which you want to load extensions or application classes.

Synopsis:

```
sajava [<options>] <class>
```

Options:

Some of these options may be enabled only when EF is built with special configuration settings. Some options allow short-form abbreviations.

- -all—Compile all methods. (abbreviation: -a)
- -breakCompile *<className> <methodName> <signature>*—Set a debug breakpoint just before compiling the specified method. Method is specified by space-separated class name, method name, and signature. (abbreviation: -bc)

- `-breakExec` *<className> <methodName> <signature>*—Set a debug breakpoint just before executing the specified method. Method is specified by space-separated class name, method name, and signature. (abbreviation: `-be`)
- `-catchHardwareExceptions`—Catch all hardware exceptions—used in the debug builds only. (abbreviation: `-ce`)
- `-classpath` *<canonical class-path>*—Specify the full class path. (abbreviation: `-c`)
- `-debug`—Enable debugging.
- `-help`—Print a help message. (abbreviation: `-h`)
- `-lib` *<libname>*—Load the specified native shared library at `init` time. Library name is specified in the usual Java canonical format. (abbreviation: `-l`)
- `-logFile` *<filename>*—Specify the log file to use for the `-log` option. Can be interspersed with `-log` options, specifying a different log file for different logs. A value of `stderr` for the *<filename>* is also accepted. (abbreviation: `-lf`)
- `-log` *<module-name> <level>*—Turn on logging for a particular module. Higher *<level>* results in more detail. Log output defaults to `stderr` unless overridden by `-logFile`.
- `-logNames`—Print out a list of all modules for which logging can be enabled. (abbreviation: `-ln`)
- `-method` *<methodName> <sig>*—Specify a method and signature on which the `-stage` option is to operate. (abbreviation: `-m`)
- `-methodName` *<methodName>*—Specify a method on which the `-stage` option is to operate. This is a simpler form of `-method`, usable when a signature is not needed to disambiguate overloaded method names. (abbreviation: `-mn`)
- `-noinvoke`—Do not invoke the compiled method. This is implied if the compile stage (`-stage`) is anything other than `i`. (abbreviation: `-n`)
- `-nosystem`—Do not initialize system classes on startup. (abbreviation: `-nosys`)
- `-stage` {r|p|g|o|i}—Specify how much processing the compiler should do:
  - `r`—Read
  - `p`—Preprocess
  - `g`—Generate primitives
  - `o`—Optimize
  - `i`—Generate instructions

  Clearly, any setting other than `i` will not run your application. This option is intended for use with the `-method` or `-methodName` options, discussed previously, to specify a method to process for debugging or analysis of `sajava` behavior. (abbreviation: `-s`)

- -trace *<className> <methodName> <signature>*—Enable tracing for the specified method. Method is specified by space-separated class name, method name, and signature. (abbreviation: -t)
- -traceAll—Enable tracing for all methods. (abbreviation: -ta)
- -verbose—Run verbosely. (abbreviation: -v)

ElectricalFire and Netscape

Is ElectricalFire to become the official Netscape JVM?

The answer from Mozilla.org is a clear *no*. But as Netscape gains the capability to support any JVM through its OJI initiative (see Chapter 11, "Choosing an Environment: 1.1 or 1.2?," in the section "Option 2: Netscape Open Java Interface"), EF will become a usable choice with Netscape Navigator and Communicator.

Summary

This chapter has discussed ElectricalFire, an open source JVM from the Netscape Mozilla project. Beside providing an alternative free JVM, ElectricalFire offers an intriguing approach to runtime bytecode compilation and a worthwhile addition to the Java performance discussion.

CHAPTER 30

SUN HOTSPOT PERFORMANCE ENGINE

Sun's HotSpot Performance Engine is another approach to improving JVM performance.

Platforms: JDK1.2

Java performance has been steadily improving since its unfortunate early days. Sun's 1999 release of its HotSpot performance engine represents a significant overhaul of the JVM—targeted specifically at improving the performance story.

Sun initially positioned HotSpot as the solution to achieving parity with native C/C++ performance. That's not really possible (see Chapter 57, "Why Is Java Slow?"), and the boldest performance claims were quickly dropped in the face of reality, but HotSpot has certainly improved the Java performance picture.

As of this writing, HotSpot is not available for Linux. But Sun has announced plans to release the source code through its Sun Community Source License, which should eventually lead to Linux availability. This chapter takes a brief look at what HotSpot has to offer.

HotSpot's Dynamic Optimization

What is HotSpot? It's another JVM, like ElectricalFire (see Chapter 29, "Mozilla ElectricalFire: A New JVM"), but it takes a nearly opposite approach to bytecode compilation. Instead of compiling immediately, HotSpot defers any compilation of Java bytecodes until it has had an opportunity to run the application for a while and see where it spends its time. This approach allows it to collect global information on how classes, methods, and resources are used, and then concentrate its compilation and optimization efforts on the ***hotspots*** in the code.

Similar approaches are already used in C/C++ development, for example in ***Profile-Based Optimization*** (PBO). A typical PBO development cycle is as follows:

1. Build an instrumented version of the application.
2. Run the application with workloads representative of real-world problems, collecting detailed statistics on control flow and resource usage.
3. Rebuild the application, applying optimizations based on the statistics.

The steps applied during the rebuild include aggressive optimization of hotspots (heavily trafficked stretches of code), intra- and intermodule inlining, and rearranging module location to improve locality.

This sort of optimization works well, often dramatically so, but suffers some shortcomings:

- It adds a lot of work to the product build-release cycle.
- There is always some concern that a test workload may not accurately represent real deployment workloads, and that PBO may even detune the application for real-world use. (This problem is more psychological than real, but it does reduce the acceptance of PBO.)

Research continues in industry and academia into better solutions, with a strong focus on moving optimization from the factory to the field.

Java, of course, presents a unique environment for dynamic optimization, and HotSpot is Sun's approach. HotSpot incorporates the steps we described previously—instrumentation and optimization—into the runtime environment and concentrates its bytecode compilation efforts on performing advanced optimizations with the greatest return.

HotSpot's greatest gains are expected to be on the server side: Long-lived server processes give HotSpot time to perform its optimizations, and the application time to amortize the costs of runtime optimization and benefit from the results.[1]

[1]Sun reinforces its HotSpot server-side focus with a claim that client application performance is determined more by native platform facilities—system libraries, kernel, and GUI—than by JVM performance. This claim does not really hold up to competitive language benchmarking. Java's client-side performance problems stem from several causes, including JVM performance, memory requirements, and less-than-efficient use of the underlying window system. But the message is clear enough: HotSpot is not the performance solution we've been waiting for on the client side.

Other HotSpot Improvements

In addition to dynamic optimization, HotSpot has redesigned many of the JVM subsystems to address current Java bottlenecks:

- Object references use actual pointers instead of handles, eliminating one level of indirection whenever objects are dereferenced.
- Thread synchronization is faster.
- A shared stack between Java and native code reduces the cost of switching language contexts.
- Aggressive inlining by the optimizer, and lower call overhead for non-inlined methods, lowers the cost of method calls—a traditionally expensive component of object-oriented programs.
- New heap management, with faster allocation, smarter garbage collection (GC), and a reduction of "choppy" performance caused by GC activity, results in faster and better GC.

For more detail, visit the HotSpot product page (`http://java.sun.com/products/hotspot`) and view the white paper.

Summary

This chapter has discussed HotSpot, Sun's current approach to Java performance improvement. HotSpot's results on Microsoft Windows platforms have been encouraging, and its eventual availability on Linux should be good news for the Java/Linux performance story.

CHAPTER 31

gcj: A COMPILED JAVA SOLUTION

Gcj is a native-language Java compiler.

Platforms: <JDK1.1

All the solutions discussed so far have fully embraced the Java application model of interpreted bytecodes and dynamic loading of classes. The model is flexible but expensive: Interpretation is slow, and dynamic compilation is still a long way from delivering native-level performance.

An obvious alternative for some applications is to embrace the language, with its many advantages for developers, but live without some of the flexibility and portability: compile down to the native platform. You still enjoy the advantages of portable source (much more portable than C++), but gain dramatically in performance.

`gcj` is the familiar GNU C compiler, with a Java front end. It actually consists of two components:

- A Java compiler (`gcj`) that reads Java source or class files
- A runtime library (`libgcj`) to provide the core classes

In its current state (as of this writing), `gcj/libgcj` is a native-only solution that supports parts of JDK1.1. Some things it does not yet do are:

- Support all of JDK1.1.
- Support the AWT.
- Support loading and interpretation of bytecoded class files.

All these areas are under active development, however, and some may be in place by the time you read this.

Obtaining gcj and libgcj

The compiler and library are published by Cygnus Solutions, which is managing the development tree. Both are a part of the gcc compiler suite, and were first released as part of the 2.95 gcc release in summer of 1999.

To obtain gcj and libgcj, visit GNU compiler repositories managed by Cygnus (http://www.cygnus.com), GNU (http://www.gnu.org), or elsewhere, and obtain the compressed tarballs for gcc and libgcj—version 2.95 or later.

The gcc distribution is available either as a single distribution (gcc-*<version>*) or in pieces (gcc-core-*<version>*, gcc-gcj-*<version>*, and so on). The simplest solution is to obtain the single distribution. Unpack the gcc and libgcj tarballs into any convenient location.

gcj and libgcj are also maintained in publicly accessible cvs trees (see Chapter 9, "Setting Up a Linux Development Environment," in the section "cvs Remote Repository Servers") at Cygnus. Unless you wish to hack the latest source, working from published distributions is the way to go.

Building gcj and libgcj

We'll show some sample build procedures here. Because we're working with new compilers whose general usability with Linux is not yet established[1], we will build everything into an isolated sandbox that will not interfere with normal compiler and library use on the system.

Building gcc

After unpacking the gcc archive, everything will be in the gcc-*<version>* subdirectory.

The Cygnus source trees are designed to be built in a separate binary directory, not in the source tree. We create a sibling directory for the binaries and configure to build there. Note the recommended options (explained in the list following the code example):

```
bash$ bzip2 -d <gcc-2.95-tar.bz2 ¦ tar xvf -
<...lots of output unpacking into gcc-2.95/...>
bash$ mkdir gcc-2.95-bin
bash$ cd gcc-2.95-bin
```

[1] As of this writing, gcc v2.95 cannot be used to build the Linux kernel.

```
bash$ ../gcc-2.95/configure -prefix=/usr/local/Java/gcj \
-enable-java-gc=boehm -enable-threads=posix \
-enable-languages=java,c++ -enable-version-specific-runtime-libs
<...lots of output...>
```

Here are the recommended options, and why:

- `-prefix=/usr/local/Java/gcj`—Because we are building prerelease compilers, we specify a sandbox installation directory that will not interfere with normal system compilers.
- `-enable-java-gc=boehm`—This specifies the garbage collection mechanism that will be used (boehm is the default).
- `-enable-threads=posix`—This specifies the threading mechanism to use. Default is no threads, so this is an important option.
- `-enable-languages=java,c++`—These are the languages we need to build `libgcj`, as well as our own applications. We cannot use the regularly installed C++ compiler: It may not be compatible with this `gcj` and its libraries.
- `-enable-version-specific-runtime-libs`—This allows us to place the runtime support libraries in the sandbox with the compiler, rather than in standard system locations.

The remaining steps are familiar:

```
bash$ make
<...lots of output...>
bash$ make install
<...lots of output...>
bash$
```

The result will be an installation of `gcj` into our target directory (`/usr/local/Java/gcj`).

Building `libgcj`

With the new `gcc` available, we can now build `libgcj`. First set some important environment variables:

```
bash$ PATH=/usr/local/Java/gcj/bin:$PATH
bash$ export LD_LIBRARY_PATH=/usr/local/Java/gcj/lib
bash$ export LD_RUN_PATH=/usr/local/Java/gcj/lib
```

The configuration step is similar to that for the `gcc` build. In a directory outside of that containing the `gcc` build, enter the following commands:

```
bash$ bzip2 -d <libgcj-2.95-tar.bz2 ¦ tar xvf -
<...lots of output unpacking into libgcj-2.95/...>
bash$ mkdir libgcj-2.95-bin
bash$ cd libgcj-2.95-bin
bash$ ../libgcj-2.95/configure -prefix=/usr/local/Java/gcj \
-enable-java-gc=boehm -enable-threads=posix
<...lots of output...>
```

The options chosen for `prefix`, `enable-java`, and `enable-threads` must match the settings for the compiler.

Build and install the usual way:

```
bash$ make
<...lots of output...>
bash$ make install
<...lots of output...>
bash$
```

Compiling and Running Java Programs

`gcj` compiles both Java source and bytecoded class files. Because it does not handle all the modern *source* constructs (such as inner classes), the compiler works best with class files.

With the environment variables set as shown in the previous section,"Building `libgcj`," we can compile and run Java programs.

Synopsis:

```
gcj [<options>] <.java and .class files>
```

Options:

Options are similar to those of any other GNU compiler front end, with two important additions:

- `—main=`*`<class>`*—Specify the main class for the application (the class name you would normally specify to the `java` application launcher).
- `—CLASSPATH` *`<classpath>`* or `—classpath` *<classpath>*—Specify a class path to search during compilation. If not specified, the `CLASSPATH` environment variable is used. Note that this is compile-time behavior, and results in creating references that must be resolved by natively compiled classes at link time.

Example:

```
bash$ gcj -O -c Hello.class
bash$ gcj -O —main=Hello -o Hello Hello.o
bash$ ./Hello
Hello world
bash$
```

As with any program built by `gcc`, objects and executables can be built with optimization (`-O`) and/or debugging flags (`-g`), and programs can be debugged with source-level native debuggers such as `gdb`.

Subtleties

Class files can, somewhat confusingly, serve two purposes at once during compilation:

- If specified on the gcj command line, class files are compiled into native object files.
- Class files in the class path serve to resolve references generated by classes being compiled.

The two roles are disjoined, and some classes may be needed both on the command line and in the class path. For example, if you compile

```
gcj Foo.class Bar.class
```

and `Foo` has dependencies on `Bar`, then `Bar.class` must be found in the class path in order for `Foo.class` to successfully compile. It is not sufficient that `Bar.class` is also being compiled.

If class `Bar` is in a package, the usual class path rules apply: It must be found in a directory structure reflecting the package name.

Additional `gcj` Components

The `gcc` enhancements for Java include more than a new front end and the `libgcj` library. Three new utilities provide support for `gcj` development.

`jvgenmain`: `main()` Procedure Generator

This utility, called by `gcj` when the `-main` option is specified, generates a `main()` procedure—a basic requirement for native executables. The job of the native `main()` is to launch the `gcj` runtime and call the `main()` entry point in the specified Java class.

Synopsis:

`jvgenmain <classname> [<outputfilename>]`

`jvgenmain` is installed in the directory containing the `gcc` pipeline components (preprocessors and such) rather than the `bin/` subdirectory of the installation.

`gcjh`: Native Header File Generator

The counterpart of `javah`, `gcjh` generates header files to support C/C++ native implementations of Java methods.

Given the differences between the native `gcj` and normal Java environments, `gcj` does *not* use Java's JNI interface for calling C/C++ methods. It employs its own unique, fast native interface (the Cygnus Native Interface) well suited to fully native applications.

Synopsis:

`gcjh [<options>] <classes>`

Options:

- `-classpath <path>` or `-CLASSPATH <path>`—Specify the class path.

- -I<*dir*>—Append the specified directory to the class path.
- -d <*dir*>—Specify output directory name.
- —help—Print a help message.
- -o <*file*>—Specify output file name.
- -td <*dir*>—Specify directory to be used for temporary files.
- -v or -verbose—Run verbosely.
- —version—Report version number and terminate.

jcf-dump: Class File Dump Utility

This utility reads and dumps the contents of a class file in a readable and highly informative format.

Synopsis:

```
jcf-dump [-o <outputfile>] [-c] <class>
```

Options:

- -c—Disassemble the bytecodes.
- -o <*outputfile*>—Send results to specified file instead of stdout.

Summary

This chapter has presented gcj and libgcj, the GNU compiler components for support of native-compiled Java applications. The compiler and runtime are under active development, and are also a part of Cygnus' commercial Code Fusion product.

Given the importance and success of gcc, there is little doubt that gcj and libgcj will achieve high quality and functionality, and become important Java development and deployment tools in Linux and other environments.

CHAPTER 32

TOWERJ: A SERVER-SIDE HYBRID JAVA ENVIRONMENT

TowerJ is a high-end commercial Java runtime designed to support server-side Java.

Platform: JDK1.1

TowerJ is a commercial Java environment targeted at enabling the middle tier in three-tier client/server architectures (see Chapter 67, "Java, Linux, and Three-Tiered Architectures"). It is available for several server platforms including Linux, and focused on delivering extremely high performance.

TowerJ uses a hybrid approach to creating an execution environment, a combination of a run-time interpreter (such as JRE, Kaffe, ElectricalFire, HotSpot, and so on), native language static compilation (such as `gcj`, discussed in Chapter 31, "`gcj`: A Compiled Java Solution," and numerous products in the Microsoft Windows world), and a proprietary runtime engine that supports Java-like dynamic loading capabilities for native code.

Figure 32.1 contrasts the TowerJ approach to other standard approaches.

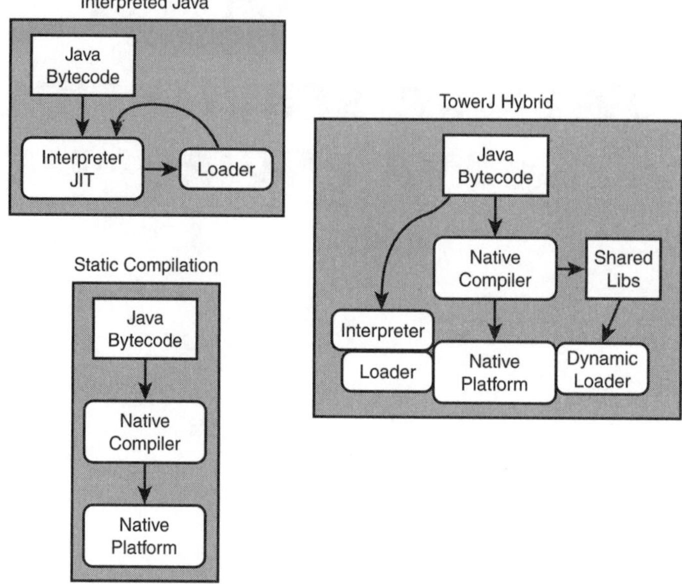

FIGURE 32.1
A comparison of three approaches to Java runtime.

The two standard approaches offer two extremes in the trade-off between performance and flexibility:

- Java interpreters offer the flexibility of the Java loading model but poor performance.
- Compiled Java offers the best performance but no dynamic loading of classes—a central Java feature.[1]

TowerJ implements a hybrid of these two approaches, targeting performance *and* flexibility. With TowerJ, the server application is statically compiled into native platform code by a fully optimizing compiler. Additional classes, outside the core application, can be compiled into their own shared libraries. The runtime can then dynamically load *class bytecodes* into an interpreter and *compiled class objects* in the form of shared libraries.

Obtaining TowerJ

TowerJ is available for download and purchase from TowerJ's Web site, `http://www.towerj.com`. You can obtain a free 15-day evaluation license if you want to test drive the product.

The product is distributed in the form of a *classball*—a single class file that encapsulates the product archives and an installer program. To install, just run the class file and answer the questions. You can install the product anywhere, although choosing a location other than the default (`/opt/TowerJ`) requires you to set an additional environment variable to run the product. The vendor supplies license keys and instructions for installation.

[1] `gcj` is moving toward supporting dynamic class loading.

TowerJ Installation Contents

The installation includes all the TowerJ executables and libraries, documentation, and binaries. The two important binaries are the following:

- `towerj`—A GUI-based project manager implemented in Java.
- `tj`—The TowerJ compiler, which can be invoked from the project manager or run from the command line.

TowerJ offers a nearly complete JDK1.1 environment, with AWT conspicuously absent—a reasonable configuration for a server-side solution. The absence of AWT is a licensing issue and may be addressed in future releases.

Product and Environment Dependencies

TowerJ has the following outside product dependencies:

- A JDK1.1 JVM and core classes (JRE1.1 is sufficient; you do not need SDK1.1).
- The `gcc` compiler.
- Swing 1.1, if you are going to use the **`towerj`** Project Manager.

The product also depends on the following environment variables:

- `TOWERJ`—Set to the directory containing the TowerJ installation; optional if TowerJ was installed in the default `/opt/TowerJ` directory.
- `PATH`—Must include the TowerJ `bin` directory (`$TOWERJ/bin/x86-linux`). (Naturally, it must also include the path components for the JDK and `gcc`.)
- `CLASSPATH`—Must include the JDK1.1 core classes. If you are going to use the TowerJ Project Manager, it must also include the Swing 1.1 classes.
- `LD_LIBRARY_PATH`—Must include the TowerJ `lib` directory (`$TOWERJ/lib/x86-linux`).
- `TOWERJ_TJLIB_PATH`—Search path for compiled class files (which are known as Tjlibs).

Running the TowerJ Project Manager

The Project Manager provides a GUI interface to drive all steps of building a server-side solution. Using the Project Manager is optional. Everything *can* be done with command-line interfaces, but we will use the Project Manager for illustration.

Synopsis:

```
towerj
```

We create a new project from the main window (see Figure 32.2) and choose a directory in which to run the project.

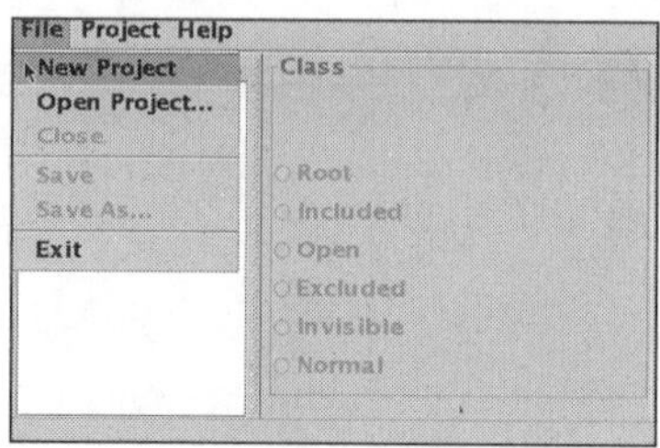

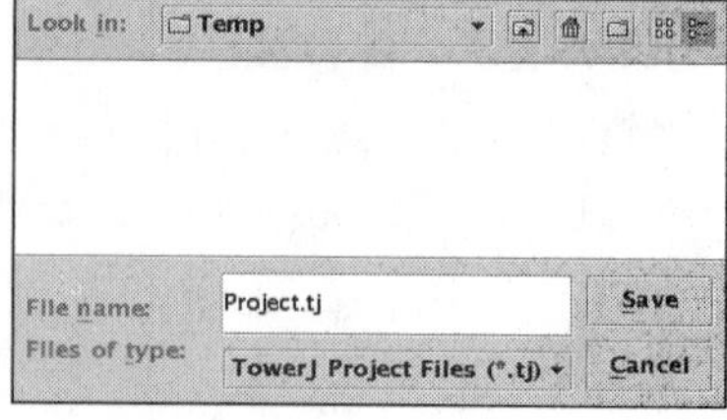

FIGURE 32.2
Starting a new project.

Sample TowerJ Projects

In the next several sections, we'll explore some simple TowerJ projects to illustrate the basic operation of the development and execution environment.

First Project: Hello World

The first project is the customary "Hello World" program, illustrating how to turn a simple Java application into a TowerJ application. In this project, as in those that follow, the application is first built as conventional Java classes by the SDK or comparable tools. The TowerJ development process will then generate TowerJ executables from the application and core Java classes.

Building the Program

After initially creating the project and its directory, TowerJ searches its entire class path and catalogs all the classes in the main window (see Figure 32.3). We see the core classes and another familiar class (built-in examples in earlier chapters) in the class path.

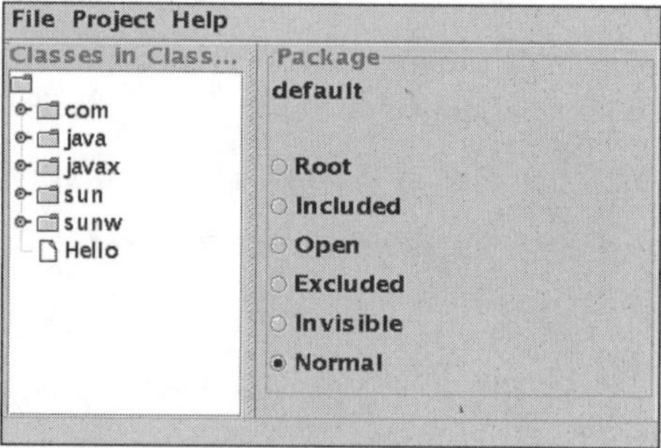

FIGURE 32.3
All the classes in our class path, displayed in a Swing JTree structure.

We are going to build a TowerJ application from the "Hello World" program, so we designate that class as the root class (see Figure 32.4).

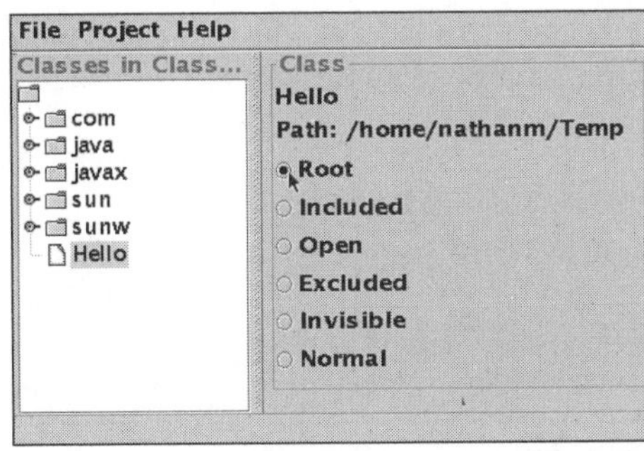

FIGURE 32.4
Specifying the root class: Select the class on the left and designate it as root.

It's now time to build the application. Selecting the `Build` button from the `Project` menu launches the process. We watch as TowerJ analyzes the root class and the class path and resolves all classes that will be loaded to run the root class. These classes are then compiled to native code, and an executable is built containing the complete application (see Figure 32.5).

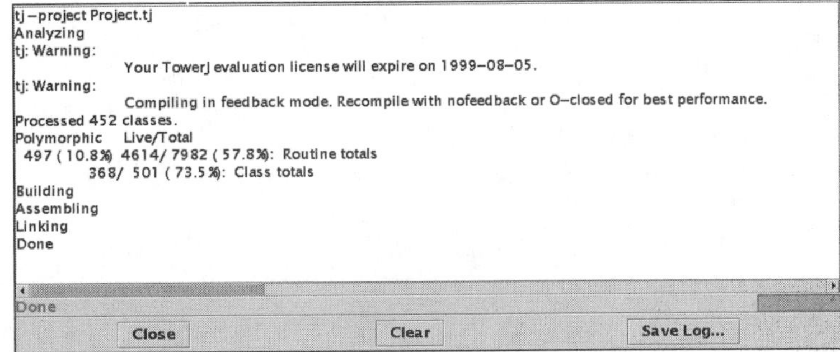

FIGURE 32.5
The build window reports on project build progress.

The result of this activity is an executable native program, `Hello`, that implements our Java program:

```
bash$ ./Hello
Hello world
```

Because all needed classes were compiled into native TowerJ components, the `Hello World` program has no dependencies on the Sun JDK. (It does, however, depend on TowerJ shared libraries that must be licensed and installed on a deployment host.)

Tuning the Program

We're not finished. The program is not yet deployable—rather, it is configured for the next phase of development, performance tuning.

We tune the program by running it under a variety of workloads and capturing runtime information. The program was built in *feedback mode*, with instrumentation to capture useful data.

Every run of the program generates a feedback file, with a `.tjp` suffix, reporting on class use. For this trivial example, the feedback files (shown in Listing 32.1) tell us that the application is already fully self-contained.

LISTING 32.1 First Project: Hello World Feedback

```
feedbackID=1
#--------------------------------------------.
# No classes were interpreted
#--------------------------------------------.
# No classes were loaded by custom class loaders
#--------------------------------------------.
# All classes were found.
#--------------------------------------------.
# No classes need be marked open
#--------------------------------------------.
# No 'dead' classes need be marked included
#--------------------------------------------.
# No invisible classes need be marked included
```

With this information on class usage, we can now rebuild the project with full optimization. Using the `Options` button in the `Project` menu, call up the options dialog, set No Feedback mode (see Figure 32.6), and rebuild. The feedback information (if any real information had been captured) is used for optimization purposes.

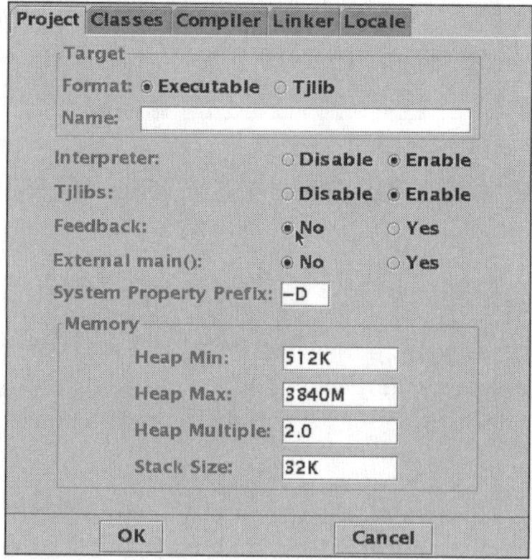

FIGURE 32.6
Preparing to build a final version.

The final version of the `Hello` executable is no longer instrumented and, of course, very fast.

Second Project: Dynamic Loading of Classes

Although the first project demonstrated basic operation, it did not exploit one of TowerJ's selling points: its capability to dynamically load classes into a running application. The second project illustrates how TowerJ identifies and optimizes additional classes needed at program runtime.

We rewrite our trivial example as shown in Listing 32.2.

LISTING 32.2 Second Project: Dynamic Loading of Classes

```
import java.util.*;

class Hello
{
    public static void main(String[] argv)
    {
        for (int i = 0; i < argv.length; i++)
        {
            Date date1 = new Date();
            Class cls;
            try { cls = Class.forName(argv[i]); }
            catch (ClassNotFoundException e)
            {
                System.out.println(e);
                continue;
            }
            Date date2 = new Date();
            System.out.println("Loaded " + cls + " in " +
                               (date2.getTime() - date1.getTime()) +
                               " msec");
        }
    }
}
```

This version loads any and all arbitrary classes requested on the command line, printing the name of and the time taken to load each class. Running under the Blackdown JDK1.1 and loading two classes from Swing gives us these results:

```
bash$ java Hello javax.swing.JFrame javax.swing.JButton
Loaded class javax.swing.JFrame in 35 msec
Loaded class javax.swing.JButton in 34 msec
bash$
```

(Note that all times reported are approximate. The Java `Date()` methods rely on the host system clock, and are not a reliable source of high-precision timing data.)

After building a TowerJ version in feedback mode, we run a sample workload (we would run many sample workloads for a less trivial example):

```
bash$ ./Hello javax.swing.JFrame javax.swing.JButton
Loaded class javax.swing.JFrame in 1177 msec
Loaded class javax.swing.JButton in 1195 msec
bash$
```

The large numbers show the time required for TowerJ to load the classes—it's obviously slow, but we're running an instrumented version that is collecting runtime data.

The resulting feedback file(s) (shown in Listing 32.3) holds information for the next phase of optimization—all the new classes loaded as a result of running the test workloads. Feedback from the test workloads identifies dynamically loaded classes that were not found when the executable was initially built.

LISTING 32.3 Second Project: Feedback from the Dynamic Loading of Classes

```
feedbackID=1
#-----------------------------------.
# The following classes were interpreted from the classpath:
interpreted= java.text.resources.LocaleElements_en \
 javax.swing.JFrame \
 java.awt.MenuContainer \
 javax.swing.AbstractButton \
 javax.swing.JButton \
 java.text.resources.LocaleElements \
 javax.swing.WindowConstants \
 java.util.ListResourceBundle \
 javax.swing.SwingConstants \
 java.text.resources.DateFormatZoneData \
 java.awt.Component \
 javax.accessibility.Accessible \
 javax.swing.JComponent \
 java.awt.Frame \
 java.awt.Container \
 java.awt.image.ImageObserver \
 java.awt.Window \
 java.awt.ItemSelectable \
 java.text.resources.DateFormatZoneData_en \
 javax.swing.RootPaneContainer
#-----------------------------------.
# No classes were loaded by custom class loaders
#-----------------------------------.
# All classes were found.
#-----------------------------------.
# The following classes pairs denote dynamic classes and their compiled
# ancestors which need to be marked open if the class remains dynamic:
open-pairs= java.util.ListResourceBundle java.util.ResourceBundle
#-----------------------------------.
# No 'dead' classes need be marked included
#-----------------------------------.
# No invisible classes need be marked included
```

Using this data, we can rebuild and process these new classes into fast TowerJ executable versions. When we rebuild, TowerJ offers us the opportunity to decide which of these new classes to compile into the application (see Figure 32.7).

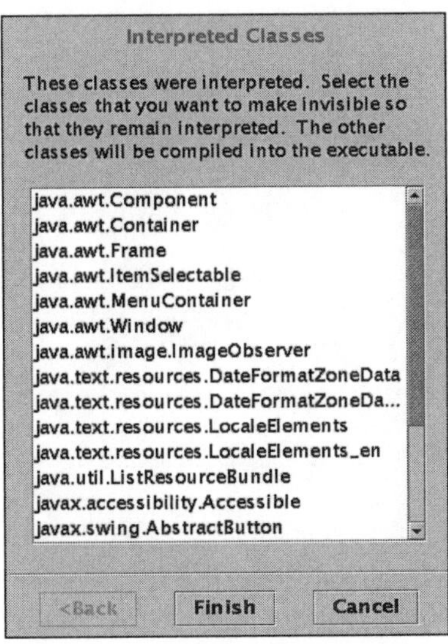

FIGURE 32.7
TowerJ offers control over the next step of optimization.

Our `Hello` executable grows by 52 percent—20 new classes have been compiled in. The results of running the final, optimized executable with one *new* class requested are as follows:

```
bash$ ./Hello javax.swing.JFrame javax.swing.JButton javax.swing.JLabel
Loaded class javax.swing.JFrame in 0 msec
Loaded class javax.swing.JButton in 0 msec
Loaded class javax.swing.JLabel in 387 msec
bash$
```

We notice fast loading for the classes we compiled in and slow loading of the new class (slower than the Blackdown JDK, faster than we would have seen in feedback mode). Because `javax.swing.JLabel` was never processed for use by TowerJ, it is loaded and interpreted as a bytecoded class.

Third Project: Building a Tjlib

The support of dynamically loaded compiled classes, which TowerJ calls *Tjlibs*, is its unique contribution as a product. The second project illustrated the need to load arbitrary new classes at runtime—a standard practice with servlets, Enterprise JavaBeans, and other Java server environments. By building compiled versions of those classes external to the application, Tjlibs provide the speed of native applications and shared libraries with the dynamic loading model of Java.

Following on the previous project, we create a new project to build a Tjlib containing a compiled version of the `javax.swing.JLabel` class. For this Tjlib, we want to build *only* that class and nothing that will already be found in the core application (which runs afoul of a current TowerJ restriction). We set up the project to build a Tjlib called `MyNewClass`, marking the target class as ***`included`*** (see Figure 32.8).

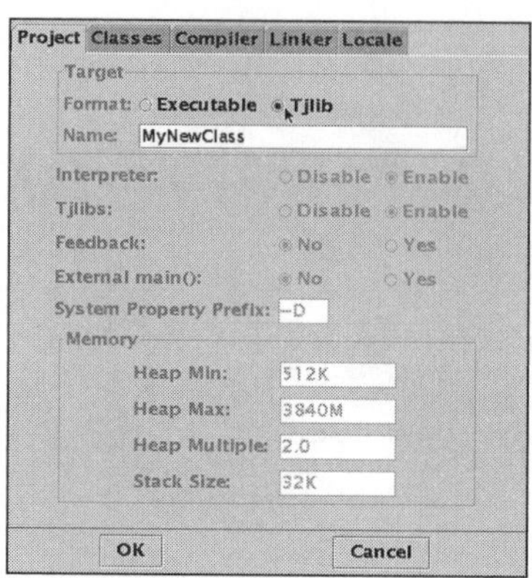

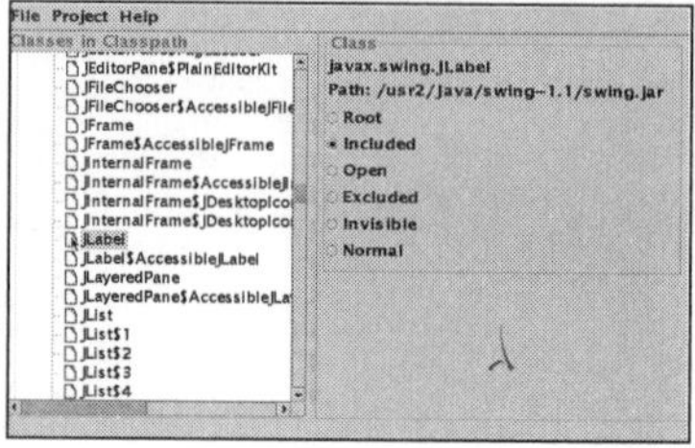

FIGURE 32.8
Setting up to build a Tjlib containing the single class `javax.swing.JLabel`.

The result of this build is `MyNewClass.tjlib`, which we install in some location in the deployment environment. The environment variable `TOWERJ_TJLIB_PATH` must be set to point to the installation directories of installed Tjlibs, allowing the TowerJ runtime to find them.

There is no change to the application: Tjlibs are loaded through the same calls (such as `Class.forName()`) that load bytecoded class files. With the new Tjlib deployed, the results of running the application are improved:

```
bash$ ./Hello javax.swing.JFrame javax.swing.JButton javax.swing.JLabel
Loaded class javax.swing.JFrame in 0 msec
Loaded class javax.swing.JButton in 0 msec
Loaded class javax.swing.JLabel in 19 msec
bash$
```

And, of course, `javax.swing.JLabel` is now a compiled class, meaning substantially improved runtime performance when we start using the class.

Note that the times reported in these examples provide some visibility into how the classes are being loaded. They do *not* reflect TowerJ's actual (and impressive) performance in deployment environments.

Summary

This chapter has discussed the TowerJ server development and deployment platform. While clearly not a tool for the average Linux user, it is a powerful and effective solution on the server. Current published results from the Volano benchmarks (`http://www.volano.com/report.html`) show that the combination of Linux and TowerJ comprises a world-beating Java server platform.

PART VII

ADDITIONAL JAVA RUNTIME COMPONENTS

Part VI discussed core runtime environments. This part moves beyond the core to examine additional runtime components available to enhance your Java/Linux installation. In particular, we explore the following two areas:

- Alternative JIT compilers—allowing you to add just-in-time compilation to Blackdown JDK1.1 or choose an alternate JIT solution for Blackdown JDK1.2.
- Native Java extensions—Linux versions of standard Java extensions, bringing 3D graphics and data communications capabilities to Java on Linux.

CHAPTER 33

JUST-IN-TIME COMPILERS

JIT compilers have been Java's first line of offense against the performance challenges of an interpreted language. The notion behind JIT is simple: Java bytecodes are compiled, on a method-by-method basis, into native-code implementations for direct execution by the underlying hardware. JIT compilation is performed by a low-priority thread concurrently with application execution. Methods that are called are compiled; methods that are not called are left alone. After the initial cost of compilation, benefits from JIT begin to appear the second time a method is called.

JIT *works*. Significant effort has gone into JIT development on the Microsoft Windows platform (Symantec is one of the technology leaders here), and there is ample evidence that it is effective. It works best in long-lived Java server applications, but JIT measurably helps all but the most trivial applications.

Does JIT work *well*? Does it deliver anything approaching the performance of compiled, optimized applications? Yes, it works well; no, it doesn't match performance available from globally optimizing static native compilers. And neither approach achieves C/C++ levels of performance (for more discussion see Chapter 57, "Why Is Java Slow?").

JIT is not confined to the Windows world, of course. After some general JIT discussion in the following section, we'll examine three free JIT compilers available today for Linux deployment.

JVM/JIT Interfacing

The JIT interface is a native Java interface published by Sun and supported with C/C++ header files included with the SDK. The interfaces differ between JDK1.1 and JDK1.2. A single JIT binary cannot serve both environments, but some JITs (`tya` and `shujit`, discussed later) can be built for either environment.

JITs, like other native components, are always supplied in the form of shared native libraries. To use it, the shared library is placed somewhere the JVM can find it, and the JVM is told which JIT to use (see Chapter 14, "Configuring the Linux SDK/JRE Environment," in the section "Installing an Alternative JIT").

In general, Java applications do not worry about the JIT—it's just there, and it just (usually) works. The core classes do provide a minimal interface that applications can use if needed:

`public final class` **`java.lang.Compiler`** `extends java.lang.Object`

- `public static native java.lang.Object command(Object any)`—Call an implementation-specific hook into the JIT compiler. The Java specification does not define anything about this call other than its existence. The JIT may choose (and presumably document) any functionality for this method.
- `public static native boolean compileClass(Class clazz)`—Compile the class specified by the `java.lang.Class` argument.
- `public static native boolean compileClasses(String string)`—Compile the class whose name matches the string argument.
- `public static native void disable()`—Disable JIT activity.
- `public static native void enable()`—Re-enable JIT activity.

The `sunwjit` Compiler

With the release of the Java 2 Platform, Sun began bundling JIT technology with the JDK.

Platform: JDK1.2

Sun's JIT, `libsunwjit.so`, is shipped in the standard SDK and JRE native shared library directories, and the use of this JIT during Java execution is enabled by default. This JIT can be disabled by using a different JIT or specifying no JIT (see Chapter 14, "Configuring the Linux SDK/JRE Environment," in the section "Adding JIT Compilers").

Controlling `sunwjit` with Environment Variables

The `sunwjit` compiler recognizes one environment variable—`JIT_ARGS`—that can be used to modify its behavior. The two documented arguments are `trace` and `exclude`, which selectively enable tracing of JIT activity.

```
bash$ export JIT_ARGS="trace [exclude(<method name> [<method name>...])]"
```

This will cause the JIT to report all procedures being compiled, excepting methods specifically excluded.

As of this writing, this option is not yet functional in the Linux port.

The tya Compiler

The tya JIT compiler is an open-source (GPL) product published by Albrecht Kleine for Linux and FreeBSD platforms.

Platform: JDK1.1/JDK1.2

Performance of tya is good and continuing to improve, the code is actively maintained, and the author is an active participant in the Blackdown community.

Obtaining and Building tya

Current tya distributions are published, as compressed source tarballs (see Chapter 8, "Installing Additional Linux Software," in the section "Compressed Tarball Source Distribution"), at ftp://gonzalez.cyberus.ca/pub/Linux/java/. tya uses GNU autoconf technology—configuration, building, and installation are straightforward.

While tya targets both JDK1.1 and JDK1.2, you cannot use the same binary on both; like any JIT, tya must be compiled for a particular Java platform. The decision about target platform is made automatically when you perform the configure step before building tya—the configuration script does this by examining the first java executable found in your $PATH.

tya is also published in RPM form and appears in some Linux distributions. Such versions are almost always out-of-date—the best source for current tya is the gonzalez.cyberus.ca FTP server.

Controlling tya with Environment Variables

tya supports one environment variable—TYA_LOGFILE. If set, this is the name of a log file tya will use. Note that tya will generate very little log output unless some debugging is enabled with compile-time options (discussed in the following section).

Configuring tya with Compile-Time Options

tya behavior can be configured, to a large extent, with some trivial hacking. The distribution includes a header file, tyaconfig.h, containing #defines to control several debugging and code generation options. The project is set up to encourage freelance hacking and accept improvements from outside developers.

Debug Options:

- DEBUG—If defined, generate voluminous debugging output.
- VERBOSE—If defined, generate statistics.

- VERBOSE_ASM86—If defined, generate voluminous output showing x86 instructions generated.
- USE_SYSLOG—If defined, tya sends log output to the Linux syslog. $TYA_LOGFILE is ignored.
- GATHER_STATS—If defined, gather and report some statistics on tya activity.

Code Generation Options:

- USE_REG_OPT—If defined, enable use of some CPU registers for holding local variables.
- INLINING—If defined, enable runtime inlining of some method calls.
- TRY_FAST_INVOKE—If set, enables a fast method invocation technique.
- EXCEPTIONS_BY_SIGNALS—If set, uses UNIX signals instead of traditional Java runtime checking to detect certain exceptions. This should speed up performance in the normal case and slow down handling of exceptional conditions.
- USEASM—If set, uses assembler code instead of C for certain generated code.
- INLINE_LONGARITM—If set, emit code for handling certain operations on long long (64-bit) integers; else use wrappers provided by the JDK.
- COMBINEOP—If set, generate combined-operation x86 opcodes when possible.
- FAST_FPARITH—If set, make low-overhead fast calls into Java math code.
- INLINE_FPARITM—If set, generate code that uses floating point processor instructions for certain math operations.

The shujit Compiler

The shujit JIT compiler is an open-source (GPL) product published by Shudo Kazuyuki for Linux and FreeBSD platforms.

Platform: JDK1.1/JDK1.2

Like tya, shujit's performance is competitive, the code is actively maintained, and the author is an active participant in the Blackdown community.

Obtaining and Building shujit

Current shujit distributions are published, as compressed source tarballs, at http://www.shudo.net/jit/. To build shujit, you need to obtain ruby, an object-oriented scripting language popular in Japan, from http://www.netlab.co.jp/ruby/. Both ruby and shujit use GNU autoconf technology—configuration, building, and installation are straightforward. As with building tya, the configuration step figures out the target Java environment (JDK1.1 or 1.2) by examining the first java executable in your $PATH.

Controlling `shujit` With Environment Variables

`shujit` uses an environment variable—`JAVA_COMPILER_OPT`—for configuration of several runtime options. Format is as follows:

```
JAVA_COMPILER_OPT="<option> [<option> ...]"
```

where the options can be space- or comma-separated. Currently recognized options are as follows:

- `cmplatload`—Compile all class methods when a class is loaded.
- `cmplclinit`—Enable compilation of class initialization methods.
- `codedb`—Build a database of compiled code to database files named `./shujit_code.*` (output is to multiple database files whose names begin with `shujit_code`).
- `codesize`—Print statistics on size of generated code to a log file named `./jit_codesize`.
- `dontcmplvmcls`—Disable initialization of already loaded core classes at JIT startup.
- `igndisable`—Ignore calls to disable JIT activity (`java.lang.Compiler.disable()`).
- `outcode`—Generate assembly language source files (`.S`) containing source for methods that are compiled. The files are named according to the C/C++ naming conventions for Java native methods.
- `quiet`—Disable normal messages from the JIT.

Future JIT Directions

Projects such as Sun's HotSpot (see Chapter 30, "Sun HotSpot Performance Engine,") and Mozilla's ElectricalFire (see Chapter 29, "Mozilla ElectricalFire: A New JVM,") suggest a future without JITs, in which new JVM architectures own the entire responsibility for native code generation and optimization. But JITs have been a rich area for research and innovation, and will undoubtedly remain so.

One of the more intriguing glimpses of future activity can be found in the OpenJIT project, at Tokyo Institute of Technology. OpenJIT incorporates computational reflection, the capability of classes to assist in their own optimization by providing their own optimizers—written in Java, of course. Details are published at `http://openjit.is.titech.ac.jp/`.

Summary

This chapter has discussed three JIT compilers available on Linux for the Blackdown JDK. The Java performance story on Linux still has much room for improvement, and future JITs from these and other sources will improve the competitiveness of the Java/Linux platform.

CHAPTER 34

JAVA3D EXTENSION

The Java3D Extension brings 3D graphics capabilities to Java on Linux.

Platform: JDK1.2

Java3D is a standard Java extension that brings native platform 3D rendering to Java applications. Unlike most standard extensions, however, you cannot obtain one for Linux from Sun Microsystems. The reason: a dependence on the native platform.

The reliance of Java's standard extensions on native platform capabilities creates three categories of extensions:

- Extensions implemented entirely in Java. This includes JNDI, JavaMail, and most other extensions.
- Extensions that *can* be implemented in entirely in Java but are also implemented with native platform support for performance reasons. An example is the Java Advanced Imaging API. Sun publishes Java-only sample implementations of these extensions, as well as some platform-specific versions.
- Extensions that can *only* be implemented with native platform support. For native platforms not supported by Sun, these extensions can be ported by third parties—vendors, volunteers, or whomever.

The latter category includes Java3D, for which Sun has delivered Solaris and NT versions.

Both implementations are built on the OpenGL graphics rendering API, and Sun is also working toward an NT implementation that uses Microsoft's Direct3D API.

Java3D has been licensed to other UNIX vendors for implementation and is being ported to Linux under the auspices of the Blackdown organization.

Obtaining and Installing Java3D for Linux

Java3D is published alongside the Blackdown JDK distributions (see Chapter 13, "Blackdown: The Official Linux Port," in the section "Supported Linux Versions for the Blackdown SDK and JRE") and can be obtained from Blackdown download sites. The distribution is in the form of a compressed binary tarball (see Chapter 8, "Installing Additional Linux Software," in the section "Compressed Tarball Binary Distribution").

The tarball is structured to unpack directly into an SDK installation and assumes that the installation is rooted in a directory named `jdk1.2/`. To unpack according to these assumptions, perform the following step from the *parent directory* of `jdk1.2/`:

```
bash$ bzip2 -d <<tarball.bz2> ¦ tar xvf -
```

where *<tarball.bz2>* is the name of the compressed archive. For example:

```
bash$ bzip2 -d <java3d.tar.bz2 ¦ tar xvf -
```

This distribution is in prerelease as of this writing; future releases may choose a different scheme. You can always examine the contents of the archive, without unpacking, by running `tar` with the `t` option instead of `x`—this will give you visibility into archive layout.

A cleaner choice than unpacking into the current SDK would be to unpack elsewhere, say `/usr/local/Java/Java3d`, and then create a few symbolic links from the SDK:

```
bash$ ln -s /usr/local/Java/Java3d/jdk1.2/demo/java3d \
/usr/local/Java/jdk1.2/demo/
bash$ ln -s /usr/local/Java/Java3d/jdk1.2/jre/lib/ext/* \
/usr/local/Java/jdk1.2/jre/lib/ext
bash$ ln -s /usr/local/Java/Java3d/jdk1.2/jre/lib/i386/* \
/usr/local/Java/jdk1.2/jre/lib/i386
```

But you're not yet ready to run. The extension depends on the presence of native 3D graphics support on your system.

Obtaining Linux 3D Support—Mesa

There is currently an open source 3D graphics library and toolkit, Mesa, that provides a fully functional 3D API modeled on the OpenGL API. The Blackdown Java3D implementation uses Mesa, so you must install Mesa to use Java3D.

Mesa is widely available in RPM and tarball form, both source and binary. You can find it at your favorite repository, or at Mesa's Web site (`http://www.mesa3d.org`). Get it, install it, and you're ready to run Java3D.

The Current State of Linux 3D Support

The state of 3D graphics support for Linux is highly fluid at the moment.

We just mentioned Mesa, but what exactly is it? Mesa is a free 3D graphics library and toolkit *modeled* on the OpenGL standard, and offering substantial source-level API compatibility with the OpenGL API. Many applications written to use OpenGL (including the Java3D sample implementation from Sun) can easily use Mesa and choose to do so because the price is right.

For those needing a true OpenGL implementation, Mesa is not such a beast. Users of the current Java3D implementation do not need one (as of this writing), but several options exist in this rapidly changing landscape:

- Commercial OpenGL implementations are available that run against commercial X servers.
- Commercial OpenGL implementations are available that run against XFree86.
- PrecisionInsight is working toward creating an open source OpenGL, based on Mesa, GLX (an open source interface from SGI), and XFree86. It's not fully cooked, as of this writing, but beta versions for certain graphics cards are starting to appear.

The best sources of current information on OpenGL status, including Linux support, are the OpenGL Web site, `http://www.opengl.org`, and the Mesa Web site, `http://www.mesa3d.org`.

Contents of the Java3D Distribution

The distribution includes three components:

- Class libraries, in the `jdk1.2/jre/lib/ext` directory. Following standard practice for JDK1.2 extensions (see Chapter 14, "Configuring the Linux JSDK/JRE Environment," in the section "Adding Standard Extensions and Application Classes Under JDK1.2"), these files (or symlinks to them) should be placed in the SDK or JRE `lib/ext` directory.
- Native support libraries, in the `jdk1.2/jre/lib/i386` directory. Following standard practice for extensions, these files (or symlinks to them) should be placed in the SDK or JRE `lib/i386` directory.
- A lot of great demos!

Running Java3D Demos

The fastest way to verify that the installation is working is to run a demo. Just `cd` to one of the demo directories (or otherwise include it in your class path) and run. If the demo fails immediately with the message `libMesaGL.so.3: cannot open shared object file: No such file or directory`, you probably didn't install Mesa. See the section "Obtaining Linux 3D Support—Mesa" earlier in this chapter.

The Java3D 1.1.1 prerelease contains 37 demos. A couple of examples are discussed in the following sections.

Text3DLoad

This is found in the `demo/java3d/Text3D` subdirectory, and demonstrates display and manipulation of 3D text.

Synopsis:

```
java Text3DLoad [-f <fontname>] <text>
```

Example:

```
bash$ java Text3DLoad -f sansserif "Hello World"
```

This results in the window shown in Figure 34.1.

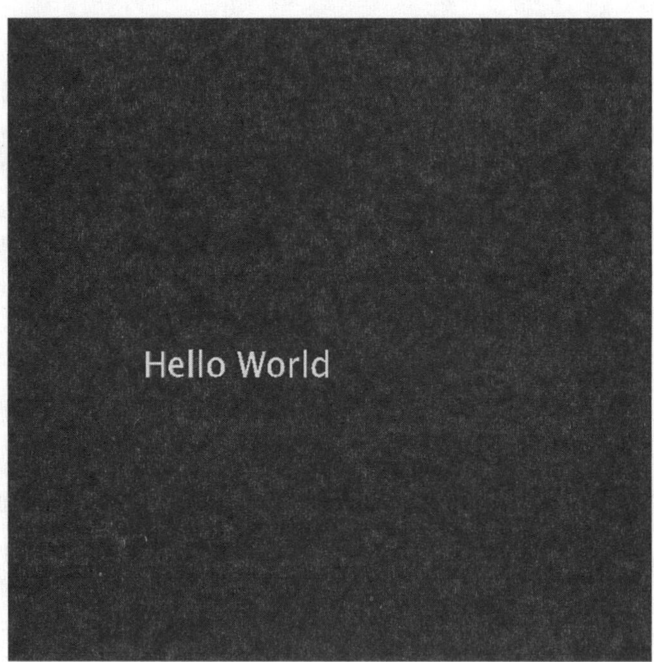

FIGURE 34.1
Text3DLoad demo window.

The left, middle, and right mouse buttons serve to rotate the image and move it along various axes. The result, after a bit of clicking and dragging, appears in Figure 34.2.

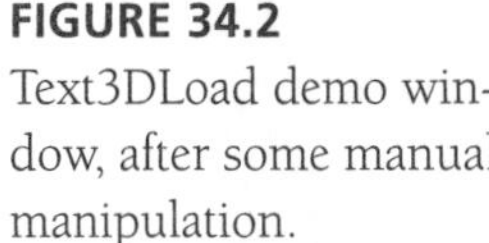

FIGURE 34.2
Text3DLoad demo window, after some manual manipulation.

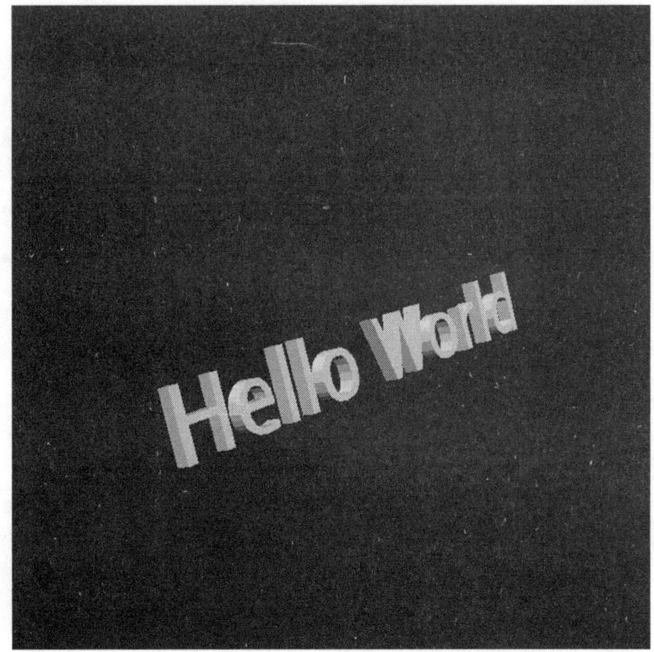

ObjLoad

Found in the `demo/java3d/ObjLoad` subdirectory, this demo shows the capability to load objects saved in the WaveFront `.obj` format.

Synopsis:

```
java ObjLoad [-s] [-n] [-t] [-c <degrees>] <.obj file>
```

Options:

- -c *<degrees>*—Sets the crease angle used when generating surface normals.
- `-n`—Suppresses triangulation.
- `-s`—Spins the model. If not specified, the user interacts with the model through mouse buttons.
- `-t`—Suppresses stripification.

Example:

Two sample objects are shipped with Java3D. We load one of them:

```
bash$ java ObjLoad ../geometry/galleon.obj
```

This results in the interactive model shown in Figure 34.3.

FIGURE 34.3
ObjLoad demo window displaying the galleon model.

Programming to the Java3D API

The Java3D API is big: 262 public classes in Java3D 1.1.1, with 671 public constructors and 2,884 public methods. Extensive documentation is provided by Sun. Visit `http://java.sun.com` and navigate to the Java3D pages for pointers to documentation.

The following section gives a quick class list.

Packages `j3d.audio` and `j3d.audioengines`

Not only does Java3D target the gaming market—a keen customer for audio capabilities—it also offers 3D spatial sound processing. Listing 34.1 lists the classes in these two packages.

LISTING 34.1 Java3D Classes Supporting Audio

```
com.sun.j3d.audio.AudioData
com.sun.j3d.audio.AudioDataStream
com.sun.j3d.audio.AudioDevice
com.sun.j3d.audio.AudioPlayer
com.sun.j3d.audio.AudioSecurityAction
com.sun.j3d.audio.AudioSecurityExceptionAction
com.sun.j3d.audio.AudioStream
com.sun.j3d.audio.AudioStreamSequence
com.sun.j3d.audio.AudioTranslatorStream
com.sun.j3d.audio.ContinuousAudioDataStream
```

```
com.sun.j3d.audio.Format
com.sun.j3d.audio.HaeNoise
com.sun.j3d.audio.HaePlayable
com.sun.j3d.audio.HaeWaveNoise
com.sun.j3d.audio.HaeWaveStream
com.sun.j3d.audio.J3DHaeClip
com.sun.j3d.audio.J3DHaeStream
com.sun.j3d.audio.JavaSoundParams
com.sun.j3d.audio.MediaInputStream
com.sun.j3d.audio.NativeAudioStream
com.sun.j3d.audio.SunAudioClip
com.sun.j3d.audioengines.AudioEngine
com.sun.j3d.audioengines.AudioEngine3D
com.sun.j3d.audioengines.AuralParameters
com.sun.j3d.audioengines.Sample
com.sun.j3d.audioengines.javasound.JavaSoundMixer
```

Package `j3d.loaders` and Subpackages

Java3D loaders handle the reading of scene graphs from files and URLs. Listing 34.2 lists the classes in these packages.

LISTING 34.2 Java3D Classes Supporting 3D Scene Loading

```
com.sun.j3d.loaders.IncorrectFormatException
com.sun.j3d.loaders.Loader
com.sun.j3d.loaders.LoaderBase
com.sun.j3d.loaders.ParsingErrorException
com.sun.j3d.loaders.Scene
com.sun.j3d.loaders.SceneBase
com.sun.j3d.loaders.lw3d.FloatValueInterpolator
com.sun.j3d.loaders.lw3d.Lw3dLoader
com.sun.j3d.loaders.lw3d.LwsPrimitive
com.sun.j3d.loaders.objectfile.ObjectFile
```

Packages `j3d.util.*`

This is a grab-bag of utilities to support Java3D behaviors, geometry computations, and world coordinates. See Listing 34.3 for a list of classes.

LISTING 34.3 Java3D Utility Classes

```
com.sun.j3d.utils.applet.MainFrame
com.sun.j3d.utils.audio.DistanceAttenuation
com.sun.j3d.utils.behaviors.interpolators.CubicSplineCurve
com.sun.j3d.utils.behaviors.interpolators.CubicSplineSegment
com.sun.j3d.utils.behaviors.interpolators.RotPosScaleTCBSplinePathInterpolator
com.sun.j3d.utils.behaviors.interpolators.TCBKeyFrame
```

continued on next page

continued from previous page

```
com.sun.j3d.utils.behaviors.interpolators.TCBSplinePathInterpolator
com.sun.j3d.utils.behaviors.keyboard.KeyNavigator
com.sun.j3d.utils.behaviors.keyboard.KeyNavigatorBehavior
com.sun.j3d.utils.behaviors.mouse.MouseBehavior
com.sun.j3d.utils.behaviors.mouse.MouseBehaviorCallback
com.sun.j3d.utils.behaviors.mouse.MouseRotate
com.sun.j3d.utils.behaviors.mouse.MouseTranslate
com.sun.j3d.utils.behaviors.mouse.MouseZoom
com.sun.j3d.utils.behaviors.picking.Intersect
com.sun.j3d.utils.behaviors.picking.PickMouseBehavior
com.sun.j3d.utils.behaviors.picking.PickObject
com.sun.j3d.utils.behaviors.picking.PickRotateBehavior
com.sun.j3d.utils.behaviors.picking.PickTranslateBehavior
com.sun.j3d.utils.behaviors.picking.PickZoomBehavior
com.sun.j3d.utils.behaviors.picking.PickingCallback
com.sun.j3d.utils.geometry.Box
com.sun.j3d.utils.geometry.ColorCube
com.sun.j3d.utils.geometry.Cone
com.sun.j3d.utils.geometry.Cylinder
com.sun.j3d.utils.geometry.GeometryInfo
com.sun.j3d.utils.geometry.NormalGenerator
com.sun.j3d.utils.geometry.Primitive
com.sun.j3d.utils.geometry.Sphere
com.sun.j3d.utils.geometry.Stripifier
com.sun.j3d.utils.geometry.Text2D
com.sun.j3d.utils.geometry.Triangulator
com.sun.j3d.utils.image.TextureLoader
com.sun.j3d.utils.internal.FastVector
com.sun.j3d.utils.internal.J3dUtilsI18N
com.sun.j3d.utils.universe.MultiTransformGroup
com.sun.j3d.utils.universe.PlatformGeometry
com.sun.j3d.utils.universe.SimpleUniverse
com.sun.j3d.utils.universe.Viewer
com.sun.j3d.utils.universe.ViewerAvatar
com.sun.j3d.utils.universe.ViewingPlatform
```

Package `javax.media.j3d`

This is the core Java3D API. Java3D presents a familiar paradigm to 3D programmers: scene graphs, with immediate- and retained-mode rendering. See Listing 34.4 for a list of classes.

LISTING 34.4 Core Java3D Classes Supporting Scenes and Rendering

```
javax.media.j3d.Alpha
javax.media.j3d.AmbientLight
javax.media.j3d.Appearance
javax.media.j3d.AudioDevice
javax.media.j3d.AudioDevice3D
javax.media.j3d.AuralAttributes
javax.media.j3d.Background
```

```
javax.media.j3d.BackgroundSound
javax.media.j3d.BadTransformException
javax.media.j3d.Behavior
javax.media.j3d.Billboard
javax.media.j3d.BoundingBox
javax.media.j3d.BoundingLeaf
javax.media.j3d.BoundingPolytope
javax.media.j3d.BoundingSphere
javax.media.j3d.Bounds
javax.media.j3d.BranchGroup
javax.media.j3d.Canvas3D
javax.media.j3d.CapabilityNotSetException
javax.media.j3d.Clip
javax.media.j3d.ColorInterpolator
javax.media.j3d.ColoringAttributes
javax.media.j3d.CompressedGeometry
javax.media.j3d.CompressedGeometryHeader
javax.media.j3d.ConeSound
javax.media.j3d.DanglingReferenceException
javax.media.j3d.DecalGroup
javax.media.j3d.DepthComponent
javax.media.j3d.DepthComponentFloat
javax.media.j3d.DepthComponentInt
javax.media.j3d.DepthComponentNative
javax.media.j3d.DepthComponentRetained
javax.media.j3d.DirectionalLight
javax.media.j3d.DistanceLOD
javax.media.j3d.ExponentialFog
javax.media.j3d.Fog
javax.media.j3d.FogRetained
javax.media.j3d.Font3D
javax.media.j3d.FontExtrusion
javax.media.j3d.GeneralizedStripFlags
javax.media.j3d.Geometry
javax.media.j3d.GeometryArray
javax.media.j3d.GeometryArrayRetained
javax.media.j3d.GeometryDecompressor
javax.media.j3d.GeometryRetained
javax.media.j3d.GeometryStripArray
javax.media.j3d.GeometryStripArrayRetained
javax.media.j3d.GraphicsConfigTemplate3D
javax.media.j3d.GraphicsContext3D
javax.media.j3d.Group
javax.media.j3d.HiResCoord
javax.media.j3d.IllegalRenderingStateException
javax.media.j3d.IllegalSharingException
javax.media.j3d.ImageComponent
javax.media.j3d.ImageComponent2D
javax.media.j3d.ImageComponent3D
javax.media.j3d.ImageComponentRetained
javax.media.j3d.IndexedGeometryArray
```

continued on next page

continued from previous page

```
javax.media.j3d.IndexedGeometryArrayRetained
javax.media.j3d.IndexedGeometryStripArray
javax.media.j3d.IndexedGeometryStripArrayRetained
javax.media.j3d.IndexedLineArray
javax.media.j3d.IndexedLineStripArray
javax.media.j3d.IndexedPointArray
javax.media.j3d.IndexedQuadArray
javax.media.j3d.IndexedTriangleArray
javax.media.j3d.IndexedTriangleFanArray
javax.media.j3d.IndexedTriangleStripArray
javax.media.j3d.InputDevice
javax.media.j3d.Interpolator
javax.media.j3d.J3dProperties
javax.media.j3d.LOD
javax.media.j3d.Leaf
javax.media.j3d.LeafRetained
javax.media.j3d.Light
javax.media.j3d.LightRetained
javax.media.j3d.LineArray
javax.media.j3d.LineAttributes
javax.media.j3d.LineStripArray
javax.media.j3d.LinearFog
javax.media.j3d.Link
javax.media.j3d.Locale
javax.media.j3d.Material
javax.media.j3d.MediaContainer
javax.media.j3d.Morph
javax.media.j3d.MultipleParentException
javax.media.j3d.Node
javax.media.j3d.NodeComponent
javax.media.j3d.NodeReferenceTable
javax.media.j3d.NodeRetained
javax.media.j3d.ObjectUpdate
javax.media.j3d.OrderedGroup
javax.media.j3d.PathInterpolator
javax.media.j3d.PhysicalBody
javax.media.j3d.PhysicalEnvironment
javax.media.j3d.PickShape
javax.media.j3d.PointArray
javax.media.j3d.PointAttributes
javax.media.j3d.PointLight
javax.media.j3d.PointSound
javax.media.j3d.PolygonAttributes
javax.media.j3d.PositionInterpolator
javax.media.j3d.PositionPathInterpolator
javax.media.j3d.QuadArray
javax.media.j3d.Raster
javax.media.j3d.RenderingAttributes
javax.media.j3d.RestrictedAccessException
javax.media.j3d.RotPosPathInterpolator
javax.media.j3d.RotPosScalePathInterpolator
javax.media.j3d.RotationInterpolator
```

```
javax.media.j3d.RotationPathInterpolator
javax.media.j3d.ScaleInterpolator
javax.media.j3d.SceneGraphCycleException
javax.media.j3d.SceneGraphObject
javax.media.j3d.SceneGraphObjectRetained
javax.media.j3d.SceneGraphPath
javax.media.j3d.Screen3D
javax.media.j3d.Sensor
javax.media.j3d.SensorRead
javax.media.j3d.Shape3D
javax.media.j3d.SharedGroup
javax.media.j3d.Sound
javax.media.j3d.SoundException
javax.media.j3d.SoundRetained
javax.media.j3d.Soundscape
javax.media.j3d.SpotLight
javax.media.j3d.Switch
javax.media.j3d.SwitchValueInterpolator
javax.media.j3d.TexCoordGeneration
javax.media.j3d.Text3D
javax.media.j3d.Texture
javax.media.j3d.Texture2D
javax.media.j3d.Texture3D
javax.media.j3d.TextureAttributes
javax.media.j3d.TextureRetained
javax.media.j3d.Transform3D
javax.media.j3d.TransformGroup
javax.media.j3d.TransparencyAttributes
javax.media.j3d.TransparencyInterpolator
javax.media.j3d.TriangleArray
javax.media.j3d.TriangleFanArray
javax.media.j3d.TriangleStripArray
javax.media.j3d.View
javax.media.j3d.ViewPlatform
javax.media.j3d.VirtualUniverse
javax.media.j3d.WakeupCondition
javax.media.j3d.WakeupCriterion
```

Package `javax.vecmath`

This package provides the vector, matrix, and colorspace manipulation support needed in 3D applications. See Listing 34.5 for a list of classes.

LISTING 34.5 Java3D Classes for Vector, Matrix, and Colorspace Arithmetic

```
javax.vecmath.AxisAngle4d
javax.vecmath.AxisAngle4f
javax.vecmath.Color3b
javax.vecmath.Color3f
```

continued on next page

continued from previous page

```
javax.vecmath.Color4b
javax.vecmath.Color4f
javax.vecmath.GMatrix
javax.vecmath.GVector
javax.vecmath.Matrix3d
javax.vecmath.Matrix3f
javax.vecmath.Matrix4d
javax.vecmath.Matrix4f
javax.vecmath.MismatchedSizeException
javax.vecmath.Point2d
javax.vecmath.Point2f
javax.vecmath.Point3d
javax.vecmath.Point3f
javax.vecmath.Point4d
javax.vecmath.Point4f
javax.vecmath.Quat4d
javax.vecmath.Quat4f
javax.vecmath.SingularMatrixException
javax.vecmath.TexCoord2f
javax.vecmath.TexCoord3f
javax.vecmath.Tuple2d
javax.vecmath.Tuple2f
javax.vecmath.Tuple3b
javax.vecmath.Tuple3d
javax.vecmath.Tuple3f
javax.vecmath.Tuple4b
javax.vecmath.Tuple4d
javax.vecmath.Tuple4f
javax.vecmath.Vector2d
javax.vecmath.Vector2f
javax.vecmath.Vector3d
javax.vecmath.Vector3f
javax.vecmath.Vector4d
javax.vecmath.Vector4f
```

Summary

This chapter has presented the Java3D standard extension and its implementation for Linux. This implementation is still a work in progress, and we can expect over time to see improved support for various 3D graphics cards.

CHAPTER 35

JAVACOMM, JCL, AND RXTX: SERIAL COMMUNICATIONS FROM JAVA

The Java Communications API (JavaComm) is a standard extension to support use of the serial and parallel ports. This chapter describes an implementation available for Linux. As of this writing, the implementation supports serial ports only.

Platforms: JDK1.1/JDK1.2

The Java Communications API provides a standard interface for serial and parallel port hardware. The capabilities of the current 2.0 release include

- Finding and enumerating available serial and parallel hardware
- Opening and asserting process ownership of a port
- Resolving port ownership between contending applications
- Performing asynchronous and synchronous I/O on ports
- Receiving events describing communication port state changes

Among the applications you can develop with such an API are

- Device drivers for custom I/O devices and protocols
- Monitors for uninterruptible power supplies
- Terminal servers for ISP environments

Like the Java3D extension discussed earlier (Chapter 34, "Java3D Extension"), JavaComm is one of the standard Sun extensions that cannot be implemented entirely in Java. It requires a native component that understands how to drive the serial and parallel port hardware on a host system.

A JavaComm solution for Linux (or any other platform) consists of three components:

- The JavaComm extension library, published by Sun.
- A platform-specific driver, in the form of a class library. This driver will necessarily include some native methods that know how to control the hardware.
- A native code shared library to implement the native methods in the driver.

For the Linux platform, these three pieces come from three different sources. The following sections describe how to obtain and build the components.

Obtaining JavaComm

The Java Communications API is distributed as a standard extension from Sun: Visit the product page (`http://java.sun.com/products/javacomm`) and download the distribution for Sparc Solaris (you *must* use this version, not those for x86 Solaris or NT).

Unpack the tarball in some convenient location:

```
bash$ gzip -d  <javacomm20-sparc.tar.Z ¦ tar xvf -
```

You need only the `comm.jar` file from the distribution, although some other files will be useful at testing time. To install `comm.jar`:

- Under JRE1.1 or SDK1.1, place the jar file (or a symbolic link to it) in the `lib` subdirectory of the installation, *and* add the jar file to your class path. Java does not require that the jar file live in this directory, but the JCL/RXTX build process (discussed in the following section) does.
- Under SDK1.2, place the jar file (or a symbolic link to it) in the `jre/lib/ext` subdirectory of the installation.
- Under JRE1.2, place the jar file (or a symbolic link to it) in the `lib/ext` subdirectory of the installation.

You also need to create a properties file, `javax.comm.properties`, containing the following single line:

```
Driver=gnu.io.RXTXCommDriver
```

This file should be installed in the usual location for properties files:

- In JRE1.1, SDK1.1, or JRE1.2: `lib/` subdirectory of the JDK installation.
- In SDK1.2: `jre/lib/` subdirectory of the JDK installation.

After we have installed the drivers (described in the next section), this file has the important job of identifying the drivers so they can be used by JavaComm.

Obtaining and Installing JCL and RXTX

The drivers needed to enable JavaComm on Linux are, for historical reasons, the product of two different authors:

- The low-level native RXTX library, published by Keane Jarvi, is a general-purpose multi-platform API for serial and parallel port interfaces.
- The JavaComm for Linux (JCL) driver, published by Kevin Hester, is an implementation of the JavaComm driver interface. When the author needed to implement the low-level code to access the hardware, he chose to use the RXTX library instead of writing his own.

Despite the diverse authorship, you can get both from a single source. The RXTX distribution, published at `http://www.frii.com/~jarvi/rxtx/`, includes a copy of JCL.

From the RXTX home page, navigate to the download page and obtain the stable or developer's version (depending on your tastes) of the compressed tarball. After unpacking it into any convenient directory, perform the following steps to build it:

```
bash$ ./configure
<...lots of output...>
bash$ make
<...lots of output...>
bash$ make jcl
<...a little output...>
bash$ make install
```

The build process identifies the Java environment in which it is running (JDK1.1 or JDK1.2), builds a version appropriate to that environment, and installs the JCL and RXTX libraries to an appropriate place:

- JRE1.1 and SDK1.1: Native libraries to `/usr/local/lib` (you can set an alternate destination at `./configure` time); `jcl.jar` to the `lib/` subdirectory in the JDK installation. You will need to add `jcl.jar` to your class path.
- JRE1.2: Native libraries to the `lib/i386/` in the JRE installation; `jcl.jar` to the `lib/ext/` subdirectory.
- SDK1.2: Native libraries to the `jre/lib/i386/` in the SDK installation; `jcl.jar` to the `jre/lib/ext/` subdirectory.

If you are building versions for both JDK1.1 and JDK1.2, you must perform the builds separately; do not perform a single build and try to install the same result into JDK1.1 and JDK1.2 installations. After building and installing for one environment, perform the following step to clean up the build tree:

```
bash$ make distclean
```

change your environment (see Chapter 14, "Configuring the Linux JSDK/JRE Environment," in the section on "Accommodating Multiple Java Installations"), and rebuild the product from the `./configure` step onward.

Testing JavaComm for Linux

The test recommended with the JCL/RXTX distribution is the BlackBox test that is bundled with the Sun JavaComm distribution. To run, include the `<javacomm_dir>/samples/BlackBox/BlackBox.jar` archive in your class path and run the BlackBox class:

```
bash$ java BlackBox
```

The BlackBox example will display a GUI for every device it can open (see Figure 35.1) and dump an exception trace for every device it cannot.

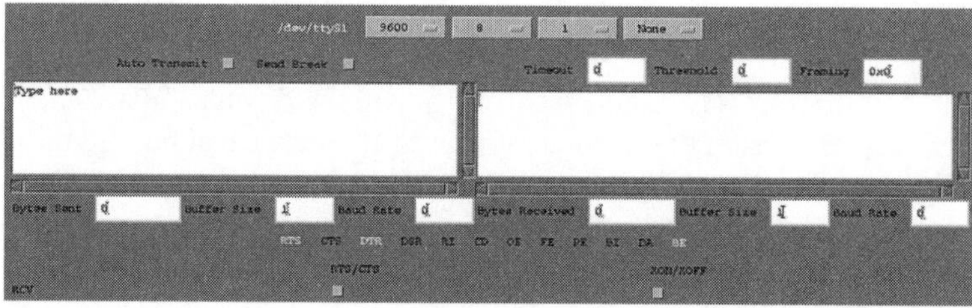

FIGURE 35.1
The GUI for the JavaComm BlackBox tester.

If you find that BlackBox fails to open all serial devices on your system, the two most likely causes are as follows:

- The permissions on the devices do not let you access them. Check the permissions on `/dev/ttyS0`, `/dev/ttyS1`, and so on. You may need to run this test as the root user.
- The interface is in use by another process. You cannot open this device—even running as the root user—until the other process has relinquished it.

The BlackBox GUI allows you to set various device parameters and to send and receive data. Obviously, an interesting testing session will require that the port be connected to a responsive device. If you have two available serial ports, you can test communications between them by connecting them with a crossover serial cable.

The JavaComm API

The Java Communications API provides 13 classes and interfaces, in the package `javax.comm`, to support serial and parallel port usage. Here is a brief summary:

- `public interface CommDriver`—This interface is implemented by loadable comm port drivers, such as JavaComm for Linux, and is not normally used from applications.

- `public abstract class CommPort`—`CommPort` is the superclass of all devices supported by this package. `CommPort` objects (and their device-specific `SerialPort` and `ParallelPort` subclasses) are not explicitly instantiated by applications but are returned by the static `CommPortIdentifier.getPortIdentifiers()` call. This superclass defines general comm-device methods for interfacing with transmit/receive buffers, timers, and framing control.
- `public class CommPortIdentifier`—This class handles access to comm ports: discovery of available devices, claiming and resolving ownership, and managing ownership-related events.
- `public interface CommPortOwnershipListener`—This interface describes an API for detection of events related to ownership of comm ports. Applications can use this interface to implement mechanisms for shared ownership of comm ports.
- `public class NoSuchPortException`—This exception is thrown when a requested port cannot be found.
- `public abstract class ParallelPort`—This is the main class for parallel port devices; it defines methods and modes for port and printer I/O.
- `public class ParallelPortEvent`—This class describes events that are reportable by the parallel port.
- `public interface ParallelPortEventListener`—This interface describes a listener for parallel port events.
- `public class PortInUseException`—This exception is thrown when a requested port is already in use.
- `public abstract class SerialPort`—This is the main class for serial ports and includes methods and modes for control of serial port word size, hardware and software flow control, parity, framing, baud rate, modem lines, buffers, break character send/detect, and error detection.
- `public class SerialPortEvent`—This class describes events that are reportable by the serial port.
- `public interface SerialPortEventListener`—This interface describes a listener for parallel port events.
- `public class UnsupportedCommOperationException`—This exception is thrown when an unsupported operation is attempted on a comm port.

Summary

This chapter discussed the Java Communications API and the components necessary to install a Linux implementation. Only serial devices are supported by the current implementation, but support of parallel devices is intended in future versions.

PART VIII

COMPILERS AND DEBUGGERS

The development tools offered with the Sun SDK are sufficient for building complete applications but, in the UNIX tradition, not highly optimized for usability. Sun vocally encourages other tool vendors to improve on their offerings, with the most visible results in the Microsoft Windows world: highly capable development environments from Symantec, Inprise, IBM, numerous smaller players, and of course (controversially) Microsoft.

But the list of quality offerings is not restricted to Windows. This and the next few parts of the book examine development tools, beginning with single-purpose tools and, later, moving into development environments.

CHAPTER 36

THE JIKES COMPILER

This chapter explores the Jikes compiler, an open source Java compiler from IBM's AlphaWorks organization.

Platform: JDK1.1/JDK1.2

One of the most popular tools to come from IBM's Java research, Jikes is a free, open source, natively implemented Java compiler. Jikes is not a product; it's a project from IBM Research and is, for IBM, as much about researching the open source model as it is about languages and compilers.

Jikes compiles `.java` sources into `.class` files, roughly 10 times faster than `javac`. The speed comes from a combination of the native implementation—it's written in C++—and a great deal of clever coding.

Jikes's speed has made it a popular tool for use in medium-size to large projects, where it saves significant time during recompilation. Perhaps its biggest downside is a lack of optimization: Jikes produces correct but poorly optimized bytecodes. Projects that use Jikes for quick turn-around during the workday often opt to use Sun's `javac` to (slowly) build final, well-optimized versions.

Obtaining Jikes

Jikes is available from IBM Research at `http://ibm.com/developerworks/opensource`. Its three components are the compiler, parser generator, and test suite. From the main project page, you can

- View current source (all three components) through a Web-based interface to the project `cvs` tree.
- Download the current development version (internal release) in source form or as an executable for Linux, Microsoft Windows, AIX, or Solaris.
- Download a stable, released version in source form or as an executable for Linux, Microsoft Windows, AIX, or Solaris.

Unless you need to hack source, it's much easier to grab the binaries. The archive consists of three files: the `jikes` executable, some brief HTML documentation, and a license. Install it anywhere.

Running Jikes

Synopsis:

`jikes [<options>] [<source files>] [@<files>]`

Compile the specified source files. The `@` option allows the compiler to read a list of source files and other options from a file instead of the command line.

General Options:

- `+1.0`—Recognize only Java 1.0.2 language constructs (for backwards compatibility).
- `+B`—Run Jikes as a syntax-checker, without generating bytecodes.
- `-classpath <path>`—Specify the class path (overrides `$CLASSPATH`). Note that Jikes follows the JDK1.1 class path model (see Chapter 14, "Configuring the Linux SDK/JRE Environment," in the section "JDK1.1 Class Path Construction"). The class path must include all core, extension, and user classes to be searched at compile time.
- `+D`—Same as option `+E` (discussed later in the list), but errors are output immediately, without buffering and sorting. This is useful primarily if Jikes is crashing before generating error messages.
- `-d <dir>`—Output class files to the specified directory. This is analogous the the `javac` `-d` option (see Chapter 19, "The Java Compiler: `javac`"): classes are placed into a hierarchy reflecting the package name.
- `-debug`—Ignored (recognized for compatibility).
- `-deprecation`—Report on use of deprecated *language features*. (Deprecated classes and methods are reported regardless of this flag.)

- `+E`—Report errors in an easy-to-parse one-line format—useful for integration with IDEs. The `+E` stands for **`emacs`**, which is often used as an IDE (see Chapter 44, "The Emacs JDE"). Without this option, error messages are reported in a longer, more human-readable format.
- `-g`—Generate the local variable table for debugging use.
- `+K<name>=<TypeKeyWord>`—Perform type substitution: all occurrences of `<name>` in the source are interpreted as the specified `<TypeKeyWord>`. The `<TypeKeyWord>` can only be a primitive data type, such as `int`. For example, the option `+Kfoo=double` will interpret variables declared as type `foo` to be declared as `double`.
- `-nowarn`—Suppress warning messages.
- `-nowrite`—Suppress writing of class files.
- `-O`—Create a small class file by suppressing writing of the line number table. Optimization? Not yet.
- `+P`—Compile pedantically, with many warnings.
- `+T<n>`—Set an alternate tab stop value. Jikes uses tab stops to align parts of its error messages; the default value is `8` if this option is not specified.
- `-verbose`—Run verbosely, listing source and class files read and written during compilation.
- `-Xstdout`—Redirect all output listings to `stdout`.
- `+Z`—Treat cautions as fatal errors. Otherwise, cautions (worse than warnings, not as bad as errors) are nonfatal.

Dependency-Related Options:

Dependencies in Java projects are difficult to describe and handle (see Chapter 48, "`JMakeDepend`: A Project Build Management Utility"). Jikes offers a number of options to control how it discovers, reports, and acts on dependencies between source and class files.

By default, Jikes performs a simple dependency check for the classes it builds—looking for class files that do not exist or are older than source, and looking for simple dependencies between class files. Depending on the results of the analysis, Jikes could compile all classes on the command line, some classes on the command line, or even some classes *not* on the command line. This check (described in more detail in the HTML page shipped with Jikes) is imperfect but is comparable to that performed by many other Java compilers.

The following options modify Jikes' default behavior in handling dependencies:

- `+F`—Enable a more thorough dependency analysis, possibly resulting in performing more compilation. This approach is more expensive than the default behavior but avoids certain perils of missing classes that should be recompiled. See `+U` later in the list for a stronger setting.

- `-depend`—Suppress dependency analysis: recompile everything.
- `+M`—Generate Makefile dependencies, one dependency file per source file. The dependency file, named `<classname>.u`, lists `classfile:source` and `classfile:classfile` dependencies in a format understood by `make`.
- `+M=<filename>`—Generate dependencies, collected into a single file. Format is different from that produced by the plain `+M` option, discussed previously.
- `+U`—Perform a more thorough dependency analysis, like `+F`, discussed previously, but also examine classes in `.zip` and `.jar` archives.
- `-Xdepend`—Recompile all used classes.
- `++`—Enable "incremental mode." This option implies the `+F` flag (discussed previously) but it causes the compiler not to terminate compilation: It sits and waits for terminal input. Enter a blank line, it recompiles; another blank line, another recompile, and so on; enter "`q`" and the compiler terminates.

  This behavior gives you a fast edit-compile cycle: make source changes in your editor and then press Enter in your Jikes terminal window to recompile only the affected modules. Edit some more, compile again with a single keystroke. This not only saves a few keystrokes, it saves the time Jikes takes to build its dependency structures. It's a worthwhile option if you find yourself in a tweak-rebuild-tweak cycle.

Setting the Environment for Jikes

The following environment variables affect Jikes' behavior:

`CLASSPATH`	Class path to search for all classes: system, extension, user.
`JIKESPATH`	Same as `CLASSPATH`; if specified, `JIKESPATH` overrides `CLASSPATH`.

Troubleshooting Jikes Problems

Jikes is a research project on compiling Java, and the team has put considerable energy into shaking out flaws and underspecifications in the language. If compiling a program with Jikes produces different results from compiling with other tools, the cause may be a bug in Jikes. But it is also likely to be a dependence on some underspecified aspect of the Java language.Useful sources of help are

- The HTML page (`jikes.html`) shipped with the Jikes distribution.
- The Jikes mailing list (see the project home page for subscription information). Lists are provided for general discussion, bugs, announcements, patches, and licensing issues.
- The Jikes discussion database (see the project home page for directions).

Summary

This chapter discussed the Jikes compiler from IBM, an open source Java compiler implemented in C++. Jikes is probably the best compiler around for speed and language compliance, but its lack of well-optimized output prevents it from being a complete, one-size-fits-all tool.

CHAPTER 37

KJC: KOPI JAVA COMPILER

This chapter discusses the Kopi Java compiler, an open source Java compiler implemented in Java.

Platforms: JDK1.1/JDK1.2

The Kopi Java compiler, by Vincent Gay-Para and Thomas Graf, is the first Java compiler, implemented in Java, to be published under GPL terms. Kopi is a four-pass optimizing compiler, distributed with all sources—a good compiler and a good study source on Java compilation and optimization techniques.

Kopi enjoys growing acceptance in the Java community. In late 1999, the Kaffe project (see Chapter 26, "Kaffe: A Cleanroom Java Environment") announced it would bundle Kopi with its distribution—replacing the older Pizza compiler.

Obtaining Kopi

Kopi is published by Decision Management Systems (DMS) and is distributed through its Web site: `http://www.dms.at/`. You can download the Kopi compiler suite, various source components, and related DMS products from the site. You can also check out sources from DMS's networked CVS repository (see Chapter 9, "Setting Up a Linux Development Environment," in the section "CVS Remote Repository Servers").

For a minimal download, you need only `kjc.jar`. This gives you everything you need to use the Kopi compiler. Install it anywhere, and include it in your class path to run the compiler.

Should you choose to obtain sources, you will need to obtain some additional technologies, used by Kopi itself, to build the Kopi class libraries:

- The GNU `getopt` utility (available from `http://www.gnu.org/software/java/java-software.html`) is a Java version of the popular C/C++ `getopt(3)`, which assists in parsing command lines.
- The ANTLR (ANother Tool for Language Recognition) generator (available from `http://www.antlr.org/`) is used to build language parsers.

The Structure of Kopi

Kopi contains four packages that encapsulate the compiler's functionality:

- `at.dms.classfile`—An API that supports reading, writing, and modification of class files. It includes a bytecode optimizer and an assembler.
- `at.dms.dis`—A disassembler that dumps class files into the assembler format (`.ksm`) used by Kopi.
- `at.dms.ksm`—An assembler that generates class files from `.ksm` source files.
- `at.dms.kjc`—The compiler itself.

Because source is available, these pieces can be adapted for other uses—subject, of course, to GPL terms (see Chapter 12, "Software Licensing," in the section "The GNU GPL").

Running Kopi

To run Kopi, include the `kjc.jar` archive in your class path. Most options are specified with the customary GNU double-dash prefix.

Synopsis:

`java at.dms.kjc.Main [<options>] <java sources>`

Options:

- `—beautify`—Generate reformatted (pretty-printed) versions of the original source. Does not generate class files. Output is to the current directory unless `-d` (discussed later in the list) is specified. Result is in `<sourcename>.gen`.
- `—classpath <path>`—Specify the compile-time class path.
- `—d <directory>`—Specify a destination directory instead of the current directory. Class files are placed in a hierarchy representing the package name, but source files (from `-beautify` or `-java`) are simply placed in the specified directory.

- `-deprecation`—Report use of deprecated classes and members.
- `-fast`—Choose the fastest modes for compilation.
- `-g`—Compile for debugging.
- `-help`—Generate a help message.
- `-java`—Generate a version of the source with all class names fully qualified (package+class). Output is to the current directory unless `-d` (discussed previously) is specified. The result for each source file appears in `<sourcename>.gen`.
- `-multi`—Run the compiler in multithreaded mode.
- `-nowrite`—Run the compiler only as a syntax-checker: do not generate code.
- `-O0`—Disable all optimization (option is the capital letter O followed by the number zero).
- `-O`—Compile with normal optimization (default).
- `-O2`—Enable maximum optimization.
- `-strict`—Strictly enforce the Java language spec.
- `-verbose`—Generate verbose compilation output.
- `-version`—Report the current compiler version number.
- `-warning`—Display warning messages. Kopi generates some good messages about unused variables and suspicious constructs.

The Extended Kopi Java Compiler

The Kopi compiler is part of a larger work by DMS, the Extended Kopi Java Compiler (`xkjc`), which extends the language for SQL database support. `xkjc` is also available in source and binary form from the DMS Web site.

Briefly, `xkjc`'s enhancements are

- Support for unnamed parameters, as in C++: `foo(int)` is permitted instead of `foo(int x)` in situations where the method signature is needed but the variable is not used.
- A simple assertion mechanism that allows you to write assertions in source. For ease of management, the assertions are automatically disabled by compiling with the `-O` option.
- Operator overloading, as in C++: standard unary and binary operators can be extended to work on any class.
- Embedded Structured Query Language (SQL)—to ease development of database applications. SQL is part of the language (not just quoted strings passed to a database) and is parsed and syntax-checked along with the Java source.

Summary

This chapter discussed the Kopi Java compiler, an open source Java compiler implemented in Java. The Kopi GPL-licensed distribution provides a high-quality optimizing compiler and components you can use to build your own compiler-related tools.

CHAPTER 38

GENERIC JAVA COMPILERS

This chapter discusses Java compilers that support generic programming—what C++ programmers call *templates*.

Platforms: SDK1.1/SDK1.2

One visible shortcoming of the Java language has been lack of support for *generic types*, specifically in the form of *parametric polymorphism*.

Para-*what*?

Parametric polymorphism is the capability to develop procedures for which the *data type* of one or more parameters is unspecified (generic), and can be used with a variety of data types. Developers working in modern environments are typically exposed to three variations on parametric polymorphism:

- In the C programming language, *macro* definitions do not specify parameter types and are thus generic.
- C++ uses templates, which allow generic types to be used with methods and procedures.
- Java considers `java.lang.Object` to be a generic type, but does not otherwise support generic programming.

The following sections explore generic programming in more detail, discuss how Java can benefit from the technique, and describe compilers that support it.

The Problem: Generic Code for Specific Data Types

Most computer languages are much more supportive of variable data than they are of variable types. We illustrate with a small example from C++.

Consider a simple data structures problem. A stack to handle objects of class `foo` might look like this:

```
class foostack
{
public:
    void push(foo obj);
    foo pop();
};
```

Using the stack is straightforward, as shown in this code fragment:

```
foo X;
foostack Y;
     .
     .
Y.push(X);
     .
     .
X = Y.pop();
```

If we want to implement a stack for objects of class `bar`, the code looks familiar:

```
class barstack
{
public:
    void push(bar obj);
    bar pop();
};
```

What is wrong with this picture?

We have written two nearly identical classes to implement a stack—truly a case of reinventing the wheel. Each implementation supports variable data (the argument to `push()` is a variable), but we had to write unique code for two different data types.

Let's look at how Java solves the problem.

The Current Java Solution

The Java answer to the preceding problem is to use the `Object` superclass. Unlike in C++, all Java classes descend from a single superclass, which suggests a generic solution to the problem:

```
public class MyStack
{
```

```
    public void push(Object obj)  { <...implementation...> }
    public Object pop()           { <...implementation...> }
}
```

If we want to implement a stack of class `Foo`, the code is simple:

```
Foo X = new Foo();
MyStack Y = new MyStack();
      .
      .
Y.push(X);
      .
      .
X = (Foo)Y.pop();
```

And what is wrong with *this* picture?

Two problems stand out:

- The need to use a typecast on the `MyStack.pop()` operation is annoying and aesthetically unsatisfactory. Programs that make heavy use of such generic approaches (including users of the Sun Collections classes) tend to make heavy use of typecasts.
- We can push *anything* onto the stack, despite our intent to use it only for objects of type `Foo`. We are relying on runtime checking—the typecast will throw an exception if it is inappropriate—to detect a problem that could easily and more appropriately be found at compile time. Wouldn't it be better and more friendly to spot such a problem, during compilation, at the site of the `MyStack.push()` call?

We look back to C++ for a possible solution.

C++ Templates

Templates are the C++ implementation of parametric polymorphism. Unlike primitive C macros, templates allow you to specify generic parameters while taking advantage of the type-safety offered by the C++ compiler. We illustrate with a reimplementation of the earlier stack example:

```
template <class T> class mystack
{
public:
    void push(T obj);
    T pop();
};
```

We have introduced a new variable to stand in for an arbitrary class, and written a class definition *parameterized* in that variable. The parameter is specified in the `<class T>` declaration and used in the individual method declarations for `push()` and `pop()`.

Here is our rewrite of the application code:

```
foo X;
```

```
mystack<foo> Y;
      .
      .
Y.push(X);
      .
      .
X = Y.pop();
```

The notation is a bit strange, but the effect is just what we need. The `mystack<foo>` declaration requests a version of `mystack` that is specialized for use with class `foo`. The resulting stack class will operate *only* on `foo` objects—`push()` will only take a parameter of that class, and `pop()`'s return type matches that class. We could, using the same "<>" notation, specialize `mystack` for any type.

Java Templates

Does Java need its own version of templates? Despite Sun's initial claim that it is unnecessary, the need is clear to users. Generic types are one of the most requested enhancements to the language, and Sun is giving it serious consideration. Given the associated costs and risks—changing the language, possibly changing the class file format, maintaining backward compatibility, preserving performance—we probably cannot expect a quick resolution to the request. But the interest is strong.

Fortunately, you do not have to wait. Compilers are available today, capable of handling parametric polymorphism and generating code that works in today's environments with today's class libraries. We will look at them in the following sections.

GJ: The Generic Java Compiler

The Generic Java (GJ) compiler is the work of a team based at the University of South Australia. Its first attempt at generic support was the Pizza compiler, which has now been largely supplanted by GJ. The GJ effort includes the participation of two engineers from JavaSoft, and it appears to be the leading model for how generic support might be added to the core language.

The next several subsections describe how to install and use the GJ compiler. In Chapter 48, "`JMakeDepend`: A Project Build Management Utility," we present a project written in Generic Java.

Obtaining and Installing GJ

GJ can be obtained from the project Web site at `http://www.cis.unisa.edu.au/~pizza/gj/`, or at mirrors referenced from the main site. Two different versions are available: one for JDK1.1 and one for JDK1.2—choose the one for your target platform. The distribution is a compressed binary tarball (see Chapter 8, "Installing Additional Linux Software," in the section "Compressed Tarball Binary Distribution"). You can install it anywhere.

To use GJ, you also need an existing JRE or SDK installation—both to run the compiler (which is a Java program) and to resolve classes at compile and runtime.

The GJ installation consists of several subdirectories:

- `classes`—The classes that make up the compiler, plus some type-parameterized versions of the Java Collections classes. (Later, in the section "Using the Collections Classes," we discuss some details of using the Collections classes for generic programming.)
- `doc`—Documentation on the parameterized versions of the Collections classes.
- `src`—Sources for some modified Sun classes. Source for the compiler is not provided and is not publicly available.

The Web site includes detailed installation information, documentation (including a tutorial), an FAQ, and some good related links. GJ has a user community and a mailing list and is actively (if spottily) maintained.

Using GJ's Language Enhancements

The full GJ language and its use are described in papers available from the GJ site. Briefly, GJ's enhancements to Java are much smaller and simpler than C++ templates: Generic classes are specified by one or more comma-separated class name(s) appearing between angle-brackets (<>), immediately to the right of the class name being parameterized. We revisit our earlier `MyStack` definition:

```
public class MyStack<T>
{
    public void push(T obj)  { <...implementation...> }
    public T pop()           { <...implementation...> }
}
```

This gives us a fully specialized implementation of a stack, with type-checking by the compiler, whenever we need one:

```
Foo X = new Foo();
MyStack<Foo> Y = new MyStack<Foo>();
      .
      .
Y.push(X);
      .
      .
X = Y.pop();
```

The subtleties of using GJ templates, including template nesting, are explored in papers available from the GJ site. If you are already familiar with templates, you will find them less general but easier to use than their C++ counterparts.

Subtleties

The differences between Java and C++ result in some interesting under-the-covers implementation differences:

- In C++, the compiler and linker manufacture new code to implement the specializations. For every specialization of class `mystack` created in the previous section "C++ Templates" (`mystack<foo>`, `mystack<bar>`), code is automatically generated and added to the application. The compiler is doing automatically what we did manually in the section "The Problem: Generic Code for Specific Data Types" earlier in this chapter.
- In Java, the same compiled code, if written using `java.lang.Object`, can run all specializations. The GJ compiler generates such code when compiling the parameterized methods, and inserts the necessary typecast operators into code using those methods. It is doing automatically what we did manually in the section "The Current Java Solution" earlier in the chapter.

Some other subtleties to note are as follows:

- The Java bytecodes generated from GJ source looks like any other Java bytecodes. The template-specific information disappears (the compiler developers describe it as *translation by erasure*), and the code is fully interoperable with ordinary Java classes. The template signatures are recorded in the class file as attributes, where they are used by the GJ compiler and ignored by everyone else.
- C++ templates are more general than GJ templates in one important respect: C++ templates can be specialized for any type; GJ templates can be specialized only for classes. You cannot create a `MyStack<int>` (but you *can* create a `MyStack<Integer>`).

Using the Collections Classes

The GJ release includes an implementation of the Sun Collections classes that supports parametric polymorphism. Documentation for these classes is included in the GJ distribution, but, in a nutshell, the classes are parameterized in an obvious way: Occurrences of the `java.lang.Object` type in class definitions are replaced with parameterized classes. For example, the `java.util.TreeSet<A>` class offers the following specialized constructors:

```
TreeSet(Collection<A>)
TreeSet(SortedSet<A>)
TreeSet(Comparator<A>)
```

and the following specialized methods:

```
public Iterator<A> iterator();
public boolean contains(A o);
public boolean add(A o);
public boolean remove(A o);
public SortedSet<A> subSet(A fromElement, A toElement);
public SortedSet<A> headSet(A toElement);
public SortedSet<A> tailSet(A fromElement);
public Comparator<A> comparator();
public A first();
public A last();
```

Listing 38.1 is a simple demonstration using `java.util.TreeSet` to read input lines and output them in sorted order, eliminating duplicate lines.

LISTING 38.1 Demonstration of Generic Programming with the Collections Classes

```
1  import java.util.*;
2  import java.io.*;
3
4  public class StringSort
5  {
6      public static void main(String[] argv) throws java.io.IOException
7      {
8          TreeSet<String> set = new TreeSet<String>();
9          BufferedReader reader =
10             new BufferedReader(new InputStreamReader(System.in));
11         String currLine;
12         while ((currLine = reader.readLine()) != null)
13             set.add(currLine);
14         Iterator<String> iterator = set.iterator();
15         while (iterator.hasNext())
16         {
17             currLine = iterator.next();
18             System.out.println(currLine);
19         }
20     }
21 }
```

The template additions are highlighted in ***bold italic***. Not shown, in line 17, is the `(String)` typecast that would be needed if this program were implemented without templates.

To use these new versions of the Collections classes, you must include them in the class path during compilation—they contain the template signatures needed by the compiler. These new versions are *not* needed at runtime, however; the application will run with the standard class libraries.

Later, in the section "Retrofitting Existing Classes for Generic Programming," we discuss the work necessary to create template-enabled versions of any existing class.

Running the Compiler

The GJ compiler is named `gjc`, and is shipped in the GJ class libraries. To use the compiler, you must include the `classes/` subdirectory of the GJ installation in your class path.

Synopsis:

```
java [<java options>] gjc.Main [<options>] <sourcefiles>
```

Options:

- `-bootclasspath` *<path>*—(**JDK1.2 only**)Set the boot class path. If you are using the parameterized versions of the Sun Collections classes, use this option to place the GJ classes ahead of the core classes in the boot class path:

```
bash$ java gjc.Main -bootclasspath /usr/local/Java/gjc/classes:\
$JAVA_HOME/jre/lib/rt.jar:\
$JAVA_HOME/jre/lib/i18n.jar ...
```

- `-classpath` *<path>*—Set the class path. If you are using the parameterized versions of the Sun Collections classes under JDK1.1, use this option to place the GJ classes ahead of the Sun versions of the classes:

  ```
  bash$ java gjc.Main -classpath /usr/local/Java/gjc/classes:$CLASSPATH ...
  ```

- `-d` *<filename>*—Specify a destination directory for the class files. As with other Java compilers, the class files are placed into a hierarchical directory tree reflecting the package name.
- `-experimental`—Enable experimental compiler features.
- `-g`—Include debugging information (line numbers and local variables) in the class files.
- `-nowarn`—Suppress warning messages.
- `-prompt`—Pause after every error, prompting you to continue or abort.
- `-retrofit` *<path>*—Retrofit existing classes for templates. See the section "Retrofitting Existing Classes for Generic Programming" later in the chapter for details.
- `-s`—Emit source. This runs `gjc` as a translator, generating plain Java source files as output. If you use the `-d` option (discussed previously), the generated `.java` files are placed into a hierarchical directory tree reflecting the package name. If you do not use `-d`, `gjc` will refuse to overwrite any source files with output files.
- `-scramble`—Obfuscate the bytecode by scrambling private identifiers.
- `-scrambleall`—Obfuscate the bytecode by scrambling private and package-visible identifiers.
- `-switchcheck`—Warn about fall-through in switch statements.
- `-unchecked`—Suppress "unchecked" warnings.
- `-verbose`—Run verbosely.
- `-version`—Output current compiler version number.

Retrofitting Existing Classes for Generic Programming

We discussed how to write parameterized classes in the section "Using GJ's Language Enhancements" earlier in the chapter, but how can you take existing classes with existing generic behavior (such as the Collections classes) and create parameterized versions of them?

`gjc` provides just such a facility: *class retrofitting*. It allows you, without benefit of source availability, to create parameterized versions of existing classes. To retrofit a class, begin by generating a list of public and protected class members with the `javap` utility. For example, Listing 38.2 shows what `javap` gives us for the `java.util.Collection` interface.

LISTING 38.2 Output from Running `javap java.util.Collection`

```
public interface java.util.Collection
    /* ACC_SUPER bit NOT set */
{
    public abstract boolean add(java.lang.Object);
    public abstract boolean addAll(java.util.Collection);
    public abstract void clear();
    public abstract boolean contains(java.lang.Object);
    public abstract boolean containsAll(java.util.Collection);
    public abstract boolean equals(java.lang.Object);
    public abstract int hashCode();
    public abstract boolean isEmpty();
    public abstract java.util.Iterator iterator();
    public abstract boolean remove(java.lang.Object);
    public abstract boolean removeAll(java.util.Collection);
    public abstract boolean retainAll(java.util.Collection);
    public abstract int size();
    public abstract java.lang.Object toArray()[];
    public abstract java.lang.Object toArray(java.lang.Object[])[];
}
```

The output shown in Listing 38.2 is almost legal Java source. With some minor editing, it can be turned into the source we need.

To take the next step, choose the members we need to parameterize and create a new, sparse parameterized class definition with just those members. We also need to edit our `javap` output into something that looks like Java source (see Listing 38.3)—adding a package specification, normalizing the class names, and adding argument names:

LISTING 38.3 `Collection.java`

```
package java.util;

public interface Collection<T>
{
    public abstract boolean add(T obj);
    public abstract boolean addAll(Collection<T> coll);
    public abstract boolean contains(T obj);
    public abstract boolean containsAll(Collection<T> coll);
    public abstract boolean equals(T obj);
    public abstract Iterator<T> iterator();
    public abstract boolean remove(T obj);
    public abstract boolean removeAll(Collection<T> coll);
    public abstract boolean retainAll(Collection<T> coll);
    public abstract T toArray(T[] array)[];
}
```

The class described in Listing 38.3 has a dependency on one other class, `java.util.Iterator`, so we create a sparse parameterized definition (see Listing 38.4) for that class.

LISTING 38.4 Iterator.java

```
package java.util;

public interface Iterator<T>
{
    public abstract T next();
}
```

Now we're ready to create parameterized versions of these classes. The `-retrofit <path>` argument runs the compiler in a special mode that generates retrofitted classes. The `<path>` argument is the class path to search for the classes being retrofitted:

```
bash$ java gjc.Main -retrofit /usr/local/Java/jdk1.2/jre/lib/rt.jar -d . \
Iterator.java Collection.java
```

The result is two class files, `java/util/Iterator.class` and `java/util/Collection.class`, that are copies of the original classes from `rt.jar`, but with signatures added to support their use as parameterized classes.

To use the parameterized versions of these classes with `gjc`, include them in your class path *before* any class libraries containing the original version of the classes (see the recommended use of `-classpath` and `-bootclasspath` in the earlier section "Running the Compiler"). You do *not* need these special versions of the classes at runtime—only when compiling.

Subtleties

Why did we choose to parameterize this method:

```
public abstract java.lang.Object toArray(java.lang.Object[])[];
```

but not this method:

```
public abstract java.lang.Object toArray()[];
```

to return an array of generic class `T`?

We know that the first function will, in fact, return the `T[]` passed to it. The second function will return an `Object[]` full of elements of class `T`, but that array is not legally castable to `T[]`—GJ's under-the-covers typecasting will not work.

There is no bulletproof workaround available to the compiler—clearly, retrofitting has its limits.

Creating Documentation Using PizzaDoc

One lasting legacy of the Pizza project—GJ's predecessor—is the PizzaDoc documentation generator. It's a good drop-in replacement for the JDK1.1 `javadoc`, and it boasts the capability to handle source files that use templates.

To use PizzaDoc, you need the Pizza compiler. You can obtain this from the Pizza Web page (`http://www.cis.unisa.edu.au/~pizza/`), or as part of a Kaffe distribution (see Chapter 26, "Kaffe: A Cleanroom Java Environment").

PizzaDoc has one idiosyncrasy in processing GJ sources: You need the `-pizza` option to process `.java` files that use templates. This option is not necessary if the files are instead named with the `.pizza` extension.

Synopsis:

`pizzadoc [<options>] <sourcefiles>`

Options:

Many of the PizzaDoc options are duplicates of options provided by Sun's `javadoc`. You can learn more about `javadoc` and its options in Chapter 23, "The Java Documentation Generator: `javadoc`."

- `-author`—Include author information in the generated documentation (also in `javadoc`).
- `-classpath <pathname>`—Specify a class path (also in `javadoc`).
- `-d <filename>`—Specify a destination directory for the generated documentation (also in `javadoc`).
- `-excludedeprecated`—Exclude classes or members marked as *deprecated*.
- `-index`—Generate an index page.
- `-linktrans`—Transform links, using information read from a `.pizzadoc` file. This is default behavior.
- `-newindex`—Generate new index files (versus updating existing files).
- `-nodeprecated`—Do not include information from `@deprecated` documentation tags (also in `javadoc`).
- `-noindex`—Do not generate a class index (also in `javadoc`).
- `-nointerface`—Do not generate pages for pure interfaces.
- `-nolinktrans`—Disable `-linktrans` (discussed earlier in the list) behavior.
- `-nosourcename`—Do not include source filenames in the pages.
- `-notree`—Do not generate a class hierarchy list (also in `javadoc`). This is default behavior.
- `-package`—Generate documentation on `public`, `protected`, and `package`-accessible classes and class members (also in `javadoc`).
- `-pizza`—Recognize the GJ template extensions. Use this flag when processing `.java` files containing Generic Java.
- `-private`—Generate documentation on all classes and class members (also in `javadoc`).
- `-protected`—Generate documentation on `protected` and `public` classes and class members (also in `javadoc`).

- `-public`—Generate documentation on public classes and class members (also in *javadoc*).
- `-since`—Include information from `@since` tags.
- `-sourceversion`—Include information from `@version` tags.
- `-tree`—Generate a class hierarchy tree (versus `-notree`).
- `-verbose`—Run verbosely.

Alternative Generic Java Compilers

GJ is not the only generic Java compiler in town. Two others are known, although they appear to receive little maintenance these days.

The JUMP Compiler

The JUMP compiler extends Java with a number of familiar C++ features:

- Operator overloading—The capability to define class operations for the unary and binary operators.
- Default parameters—The capability to underspecify a method call and allow default values to fill in the blanks.
- Parametric polymorphism—This version uses a template instantiation code generation mechanism similar to C++.
- Global variables and functions—As in C++, globals can be defined outside a class context.
- Namespaces—As in C++, the variable namespace can be segmented into multiple spaces to avoid name collisions.

The compiler is a native program—much faster than Java-based compilers—and generates standard Java bytecodes that can be interpreted by standard JVMs.

You can obtain JUMP from `http://ourworld.compuserve.com/homepages/DeHoeffner/jump.htm`.

The PolyJ Compiler

A product of the MIT Laboratory for Computer Science, PolyJ is also heavily mentioned in the Sun discussions supporting parametric polymorphism. The language and implementation approach is different from that of GJ. An extensive comparison is provided at the PolyJ Web site.

PolyJ is implemented on top of the `guavac` compiler, a free natively implemented Java compiler. As of this writing, PolyJ supported JDK1.02 but not JDK1.1. Current evidence suggests that `guavac` is no longer maintained (probably put out of business by the Jikes compiler) and that PolyJ is not getting much attention.

The PolyJ home page is at `http://www.pmg.lcs.mit.edu/polyj/`.

Summary

This chapter explored generic programming in Java and the compilers that support it through the use of templates. Support for generic types may someday appear in Sun's JDK, but there is currently no indication when (or if) that will occur.

CHAPTER 39

THE JIKES DEBUGGER

From IBM's AlphaWorks, the people who brought you the Jikes compiler (see Chapter 36, "The Jikes Compiler"), comes the Jikes Debugger (JD).

Platforms: SDK1.1

JD is a GUI-based Java debugger written in Java. It does not enjoy the level of success or support of the Jikes compiler, but it's a useful and powerful tool.

Obtaining the Jikes Debugger

To obtain JD, visit the AlphaWorks home page (`http://alphaworks.ibm.com`), navigate to the technology page for the Jikes Debugger, and download. The download is in the form of a zip file, which you can install anywhere.

The documented system requirements are a JDK1.1.5 or greater installation. JD has never been ported to SDK1.2, and its heavy SDK1.1 dependencies prevent its reliable use in that environment.

Contents of the JD Distribution

The distribution contains:

- A `.zip` application archive containing all the JD class files; add this to your class path to run JD.
- Source for *most* of JD (except, for licensing reasons, some classes created by modifying Sun sources). The source is included in the `.zip` archive.
- Some sample invocation scripts.
- Bits of documentation, including an HTML page.

Running JD

The first requirement for debugging with JD, or any debugger, is to compile the application with the debug flag. For Sun's `javac` compiler, as for most compilers, this is the `-g` flag.

To use JD, you must include the JD archive, `jd.zip`, in your class path.

Launching JD

Two different debugger invocations are provided—one to start a new process under the debugger, and one to attach the debugger to a process that is already running.

Synopsis:

```
java jd.Main [<jd_args>] [<jvm_args>] [<classname> [<class_args>]]
```

```
java jd.Main [<jd_args>] -host <hostname> -password <password>
```

The first form starts a new application under the debugger. The three groups of arguments are:

- *<jd_args>*—arguments passed to JD. The recognized arguments are described later in this section.
- *<jvm_args>*—arguments passed to the `java` launcher starting the application. The first argument on the command line that is not recognized as a JD argument is interpreted as the end of the *<jd_args>* and the start of the *<jvm_args>*.

  Arguments recognized by the `java` launcher are described in Chapter 17, "The Java Application Launchers: `java`, `jre`, and `oldjava`," in the section "java Launcher."
- *<class_args>*—arguments passed to the class being debugged, just as they would be specified if the class were run from a normal `java` launch command.

The second form attaches JD to a running application that was started with the `-debug` option. *<jd_args>* has the same meaning as for the first form.

Both forms of debugger invocation usage exactly mirror those provided by the Sun Java Debugger (see Chapter 20, "The Java Debugger: `jdb`").

Arguments:

These arguments are recognized as valid `<jd_args>`:

- `-classpath <classpath>`—Specify the class path JD searches for classes.
- `-help`—Print a usage message.
- `-noversioncheck`—You must specify this option if you are running in any environment other than JDK1.1.6; otherwise, the compiler will check the environment and refuse to run.
- `-sourcepath <sourcepath>`—Specify the path JD searches for source files. JD expects to find sources in a directory hierarchy reflecting the full *package+class name*. In other words, a source living in the same directory as its class file will be found.

These arguments are used with the second form of the JD invocation:

- `-host <hostname>`—Specify the host on which the application is running.
- `-password <password>`—Specify the password that was reported by the `java` launcher when the application was started with the `-debug` option.

Using The JD GUI

Figure 39.1 shows the Jikes Debugger GUI.

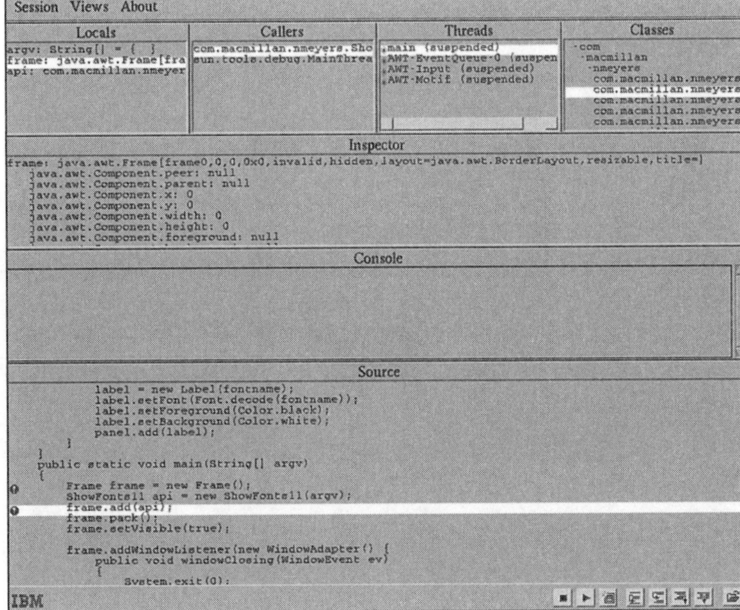

FIGURE 39.1
The Jikes Debugger interface is clear and intuitive.

The interface is well designed and easy to use. Table 39.1 itemizes the panels. The top four panels provide navigation through the program being debugged, whereas the bottom three provide visibility and interaction with the program.

TABLE 39.1 Panels in the Jikes Debugger GUI

Panel	Purpose
`Locals`	Shows the value of local variables. If you are not seeing your local variables, the class was probably compiled without the `-g` option.
`Callers`	Navigates the call stack.
`Threads`	Allows you to inspect the application threads.
`Classes`	Allows you to inspect code in various classes.
`Inspector`	Provides detailed information on the currently selected local variable. You can use the mouse to explore the data structure in depth, increasing detail by clicking on fields of interest.
`Console`	Handles input to and output from the application. You can type input into this panel if any input is needed.
`Source`	Displays source in the currently selected stack frame.

A few menus and buttons provide the rest of the interface:

- Pull-down menus from the menu bar allow you to set the class path and source path, restart the program, and selectively show or hide the panels.
- The buttons on the lower right take care of stopping; starting; single-stepping; and stepping into, out of, and over method calls. These buttons display ToolTips (hints about what they do) when the mouse hovers overhead.

JD Bugs

- There is apparently some functionality associated with the right mouse button in the panels, but the pop-up window disappears so quickly that it remains a mystery.
- The interface is strange and confusing if JD cannot allocate enough colors, the highlighted lines (refer to Figure 39.1) are not highlighted, making it difficult to figure out where you are. There is no warning message under JDK1.1 to indicate that not enough colors were available. For an X server trick that works around this problem, see Chapter 56, "X Window System Tips and Tricks" in the section "`xwinwrap`: Controlling Colormap and Visual Usage."

Running a Sample Session

We'll take a quick test drive, using the `ShowFonts11` example from Chapter 14, "Configuring the Linux JSDK/JRE Environment," in the section "Adding, Changing, and Configuring Fonts in JDK1.1." Starting up the debugger

```
bash$ jd.Main -noversioncheck com.macmillan.nmeyers.ShowFonts11
```

starts the session. Referring to Figure 39.1, clicking the mouse on the third line of the main program sets a breakpoint at the `frame.add()` call.

Now we are ready to run. The buttons in the lower right of the GUI (see Figure 39.2) control execution. From left to right, these buttons do the following: stop execution, start execution, refresh the GUI windows, step over method calls, single-step, step out of current method, and debug a single thread.

Pressing the button to release all threads (in Figure 39.2) starts execution; the program runs until it reaches the breakpoint.

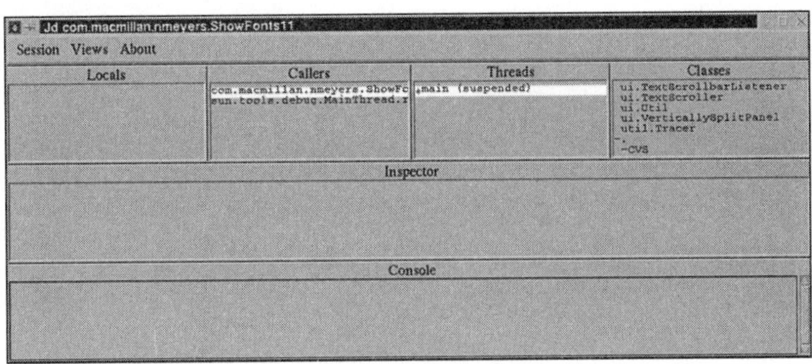

FIGURE 39.2
The stop/start controls; the currently highlighted button starts or continues execution.

Having reached the breakpoint, we can use the `Locals` and `Inspector` panels to examine data. In Figure 39.3, we have chosen in the `Locals` panel to inspect the variable `frame`. We can navigate in the `Inspector` panel to view `frame`'s contents.

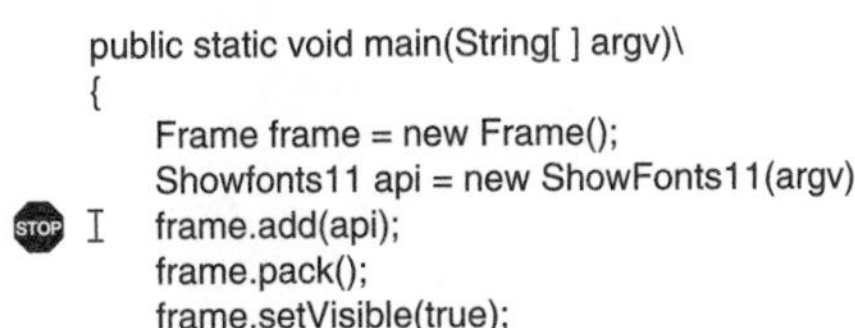

```
public static void main(String[ ] argv)\
{
    Frame frame = new Frame();
    Showfonts11 api = new ShowFonts11(argv)"
STOP I  frame.add(api);
    frame.pack();
    frame.setVisible(true);
```

FIGURE 39.3
Inspecting the `frame` variable.

You can continue running and debugging using the controls we've shown in this section.

Summary

This chapter discussed the Jikes Debugger, from IBM's AlphaWorks. Jikes is not only free, it is a first-rate GUI debugger. Unfortunately, it has not been ported to JDK1.2 and appears to be receiving no further development.

CHAPTER 40

DDD: THE DATA DISPLAY DEBUGGER

The *Data Display Debugger* (DDD) is a free GUI front end for non-GUI debuggers such as Sun's JDK debugger.

Platforms: SDK1.1/SDK1.2

DDD is not itself a debugger, but it makes many popular text-oriented debuggers much easier to use. In addition to supporting such classic UNIX native-code debuggers as `gdb`, `dbx`, and `xdb`, it has grown in recent years to support debuggers for Perl, Python, and Java.

DDD's magic is to present a well-designed debugger GUI and translate the user's actions into the text commands recognized by the underlying tool. Its ability to drive Sun's `jdb` (see Chapter 20, "The Java Debugger: `jdb`") gives Java developers a powerful graphical debugger.

Obtaining DDD

DDD is widely available from Linux and UNIX repositories. It is published in source and binary form (for libc5 and glibc systems), as both RPMs and tarballs. Pick your favorite installation method and choose the distribution appropriate to your environment.

Binary distributions of DDD come in three variants:

- `ddd-dynamic`—A dynamically linked version of DDD, with dependencies on many X libraries, and on the Motif (or Lesstif clone) library.

- `ddd-semistatic`—A version with the Motif library statically linked in, eliminating dependence on a local Motif installation. This version still has dependencies on many X libraries.
- `ddd-static`—A fully statically linked executable, with no dependencies on any shared libraries (not even libc).

For systems with Motif or Lesstif installed, `ddd-dynamic` is the sensible choice; for systems without Motif or Lesstif, `ddd-semistatic` is the sensible choice.

Running DDD

Basic DDD use is straightforward, and we will list just the basic options and operations relevant to Java debugging. Full DDD functionality is extensive: the man page (run `man ddd`) is 112 pages long.

Synopsis:

```
ddd --jdb [<options>] <class>
```

Options:

- `--font` *<font>*—Specify an X font to use for the GUI.
- `--fontsize` *<size>*—Specify font size, in 1/10-point units.
- `--trace`—Send a running log of `DDD<->`*jdb* interaction to `stderr`.
- `--tty`—Use the terminal from which `ddd` is launched as a text debugging console. The default behavior is to provide the console in one of the windows of the DDD main GUI.
- `--version`—Report DDD version number, then exit.
- `--configuration`—Report DDD configuration flags, then exit.
- `--manual`—Run `man ddd` to view the documentation.
- `--license`—Display the DDD license.

As an X Toolkit program, the `ddd` executable also supports the X toolkit options described on the X Window System man page (`man X`).

Notice the lack of a `--classpath` option. You should set your class path with the `CLASSPATH` environment variable.

As with the Jikes Debugger, DDD becomes difficult to use if it doesn't manage to allocate all the colors it needs. The workaround in Chapter 56, "X Window System Tips and Tricks," in the section "`xwinwrap`: Controlling Colormap and Visual Usage" can be useful here.

The DDD GUI

Figure 40.1 shows the basic DDD interface.

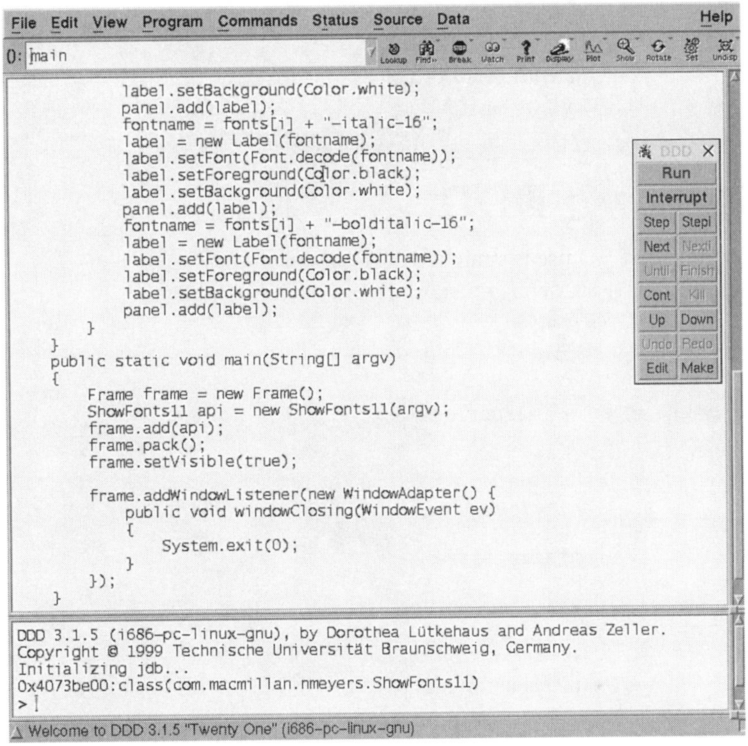
File Edit View Program Commands Status Source Data Help
0: main
Lookup Find» Break Watch Print Display Plot Show Rotate Set Undisp
label.setBackground(Color.white);
panel.add(label);
fontname = fonts[i] + "-italic-16";
label = new Label(fontname);
label.setFont(Font.decode(fontname));
label.setForeground(Color.black);
label.setBackground(Color.white);
panel.add(label);
fontname = fonts[i] + "-bolditalic-16";
label = new Label(fontname);
label.setFont(Font.decode(fontname));
label.setForeground(Color.black);
label.setBackground(Color.white);
panel.add(label);
}
}
public static void main(String[] argv)
{
Frame frame = new Frame();
ShowFonts11 api = new ShowFonts11(argv);
frame.add(api);
frame.pack();
frame.setVisible(true);
frame.addWindowListener(new WindowAdapter() {
public void windowClosing(WindowEvent ev)
{
System.exit(0);
}
});
}
DDD
Run
Interrupt
Step Stepi
Next Nexti
Until Finish
Cont Kill
Up Down
Undo Redo
Edit Make
DDD 3.1.5 (i686-pc-linux-gnu), by Dorothea Lütkehaus and Andreas Zeller.
Copyright © 1999 Technische Universität Braunschweig, Germany.
Initializing jdb...
0x4073be00:class(com.macmillan.nmeyers.ShowFonts11)
>
Welcome to DDD 3.1.5 "Twenty One" (i686-pc-linux-gnu)

FIGURE 40.1
DDD GUI, with source window, console window, and command tool.

Table 40.1 lists the functions available with the windows shown in Figure 40.1.

TABLE 40.1 DDD's Windows and Their Functions

Window	Function
Source Window	Navigate through source. Also set breakpoints and examine data.
Console Window	View the interaction between DDD and `jdb`. You can also type in your own `jdb` commands. If you run DDD with the `--tty` option, the terminal from which you launched the debugger acts as the console.
Data Window	Examine data structures in detail (not shown in the figure).
Command Tool	Basic run, stop, single-step, step-over, and similar functionality.

The right mouse button provides pop-up functionality in the source window, allowing you to manage breakpoints and examine variables (see Figure 40.2). The pop-ups are context-sensitive—the available functions depend on the location of the mouse when the mouse button is pressed.

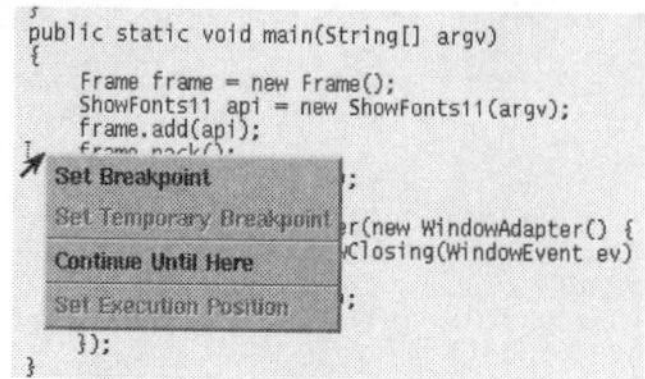

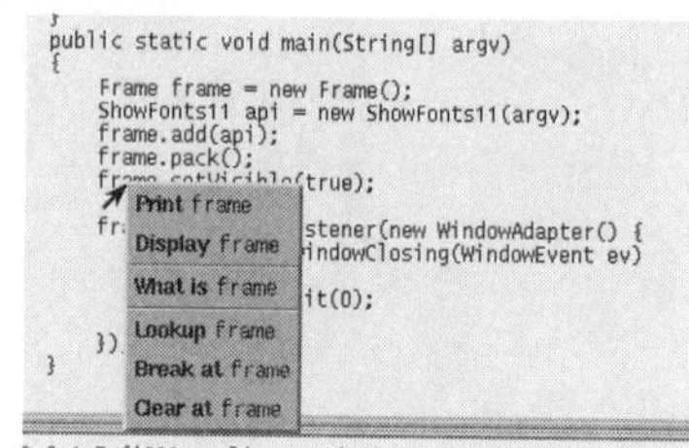

FIGURE 40.2
Pop-up menus from the right mouse button allow you to control breakpoints and examine variables.

The remainder of DDD's extensive functionality—configuration, search, execution control—is offered in the various pull-down menus on the menu bar (see Figure 40.3).

FIGURE 40.3
DDD's pull-down menus.

Running a Sample Session

We'll test drive the `ShowFonts11` example, as we did with the Jikes Debugger (see Chapter 39, "The Jikes Debugger," in the section "Running a Sample Session"). This command launches the session:

```
bash$ ddd -jdb com.macmillan.nmeyers.ShowFonts11
```

After startup, the `ShowFonts11` source appears in the Source window. By right-clicking to the left of the third line of `main()` in the Source window and choosing `Set Breakpoint` from the pop-up window, we can set a breakpoint(see Figure 40.4).

FIGURE 40.4

A breakpoint (indicated with the stop sign) at the `frame.add()` call.

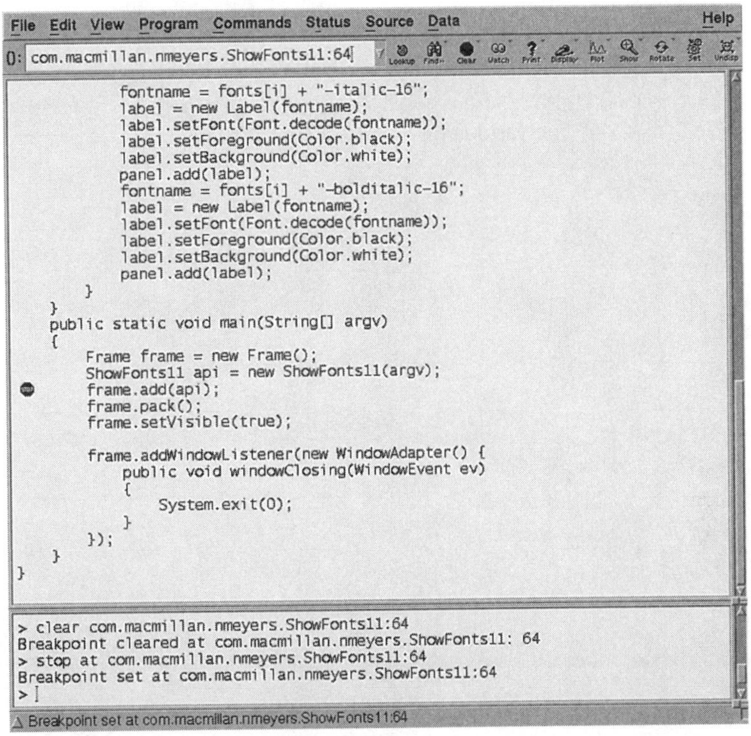

```
File Edit View Program Commands Status Source Data Help
(): com.macmillan.nmeyers.ShowFonts11:64

            fontname = fonts[i] + "-italic-16";
            label = new Label(fontname);
            label.setFont(Font.decode(fontname));
            label.setForeground(Color.black);
            label.setBackground(Color.white);
            panel.add(label);
            fontname = fonts[i] + "-bolditalic-16";
            label = new Label(fontname);
            label.setFont(Font.decode(fontname));
            label.setForeground(Color.black);
            label.setBackground(Color.white);
            panel.add(label);
        }
    }
    public static void main(String[] argv)
    {
        Frame frame = new Frame();
        ShowFonts11 api = new ShowFonts11(argv);
        frame.add(api);
        frame.pack();
        frame.setVisible(true);

        frame.addWindowListener(new WindowAdapter() {
            public void windowClosing(WindowEvent ev)
            {
                System.exit(0);
            }
        });
    }
}

> clear com.macmillan.nmeyers.ShowFonts11:64
Breakpoint cleared at com.macmillan.nmeyers.ShowFonts11: 64
> stop at com.macmillan.nmeyers.ShowFonts11:64
Breakpoint set at com.macmillan.nmeyers.ShowFonts11:64
>
Breakpoint set at com.macmillan.nmeyers.ShowFonts11:64
```

We start the program with the `Run` button in the command tool or the `Program` pull-down menu. A green arrow (see Figure 40.5) indicates that we've reached the line of interest.

Now, by right-clicking on an instance of the `frame` variable, we can ask to `Display frame`. This brings up a detailed view in the Data window (see Figure 40.6).

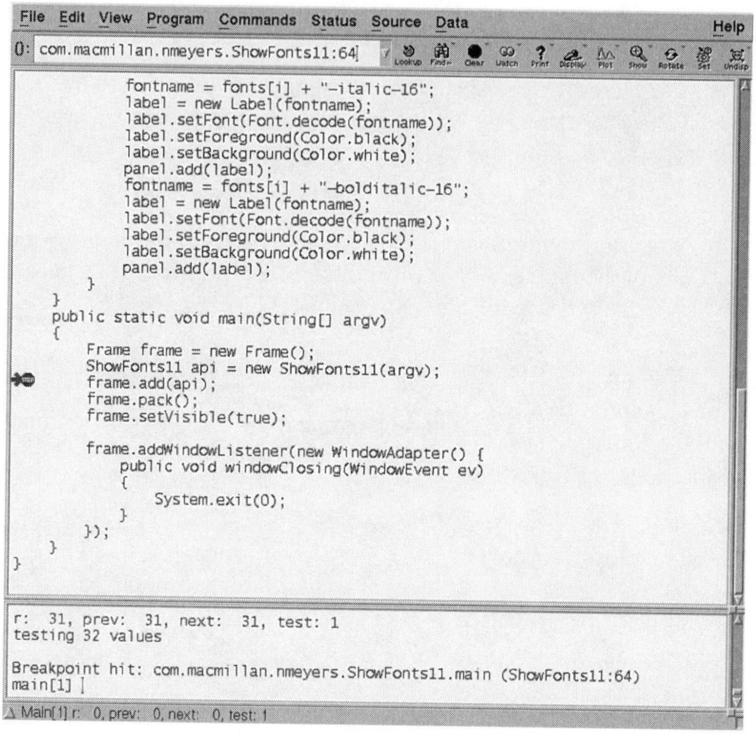

FIGURE 40.5
The green arrow shows our position—we've hit the breakpoint.

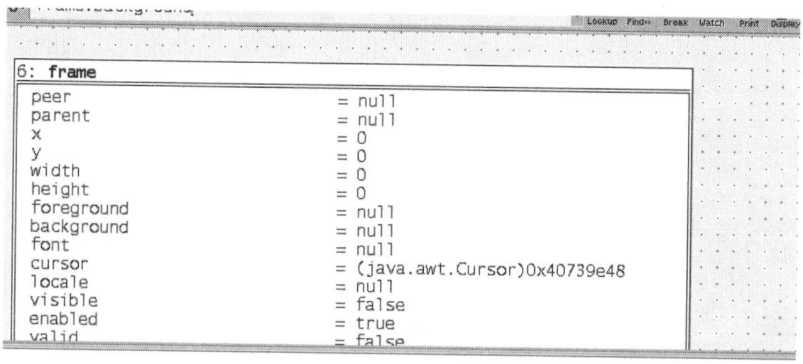

```
File Edit View Program Commands Status Source Data                Help
0: com.macmillan.nmeyers.ShowFonts11:64
            fontname = fonts[i] + "-italic-16";
            label = new Label(fontname);
            label.setFont(Font.decode(fontname));
            label.setForeground(Color.black);
            label.setBackground(Color.white);
            panel.add(label);
            fontname = fonts[i] + "-bolditalic-16";
            label = new Label(fontname);
            label.setFont(Font.decode(fontname));
            label.setForeground(Color.black);
            label.setBackground(Color.white);
            panel.add(label);
        }
    }
    public static void main(String[] argv)
    {
        Frame frame = new Frame();
        ShowFonts11 api = new ShowFonts11(argv);
        frame.add(api);
        frame.pack();
        frame.setVisible(true);

        frame.addWindowListener(new WindowAdapter() {
            public void windowClosing(WindowEvent ev)
            {
                System.exit(0);
            }
        });
    }
}

r:  31, prev:  31, next:  31, test: 1
testing 32 values

Breakpoint hit: com.macmillan.nmeyers.ShowFonts11.main (ShowFonts11:64)
main[1]
Main[1] r: 0, prev: 0, next: 0, test: 1
```

FIGURE 40.6
Details on the `frame` variable in the Data window.

```
6: frame
peer          = null
parent        = null
x             = 0
y             = 0
width         = 0
height        = 0
foreground    = null
background    = null
font          = null
cursor        = (java.awt.Cursor)0x40739e48
locale        = null
visible       = false
enabled       = true
valid         = false
```

Examining the data, we can right-click on individual components and ask to **`Display()`** their contents (see Figure 40.7).

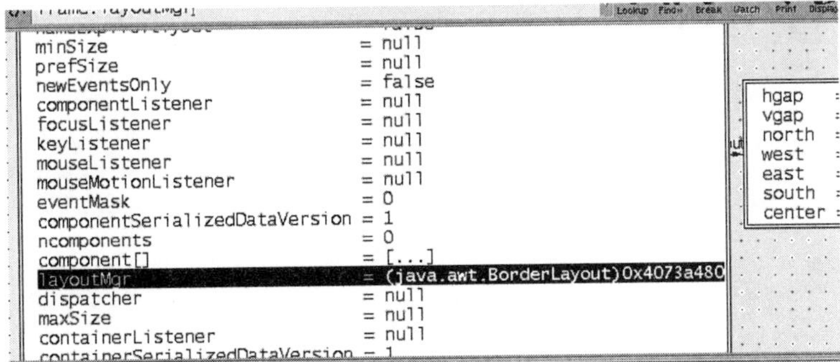

FIGURE 40.7
Right-clicking on `layoutMgr` allows us to descend and explore its contents.

Finally, we can generate a more permanent record with the **`File`**, **`Print Graph`** menu button, which allows us to generate a PostScript ® version of the information in the Data window (see Figure 40.8).

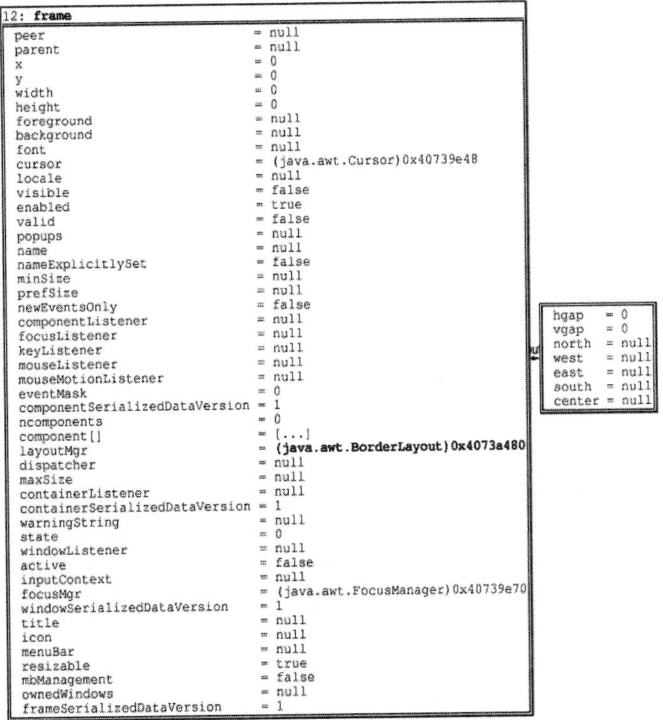

FIGURE 40.8
PostScript rendition of the contents of the Data window.

DDD Quality

DDD is a fine tool. Experience suggests that it works well with every debugger it uses—except the SDK1.2 `jdb`. The problem isn't DDD, it is the instability of that debugger. Its unpredictable behavior makes the SDK1.2 `jdb` difficult to use by itself, and it badly confuses DDD. Until that debugger functions more reliably (perhaps in an upcoming Blackdown JDK release), you may not want to use it with DDD.

Summary

This chapter explored DDD, a powerful GUI front end to text-oriented debuggers such as `jdb`. DDD drives many different debuggers, giving you the opportunity to use a consistent debugging interface with Java, C/C++, and numerous other languages and environments.

PART IX

IDES, GUI BUILDERS, AND RAD TOOLS

Integrated Development Environments (IDEs), GUI Builders, and *Rapid Application Development* (RAD) tools are all GUI-based development tools, and the distinctions between them can be a bit fuzzy. In this part, we examine some of the available offerings, including both Linux native apps and some Java apps that are usable on Linux.

The story for advanced development tools on Linux has been weak to date, with most of the interesting offerings targeted at the huge Microsoft Windows market. This doesn't mean that you cannot develop significant Java applications on Linux: There is really very little you can do with the most advanced RAD tool that you cannot do with the Sun SDK or some of the other tools we've examined. But the best advanced tools can offer significant productivity gains, and their availability for Linux is steadily improving.

So what are these products and what do the names mean? Here are some brief definitions:

- IDEs combine the most common components of application development—editing, compiling, running, and debugging—into a single GUI-based environment. Additional capabilities often include project management, revision control, and *wizards* that help automate the creation of new components.
- GUI Builders are specialized tools: Their purpose is to speed you through one of the most dreary steps of creating a GUI application—laying out and customizing the UI components.

  After creating the layout, GUI builders generate skeleton application code from which you can build the rest of the program. At that point, a typical GUI-builder's usefulness ends. But many modern IDEs incorporate GUI-building among their other features, allowing you to move freely between GUI design and application development.
- Rapid Application Development is not really a type of tool, it's a methodology for speeding up software product development cycles. RAD tools are designed to support the methodology by assisting in some of the project phases—gathering requirements, prototyping, computer-aided software engineering, supporting collaboration, and testing—comprising RAD.

CHAPTER 41

vTcLava: A TCL-BASED JAVA GUI BUILDER

VTcLava is a GUI builder, based on the Tcl scripting language, supporting generation of Java GUIs.

Platforms: SDK1.1/SDK1.2

Visual Tcl (vTcl) is a GUI builder for the Tcl scripting language and its companion Tk GUI toolkit. The tool is implemented entirely in Tcl/Tk and is designed to generate new GUIs in the form of Tcl/Tk scripts. The tool is also extensible, allowing developers to create new functionality with add-on modules.

One such module is vTcLava, developed by Constantin Teodorescu, that turns vTcl into a GUI builder for Java. The result is a basic tool that can get you quickly into the Swing-based GUI business. The tool is distributed under GPL terms.

Obtaining vTcLava

The home page for vTcLava is http://www.java.ro/vtclava. The author distributes it in the form of a modified vTcl distribution, so you do not need to separately obtain vTcl. (But, for the record, the vTcl home page is http://www.neuron.com/stewart/vtcl.)

The vTcLava distribution is in the form of a compressed tarball. To install it, unpack it into any convenient directory. Because the implementation is entirely in the form of scripts, no further building needs to be done.

Resolving vTcLava Platform Dependencies

vTcLava is a portable tool implemented entirely with Tcl scripts. It requires the following components (which are available for Linux and for many other platforms, including Windows):

- Tcl, v8.0 or later. This is included with almost all Linux distributions and can also be widely found at software repositories. For Red Hat users, the RPM is tcl. Tcl can also be obtained from the publisher of the technology, Scriptics, at http://www.scriptics.com.
- Tk, v8.0 or later. This is the graphical toolkit associated with Tcl and is distributed through the same channels. The RPM is named tk. Tk includes the wish (WIndowing SHell) executable, which is the environment under which vTcLava runs.
- SDK1.2, or SDK1.1 + Swing.

Running vTcLava

You need to set two environment variables to run vTcLava:

- PATH_TO_WISH—the full pathname of the wish executable.
- VTCL_HOME—the directory in which vTcLava is installed.

Then run the wish script $VTCL_HOME/vt.tcl.

For convenience, the vTcLava installation includes a shell script, $VTCL_HOME/vtcl, that can be used to launch vTcLava after the appropriate edits have been made to the PATH_TO_WISH and VTCL_HOME assignments at the beginning of the script.

Synopsis:

```
wish $VTCL_HOME/vt.tcl
```

Using vTcLava

Figure 41.1 shows most of the vTcLava windows (clockwise from upper-left): main window, list of top-level windows, view of widget tree hierarchy, workspace, tools palette, attribute editor, and (center) function list.

To start creating a new GUI, select File, New from the menu. This creates a new empty workspace, which you can begin to populate with objects from the tools palette. The palette offers some basic widgets—boxes, buttons, scrollbars, labels, lists—with some more advanced items (scrolled text areas and such) available by choosing Compound, Insert, System from the menu.

To add a new component, choose it from the tools palette or the Compound menu. It will appear in the workspace, where you can move and/or resize it. To change the component, select that component (the top button is selected in Figure 41.1) and make changes in the attributes editor. For example, by changing the text (see Figure 41.2), we change the label that appears on the button (see Figure 41.3).

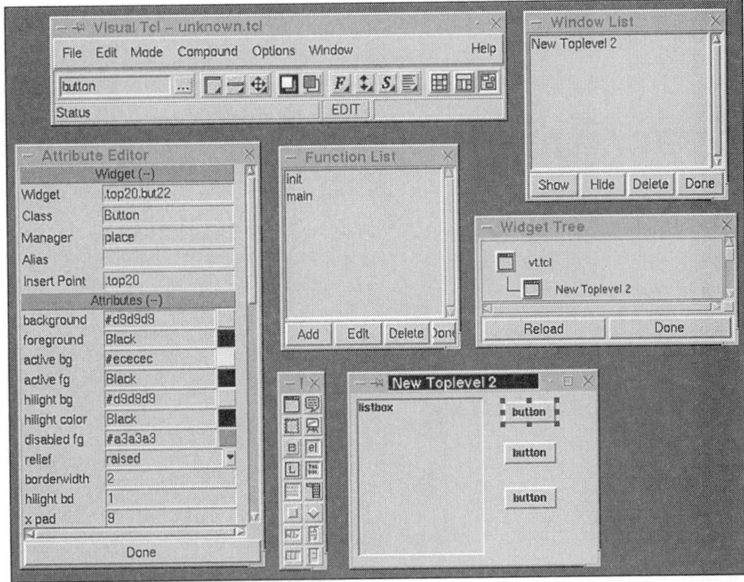

FIGURE 41.1
vTcLava windows.

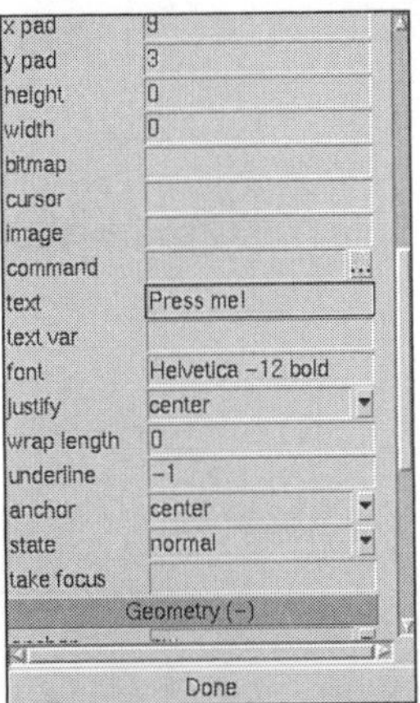

FIGURE 41.2
Editing the text attribute for our button.

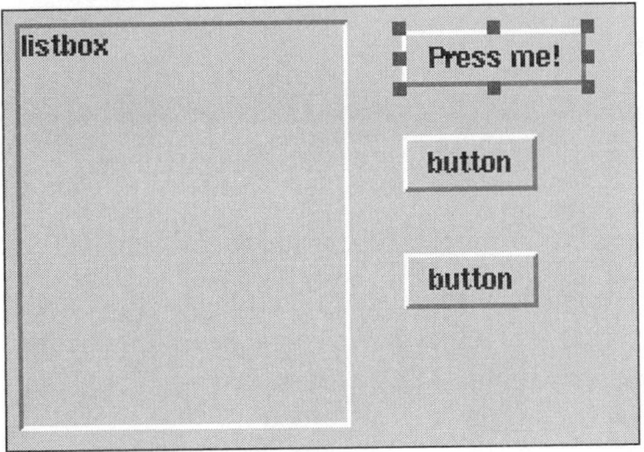

FIGURE 41.3
New text for the button.

To test-drive the interface, choose test mode (select `Mode`, `Test Mode`) from the menu bar. Interface behavior will be simulated under the Tcl interpreter.

Generating Java Code

To start generating Java code, right-click in the workspace and select `Generate Java UI`. This brings up a new Java Console window (see Figure 41.4).

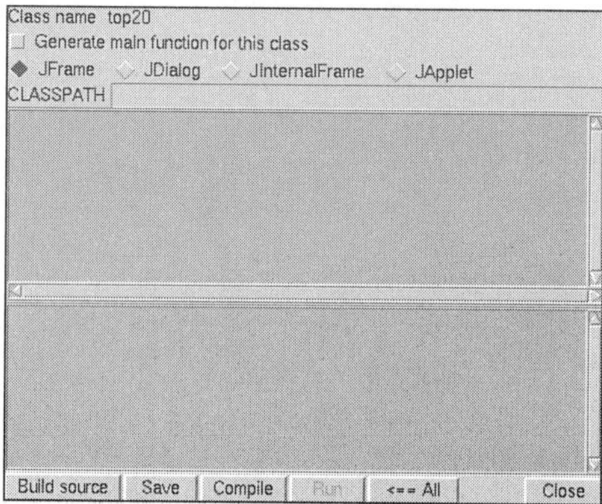

FIGURE 41.4
The Java Console—used for GUI generation.

Choose your top-level class (`JFrame`, `JDialog`, `JInternalFrame`, or `JApplet`) and, if necessary, choose to generate a `main()` procedure. Choosing the `Build Source` button generates the code (see Figure 41.5), which uses Swing components.

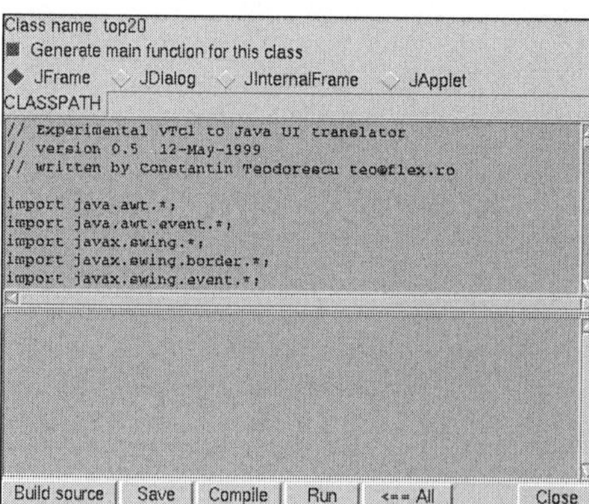

FIGURE 41.5
After generation of the GUI.

Additional buttons on the interface allow you to save, compile, and run the code.

Examining the generated skeleton code (see Listing 41.1), you see a fully functional program that creates, initializes, and places all the components (cryptic component names, such as `top`, `lis`, and `but`, are derived from Tk component names). The skeleton also includes empty callbacks for various events—button-clicking and list selection—that can occur on the components.

LISTING 41.1 Java Code Generated by vTcLava

```
// Experimental vTcl to Java UI translator
// version 0.5  12-May-1999
// written by Constantin Teodorescu teo@flex.ro

import java.awt.*;
import java.awt.event.*;
import javax.swing.*;
import javax.swing.border.*;
import javax.swing.event.*;
//import com.sun.java.swing.*;
//import com.sun.java.swing.event.*;
//import com.sun.java.swing.border.*;

// user defined import taken from
// proc top20:import (if any)


public class top20 extends JFrame {
  JList lis21 = new JList ();
  JScrollPane jsp_lis21 = new JScrollPane();
  JButton but22 = new JButton ();
  JButton but23 = new JButton ();
  JButton but24 = new JButton ();

  Font sansserif_font = new Font("SansSerif",0,12);
  Color black_color = new Color(0);
  // User defined variables
  // from proc top20:variables (if any)


  // Construct the frame
  public top20 () {

          enableEvents(AWTEvent.WINDOW_EVENT_MASK);
          try {
                  widgetinit();
          } catch (Exception e) {
                  e.printStackTrace();
          }
  }

  // component initialization
  private void widgetinit() throws Exception {
          this.getContentPane().setLayout(null);

          this.setSize(new Dimension(289,219));
          this.setLocation(595,542);
          this.setResizable(true);
          this.setTitle("New Toplevel 2");
```

continued on next page

continued from previous page

```

    jsp_lis21.getViewport().add(lis21);
    jsp_lis21.setBounds(new Rectangle(5, 5, 148, 176));
    this.getContentPane().add(jsp_lis21, null);
    lis21.addListSelectionListener(new ListSelectionListener() {
            public void valueChanged(ListSelectionEvent e) {
                    lis21_state_changed (e);
}
    });
    but22.setBounds(new Rectangle(175, 10, 84, 26));
    but22.setText("Press me!");
    but22.setMargin(new Insets(0,0,0,0));
    but22.addActionListener(new java.awt.event.ActionListener() {
            public void actionPerformed(ActionEvent e) {
                    but22_click (e);
            }
    });
    this.getContentPane().add(but22, null);
    but23.setBounds(new Rectangle(175, 55, 62, 26));
    but23.setText("button");
    but23.setMargin(new Insets(0,0,0,0));
    but23.addActionListener(new java.awt.event.ActionListener() {
            public void actionPerformed(ActionEvent e) {
                    but23_click (e);
            }
    });
    this.getContentPane().add(but23, null);
    but24.setBounds(new Rectangle(175, 105, 62, 26));
    but24.setText("button");
    but24.setMargin(new Insets(0,0,0,0));
    but24.addActionListener(new java.awt.event.ActionListener() {
            public void actionPerformed(ActionEvent e) {
                    but24_click (e);
            }
    });
    this.getContentPane().add(but24, null);

            // User defined init statements

    }


  // Overriden so we can exit on System Close

    protected void processWindowEvent(WindowEvent e) {
            super.processWindowEvent(e);
            if (e.getID() == WindowEvent.WINDOW_CLOSING) {
                    System.exit(0);
            }
    }

     void lis21_state_changed (ListSelectionEvent e) {
```

```
            if ((! e.getValueIsAdjusting()) && (lis21.getSelectedValue()!=
➥null)) {
            // Code for lis21 click event

            }
      }

      void but22_click (ActionEvent e) {
      // Code for but22 click event

      }

      void but23_click (ActionEvent e) {
      // Code for but23 click event

      }

      void but24_click (ActionEvent e) {
      // Code for but24 click event

      }


      // User defined methods for top20 class from
      // proc top20:methods (if any)


      public static void main(String argv[]) {
                 top20 _top20 = new top20 ();
                 _top20.setVisible(true);
      }

}
```

Figure 41.6 shows the Java program in operation: an empty list and three buttons.

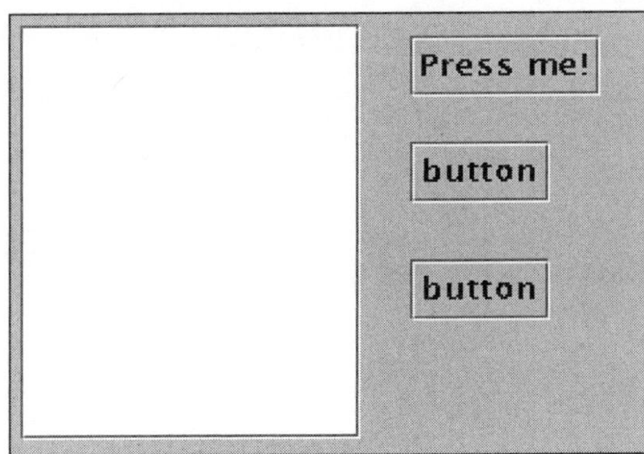

FIGURE 41.6
Running the generated program.

Improving `vTcLava` Capabilities

The `vTcLava` tool is an early work, written to solve the author's problem and then released for public consumption. It is still very Tk-flavored, trying (not always successfully) to map Tk components to Swing components and not yet supporting many of the components or layout managers in Swing. It also does not generate any non-Swing AWT interfaces, although the author would like to add that capability.

`vTcLava` is a GPL project and, like many GPL projects, welcomes contributed engineering. If it looks like a good solution, or half of a good solution, you are welcome to make improvements and send them to the author for future releases.

Summary

This chapter explored `vTcLava`, a Java GUI builder implemented in the portable Tcl scripting language. Built on the extensible `vTcl` GUI builder, `vTcLava` offers basic Swing-based GUI creation and skeleton code generation.

CHAPTER 42

KORFE: A PYTHON-BASED JAVA GUI BUILDER

Korfe, published by the JavaLobby, is a GUI builder implemented in the Python scripting language.

Platforms: SDK1.2

This chapter takes a look at a Java GUI builder, Korfe, implemented in the Python scripting language. Although this particular builder is not yet well cooked (it still needs some sustained development attention), it is interesting as an example of the integration of Java with scripting.

This chapter looks at two technologies:

- JPython, a Java implementation of the Python scripting language
- Korfe, a GUI builder implemented in JPython

Python and JPython

Python is one of the powerful scripting languages enjoying heavy use in the Internet world, the other two best-known being Perl and Tcl. These languages are successful for several reasons:

- All enjoy wide acceptance and support, open source distribution, and active user communities.

- They can be used to solve problems that are much slower and more difficult to solve in programming languages—Java included.
- They can be used to implement significant GUI applications. We saw one example in Chapter 41, "`vTcLava`: A Tcl-Based Java GUI Builder." Another (possibly extreme) example is Grail, a full-featured Web browser implemented entirely in Python.
- All support object-oriented constructs. Python was originally designed as an object-oriented scripting language, whereas object-orientation was grafted onto the other two languages (a heritage they share, incidentally, with C++).

All three languages have their vocal supporters, and choosing one is largely a matter of personal taste. But Python enjoys a unique affinity with Java—an implementation called ***JPython***.

JPython is a 100% Pure Java implementation of the Python interpreter, and it interprets Python the way JIT compilers interpret Java: by compiling down to something more natural. In other words, it's not a script interpreter implemented in Java (which would be unspeakably slow) but a script compiler that generates and then runs Java bytecodes.

This close coupling between a scripting language and a programming language creates some remarkable synergies between the two:

- JPython and Java classes can fully interact, calling each other's methods and even subclassing each other's classes.
- Portions of a Java application can be implemented with Python scripts.
- Python scripts can be compiled into class files.

The result is a flexible development and applications environment that allows a mix of scripting and Java coding, supporting (say the JPython backers) whatever combination of the two meets your project's needs for rapid prototyping, development, and runtime performance.

The next section of this chapter explores an application of this scripting/Java combination. Building on the idea explored with `vTcLava`, we explore another script-based GUI builder whose use of JPython gives it the unique ability to directly run the GUIs it creates.

For more information about JPython, or to obtain a distribution, visit `http://www.jpython.org`. JPython is most commonly distributed as a ***classball***, a single class file that encapsulates an archive and installation GUI—just run the class to install.

The Korfe Builder

Korfe is being developed under the auspices of JavaLobby (`http://www.javalobby.com`), as part of its JavaLobby Foundation Applications suite.

Korfe is a GUI builder, implemented in Python and Java, and runnable under JPython and JDK1.2. Like `vTcLava` (see Chapter 41), Korfe is an early offering with some growing yet to do. Also like `vTcLava`, it generates Swing-based GUIs.

Obtaining Korfe

The Korfe home page is `http://www.javalobby.com/jfa/projects/korfe.html`, and Korfe is available as source and binary distributions and also via a networked `cvs` repository. The easiest way to use Korfe is to download the self-executable jar file. Instructions and links for all these can be found on the home page.

The Korfe distribution includes bundled JPython classes, so you do not need to separately install JPython.

Running Korfe

The easiest way to use Korfe is from the self-executable jar file, `korfe-bin.jar`, distributed on the Korfe home page.

Synopsis:

```
java -jar korfe-bin.jar
```

Figure 42.1 shows the Korfe desktop. Running within a Swing-based desktop are the design workspace, a view of the hierarchy, and a properties editor.

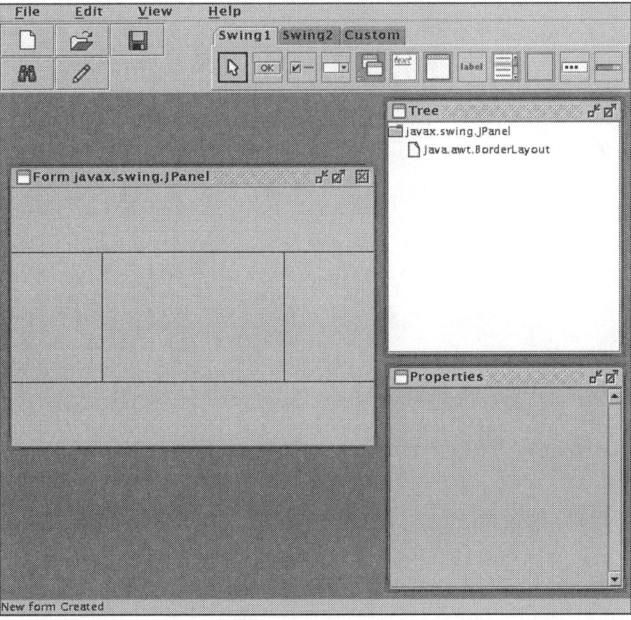

FIGURE 42.1
The Korfe desktop.

All the available components are provided in a tabbed toolbar (upper right of Figure 42.1). Of the AWT and Swing layout managers, Korfe currently supports only the `BorderLayout`—whose regions are clearly labeled in the design workspace.

To create a new workspace, choose File, New from the menu.

To add components to the workspace, select the component from the toolbar and click in a region in the workspace. Figure 42.2 shows the results of some editing.

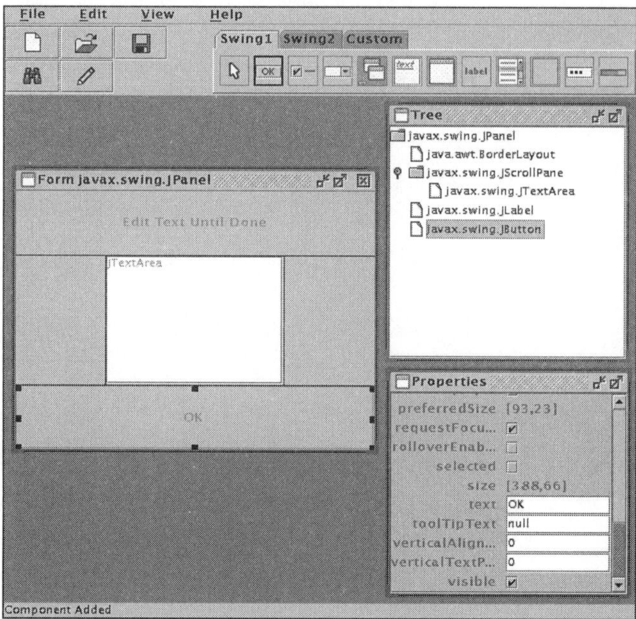

FIGURE 42.2
A new text editing application in Korfe.

The application in Figure 42.2 was built with the following steps:

1. Select the `JScrollPane` (from the `Swing2` tab) and click in the middle region of the layout.
2. Select `JTextArea` (from the `Swing2` tab) and click in the middle region of the layout.
3. Select the `JLabel` (from the `Swing1` tab) and click in the top region of the layout. The properties editor was then used to change the text of the label to "`Edit Text Until Done`" and the horizontal alignment to center the text.
4. Select the `JButton` (from the `Swing1` tab) and click in the bottom region of the layout. The properties editor was then used to change the text of the button to `OK`.

To test-drive the GUI, select View, Show Run Time Version from the menu—the interface will be run directly by the JVM running Korfe.

The File menu offers choices to save work-in-progress and to generate code. Listing 42.1 shows the code generated for this example.

LISTING 42.1 Application Code Generated by Korfe

```
/*
 * Written by Korfe version 0.2.8
 */

import java.awt.*;
import javax.swing.*;

class korfetest extends javax.swing.JPanel
{

   public korfetest()
   {
          super();
          setupGUI();
   }


   //Call this method to set up the GUI
   public void setupGUI()
   {
          BorderLayout layout1 = new BorderLayout();
          setLayout(layout1);
          variable0 = new JScrollPane();
          variable1 = new JTextArea();
          variable1.setText("JTextArea");
          variable0.setViewportView(variable1);

          add(variable0 , "Center");

          variable2 = new JLabel();
          variable2.setText("Edit Text Until Done");
          variable2.setHorizontalAlignment(0);
          add(variable2 , "North");

          variable3 = new JButton();
          variable3.setText("OK");
          add(variable3 , "South");

   }

   //Variables
   private JButton variable3;
   private JLabel variable2;
   private JTextArea variable1;
   private JScrollPane variable0;
}
```

As seen in the code, Korfe sets up a single GUI component, subclassed from `javax.swing.JPanel`, without additional skeleton code and without a `main()` procedure. Figure 42.3 shows the component in action.

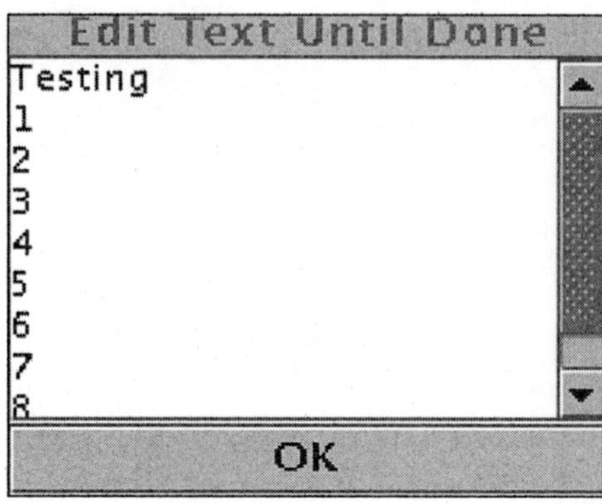

FIGURE 42.3
Running the component built by Korfe.

Summary

This chapter examined Korfe, a GUI-builder, and JPython, the Java-based scripting package in which it is implemented. While Korfe needs more attention before it can be considered a highly functional builder, it demonstrates the unique potential JPython offers in integrating a powerful scripting language with Java.

CHAPTER 43

INPRISE JBUILDER

Inprise JBuilder is a pure-Java integrated development environment.

Platform: SDK1.2

Macmillan Computer Publishing has proudly partnered with Inprise Corporation (formerly Borland) to bundle its new JBuilder product with this book. JBuilder, a successor to the popular Borland C++ line of IDEs, is a full-featured offering whose capabilities and features include

- Wizard-based creation of projects, applications, applets, classes, JavaBeans, and more.
- A visual designer supporting AWT, Swing, and a collection of value-added GUIs from Inprise.
- An integrated debugger.
- JavaBean development support, with GUI-based management of properties, events, and advanced beaninfo and property editor support.
- Integrated support of javadoc documentation.
- Extensive support of database applications, with a number of value-added GUI and non-GUI components. This plays to an existing Inprise strength: the company already ships a professional SQL Database Management System, InterBase, on Linux.
- Support of enterprise component development, with Java servlets, JavaServer Pages, Enterprise JavaBeans, and CORBA wizards and support.

In addition to JBuilder and InterBase, Inprise has thrown its support behind Linux in some significant and visible ways, notably:

- Its Just-In-Time compiler technology, based on an existing Microsoft Windows-based product, is available in a version for Linux.
- A new rapid application development suite, code-named Kylix, has been announced for release on Linux in 2000. Kylix will support development in C, C++, and Delphi.

Obtaining and Installing JBuilder

The CD-ROM with this book includes the JBuilder distribution and installation instructions. To use JBuilder, you need an SDK1.2 installation.

As of this writing, four issues had been identified with the use of JBuilder on Linux:

- It requires green threads to run correctly.
- Due to bugs in Swing (under JDK1.2), JBuilder requires a special version of its own GUI classes. When JDK1.2.2 becomes available on Linux, the special classes will no longer be needed.
- Due to bugs in the generation or use of font metrics, the use of the bold font in IDE text editors causes cursor placement problems. It may be necessary to modify some JBuilder font settings.
- JBuilder depends on Sun's Java Platform Debugging Architecture (JPDA) to support integrated debugging. Until JPDA becomes available for Linux (it is a collection of Java and native components that are not part of the JDK), JBuilder cannot support debugging and may require installation of a workaround.

See the CD-ROM for installation instructions and any required workaround instructions. You can also check the JBuilder home page (`http://www.borland.com/jbuilder/`) for current Linux support information.

Running JBuilder

After installation, JBuilder occupies a directory hierarchy containing tools and sample applications. The launch script for the IDE can be found in the `bin/` subdirectory for the tools.

Synopsis:

```
<path to JBuilder installation>/jbuilder/bin/jbuilder
```

Figure 43.1 shows the main JBuilder GUI visible after startup.

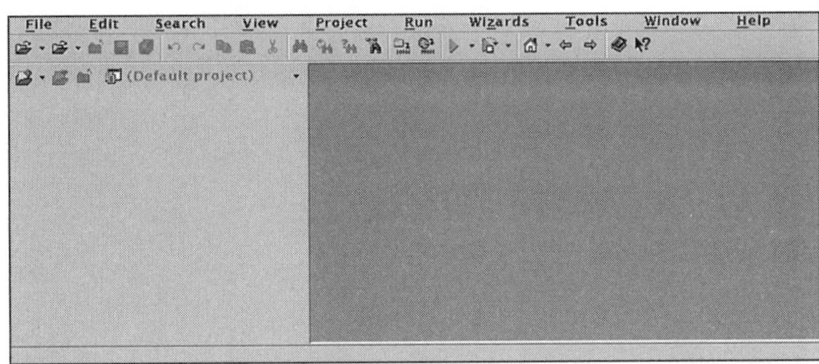

FIGURE 43.1
The main JBuilder GUI.

Creating a Sample JBuilder Project

JBuilder's extensive capabilities are described in documentation with the product. Although there is far too much to try to discuss in a single chapter, we will build a simple project—a text editor—to illustrate basic JBuilder usage.

Starting the Project

We start the project by selecting `File`, `New` from the menu, which brings up a dialog offering a choice of projects and objects (see Figure 43.2). Many entries in the list are not meaningful, and are grayed out, until a project has been started.

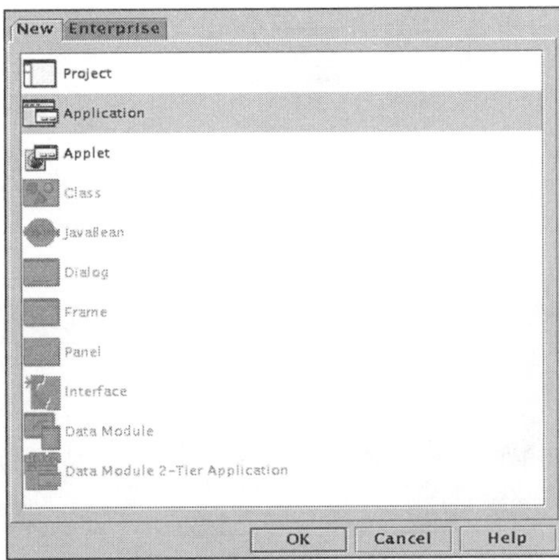

FIGURE 43.2
This dialog lets you choose new projects and objects.

From this dialog, choosing to create an `Application` brings up the New Project Wizard, in which you specify a directory to contain the project (see Figure 43.3) and general project identification (see Figure 43.4).

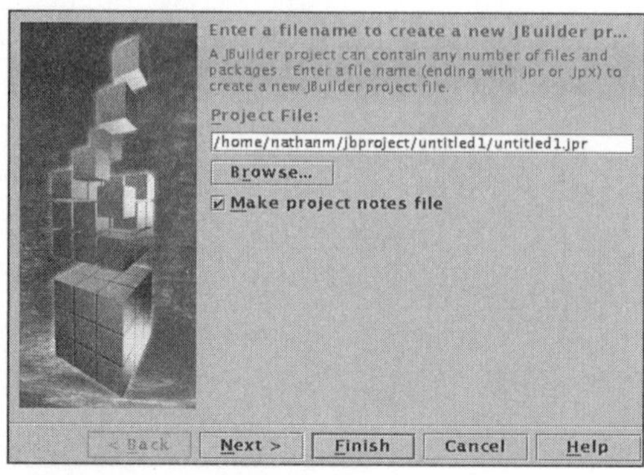

FIGURE 43.3
Setting up a destination directory for project files.

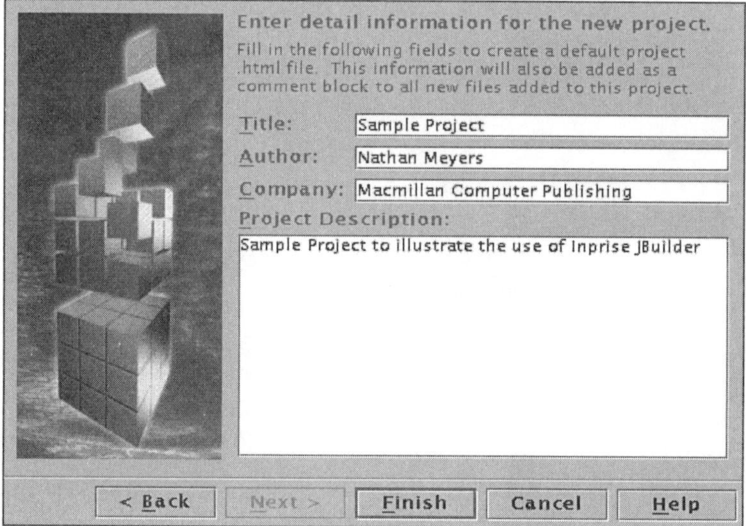

FIGURE 43.4
Specifying general project identification.

After the New Project Wizard, JBuilder presents the Application Wizard dialog, in which you specify top-level class information (see Figure 43.5) and create an initial GUI (see Figure 43.6).

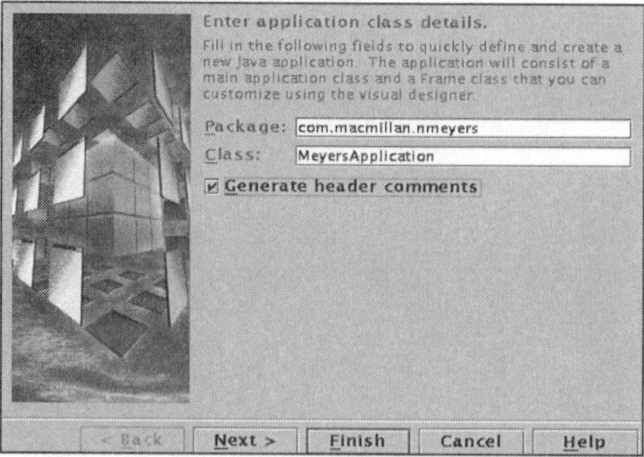

FIGURE 43.5
Specifying the top-level class.

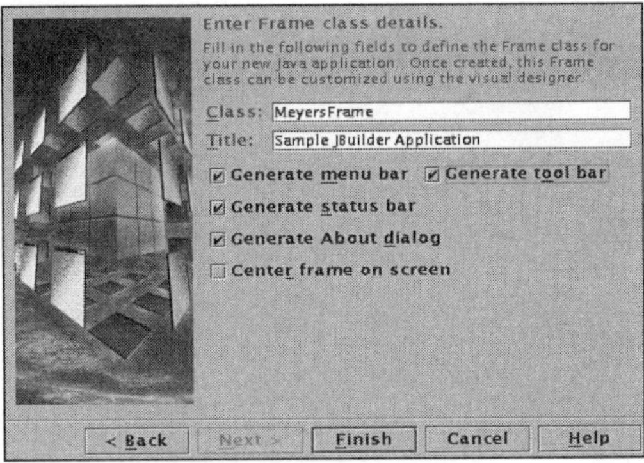

FIGURE 43.6
Creating the initial GUI, including an optional top-level menu and toolbar.

After you finish with the wizards, JBuilder constructs and compiles the application. The main JBuilder GUI (see Figure 43.7) provides several different views of the project.

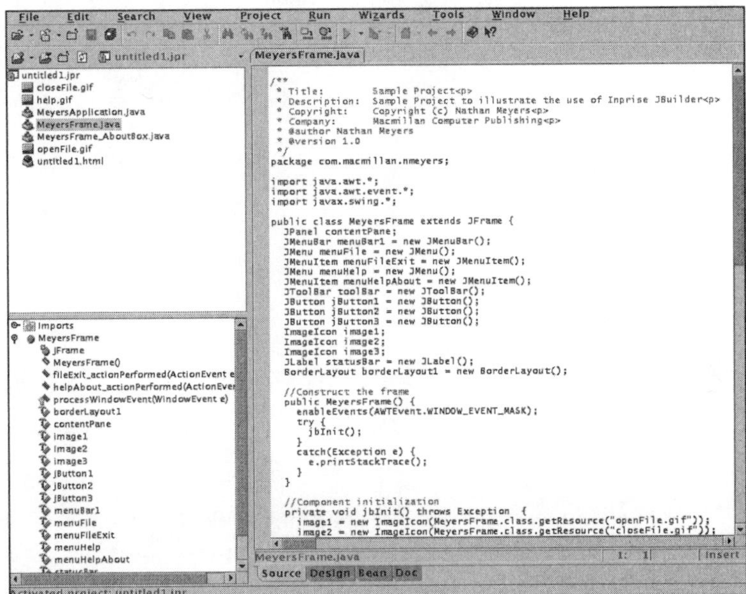

FIGURE 43.7
The main GUI shows multiple views of the project and its classes.

The upper-left panel in Figure 43.7 catalogs the various files associated with the project—three `.java` files, three GIF images for the toolbar, and an HTML file for project-level notes. You can edit any of these files by double-clicking on it in this panel.

The right-hand panel is the editor. In Figure 43.7, it contains a text editor currently being used to edit `MeyersFrame.java`—the main GUI class. Tabs at the bottom of the editor choose other editing modes: the visual designer, a JavaBeans properties editor, and an HTML documentation editor.

The lower-left panel is a navigator used in conjunction with the editor—its format and contents depend on what editor is in use in the editor panel. With the text editor shown in Figure 43.7, the navigator shows procedures and variables declared in the file. You can click on entries in the navigator to jump to the declarations.

With the basic project defined, the next section explores the use of the visual designer to build the GUI.

Building the GUI

Selecting the Design tab at the bottom of the editor starts the visual designer (see Figure 43.8).

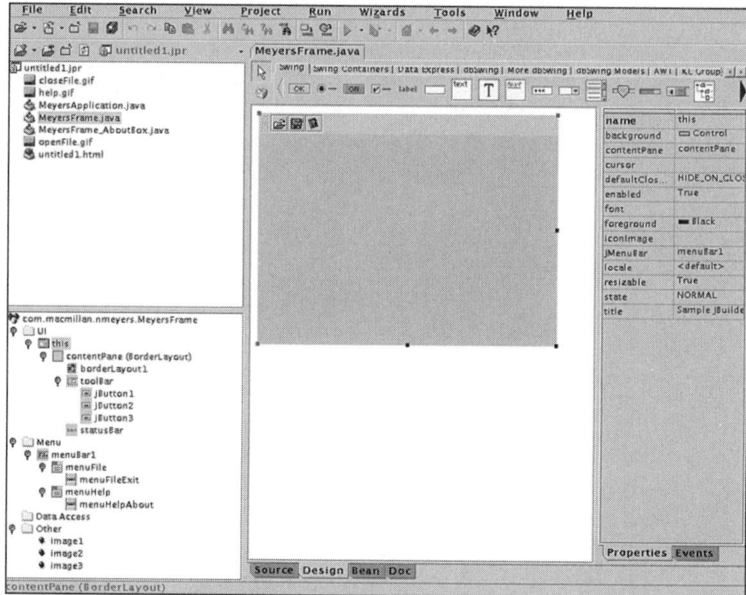

FIGURE 43.8
Running the visual designer.

The editor now displays a GUI designer, a wide selection of GUI and non-GUI components (top of the visual designer window), and a properties and events editor (panel on the far right). The navigator in the lower left panel now displays a hierarchical view of the GUI, the menus, and other project resources that can be configured from the visual designer. You can edit any object in the navigator by first selecting the object (with a single-click) and then right-clicking and selecting `Activate Designer` from the pop-up menu.

This project needs two new GUI components to implement the text editor: a scroll pane and an editor pane. To add the scroll pane, select the `JScrollPane` from the `Swing Containers` tab above the editor (see Figure 43.9) and click inside the GUI to insert it. Then select the `JEditorPane` from the `Swing` tab (see Figure 43.10) and click inside the GUI to insert it.

FIGURE 43.9
Selecting the scroll pane.

FIGURE 43.10
Selecting the editor pane.

After the new components have been inserted, they appear in the GUI designer (see Figure 43.11) and in the hierarchical navigator panel at the lower left.

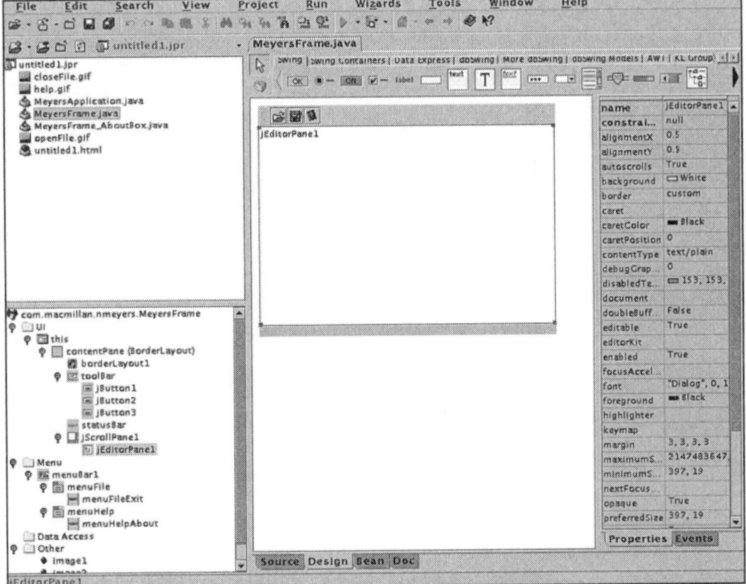

FIGURE 43.11
The visual editor and navigator show the results of adding the new components.

More GUI components are required: the **`File`** menu needs buttons defined for opening and saving files. To edit the menu bar, select **`menuBar1`** in the navigator; then right-click and select **`Activate Designer`** from the pop-up menu (see Figure 43.12).

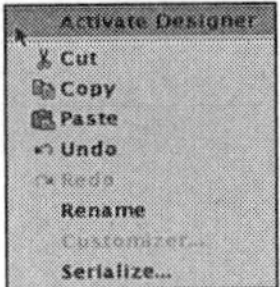

FIGURE 43.12
Selecting the pop-up menu for editing.

The visual designer now provides a view of the application's menu bar (see Figure 43.13).

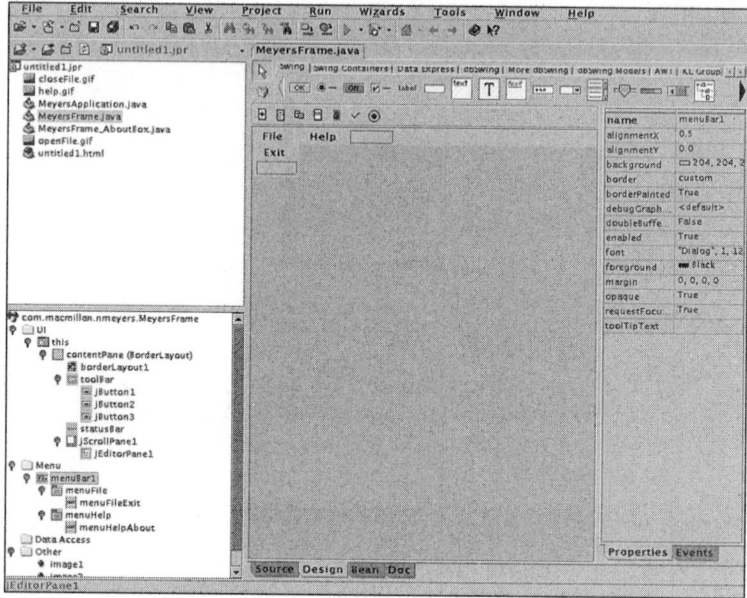

FIGURE 43.13
The visual designer edits the application's top-level menu bar.

To add a new menu item, right-click on the existing `Exit` menu item and select `Insert Menu item` from the pop-up menu (see Figure 43.14).

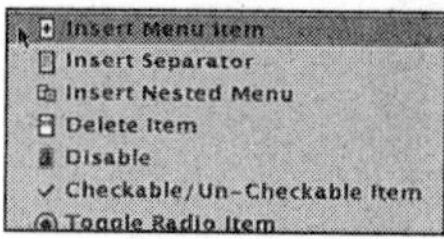

FIGURE 43.14
Inserting a new menu item.

After creating the new item, double-click on that item for editing (see Figure 43.15). You can also change the object's name in the properties editor (see Figure 43.16) to something more descriptive (`menuFileOpen`, in this case) than the default.

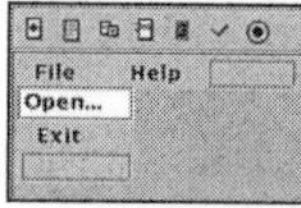

FIGURE 43.15
Editing the menu button text.

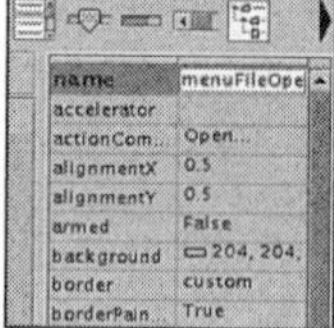

FIGURE 43.16
Changing the name of the `Open` menu button in the properties editor.

You can add a `Save` button in the same way.

Adding Behaviors

By now the project has all its GUI components defined; now we must define behaviors. For this step, we will define a procedure for opening files.

Returning to the `Open` button added in the previous section, select the `Events` tab at the lower right to activate the events editor (see Figure 43.17).

FIGURE 43.17
The events editor (right side) allows us to define event handlers for, in this case, the `Open` key.

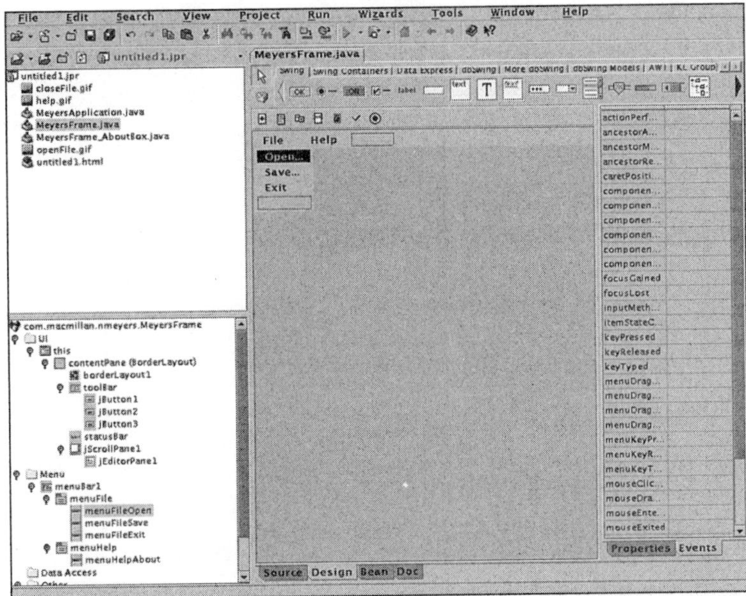

The application needs an event handler for the `actionPerformed` event; clicking the mouse inside the empty text box for that event causes JBuilder to create and automatically name such a handler (see Figure 43.18). Double-clicking on the new handler name automatically switches us to the text editor (see Figure 43.19), with the cursor positioned in the new code to allow editing.

FIGURE 43.18
Creating a new handler with a single click.

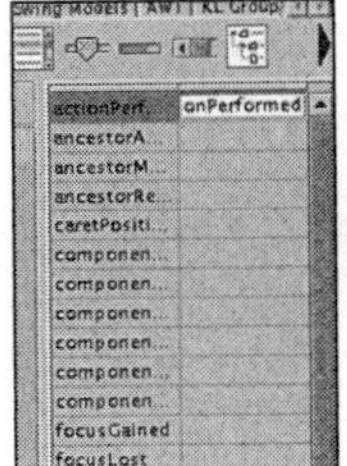

FIGURE 43.19
Editing the new action handler code (at bottom of the text editor).

For this example, we'll type in the code for a short event handler that opens and loads a file. JBuilder provides a context-sensitive pop-up menu with possible name completions (see Figure 43.20) while you edit the text.

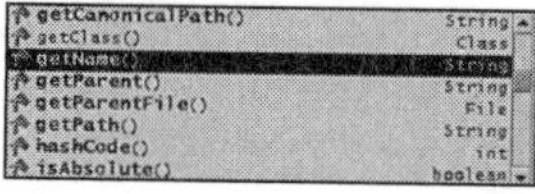

FIGURE 43.20
The name-completion pop-up menu (cursor is above left of the pop-up).

Figure 43.21 shows the completed handler code. (The code also requires the addition of an `import java.io.*` statement at the beginning of the module.)

FIGURE 43.21
The completed handler code displays and handles a `JFileChooser` dialog.

```
void menuFileOpen_actionPerformed(ActionEvent e) {
  // Frame for our dialog
  final JFrame frame = new JFrame("Select File to Open");
  // Create an anonymous class derived from JFileChooser for our use
  JFileChooser chooser = new JFileChooser() {
    public void approveSelection()
    {
      // User hit Open button; open the file
      File file = getSelectedFile();
      // Kill the dialog
      frame.dispose();
      // Load the file; report success or errors to the status bar
      try {
        InputStream stream = new FileInputStream(file);
        jEditorPane1.read(stream, file.getName());
        statusBar.setText("Opened file " + file.getName());
      }
      catch (IOException e) {
        statusBar.setText(e.toString());
      }
    }
    public void cancelSelection()
    {
      // User hit cancel button; give up
      frame.dispose();
    }
  };
  // Customize dialog for opening an existing file
  chooser.setDialogType(JFileChooser.OPEN_DIALOG);
  // Place the file chooser in the dialog and display
  frame.getContentPane().add(chooser);
  frame.pack();
  frame.setVisible(true);
}
```

At this point, the application has defined one behavior—opening a file for editing—and associated it with the `Open` button in the `File` menu. We must also associate that behavior with the relevant button in the toolbar.

To add the missing behavior, return to the design editor, select the first icon (the open-file icon) in the toolbar and edit its events (see Figure 43.22). Select the `actionPerformed` event and change the default method name to the method that was recently created for the `Open` button: `menuFileOpen_actionPerformed()`.

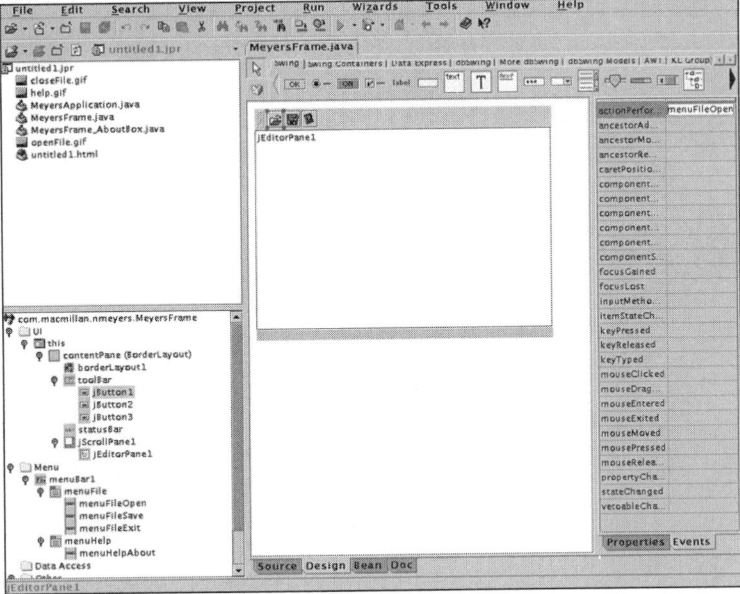

FIGURE 43.22
Adding an event handler for the toolbar open-file icon.

With this behavior defined, the project now *does* something. We're not finished, of course; the application must add behaviors for saving files, providing online help, and so on. The necessary buttons and menu items are already in place. You can apply the steps described in this section to add their behaviors.

Building the Project

If you have not yet saved your files, now is a good time. Select `File`, `Save All` from the menu to save all project and source files.

To build the project, select `Project`, `Make project "<projectname>"` from the menu. If any errors occur during compilation, a new JBuilder pane will be created displaying the error messages. Clicking the mouse on any message will display the offending line in the text editor, allowing you to make corrections.

Running the Project

To run the project, select `Run`, `Run Project` from the menu. If the project generates any `stdout` or `stderr` output, a new JBuilder pane will be created displaying the output (see Figure 43.23). All output panes can be selected by tabs (along the bottom). To remove one or more output panes, right-click on a tab and select the desired `Remove` command from the popup menu.

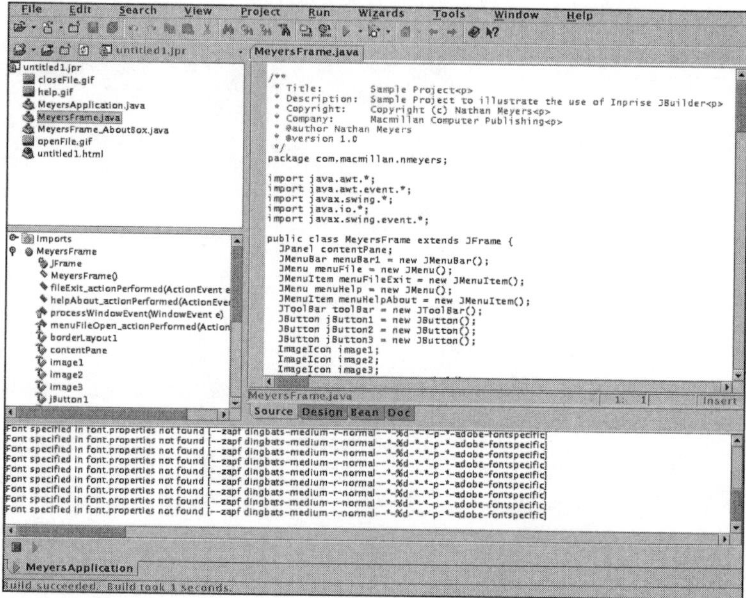

FIGURE 43.23 Running or building the project can create a new tabbed pane at the bottom of the IDE.

Figure 43.24 shows the application at startup. To load a file for editing, select the open-file icon from the toolbar, or choose `File`, `Open` from the menu and use the file chooser (see Figure 43.25) to select a file. Figure 43.26 shows the running application with the file loaded.

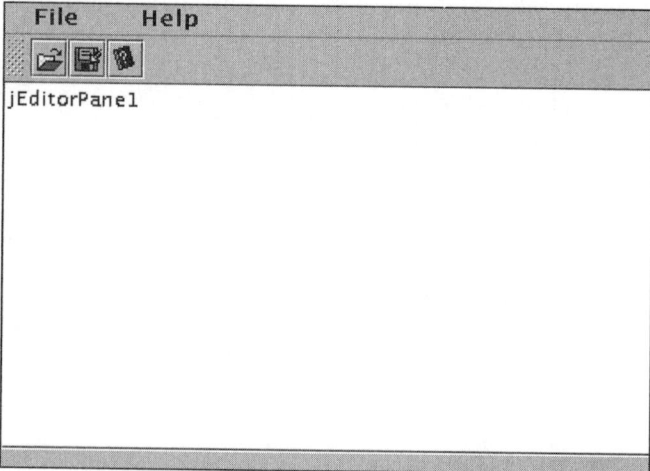

FIGURE 43.24 The running application, showing the default editor contents (`jEditorPane1`) configured by the application.

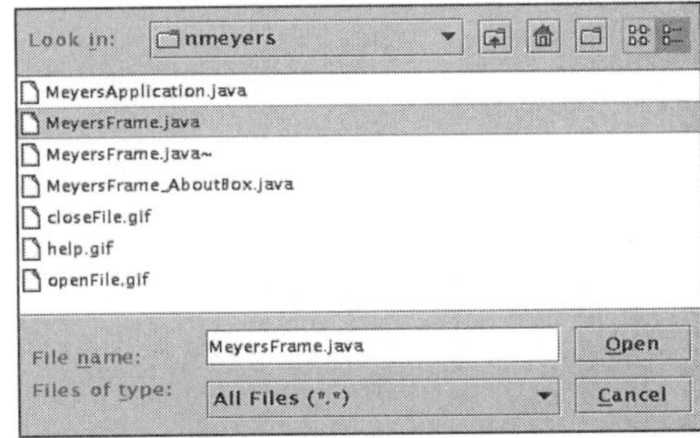

FIGURE 43.25
Using the Swing file chooser (in the project source directory) to select a file to edit.

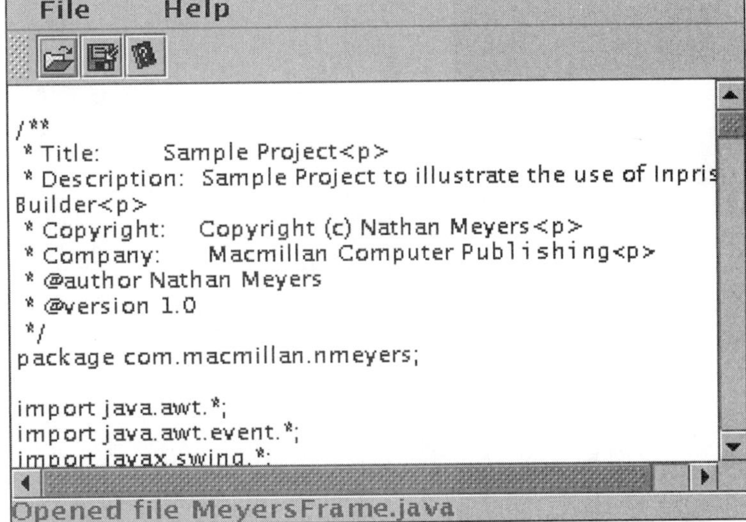

FIGURE 43.26
The working application now contains a text file to edit.

Debugging the Project

JBuilder includes a debugger, but Linux does not (as of this writing) support the Java Platform Debugging Architecture. Until a Linux JPDA port is released, you cannot debug under JBuilder. For current status of the JPDA, visit the Sun JPDA page at `http://java.sun.com/products/jpda/`.

Summary

This chapter presented Inprise JBuilder, the full-featured Java IDE bundled with this book. The sample project presented here should familiarize you with JBuilder's basic operation. Much more detail, and information on JBuilder's many other capabilities, is available in the product documentation on the CD-ROM.

CHAPTER 44

THE EMACS JDE

This chapter discusses the Emacs JDE, a Java integrated development environment built with the Emacs text editor.

Platforms: SDK1.1/SDK1.2

Figure 44.1 shows one of the icons shipped with the XEmacs editor. It is an overflowing kitchen sink, and it faithfully represents the ethos of the Emacs (GNU Emacs and XEmacs) editors: they contain everything but the kitchen sink.

FIGURE 44.1
XEmacs: The kitchen sink.

Emacs may be the first text editor whose power and complexity rivals that of many operating systems. This is due to an embedded Lisp interpreter that turns Emacs into a general-purpose computer and a huge collection of published Elisp packages that customize the editor into whatever you want it to be. It is not uncommon for serious Emacs users to completely eschew all other interfaces—GUIs, command shells, and so on—and use their systems entirely from within Emacs sessions. Indeed, if Emacs enjoyed the marketing muscle that Java does, it might well eclipse Java as a portable programming environment.

An Emacs overthrow of Java is unlikely, given present realities, but Emacs does have a presence in the Java world[1]: The Emacs Java Development Environment, published by Paul Kinnucan. This free IDE, distributed under GPL terms, includes all the features you expect in an IDE: source editing with syntax coloring and automatic indentation, tight compiler integration, source-level debugging, source code browsing, support of Makefiles, automatic generation of application skeleton code—even an interactive command interpreter that speaks Java.

Emacs is not for everyone; people either love it or hate it. Emacs offers a GUI of sorts (we have many screen dumps in this chapter to prove it), but its design is largely text-based. Of the two major Emacs versions, XEmacs embraces the X Window System more than does GNU Emacs, but neither is an easy leap from the rich GUI toolsets normally used in X, Microsoft Windows, Macintosh, and Java platforms.

On the other hand, for those who embrace the Emacs view of human-computer interaction, it has proven to be a capable IDE, and the package described in this chapter adds Java to those capabilities.

Obtaining Emacs JDE

The Emacs JDE home page is `http://sunsite.auc.dk/jde/`. Links are provided on the home page to download the current software, either as a compressed tarball or a zip file.

Additional requirements for using Emacs JDE are as follows:

- A GNU Emacs or XEmacs editor of recent vintage (see Chapter 9, "Setting Up a Linux Development Environment," in the section "emacs").

  Emacs has traditionally shipped with a huge collection of packages that add functionality. GNU Emacs still does so, but XEmacs recently chose to unbundle the packages and make them available for individual installation. If you install such an unbundled distribution, you need to obtain the following add-on packages to support JDE: `cc-mode`, `debug`, `edit-utils`, `mail-lib`, and `xemacs-base`. Details on installation and package management are provided at `http://www.xemacs.org/Install/index.html`.
- An SDK.
- A Web browser for viewing documentation.

Examining the Contents of Emacs JDE

The JDE distribution includes the components shown in Table 44.1. Components suffixed `.el` are *ELisp* programs recognized by the Emacs Lisp interpreter.

---

[1] Emacs and Java also enjoy an incidental historical affinity. James Gosling, the chief architect behind Java, was the author of Gosling Emacs—the first Emacs for UNIX and a commercial predecessor of GNU Emacs.

TABLE 44.1 Components of the Emacs JDE Distribution

Components	Description
`jde.el`	An Emacs Lisp script defining an Emacs editing mode for Java development.
`jde-run.el`	Script to launch applications and applets.
`jde-db.el`	Script to interface with `jdb` for debugging.
`jde-gen.el`	Script with code generation templates.
`speedbar.el`	Script providing a tree-structured source code browser.
`imenu.el`	Script providing an indexing utility for `speedbar.el`.
`bsh.jar`	The BeanShell—an interactive Java source code interpreter. Source is not included.
`beanshell.el`	Script to interface with the BeanShell.
`jde.jar`	Classes to support generation of skeleton source code. Source is included.
`jde-wiz.el`	Script to interface with `jde.jar` functionality.

Installing Emacs-JDE

Installation from the compressed tarball or zip file is straightforward: Choose an installation directory and unpack the archive.

You will then need to add information to your `~/.emacs` initialization file to add the Emacs-JDE to your environment:

```
(setq load-path (nconc '( "<installation directory>" ) load-path))
(require 'jde)
```

where *`<installation directory>`* specifies the top-level directory unpacked by the archive.

Developing with Emacs JDE

The full power of Emacs has been described in books—very thick books—that we avoid trying to duplicate. Instead, we will illustrate some basic operations to get you started with Emacs JDE.

Synopsis:

```
emacs <source file>
xemacs <source file>
```

If you edit a source file with the suffix `.java` (or create one, as in the section "Generating Code from JDE" later in this chapter), Emacs enables Java editing and JDE features. The display (we will use XEmacs in these examples) includes an edit buffer and some menus to support Java development (see Figure 44.2).

File Edit Apps Options Buffers Tools Java JDE
Help
Open Dired Save Print Cut Copy Paste Undo Spell Replace Mail Info Compile Debug News
import java.io.*;
public class Hello
{
public static void main(String[] argv) throws IOException
{
System.out.printlx("Hello World");
}
}
--**-XEmacs: Hello.java (JDE Font)----All----

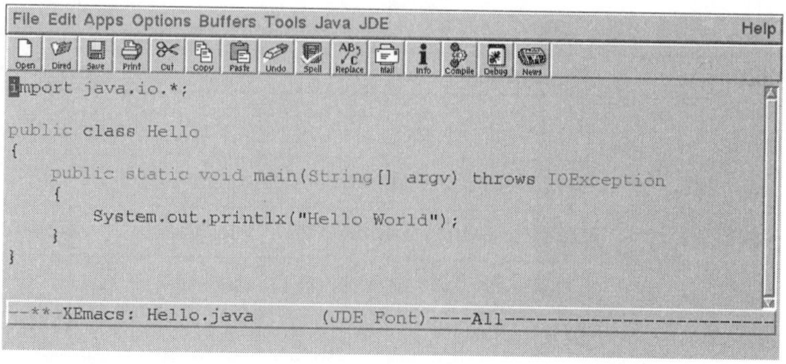

FIGURE 44.2
Editing a Java application in XEmacs.

For those viewing Figure 44.2 in black and white, the keywords, variables, package names, and other items are distinguished with various shades of red, green, blue, brown, and black.

Compiling and Running

A pull-down JDE menu gives us a choice of compilation, debugging, and other development steps (see Figure 44.3).

JDE
Help
Compile C-c C-v C-c
Run App C-c C-v C-r
Debug App C-c C-v C-d
Run Applet C-c C-v C-a
Debug Applet C-c C-v C-t
Build C-c C-v C-b
Interpret C-c C-v LFD
Templates
Wizards
Speedbar C-c C-v C-s
Browse JDK Doc C-c C-v C-n
Options
Help

FIGURE 44.3
The JDE menu.

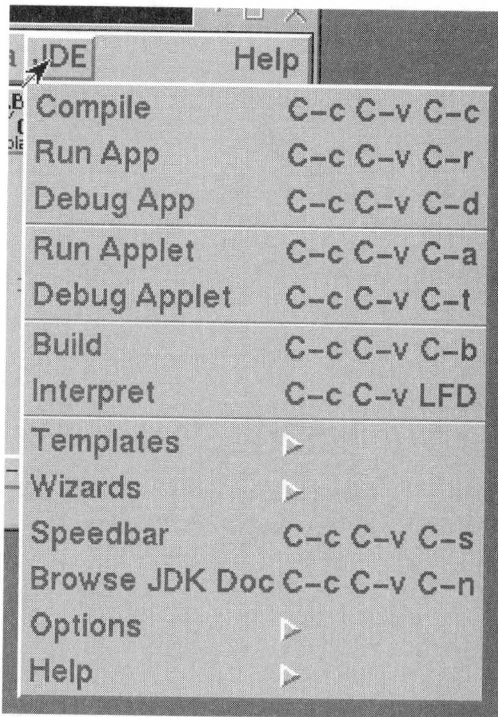

We begin by compiling our program, which reveals a problem (see Figure 44.4).

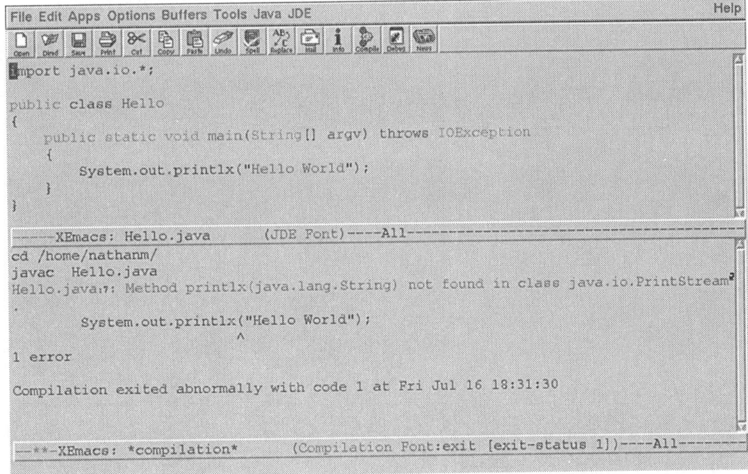

FIGURE 44.4
The `javac` compiler complains about a bad method name.

By placing the cursor on the complaint, right-clicking, and choosing `Goto Error` (see Figure 44.5), we move the cursor to the offending line of code in the top window, where we can correct the error.

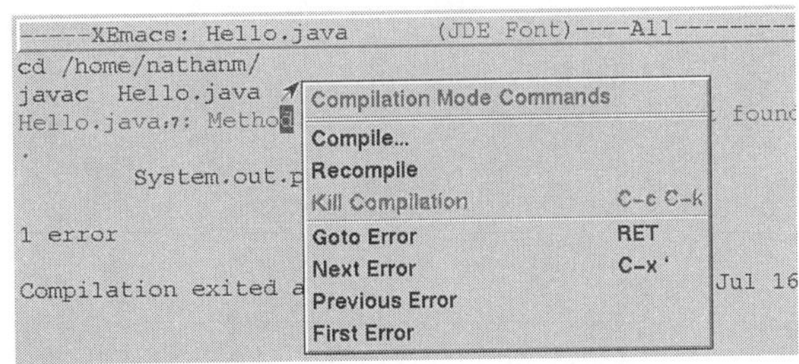

FIGURE 44.5
Right-click on the compiler error to edit the bad code.

After successfully compiling, we choose to run (select the `Run App` choice in Figure 44.3) and see the results in the lower buffer window (see Figure 44.6).

Customizing Emacs JDE

We will shortly debug, but we must first change some settings. Using the menu choice to customize the compiler (see Figure 44.7) brings up the customization screen (see Figure 44.8), which allows us to change settings.

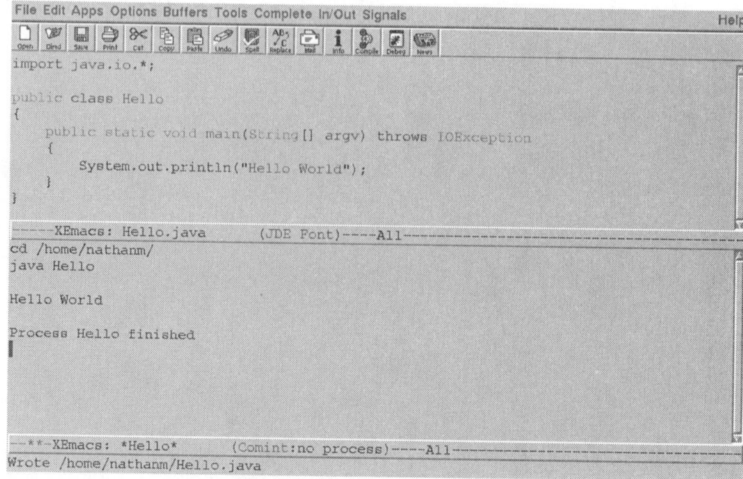

FIGURE 44.6
Running the program uses an Emacs buffer (bottom) as a console.

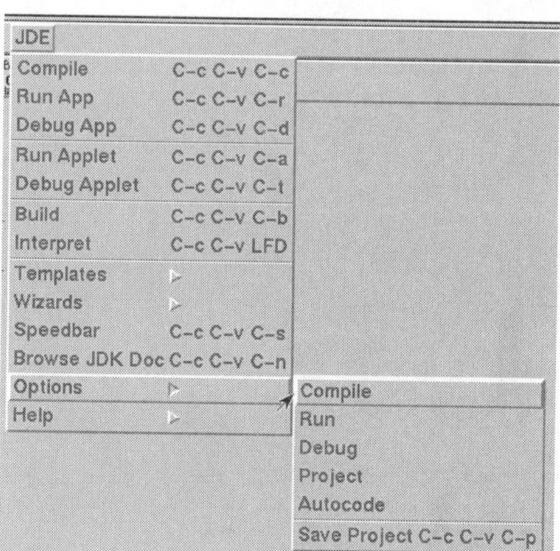

FIGURE 44.7
The menus to select customization options.

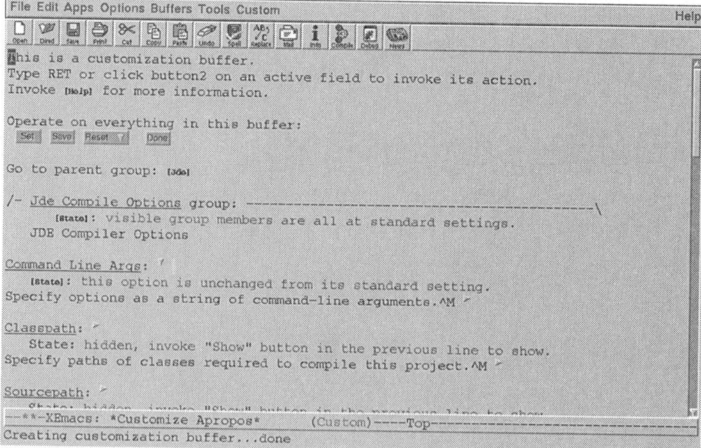

FIGURE 44.8
The customization buffer for the compilation step.

We change the debug setting to compile with full debugging (see Figure 44.9) and right-click to set the option.

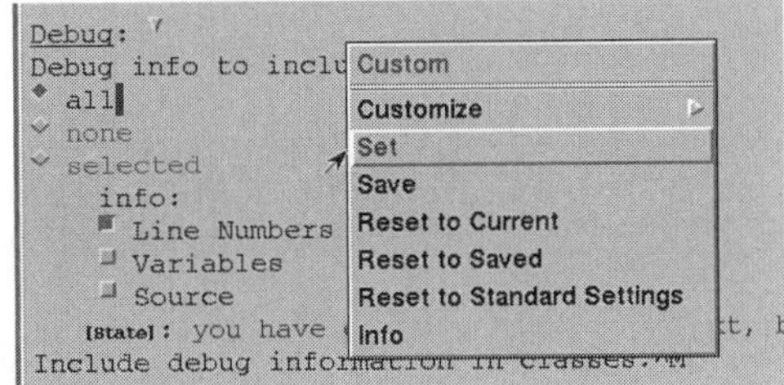

FIGURE 44.9
Turn on the debugging option.

We also customize the project settings by adding the current directory, "`.`", to the debugger source path (see Figure 44.10).

FIGURE 44.10
Add "`.`" to the debugger source path.

Many settings can be customized, beyond these two examples—Emacs JDE is infinitely configurable. For example, although the defaults assume that you are using a Sun SDK, the system can be configured to use any choice of JVM (Kaffe, for example), any choice of compiler (Jikes, for example), any source path, class path, and so on. After customizing, save the choices in a project file (choose `Save Project` as shown in Figure 44.7) for future use.

Emacs project files, in which customizations are saved, are specified in ELisp—the same language in which Emacs extensions are programmed. While perhaps not understandable to the casual reader, these files can be understood by Emacs wizards, who will often choose to edit them directly rather than deal with the ponderous interface shown in Figures 44.8[nd]44.10. Here is a small excerpt from the JDE project file, reflecting the customizations we just performed:

```
(jde-set-variables
       .
       .
       .
'(jde-compile-option-debug (quote ("all" (t nil nil))))
'(jde-db-source-directories (quote ("./")) t)
       .
       .
       .
```

Debugging with Emacs JDE

After recompiling for debugging, we choose to **Debug App** (refer to Figure 44.3). Emacs gives us a debugger console window and uses a pointer (=>) to track program location in the source window (see Figure 44.11).

FIGURE 44.11
Start of a debugging session; => points to the current source line.

```
File Edit Apps Options Buffers Tools Complete In/Out Signals                Help
Open Dired Save Print Cut Copy Paste Undo Spell Replace Mail Info Compile Debug News
import java.io.*;

public class Hello
{
    public static void main(String[] argv) throws IOException
    {
=>      System.out.println("Hello World");
    }
}
-----XEmacs: Hello.java      (JDE Font)----All---------------------
cd /home/nathanm/
jdb Hello

Initializing jdb...
0x40738ec0:class(Hello)
> Breakpoint set in Hello.main
> run Hello
running ...
main[1]
Stopped at line 7 in Hello.java
main[1]
--**-XEmacs: *debugHello*      (Debugger: run)----All-------------
```

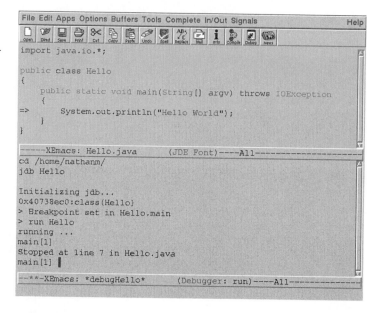

A debugging menu (see Figure 44.12) appeared when we began debugging, providing the necessary buttons to run, single-step, set breakpoints, and print variable values. For operations such as managing breakpoints and inspecting variables, you first place the cursor at an appropriate location in the source window (for example, on a variable name) and then request the desired action from the debugging menu.

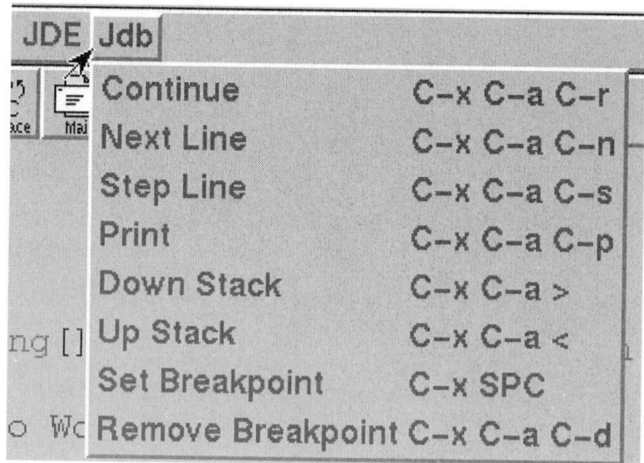

FIGURE 44.12
A debugger menu offers the usual debugging choices.

Generating Code from JDE

Emacs can create class files from scratch. A choice from the File menu (see Figure 44.13) creates a new `.java` file, with a `javadoc` skeleton (see Figure 44.14) and assistance in building the class.

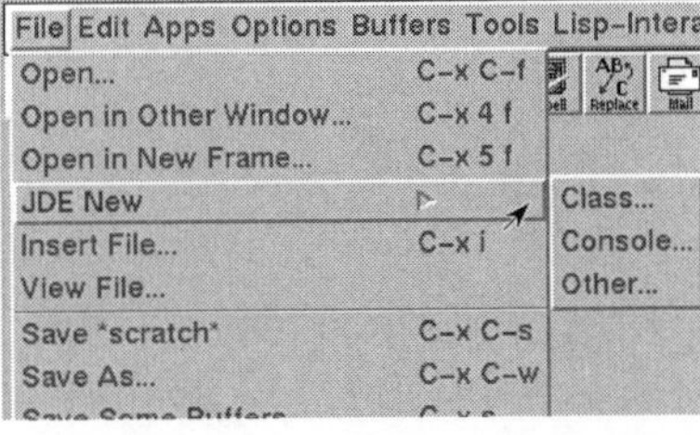

FIGURE 44.13
Emacs JDE creates a new class.

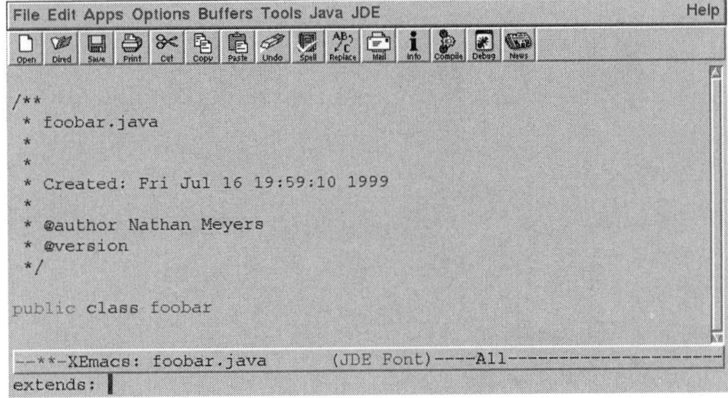

FIGURE 44.14
The Skelton Class code includes skelton `javador` comments.

Our new class includes some `javadoc` skeleton documentation and prompts us for basic class information. (The `extends:` prompt, at the bottom of Figure 44.14, is requesting the name of a superclass.)

Beyond skeleton creation, Emacs JDE offers several wizards and templates (through the JDE menu, shown in Figure 44.3) that assist in defining a class, including those shown in Table 44.2.

TABLE 44.2 JDE Wizards and Templates

Wizard/Template	Purpose
`Get/Set Pair`	Declares a class member variable and creates get and set skeleton calls for manipulating the variable—useful for developing JavaBeans.
`Listener`	Creates skeleton implementations of event adapters for Action, Window, and Mouse events.
`Override Method`	Creates a skeleton implementation of a method to be overridden from a parent class.
`Implement Interface`	Creates a skeleton implementation of a specified interface.

For example, starting with our new class (see Figure 44.15), invoking the `Implement Interface` wizard prompts for an interface name (see Figure 44.16) in the bottom minibuffer and adds the necessary skeleton code (see Figure 44.17), complete with `javadoc` comments and some "TODO" reminder comments.

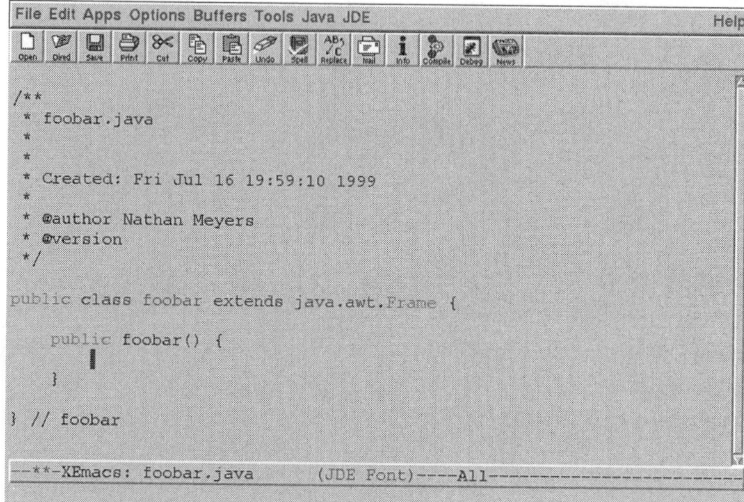

FIGURE 44.15 The skeleton implementation of class `foobar`.

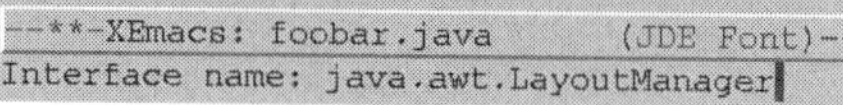

FIGURE 44.16 The `Implement Interface` wizard prompts for an interface name.

FIGURE 44.17 The skeleton methods created by the wizard await implementation.

```
File Edit Apps Options Buffers Tools Java JDE                         Help
/**
 *
 * @param param1 <description>
 * @param param2 <description>
 */
public void addLayoutComponent(String param1, Component param2) {
  // TODO: implement this java.awt.LayoutManager method
}

/**
 *
 * @param param1 <description>
 */
public void removeLayoutComponent(Component param1) {
  // TODO: implement this java.awt.LayoutManager method
}

/**
 *
 * @param param1 <description>
 * @return <description>
 */
public Dimension preferredLayoutSize(Container param1) {
  // TODO: implement this java.awt.LayoutManager method
  return null;
}
--**-XEmacs: foobar.java      (JDE Font)----29%--------------------
```

Using the Interactive BeanShell Command Shell

The Emacs JDE distribution includes an interactive shell, the *BeanShell* (`bsh`), that speaks Java. `bsh` is a command interpreter, like `bash` or `csh`, that runs inside a Java environment. You can interactively run single Java commands or write small Java scripts for interpretation.

BeanShell is usable as a standalone scripting tool (visit the product's home page at `http://www.beanshell.org` to learn more), and is also usable from Emacs. `bsh` is activated with the JDE `Interpret` menu selection (refer to Figure 44.3), which opens a new Emacs buffer providing the `bsh` interface (see Figure 44.18). Extensive documentation on `bsh` usage is available at the Emacs JDE Web site.

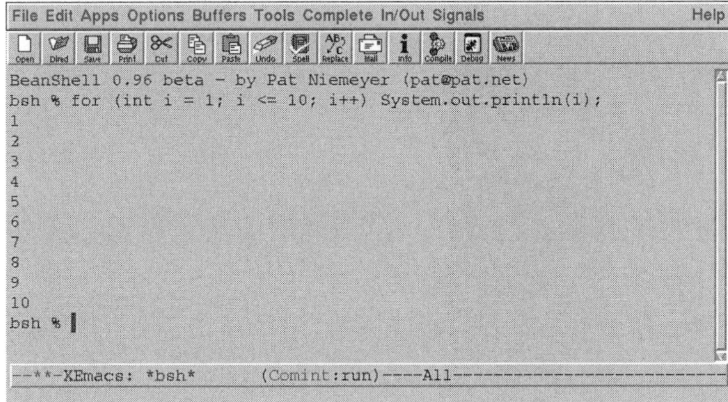

FIGURE 44.18
Some Java interpreted by the BeanShell.

Summary

This chapter examined Emacs JDE, a Java integrated development environment built on the Emacs text editor. Thanks to Emacs's legendary extensibility, JDE provides a full-featured IDE for use with Java.

CHAPTER 45

ARGOUML MODELING TOOL

ArgoUML is a tool for rapid application development based on User Model Language.

Platform: JDK1.1/JDK1.2

The Unified Software Development Process, developed Ivar Jacobson, Grady Booch, and James Rumbaugh, uses the graphical User Modeling Language (UML) to model software systems. Tools to support this process, from modeling through code generation and implementation, are one of the current frontiers in RAD tool development.

The major player in this business is Rational Software, but competition in the field is growing. Several of these systems are implemented in Java, some exclusively Java-centric: You can use them today on Linux.

One such tool is *ArgoUML*, an open source project from the University of California at Irvine. Although not as fully cooked as the high-priced commercial products, it offers an inexpensive glimpse into this important area. And, like all open source products, ArgoUML gives you the opportunity to be a contributor.

Obtaining ArgoUML

The ArgoUML home page can be found at `http://www.ics.uci.edu/pub/arch/uml/` and has pointers to distributions. Two streams are available, one based on JDK1.1 and an old Swing toolkit (with early package names), and a new version usable with JDK1.1/Swing1.1 and JDK1.2. The examples and instructions presented in this chapter are generated with the v0.7.0 preview release for JDK1.1/JDK1.2.

ArgoUML has a dependency on one external package, the XML parser for Java from IBM's Alphaworks: the UML download site includes a link to download the class library.

Both libraries are shipped as ZIP files that each encapsulate one jar file. To install, unzip both files into the same directory.

Running ArgoUML

ArgoUML can be invoked by including its jar file in the class path and invoking the main class, or, under JDK1.2, using the `java -jar` option.

Synopsis:

```
java uci.uml.Main
java -jar <argo jarfile> (JDK1.2 only)
```

The XML parser jar file must be resident in the directory containing the ArgoUML jar file. The only other dependencies are on the core classes and, if you are running JDK1.1, the Swing1.1 library.

Starting a New UML Project

When you start ArgoUML, you are automatically working on a new, empty project. If you want to work on an existing project saved earlier, you can open it with the `Open Project` button in the `File` menu.

The main window (see Figure 45.1) shows some views of the project. The collection of pull-downs and tabs throughout the interface provides different views of the project to meet the varied needs of UML design.

The upper-left window contains the navigator, which allows you to move through the project's components. The lower-left window contains a to-do list. You can add items to the list, but, most interestingly, ArgoUML critiques the project and adds its own to-do items. At the beginning of the project, the to-do list tells you (see Figure 45.2) that you need to get started. Throughout the project, items appear in and disappear from this list, guiding you through the project and, to a degree, acting as a tutorial on the process.

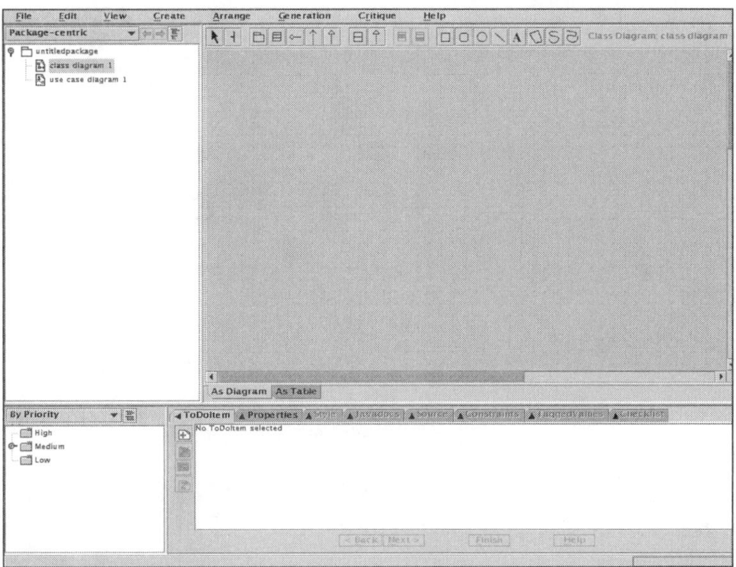

FIGURE 45.1
The main ArgoUML window.

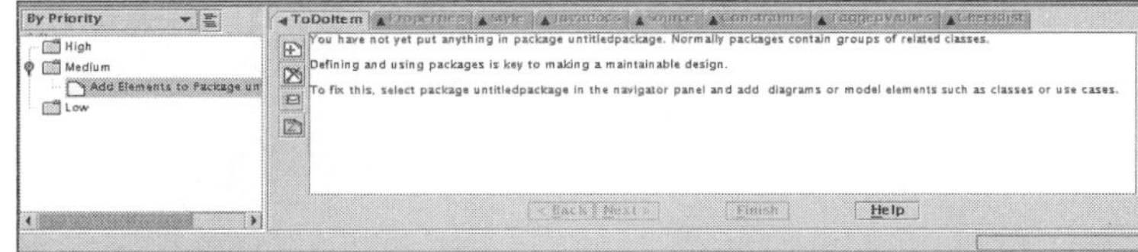

FIGURE 45.2
The to-do list for a fresh project.

Adding Classes to a Project

After assigning a package name to the project by editing some properties (see Figure 45.3), select the class diagram in the navigator to edit the class diagram. Choosing the class button (see Figure 45.4) allows you to drop a new class into the diagram (see Figure 45.5).

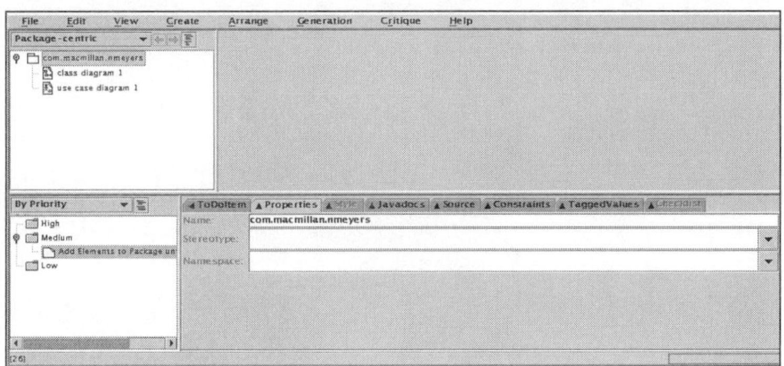

FIGURE 45.3
Editing properties of the package name to give it a suitable Java package name.

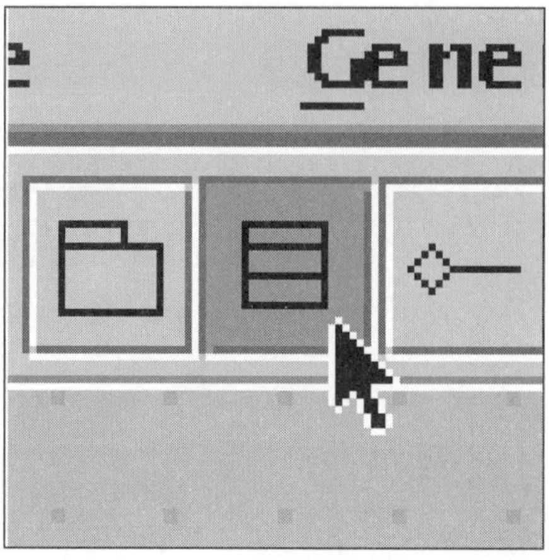

FIGURE 45.4
Select this button to add a new class.

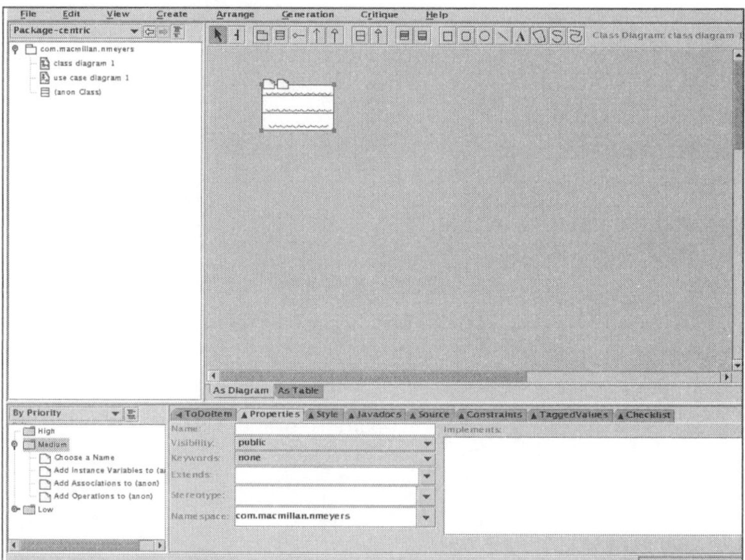

FIGURE 45.5
A new class is added.

Right-clicking on the object exposes some editing choices (see Figure 45.6). By editing properties and adding attributes and operations, we begin to fill out the class (see Figure 45.7).

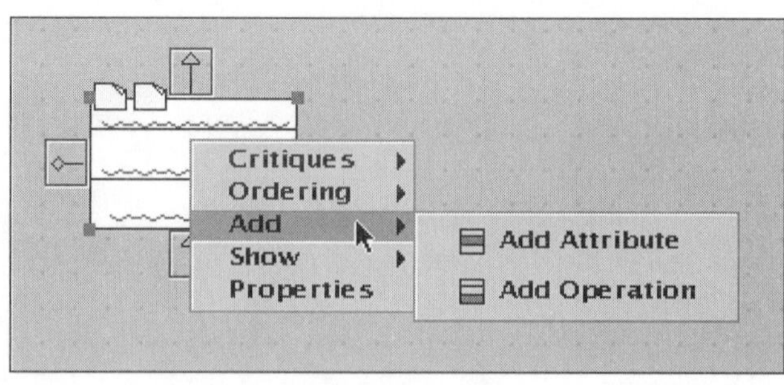

FIGURE 45.6
Right-clicking exposes choices to add functionality to the class.

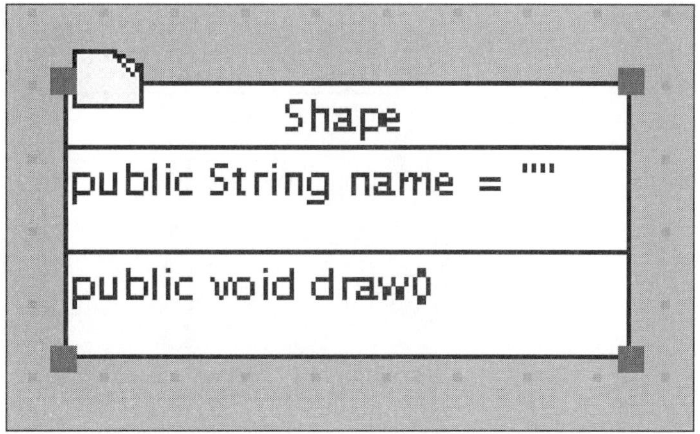

FIGURE 45.7
Defining some class attributes and operations.

Through a similar set of operations, we define another class (see Figure 45.8) and use the generalization operator (see Figure 45.9) to define an inheritance relationship (see Figure 45.10). The navigator shows the growth of our project (see Figure 45.11).

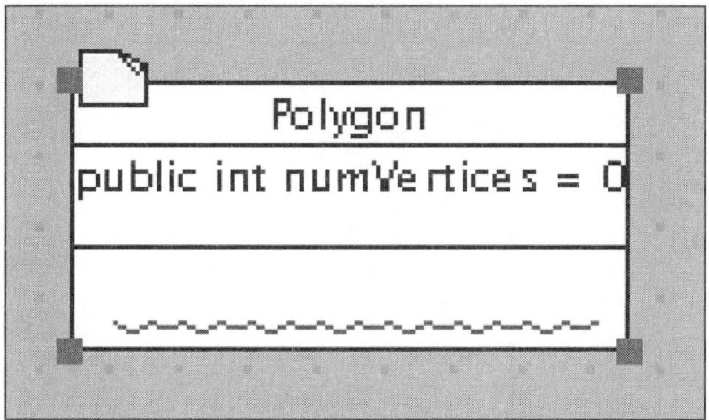

FIGURE 45.8
A new class: Polygon.

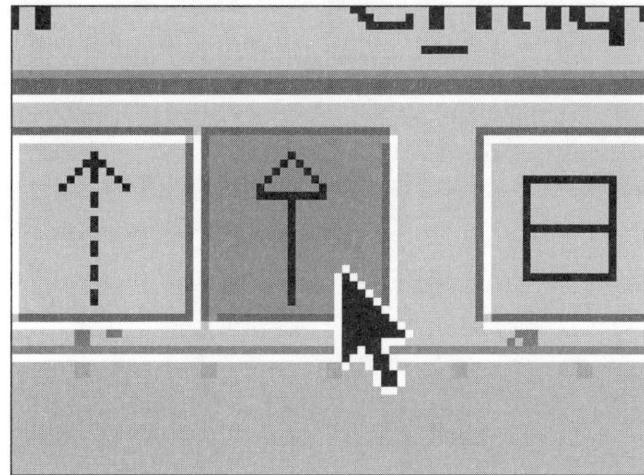

FIGURE 45.9
The generalization button.

FIGURE 45.10
Defining the new inheritance relationship.

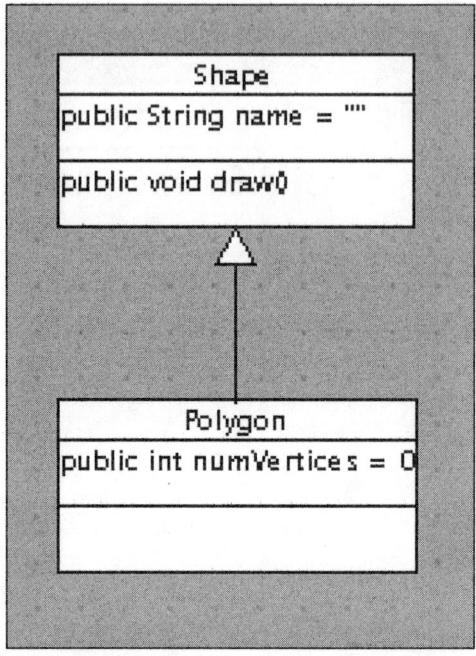

FIGURE 45.11
Current view of the project.

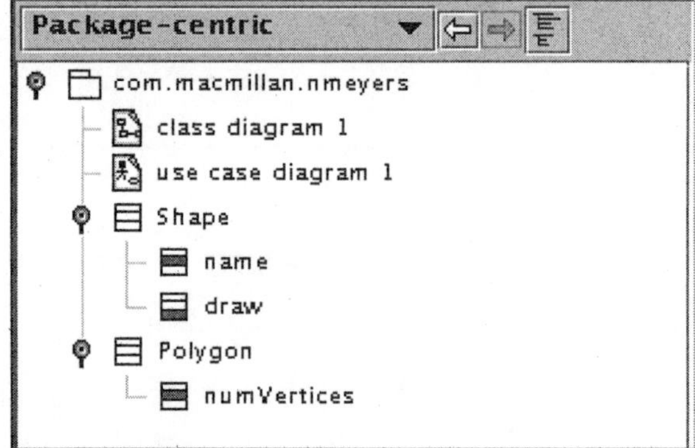

Not to overlook the all-important documentation, you can edit the `javadoc` comments for the various classes, methods, and fields (see Figure 45.12) in the tabbed pane at the bottom.

FIGURE 45.12
Editing `javadoc` comments for the Polygon class.

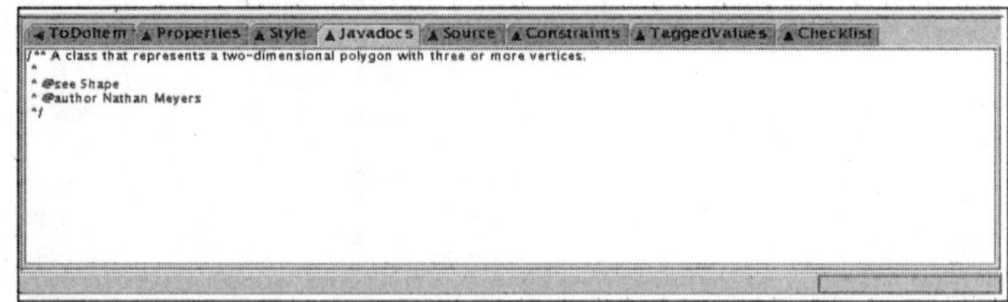

Saving Output and Generating Code

At this point, you've seen about 40% of what you can do in a class diagram and 2% of what you can do in UML. Use cases, state diagrams, activity diagrams, and collaboration diagrams are well beyond the scope of this chapter.

To name and save the project, use the **`Save Project As`** button in the **`File`** menu. You specify a single destination name, but several files are saved describing the project and the diagrams. All class and use case information is saved in XML format, using (where appropriate) standard Document Type Definitions that are or will be supported by all UML tools.

To generate code, use the **`Generate All Classes`** button in the **`Generation`** menu to call up the code generation dialog (see Figure 45.13).

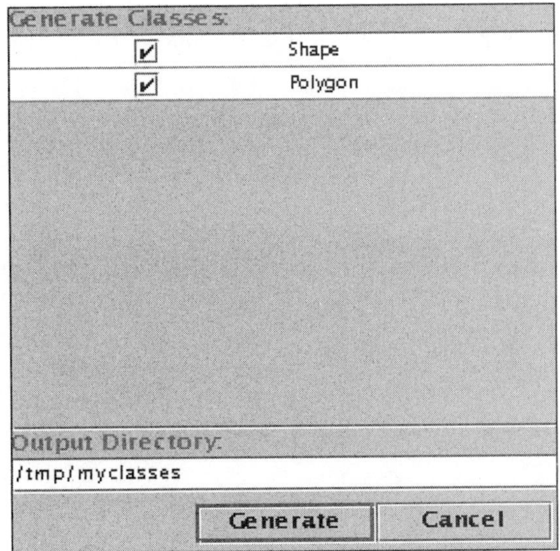

FIGURE 45.13
Code generation dialog.

Specify a directory: ArgoUML will generate the Java source into a hierarchical tree representing the package name. Listings 45.1 and 45.2 show the contents of the two files generated from our simple project.

LISTING 45.1 `Shape.java`, a Java Source File Generated by ArgoUML

```
// FILE: /tmp/myclasses/com/macmillan/nmeyers/Shape.java

package com.macmillan.nmeyers;
import java.util.*;

/** A class that represents ...
 *
```

continued on next page

continued from previous page

```
 * @see OtherClasses
 * @author your_name_here
 */
public class Shape {

  // Attributes
  /** An attribute that represents ...
 */
  public String name = "";

  // Associations

  // Operations
  /** An operation that does ...
 *
 * @param firstParamName  a description of this parameter
 */
  public void draw() {
  }
} /* end class Shape */
```

LISTING 45.2 Polygon.java, the ArgoUML-generated Source for the `Polygon` Subclass of `Shape`

```
// FILE: /tmp/myclasses/com/macmillan/nmeyers/Polygon.java

package com.macmillan.nmeyers;
import java.util.*;

/** A class that represents a two-dimensional polygon with three or more vertices.
 *
 * @see Shape
 * @author Nathan Meyers
 */
public class Polygon extends Shape {

  // Attributes
  /** An attribute that represents ...
 */
  public int numVertices = 0;

  // Associations

  // Operations

} /* end class Polygon */
```

Future of ArgoUML

The to-do list is still long, but ArgoUML is under active development, with dozens of contributors and several thousand users. Despite its low version number, ArgoUML's capabilities and robustness are impressive. It should continue to serve as a powerful learning tool and a good Java development aid for those who do not need the costly, enterprise-class features of commercial products.

Summary

This chapter has presented ArgoUML, an open source UML modeling tool from the University of California at Irvine. The Unified Software Development Process and its predecessor software engineering methodologies (such as Structured Analysis and Design) have been around for years—enthusiastically embraced by some development organizations and ignored by many others. Adopting the Process and UML is a big decision: An organization must fully commit to using it and must structure its development processes around it. ArgoUML gives you an excellent and low-cost way to explore UML and what it offers for the software development process.

PART X

MISCELLANEOUS DEVELOPMENT TOOLS

This part looks at some development tools that do not fit neatly into the standard categories of compilers, debuggers, development environments, and so on. This is not the book's last word on tools. Later, in discussion of deployment, platform, and performance issues, we look at tools, projects, and products specifically focused on those areas.

CHAPTER 46

jad: A JAVA DECOMPILER

Jad (JAva Decompiler) is a natively implemented decompiler for Java class files.

Platform: Linux JDK1.1/JDK1.2

The tortured history of Java decompilers began in 1996, when the late Hanpeter Van Vliet published *Mocha*, a decompiler that generated Java source files from bytecoded class files. A great uproar ensued after its publication, and Mocha has, at various times, been withdrawn from and returned to distribution.

Why the fuss? The controversy about decompilers is the ease with which they allow you to construct unpublished source from published binary code—a potential threat to the intellectual property rights of software authors. Over time, the controversy died down, and several commercial decompilers are now available as standalone products or part of development suites.

A few general observations about decompilers before we describe `jad`:

- The best reason to have a decompiler is to recover classes to which you have mislaid the source, or to study how Java is compiled and optimized into bytecodes. The worst reason is to steal someone else's code—you're creative enough to build your own masterpieces.
- All decompilers work to some degree; none works perfectly, and most can be made to trip up on some example of ordinary, unobfuscated code.

- It is impossible to completely protect software from reverse engineering. Java is easier to decompile than most, but not even native code is immune. You can only make the job more or less difficult.
- The best way to protect valuable code assets is to run them on a secure server and not let them anywhere near users' machines. Java offers a rich collection of mechanisms (RMI, CORBA, servlets, and so on) to support this model.

We will look at the other side of the coin—tools for obfuscating code to discourage decompilation—when we examine deployment-related tools in later chapters.

Obtaining `jad`

`jad` is a natively implemented decompiler published as freeware by Pavel Kouznetsov. `jad` is distributed, in binary form only, for several platforms including Linux. As a native application, it runs several times faster than decompilers (such as Mocha) that are implemented in Java. The source for `jad` is unpublished, and it is free for noncommercial use only.

Home for `jad` is `http://www.geocities.com/SiliconValley/Bridge/8617/jad.html`, which contains links to executables for Linux and other platforms.

Installation is trivial: Unzip the file anywhere to produce a `jad` executable and a `Readme.txt` file. `jad` has no dependencies on any installed Java environment.

Running `jad`

The `jad` invocation generates decompiled sources from one or more class files.

Synopsis:

`jad [<options>] <classfiles>`

Options:

- `-a`—Include Java bytecodes, as comments, in the decompiled output.
- `-af`—Include Java bytecodes, as with `-a`, but use full package+class names for all class references.
- `-b`—Output redundant braces around code blocks.
- `-clear`—Clear automatic prefixes. When `jad` encounters mangled names that are not legal Java identifiers, it generates automatic prefixes for those names (see the `-pa`, `-pc`, `-pe`, `-pf`, `-pl`, `-pm`, and `-pp` options later in this list). This option clears all automatic prefixes.
- `-d <dir>`—Specify destination directory for output files.
- `-dead`—Try to decompile dead code. (Dead code may be a result of writing unreachable code, or intentionally inserted by obfuscators to thwart decompilers. Note that `jad` may crash when trying to decompile intentionally bad code.)

- `-disass`—Generate a disassembly listing (like `-a`) but with no source listing.
- `-f`—Output full package+class names for classes and members.
- `-ff`—Output class fields before methods.
- `-i`—Output default initializers for all non-final fields.
- `-l`*<num>*—Split string constants into chunks of the specified size, adding concatenation operators as needed.
- `-nl`—Split string constants at newline characters, adding concatenation operators as needed.
- `-nocast`—Disable generation of auxiliary casts.
- `-nocode`—Disable generation of source code for methods.
- `-noconv`—Disable conversion of Java identifiers.
- `-noctor`—Disable generation of empty class constructors.
- `-nodos`—Disable checking for class files in DOS mode.
- `-noinner`—Disable support of inner classes.
- `-nolvt`—Ignore local variable table.
- `-nonlb`—Disable output of newline before opening brackets.
- `-o`—Overwrite output files without requesting confirmation.
- `-p`—Send decompiled code to `stdout` instead of writing to `.jad` file.
- `-pa` *<pfx>*—Specify prefix for packages in generated source files.
- `-pc` *<pfx>*—Specify prefix for classes with numerical names (default: `_cls`).
- `-pe` *<pfx>*—Specify prefix for unused exception names (default: `_ex`).
- `-pf` *<pfx>*—Specify prefix for fields with numerical names (default: `_fld`).
- `-pi`*<num>*—Pack imports into one line after the specified number of imports.
- `-pl` *<pfx>*—Specify prefix for locals with numerical names (default: `_lcl`).
- `-pm` *<pfx>*—Specify prefix for methods with numerical names (default: `_mth`).
- `-pp` *<pfx>*—Specify prefix for method parms with numerical names (default: `_prm`).
- `-pv`*<num>*—Pack fields with identical types into one line.
- `-r`—Restore package directory structure.
- `-s` *<ext>*—Use specified extension for output file instead of `.jad`.
- `-stat`—Display summary statistics on classes/methods/fields processed.
- `-t`—Use tabs for indentation.

- `-t<num>`—Use specified number of spaces for indentation.
- `-v`—Run verbosely by displaying method names as they are being decompiled.

The single-word options can be specified in several ways:

- `-<option>`—Toggle option
- `-<option>+`—Enable option
- `-<option>-`—Disable option

Decompiling a Sample Project Using `jad`

Using the "Hello world" example, we invoke **`jad`** with the **`-a`** option to include bytecodes in the output:

```
bash$ jad -a Hello.class
Parsing Hello.class... Generating Hello.jad
bash$
```

The results are shown in listing 46.1. The decompiled bytecodes appear as comments.

LISTING 46.1 A Decompiled Version of the "Hello World" Program Generated by **`jad`**

```
// Decompiled by Jad v1.5.7. Copyright 1997-99 Pavel Kouznetsov.
// Jad home page: http://www.geocities.com/SiliconValley/Bridge/8617/jad.html
// Decompiler options: packimports(3) annotate
// Source File Name:   Hello.java

import java.io.PrintStream;

class Hello
{

    Hello()
    {
    //    0    0:aload_0
    //    1    1:invokespecial   #6    <Method void Object()>
    //    2    4:return
    }

    public static void main(String argv[])
    {
        System.out.println("Hello world");
    //    0    0:getstatic       #7    <Field PrintStream System.out>
    //    1    3:ldc1            #1    <String "Hello world">
    //    2    5:invokevirtual   #8    <Method void PrintStream.println(String)>
    //    3    8:return
    }
}
```

Summary

This chapter has presented `jad`, a Java decompiler implemented as a native executable for Linux and other platforms. With the easy availability of `jad` and similar tools—in other words, the ease with which Java can be decompiled—relying on "security through obscurity" is risky. Alternative approaches to protecting software are to limit its deployment and to understand the protections offered by national and international copyright law.

CHAPTER 47

DUMPCLASS: A TOOL FOR QUERYING CLASS STRUCTURE

`DumpClass` is a tool for viewing class contents and a demonstration of how to use the Reflection API classes and methods.

Platform: JDK1.1/JDK1.2

This is a personal tool, written out of frustration with the limitations of the SDK `javap` tool. My favorite `javap` functionality is the default (no-option) functionality, which simply dumps information about class members. My frustration is that it only describes members defined by the class and not inherited members.

`DumpClass` displays the structure of a class—methods, initializers, and fields—including members inherited from superclasses. Personal experience suggests that that looking at such information—C++ header files or Java class dumps—is often of more value and convenience than diving into the documentation. This tool generates the Java class dumps I find most useful.

Obtaining DumpClass

`DumpClass` is provided, in source and binary form, on the enclosed CD-ROM. Different versions are provided for JDK1.1 and JDK1.2. A listing is also provided in Appendix B, "Miscellaneous Program Listings."

The JDK1.1 version relies on the external Sun v1.1 Collections classes (see Chapter 11, "Choosing an Environment: 1.1 or 1.2?," in the section "Java Collections Classes"), which must be included in the class path.

The JDK1.2 version has no dependencies outside the core classes and uses a more robust class loader (built on JDK1.2's class-loading model) that is less likely to fail when examining classes with unresolved references.

Running DumpClass

The `DumpClass` invocation specifies one or more classes on which you want information.

Synopsis:

```
java com.macmillan.nmeyers.DumpClass [<options>] <classes> (JDK1.2 only)
java com.macmillan.nmeyers.DumpClass11 [<options>] <classes> (JDK1.1 only)
```

To specify inner classes, use Java's internal `$` separator (for example, `java com.macmillan.nmeyers.DumpClass javax.swing.text.AbstractDocument$Content`). When dumping a class, `DumpClass` will not dump its inner classes.

Options:

- `-public`—Display only public class members.
- `-protected`—Display public and protected class members (default behavior).
- `-package`—Display public, protected, and package-visible class members.
- `-private`—Display all class members.
- `-suppress:{name,interfaces,hierarchy,headings,keys, all}`—Suppress certain output features. The next section, "Running a DumpClass Example," describes the optional output features controlled by this option.
- `-noancestors`—Do not show ancestors' class members.
- `-inaccessible`—Display inaccessible members: ancestor constructors, ancestor private members, ancestor package-visible members from a different package. Default is not to display.

Running a DumpClass Example

Listing 47.1 shows an example `DumpClass` invocation and the resulting output:

LISTING 47.1 Example `DumpClass` Invocation and Output

```
bash$ java com.macmillan.nmeyers.DumpClass java.lang.System
public final class java.lang.System
  class java.lang.Object
```

```
Fields

err: public static final java.io.PrintStream java.lang.System.err
in: public static final java.io.InputStream java.lang.System.in
out: public static final java.io.PrintStream java.lang.System.out

Methods

arraycopy: public static native void
➥java.lang.System.arraycopy(java.lang.Object,int,java.lang.Object,int,int)
clone: protected native java.lang.Object java.lang.Object.clone() throws
➥java.lang.CloneNotSupportedException
currentTimeMillis: public static native long java.lang.System.currentTimeMillis()
equals: public boolean java.lang.Object.equals(java.lang.Object)
exit: public static void java.lang.System.exit(int)
finalize: protected void java.lang.Object.finalize() throws java.lang.Throwable
gc: public static void java.lang.System.gc()
getClass: public final native java.lang.Class java.lang.Object.getClass()
getProperties: public static java.util.Properties java.lang.System.getProperties()
getProperty: public static java.lang.String
➥java.lang.System.getProperty(java.lang.String)
getProperty: public static java.lang.String
➥java.lang.System.getProperty(java.lang.String,java.lang.String)
getSecurityManager: public static java.lang.SecurityManager
➥java.lang.System.getSecurityManager()
getenv: public static java.lang.String java.lang.System.getenv(java.lang.String)
hashCode: public native int java.lang.Object.hashCode()
identityHashCode: public static native int
➥java.lang.System.identityHashCode(java.lang.Object)
load: public static void java.lang.System.load(java.lang.String)
loadLibrary: public static void java.lang.System.loadLibrary(java.lang.String)
mapLibraryName: public static native java.lang.String
➥java.lang.System.mapLibraryName(java.lang.String)
notify: public final native void java.lang.Object.notify()
notifyAll: public final native void java.lang.Object.notifyAll()
runFinalization: public static void java.lang.System.runFinalization()
runFinalizersOnExit: public static void
➥java.lang.System.runFinalizersOnExit(boolean)
setErr: public static void java.lang.System.setErr(java.io.PrintStream)
setIn: public static void java.lang.System.setIn(java.io.InputStream)
setOut: public static void java.lang.System.setOut(java.io.PrintStream)
setProperties: public static void
➥java.lang.System.setProperties(java.util.Properties)
setProperty: public static java.lang.String
➥java.lang.System.setProperty(java.lang.String,java.lang.String)
setSecurityManager: public static synchronized void
➥java.lang.System.setSecurityManager(java.lang.SecurityManager)
toString: public java.lang.String java.lang.Object.toString()
wait: public final void java.lang.Object.wait() throws
➥java.lang.InterruptedException
wait: public final native void java.lang.Object.wait(long) throws
➥java.lang.InterruptedException
wait: public final void java.lang.Object.wait(long,int) throws
➥java.lang.InterruptedException
```

The first lines display the class name and hierarchy. This can be suppressed with the -suppress:name option. To suppress the hierarchy but not the class name, use -suppress:hierarchy.

If the class implements any interfaces, they are also shown as an **implements** clause in the first line (none in this example). To suppress this information, use **-suppress:interfaces**.

To suppress the headings that describe each section (**Constructors**, **Fields**, **Methods**), use -suppress:headings.

To suppress the keys shown for each member (**<*membername*>:** at the beginning of each line), use -suppress:keys.

Summary

This chapter has presented **DumpClass**, a utility for dumping the contents of a class. In addition to its utility as a development tool, **DumpClass** serves as an illustration of how the Reflection API can be used to discover detailed information about class structure.

CHAPTER 48

JMAKEDEPEND: A PROJECT BUILD MANAGEMENT UTILITY

JMakeDepend is a project build utility, used in conjunction with GNU make to manage Java projects.

Platform: JDK1.1/JDK1.2

This is a personal tool, written to address some of the difficulties of managing Java development with UNIX/Linux tools such as GNU make. Before exploring JMakeDepend, we'll take a look at the challenges of building Java projects with make.

The Java make Problem

The make utility, which has long proven its value in managing the building of software projects, is not well suited to managing Java projects. Java presents unique challenges—relationships between sources and objects, relationships between objects and other objects—not found in most languages and not easily managed by make.

A Closer Look at make

The purpose of make is to bring a software project up to date. At every step of a project, make identifies and executes the actions required to bring a project to a known state: which sources to recompile for an up-to-date executable, which executables to rebuild for an up-to-date project, which files to remove to clean up your project area, and so on.

`make` does its job by reading dependency rules and actions that you provide (in a `Makefile`), building a dependency graph for the project, and performing whatever actions are needed to reach a desired node in the graph—for example, building an executable that is up-to-date with regard to the latest sources. A simple `Makefile` to build a shared library from two C sources might look like this:

```
libfoobar.so:  foo.o bar.o
        gcc -o libfoobar.so -shared foo.o bar.o

foo.o:  foo.c
        gcc -fpic -c foo.c

bar.o:  bar.c
        gcc -fpic -c bar.c
```

This `Makefile` describes a relationship between two C-language source files, their corresponding object files, and the final shared library. Whenever you run `make`, it recompiles or relinks (using various invocations of `gcc`) as needed—based on what files are missing and on what objects are out-of-date with respect to the sources and objects on which they depend.

How Java Breaks `make`

In examining the `Makefile` shown in the previous section, you can discern a clear chain of dependencies between sources and objects: The library (`.so`) depends on two compiled modules (`.o`), and each module depends on one C source file (`.c`). You can, whatever the current project state, use these relationships to determine what steps are needed, in what order, to bring the project up to date.

All `Makefiles`, no matter how large or complex, must describe relationships that can be represented in this way (in other words, the dependencies are representable in a directed acyclic graph). Unfortunately, Java breaks this requirement in several ways:

- `make` assumes that there are no cycles in the dependency graph (if `foo.o` depends on `bar.o`, then `bar.o` cannot depend on `foo.o`), but Java allows mutual dependencies between classes.
- `make` assumes that separate modules can be built independently (you can safely build `foo.o` and `bar.o` in two separate compilation steps). In Java, you must sometimes build multiple objects in a single compilation step.
- `make` assumes that there is a straightforward mapping from provider to dependent (compiling `foo.c` generates the single file `foo.o`). Java, with its inner and anonymous classes, can generate many class files from a single source—and the developer might not know the names of the files to be generated.

Listings 48.1-48.4 illustrate the problem with a small set of Java classes.

LISTING 48.1 `A.java`

```


class A {
```

```
    A()
    {
    }
    static class C extends B
    {
    }
    interface D
    {
    }
    void foobar(E e)
    {
    }
}
```

LISTING 48.2 `B.java`

```
package com.macmillan.nmeyers;

class B extends A implements A.D
{
}
```

LISTING 48.3 `E.java`

```
package com.macmillan.nmeyers;

class E implements A.D, F
{
}
```

LISTING 48.4 `F.java`

```
package com.macmillan.nmeyers;

interface F
{
}
```

This is legal Java and shows (perhaps to excess) a common practice: mutual dependencies among Java classes[1]. There are no illegal cycles in the inheritance hierarchy (no class attempts to be its own ancestor), but there *are* cycles in the dependency graph: A change to class `A` affects class `B`, and a change to class `B` affects class `A` (in this case, an inner class under `A`). By the time you tease out all the dependencies, a change to almost any class affects almost everything.

---

[1] This, by the way, is another Java advantage over C/C++. Dependencies like this are not unreasonable in complex projects, but are nearly impossible to support in C/C++. Large projects sometimes take extraordinary steps, such as multiple compilation cycles, or take great pains to architect such dependencies *out* of the product.

How would you express these relationships in a `Makefile`? You might try the traditional C/C++ approach of expressing source and object dependencies:

```
A.class:        A.java B.class E.class
        javac A.java

B.class:        B.java A.class
        javac B.java

E.class:        E.java A.class F.class
        javac E.java

F.class:        F.java
        javac F.java
```

Unfortunately, this will fail for several reasons:

- `make` will complain about the cycles (such as the mutual dependence between `A.class` and `B.class`) and remove the offending edges from the graph. The result is missing dependencies.
- If mutually dependent class files are to be rebuilt, they must be rebuilt together in a single invocation of the Java compiler. `make` gives us no easy way to execute such a command.
- The dependencies shown are not really correct. Class `E` does not really depend on a class found in the class file `A.class`, it depends on an inner class (`A.D`) that comes from a different class file: `A$D.class`.

Clearly, the difficulties of expressing these relationships in a `Makefile` can be extreme for complex projects. Easier solutions are to rebuild the entire project every time (a slow alternative), or to rely on compiler detection of dependencies (not supported, or not supported properly, on most compilers).

Identifying a Solution

`make` may not be the solution to managing Java development, but it can be 90 percent of the solution—it's too good a tool *not* to use. This conclusion is borne out by UNIX history, in which tools such as `Imake` and `makedepend` were developed specifically to adapt `make` to project requirements.

`JMakeDepend` serves such a role: It was written to adapt GNU `make` for Java development. It employs a handful of `make` tricks to work around the limitations, accurately record and act on the dependencies, and rebuild a minimal number of class files to bring a project up-to-date.

I am not the first to attack this problem: Other approaches have been published online. I have not found them particularly workable, and they are too often dependent on the features provided by a particular compiler. So I offer my compiler-neutral approach in this chapter.

The solution to be described is implemented in two parts: The `JMakeDepend` program itself and some rules in the `Makefile` to run the program and use the rules it generates. The next several sections describe and illustrate the use of `JMakeDepend`.

Obtaining JMakeDepend

`JMakeDepend` is provided, in source and compiled form for JDK1.1 and JDK1.2, on the CD-ROM. It consists of two pieces: a class to read class files and the `JMakeDepend` class—the latter is written in Generic Java and must be compiled with `gjc` (see Chapter 38, "Generic Java Compilers," in the section "GJ: The Generic Java Compiler"). Source listings also apppear in Appendix B, "Miscellaneous Program Listings."

The JDK1.2 version of `JMakeDepend` has no external dependencies. The JDK1.1 version depends on the Sun 1.1 Collections classes (see Chapter 11, "Choosing an Environment: 1.1 or 1.2?," in the section "Java Collections Classes").

Running JMakeDepend

We'll first describe operation of the program and, in the next section, show how to use it from a `Makefile`.

Synopsis:

```
java com.macmillan.nmeyers.JMakeDepend [-noinner] [<classfiles>] (JDK1.2 only)
java com.macmillan.nmeyers.JMakeDepend11 [-noinner] [<classfiles>] (JDK1.1 only)
```

Class file names are specified on the command line; if none is specified, they are read (one per line) from `stdin`. Output is sent to `stdout` and consists of dependencies and commands designed to be included (via the `include` directive) in a `Makefile`.

Options:

- `-noinner`—Normally, `JMakeDepend` creates `Makefile` dependencies for all class files it examines. If this option is specified, dependencies for inner classes are hidden and their dependent relationships folded into the dependency listings for the corresponding outer class.

Using JMakeDepend from a Makefile

Listing 48.5 presents a sample prescription for a `Makefile`, with detailed discussion (line numbers added for clarity). This is based on the example classes shown in Listings 48.1–48.4 and assumes that we are building the class files in a subdirectory named `classes`, using SDK1.2.

LISTING 48.5 Sample `Makefile` Prescription

```
.PHONY: all clean buildall depend

SOURCES=A.java B.java E.java F.java
```

continued on next page

continued from previous page

```
4
5   all:
6           rm -f .targets
7           $(MAKE) .targets
8           [ -f .targets ] && javac -classpath $CLASSPATH:classes -d classes
➥@.targets || true
9
10  clean:
11          rm -rf classes .depend
12
13  ifneq ($(MAKECMDGOALS),buildall)
14  ifneq ($(MAKECMDGOALS),clean)
15  include .depend
16  endif
17  endif
18
19  .depend:
20          $(MAKE) buildall
21          find classes -type f -print | java com.macmillan.nmeyers.JMakeDepend
➥>.depend
22
23  depend:
24          rm -f .depend
25          $(MAKE) .depend
26
27  buildall:
28          rm -rf classes
29          mkdir classes
30          javac -d classes $(SOURCES)
```

Here is how the `Makefile` runs `JMakeDepend` and uses the rules it generates:

1. `make` builds a `.depend` file containing dependency rules (lines 19-21). The file is created by first building the entire project (line 20) and then running `JMakeDepend` to examine the resulting class files (line 21).

2. `make` includes (reads in) the `.depend` file (line 15), whose rules will be used in the next step. Inclusion is conditional; `.depend` is not included if we are performing a `make clean` or are rebuilding the entire project. (The latter condition is needed to prevent infinite `make` recursion when building a new `.depend` file.)

3. `make` builds the project (lines 5-8) by first creating a temporary `.targets` file containing a list of sources to be recompiled (line 7, using rules that were included from `.depend`) and then invoking the Java compiler with that information (line 8). The compiler invocation specifies `-d` for placement of the class files being built and `-classpath` to find those that already exist. If no `.targets` file exists (nothing needs to be rebuilt), the compiler is not invoked.

The first step is the most time-consuming—it rebuilds the entire project and then runs `JMakeDepend`. It occurs automatically if the `.depend` file is missing, but you will need to perform your own `make depend` (lines 23–25) to update if you add new classes or otherwise change dependency relationships. In general, this step is infrequently performed.

The third step is the most frequent: change your source, run `make`, and the minimal set of files is rebuilt.

The key logic behind building the project comes from the `.depend` file generated by `JMakeDepend` and shown in Listing 48.6 for this project (again with line numbers added):

LISTING 48.6 Sample `.depend` File Generated by `JMakeDepend`

```
1   classes/com/macmillan/nmeyers/A$$D.class: A.java B.java E.java F.java
2           echo $< $? >>.rawtargets
3
4   classes/com/macmillan/nmeyers/A$$C.class: A.java B.java E.java F.java
5           echo $< $? >>.rawtargets
6
7   classes/com/macmillan/nmeyers/F.class: F.java
8           echo $< $? >>.rawtargets
9
10  classes/com/macmillan/nmeyers/E.class: E.java A.java B.java F.java
11          echo $< $? >>.rawtargets
12
13  classes/com/macmillan/nmeyers/B.class: B.java A.java E.java F.java
14          echo $< $? >>.rawtargets
15
16  classes/com/macmillan/nmeyers/A.class: A.java B.java E.java F.java
17          echo $< $? >>.rawtargets
18
19  JSOURCES = A.java B.java E.java F.java
20
21  JOBJECTS = classes/com/macmillan/nmeyers/A$$D.class
classes/com/macmillan/nmeyers/F.class
classes/com/macmillan/nmeyers/A.class
classes/com/macmillan/nmeyers/E.class
classes/com/macmillan/nmeyers/B.class
classes/com/macmillan/nmeyers/A$$C.class
22
23  .rawtargets:    $(JOBJECTS)
24
25  .targets:
26          rm -f .rawtargets
27          $(MAKE) .rawtargets
28          [ -f .rawtargets ] && tr -s ' ' '\012' <.rawtargets ¦ sort -u >
➥.targets ¦¦ true

29          rm -f .rawtargets
```

For every class file, `JMakeDepend` has created a dependency relationship to all *sources* on which it ultimately depends. By specifying a relation to sources instead of class files, it avoids the cycles that `make` cannot handle.

When `make` is asked to build `.targets` (line 7 of the original `Makefile`), it triggers the rule at line 25 of `.depend`. Line 27 creates `.rawtargets` by triggering dependency rules for the various class files (lines 1–17) to name the sources that need to be rebuilt. That list of names is filtered (line 28) to remove duplicates and generate the `.targets` file. With that information, the build can proceed (line 8 of the original `Makefile`).

This technology has dependencies on the UNIX/Linux utilities `tr` and `sort`, but none on the choice of compiler. For compilers that (unlike the SDK1.2 `javac`) cannot read arguments from a file, you can pull the contents of the file into the command line with shell command substitution:

```
javac ... `cat .targets`
```

JMakeDepend Caveats

Two cautions about `JMakeDepend` deserve mention:

- Although `JMakeDepend` tries to minimize the number of files that must be rebuilt after a change, it does not always succeed. Because it cannot detect the difference between substantive modifications (such as API changes) and trivial changes (such as editing comments), `JMakeDepend` errs on the side of caution and recompiles all classes with dependencies on a changed source file.
- `JMakeDepend` does not handle any dependencies outside the class files being examined. It will not record dependencies on the core classes, extension classes, other application class libraries, or anything else that happens to be in the class path. If necessary, you can express those inter-project dependencies in the `Makefile`.

Summary

This chapter has presented `JMakeDepend`, a utility to assist GNU `make` in managing Java projects. `JMakeDepend` allows you to exploit the power of `make`—keeping projects up-to-date and minimizing compilation time—while coping with the new, unique requirements of Java development.

PART XI

JAVA APPLICATION DISTRIBUTION

The portability of the Java platform is one of its major attractions as an applications target. In a perfect Java world, that portability would extend all the way from the source code to the end-user environment: Drop in the application, and it just works.

That world does not exist, of course, and distributing Java applications and applets puts you face-to-face with a few real-world challenges:

- End users may not have a Java environment.
- End users may have an old Java environment.
- End users may have the wrong current Java environment (for example, a Microsoft JVM without RMI support).
- Many generations of Web browsers are in use, with varying degrees of Java support and with their own platform-specific requirements and capabilities.

To date, these problems have created formidable barriers to application distribution, making publication of platform-neutral Java applications a challenging discipline in itself.

These problems will always be with us as Java evolves, but the situation is improving: The (hoped-for) stability offered by the Java 2 Platform, the availability of free and commercial distribution technologies, and technologies such as Java Plug-in and Netscape OJI (Chapter 11, "Choosing an Environment: 1.1 or 1.2?," section "Option 2: Netscape Open Java Interface") offer hope.

The chapters in this part explore the issues, tools, and technologies relevant to the problem of getting your Java creations to your users. We focus on two major aspects of application distribution:

- Ensuring a match between your application's requirements and the end-user environment. Because your deployment environments will undoubtedly include many boxes running Microsoft, we lavish some detail on that part of the delivery/distribution problem.
- Technologies for optimization and delivery of applications: optimizers, packagers, and obfuscators.

CHAPTER 49

DISTRIBUTING JAVA APPLICATIONS AND JRES

The two components a user needs to run your Java applications are a runtime environment and the application itself. Because you are presumably writing software for users on many different platforms, we must examine the question of how to get them up and running.

Sun publishes *Java Runtime Environments* (JREs) for two platforms: Solaris and Microsoft Windows. They can be obtained from the Sun JDK product pages at the main Java Web site (`http://java.sun.com`). JREs are available for other platforms that support the JDK (HP, IBM, and others), and are distributed by the individual platform vendors. Blackdown also distributes JREs for Linux from its download sites.

As we discussed in Chapter 10, "Java Components for Linux," in the section "A Glossary of Sun Java Terminology," these runtime environments are not full SDKs—just a minimal set of components to support runtime Java. Unlike the SDK, which you are not allowed to redistribute, JREs have liberal redistribution terms. They also do not charge any licensing fees. They are published for the sole purpose of enabling Java on more platforms.

The business model behind JREs is unquestionably weird but necessary to world domination. Sun publishes, for no licensing fee, an optimized JRE, JIT, and HotSpot for the arch-rival Windows operating system. It's important for Java's acceptance even if it hurts Solaris. Sun's competitors, such as HP, license and publish optimized JRE ports because they cannot afford *not* to be in the Java business. And although Sun collects licensing fees for commercial ports such as HP's, it derives no income from the Linux port—another OS that competes with Solaris.[1]

The details on how JREs can be deployed are provided in README files shipped with the JREs. These details can vary between Java releases, but this chapter provides a general picture of how it works. For more detail, refer to the READMEs accompanying any JRE you want to ship.

Shipping a JRE with Your Application

The easiest way to deploy the JRE is to ship it, complete, with your application. For customers deploying on Windows platforms, the JRE is available as a self-installing executable. You can ship that executable and, as part of your product installation procedure, simply run it.

For UNIX and Linux platforms, customers face the same procedure *you* faced when installing the Blackdown port: no auto-installation, just a large compressed archive file (a tarball). Your options for shipping the JRE include the following:

- Bundling it with your application and giving the customer instructions on installing from a compressed archive.
- Not bundling the JRE and directing the customer to platform-vendor Web sites to obtain one (or relying on whatever the customer has already installed).
- Installing it as part of your product installation process, either in some central location or a location specific to your product. Installing in a central location incurs the risk that you may damage an existing Java installation or applications that depend on particular Java versions, so consider such a step carefully. Some reasonable precautions include:
    - Allowing the user to choose whether or not to replace an existing JRE.
    - Allowing the user to choose between a global and a product-specific installation location.
    - Providing an uninstall capability that will recover an older JRE installation.

  In light of the risks and difficulties of shipping a JRE, Sun suggests an alternate approach—discussed in the next section.

[1]Like many high-tech companies, Sun has no shortage of Linux partisans roaming the hallways. Their presence is visible in the activities of the Blackdown organization.

Incorporating Minimal JRE Functionality into Your Application Installation

An alternative approach promoted by Sun is not to ship an entire JRE, but just to ship some minimal components in your own product's directories: Your application has its own private JRE. This avoids the risks of polluting the user's system or depending on the user's installed versions, at the cost of some disk space.

If you take this approach, Sun strictly prescribes what you ship. You cannot arbitrarily subset Java functionality. According to the current JRE1.2 requirements for Solaris and Windows, the following components *may* be excluded from a redistributed JRE:

- I18N support classes (`i18n.jar`)
- JIT compiler
- The `ext/` extensions subdirectory
- RMI components `rmid` and `rmiregistry`
- CORBA component `tnameserv`
- Security components `keytool` and `policytool`
- Font properties files other than the default `lib/font.properties`
- Java Plug-in classes and plug-in ActiveX control (`jaws.jar` and `beans.ocx`) in the Win32 version

All other components are required. You can choose to ship green-only or native-only threading implementations.

Most of the required files can be shipped in your product directories. For Windows deployments, the required `msvcrt.dll` included in the JRE needs to be installed into the Windows system directory (unless a newer version of that library is already installed).

To repeat an earlier warning: Be *sure* to consult the README and other documentation that comes bundled with any JRE you want to redistribute.

What About Applet Support?

This chapter has focused on applications. For applets, the story is still in flux. The old answer to the question was to leave it to the browser. Netscape bundles its own JRE, and Internet Explorer uses the Microsoft JRE.

With the advent of Java Plug-in (see Chapter 50, "Deploying Applets with Java Plug-In"), applets can find and install their own replacement JRE.

The story will undoubtedly be different for the Netscape Open Java Interface, but those answers are not yet available.

For Further Reading

A good source of information, in the form of developers' notes on the JRE, can be found on the main Java Web site at `http://java.sun.com/products/jdk/1.2/runtime.html`.

Summary

This chapter has discussed the problem of shipping Java Runtime Environments with your applications. Until the time that we can reliably count on finding current Java environments installed on current operating systems, JRE distribution will remain an unavoidable part of application distribution.

CHAPTER 50

DEPLOYING APPLETS WITH JAVA PLUG-IN

The Java Plug-in extends existing Web browsers to use new Java Runtime Environments, enabling the deployment of applets that might otherwise not be usable with noncompliant browsers.

Platforms: JDK1.1/JDK1.2

One of the early and, in retrospect, unfortunate architectural decisions in the Java world was the bundling of the Java Runtime Environment (JRE) with Web browsers.

Netscape was an early Java partner and champion, and its work on bundling Java with the Navigator product brought JVMs to many platforms quickly. Unfortunately, it created huge ongoing maintenance and performance headaches for Netscape on many platforms. The Java sources are not particularly portable to begin with, and Netscape had to create threading mechanisms on many operating systems that lacked native threading support. Netscape's JDK1.1 was not fully compliant until well into 1999, and there is no Netscape JDK1.2 anywhere on the horizon.

Microsoft's solution on the Windows platform was architecturally much cleaner: a separate Java runtime, usable by Microsoft's browser or by any other Java consumer. Unfortunately, as the ongoing Sun/Microsoft legal battles show, Microsoft's JDK1.1 compliance is in dispute, and its JDK1.2 may never happen.

The end result of both approaches is that browser applets, the original purported killer app for Java technology, have turned out to be an unhappy place to do business. Add such incompatibilities as different security certification requirements, plug-in technologies, HTML and JavaScript enhancements, and LiveConnect[1], and you realize that developers and users have not been the victors in the browser wars.

The good news: Things are looking up.

Technologies are now available to bring current JDK environments to browsers on at least *some* platforms. This chapter looks at today's solutions for full JDK1.1 and JDK1.2 applet support in Netscape Navigator and Microsoft Internet Explorer.

Java Plug-in for JDK1.1

Early versions of this product were called *Java Activator*, and the term is sometimes still encountered. If you're looking for Java Activator—you've found it. The Java Plug-in is an add-on for current browsers that provides a fully compliant JDK1.1 Java environment for applet execution.

The Plug-in employs a clever back door for adding new Java support to old browsers: expandability that is already provided by Netscape Navigator and Internet Explorer. Plug-ins are simply pieces of native code designed to expand browser functionality. Typical plug-ins on the market include streaming audio players, multimedia viewers, and PDF file readers. The Java Plug-in is *just another* native-code plug-in: It happens to implement a Java Virtual Machine![2]

To use the Java Plug-in from a Web page, you must include special HTML tags in the page that invokes it and, if necessary, download it into a machine that does not have one installed. Details are discussed later in this chapter, in the section "Invoking the Java Plug-in from HTML."

Sun ships the Java Plug-in for Solaris and Windows, and versions for some other platforms are available from other vendors. Not all platforms are represented, unfortunately; there is not yet one for Linux. But the availability of the product for Windows means that you can still deploy modern applets to a very large customer base.

Sun has positioned the JDK1.1 Plug-in as a solution for Enterprise customers, rather than for general Web deployment. One can surmise several possible reasons:

- Corporate intranets tend to deploy more conservatively than home users. Whereas you and I run current browser releases with good JDK1.1 support, the typical cubicle dweller runs older code.

---

[1]A Netscape-specific bridge between Java, JavaScript, and native code.

[2]To be more precise, the Java Plug-in implements the glue between a JRE1.1 installation and the browser. This new browser/JVM architecture looks much more like Microsoft's approach to JVM integration.

- Corporate intranets tend to settle on one or two browser, platform, and version choices, which simplifies the problem of plug-in deployment.
- Microsoft Internet Explorer (IE) enjoys significant market penetration in corporate intranets; the Plug-in offers full JDK1.1 compliance where MSIE does not.
- Installing the Plug-in involves an interruption to your surfing and a big download to your PC. It's not clear whether home users will tolerate this as patiently as corporate users on a fast LAN. And the Plug-in doesn't make exceptions for browsers that are already JDK1.1-compliant: If you browse a page requiring the Plug-in, you *must* use the Plug-in.

All things considered, the presence of a Web page requiring the JDK1.1 Java Plug-in makes sense on a high-speed corporate intranet, but would probably not be appreciated on the Web.

Obtaining the JDK1.1 Java Plug-in

If you need to obtain the Java Plug-in for deployment on an intranet, it is available for free download from Sun. Visit the Java Plug-in product pages at `http://java.sun.com` for details.

Invoking the Java Plug-in from HTML

Use of the Java Plug-in requires different HTML tags than the customary `<APPLET>`. The page must use tags that are normally used for Netscape plug-ins (the `<EMBED>` tag) or MSIE ActiveX controls (the `<OBJECT>` tag).

To illustrate (see Listings 50.1 and 50.2), we create a trivial applet and corresponding traditional HTML code (this is similar to the example in Chapter 28, "GNU Classpath: Cleanroom Core Class Libraries," but specific to JDK1.1 and its Plug-in):

LISTING 50.1 Simple Demonstration Applet

```
import java.awt.*;
import java.applet.*;

public class Hello extends Applet
{
    Label label;
    public Hello()
    {
        label = new Label();
        add(label);
    }
    public void init()
    {
        label.setText(getParameter("LabelText"));
    }
}
```

LISTING 50.2 Standard HTML Applet Invocation, Which Uses the Default Browser JVM

```
<html>
<body>
<h1>Hello World Applet</h1>
<applet code="Hello.class"
        LabelText="Hello World"
        width="200"
        height="100">No Applet?</applet>
</body>
</html>
```

Invoking the Java Plug-in in Netscape Navigator

The traditional HTML will run the applet with Navigator's built-in Java interpreter. To invoke the Java Plug-in, the HTML must instead describe an embedded Java object. Those deploying on intranets are encouraged to replace the `java.sun.com` reference with links to locally installed copies of the downloadable code shown in Listing 50.3.

LISTING 50.3 HTML Applet Invocation to Use the Java Plug-in Under Netscape Navigator

```
<html>
<body>
<h1>Hello World Applet</h1>
<EMBED type="application/x-java-applet;version=1.1"
code = "Hello.class"
WIDTH = "200"
HEIGHT = "100"
LabelText="Hello World"
pluginspage="http://java.sun.com/products/plugin/1.1/plugin-install.html">
<NOEMBED>
No Applet?
</NOEMBED></EMBED>
</body>
</html>
```

When this page is browsed from Navigator, the Plug-in will be installed (if not already installed), and the applet will run under a full JRE1.1. The installation can be large: it includes the full JRE1.1 in addition to the small Plug-in code.

Invoking the Java Plug-in in Internet Explorer

Under MSIE, the traditional HTML will run the applet with Microsoft's JVM. To instead invoke the Java Plug-in and use the Sun JVM, the HTML must describe an embedded ActiveX object. Those deploying on intranets are encouraged to replace the `java.sun.com` reference with links to locally installed copies of the downloadable code shown in Listing 50.4.

LISTING 50.4 HTML Applet Invocation to Use the Java Plug-in Under Microsoft Internet Explorer

```
<html>
<body>
<h1>Hello World Applet</h1>
<OBJECT classid="clsid:8AD9C840-044E-11D1-B3E9-00805F499D93"
WIDTH = "200"
HEIGHT = "100"
codebase="http://java.sun.com/products/plugin/1.1/jinstall-11-
➥win32.cab#Version=1,1,0,0">
<PARAM NAME = CODE VALUE = "Hello.class" >
<PARAM NAME="type" VALUE="application/x-java-applet;version=1.1">
<PARAM NAME="LabelText" VALUE="Hello World">
No Applet?
</OBJECT>
</body>
</html>
```

When browsed with MSIE, the page will install the Plug-in (if it is not already installed), and the applet will run under a full JRE1.1.

Invoking the Java Plug-in for Both Browsers

You can target both browsers with an HTML trick: Hide the Navigator code inside a `<COMMENT>` in the MSIE `<OBJECT>` code as shown in Listing 50.5.

LISTING 50.5 HTML Applet Invocation to Use the Java Plug-in Under Either Netscape or MSIE

```
<html>
<body>
<h1>Hello World Applet</h1>
<OBJECT classid="clsid:8AD9C840-044E-11D1-B3E9-00805F499D93"
WIDTH = "200"
HEIGHT = "100"
codebase="http://java.sun.com/products/plugin/1.1/jinstall-11-
➥win32.cab#Version=1,1,0,0">
<PARAM NAME = CODE VALUE = "Hello.class" >
<PARAM NAME="type" VALUE="application/x-java-applet;version=1.1">
<PARAM NAME="LabelText" VALUE="Hello World">
<COMMENT>
  <EMBED type="application/x-java-applet;version=1.1"
  code = "Hello.class"
  WIDTH = "200"
  HEIGHT = "100"
  LabelText="Hello World"
  pluginspage="http://java.sun.com/products/plugin/1.1/plugin-
➥install.html">
  <NOEMBED>
No Applet?
</COMMENT>
  </NOEMBED></EMBED>
</OBJECT>
</body>
</html>
```

Now, either browser can read this page and load the Java Plug-in. Netscape finds its HTML (lines 12–21) amid MSIE tags it ignores, while MSIE doesn't see the Netscape tags hidden between `<COMMENT></COMMENT>` delimiters (lines 11 and 20).

Subtleties

This last example (Listing 50.5) contains an interesting bit of poorly formed HTML: interleaving of the `<COMMENT></COMMENT>` tags with `<EMBED></EMBED>` and `<NOEMBED></NOEMBED>`. The exact order of these tags—`<COMMENT>`, `<EMBED>`, `<NOEMBED>`, `</COMMENT>`, `</NOEMBED>`, `</EMBED>`—is not, strictly speaking, good HTML coding. How can you get away with it?

Because Navigator ignores `<OBJECT>` and `<COMMENT>` tags, MSIE ignores everything inside a `<COMMENT>`, and both browsers ignore unmatched end-tags, this code appears to each browser to be more or less well-formed HTML. The effect of this trick is a neat convenience for the Web page author: The HTML executed when the applet cannot be run (the text "No Applet?" on line 19) need only be specified once.

`htmlconv`: Automatic Generation of Java Plug-in Tags

Sun provides a free tool for conversion of HTML `<APPLET>` tags to the new tags needed for the Java Plug-in. You can obtain the tool, `htmlconv`, from the Java Plug-in product pages. We describe the JDK1.2 version, which you are more likely to find of interest, in detail in the following section.

Java Plug-in for JDK1.2

Java Plug-in v1.2 is the JDK1.2 counterpart to the Plug-in discussed previously. Unlike the earlier version, Sun is encouraging wide deployment of this product. The reason is clear: There is currently no other way to support JDK1.2 applets in browsers. Future developments (Netscape OJI) will improve the story for Netscape Navigator, but there is currently no other known route to JDK1.2 support by MSIE.

Multiplatform availability is still a weak link; there is no version for Linux or many other OSes. But the Windows version opens up many target browsers to JDK1.2 applets—and you always have the capability to test-drive your applets in Linux under `appletviewer` (see Chapter 18, "The Java Applet Viewer: `appletviewer`").

Obtaining Java Plug-in 1.2

The Plug-in is included with the SDK1.2 and JRE1.2 installations for the Windows platforms. If it is not installed, it can be installed automatically when the relevant HTML tags are encountered.

Invoking the Java Plug-in from HTML

The HTML required to invoke the 1.2 Plug-in is almost identical to that used for 1.1. The two changed fields are as follows (for the MSIE-related tags):

```
codebase="http://java.sun.com/products/plugin/1.2/jinstall-12-
➥win32.cab#Version=1,2,0,0"

<PARAM NAME="type" VALUE="application/x-java-applet;version=1.2">
```

and (for the Navigator-related tags):

```
EMBED type="application/x-java-applet;version=1.2"

pluginspage="http://java.sun.com/products/plugin/1.2/plugin-install.html"
```

Supporting Multiple Platforms

The HTML changes described so far are focused entirely on delivering the Java Plug-in to browsers running on Microsoft and Solaris platforms. Sun also recommends a set of tags you can use to support a wider range of browsers—which we will now explore.

The code in Listings 50.6 and 50.7 adds some logic that identifies the browser and platform, installs the Java Plug-in for Windows and Solaris platforms, and just runs the normal `<APPLET>` tag on all other platforms (where it will fail until the browser has JDK1.2 support). With some JavaScript hacking, it is extensible to support other Java Plug-in implementations as they become available.

The first part of the solution (Listing 50.6) is placed at the beginning of the document body (immediately after the `<BODY>` tag). Its purpose is to identify browsers and versions capable of hosting a Java Plug-in, and it sets some variable values that will be used later.

LISTING 50.6 Part 1 of the Multiplatform HTML Java Plug-in Code

```
<SCRIPT LANGUAGE="JavaScript"><!--
    var _info = navigator.userAgent; var _ns = false;
    var _ie = (_info.indexOf("MSIE") > 0 && _info.indexOf("Win") > 0
        && _info.indexOf("Windows 3.1") < 0);
//--></SCRIPT>
<COMMENT><SCRIPT LANGUAGE="JavaScript1.1"><!--
    var _ns = (navigator.appName.indexOf("Netscape") >= 0
        && ((_info.indexOf("Win") > 0 && _info.indexOf("Win16") < 0
        && java.lang.System.getProperty("os.version").indexOf("3.5") < 0)
        || _info.indexOf("Sun") > 0));
//--></SCRIPT></COMMENT>
```

The other part of the solution (shown in Listing 50.7) replaces each `<APPLET>` tag (again using our trivial applet example) with tags that enable the Java Plug-in. This code includes references to variables that were defined in Listing 50.6.

LISTING 50.7 HTML to Invoke Our Trivial Applet Under the Java Plug-in on Platforms That Support the Plug-in

```
<SCRIPT LANGUAGE="JavaScript"><!--
    if (_ie == true) document.writeln('<OBJECT
    classid="clsid:8AD9C840-044E-11D1-B3E9-00805F499D93"
    width="200" height="100" align="baseline"
codebase="http://java.sun.com/products/plugin/1.2/jinstall-12-
➥win32.cab#Version=1,2,0,0">
    <NOEMBED><XMP>');
    else if (_ns == true) document.writeln('<EMBED
    type="application/x-java-applet;version=1.2" width="200" height="100"
    align="baseline" code="Hello.class"
    LabelText="Hello World"
    pluginspage="http://java.sun.com/products/plugin/1.2/plugin-
➥install.html">
    <NOEMBED><XMP>');
//--></SCRIPT>
    <APPLET code="Hello.class" align="baseline"
        width="200" height="100"></XMP>
    <PARAM NAME="java_code" VALUE="Hello.class">
    <PARAM NAME="java_type" VALUE="application/x-java-applet;version=1.2">
    <PARAM NAME="LabelText" VALUE="Hello World">
    No applet?
</APPLET></NOEMBED></EMBED></OBJECT>

<!--
    <APPLET code="Hello.class" align="baseline"
        width="200" height="100">
    <PARAM NAME="LabelText" VALUE="Hello World">
    No applet?
    </APPLET>
-->
```

If this collection of HTML and JavaScript seems like a convoluted mess (compare it to the original code in Listing 50.2), it at least serves as a vivid example of the portability nightmares that have resulted from the browser wars.

`htmlconv` v1.2: Automatic Generation of HTML Tags

Sun provides a Java utility to assist in converting HTML source to use the Java Plug-in. You can obtain the JDK1.2 version of **`htmlconv`** from the product page for Java Plug-in 1.2; just unzip it anywhere and add its top-level directory to the class path.

Using the `htmlconv` GUI

This invocation starts up the GUI version of **`htmlconv`** (see Figure 50.1).

Synopsis:

```
java HTMLConverter
```

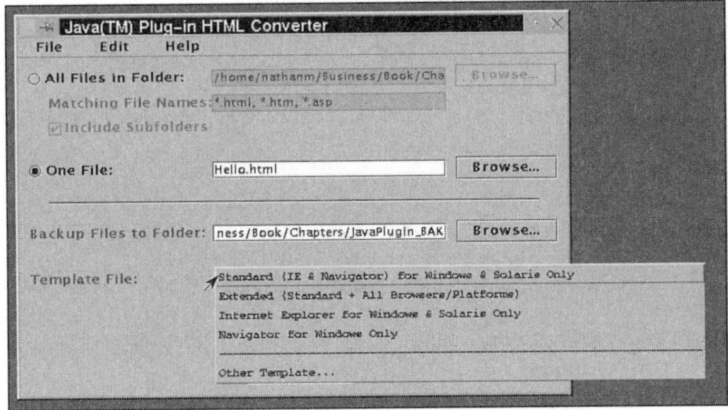

FIGURE 50.1
The HTML converter for Java Plug-in 1.2.

A simple GUI allows you to convert single HTML files or directory trees full of HTML files. A choice of *templates* handles the four cases described in the earlier code examples: targeting Netscape, targeting MSIE, targeting both on Solaris and Windows, or targeting all platforms. If none of these is suitable, you are free to define your own template.

Running the converter on our original `Hello.html`, with the *extended* template (which targets all platforms), produces the multibrowser HTML shown in Listing 50.8.

LISTING 50.8 HTML Code to Use the Java Plug-in

```
<html>
<body>
<h1>Hello World Applet</h1>
<!--"CONVERTED_APPLET"-->
<!-- CONVERTER VERSION 1.0 -->
<SCRIPT LANGUAGE="JavaScript"><!--
    var _info = navigator.userAgent; var _ns = false;
    var _ie = (_info.indexOf("MSIE") > 0 && _info.indexOf("Win") > 0 &&
➥_info.indexOf("Windows 3.1") < 0);
//--></SCRIPT>
<COMMENT><SCRIPT LANGUAGE="JavaScript1.1"><!--
    var _ns = (navigator.appName.indexOf("Netscape") >= 0 &&
➥((_info.indexOf("Win") > 0 && _info.indexOf("Win16") < 0 &&
➥java.lang.System.getProperty("os.version").indexOf("3.5") < 0) ||
➥(_info.indexOf("Sun") > 0) || (_info.indexOf("Linux") > 0)));
//--></SCRIPT></COMMENT>

<SCRIPT LANGUAGE="JavaScript"><!--
    if (_ie == true) document.writeln('<OBJECT classid="clsid:8AD9C840-
044E-11D1-B3E9-00805F499D93" WIDTH = "200" HEIGHT = "100"
codebase="http://java.sun.com/products/plugin/1.2/jinstall-12-
win32.cab#Version=1,2,0,0"><NOEMBED><XMP>');
```

continued on next page

continued from previous page

```
16        else if (_ns == true) document.writeln('<EMBED type="application/x-java-applet;version=1.2" java_CODE = "Hello.class" WIDTH = "200" HEIGHT = "100" pluginspage="http://java.sun.com/products/plugin/1.2/plugin-install.html"><NOEMBED><XMP>');
17    //--></SCRIPT>
18    <APPLET CODE = "Hello.class" WIDTH = "200" HEIGHT = "100" ></XMP>
19    <PARAM NAME = CODE VALUE = "Hello.class" >
20
21    <PARAM NAME="type" VALUE="application/x-java-applet;version=1.2">
22
23    </APPLET>
24    No Applet?
25    </NOEMBED></EMBED></OBJECT>
26
27
28    <!—
29    <APPLET  CODE = "Hello.class" WIDTH = "200" HEIGHT = "100" >
30    No Applet?
31
32    </APPLET>
33    -->
34    <!--"END_CONVERTED_APPLET"-->
35
36    </body>
37    </html>
```

The result is similar to the version we produced manually in Listings 50.6 and 50.7, with two notable differences:

- Line 11 contains, optimistically, a reference to another supported operating system. As of this writing, Linux does not yet have the Java Plug-in.
- The `LabelText` applet parameter has been lost. The code is now broken and requires manual editing to reinsert the applet parameter(s).

The converter can save considerable tedium in creating these files, but the results are still clearly a bit fragile. Use with care.

`htmlconv` Batch Operation

A non-GUI mode allows you to use **`htmlconv`** as a batch processor.

Synopsis:

```
java HTMLConverter <filespecs> [-simulate] [<options>]
```

The ***`<filespecs>`*** specifies the names of HTML files to be converted. If you use wildcards, quoted to prevent interpretation by your shell, they will be interpreted by the converter. For example:

```
java HTMLConverter '*.html' '*.htm'
```

will process all HTML files in the directory (and subdirectories, if you specify recursion).

Options:

- `-simulate`—List files that will be converted, and current option values, but do not perform conversions.
- `-source` *<directory>*—Specify the path to the source files.
- `-backup` *<directory>*—Specify the directory in which to back up original files.
- `-subdirs` {TRUE|FALSE}—Process directories recursively if `TRUE`.
- `-template` *<filename>*—Use the specified template file for the conversion. (The standard four files can be found in the `templates/` subdirectory of the `htmlconv` installation directory.)
- `-log` *<logfile>*—Specify a log file for recording conversions performed.
- `-progress` {TRUE|FALSE}—Display progress messages to `stdout` if `TRUE`.

Future Applet Support in JDK1.2 and Beyond

The Java Plug-in solutions discussed in this chapter are incomplete. They support only a few platforms, and experimentation suggests that they are not entirely robust. At this stage, betting the business on JDK1.2 applets is risky.

The only future JDK1.2 browser support that looks reasonably certain, as of this writing, is the Netscape Open Java Interface (see Chapter 11 "Choosing an Environment: 1.1 or 1.2?," in the section "Option 2: Netscape Open Java Interface"), scheduled for introduction with Netscape's 5.0 release. Will it work well and robustly? Will MSIE offer a compatible solution? My crystal ball is cloudy on these questions.

For Further Reading

The product pages for the Java Plug-in at `http://java.sun.com` include good documentation, with more extensive examples than those in this chapter and detailed instructions on how to handle many applet parameters not shown here.

Summary

This chapter has discussed the Java Plug-in and its use in deploying applets. In the aftermath of the brutal Netscape/Microsoft browser wars, the Java Plug-in creates some hope that applets may yet become a viable and reliable way to deliver functionality to users on the Web.

CHAPTER 51

CROSSING PLATFORM COMPONENT MODELS: BRINGING JAVA TO ACTIVEX

This chapter discusses delivery of Java Beans into Microsoft's ActiveX component framework.

Platforms: JDK1.1/JDK1.2

If you deliver components to users in the Microsoft Windows space, you inevitably face the issue of whether and how to adopt Microsoft's *Component Object Model* (COM) and its *ActiveX* component framework.

ActiveX is, to a reasonable approximation, Microsoft's counterpart to Sun's JavaBeans specification—a way to deliver reusable components for use in a wide variety of Windows applications, not just browsers, but any application that subscribes to the Component Object Model.

In the past, supporting ActiveX and Java has been an either/or proposition: Java developers could not deliver ActiveX components, and ActiveX components were not usable from Java. The situation has improved, with (predictably) both Microsoft and Sun providing different advice and techniques for integrating the two technologies. This chapter focuses on the question you face as a Java developer on Linux: how to deliver Java components into the ActiveX framework.

What's a Component?

This is one of those Big Questions that can send developers and development organizations to the brink of war. A *component* is a reusable, modular piece of functionality intended for use as a building block in larger applications. What's reusable? What's modular? What's the right type and amount of functionality to package into a component? If a component is published on the Internet and nobody reuses it, does it still make a sound?

Sun's answer, the JavaBeans component model, avoids many of the troublesome questions and creates a clean and simple specification for what constitutes a Java Bean. Briefly, the attributes listed in Table 51.1 define a Bean.

TABLE 51.1 Characteristics of Java Beans

Attribute	Description
Introspection	Beans allow other applications to analyze and understand their function.
Customization	Beans can be customized in appearance and behavior.
Events	Beans support events as a means of communication between components.
Properties	Beans provide access to properties, both for customization when they are configured and for runtime use.
Persistence	Beans can be saved, in serialized form, and reconstituted for later use.

These attributes are expressed through conventions on how Bean methods are named, rules on how Beans are packaged, and the availability of `java.beans.*` support classes to assist in creating and implementing Beans.

Creating a Java Bean

To illustrate how the JavaBeans characteristics translate into practice, we create a small Bean from some example code provided by Sun.

Listing 51.1 is an example of a component, a Java Bean distributed by Sun in its *Bean Development Kit* (BDK)[1]:

[1]The BDK is available from the Java product pages but is not intended for serious development work. Sun publishes it primarily as a template to help IDE vendors understand the requirements for supporting Beans.

LISTING 51.1 Example Bean From Sun's Bean Development Kit

```

package sunw.demo.buttons;

import java.awt.*;
import java.awt.event.*;
import java.beans.*;
import java.io.Serializable;
import java.util.Vector;


/**
 * A simple Java Beans button.  OurButton is a "from-scratch"
 * lightweight AWT component.  It's a good example of how to
 * implement bound properties and support for event listeners.
 *
 * Parts of the source are derived from sun.awt.tiny.TinyButtonPeer.
 */

public class OurButton extends Component implements Serializable,
                                MouseListener, MouseMotionListener {

    /**
     * Constructs a Button with the a default label.
     */
    public OurButton() {
        this("press");
    }

    /**
     * Constructs a Button with the specified label.
     * @param label the label of the button
     */
    public OurButton(String label) {
        super();
        this.label = label;
        setFont(new Font("Dialog", Font.PLAIN, 12));
        setBackground(Color.lightGray);
        addMouseListener(this);
        addMouseMotionListener(this);
    }

    //----------------------------------------------------------------------

    /**
     * Paint the button: the label is centered in both dimensions.
     *
     */
    public synchronized void paint(Graphics g) {
```

continued on next page

continued from previous page

```
            int width = getSize().width;
            int height = getSize().height;

            g.setColor(getBackground());
            g.fill3DRect(0, 0, width - 1, height - 1, !down);

            g.setColor(getForeground());
            g.setFont(getFont());

            g.drawRect(2, 2, width - 4, height - 4);

            FontMetrics fm = g.getFontMetrics();
            g.drawString(label, (width - fm.stringWidth(label)) / 2,
                                   (height + fm.getMaxAscent() - fm.getMaxDescent())
➥/ 2);
        }

        //------------------------------------------------------------------

        // Mouse listener methods.

        public void mouseClicked(MouseEvent evt) {
        }

        public void mousePressed(MouseEvent evt) {
            if (!isEnabled()) {
                return;
            }
            down = true;
            repaint();
        }

        public void mouseReleased(MouseEvent evt) {
            if (!isEnabled()) {
                return;
            }
            if (down) {
                fireAction();
                down = false;
                repaint();
            }
        }

        public void mouseEntered(MouseEvent evt) {
        }

        public void mouseExited(MouseEvent evt) {
        }

        public void mouseDragged(MouseEvent evt) {
            if (!isEnabled()) {
```

```
                return;
            }
            // Has the mouse been dragged outside the button?
            int x = evt.getX();
            int y = evt.getY();
            int width = getSize().width;
            int height = getSize().height;
            if (x < 0 || x > width || y < 0 || y > height) {
                // Yes, we should deactivate any pending click.
                if (down) {
                    down = false;
                    repaint();
                }
            } else if (!down) {
                down = true;
                repaint();
            }
        }

        public void mouseMoved(MouseEvent evt) {
        }

        //----------------------------------------------------------------

        // Methods for registering/deregistering event listeners

        /**
         * The specified ActionListeners <b>actionPerformed</b> method will
         * be called each time the button is clicked.  The ActionListener
         * object is added to a list of ActionListeners managed by
         * this button, it can be removed with removeActionListener.
         * Note: the JavaBeans specification does not require ActionListeners

         * to run in any particular order.
         *
         * @see #removeActionListener
         * @param l the ActionListener
         */

        public synchronized void addActionListener(ActionListener l) {
            pushListeners.addElement(l);
        }

        /**
         * Remove this ActionListener from the buttons internal list.  If the

         * ActionListener isn't on the list, silently do nothing.
         *
         * @see #addActionListener
         * @param l the ActionListener
```

continued on next page

continued from previous page

```
     */
    public synchronized void removeActionListener(ActionListener l) {
        pushListeners.removeElement(l);
    }

    /**
     * The specified PropertyChangeListeners <b>propertyChange</b> method will
     * be called each time the value of any bound property is changed.
     * The PropertyListener object is addded to a list of PropertyChangeListeners
     * managed by this button, it can be removed with removePropertyChangeListener.
     * Note: the JavaBeans specification does not require PropertyChangeListeners
     * to run in any particular order.
     *
     * @see #removePropertyChangeListener
     * @param l the PropertyChangeListener
     */
    public void addPropertyChangeListener(PropertyChangeListener l) {
        changes.addPropertyChangeListener(l);
    }

    /**
     * Remove this PropertyChangeListener from the buttons internal list.
     * If the PropertyChangeListener isn't on the list, silently do nothing.
     *
     * @see #addPropertyChangeListener
     * @param l the PropertyChangeListener
     */
    public void removePropertyChangeListener(PropertyChangeListener l) {
        changes.removePropertyChangeListener(l);
    }

    //----------------------------------------------------------------------


    /**
     * This method has the same effect as pressing the button.
     *
     * @see #addActionListener
     */
    public void fireAction() {
        if (debug) {
            System.err.println("Button " + getLabel() + " pressed.");
        }
        Vector targets;
        synchronized (this) {
```

```
                targets = (Vector) pushListeners.clone();
            }
            ActionEvent actionEvt = new ActionEvent(this, 0, null);
            for (int i = 0; i < targets.size(); i++) {
                ActionListener target = (ActionListener)targets.elementAt(i);

                target.actionPerformed(actionEvt);
            }

        }

        /**
         * Enable debugging output.  Currently a message is printed each time

         * the button is clicked.  This is a bound property.
         *
         * @see #getDebug
         * @see #addPropertyChangeListener
         */
        public void setDebug(boolean x) {
            boolean old = debug;
            debug = x;
            changes.firePropertyChange("debug", new Boolean(old), new
➥Boolean(x));

        }

        /**
         * Returns true if debugging output is enabled.
         *
         * @see #setDebug
         */
        public boolean getDebug() {
            return debug;
        }

        /**
         * Set the font size to 18 if true, 12 otherwise.  This property
➥overrides

         * the value specified with setFontSize.  This is a bound property.
         *
         * @see #isLargeFont
         * @see #addPropertyChangeListener
         */
        public void setLargeFont(boolean b) {
            if (isLargeFont() == b) {
                return;
            }
            int size = 12;
            if (b) {
```

continued on next page

continued from previous page

```
                size = 18;
            }
            Font old = getFont();
            setFont(new Font(old.getName(), old.getStyle(), size));
            changes.firePropertyChange("largeFont", new Boolean(!b), new
➥Boolean(b));
        }

        /**
         * Returns true if the font is "large" in the sense defined by
➥setLargeFont.
         *
         * @see #setLargeFont
         * @see #setFont
         */
        public boolean isLargeFont() {
            if (getFont().getSize() >= 18) {
                return true;
            } else {
                return false;
            }
        }


        /**
         * Set the point size of the current font.  This is a bound property.
         *
         * @see #getFontSize
         * @see #setFont
         * @see #setLargeFont
         * @see #addPropertyChangeListener
         */
        public void setFontSize(int x) {
            Font old = getFont();
            setFont(new Font(old.getName(), old.getStyle(), x));
            changes.firePropertyChange("fontSize", new Integer(
➥old.getSize()), new Integer(x));
        }

        /**
         * Return the current font point size.
         *
         * @see #setFontSize
         */
        public int getFontSize() {
            return getFont().getSize();
        }
```

```

    /**
     * Set the current font and change its size to fit.  This is a
     * bound property.
     *
     * @see #setFontSize
     * @see #setLargeFont
     */
    public void setFont(Font f) {
        Font old = getFont();
        super.setFont(f);
        sizeToFit();
        changes.firePropertyChange("font", old, f);
        repaint();
    }

    /**
     * Set the buttons label and change its size to fit.  This is a
     * bound property.
     *
     * @see #getLabel
     */
    public void setLabel(String newLabel) {
        String oldLabel = label;
        label = newLabel;
        sizeToFit();
        changes.firePropertyChange("label", oldLabel, newLabel);
    }

    /**
     * Returns the buttons label.
     *
     * @see #setLabel
     */
    public String getLabel() {
        return label;
    }

    public Dimension getPreferredSize() {
        FontMetrics fm = getFontMetrics(getFont());
        return new Dimension(fm.stringWidth(label) + TEXT_XPAD,
                             fm.getMaxAscent() + fm.getMaxDescent() +
➥TEXT_YPAD);
    }

    /**
     * @deprecated provided for backward compatibility with old layout
➥managers.
     */
```

continued on next page

continued from previous page

```
        public Dimension preferredSize() {
            return getPreferredSize();
        }

        public Dimension getMinimumSize() {
            return getPreferredSize();
        }

        /**
         * @deprecated provided for backward compatibility with old layout
➥managers.
         */
        public Dimension minimumSize() {
            return getMinimumSize();
        }

        private void sizeToFit() {
            Dimension d = getSize();
            Dimension pd = getPreferredSize();

            if (pd.width > d.width || pd.height > d.height) {
                int width = d.width;
                if (pd.width > width) {
                    width = pd.width;
                }
                int height = d.height;
                if (pd.height > height) {
                    height = pd.height;
                }
                setSize(width, height);

                Component p = getParent();
                if (p != null) {
                    p.invalidate();
                    p.validate();
                }
            }
        }

        /**
         * Set the color the buttons label is drawn with.  This is a bound
➥property.
         */
        public void setForeground(Color c) {
            Color old = getForeground();
            super.setForeground(c);
            changes.firePropertyChange("foreground", old, c);
            // This repaint shouldn't really be necessary.
            repaint();
        }


```

```
378        /**
379         * Set the color the buttons background is drawn with.  This is a bound
➥property.
380         */
381        public void setBackground(Color c) {
382            Color old = getBackground();
383            super.setBackground(c);
384            changes.firePropertyChange("background", old, c);
385            // This repaint shouldn't really be necessary.
386            repaint();
387        }
388
389
390        private boolean debug;
391        private PropertyChangeSupport changes = new PropertyChangeSupport(
➥this);
392        private Vector pushListeners = new Vector();
393        private String label;
394        private boolean down;
395        private boolean sized;
396
397        static final int TEXT_XPAD = 12;
398        static final int TEXT_YPAD = 8;
399    }
```

Some of the characteristics that make this recognizably a Bean:

- The class has a no-argument constructor (lines 25–27).
- The class includes properly named methods to get and set properties—`getFontSize()` (lines 278–280) and `setFontSize()` (lines 267–271), among many others.
- The class uses property change events to report (for example, line 384) and detect changes to Bean properties. Listeners can register their interest in property changes in lines 163–165.
- The class can be serialized (declared in line 19).

This class compiles to the file `sunw/demo/buttons/OurButton.class`. To properly package this class as a Bean, we create a custom manifest file, `mymanifest`, containing

```
Name: sunw/demo/buttons/OurButton.class
Java-Bean: True
```

and package it with the compiled class into a jar file, `OurButton.jar`:

```
bash$ jar cvfm OurButton.jar mymanifest sunw/
added manifest
adding: sunw/ (in=0) (out=0) (stored 0%)
adding: sunw/demo/ (in=0) (out=0) (stored 0%)
adding: sunw/demo/buttons/ (in=0) (out=0) (stored 0%)
adding: sunw/demo/buttons/OurButton.class (in=6104) (out=2979) (deflated 51%)
bash$
```

We now have a Bean—Java's notion of a component. The following sections discuss how to package it into Microsoft's notion of a component, an ActiveX control.

For the next steps, we must move the action to a Windows box: the solutions delivered by both Sun and Microsoft run only under Win32.

The Sun JavaBeans Bridge for ActiveX

Sun's early attempt to package Beans for ActiveX was a Beans/ActiveX bridge distributed with the Bean Development Kit (BDK). ActiveX components created by this tool could be distributed with an accompanying Sun runtime component that provided the bridging glue to ActiveX.

More recently, Sun moved the Bridge into its Java Plug-in (see Chapter 50, "Deploying Applets with Java Plug-in"). This new approach encourages deployment of the Plug-in, leverages the Plug-in when the component is used, and simplifies distributing your component.

To turn your Bean into an ActiveX component, you use the packager shipped with the Java Plug-in for Windows. We will illustrate with the Plug-in 1.2 version.

Running the JavaBeans ActiveX Packager

The packager, bundled with the Java Plug-in, turns a Bean into an ActiveX control. It is launched from an MS-DOS command shell by running the `java` application launcher on the `jaws.jar` archive installed with the Plug-in.

In the following synopsis, we use the Windows variable `%JRE%` to designate the location of the Java Plug-in installation (a typical value might be `c:\Program Files\JavaSoft\JRE\1.2`).

Synopsis:

```
java -cp %JRE%\lib\jaws.jar sun.beans.ole.Packager
```

This starts up the packager GUI—Figure 51.1 shows the startup screen. For this demonstration, we assume that the `OurButton.jar` file created previously (in the section "Creating a Java Bean") has been copied to the `c:\temp` directory on the Windows machine.

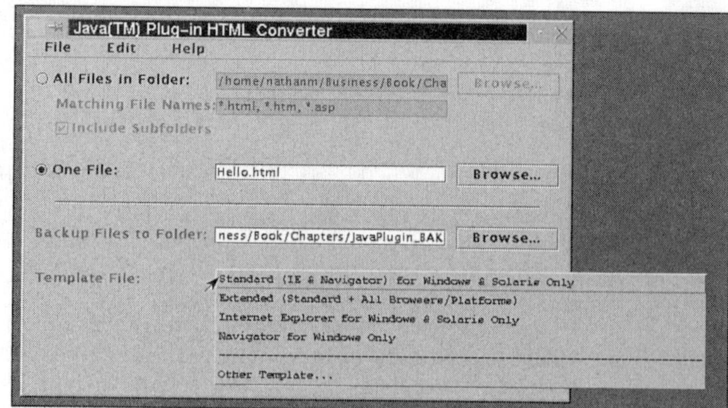

FIGURE 51.1
Packager startup screen.

The next screen allows us to choose which Bean to package (see Figure 51.2).

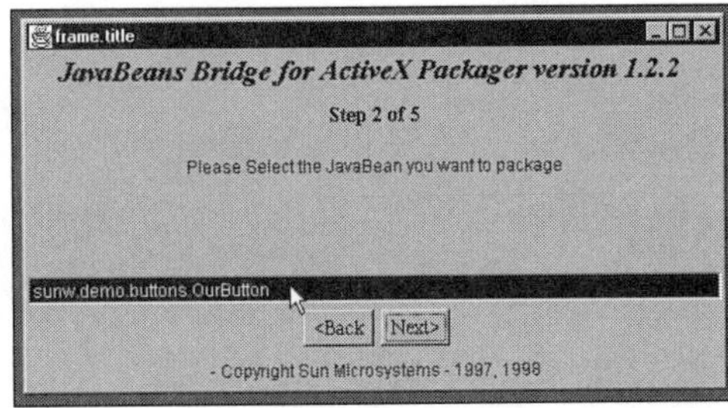

FIGURE 51.2
Choose the Bean. In this case, we only have one.

Next we name the object (see Figure 51.3).

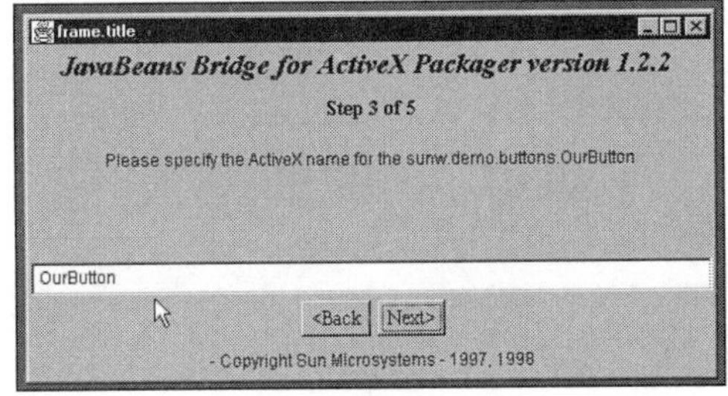

FIGURE 51.3
The third screen names the ActiveX object being built.

We will be generating two new files in a specified destination directory (see Figure 51.4).

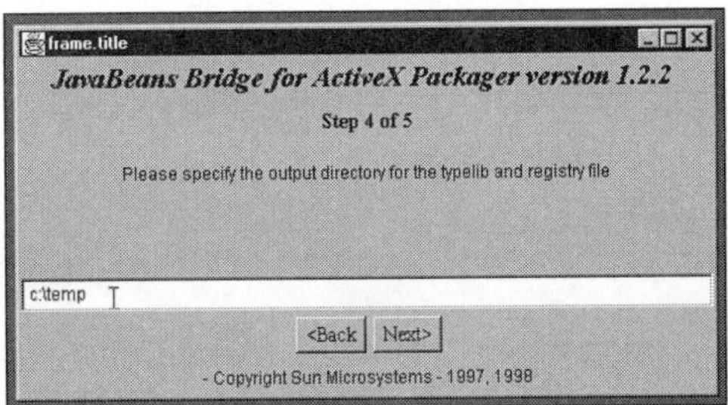

FIGURE 51.4
Specify a destination for generated files.

Finally, we generate the new files and, optionally, register the new control on our development system (see Figure 51.5). A status dialog informs us of progress and success or failure.

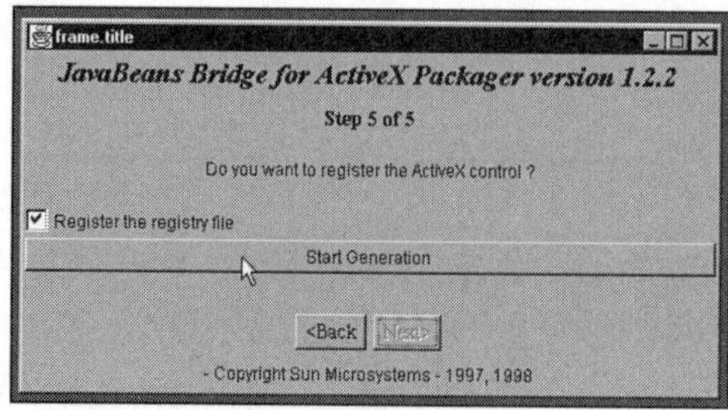

FIGURE 51.5
Ready to create the new ActiveX control.

Examining the Packaged Bean

The end result of running the packager is two new files: a type library file (`OurButton.tlb`) and a file of Windows Registry entries (`OurButton.reg`). The Registry entries (excerpted in Listing 51.2) provide the glue to integrate the Bean with Windows—the new object's Class ID (CLSID), instructions to run the JRE when the object is referenced, and other relevant information.

LISTING 51.2 Registry Entries (Excerpted) for the New ActiveX Object

```
REGEDIT4
[HKEY_CLASSES_ROOT\OurButton.Bean]
@= "OurButton Bean Control"
[HKEY_CLASSES_ROOT\OurButton.Bean\CLSID]
@= "{7FB22CF0-50F8-11D3-B327-005056FDBDB1}"
[HKEY_CLASSES_ROOT\OurButton.Bean\CurVer]
@= "1"
.
.
.
[HKEY_CLASSES_ROOT\CLSID\{7FB22CF0-50F8-11D3-B327-005056FDBDB1}\
➥JarFileName]

@= "C:\\TEMP\\OurButton.jar"
[HKEY_CLASSES_ROOT\CLSID\{7FB22CF0-50F8-11D3-B327-005056FDBDB1}\
➥JavaClass]

@= "sunw.demo.buttons.OurButton"
[HKEY_CLASSES_ROOT\CLSID\{7FB22CF0-50F8-11D3-B327-005056FDBDB1}\
➥InterfaceClass]

@= "sun/beans/ole/OleBeanInterface"
.
.
.
[HKEY_CLASSES_ROOT\TypeLib\{7FB22CF1-50F8-11D3-B327-005056FDBDB1}]
@= "OurButton Bean Control Type Library"
[HKEY_CLASSES_ROOT\TypeLib\{7FB22CF1-50F8-11D3-B327-005056FDBDB1}\1.0]
@= "OurButton Bean Control "
[HKEY_CLASSES_ROOT\TypeLib\{7FB22CF1-50F8-11D3-B327-005056FDBDB1}\1.0\
➥0\win32]
```

```
@= "c:\\temp\\OurButton.tlb"
[HKEY_CLASSES_ROOT\TypeLib\{7FB22CF1-50F8-11D3-B327-005056FDBDB1}\1.0\
➥FLAGS]

@= "2"
[HKEY_CLASSES_ROOT\TypeLib\{7FB22CF1-50F8-11D3-B327-005056FDBDB1}\1.0\
➥HELPDIR]

@= "c:\\temp"
```

Our little Java Bean has generated 74 lines of entries for the Windows Registry. These entries, along with `OurButton.tlb` and the original jar file (`OurButton.jar`), constitute the ActiveX control to be installed.

One modification is needed before installation. The Registry entries reflect our use of the `c:\temp` directory when we ran the packager. These references must, as part of installation, be changed to reflect the actual product installation directory.

Using the New Component

With the new ActiveX component installed, the `OurButton` Bean is available for use.

We demonstrate the new component by running Microsoft Word in Visual Basic Design Mode (see Figure 51.6). To start this mode from Word, launch the Visual Basic editor (under the `Tools` menu, `Macro` submenu) and, in the Visual Basic editor, select `Design Mode` from the `Run` menu. This will bring up two floating tool bars, usable from Word, offering access to ActiveX controls—including the control we just added.

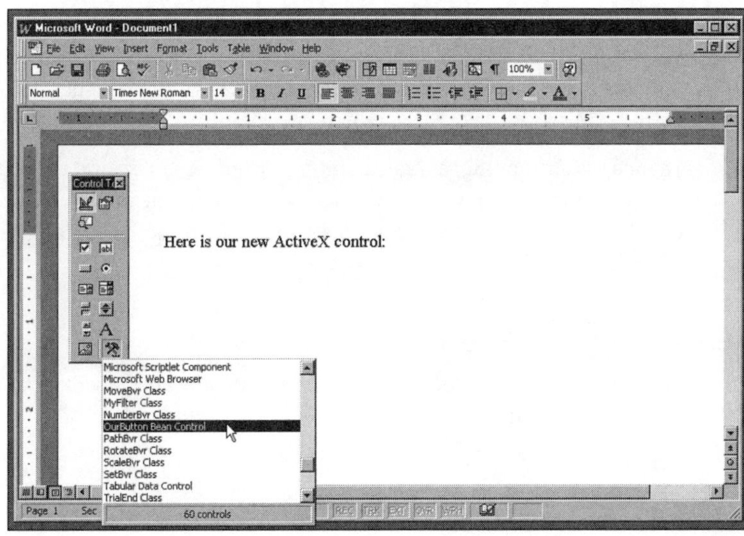

FIGURE 51.6
Adding ActiveX controls to a Word document. Our new control is one of the available choices.

After the Bean is added, the properties editor (see Figure 51.7) gives us access to the various properties we exposed through the JavaBeans methods. The component is blacked out during this step (a Visual Basic feature), but appears afterward showing the proper settings (see Figure 51.8).

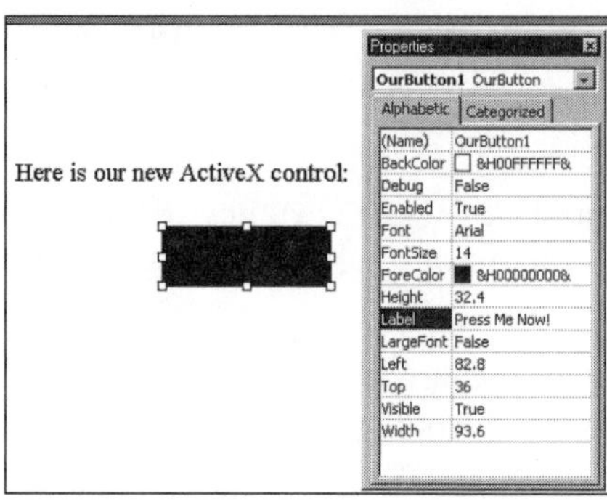

FIGURE 51.7
The control has been added, and we can edit its properties.

Here is our new ActiveX control:

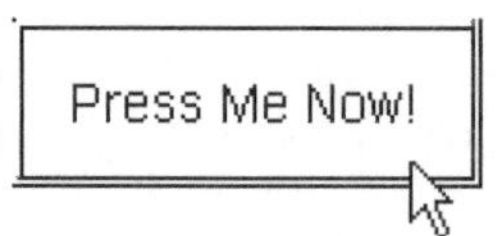

FIGURE 51.8
The control after it has been customized.

The Microsoft `javareg` Tool

`javareg` is Microsoft's answer to the Sun packager. Not surprisingly, it generates ActiveX components that run on the Microsoft JVM instead of the installed Sun JRE. `javareg` is shipped with the Microsoft Java SDK, which is available as a free download from Microsoft.

`javareg` is a bit more general than the Sun packager in one respect: Its input is not confined to Beans, and its output is not confined to ActiveX controls. It can package other Java classes as COM or DCOM objects. We will use it here with the Java Bean used previously (in the section "The Sun JavaBeans Bridge for ActiveX").

Running `javareg`

`javareg` is launched from an MS-DOS command window. It has no GUI—you use options to control its activities.

Synopsis:

```
javareg <options>
```

Options:

- `/class:<classname>`—Specify the class to be registered or unregistered.

- `/clsid:<CLSID>`—Specify the CLSID to use for the registered class. If unspecified, one is automatically generated. Typically, you would automatically generate one when you first release the Bean and then explicitly use that same CLSID with this option when the Bean is deployed.
- `/codebase:<path>`—Specity the path, a URL or directory name, in which the class being registered can be found. Evidently, this can be a directory or a Microsoft cabinet (`.cab`) file, but cannot be a jar file.
- `/control`—Register this object as an ActiveX control (used when creating ActiveX but not COM objects).
- `/nomktyplib`—Register an existing typelib file (specified by `/typelib`) instead of generating a new one.
- `/progid:<PROGID>`—Specify a COM ProgID for the class being registered.
- `/q`—Run quietly.
- /register **or** `/regserver`—Register the class specified by `/class`.
- `/remote:<RemoteServerName>`—Activate the class remotely using DCOM.
- `/surrogate`—Write the Registry entries for the Java class. Typically used to support DCOM.
- `/typelib:<filename>`—Specify the location of the typelib to be written or, if `/nomktyplib` is specified, to be read.
- /unregister **or** `/unregserver`—Unregister the class specified by `/class`.
- `/?`—Display a help dialog.

Example:

Assuming that the class file has been placed in `c:\temp\sunw\demo\buttons\OurButton.class`, this invocation will register it as an ActiveX control:

```
c:\> javareg /class:sunw.demo.buttons.OurButton /register /control
➥/codebase:c:\temp /typelib:c:\temp\OurButton.tlb
```

After successful execution, `javareg` will display a dialog providing the CLSID. The Bean should now be usable as an ActiveX control.

A Comparison of `javareg` Versus Sun's Packager Procedures

`javareg` differs radically from the Sun packager in two respects:

- It is command-line driven.

- Its purpose is to register (or unregister) Java-based controls, not to create a `.reg` file that will allow others to do so.

Unlike the Sun approach, in which you generate Registry entries to ship with the control, `javareg` *directly* manipulates the Registry at installation time. You run it when *you* need to register a control; end users run it when *they* need to register a control. So the steps (see Table 51.2) of shipping a Java Bean as an ActiveX control are markedly different between the two tools:

TABLE 51.2 Comparison of the Steps to Shipping ActiveX Controls

Step	Sun Packager	Microsoft javareg
Creating the file Control	Run Packager on your jar file to generate `.tlb` and `.reg` files. Packager also generates a unique CLSID at this time.	Run `javareg` on your class to generate a `.tlb` file, generate a unique CLSID, and register the results in the Windows Registry.
Shipping Bits	Ship your jar file, the `.tlb` file, and the `.reg` file - with the `.reg` file modified to reflect where everything will be placed.	Ship your class file and a copy of the `javareg` executable.
Installing	Install the jar file and the `.tlb` file. Add the `.reg` file entries to the Windows Registry by running `regedit.exe`.	Install the class file and run `javareg` on the deployment machine to create a `.tlb` and add the control to the Registry. Specify the CLSID explicitly to match the original value.
Removing the Control	Edit the Windows Registry by hand.	Run `javareg` with the `/unregister` option to remove (some of) the Registry entries.

Summary

We have examined two approaches to delivering Java components as ActiveX control to users in the Windows environment:

- The solution from Sun, bundled with the Java Plug-in, is particularly well suited to shipping JDK1.2 functionality in an ActiveX control. Given Sun's limited deployment message about Java Plug-in 1.1 (discussed in Chapter 50, "Deploying Applets with Java Plug-in"), using Plug-in v1.2 for this job seems a better choice.

- The solution from Microsoft is suitable for delivering controls that are closely tied to execution only on Microsoft's JVM.

CHAPTER 52

INSTALLSHIELD: CREATING SELF-INSTALLING JAVA APPLICATIONS

InstallShield Java Edition is a commercial tool for creating multiplatform Java application installation packages.

Platforms: JDK1.1/JDK1.2

One of the downsides of Java's promise of platform neutrality is the delivery problem: How do you ship something platform-neutral to platforms that are not…well, neutral? Some examples of application delivery difficulties are as follows:

- UNIX systems employ different package management technologies that vary by vendor and even by operating system release.
- Linux systems employ different package management technologies that vary by distribution. Even distribution vendors using the same package management technology (such as Red Hat's and SuSE's use of RPM) cannot necessarily use the same product installation packages.
- You can bypass package management and simply install products in a convenient directory—but then you've saddled the user with the problem of keeping detailed track of product installations.

- There are no standards for installing graphical components into an X-based desktop. How and where do you install an icon to launch an application? How do you associate file types with applications? The answer varies between CDE, KDE, Gnome, and other desktops.
- Although Microsoft Windows offers more GUI consistency than do X desktops, application installation is a complex and fragile process involving the Windows Registry and various application and system directories scattered throughout the file system.

InstallShield is a commercial product that is long-established in the area of delivering applications to Windows platforms. Its more recent Java Edition is focused on delivering Java applications to multiple platforms.

The product is, at present, more strongly focused on the complexities of delivering to Windows platforms. For UNIX and Linux, it creates usable self-installers that do not try to solve the (perhaps hopeless) package management and desktop integration problems, but do provide for easy product installation and removal.

Obtaining InstallShield

The Java version of InstallShield is available for download, evaluation, and purchase from `http://www.installshield.com/java`. You can use the version for "other Unix platforms," which is provided either as a self-installing shell script, a self-installing *classball* (`.class` file) that can be run by a JVM, or an applet that will install through a browser.

Install the product in any convenient directory.

Running InstallShield

The InstallShield installation includes a launcher, `isjava`, in the `bin` subdirectory.

Synopsis:

```
isjava
```

This starts the GUI (see Figure 52.1), which you can navigate linearly or, using the optional navigation pane, randomly. The product requires a JDK1.1 or JDK1.2 installation to run.

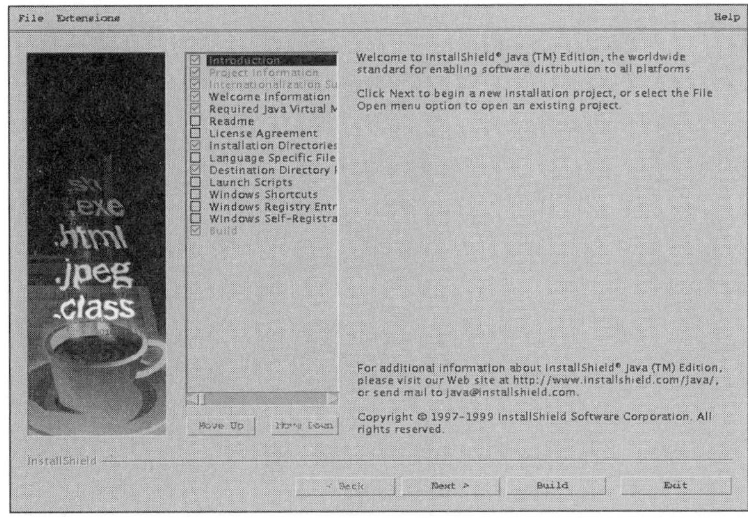

FIGURE 52.1
InstallShield GUI welcome screen. The navigation pane is enabled with the `View` button in the `Extensions` menu.

The next screen (see Figure 52.2) allows you to customize the welcome screen.

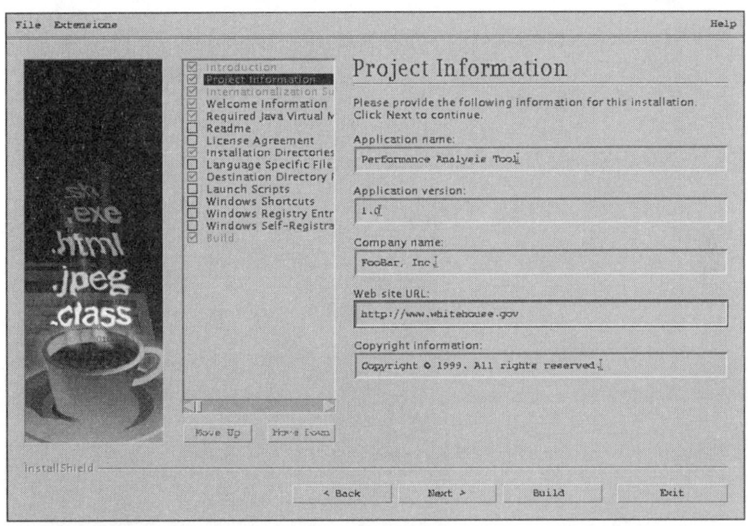

FIGURE 52.2
Design your own welcome screen.

Subsequent screens allow you to specify supported languages, preview the welcome screen, and specify a target environment (see Figure 52.3).

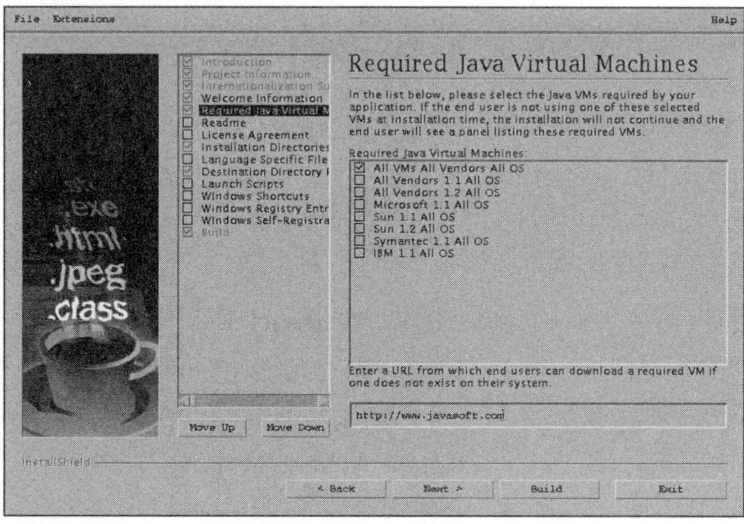

FIGURE 52.3
You can target your application for specific Java revisions and/or specific platforms—or allow it to run wherever a JRE can be found.

You can construct a custom Readme panel for displaying introductory textual information, and a License panel that the user must read and accept during installation.

The destination directory structure is designed in the Installation Directories dialog (see Figure 52.4), in which you map portions of your development tree or staging area into the destination directories. Each of these components can be designated as required or optional, components can be associated with particular locales, and you can control how much flexibility the user has in placing the directories.

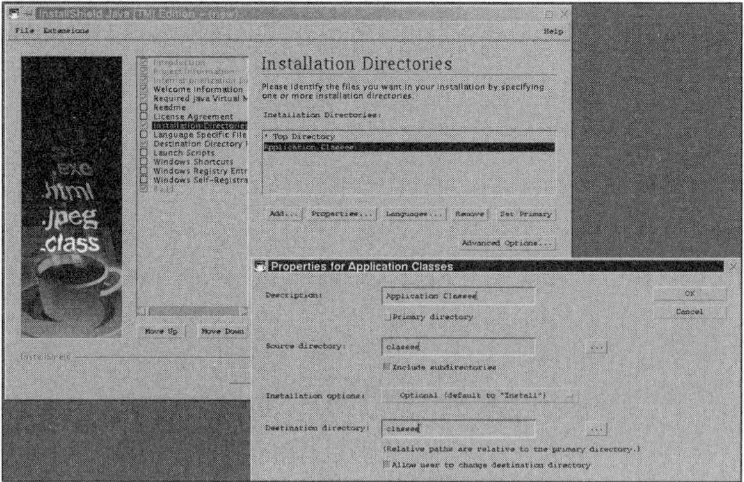

FIGURE 52.4
Designing the destination directory structure.

Subsequent screens allow you to designate language-specific configurations and to designate scripts (Java classes, actually) to be run during installation. Finally, a series of three screens helps you through the complexities of delivering into Windows environments—setting up shortcuts and dealing with the Registry.

After all configuration is completed, InstallShield lets you build a deliverable package (see Figure 52.5) in formats usable on various destination platforms. The packages can include JREs that the customer can install, as part of product installation, if the target machine has none.

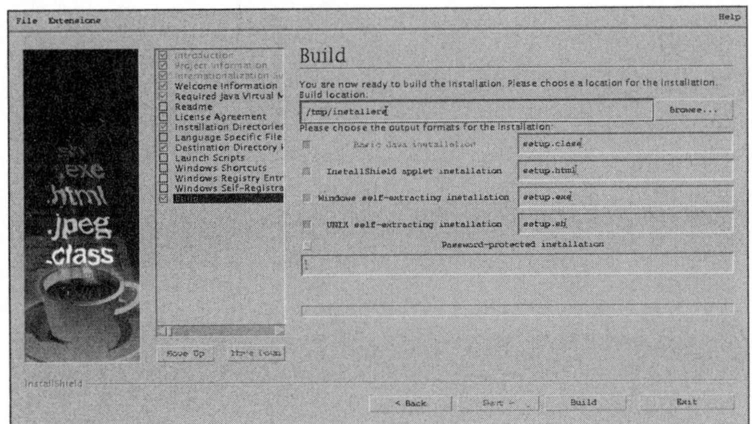

FIGURE 52.5
You can build a deliverable classball, applet, .EXE, and/or a self-installing shell script.

Summary

Building delivery packages for users on Java's many platforms is a difficult exercise in non-portability. InstallShield addresses the problem and, judging from various Java applications found on the Web, enjoys good success in the marketplace.

CHAPTER 53

DASHO: OPTIMIZING APPLICATIONS FOR DELIVERY

DashO is an optimizer and obfuscator used to prepare Java applications for delivery.

Platforms: JDK1.1/JDK1.2

DashO is a professional tool from Preemptive Solutions, targeted at optimizing Java applications for delivery. The name (the last character is the letter O, not zero) is suggestive of the compiler option, `-O`, often used for optimization, and it reflects the product's mission: to create highly optimized versions of Java applications.

DashO's capabilities include

- Bytecode optimization for improved runtime performance
- Obfuscation of bytecodes to discourage reverse engineering
- Shrinking application and library archives to create applications that download more quickly and consume less disk space

Preemptive's product line includes versions at various price points. Less expensive versions provide obfuscation and size reduction; more expensive versions can optimize.

This type of optimization—performed when packaging the product rather than when compiling—is analogous to link-time optimizations provided in some commercial C/C++ compilers.

By using global application information that is not available at compile time, it can detect optimization opportunities that would otherwise be missed.

Post-compilation optimization has also gained favor among some Java developers because optimization support is uneven, and sometimes buggy, among different Java compilers.

Obtaining DashO

DashO can be downloaded and purchased from Preemptive's main Web site (`http://www.preemptive.com`). Available versions include the full-featured DashO-Pro and the less expensive DashO-OE (Optimization Edition). A no-charge non-GUI evaluation version is also available, with most of the DashO-Pro capabilities, and with a license that disallows anything but personal use.

DashO is shipped in a self-installing shell script: run the script and install to some convenient location.

This chapter looks at the DashO-Pro capabilities. The product ships with excellent and extensive documentation; our goal here is to briefly examine what the product can do for you, not to duplicate the wealth of information found in the manual.

Running DashO

The DashO-Pro installation provides a jar file, `DashoPro.jar`, that you must add to your class path.

Synopsis:

```
java DashoPro [<options>] <configfile>
java DashoProGui
```

The first invocation runs the command-line version; the second runs the GUI.

Both versions use a configuration file, whose suffix is conventionally `.dop`, and whose contents are discussed in the later section "Configuration File Directives."

The GUI provides a friendly front end to DashO configuration and to managing the `.dop` file. The command-line version can be used to batch-run a configuration file saved by the GUI or created by you in a text editor.

Command-line Mode Options:

- `-f`—Force execution. Normally, DashO will refuse to run if it detects the use of methods for dynamic loading of classes (for example, `Class.forName()`). DashO *must* know all classes that can ever be loaded to do its job correctly. After explicitly telling DashO (in the configuration file) of all classes that can be loaded, running with `-f` will cause it to complete.

- `-i`—Run in "investigation" mode, generating a report but not an output archive.
- `-l`—Use less memory (but run slower).
- `-q`—Run quietly.
- `-v`—Run verbosely.

The DashO-Pro GUI

When you create a new project in DashO-Pro, a New Project Wizard helps you build the initial project configuration. The first screen (see Figure 53.1) sets up the class path and some global options. For this example, we use the **`PerfAnal`** project from Chapter 60, "PerfAnal: A Free Performance Analysis Tool."

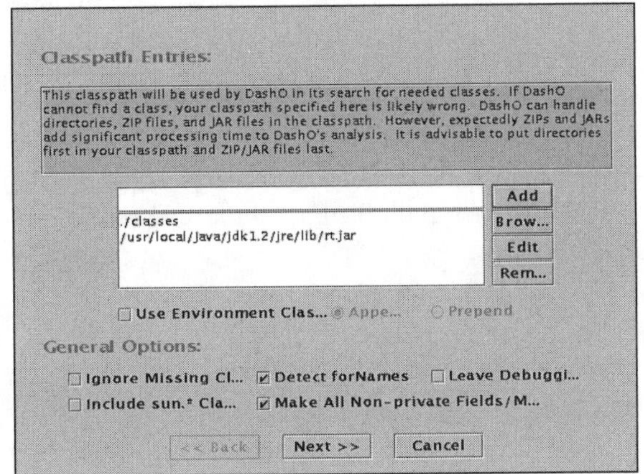

FIGURE 53.1
Initial setup of the class path and global options under the DashO-Pro Project Wizard.

Choosing the **`Use Environment Classpath`** option will add the current JVM's class path. Everything else, including application class paths and the bootclasspath (if you are running under JDK1.2), must be explicitly specified.

Other options selected in this example are **`forName detection`** (look for invocations of **`Class.forName()`** in the code) and making many class members public. See the discussion of the **`General`** directive (in the section "Configuration File Directives") for more explanation of these options.

The next screen (see Figure 53.2) allows you to specify a project type. For all projects types, you will then need to specify *triggers*—the interfaces that the outside world needs. Triggers include all advertised `main()` methods (if you are packaging an application), `init()` methods lif packaging applets), and all public methods and packages (if packaging libraries).

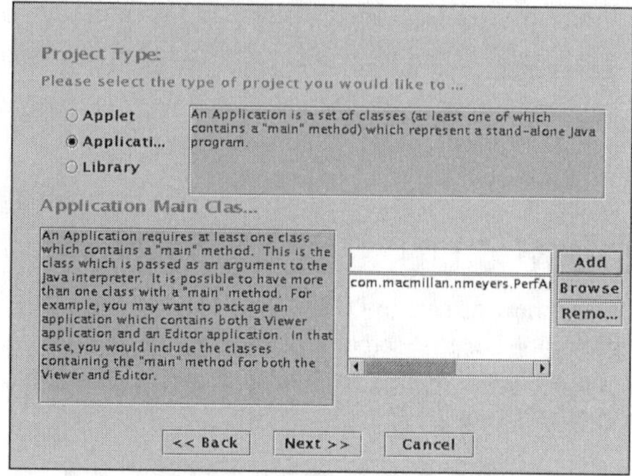

FIGURE 53.2
Specifying the project type and the trigger methods.

DashO-Pro will build a dependency graph, from the triggers, to identify all classes that are needed by the project. But it will need some help in identifying situations not explicitly found in the code: Any classes loaded dynamically, or classes whose serialization should not be modified by the optimization process. The next dialog (see Figure 53.3) solicits this necessary information. See Subtleties (later in the chapter) for further discussion of this problem.

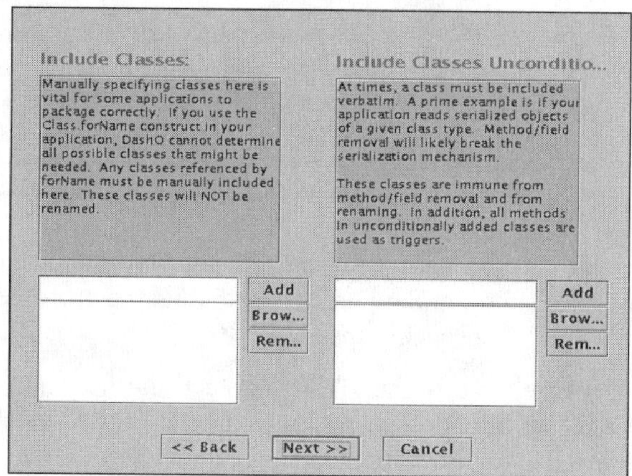

FIGURE 53.3
Identifying dependencies that cannot be detected by examining code.

Finally, you can specify any packages to be automatically excluded from the analysis and the final output (see Figure 53.4). For this example, we exclude `javax.*`—following DashO's recommended settings for packaging Swing-based applications.

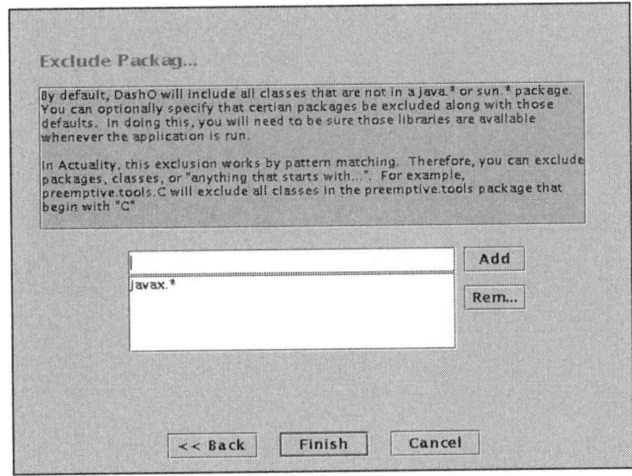

FIGURE 53.4
Identifying classes to exclude.

After you complete initial configuration, DashO-Pro closes the wizard and analyzes the results to ensure that all classes are found. You can then interact with the main screen (see Figure 53.5) to further tune the settings.

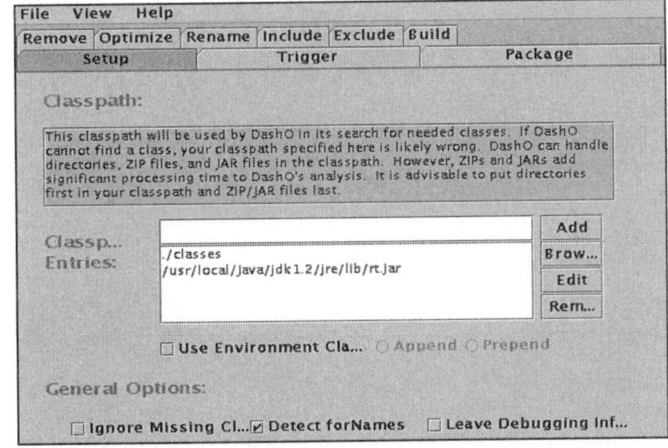

FIGURE 53.5
The main DashO-Pro GUI. A selection of tabbed pages gives you access to choices for optimization and obfuscation options.

All options seen in the various screens correspond to settings in the configuration file, which are described in the next section, "Configuration File Directives."

The results of running our particular example: All classes except the main class were renamed to short one- or two-letter names, most methods were renamed, and the size of the application jar file shrunk by 42 percent.

Configuration File Directives

If you run DashO without the GUI, you must provide a configuration file. You can write one in a text editor or create one by saving configuration settings from the DashO GUI.

Directives are specified across multiple lines, beginning with a dash and a directive name followed by a colon, with parameters specified on subsequent lines. The general form is

```
-<directive>:
<parameters>
```

For example:

```
-Version:
1.2
```

Here is the full list of configuration directives:

```
-Version:
<version>
```

Identify the version of DashO targeted by this configfile.

```
-MapFile:
<filename>
```

Create a map file identifying classes and members that have been renamed.

```
-ReportFile:
<filename>
```

Generate a report file with summary and details on what has been removed.

```
-ClassPath:
<classpath components>
```

Specify the class path to search. The components can be specified on a single line, with delimiters, or spread over multiple lines without delimiters.

```
-Destination:
<directory or jarfile>
```

Specify where the output hierarchy is to be built, either a directory tree or a Java Archive.

```
-TriggerMethods:
<methodnames>
```

Specify the method(s), in the form *class:method:parameters*, that launches the application.

```
-RemoveUnusedElements:
{all¦none¦onlynonpublics}
```

Control the extent of what elements are removed. A good value for applications containing no classes that will be subclasses is `all`.

```
-ExcludePackages:
<packagenames>
```

Specify packages not to be included in the output classes.

```
-General:
<option>
```

Specify certain global options that control overall behavior. Possible options are:

- `makepublic`—Make all classes and non-private members public, for faster runtime loading.
- `includesun`—Include `sun.*` classes, normally excluded.
- `fornamedetection`—Enable DashO heuristics to try to detect classes dynamically loaded by `Class.forName()` calls.
- `ignorenotfoundclasses`—Do not fail if some referenced classes are not found.
- `leavedebugginginfo`—Do not remove debugging info from class files.

`-IncludeClasses:`
`<classfile names>`

Specify classes to include that DashO might not otherwise detect as live classes. This is typically used to specify classes that will be dynamically loaded.

`-IncludeClassesUnconditionally:`
`<classfile names>`

Do not remove any members from specified classes that would break serialization compatibility with versions of the class that have not been processed by DashO.

`-IncludeNonClassFiles:`
`<filenames>`

Specify non-class files to include in the output—resource files. Used to specify images and other such resources to including in the output.

`-RenameOptions:`
`{on¦off¦onlynonpublics}`

Specify which classes and members are candidates for renaming to short, cryptic names.

`-RenamePrefix:`
`<prefix>`

Specify a distinctive prefix to be prepended to all renamed classes. Used to avoid collision when separate components of the same project are processed in different DashO invocations.

`-NoRenameClasses:`
`<classfile names>`

Specify classes not to be renamed.

`-NoRenameMethods:`
`<methods>`

Specify methods not to be renamed, in the format *class:method:parameter*.

`-OptimizationType:`
`{none¦speed¦size}`

Specify preferred optimization mode. If none, DashO only performs obfuscation.

Sample Configuration File

Listing 53.1 shows an example of a configuration file saved from the DashO GUI. These are the settings from the PerfAnal example shown in the section "The DashO-Pro GUI."

LISTING 53.1 Configuration Settings for the PerfAnal Project

```
-Version:
1.2
-MapFile:
-ReportFile:
-ClassPath:
./classes
/usr/local/Java/jdk1.2/jre/lib/rt.jar
-TriggerMethods:
com.macmillan.nmeyers.PerfAnal:main:java.lang.String[]
-Destination:
/home/nathanm/Business/Book/Projects/PerfAnal/build
-ExcludePackages:
javax.*
-ExcludeClasses:
-IncludeClasses:
-NoRenameMethods:
-NoOptimizeClasses:
-NoOptimizeMethods:
-NoRenameClasses:
-OptimizationType:
SPEED
-Optimizations:
-RemoveUnusedElements:
ALL
-RenameOptions:
ON
-RenamePrefix:
-IncludeClassesUnconditional:
-IncludeNonClassFiles:
-General:
MAKEPUBLIC
FORNAMEDETECTION
```

Understanding DashO Operation

Starting with knowledge of an application's *trigger methods*—the methods that commence execution—DashO analyzes an application for all dependencies, ascertaining what classes and class members are referenced. With this information, it can perform a number of space and speed optimizations:

- Rename classes and class members with short names, shortening many entries in constant pools in all the application's class files.

- Remove unused entries or combine equivalent entries in class file constant pools to save space.
- Remove unused classes and class members.
- Discover methods and classes that can be declared final, resulting in fewer virtual method calls.
- Discover virtual method calls that can be transformed into direct calls, saving a level of indirection.
- Change the access level on classes and class methods to public, creating a shorter path through class-loading security mechanisms.

The result is a smaller archive of faster code. DashO can also be used on class libraries, restricting its behavior to transformations that do not damage the capability of classes to be inherited, have their methods overridden, or be serialized.

Subtleties

Performance and space optimizations, such as devirtualizing virtual method calls and removing class members, depend on a thorough understanding of how classes and members are used. Members that are never touched can be removed, methods that are never overridden can be declared final, and so on.

Building this understanding is a difficult problem in an environment such as Java, where dynamic class-loading (for example, `Class.forname()`) and reflective methods (for example, `Method.invoke()`) can make it impossible to completely determine what classes and members will end up being used when the application runs.

DashO includes optional heuristics that try to derive such information from the class files—but the problem is not easy. In some cases, ascertaining the class or member being referenced is trivial:

```
Class.forName("Foo")
```

In others, it is implied by context:

```
String s;
Foo foo = (Foo)Class.forName(s).newInstance();
```

or can be derived from the control flow:

```
String s = "Foo";
Class.forName(s);
```

or is hopelessly unsolvable:

```
BufferedReader r;
Class.forName(r.readLine());
```

DashO and similar tools can help you discover these cases, but it will take some configuration and testing on your part to ensure that you end up with a usable and deliverable optimized application.

Subtleties

Another subtle problem created by optimization is that of preserving the serialized representation of a class. If any data fields are identified as unused and are removed from a class, the serialized representation of the class is changed.

This change can introduce incompatibilities if serialization is used (objects of this class are saved to a file, sent across a network, or whatever) and another application uses the serialized version. The `IncludeClassesUnconditionally` directive is provided specifically to let you preserve the serialized representation of a class.

Summary

This chapter examined DashO, a commercial offering for packaging Java applications for distribution. DashO specifically addresses three aspects of application delivery: space optimization, obfuscation, and bytecode performance optimization.

PART XII

LINUX PLATFORM ISSUES

As compelling as is Java's vision of a platform-neutral world, we will always face platform-specific issues. Where differences occur among Java's various host environments, Java takes four different approaches:

- Abstract out the differences between platforms—as the AWT does for GUIs.
- Replace native functionality with Java and/or native code—as Graphics2D does for graphical rendering and Swing does for GUIs.
- Underspecify behavior—threading behavior is sufficiently underspecified to allow implementation on all platforms.
- Ignore platform capabilities—deprive developers of access to the unique strengths and capabilities of a particular host platform.

This part of the book focuses on some of these issues—using Java on Linux, issues unique to Linux, accessing platform-specific capabilities, and issues specific to running under the X Window System.

CHAPTER 54

JAVA, LINUX, AND THREADS

Multithreaded programming has long lurked as a mysterious art in application development: rarely practiced, and more rarely practiced well. Support has varied widely among languages and environments, and standardization efforts in the UNIX community have been slow and controversial.

The early major successes in providing widely available multithreaded capabilities came from two organizations—Microsoft and Sun Microsystems—that proceeded with their own designs while standardization efforts muddled along. Those two approaches, NT threads and Solaris threads, are very much core components of their respective operating systems and are used under the covers of the Java implementations on those two platforms.

Other platforms have caught up, thanks to standardization of threading APIs and to implementation efforts by the various vendors. Combined with other factors—Java's success as the first mainstream language to provide a good threading interface, the increasing availability of multiprocessor machines—multithreaded programming is finally moving from the domain of wizards into the mainstream.

This chapter undertakes a brief exploration of some threading-related topics relevant to Java development, particularly on Linux. The topic of parallel programming is broad and deep, touching on fundamental operating system and architectural design issues. We can only scratch the surface here and will concentrate the discussion on programming models and problems faced by Java developers on Linux and elsewhere.

What Is Multithreaded Programming?

Multithreaded programming is a form of *parallel programming*: the use of independent, cooperating streams of execution to solve a problem.

Any discussion of parallel programming quickly delves into terms such as *parallel processing*, *multiprogramming*, *multitasking*, and *multiprocessing*, all of which have specific and historical connotations in computer science. The topic also leads to architectural design concepts such as MIMD (*Multiple Instruction, Multiple Data*), SMP (*Symmetric Multiprocessing*), and MPP (*Massively Parallel Processing*), and to distribution/communications mechanisms such as PVM (*Parallel Virtual Machine*) and MPI (*Message-Passing Interface*).

All are interesting topics, particularly for solving large computation problems—but we aren't going to go there because Java doesn't take us there. All you really need to understand multithreaded programming, at this level of abstraction and function, is to wrap your mind around *heavyweight processes* and *lightweight processes*.

Heavyweight Processes

Heavyweight processes are what UNIX programmers have traditionally called simply *processes*—separate streams of execution that run in isolation from each other. Processes run in their own address spaces, interacting (in general) with the kernel but not usually with other processes (see Figure 54.1).

FIGURE 54.1
Typical heavyweight processes.

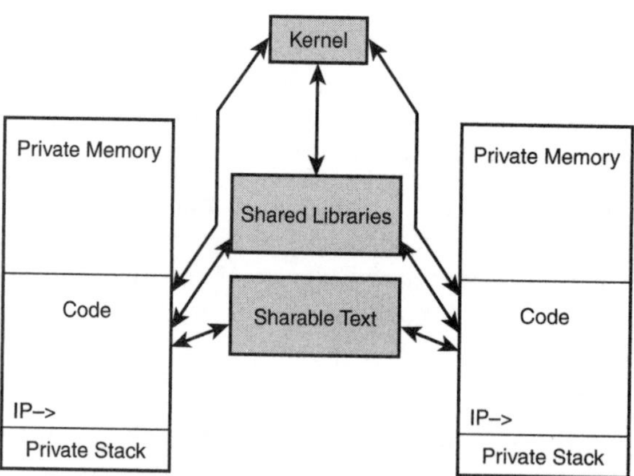

The heavyweight processes in Figure 54.1 run in isolation, and are prevented by the hardware and the operating system from interfering with each other. Each process has its own data memory, code, instruction pointer (IP) and stack. *Some* memory is shared (in the interest of conservation) by heavyweight processes:

- All processes share read-only access to native code in shared libraries.
- If more than one instance of a particular program is running, the instances share read-only access to the *text* (code) segment of the program.

Some implementation details are associated with processes, such as how they share limited CPU resources, but developers do not usually have to worry about them.

Where processes do need to interact, several enabling mechanisms are provided (see Figure 54.2).

FIGURE 54.2
Heavyweight process interaction.

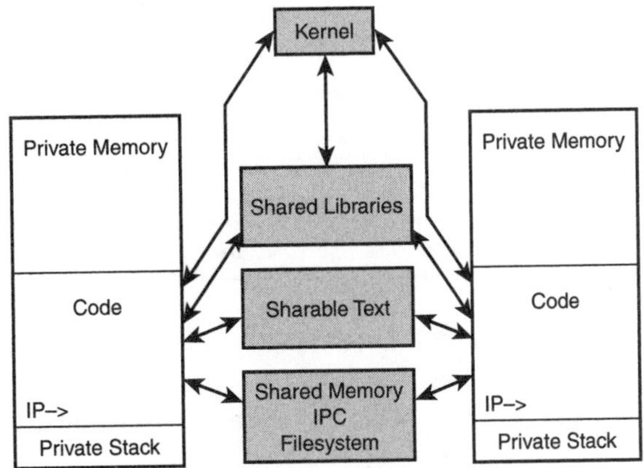

Among the mechanisms heavyweight processes typically use to interact (see Figure 54.2) are shared memory, interprocess communication mechanisms (pipes, semaphores, signals, networking), and shared access to the the file system.

Three factors make heavyweight processes heavy:

- Significant amounts of resources (most notably, private memory to hold data) are uniquely associated with each process.
- When limited resources, such as a single CPU, must be shared among processes, the context switch between processes is costly.
- The interaction mechanisms are costly, requiring kernel activity and protocol overhead. Shared memory is much cheaper than the other mechanisms but is a precious and limited systemwide resource.

Lightweight Processes

Lightweight processes is a synonym[1] for *threads*. The important difference between processes and threads is that, in the latter, the multiple streams of execution share code, memory, and address space (see Figure 54.3).

[1]This is an approximate synonym, as noted in the section "Hybrid Threading Models," later in this chapter.

FIGURE 54.3
Comparing lightweight and heavyweight processes.

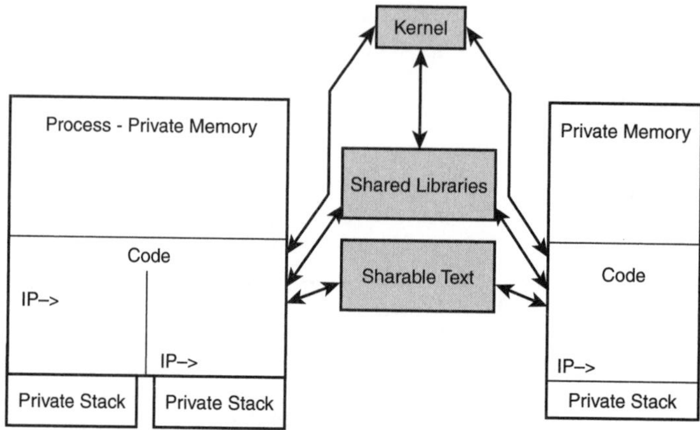

On the right (in Figure 54.3) is a traditional heavyweight process. On the left are two threads, sharing the data memory and address space, running the same code, but with private stacks and IPs: each has its own flow of control, local variables, and call stack.

There are two crucial distinctions between lightweight and heavyweight processes buried in Figure 54.3:

- Private memory allocated for data is often a process's largest resource demand on a system. By sharing this resource, the two threads have reduced their memory demand to that of a single process.
- In addition to sharing memory, the threads share *address space*—a critical difference from how heavyweight processes can share memory. A memory pointer (or object reference) in one thread has the same meaning in all threads, increasing the ability of threads to cooperate on the same problem.

Indeed, it is often useful, if sometimes simplistic, to think of the threads as multiple streams of execution *within the same process*.

Because of the differences imposed by the shared memory and address space, threads offer new opportunities and challenges in software design and development:

- Fully shared access to the address space vastly opens up communications between the streams of execution.
- New, low-cost synchronization mechanisms are needed to allow the streams to share memory without clobbering each other: mutexes, condition variables, monitors, and such.
- New levels of developer discipline are required to use the synchronization mechanisms, and it is difficult to detect when you've done it wrong.
- Developers must find a workable balance between coarse-grained parallelism (threads work largely independently) and fine-grained parallelism (threads communicate and coordinate extensively) that fairly divides the work among threads but does not bog them down in endless synchronization and communication tasks.

- Threading implementations present many new and different implementation details (see the next section, "Lightweight Process Implementation Details"), which unavoidably intrude on the design of multithreaded software.

Lightweight Process Implementation Details

When implementing threads in any environment, the devil is in the details. Here are some of the details you need to understand and how they can affect you.

Threading in Which Space?

The use of multiple streams of execution within a process did not begin with the advent of standard threading mechanisms. Long before, inventive developers were finding other ways to do the job. Figure 54.4 illustrates such a mechanism.

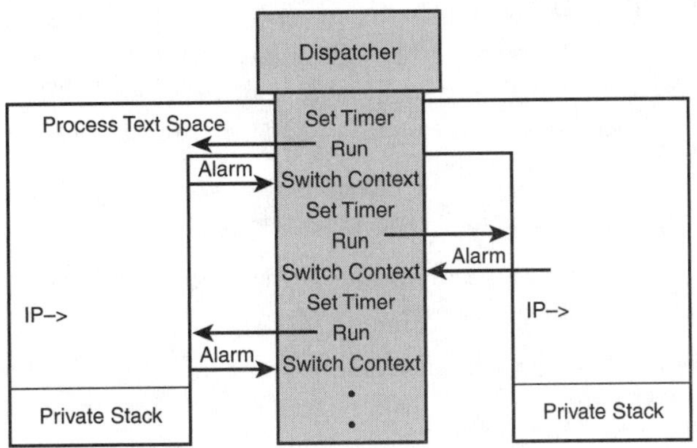

FIGURE 54.4
An example dispatching mechanism for multiple streams of execution with a process.

In this example, the dispatcher is responsible for switching process context—CPU registers and run stack—and for allocating time slices to the different streams.

User-Space Threads

The example in Figure 54.4 is a simplified version of user-space threads. The mechanism is implemented entirely by the application in user space, and the kernel is not responsible for switching contexts. In essence, the application has implemented its own mechanism for scheduling threads, modeled on the kernel's mechanism for scheduling processes.

One of Sun's important contributions to the early acceptance of Java was a threading library, ***green threads***, that creates a user-space threading mechanism. Long before all the UNIX vendors were supporting threading APIs, green threads allowed Netscape to deliver working JVMs to many different platforms.

Even today, with extensive threading support available on most systems, green threads are still important. The first working implementation of the JDK on a new platform is usually based on green threads.

Subtleties

Building a user-space threading mechanism presents some interesting programming challenges:

- Implementing the context-switch itself requires architecture-dependent code to handle the details of switching stacks and registers. Some assembly-language coding is usually required.
- A single thread must not be allowed to block the entire process. If one thread wants to issue a `read()` call, for example, it must not stop the other threads while it waits for available data. A user-space threading implementation will typically provide its own implementation of `read()`, blocking the calling thread but continuing to dispatch other threads until data becomes available.
- The threading mechanism must do something sensible when signals are received, dispatching them to whichever thread is equipped to handle them. This typically requires the implementation to build its own signal-handling mechanism to keep track of which threads have registered signal handlers.

Kernel-Space Threads

Kernel-space threads put control of thread dispatching in the kernel, where the same logic that switches between processes also switches between threads ***within*** processes. It is often the case that kernel threads are more expensive than user threads, but they also offer important advantages:

- They leverage existing kernel scheduling code, creating a cleaner solution.
- In multiprocessor environments, kernel threads can assign different threads to different CPUs, user threads cannot.

The latter point is the most important. Without kernel threads, multithreaded applications cannot enjoy any of the performance advantages of multiprocessor systems.

Hybrid Threading Models

Some systems implement hybrid models—kernel-scheduled clusters of user-scheduled threads. Solaris threads offer such a model and, contrary to our simplistic definition in the section "Lightweight Processes," Solaris distinguishes between the terms ***lightweight processes*** (scheduled by the kernel) and ***threads*** (scheduled in user space within lightweight processes).

Java's Threading Model

Understanding operating system threading models is important to using them properly, but you also face one unsettling certainty with Java: You have no control over the threading model. The details are settled between the JVM and the operating system. Your application may run in an environment that offers only one threading model, or the choice of model may be imposed on you by a user who launches the application with the `-green` or `-native` option specified.

The good news is that this forces you to write more portable code. The bad news is that this forces you to write more portable code.

API ≠ Threading Space

Java provides two threading models on Linux and many other platforms, ***green*** and ***native***. These terms are often interpreted as meaning, respectively, ***user-space*** and ***kernel-space***—but that is not necessarily the case. When discussing Java implementations, ***native*** simply means using a native threading API provided by the platform (see Figure 54.5).

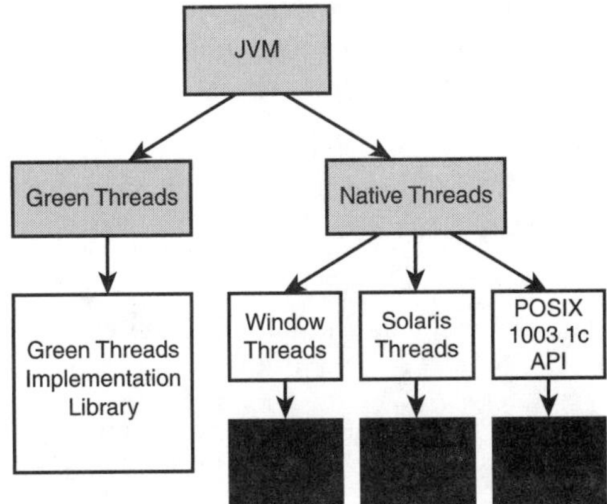

FIGURE 54.5
Green versus native threads on different architectures.

"Green" threads (on the left-hand side of Figure 54.5) have an API defined by Sun—the same API on all platforms—and are implemented with user-space threads.

By contrast, "native" threads (on the right-hand side of Figure 54.5) are implemented with APIs provided by the native platform. Microsoft Windows and Solaris provide proprietary native APIs, and other UNIX platforms provide the POSIX P1003.1c ***pthreads*** API defined by the International Standards Organization. But defining an API does not mean defining an implementation. What lives on the other side of an API is, as shown in Figure 54.5, a black box—it may or may not be a kernel-based thread implementation. It may even change over time: Some operating systems, such as HP-UX, shipped user-space implementations of P1003.1c before they offered kernel threads, and then shipped kernel-space implementations after the necessary support was in place.

Under Linux, the POSIX P1003.1c API ***does*** use kernel threads. We peek inside the black box in the section "Linux Threading Specifics" later in the chapter.

Preemption

Preemption—the capability of the thread scheduler to interrupt one thread to schedule another—is a feature of many threading implementations, but not all. Java does not require preemption in threading, and some Java implementations do not preempt.

As a result, Java applications may run in an environment that passes control between threads at ***any*** time. Or, alternatively, a running thread might give up control to other threads only when it initiates a blocking operation (such as a `read()`) or explicitly yields control with the `Thread.yield()` or `Thread.sleep()` call.

So an application that needs to run well in all environments must allow for operation with and without preemption. If your application includes a stretch of compute-intensive code, for example, that code could potentially hog the CPU in a non-preemptive environment. This could block out all other threads, including GUI threads, making the application unresponsive and difficult to use. You may need to add `Thread.yield()` calls at strategic places to ensure that important threads are not starved.

Preemptive threading avoids the CPU-hog problem, but it introduces another risk to Java programs. A thread can be interrupted at *any* time. Any objects that are being shared between threads must make use of Java's synchronization mechanisms to ensure that different threads do not interfere with each others' use of the object.

The bottom line is summed up in this warning: Assume that code can be preempted at any time, ***and*** assume that preemption will never occur. This leads to two prescriptions for multi-threaded development:

- Use the `Thread.yield()` call in compute-intensive code to ensure that other threads can run.
- Use Java's synchronization capabilities to prevent threads from interfering with each other. This means using the **`synchronized`** keyword and taking advantage of `Object.wait()` and `Object.notify()` to coordinate activities between threads.

Finally, it's important to test an application under both models. Those that work well under only one threading model are probably suffering from thread starvation, deadlock, or a failure to properly synchronize access to shared objects.

Thread Scheduling

Java makes no guarantees about the order in which threads will be scheduled, which threads will run concurrently on multiple CPUs, or how big a timeslice threads will get in a preemptive threading environment. Java applications should not make any assumptions about the scheduling of threads.

Thread Priorities

Java supports thread priorities. The `Thread.setPriority()` call can be used to mark the relative importance of threads. Priorities are useful, but they are basically ***suggestions***. There is no guarantee that the underlying threading system supports priorities, or that it supports as many priority levels as Java offers, or how priorities actually map to thread scheduling.

Linux Threading Specifics

Having explored the threading questions Java faces on any platform, we take a look at how Linux answers those questions.

Modern Linux implementations include a fully functional POSIX *pthread* library. Any application using the pthread API is using kernel threads with preemption. The JDK, when running with native threads, falls into this category.

Linux threading is, however, unique. Two factors distinguish the Linux implementation of threading from that of many other operating systems supporting multithreading:

- It is fast. Kernel-switched threads are reputed to perform as well as user-space threads (a rarity), obviating the usual rationale for favoring user-space threads or hybrid thread models.
- The thread mechanism is built on a unique system call, `__clone()`, that generalizes the traditional `fork()` call for support of lightweight processes.

The `__clone()` call is not visible to Java developers, nor is it recommended for use by C/C++ developers (it's highly nonportable!); but it is used under the covers of the pthread implementation, and has important implications for multithreaded programs.

In a nutshell, the `__clone()` call spawns a new system process, similar to the `fork()` system call, but allows fine-grained control over whether the parent and child processes share private memory, file system information, file descriptors, signal handlers, and process ID. Heavyweight processes share very little, lightweight processes share a lot, and the standard mechanisms for managing processes work on both.

The upshot of Linux's kernel-space threading model, and the behavior of the `__clone()` call, is that threads take up entries in the process table and have unique per-thread process IDs[2]. The consequences are as follows:

- There is a disconcerting tendency for multithreaded processes to show up as many entries in the process list (see the section "Identifying Related Thread Processes" later in this chapter.
- Because the process table is a finite resource, there is a limit on your ability to create huge numbers of threads. By default, Linux limits a single user to no more than 256 entries in the process table—although you can increase that number if necessary (see the section on "Increasing the Maximum Number of Processes" later in this chapter).

Identifying Related Thread Processes

How do you distinguish threads from processes running on your system? This question was asked in Chapter 15, "Troubleshooting The Blackdown JRE/JSDK Installation," in the section "Java Use of the Linux Process Table," and is often the reason for panicked questions from new users of the Blackdown JDK on Linux.

Consider this output generated by the Linux `ps` (process status) utility:

---

[2]The `__clone()` call permits parent and child processes to share a PID, but this is highly discouraged. There are too many places in the OS where such a practice would break important assumptions. Perhaps the existence of this capability implies future plans to make it work properly.

```
PID TTY      STAT   TIME  MAJFL   TRS   DRS   RSS %MEM COMMAND
23250 ttyp2   S     0:07   3573     9 30066 12996 10.1 java
23274 ttyp2   S     0:00      0     9 30066 12996 10.1 java
23275 ttyp2   S     0:00      0     9 30066 12996 10.1 java
23276 ttyp2   S     0:00      0     9 30066 12996 10.1 java
23277 ttyp2   S     0:00      0     9 30066 12996 10.1 java
23278 ttyp2   S     0:01     52     9 30066 12996 10.1 java
23279 ttyp2   S     0:00      0     9 30066 12996 10.1 java
23280 ttyp2   S     0:00      5     9 30066 12996 10.1 java
23281 ttyp2   S     0:00      0     9 30066 12996 10.1 java
```

To anyone familiar with using `ps`, this output clearly describes 9 processes, all running the command `java` and consuming (according to the numbers in the `DRS` column) a total of 270MB of memory.

But the output is deceptive: In reality, these are all threads sharing the same 30MB of memory.

How can you ascertain the truth from the `ps` output? The short answer is that you can't—there is nothing in the output identifying these processes as lightweight.

There is a powerful hint, of course: all nine processes have identical memory size. But that is not proof, it's just a strong suggestion. A more powerful hint is available in the `/proc` file system. The `/proc/`*`<pid>`*`/` directory (where *`<pid>`* is a process ID, and a directory exists for every current process) contains a number of files whose contents will be identical for related threads:

- `/proc/`*`<pid>`*`/maps` contains a map of a process's memory regions: related threads will have identical maps. So, using the process IDs that appeared in the `ps` output, you will see identical contents in `/proc/23250/maps`, `/proc/23274/maps`, `/proc/23275/maps`, and so on.
- For related threads, the information in `/proc/`*`<pid>`*`/status` will report identical values for all the `Vm*` fields.
- Several other per-process items, such as `/proc/`*`<pid>`*`/environ` and the contents of the `/proc/`*`<pid>`*`/fds` directory, will match for related threads.

These approaches are not foolproof, but they are fool-resistant. You can use them to ascertain, with reasonable certainty, whether two process IDs belong to related threads.

If these instructions seem terribly imprecise, it reflects the non-goal of Linux to provide this information. Yes, you can identify related threads if it is *really* important to you, but simply understanding the reason for so many process entries is the most important knowledge.

Increasing the Maximum Number of Processes

In its default configuration, Linux allows a maximum of about 512 total processes and a maximum of 256 per user. What if your Java application wants to create thousands of threads?

The first question to ask is whether you really need thousands of threads. Threads are sometimes the simplest way to solve a problem—a busy Web server might, for example, spawn a thread to handle every request—but not always the most efficient. Too many threads can quickly lead to thrashing, and you may find that some creative queuing is a better solution than is assuming infinite resources. In the succinct words of one instructive Java Web site, too many threads is usually a sign of "lazy programming."

That said, you can increase Linux's process limits by building a custom kernel. In the kernel source tree, the file `include/linux/tasks.h` contains the relevant constants. By adjusting the values of `NR_TASKS` and `MAX_TASKS_PER_USER`, you can support up to 4,092 processes on an x86-based Linux system.

Thread Preemption on Linux

The Blackdown JDK port offers green and native-threaded versions of the JVM. Barring the unlikely possibility that you are not using the standard `libpthread`, the native-threading version uses preemptive scheduling. The green-threaded version does not.

For other Java environments, such as Kaffe and gcj, the behavior can vary with the implementation and with configuration-time choices.

Thread Priorities

Thread priorities have no effect under the JDK on Linux. Although Linux offers applications a certain amount of control over process and thread priority, that control is available only to processes running as the root user. The Blackdown JDK does not try to set thread priorities.

Summary

We have looked at some of the intricacies of Java thread usage under Linux. Applications running with native threads are supported by a preemptive, kernel-space threading mechanism. Limitations imposed by the Linux environment include a limit on the allowable number of threads and no support for thread priorities.

CHAPTER 55

JNI: MIXING JAVA AND NATIVE CODE ON LINUX

The capability to interface between Java and native platform code has been indispensable since Java's early days. It has also been changeable and contentious, as one might expect at the boundary to native platform functionality. JNI compliance is one of the issues in the Sun/Microsoft dispute.

The current Java Native Interface—introduced with JDK1.1—is being touted as the final and correct way to mesh portable code with platform code, and it certainly addresses many painful problems encountered with earlier interfaces. This chapter takes a look at the use of JNI in the Linux environment.

The good news is that JNI is a reasonably portable specification, and the ample Sun documentation about using it on other platforms applies nearly verbatim to Linux. This chapter focuses on Linux specifics: Why and how to use native components with your Java programs on Linux.

Why Use Native Code?

Writing native code is unquestionably a chore; you must deal with new tools and with languages that are less object-oriented and, well, less fun than developing in Java. But there are good reasons to add native components to a Java application, which we discuss in the next two subsections.

The Need for Speed

The most compelling reason to use native code is performance. Java is slow for many good reasons (see Chapter 57, "Why Is Java Slow?"), and relying entirely on Java code for heavy processing creates a guaranteed disadvantage.

Compute-intensive and memory-intensive applications can particularly benefit from using native components. Java's extensive runtime checking, its heavy use of indirection, and its far-from-optimal use of memory can inflict a heavy toll on hard-working applications. Sometimes, only the facilities of a dangerous language such as C or C++ can deliver the performance you need.

Native Platform Capabilities

In its ongoing quest for acceptance, Java is eagerly embracing most of the native platform functionality that the market cares about. Extensions such a Java3D, Java Media Framework, JavaComm, and Java Advanced Imaging provide portable access to many specialized hardware and platform capabilities that might otherwise be out of reach.

But there is still a big hole when it comes to supporting native platform functionality. UNIX/Linux developers adopting Java will quickly discover some of the things you *cannot* do, in the name of portability:

- You cannot fully exploit the file system—Java has no support for symbolic links, file permissions, user IDs and file ownership, named pipes, full file status information, and other unique features found in UNIX/Linux file systems.
- You cannot interact with the environment—Java gives you no access to UNIX/Linux environment variables.
- You cannot control devices—Java offers no basic device control capabilities comparable to the `ioctl()` and `fcntl()` facilities in UNIX/Linux. Need to disable terminal echo so that the user can type in a password? Not possible.
- You cannot interact with other processes—You cannot learn anything about UNIX/Linux processes, or use such interprocess communications mechanisms as signals and UNIX-domain sockets.
- You cannot interact with the X Window System, other X clients, and the window manager—You cannot control window decorations, read selection buffers, choose nondefault visuals, launch a browser, iconify or uniconify windows, or perform many other actions available to normal X clients.

The list goes on.

Are these limitations considered faults with Java or unreasonable expectations by UNIX/Linux developers? Probably some of both. Java was certainly not designed to support development of UNIX system utilities or X window managers. But, on occasion, the Java definition of portability is simply too constricting, and you need to take advantage of the strengths of the underlying platform.

JNI offers you a route to as much native platform functionality as you need.

JNI History

JNI has four predecessor technologies:

- JDK1.0 *Native Method Interface* (NMI)—The original native interface, NMI directly mapped Java structures into C structures to be passed to native code. This resulted in a fragile interface because Java does not specify how its objects are to be laid out. NMI code was, as a consequence, tightly bound to a particular JVM implementation and could be incompatible with other JVMs or even with different releases of the same JVM.

  NMI also interacted poorly with garbage collection (GC), and using it imposed severe limitations on the type of GC algorithms that could be used.

- Netscape *Java Runtime Interface (JRI)*—A more portable solution from Netscape that was used in the Navigator product, JRI was subsequently enhanced into the current JNI.

- Microsoft *Raw Native Interface (RNI)*—Like NMI, RNI provides direct native access to Java object structures. Although RNI is more GC-aware than NMI, it suffers from similar concerns and shortcomings.

- Microsoft *Java/COM interface*—Microsoft's *Component Object Model* (COM) offers a higher-level interface to Java objects than do NMI or RNI. The COM interface is a force-fit to Java's requirements, but an even greater concern is that COM is still a single-platform specification that shows no signs of acceptance outside the Microsoft Windows environment.

Building on the experience of the past interfaces, JNI tries to strike a balance between speed, portability, and supportability. Sun requires JNI support as a condition of conformance in JDK implementations and has indicated that JNI-based code will enjoy support in future JVMs long after support has disappeared for other approaches.

In a nutshell, the three main features that distinguish JNI from NMI and others are the following:

- JNI is portable across JVM implementations. The same binaries should work with any JVM on a particular platform. (See the section "Understanding Version Sensitivities of Linux JNI Components," later in this chapter, for some exceptions specific to Linux.)

- JNI handles data in a portable manner: Rather than passing raw Java structures directly to native code, access to Java structures is indirect. JNI defines native calls through which the native code can read and write class and object members.

- JNI is friendly to garbage collection, providing new techniques for managing dynamic objects that do not interfere with advanced GC techniques.

Clearly, JNI increases portability at the expense of performance. Indirect access to objects and their contents is not free, and JNI will lead to performance gains only if your native code is doing some non-trivial amount of processing. But JNI also offers the best design, to date, for building native components that will work with current, future, and multivendor Java implementations.

Connecting Java Methods to Native Functions

To build JNI-based code, you need the `javah` tool from the SDK (see Chapter 22, "The Java Native Code Header and Stub File Generator: `javah`"), and a C or C++ compiler such as `gcc` (see Chapter 9, "Setting Up a Linux Development Environment," in the section "`gcc`—the GNU C Compiler").

The gateway from Java into native code is through individual Java methods. For every Java method declared to be `native`, there is a corresponding C/C++ entry point whose mangled name reflects the corresponding Java signature. The rules for deriving the C/C++ name from the Java name are well-documented, but all you really need to know is how to use `javah`.

This section describes how to use `javah` to generate header files and derive the C/C++ entry point names. And it introduces a project, `FileStatus`, that demonstrates the use of JNI from the Java side. The next section, "Accessing Java Classes from Native Code," discusses the native side of the Java/JNI relationship.

JDK1.2 JNI Header Generation

`javah` generates JNI header files from class files—see Chapter 22. The SDK1.2 `javah` generates JNI headers by default, so usage is simple:

```
javah <classes>
```

The result will be one `.h` file for each class containing native methods, with a function prototype declared for each native function in the class. The filename reflects the full package+classname, so a class named `foo.bar.Baz` would generate a header file named `foo_bar_Baz.h`.

JDK1.1 JNI Header Generation

Generating JNI headers under JDK1.1 differs from JDK1.2 in one minor respect: `javah` generates old NMI-style headers by default and must be explicitly told to generate JNI headers:

```
javah -jni <classes>
```

The result is the same as with the JDK1.2 `javah`.

FileStatus: A Sample JNI Project

As a sample JNI project, we create a class, extending `java.io.File`, that reports some UNIX/Linux-specific details about a file: user ID, group ID, access modes, and information on symbolic links.

Listing 55.1 contains the Java portion of the project, including the declaration of the native methods to be implemented in a separate C source file.

LISTING 55.1 `FileStatus.java`

```
package com.macmillan.nmeyers;

// This class reports some Unix/Linux-specific information about
```

```
4   // files
5   public class FileStatus extends java.io.File
6   {
7       public String uid = null;    // UID in text form
8       public String gid = null;    // GID in text form
9       public int mode = 0;         // Mode bits
10      public String target = null;        // Target of symlink
11
12      static
13      {
14          System.loadLibrary("FileStatus");
15      }
16
17      public FileStatus(String path)
18      {
19          super(path);
20          getExtendedInformation();
21      }
22      public FileStatus(String path, String name)
23      {
24          super(path, name);
25          getExtendedInformation();
26      }
27      public FileStatus(java.io.File dir, String name)
28      {
29          super(dir, name);
30          getExtendedInformation();
31      }
32      private native void getExtendedInformation();
33
34      public static void main(String[] argv)
35      {
36          for (int i = 0; i < argv.length; i++)
37          {
38              FileStatus file = new FileStatus(argv[i]);
39              System.out.print(file.toString() +
40                               ": owner = " + file.uid +
41                               ", group = " + file.gid +
42                               ", mode = " + file.mode);
43              if (file.target != null)
44                  System.out.print(", symlink to " + file.target);
45              System.out.println("");
46          }
47      }
48  }
```

Lines 7–10 contain the platform-specific data. These fields are filled in by the `getExtendedInformation()` code during class construction. The user and group ID are returned as strings, and the permissions as a number. If the file turns out to be a symbolic link, `target`'s non-null String value indicates the target of the link.

Lines 12–15 contain a static initializer that loads the native portion of the code from a shared library named `libFileStatus.so`.

Lines 17–31 extend the constructors found in the superclass. After superclass construction, they call the `getExtendedInformation()` native method to fill in the object fields with platform-specific data.

Line 32 contains the declaration of our native method, to be implemented elsewhere in C.

Lines 34–47 contain a simple `main()` procedure that tests this class by applying it to filenames requested on the command line.

Sample Header File Generation

Having written and compiled the Java portion of this project, we can generate the headers needed by the native component of the project. Running the SDK1.2 `javah` on the compiled class

```
bash$ javah com.macmillan.nmeyers.FileStatus
```

generates the header file `com_macmillan_nmeyers_FileStatus.h`. The file includes a function prototype with the signature needed for the native method:

```
JNIEXPORT void JNICALL Java_com_macmillan_nmeyers_FileStatus_
  getExtendedInformation(JNIEnv *, jobject);
```

Notice reference to several types and macros, `JNIEXPORT`, `JNICALL`, `Java`, `JNIEnv`, and `jobject`, whose definitions are provided by header files included by this header file.

Native Code Access from Java

A native method call looks like any other method call. Referring to Listing 55.1, lines 20, 25, and 30 all contain invocations of the native `getExtendedInformation()` method—no additional magic is required from the Java side to use it.

Accessing Java Classes from Native Code

Having discussed the Java side of JNI in the previous section, "Connecting Java Methods to Native Functions," this section focuses on the native side of the problem.

All native-side access to Java classes, objects, and members is indirect. Your native code must jump through a few hoops to touch the class contents. As previously mentioned in the section "JNI History," this is a speed/portability trade-off that makes JNI a reasonably robust interface. To illustrate access, Listing 55.2 shows the native component of our sample project.

LISTING 55.2 `FileStatus.c`

```
#include "com_macmillan_nmeyers_FileStatus.h"
#include <sys/stat.h>
#include <unistd.h>
#include <pwd.h>
#include <grp.h>
```

```
#include <sys/types.h>
#include <limits.h>
#include <stdio.h>

void Java_com_macmillan_nmeyers_FileStatus_getExtendedInformation
  (JNIEnv *env, jobject obj)
{
    struct stat statbuf;
    /* Get our class */
    jclass cls = (*env)->GetObjectClass(env, obj);
    /* Get a method ID for toString() */
    jmethodID mid =
        (*env)->GetMethodID(env, cls, "toString",
➥"()Ljava/lang/String;");
    /* Get the full file path */
    jstring filename = (*env)->CallObjectMethod(env, obj, mid);
    /* Extract the name into a buffer */
    const char *filename_str = (*env)->GetStringUTFChars(env,
➥filename, 0);
    /* Get file status */
    int result = lstat(filename_str, &statbuf);
    /* Did the lstat succeed? */
    if (!result)
    {
        /* Yes. Get the name for the UID */
        struct passwd *passwd_entry = getpwuid(statbuf.st_uid);
        char pwbuf[64], *pwname;
        jstring uid_string = 0;
        jfieldID uid_fieldid;
        /* Yes. And the name for the GID */
        struct group *group_entry = getgrgid(statbuf.st_gid);
        char grbuf[64], *grname;
        jstring gid_string = 0;
        jfieldID gid_fieldid;
        /* And the target of the link */
        char *linktarget = 0;
        char linkbuf[NAME_MAX + 1];
        jstring target_string = 0;
        jfieldID mode_fieldid;
        /* Did we find a password entry? */
        if (passwd_entry)
        {
            /* Yes. point to it. */
            pwname = passwd_entry->pw_name;
        }
        else
        {
            /* No. print out the number to a tempbuf and use that */
            sprintf(pwbuf, "%ld", (long)statbuf.st_uid);
            pwname = pwbuf;
        }
        /* Did we find a group entry? */
```

continued on next page

continued from previous page

```
        if (group_entry)
        {
            /* Yes. point to it. */
            grname = group_entry->gr_name;
        }
        else
        {
            /* No. print out the number to a tempbuf and use that */
            sprintf(grbuf, "%ld", (long)statbuf.st_gid);
            grname = grbuf;
        }
        /* Do we have a link? */
        if (S_ISLNK(statbuf.st_mode))
        {
            /* Yes. Resolve the name. */
            int namelen = readlink(filename_str, linkbuf, NAME_MAX);
            /* If success, null-terminate the string and point at it */
            if (namelen > 0)
            {
                linkbuf[namelen] = 0;
                linktarget = linkbuf;
            }
        }
        /* We have everything. Time to start filling in our object.
➥First
           create the strings */
        uid_string = (*env)->NewStringUTF(env, pwname);
        gid_string = (*env)->NewStringUTF(env, grname);
        if (linktarget)
            target_string = (*env)->NewStringUTF(env, linktarget);
        /* Find the field ID for the uid */
        uid_fieldid =
            (*env)->GetFieldID(env, cls, "uid", "Ljava/lang/String;");
        /* Set the string */
        (*env)->SetObjectField(env, obj, uid_fieldid, uid_string);
        /* Find the field ID for the gid */
        gid_fieldid =
            (*env)->GetFieldID(env, cls, "gid", "Ljava/lang/String;");
        /* Set the string */
        (*env)->SetObjectField(env, obj, gid_fieldid, gid_string);
        if (linktarget)
        {
            jfieldID target_fieldid =
                (*env)->GetFieldID(env, cls, "target",
➥"Ljava/lang/String;");
            (*env)->SetObjectField(env, obj, target_fieldid, target_
➥string);
        }
        /* Finally, find the field ID for the mode */
        mode_fieldid = (*env)->GetFieldID(env, cls, "mode", "I");
        /* And set it */
        (*env)->SetIntField(env, obj, mode_fieldid, (jint)statbuf.
➥st_mode);
```

```
105         }
106         /* Release the name buffer */
107         (*env)->ReleaseStringUTFChars(env, filename, filename_str);
108     }
```

Three steps are required to access a class member:

1. Identify the class (line 15 derives the class ID from the current `FileStatus` object).
2. Obtain a member identifier (lines 17–18 obtain a `methodID` for the `toString()` method). This step requires us to specify the full signature of the member—notice the fourth argument to `GetMethodID()`—a method signature we obtained with help from the SDK `javap` utility.
3. Use the member identifier to get access to the object. Line 20 uses the `methodID` to invoke the `toString()` method to obtain the file path.

When not busy accessing class members, the code collects some platform-specific information about the file of interest. Line 24 issues an `lstat()` call against the file whose path was obtained in line 20, which returns much of the information of interest.

Lines 29 and 44–54 find or derive a string describing the file's user ID, mapping (if possible) the numeric ID to the user's name on the system. Lines 34 and 56–66 do the same for the file's group ID.

Lines 68–78 determine whether the file is a symbolic link and, if so, derive the string describing the link's target. Lines 81-84 create new `java.lang.String` objects that will be written into the `FileStatus` object.

Lines 86–104 write the results of our activities into the object fields. The operations to write out values are similar to the earlier activities in lines 16–20 to read in one of the fields.

Building the JNI Native Component Objects

Using `gcc`, the following steps build this project:

```
bash$ javac -d . FileStatus.java
bash$ javah com.macmillan.nmeyers.FileStatus
bash$ gcc -O -D_REENTRANT -fpic -I$JAVA_HOME/include \
-I$JAVA_HOME/include/linux -I$JAVA_HOME/include/\
genunix -c FileStatus.c
bash$ gcc -shared -o libFileStatus.so FileStatus.o
```

After creating the class file and header file with the first two commands, the third command compiles the native implementation. The important options are as follows:

- `-D_REENTRANT`—Sets a flag causing C/C++ to issue thread-safe calls where needed.
- `-fpic`—Compile *position-independent code* suitable for use in a shared library.
- `-I`*`<directories>`*—These three `-I` options cover building against either SDK1.1 or SDK1.2. The `include/linux` subdirectory is found in the SDK1.2 tree, `include/genunix` in the SDK1.1 tree.

Finally, the link step, with the important `-shared` option, builds the shared `libFileStatus.so` library.

Listing 55.3 shows the results of running the test `main()` program to list the contents of the SDK1.2 `bin/` directory. (Notice the use of the `java.library.path` property to specify the location of the shared library, `libFileStatus.so`.)

LISTING 55.3 Running the JNI `FileStatus` Project

```
bash$ java -Djava.library.path=. com.macmillan.nmeyers.FileStatus /usr/
➥local/Java/jdk1.2/bin/*
/usr/local/Java/jdk1.2/bin/appletviewer: owner = root, group = root,
➥mode = 41471, symlink to .java_wrapper
/usr/local/Java/jdk1.2/bin/extcheck: owner = root, group = root, mode =
➥41471, symlink to .java_wrapper
/usr/local/Java/jdk1.2/bin/i386: owner = nathanm, group = 401, mode =
➥16877
/usr/local/Java/jdk1.2/bin/jar: owner = root, group = root, mode =
➥41471, symlink to .java_wrapper
/usr/local/Java/jdk1.2/bin/jarsigner: owner = root, group = root, mode =
➥ 41471, symlink to .java_wrapper
/usr/local/Java/jdk1.2/bin/java: owner = root, group = root, mode =
➥41471, symlink to .java_wrapper
/usr/local/Java/jdk1.2/bin/java-rmi.cgi: owner = nathanm, group = 401,
➥mode = 33261
/usr/local/Java/jdk1.2/bin/java_g.bak: owner = nathanm, group = users,
➥mode = 33261
/usr/local/Java/jdk1.2/bin/javac: owner = root, group = root, mode =
➥41471, symlink to .java_wrapper
/usr/local/Java/jdk1.2/bin/javadoc: owner = root, group = root, mode =
➥41471, symlink to .java_wrapper
/usr/local/Java/jdk1.2/bin/javah: owner = root, group = root, mode =
➥41471, symlink to .java_wrapper
/usr/local/Java/jdk1.2/bin/javap: owner = root, group = root, mode =
➥41471, symlink to .java_wrapper
/usr/local/Java/jdk1.2/bin/jdb: owner = root, group = root, mode =
➥41471, symlink to .java_wrapper
/usr/local/Java/jdk1.2/bin/keytool: owner = root, group = root, mode =
➥41471, symlink to .java_wrapper
/usr/local/Java/jdk1.2/bin/native2ascii: owner = root, group = root,
➥mode = 41471, symlink to .java_wrapper
/usr/local/Java/jdk1.2/bin/oldjava: owner = root, group = root, mode =
➥41471, symlink to .java_wrapper
/usr/local/Java/jdk1.2/bin/policytool: owner = root, group = root, mode
➥= 41471, symlink to .java_wrapper
/usr/local/Java/jdk1.2/bin/rmic: owner = root, group = root, mode =
➥41471, symlink to .java_wrapper
/usr/local/Java/jdk1.2/bin/rmid: owner = root, group = root, mode =
➥41471, symlink to .java_wrapper
/usr/local/Java/jdk1.2/bin/rmiregistry: owner = root, group = root, mode
➥= 41471, symlink to .java_wrapper
```

```
/usr/local/Java/jdk1.2/bin/serialver: owner = root, group = root, mode = 41471, symlink to .java_wrapper
/usr/local/Java/jdk1.2/bin/tnameserv: owner = root, group = root, mode = 41471, symlink to .java_wrapper
```

This output shows you something you probably already knew: that most of the scripts in the JDK `bin/` directory are links to a single script.

Running Java from Native Code: The Java Invocation API

The JVM can be started up from a native application through the *Invocation API*, which launches the JVM—provided as a shared library—through a simple sequence of C/C++ calls. The `java` launcher executable is, itself, a small native application that uses this API to start the JVM.

The Invocation API works under Linux as elsewhere and is covered in existing Sun SDK documentation. The source for the `java` launcher is shipped as part of the SDK itself: the file `src/launcher/java.c`, in the `src.jar` archive in the top-level directory of the JDK1.2 installation, provides a good example of how to launch the JVM from native code.

Debugging JNI Code

Debugging JNI code is possible, if a bit tricky. You need to run a native debugger, such as the GNU Debugger (`gdb`), and you need to jump through a few hoops—a (currently) unavoidable problem when debugging code resident in dynamically loaded libraries.

Here is a sequence of steps that works for me:

1. Compile and link the native components with the `-g` (debug) option.
2. Set `LD_PRELOAD` to point to native shared libraries you want to debug.
3. Set `DEBUG_PROG` to a command string that will launch a debugger.
4. Run the Java green-threads launcher: `java -green`. This will start up the debugger (the launch script uses `$DEBUG_PROG` for this purpose).
5. In the debugger, set a breakpoint at `main()`.
6. Run the program, specifying the Java command-line arguments in the `run` command.
7. After the debugger hits the `main()` breakpoint, set a breakpoint in your native code and continue execution.
8. After the debugger hits your breakpoint, start debugging.

Example Debugging Session

After recompiling the native code with the -g debugging flag, we set up to run with the ddd debugger:

```
bash$ LD_PRELOAD=./libFileStatus.so DEBUG_PROG="ddd -gdb" java -green
```

This starts ddd, running the Java green-threads executable. We set a breakpoint at main() by pressing the Break button (see Figure 55.1).

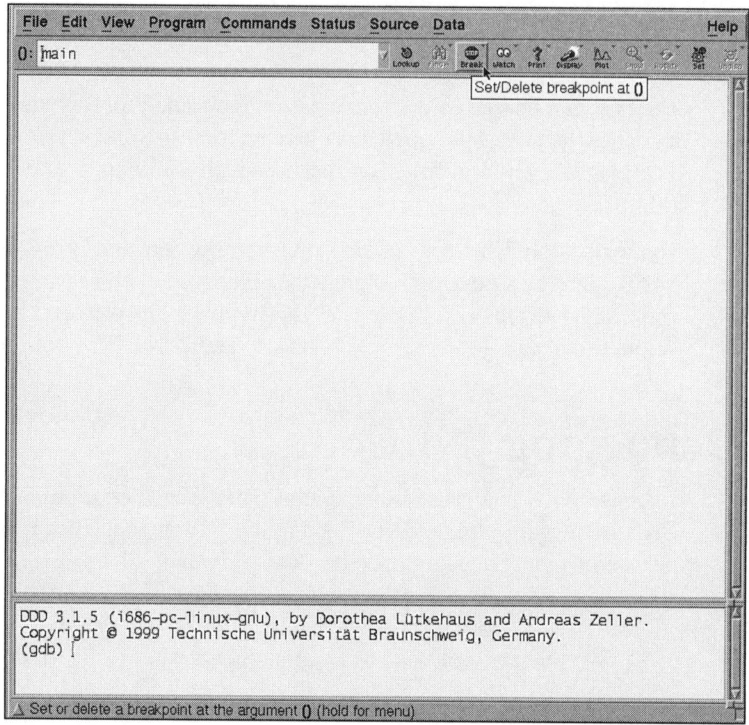

FIGURE 55.1
ddd startup, running the Java launcher executable

We start the debugger by choosing Program, Run from the menu and specifying the Java command-line arguments in the Arguments dialog (see Figure 55.2).

The arguments, which are partly obscured in the text box, are

-Djava.library.path=. com.macmillan.nmeyers.FileStatus.

Launching the application from this debugger dialog is a bit more cumbersome than launching from a shell. Unlike a shell, the debugger does not perform command-line expansion—we cannot use wildcards or other shell conveniences to construct the command.

After pressing the Run button, the program starts, and the command window (see Figure 55.3) shows that we have hit the breakpoint in main().

FIGURE 55.2
Specify the Java launch arguments in the Arguments dialog.

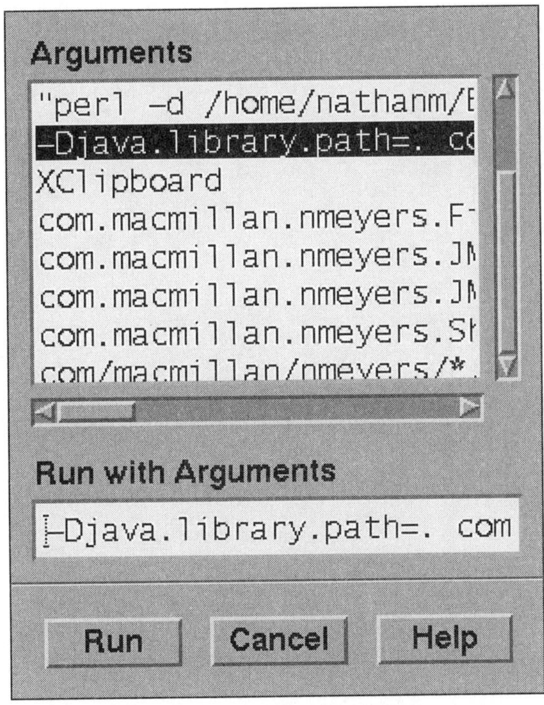

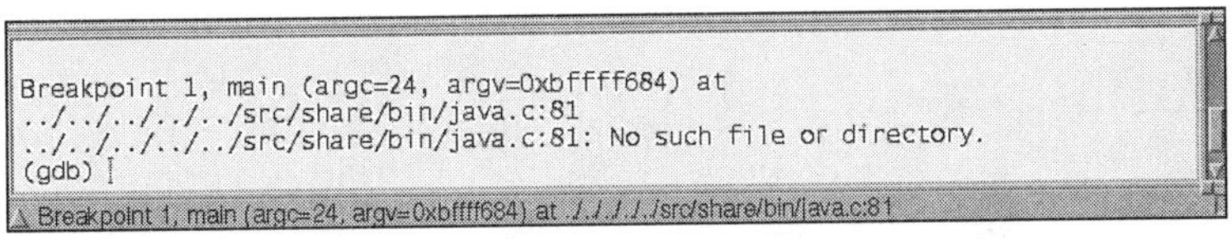

FIGURE 55.3
The debugger has hit the breakpoint in `main()`.

```
Breakpoint 1, main (argc=24, argv=0xbffff684) at
../../../../../src/share/bin/java.c:81
../../../../../src/share/bin/java.c:81: No such file or directory.
(gdb)
Breakpoint 1, main (argc=24, argv=0xbffff684) at ../../../../src/share/bin/java.c:81
```

The breakpoint encountered by the debugger in Figure 55.3 is the `java` launcher's `main()` procedure. Notice that the debugger is complaining that it cannot find the source.

Having reached a breakpoint in native code, we can finally set a breakpoint in our shared-library code. Because the library is already loaded (recall that it was preloaded) we can set the breakpoint by typing or pasting the name in the text window (see Figure 55.4, left-hand side) and pressing the `Break` button. We continue execution by choosing `Program`, `Continue`.

FIGURE 55.4
Setting a breakpoint for the JNI code.

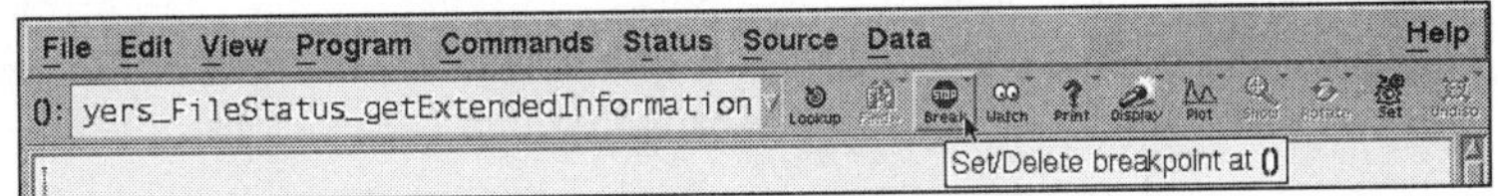

After continuing, we hit our breakpoint (see Figure 55.5) and continue into a normal debugging session.

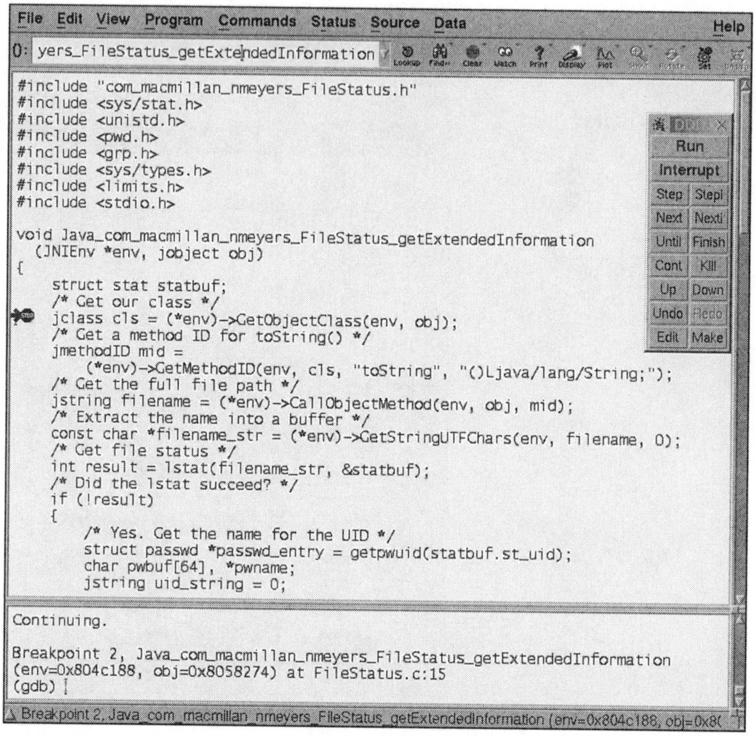

FIGURE 55.5
Ready for native debugging.

Variations in Debugging Startup

The challenge in debugging with dynamically loaded libraries is to reach a state in which you can set an initial breakpoint. The two necessary components of this state are:

- Program execution has commenced.
- The library has been loaded.

Our first technique was to preload the library with the `LD_PRELOAD` environment variable. The following sections discuss a couple of alternative approaches that do not require preloading.

Set a Breakpoint at Library Loading

The `dlopen()` procedure is responsible for loading all dynamically loaded libraries. By stopping before and after every execution of `dlopen()`, you can watch libraries being loaded. After you see your JNI library being loaded, you're ready to set a breakpoint and debug.

The sequence is this:

1. At debugging session startup, set a breakpoint at `dlopen` and continue execution.
2. When you hit a `dlopen()` breakpoint, type the `finish` command into the interactive window (see Figure 55.6) to skip past the rest of `dlopen()` execution. `dlopen()` will load the library and stop immediately after completion.

FIGURE 55.6
Using finish to skip past `dlopen()` execution.

```
Breakpoint 3, 0x8048a78 in dlopen ()
(gdb) finish
Run till exit from #0  0x8048a78 in dlopen ()
0x40024757 in sysLoadLibrary (name=0x8172450
"/usr2/Java/jdk1.2.rh6/jre/lib/i386/libsunwjit.so", err_buf=0xbffff1e0
"\210Å\004\b<ðÿ¿=P\005@\210Å\004\b", err_buflen=512) at
../../../../../src/linux/hpi/src/linker_md.c:99
../../../../../src/linux/hpi/src/linker_md.c:99: No such file or directory.
(gdb)
0x40024757 in sysLoadLibrary (name=0x8172450 "/usr2/Java/jdk1.2.rh6/jre/lib/i386/libsunwjit.so", err_buf=0xbffff1e(
```

After completion of the **`dlopen()`** procedure, **`gdb`** prints out information about its procedure, which includes (by a certain amount of luck) the name of the library just loaded. In Figure 55.6, you have just loaded the library providing the JIT compiler.

This isn't the library you want to debug, so you must repeat step 2 until you have loaded your native library. Now you can set a breakpoint.

Insert a Breakpoint in Source

The easiest solution to setting a debugging breakpoint is a shameless hack: Insert a breakpoint directly into the native source code. This avoids the tedious steps we previously prescribed.

The following C/C++ inline x86 assembly-code (recognized by `gcc` and `g++`)

```
__asm__("int $0x3");
```

inserts the code for a breakpoint directly into the native code: Place it wherever you want to break and recompile the native code. You can run your application under a debugger without the elaborate preparations given previously: This is a permanent breakpoint.

But beware: Do *not* try running this code outside a debugger—it will abort and dump core.

Understanding Version Sensitivities of Linux JNI Components

Although JNI offers excellent binary portability across JVM versions, there are two sensitive areas in which JNI cannot offer much versionitis protection. These are discussed in the following sections.

libc Version

As discussed in Chapter 13, "Blackdown: The Official Linux Port," in the section "An Important Note About libc," evolution of the GNU C library has created some prickly compatibility issues under Linux. A JNI native component built against libc5 is not usable with a glibc-based JVM, and vice versa. Just as the JVM is published in versions for multiple libraries, so too must JNI components be run in an environment that matches the build environment.

If your JNI component targets JDK1.2, the good news is that the Blackdown JDK1.2 is published only for the glibc environment—you will not have to create a libc5-based version.

Threading Model

If you need to use the POSIX pthread API, *do not* use it from code that will be run under a JVM with green threads. Mixing pthread calls with green threads is an absolute incompatibility.

Building Old NMI Code

The old Native Method Interface is still supported in the "classic" JVM under JDK1.2, but not in HotSpot, and possibly not in future JDK releases.

NMI is clearly a dead end, but here's what you need to know if you need to build NMI source under current SDKs.

Building NMI Under SDK1.1

`javah` generates NMI headers and stubs by default. To generate headers:

```
javah <classes>
```

To generate C stub files:

```
javah -stubs <classes>
```

To compile NMI native modules, add the SDK's `include/` subdirectory to the compiler's include path (using the `gcc -I` option).

Building NMI Under SDK1.2

JNI is the default native interface under JDK1.2. To generate old NMI-style headers:

```
javah -old <classes>
```

To generate C stub files:

```
javah -old -stubs <classes>
```

To compile NMI native modules, add the SDK's `include-old/` subdirectory to the compiler's include path (using the `gcc -I` option).

For Further Reading

The JDK1.1 and JDK1.2 documentation bundles include detailed instructions on using JNI. The JNI spec can be found in document `docs/guide/jni/spec/jniTOC.doc.html` in either bundle.

Summary

JNI is your entry to platform-specific code, both to improve application performance and to access native capabilities that Java might not give you. The current JNI design replaces some older, faster, but more fragile techniques with a robust design that should support you through future JDK releases and with JVMs from other vendors.

JNI usage from Linux is similar to usage from other platforms. Other than a handful of compilation options (see the section "Building the JNI Native Component Objects" earlier in this chapter) and version concerns (see the section "Understanding Version Sensitivities of Linux JNI Components" earlier in this chapter), the instructions for using JNI from Solaris are usable, verbatim, for JNI development under Linux.

CHAPTER 56

X WINDOW SYSTEM TIPS AND TRICKS

The Java AWT enjoys a close, personal relationship with the underlying graphics display system on its host machine, and in the Linux environment this means the X Window System. This chapter probes that relationship in some detail, concentrating on the areas that affect Java application behavior and interaction with other X applications.

There are many varied topics ahead. In a nutshell, this chapter covers:

- Understanding X visuals and Java AWT support/nonsupport (see "X Server Depth, Visuals, and Java Support").
- Requesting private colormaps and nonstandard visuals from Java—with code (see "`xwinwrap`: Controlling Colormap and Visual Usage").
- Changing X Server settings to work around AWT limitations (see "Experimenting with X Server Settings").
- Using X Window System capabilities not exposed by the AWT—with code (see "Exercising Full X Capabilities").
- Using the AWT on hosts (that is, servers) without displays (see "Server-Side AWT: Using AWT/X Without a Display Device").

X Server Depth, Visuals, and Java Support

Users of the Blackdown JDK1.2 port, running on Linux boxes with advanced displays, have sometimes been surprised to learn that they cannot run Java graphical or GUI applications (see Chapter 15, "Troubleshooting The Blackdown JRE/JSDK Installation," in the section "Limited Support of X Visuals"). The X Window System is capable of supporting many display depths and visuals, and the complex JDK1.2 Graphics2D pipeline cannot (yet) deal with all the choices.

This section looks at the problems of understanding X's capabilities and what Java can and cannot do with these capabilities.

Understanding Display Depth

Display *depth* is a familiar concept: It's the number of bits devoted to representing each pixel in a display device.

In the early days of expensive memory and bitonal displays, display devices had a depth of 1—a pixel was on or off, it occupied a single bit of memory, and the contents of a full 320x240 screen could fit in less than 10KB of memory.

Such devices are now rare. Most common display devices today have a depth of at least 8, and depths of 16 and 24 are common. Many display devices allow flexible memory usage, letting you trade off depth and resolution—high-res at low-depth, or low-res at high-depth. The available choices are staggering, and a huge challenge for the Java AWT.

Understanding Display Class

The X Window System uses the term *display class* to describe six different models for how pixel values in display memory map to colors on the screen. In all these models, pixel values serve as indices into color tables. The difference between the models is in how the pixel values are interpreted, how many tables are used, and how the tables are populated.

Figure 56.1 shows the six display classes used by X.

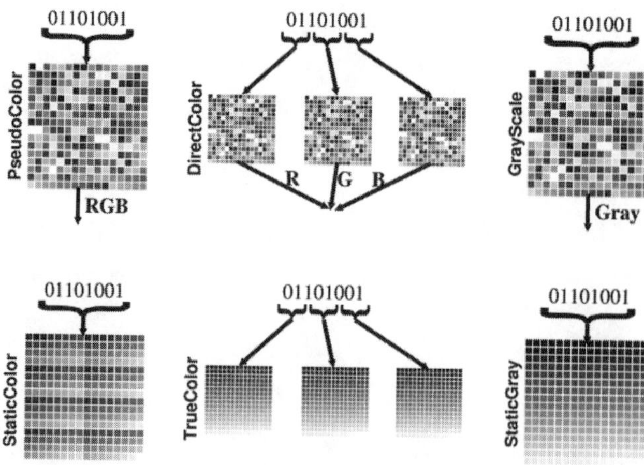

FIGURE 56.1
The six X Window System display classes.

The three classes in the top row, PseudoColor, DirectColor, and GrayScale, are read/write classes: the contents of the tables are set by X clients. Two of these models, PseudoColor and GrayScale, index into a single table of RGB or Gray values (respectively). DirectColor packs three indices into a pixel value. Each acts on one primary color table, and the resulting primaries are combined to generate the final color value.

The three classes in the bottom row, StaticColor, TrueColor, and StaticGray, are read-only versions of the first three classes. The contents of the color tables cannot be set by X clients but are instead initialized to fixed color ramps that span the color space or the gray levels.

Subtleties

In all the display classes described here, the size of the *individual* color table entries is the same. Color values in X are specified with 16-bit quantities, so you can describe 2^{16} distinct gray values and 2^{48} distinct RGB values. That is well beyond the capability of hardware to handle, or the human eye to perceive. The X server quantizes them down to whatever the hardware supports.

Understanding X Visuals

In X Window System terminology, a ***visual*** is a combination of a display depth and a display class. Examples are 8-bit PseudoColor and 24-bit TrueColor.

X can, in theory, allow any combination of depth and class, although some combinations make more sense than others. The most frequently used visual on 8-bit color displays is 8-bit PseudoColor—a sensible way for multiple applications to share scarce entries in the color table.

On 24-bit displays, the DirectColor and TrueColor classes are the most commonly used.

Whatever the capabilities of the display, the X server offers some set of visuals, and it offers a ***default visual*** that is used by the root window and by most applications. You can find out what is available from your X server, and the default values, by running the `xdpyinfo` utility. Listing 56.1 shows a typical excerpt of `xdpyinfo` output for an 8-bit XFree86 server.

LISTING 56.1 The `xdpyinfo` Output for an 8-Bit Display Device Shows That Six Different Visuals Are Supported

```
number of visuals:    6
default visual id:  0x22
visual:
  visual id:    0x22
  class:    PseudoColor
  depth:    8 planes
  available colormap entries:    256
  red, green, blue masks:    0x0, 0x0, 0x0
  significant bits in color specification:    8 bits
```

continued on next page

continued from previous page

```
visual:
  visual id:    0x23
  class:    DirectColor
  depth:    8 planes
  available colormap entries:    8 per subfield
  red, green, blue masks:    0x7, 0x38, 0xc0
  significant bits in color specification:    8 bits
visual:
  visual id:    0x24
  class:    GrayScale
  depth:    8 planes
  available colormap entries:    256
  red, green, blue masks:    0x0, 0x0, 0x0
  significant bits in color specification:    8 bits
visual:
  visual id:    0x25
  class:    StaticColor
  depth:    8 planes
  available colormap entries:    256
  red, green, blue masks:    0x7, 0x38, 0xc0
  significant bits in color specification:    8 bits
visual:
  visual id:    0x26
  class:    TrueColor
  depth:    8 planes
  available colormap entries:    8 per subfield
  red, green, blue masks:    0x7, 0x38, 0xc0
  significant bits in color specification:    8 bits
visual:
  visual id:    0x27
  class:    StaticGray
  depth:    8 planes
  available colormap entries:    256
  red, green, blue masks:    0x0, 0x0, 0x0
  significant bits in color specification:    8 bits
```

This server offers 8-bit visuals for all six display classes. Notice that for DirectColor and TrueColor, 3 bits of the pixel value are used as a red index, 3 for green, and 2 for blue. It's a weird visual, but it's available to X clients that need it.

Listing 56.2 shows some typical `xdpyinfo` output for a 24-bit server.

LISTING 56.2 The `xdpyinfo` Output for a 24-Bit Display Device Shows Two Dupported Visuals

```
number of visuals:    2
default visual id:  0x22
visual:
  visual id:    0x22
  class:    DirectColor
  depth:    24 planes
  available colormap entries:    256 per subfield
```

```
    red, green, blue masks:    0xff, 0xff00, 0xff0000
    significant bits in color specification:    8 bits
  visual:
    visual id:    0x23
    class:    TrueColor
    depth:    24 planes
    available colormap entries:    256 per subfield
    red, green, blue masks:    0xff, 0xff00, 0xff0000
    significant bits in color specification:    8 bits
```

This server offers only two visuals; clients do not even have the option of running with 8-bit PseudoColor windows. Some commercial UNIX X servers offer multiple depths. The choices for the 24-bit server might also include some 8-bit choices, and XFree86 is planning to do the same in a future release.

Understanding X Colormaps

The section "Understanding Display Class" earlier in this chapter described X's use of color tables. A *colormap* is an X resource containing the set of tables needed to implement a visual. A colormap for 8-bit PseudoColor is a table with 256 entries; a colormap for 24-bit TrueColor is three tables of 256 entries each (assuming the usual division of 8 bits/color).

The X server starts up with one colormap per screen—a default colormap used by the root window and used by most X clients. But clients have the option of requesting private colormaps, which they may do for either of two reasons:

- To avoid crowding the colormap used by everyone else. As an example, Netscape Navigator's `-install` option installs a private colormap.
- To use a nondefault visual.

When clients use private colormaps, the X window manager is responsible for installing and uninstalling that colormap when that client gains or loses the focus. The familiar result of this is the "technicolor" flashing that shows all other applications with false colors.

Subtleties

X can manage as many colormaps as fit in memory. It's possible for hundreds of different clients to have custom colormaps. Unlike the software, most display *hardware* supports a single colormap, so X must *install* the currently relevant colormap from its own buffers into the display hardware. As the focus moves from window to window in an X display, X ensures that the hardware is using the colormap created for that window.

Some display hardware in the UNIX workstation market includes support for multiple colormaps, allowing several clients to have private colormaps without causing color flashing. It is the X server's job, in its device-specific code, to properly manage such hardware.

How Does This Affect Java?

X applications face a huge universe of choices: six different display classes, many possible depths, and the capability to choose nondefault visuals and colormaps.

The Sun AWT, at present, does not take advantage of these choices. It either works with the X server's default settings or it doesn't work at all—and there are many settings with which it doesn't work.

To run Java on X servers with default settings the AWT does not support (in general, this means visuals not found on Solaris), you must work around the limitations: Either select non-default visuals the AWT *can* handle, or change X server settings to provide new visuals the AWT can handle. The next two sections describe steps you can take to run Java on uncooperative display devices.

`xwinwrap`: Controlling Colormap and Visual Usage

Most UNIX/Linux users are familiar with Netscape's **`-install`** option. It causes Navigator to install a private colormap to avoid sharing a crowded colormap with other X clients. Also available, but not as widely used, is a **`-visual`** option that lets you run Navigator with any visual offered by the X server.

Unfortunately, this flexibility is not a universal practice. Many X clients give you no choice but to run with the default visual and to share the crowded default colormap. Sun's Java AWT falls into this category.

We present a small project, `xwinwrap`, that gives you a workaround. It allows you to run any X client with its own colormap and with a nondefault visual. It can help the Sun AWT in a couple of ways:

- By installing a private colormap, the AWT will not run out of colors due to the demands of other X clients.
- By specifying a nondefault visual, the AWT may be usable on displays for which it cannot handle the default visual. This will become especially useful after XFree86 has added support for multiple depths (as discussed previously in the section "Understanding X Visuals").

Theory of `xwinwrap` Operation

When X clients open a network connection to the X server, they are given information about the current X server configuration, including the default visual and colormap. Clients not interested in private colormaps or nondefault visuals simply use these values when creating new top-level windows.

`xwinwrap` provides an onionskin library (a thin wrapper between the real X library and the client) that intercepts calls to the Xlib functions `XOpenDisplay()` and `XCreateWindow()`, substituting nondefault values as needed. Without making any change to the application itself, `xwinwrap` allows you to make choices, not otherwise offered by the application, about the application's colormap and choice of visual.

Usage

`xwinwrap` is provided as a shared library, which you preload using the `LD_PRELOAD` environment variable. This step interposes `xwinwrap` between the application and the X library, where it can do its work.

Input is provided to `xwinwrap` through a single environment variable: `XWINWRAP_VISUALID`. Set it to the number (reported by `xdpyinfo`) of the visual you want to use. If this variable is not used, `xwinwrap` installs a private colormap using the default visual.

Example:

Using the 8-bit server shown in the section "Understanding X Visuals" earlier in the chapter, we run Java with a GrayScale visual:

```
bash$ LD_PRELOAD=xwinwrap.so XWINWRAP_VISUALID=0x24 java ...
```

Building `xwinwrap`

`xwinwrap` is implemented in a single C source file, which is provided on the CD-ROM and also shown in Appendix B. The following steps will build the `xwinwrap` library from source:

```
bash$ gcc -D_REENTRANT -c -fpic xwinwrap.c
bash$ gcc -o xwinwrap.so -shared -nostdlib xwinwrap.o -ldl
```

Caveats

`xwinwrap` is a low-risk tool, but a few warnings are in order:

- Like all other native code, it depends on the libc version it was built against (see the discussion in Chapter 13, "Blackdown: The Official Linux Port" in the section "An Important Note About libc"). If you build it under glibc, it will work only with glibc-based X clients. If you build it under libc5, it will work only with libc5-based clients.
- `xwinwrap` performs its magic by meddling with the supposedly opaque X Screen data structure. This can, theoretically, be broken by future changes to X data structures. But such changes would also break many X clients and are unlikely to occur in X11R6.
- `xwinwrap` violates the assumption that the "default" visual is the one used by the root window. In the *unlikely* event that the X client renders to the root window with the default GC, this could lead to incorrect colors or a BadMatch X protocol error.

Finding the Right Visual

`xwinwrap` gives you two capabilities not found in the Java AWT: installing a private colormap and choosing a non-default visual. With the latter, you can select any visual available from the X server (as we discussed previously in the "Usage" section). But there is no guarantee that any available visual will be one the AWT can handle—you may truly be unable to run Java GUI applications.

In that case, the next step is to try running the X server with different settings. The next section discusses how you can experiment with settings that control available display depths.

Experimenting with X Server Settings

As noted in the section "Understanding X Visuals" earlier in this chapter, X servers offer a limited collection of visuals, generally restricted to a single depth. That's a problem with current X servers and current releases of the Sun JDK1.2: There are many visuals with which the AWT simply does not work.

Fortunately, most X servers give you a choice. Even when running with very capable deep hardware, most X servers have the option of running in an 8-bit mode or some other mode that the AWT can handle. It's not a happy solution to give up the capabilities of a deep display, but it is sometimes a necessary one until better AWTs are available.

X Server Options

Two options in the X server command line allow you to experiment with depths and visuals:

```
X -bpp <depth> -cc <class> ...
```

Options:

- `-bpp <depth>`—Set the *bits-per-pixel* display depth.
- `-cc <class>`—Set the default visual class. This doesn't affect which visuals are available, but it does control the choice of default visual. The possible values for <class> are as follows:
  - `0`—StaticGray
  - `1`—GrayScale
  - `2`—StaticColor
  - `3`—PseudoColor
  - `4`—TrueColor
  - `5`—DirectColor

How to Safely Experiment with X Server Invocation

Few users invoke the X server directly. The most common invocations are by the display manager (when the system automatically starts X) or with the `startx` or `xinit` commands (when you start X from the console). This section discusses how to experiment with settings without rendering your console unusable or inaccessible.

X Display Manager

If your X server starts up automatically and presents you with a login screen, you are running an X *display manager*. Every display manager has its own unique configuration procedures. If you are running the classic `xdm` (from the MIT sample implementation), or something based on `xdm`, it is probably relying on a file called `/etc/X11/Xservers` or `/etc/X11/xdm/Xservers` to specify the X server startup command.

If you are a Red Hat 6.0 user, you are probably running the newer `gdm`, which usually takes its X server startup command from `/etc/X11/gdm/gdm.conf`.

Whichever display manager you run, you will need to locate the appropriate configuration file, find the X server launch command, and add the appropriate options. This file is not writable by ordinary users—you must be running as the `root` user to edit it.

But *don't do it yet*! If you put bad values into this file, you may end up with an X server that will not start up and a console that is difficult to log in to. For purposes of experimentation, the following procedure should keep you from getting locked out (most of these operations require you to be running as root; we will use the customary `#` prompt to indicate that root is running the command shell):

1. Change your *init state* to 3 so you can start experimenting, with the following command:

   ```
   bash# /sbin/telinit 3
   ```

   This will immediately kick you out of the X server into a text-mode console. You should be able to log into the console and use the command shell.

   If you get into trouble, see the "Emergency Reboot" section later in the chapter.

2. Knowing now that you can safely work in init state 3, edit the `/etc/inittab` file (again, running as root) and look for a line like this:

   ```
   id:5:initdefault:
   ```

   and change the `5` to a `3`. This ensures that you will automatically enter init state 3 (no X server login) after rebooting.

3. Experiment with X server startup values using `startx` or `xinit` (see the later section "Trying X Server Settings").

4. After you have found X server options that work for you, try them with the X display manager. Edit the appropriate configuration file (again, running as root). For example, if your display manager is using `gdm`, you may need to add options to a line in `/etc/X11/gdm/gdm.conf` that looks like this:

   ```
   0=/usr/bin/X11/X <options...>
   ```

5. Try returning to init state 5, with the following command:

   ```
   bash# /sbin/telinit 5
   ```

   If all goes well, you will see the X login screen and you can start a desktop session. If there is a problem, X may fail to come up or stay up. See the "Emergency Reboot" section. After reboot, you will be back in init state 3 (no X server) and can straighten things out.

6. Everything works? Your desktop is still functional? Edit `/etc/inittab` (again, running as root), change the default init state from `3` back to `5`. You're finished!

These procedures are admittedly overcautious and paranoid, but they should keep you out of trouble.

Trying X Server Settings

If you are not running an X display manager, you probably start up your X server with the `startx` or `xinit` command. The two are similar—`startx` is a small shell wrapper around an `xinit` invocation and is the preferred invocation.

If you normally run an X display manager, but have disabled it for experimentation, **startx** is the command you need to launch an X server.

Synopsis:

```
startx [— <X server options>]
```

The *<X server options>* are passed to the X server; you can use this to try the **-cc** and **-bpp** options described in the section "X Server Options." To try this for the first time, just invoke it by itself:

```
bash$ startx
```

It should start up an X session with a desktop (possibly not the same desktop that runs under your display manager). You should be able to start up a terminal window and to experiment with running Java programs to see whether they work. When you're satisfied that you can use the desktop and run Java programs, exit the X server with the Ctrl+Alt+Backspace key combination and start experimenting with X server settings.

Here are some `startx` invocations worth trying:

```
bash$ startx – -bpp 8
```

This runs the X server in 8-bit mode. It is virtually guaranteed to work and to allow Java AWT applications to run.

```
bash$ startx – -bpp 16
```

This runs the X server in 16-bit mode. This typically offers just one or two visuals. the XFree86 SVGA server currently offers only a TrueColor visual with 5 bits of red, 6 bits of green, and 5 bits of blue. If the AWT is unable to run in this mode, try the next one:

```
bash$ startx – -bpp 15
```

This invocation also runs a 16-bit server but with a visual that (it is reported) makes the AWT happier. The 15-bit TrueColor visual uses 5 bits per primary color and ignores the upper bit of each 2-byte pixel value.

```
bash$ startx – -bpp 24
```

On some server/hardware combinations, this runs a 24-bit server with TrueColor and/or DirectColor visuals with 8 bits per primary color. On some hardware, the result looks strange and terrible and unusable. Try the next option:

```
bash$ startx – -bpp 32
```

When you ask for a 32-bit server, you generally get a 24-bit server that puts its pixels on 32-bit address boundaries. For some types of display hardware, this is exactly the setting you need to get a working 24-bit server.

The other relevant X server option is `-cc`, which sets the default visual class using the values described in the section "X Server Options." You don't usually need this option; it generally defaults to a reasonable value. But it is available for experimentation. By combining it with the `-bpp` option, you fully specify a default visual. For example:

```
bash$ startx -- -bpp 8 -cc 3
```

This invocation runs the X server with a depth of 8 bits per pixel and a default visual of 8-bit PseudoColor.

If you request a default visual that is not available with the requested depth, the server will complain and fail to start up.

With all these options, you should be able to find an X server setting that will support Java applications on your system.

In Case of Emergency

Experimenting with the X server is not dangerous, but it is possible—especially if you use a display manager—to put the machine into a mode that makes it difficult or impossible to log in from the console. If, for example, you choose settings that your desktop cannot handle, you may not be able to proceed past the display manager login screen.

Here are some emergency procedures that should help you out of such a bind. By testing desktop startup, and falling back on these procedures as necessary, you can ensure that your desktop works with new settings before you re-enable automatic X login.

Network Access

Even if you lock yourself out of the console, the rest of your system is fully functional. If your machine is networked and you can log in to it remotely, you can always log in and clean up from a remote terminal.

X Failsafe Mode

You may find that X runs, and the login screen runs, but the desktop will not start up. Perhaps it is unhappy with the default visual. In this case, use the display manager's option to select a "failsafe" session (see Figure 56.2). This starts up a basic X session with a single terminal and no window manager. Failsafe mode is not very friendly, but it is robust and allows you to make fixes to your environment.

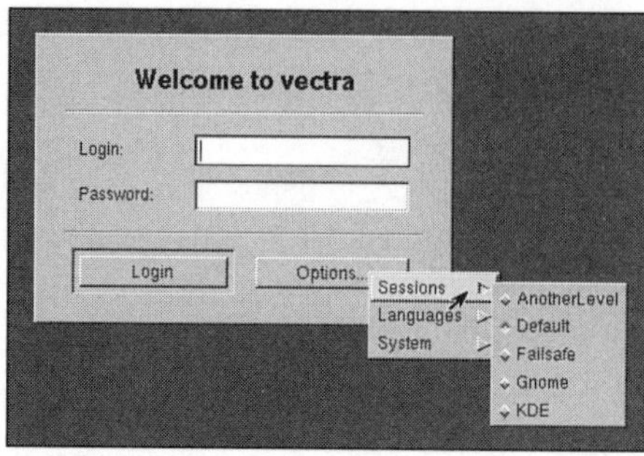

FIGURE 56.2
Most display managers offer you a "failsafe" session.

Emergency Reboot

The two most import key combinations to know in Linux are

- Ctrl+Alt+Delete—This reboots your system. On any reasonably modern Linux, this executes a clean reboot that shuts down your system in an orderly manner before restarting.
- Ctrl+Alt+Backspace—This aborts the X server. The Ctrl+Alt+Delete combination doesn't work when the X server is running—it is intercepted by the server. But you can use Ctrl+Alt+Backspace to abort the X server and then press Ctrl+Alt+Delete to reboot.

If a display manager is running, it will start a new X server moments after you abort. If you are trapped by an X server you cannot use but cannot stop from restarting, you must act quickly: abort the X server and, as soon as it terminates, quickly use Ctrl+Alt+Delete before a new server starts up.

Exercising Full X Capabilities

In its approach to portability, the Java AWT ignores many X Window System capabilities. This isn't a problem for most software most of the time, but sometimes you really need to get beyond the AWT to use X's many ignored capabilities.

You can do this, of course—it's a simple matter of writing Java Native Interface (JNI) code. Java does present a couple of roadblocks, however:

- You cannot get the X Display pointer from Java; you must open your own private connection to the X server.
- You cannot obtain any window IDs from Java. If you want to interact with any of your AWT windows, you will need to search the server's window hierarchy and try to find them.

Sun has indicated, in a FAQ, an intention to address these shortcomings in the future. Until such a future, Java is basically unsupportive of native X Window System access. Any X functionality you implement in native code is, essentially, an independent X client.

The following subsection presents a tool written to solve a specific problem: access to a native X data transfer capability that the AWT does not support. It serves as an illustration of how you can get to non-portable X Window System capabilities ignored by Java.

XClipboard: A JNI-Based Cut-and-Paste Tool

X Window System users are accustomed to two common techniques for transferring data between GUI applications:

- Cut/Copy/Paste—Select text and/or data in one application, press the `Cut` or `Copy` button to copy it to the Clipboard, and transfer it to another application with the `Paste` button. This is identical to a standard technique in the Microsoft Windows environment.
- Selection—Select text and/or data in one application and transfer it to another application (without copying it to the Clipboard) by pressing the middle mouse button. There is no counterpart in the Microsoft Windows environment. Under the X Window System, this technique is commonly used to move data to/from terminal emulators and other X clients without Cut/Copy/Paste capabilities.

From an X programming perspective, these two operations are virtually identical: the only difference is the name of the buffer—`CLIPBOARD` versus `PRIMARY`—used to hold the data.

For Java users, there is another difference: Java supports the first capability (in the `java.awt.datatransfer` package) and ignores the second. `XClipboard` is a JNI-based class that provides some of the missing functionality. You can use `XClipboard` to read text that has been selected, but not copied to the Clipboard, by another X application.

Using XClipboard

The `XClipboard` source supplied on the CD-ROM includes full API `javadoc` information. Briefly, the most interesting methods are as follows:

- `XClipboard()`—The `XClipboard` constructor opens a connection to the X server and allocates resources needed to support the read methods. The finalizer closes the connection.
- `String readPrimarySelectionString()`—This method returns the primary selection: a text string that has been selected by an X application but not necessarily copied to the Clipboard.

Using `XClipboard` from Java is straightforward. This code fragment shows how it can be used to read the current primary selection string:

```
// Create an XClipboard object
XClipboard xc = new XClipboard();
// Read the primary selection string
String selection = xc.readPrimarySelectionString();
```

As with any JNI-based class, you need to ensure that Java can find the native library (`libXClipboard.so`) associated with the class. This is discussed in Chapter 15 in the section "Finding JNI Libraries."

Building XClipboard

`XClipboard` consists of two source files, a `.java` file defining the Java interface and a `.c` file providing the native functionality. Both are provided on the CD-ROM, and listings are provided in Appendix B.

The following sequence of commands can be used to build `XClipboard`:

```
bash$ javac -d . XClipboard.java
bash$ javah -jni com.macmillan.nmeyers.XClipboard
bash$ cc -O -D_REENTRANT -fpic -I$(JAVA_HOME) \
-I$(JAVA_HOME)/include/linux \
-I$(JAVA_HOME)/include/genunix -c XClipboard.c
bash$ cc -O -shared -o libXClipboard.so XClipboard.o -L /usr/X11R6/lib \
-lX11
```

These commands compile the Java source, create a JNI header file, and compile and link the native library.

Server-Side AWT: Using AWT/X Without a Display Device

The UNIX/Linux Java AWT is dependent on the presence of an X server: If you use AWT, you use X. This is true even if you do not create any windows.

The reliance on a graphical device is no different from AWT requirements on Microsoft Windows—except that Windows always has a display. Even Microsoft NT Server, unlike UNIX or Linux servers, requires a display.

AWT's reliance on X has turned out to be a problem for server-side Java. Server-side applications that use the AWT for, say, generation of bitmapped images, cannot run without an X server—even though they do not use a GUI, create any windows, or use any X capabilities at all.

Fortunately, the problem has a simple solution: the X Virtual Frame Buffer server (`Xvfb`), an X server that uses a virtual memory frame buffer instead of a physical graphics device. From the `Xvfb` man page (emphasis added):

> The primary use of this server was intended to be server testing. The mfb or cfb code for any depth can be exercised with this server without the need for real hardware that supports the desired depths. The X community has found many other novel uses for `Xvfb`, including testing clients against unusual depths and screen configurations, doing batch processing with `Xvfb` as a background rendering engine, load testing, as an aid to porting the X server to a new platform, and *providing an unobtrusive way to run applications that don't really need an X server but insist on having one anyway.*

In other words, `Xvfb` is (unintentionally) a made-to-order solution to the server-side AWT problem! `Xvfb` is a standard XFree86 component, available wherever XFree86 is available and found in virtually all Linux distributions.

Running Xvfb

Synopsis:

```
Xvfb [:<display>] [<options>]
```

The `<display>` is the X display number, an integer ≥ 0. Whatever you specify here must also be specified in the `DISPLAY` environment variable read by the Java AWT/X client. Default is 0.

Options:

`Xvfb` has many options, most of them standard X server options. Running it without any options will give you a perfectly usable default—an X server with a depth of 8. But if the defaults are not adequate, the main option of interest is:

- `-screen` *<number>* *<WxHxD>*—Specify the width, height, and depth of a screen in the server. `Xvfb` defaults to driving a single screen of 1280x1024x8. A server can have multiple screens, with different dimensions and depths for each one.

Once started, the `Xvfb` server looks and feels to X clients like any other X server and can easily be used by the AWT for non-GUI applications.

Subtleties

The details of X terminology and how clients find servers on networks can be a bit arcane, and you don't usually have to think about them; when you use the X Window System on a workstation, it all *just works*.

But using `Xvfb` for server-side graphics is different from working at a graphical workstation. These details will help you understand how to run Java in a way that it knows how to find and talk to the `Xvfb` X server.

An X server is, in X terminology, a single *display*, listening at a single network address, controlling one or more *screens*. The TCP address at which an X server listens is 6000+*x*, where *x* is the display number. You probably run your workstation X server at display 0, meaning that it is listening at TCP port 6000. (It may also be listening to single addresses for other protocols, such as UNIX-domain sockets or DECnet addresses.)

X *clients* talk to X *servers* over the network, and they discover how to find X servers through information conveyed in the `DISPLAY` environment variable. All X clients, including the Java AWT, use this variable to figure out how to contact the X server. (When you run an X server on a graphical workstation, this variable is automatically set for use by applications.)

The `DISPLAY` variable value specifying a TCP-based X connection consists of three parts: *<host>*`:`*<display>*`.`*<screen>*, so a `DISPLAY` variable of `foo.bar.com:0.0` will connect to an X server listening at port 6000 on host `foo.bar.com` and use screen #0.

If *<host>* is omitted, the local host is assumed, and the client may connect by TCP, UNIX-domain socket, or any other protocol it chooses.

If `.`*<screen>* is omitted, the X server assumes a default value.

Using `Xvfb` on Servers

To use `Xvfb` on a server

1. Run `Xvfb` at some chosen display number.
2. Set `$DISPLAY` for any clients that will need to use the server.

For example, to support an Apache Web server running servlets, use these commands:

```
bash$ Xvfb :0 &
bash$ export DISPLAY=:0
bash$ /usr/sbin/httpd &
```

Whenever Apache spawns a JVM, that JVM will connect to the X server the first time the AWT is used and remain connected until it terminates.

How Not to Use `Xvfb`

`Xvfb` will work well as a persistent daemon, as shown in the previous Apache example. Do *not* try to start or stop `Xvfb` from individual servlets, JSPs, EJBs, or whatever, because

- It's expensive.
- A running X server requires a unique listener address; you cannot run two display :0 X servers from two concurrent servlets.
- The X connection from AWT to the X server persists for the lifetime of the JVM process, not for the lifetime of a single transaction.

Summary

We have examined a variety of topics related to the use of Java with the X Window System display server. Where Java's portability model abstracts out many details of dealing with X, we must sometimes delve into platform-specific details to get the functionality we need from Java applications on UNIX and Linux.

PART XIII

JAVA PERFORMANCE

This part of the book focuses on the crucial issue of Java runtime performance. We look at the reasons behind Java's well-known performance problems and explore remedies and tools you can use to improve the performance of your own applications.

CHAPTER 57

WHY IS JAVA SLOW?

The reality of Java performance has always lagged the promise—a painful lesson learned by some businesses that made early bets on Java technology. The situation is improving, especially on the commercially important Microsoft Windows platform, but it still has a long way to go. And Linux, which has not enjoyed the focused, expensive tuning efforts lavished on other platforms, lags considerably.

The situation will continue to improve for Linux on several fronts. The free JIT compilers, `tya` and `shujit` (see Chapter 33, "Just-In-Time Compilers"), are constantly being improved. Other JITs are on the way from commercial vendors such as Inprise. The entry of IBM into the Linux JVM arena (see Chapter 25, "The IBM SDK Port") is encouraging. Sun's planned SCSL release of HotSpot (discussed in Chapter 30, "Sun HotSpot Performance Engine") means that it will be ported to Linux. And Linux's growing importance as a strategic platform will undoubtedly attract some new participants to the performance game.

But, for now, Java is slow, and Java on Linux is slower. Why?

Perhaps a better question is, *why not*? Every worthwhile innovation in computer science has extracted a price in performance: there is no shame in this. Table 57.1 shows a few examples from history.

TABLE 57.1 Some Indispensable Software Technologies and Their Costs

Innovation	Performance Penalty
High-level Languages	Less efficient than hand-coded assembler
Time-Sharing	Costs of task-switching
Virtual Memory	Costs of paging
Graphical User Interfaces	Significantgraphical user interfaces. See GUIs (graphical user interfaces) in computation, demands on graphics hardware, and (for networked systems like X) network bandwidth
Object-Oriented Programming	Significant increase in procedure calls, indirect references, and late binding

In all the examples in Table 57.1, the performance penalty has been accepted as a normal cost of progress. Or, to paraphrase the second law of computing: "There Ain't No Such Thing as a Free Lunch."[1]

Java, like other worthwhile innovations, suffers the same problem. The problem has been exacerbated by several factors:

- *Many* of the most interesting research topics from decades of computer science—garbage collection, architecture-neutral code, on-the-fly optimization, runtime validation, object-oriented programming, type safety, and so on—have been crammed into Java.
- Java's rapid acceptance has given it little opportunity to mature.
- Java's rapid growth into the huge, all-encompassing Java 2 platform has afforded little opportunity to focus on the basics.

The result is that Java, like a child prodigy, has been thrust into the limelight at a tender young age. And Sun Microsystems, like an anxious stage parent, has been aggressively overselling Java's strengths long before the product could really deliver. Only recently has Java shown signs of settling down enough to gain some maturity.

One unfortunate promise that continually reappears is that of "native-like" performance—the notion that Java code can reach performance parity with native, compiled, optimized C and C++ applications. This is unlikely; Java is slow for many reasons, two (see Table 57.2) of which are irreducible and fundamental to Java's runtime contract with applications.

[1]The first law, of course, is "Garbage In, Garbage out."

TABLE 57.2 The Two Irreducible Reasons Java Is Slower than C++

Reason	Result
Runtime Checking	Java performs runtime checks on *many* error conditions, including bad array indices, null pointers, and illegal typecasts. C++ does not.
Garbage Collection	No matter how clever and efficient garbage collection algorithms become, they are still not free. CPU cycles spent collecting garbage are cycles not spent running the application. This is more of a problem for busy programs—servers or compute-intensive apps—than for GUI-intensive apps with a lot of idle time.

This *doesn't* mean that you can't write some fast loops or run some impressive benchmarks in Java. But there will always be code for which Java cannot run as fast as compiled languages, and few real-world applications can avoid triggering any runtime checking or garbage collection.

That said, if Java can manage to pioneer some innovative optimization technologies that are beyond the reach of anything achievable by compiled languages, it may manage to overcome these handicaps and achieve the mythical free lunch of performance parity with compiled languages.

In the next sections, we will discuss some of the ***reducible*** reasons for Java performance problems and discuss what (if anything) is being done to address them. The following chapters will offer some hints, tips, and tools to help you overcome some of the problems.

Our intent here is expository, not competitive. This chapter is ***not*** titled "Why C++ Is Better than Java." There are many reasons Java suffers performance problems, some based in design, some in implementation. Understanding those reasons can help you design faster Java applications.

Java Is Interpreted

Bytecode interpretation is slow. This is a reducible problem, thanks to JIT compilation and the more advanced techniques being applied by HotSpot (see Chapter 30, "Sun HotSpot Performance Engine"). But it leads us to another irreducible problem: the time required to perform the compilation and optimization.

Long-lived server processes benefit the most from on-the-fly compilation and optimization, primarily because they are around long enough to effectively amortize the costs of the compilation and to benefit from its results. Server apps also do not present some of the client-side difficulties that are beyond the reach of optimization techniques (see the section "Java AWT's Inefficient Graphics" later in this chapter).

One remaining approach can reduce the problem of dynamic optimization time: ahead-of-time compilation. Examples include `gcj` (see Chapter 31, "`gcj`: A Compiled Java Solution"), which compiles to native code, and TowerJ (discussed in Chapter 32, "TowerJ: A Server-Side Hybrid Java Environment"), which combines native-code compilation and a proprietary runtime engine.

Java's Use of Object References

As discussed in Chapter 2, "Moving from C++ to Java," Java object references feel much like C++ references. They are used in the source code without explicit dereferencing but are handled as pointers under the covers. This does not mean, however, that they *are* pointers. The only guarantee about a reference is that it resolves, somehow, to an object. The devil is in the details.

In the traditional Sun JVM, object references are *not* pointers. They are entities that resolve to pointers (through a map maintained by the JVM), which are then resolved to actual objects. Why the additional indirection? It gives the garbage collector the freedom to move objects: Only the reference map must be updated when an object is moved.

You pay the price of this every time you use an object: two dereferences to get to the data. By contrast, C/C++ data access requires zero dereferences (if you are directly manipulating objects) or one dereference (if you are using pointers or references). The costs rapidly escalate when you use arrays. Consider two comparable situations in C/C++ and Java. This statement (which is valid in both C/C++ and Java) reads a single field from an element in an array of class objects:

```
int y = x[n].number;
```

Here is the cost in the two environments:

- C++—An address calculation and a single dereference.
- Java—Four dereferences: two for the array itself, two for the nth element. Also, additional address calculations, a null-pointer check, and a bounds check.

Sun's HotSpot reduces this cost by removing a level of indirection: Pointers are directly used as object references. This complicates garbage collection, of course. When an object is moved, all live pointers to it must be found and updated.

Java's Limitations on Pointer Use

Java's prohibition against manipulation of data pointers is one of its most important reasons for programmer productivity gains. It eliminates a huge class of errors that cause C/C++ developers countless hours of debugging.

Unfortunately, this comes at a cost. C/C++ programmers have developed an arsenal of pointer-based techniques for enhancing performance, and these techniques are simply not available in Java. Let us consider a simple example: use of pointers to step through an array.

A C/C++ programmer wanting to copy a null-terminated array of bytes might write a loop like this:

```
register char *dest, *source;
.
.
.
while (*dest++ = *source++);
```

An optimizing x86 compiler can implement the while-loop in six instructions: four data instructions (two of which access memory), a test, and a branch. No Java loop, compiled or otherwise, can come remotely close.[2]

There are, of course, several potential errors lurking in this loop: bad pointers, missing null-terminator, writing off the end of allocated memory—any one of which may have root cause or may create havoc in some distant location. Java ends this debugging nightmare but not without depriving developers of valuable performance tools.

Java AWT's Inefficient Graphics

Before the Java 2 Platform, Java relied heavily on the native capabilities of the host graphics platform. This engendered no shortage of problems (as discussed in Chapter 3, "A Look at the Java Core Classes," in the section "Package `javax.swing`"), but it at least had the effect of delegating the heavy lifting to reasonably well-tuned, optimized, native-code graphics and GUI libraries and window systems.

With the advent of Java2D and Swing, Java has assumed a substantial portion of the graphics and GUI burden. Some of the results follow:

- Much of the rendering formerly performed by the underlying window system is now performed on memory buffers by slower algorithms running in the JVM and then blitted (bit-for-bit copied) over the network to the display. This leads to higher computation, memory, and (for X environments) higher network costs for graphics. For some operations, like rendering of text, the slowdown is dramatic.
- Swing's "lightweight"[3] approach to GUI components moves the burden of event dispatching (and other window system responsibilities) from native X server code to slower Java code in the JVM. It also increases network traffic between X server and client.
- Various inefficiences lurk in event-handling: It's not uncommon to see an excessive number of repaint requests.

Listing 57.1 shows a small benchmark that dramatically illustrates the changes between releases. FontPerf is a JDK1.1/JDK1.2 Swing-based utility that measures text refresh performance.

---

[2]Experimentation with gcj suggests that a best-case, optimized, compiled version of comparable Java code would take about 3x the time of this loop—the additional cost coming from increased indirection and run-time checking.

[3]The term lightweight to describe toolkit architectures such as Swing has been badly misused in recent years. We will explore the costs of lightweight toolkits in more detail in Chapter 58, "A Heavy Look at Lightweight Toolkits."

LISTING 57.1 FontPerf.java

```
package com.macmillan.nmeyers;
import java.awt.*;
import javax.swing.*;
import java.awt.event.*;
import java.util.*;

class FontPerf extends JFrame
{
    int nReps;
    int countdown = 0;
    Date starttime;
    FontPerf(String fontname,
             int nCols,
             int nRows,
             int nr,
             boolean doublebuffer)
    {
        super("Font Rendering Performance Test");
        nReps = nr;
        if (!doublebuffer)
        {
            // Turn off double-buffering so we can watch rendering
            getRootPane().setDoubleBuffered(false);
            ((JComponent)getContentPane()).setDoubleBuffered(
          ➥false);
        }

        // Get all available font families for JDK1.2
        try
        {
            GraphicsEnvironment.getLocalGraphicsEnvironment().
                getAvailableFontFamilyNames();
        }
        catch (NoClassDefFoundError e)  {}

        JTextArea textarea = new JTextArea(nRows, nCols);
        textarea.setFont(Font.decode(fontname));
        getContentPane().add(textarea,
                             BorderLayout.CENTER);
        JButton start = new JButton("Run Test");
        getContentPane().add(start, BorderLayout.SOUTH);
        String testString = "";
        while (testString.length() < nCols)
            testString += "ABCDEFGHIJKLMNOPQRSTUVWXYZ0123456789";
        testString = testString.substring(0, nCols);
        for (int row = 0; row < nRows; row++)
            textarea.append(testString + "\n");
        start.addActionListener(new ActionListener() {
            public void actionPerformed(ActionEvent e)
            {
                countdown = nReps;
                starttime = new Date();
```

```
                repaint();
            }
        });
        addWindowListener(new WindowAdapter() {
            public void windowClosing(WindowEvent ev)
            {
                System.exit(0);
            }
        });
    }
    public void paint(Graphics g)
    {
        super.paint(g);
        if (countdown > 0)
        {
            if (—countdown > 0) repaint();
            else
            {
                System.out.println("Time for " + nReps + " repaints: " +
                                   (new Date().getTime() -
                                    starttime.getTime()) + " ms");
                System.out.flush();
            }
        }
    }
    private static void usage()
    {
        System.err.println("Usage: FontPerf [-nodoublebuffer] fontname" +
                           " columns rows repetitions");
        System.exit(1);
    }
    public static void main(String[] argv)
    {
        boolean doublebuffer = true;
        int startArray = 0;
        if (argv.length > 0 && argv[0].equals("-nodoublebuffer"))
        {
            doublebuffer = false;
            startArray++;
        }
        if (argv.length - startArray !=  4) { usage(); }
        int nCols = Integer.parseInt(argv[startArray + 1]);
        int nRows = Integer.parseInt(argv[startArray + 2]);
        int nReps = Integer.parseInt(argv[startArray + 3]);
        FontPerf fontperf = new FontPerf(argv[startArray], nCols, nRows,
                                         nReps, doublebuffer);
        fontperf.pack();
        fontperf.setVisible(true);
    }
}
```

Synopsis:

```
java com.macmillan.nmeyers.FontPerf [-nodoublebuffer] <font> <columns> \
<rows> <repetitions>
```

This creates a Swing text editor, in the specified font, with the specified number of rows and columns. Below the text editor, a `Run Test` button is used to start the test. The test repaints the text editor for the specified number of repetitions, timing the activity and sending the result to stdout.

The optional `-nodoublebuffer` argument disables Swing's default double-buffering behavior.

Dependencies:

When running under JDK1.1, there is an additional dependency on the Swing 1.1 toolkit.

Example:

```
java com.macmillan.nmeyers.FontPerf serif-plain-20 30 10 50
```

This example creates a 30x10-character text editor (see Figure 57.1). Clicking the `Run Test` button will repaint the editor 50 times and send the elapsed time to stdout.

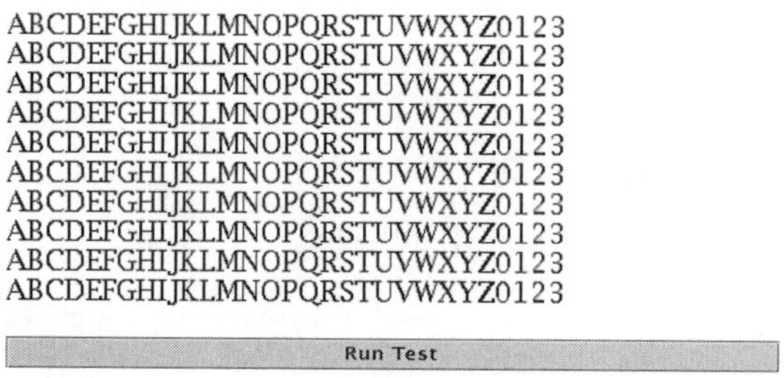

ABCDEFGHIJKLMNOPQRSTUVWXYZ0123
ABCDEFGHIJKLMNOPQRSTUVWXYZ0123
ABCDEFGHIJKLMNOPQRSTUVWXYZ0123
ABCDEFGHIJKLMNOPQRSTUVWXYZ0123
ABCDEFGHIJKLMNOPQRSTUVWXYZ0123
ABCDEFGHIJKLMNOPQRSTUVWXYZ0123
ABCDEFGHIJKLMNOPQRSTUVWXYZ0123
ABCDEFGHIJKLMNOPQRSTUVWXYZ0123
ABCDEFGHIJKLMNOPQRSTUVWXYZ0123
ABCDEFGHIJKLMNOPQRSTUVWXYZ0123

Run Test

FIGURE 57.1
FontPerf test window. The button starts a font-drawing benchmark.

The results tell us a great deal about Graphics2D. Because JDK licensing terms set limits on publication of benchmark results, you will need to run this test (found on the CD-ROM) yourself to get numbers. You will discover a performance range of approximately two orders of magnitude. Table 57.3 ranks the performances of different environments.

TABLE 57.3 Relative Performance of JDK1.1 and JDK1.2 Text Rendering

Environment	Speed	Comment
JDK1.1, no double-buffering	Fastest	
JDK1.1, double-buffering		Double-buffering involves writing to an offscreen X buffer, then blitting to the window. It creates the appearance of smoother graphics but at a performance cost.

JDK1.2, double-buffering		Graphics2D renders to a buffer in the JVM, then blits the result to the window.
JDK1.2, no double-buffering	Slowest	Graphics2D is optimized around client-side rendering and renders inefficiently directly to the X server. This case is far outside Graphics2D's design center.

The next few chapters will explore related issues, workarounds, and tools you can apply to this problem.

Java's Increased Memory Use

Java objects take more space than equivalent C++ objects. More space means more memory bandwidth demand, more cache stress, more paging. The cost goes directly to the bottom line in performance. Table 57.4 shows some causes of heavy Java memory use.

TABLE 57.4 Java Memory Demands

Cause	Cost
Headers associated with every object	3 machine-words for every object in classic JVM, 2 in HotSpot.
Object reference map	In the classic JVM (but not HotSpot), every object requires an entry in the object reference map.
Arrays are expensive: Java demands an extra level of indirection in allocating and referencing array elements.	Compare costs of allocating a 100-element array of object Foobar: C++: A single heap allocation 100*sizeof(Foobar) bytes long. Heap overhead for managing a single allocation. Java: 101 heap allocations, consisting of • A 100-element array of Foobar references. • 100 Foobar objects with their headers. Additional costs are 101 entries in the object reference map and heap overhead for managing 101 allocations. Another cost, decreased locality, is discussed in the following section, "Poor Memory Locality."

Java's Poor Memory Locality

When applications grow to consume any significant amount of memory, they encounter the awful truth of modern computer programming: CPUs are fast; memory is slow. A substantial amount of engineering has gone into modern caching architectures to solve the problem and to ensure that the memory you are using, and are about to use, is cached near the CPU in fast (and expensive) RAM.

The principle behind modern memory architectures and memory management code is *locality*: the notion that the memory you are going to use is not far from memory you have recently used. Programs that violate this principle tend to suffer terrible problems with memory latency.

How much does locality matter? In Appendix B we present a simple C program, `memstress`, that stresses a block of memory by accessing it in optimal and nonoptimal patterns. Figure 57.2 shows some results from test runs on a 200Mhz PPro Linux system with 128MB of RAM.

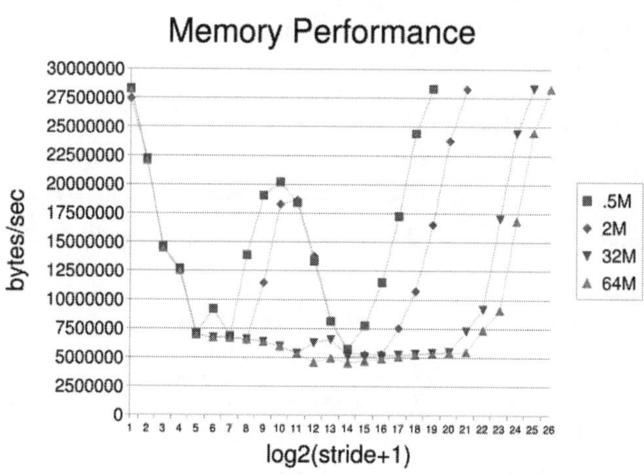

FIGURE 57.2
Results of running `memstress` on a 128MB 200Mhz PPro system.

Each curve in figure 57.2 represents a different allocated memory block size; points on the X axis represent different stride values used in stepping through memory. Everything fits in RAM—there is no paging happening—so results reflect the effectiveness of caching on memory latency.

The effect of caching based on locality is clearly evident: Optimal memory access patterns run nearly *6x* faster than worst-case memory access patterns. The differences become much more dramatic, of course, when memory size increases beyond available RAM and paging occurs.

In C/C++ environments, where programs own a great deal of memory management responsibility, developers can exert control over memory layout to favor locality. It is not uncommon for large-memory programs to implement their own heap management (C++ offers excellent facilities to support this), leading to big improvements in locality and memory performance.[4]

Java's approach to memory management runs afoul of locality in at least three ways:

- Arrays of objects are allocated much less optimally. An array of C++ objects is allocated with a single `new()` call, resulting in a tight, contiguous block of objects. Java's approach to populating arrays, with one `new()` per object, can scatter array contents through the address space.
- The lack of automatic object allocation means that the contents of individual objects can be scattered through the address space. A C++ object containing a 100-integer array might look like this:

```
class foo
{
    .
    .
    int X[100];
    .
    .
};
```

  resulting in a 100-word block of memory contiguous with the object's other storage. The Java equivalent

```
class Foo
{
    .
    .
    int[] X;
    .
    .
}
```

  requires the array to be separately allocated at construction (or later), resulting in non-contiguous storage of object data.
- Java is hostile to custom heap management. Memory layout is under the control of the allocators and the garbage collection system, and Java programmers are deprived of another technique available to C/C++ programmers.

---

[4]How big? In some businesses, where deals are made and broken by competitive benchmarking, .5% is substantial. But better results are common, and it is not unheard of for clever heap management to result in gains on the order of 2x, 10x, or 100x. Exact details are generally closely guarded secrets in competitive businesses.

There is an opportunity lurking here for Java: The garbage collector routinely relocates blocks of memory to squeeze out dead memory. If it could also base such decisions on locality, it could achieve a unique form of dynamic optimization beyond the reach of compiled languages.

Java Class-Loading Expense

Java application startup involves loading application classes and core classes. Of the 4,273 public and nonpublic classes that make up the JDK1.2 core, 180 must be loaded to run "Hello World" (44 under JDK1.1), and approximately 450 must be loaded for a simple AWT application (about 140 under JDK1.1).

Loading of core classes is analogous to a native application's loading of shared libraries, but with some handicaps:

- With native applications, many commonly used shared libraries are already loaded and mapped into shared memory before an application starts. There is not (currently) any comparable scheme for Java. The JVM must load all classes it needs from the class path into memory.
- Typical native applications depend on, at most, a dozen or two shared libraries. Java must load hundreds of classes, each involving retrieval and possible decompression from a file system or archive.

The process is impressively fast and well-tuned, given the magnitude of the problem. But there is a startup delay, much more noticeable with JDK1.2 than JDK1.1, as classes are loaded.

CHAPTER 58

A HEAVY LOOK AT LIGHTWEIGHT TOOLKITS

It's no secret that Swing is a *lightweight GUI toolkit*. Lightweight toolkits are not new: Swing is not the first for Java (Biss-AWT, a toolkit from the authors of Kaffe, has been around for a while—and Kaffe's AWT *is* lightweight), and it's not the first for the X Window System.

The term *lightweight* implies that resources of some sort—space, computational, or whatever—are saved by using such an architecture. This is true to an extent, although the term has lost much of its original meaning.

This chapter explores lightweight toolkits: what they are, why they are used, and why they can be so expensive.

Subtleties

Throughout this chapter we use the terms *client* and *server* in the X Window System sense. A *client* is an application needing graphical display services; a *server* is the device providing graphical display services.

This definition makes perfect semantic sense, but it also creates some confusion. In many internet and intranet environments, a *server* is a large central host and a *client* is an inexpensive desktop computer. In typical X environments, the *X server* runs on an inexpensive desktop computer while large *X clients* (such as high-powered design tools) often run on large computation servers.

Definition and History

A lightweight GUI component is one that does not consume window resources in the underlying window system. A lightweight GUI toolkit is a toolkit populated by lightweight GUI components.

Notice that we have defined "lightweight" in terms of window system resources. As we will see in the discussion to follow, lightweight GUIs work by moving some resource requirements from the window system to the application—sometimes at considerable expense.

Let us illustrate with an example from the Motif toolkit. Listings 58.1 and 58.2 are two nearly identical Motif programs—with only the differences shown for the second one.

LISTING 58.1 `motif1.c`, a Simple Motif-based X Application

```
#include <Xm/Form.h>
#include <Xm/PushB.h>
#include <Xm/Label.h>
#include <Xm/Separator.h>

int main(int argc, String *argv)
{
    XtAppContext context;
    Arg args[20];
    Widget top, form, label, sep, button;
    XmString str;
    int i;

    top = XtAppInitialize(&context, "MotifDemo", 0, 0, &argc,
➥argv, 0, 0, 0);

    form = XmCreateForm(top, "mainform", args, 0);
    XtManageChild(form);

    i = 0;
    XtSetArg(args[i], XmNtopAttachment, XmATTACH_FORM); i++;
    XtSetArg(args[i], XmNleftAttachment, XmATTACH_FORM); i++;
    XtSetArg(args[i], XmNrightAttachment, XmATTACH_FORM); i++;
    str = XmStringCreateSimple("Please Press Button");
    XtSetArg(args[i], XmNlabelString, str); i++;
    label = XmCreateLabel(form, "label", args, i);
    XmStringFree(str);
    XtManageChild(label);

    i = 0;
    XtSetArg(args[i], XmNtopAttachment, XmATTACH_WIDGET); i++;
    XtSetArg(args[i], XmNtopWidget, label); i++;
    XtSetArg(args[i], XmNleftAttachment, XmATTACH_FORM); i++;
    XtSetArg(args[i], XmNrightAttachment, XmATTACH_FORM); i++;
    sep = XmCreateSeparator(form, "separator", args, i);
    XtManageChild(sep);

```

```
    i = 0;
    XtSetArg(args[i], XmNtopAttachment, XmATTACH_WIDGET); i++;
    XtSetArg(args[i], XmNtopWidget, sep); i++;
    XtSetArg(args[i], XmNleftAttachment, XmATTACH_FORM); i++;
    XtSetArg(args[i], XmNrightAttachment, XmATTACH_FORM); i++;
    str = XmStringCreateSimple("OK");
    XtSetArg(args[i], XmNlabelString, str); i++;
    button = XmCreatePushButton(form, "pushbutton", args, i);
    XmStringFree(str);
    XtManageChild(button);

    XtRealizeWidget(top);
    XtAppMainLoop(context);
}
```

LISTING 58.2 `motif2.c`, Showing Only Differences (Highlighted) from the Preceding `motif1.c`

```
#include <Xm/Form.h>
#include <Xm/PushBG.h>
#include <Xm/LabelG.h>
#include <Xm/SeparatoG.h>
,
,
,
    label = XmCreateLabelGadget(form, "label", args, i);
,
,
,
    sep = XmCreateSeparatorGadget(form, "separator", args, i);
,
,
,
    button = XmCreatePushButtonGadget(form, "pushbutton", args,
➥i);
,
,
,
```

Figure 58.1 shows the GUI for both programs: A label, a thin horizontal separator, and a pushbutton.

FIGURE 58.1
GUIs from the two programs, run with the Lesstif library.

The two GUIs are virtually indistinguishable, but there is a big difference. The first is built from heavyweight Motif *widgets*, the second from lightweight Motif *gadgets*. Listings 58.3 and 58.4 show the results of running the `xwininfo` utility on the two GUIs.

LISTING 58.3 Using `xwininfo` to Reveal `motif1`'s Window Hierarchy Shows One Window Per Component

```
bash$ xwininfo -tree

xwininfo: Please select the window about which you
          would like information by clicking the
          mouse in that window.

xwininfo: Window id: 0x300001a "motif1"

  Root window id: 0x2a (the root window) (has no name)
  Parent window id: 0x2401e86 "kwm"
     1 child:
     0x300001b (has no name): ()  118x44+0+0  +183+55
        3 children:
        0x300001e (has no name): ()  118x17+0+0  +183+55
        0x300001d (has no name): ()  118x2+0+17  +183+72
        0x300001c (has no name): ()  118x25+0+19  +183+74
```

LISTING 58.4 Using `xwininfo` to Reveal `motif2`'s Window Hierarchy Shows a Single Window Holding All Components

```
bash$ xwininfo -tree

xwininfo: Please select the window about which you
          would like information by clicking the
          mouse in that window.

xwininfo: Window id: 0x4c0001a "motif2"

  Root window id: 0x2a (the root window) (has no name)
  Parent window id: 0x2401e94 "kwm"
     1 child:
     0x4c0001b (has no name): ()  118x44+0+0  +347+57
```

We see that `motif1` has a relatively deep and complex window hierarchy. Every component—label, separator, and pushbutton—occupies a window in the X server. By contrast, all the `motif2` components live in a single window. In `motif2`, the GUI components are manipulated as separate components on the client side, but are drawn into a single window on the X server.

What makes `motif2` a *lightweight* solution? Is it lightweight because fewer X server resources are used? By the definition at the beginning of this section, the answer is yes. But in terms of overall resource use, it doesn't seem any lighter. Now the client must track a window hierarchy that the server *was* tracking. Overall system resource use is unchanged.

So where *is* the light in lightweight? The answer comes from the early days of Motif, when the X Window System was much less mature and developers were first starting to build complex GUIs with Motif. These GUIs, like today's complex GUIs, were loaded with menus, text areas, buttons, labels—the usual plethora of components. Whenever such an application would start up, a terrible thing happened: The X server was brought to its knees as hundreds of windows were created. Users watched in helpless rage as many KB of X protocol were exchanged, many KB of data structures were allocated in the X server, and the workstation started to thrash.

The answer was the invention of Motif gadgets, lightweight counterparts to the heavyweight widgets. Gadget versions were defined for a handful of heavily used Motif components (label, separator, and four types of buttons), and applications were able to reduce the horrendous startup costs by reducing window usage on the X server.

The early results were promising, but a funny thing happened on the way to lightweight toolkits: memory became more plentiful, CPUs got faster, VM management got better, networking code improved, and many bloated data structures in the X server went on a diet. Lightweight components lost some of their lustre, and their other costs (see "The Costs of Lightweight Components" later in this chapter) were beginning to become evident.

Now, years later, Motif still supports only a handful of lightweight components (a recent release added an icon gadget), and it and many other X toolkits (Tk, Qt, GTK+, and so on) thrive as heavyweight GUI toolkits.

Subtleties

Sun's AWT component set on UNIX/Linux is built on top of the Motif toolkit and uses the term *peer* to describe the Motif component that corresponds to an AWT component—`java.awt.Button` uses an `XMPushButton` as a peer, `java.awt.TextArea` uses `XMText`, and so on. Similar peer relationships exist with other windowing systems. By contrast, Swing components do not have peers.

On a quick reading, it would seem that the presence or absence of peers makes a Java toolkit heavyweight or lightweight. Not so: What makes AWT "heavyweight" is that the underlying toolkit uses server-side windows for each of its components. If Motif offered enough lightweight components, AWT/Motif could have been fully lightweight.

Conversely, Swing *could* have been implemented as a heavyweight toolkit by building its components with raw native windows instead of trying to use existing GUI components. This would have imposed some design constraints, but many fewer than are imposed by Motif and Win32 GUIs. That was not done; Swing was designed with features unavailable in many windowing systems (such as the glass pane), and is thus irreversibly a lightweight toolkit.

The Costs of Lightweight Components

Lightweight GUI components were not exactly discredited as X matured—they offer some interesting advantages—but their benefit to window system performance has turned out to be minimal. They also turn out to have some significant additional costs. This section explores those costs by describing some typical window system activities and how they are handled by heavyweight versus lightweight GUI components.

For purposes of this discussion, we create a simple GUI component, consisting of a main window containing a text field and a pushbutton (see Figure 58.2). Additional semantics are that the cursor changes to a text cursor when the mouse enters the text field, and the pushbutton border lights up when the mouse enters the button area.

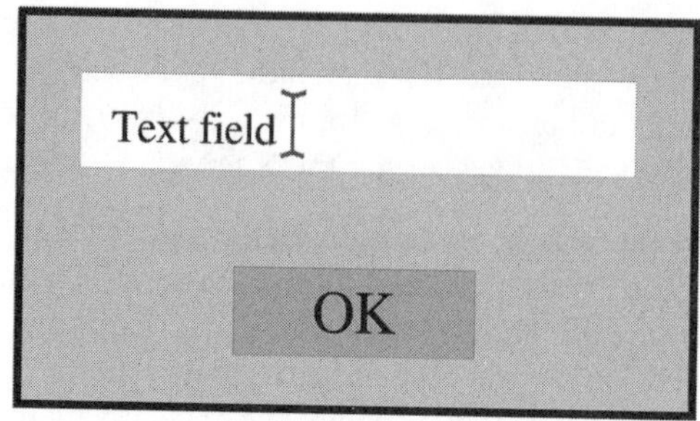

FIGURE 58.2
A simple GUI for illustration of lightweight components.

One additional assumption for this comparison is that the lightweight toolkit renders with normal X protocol and does not (as in Swing) render into a client-side buffer that is then blitted (copied bit-for-bit) over the network to the server. (The Swing approach adds an additional performance hit beyond this discussion.)

Repainting Window Backgrounds

The three components shown here—main window, text field, and pushbutton—have different backgrounds. Table 58.1 shows what occurs if the background needs to be repainted (perhaps as a result of exposing the window).

TABLE 58.1 Heavyweight Versus Lightweight Repainting Backgrounds

Heavyweight Toolkit	Lightweight Toolkit
Each window has a background color or image associated with it in the X server. The X server paints each background without any client interaction.	Window background is repainted by protocol requests sent by the client. Possible side effect is to disturb other windows (see "Rendering to Obscured Windows" in this chapter).

The increased costs of the lightweight toolkit are additional protocol requests on the network, increased latency, and a slower path through the X server (processing of a client drawing request) to repaint the background.

Rendering to Obscured Windows

In our example, the main window is partially obscured by two other components. Table 58.2 shows what occurs when rendering to that window—whether painting the background or rendering more interesting contents:

TABLE 58.2 Heavyweight Versus Lightweight Rendering to Obscured Windows

Heavyweight Toolkit	Lightweight Toolkit
For all rendering, the X server uses a clipping mask (typically with help from hardware) that prevents it from disturbing other windows. X clients painting into the main window cannot disturb the text field or the pushbutton.	When painting to the main window, the client must either avoid disturbing the other components or repaint them. Options include: • Setting a clipping mask in the server • Client-side logic to avoid drawing over the other components, possibly by painting in sections • Repainting the other components after rendering to the main window

The increased costs of the lightweight toolkit are additional protocol requests on the network, management of client clipping masks, and possible repaints of components that would not otherwise require repainting.

Typing into Text Areas

The text field accepts keyboard input according to one of two models:

- Implicit focus—Keyboard input is accepted while the mouse is in the text area.
- Explicit focus—Keyboard input is accepted when the client gives the text area the focus, regardless of mouse position.

Table 58.3 shows how keyboard input is handled.

TABLE 58.3 Heavyweight Versus Lightweight Keyboard Input

Heavyweight Toolkit	Lightweight Toolkit
For either focus model, keyboard input is sent to the client only when the text field is accepting input.	All keyboard input is sent to the client, which must implement the focus model and decide whether to accept the input and dispatch it to the text field.

The increased costs of the lightweight toolkit are unneeded keypress events on the network and additional client-side logic to process the keys.

Handling Exposure Events

An exposure event is a message from server to client that part or all of a window has been uncovered and needs to be repainted. For windows with a background, the X server will repaint the background before sending the event. Table 58.4 shows how exposure events are handled.

TABLE 58.4 Heavyweight Versus Lightweight Handling of Exposure Events

Heavyweight Toolkit	Lightweight Toolkit
An exposure event is sent for each window that has been exposed. Each event results in dispatching a repaint to the corresponding component.	An exposure event is sent for the single application window. The client must ascertain which components are affected (based on the position and size of the exposed area) and dispatch repaints accordingly.

The increased costs of the lightweight toolkit are complex dispatching logic on the client side, mimicking behavior that is already provided by the X server. Can the client do it as efficiently as an X server that's been continuously tuned for years?

The increased costs of the heavyweight toolkit are additional exposure events on the network.

Handling Mouse Clicks

The user activates the GUI pushbutton with a click of the mouse. Table 58.5 shows how it's done.

TABLE 58.5 Heavyweight Versus Lightweight Handling of Mouse Clicks

Heavyweight Toolkit	Lightweight Toolkit
The client registers interest in mouse events for the window containing the button. If the mouse is clicked in that window (but not outside it), an event is sent to the client for dispatching to the corresponding component.	The client registers interest in mouse events for the entire application window. When an event is received, the client compares the location of the click to the dimensions of the button, deciding whether to accept it and dispatch to the component, or ignore it.

The increase costs of the lightweight toolkit are additional protocol on the network and complex dispatching logic on the client side, mimicking behavior that is already provided by the X server.

Associating Cursors with Windows

When the mouse moves into the text field, the cursor changes to the familiar text "I-beam" and changes back to the default cursor when it leaves. Table 58.6 shows how it's done.

TABLE 58.6 Heavyweight Versus Lightweight Associating Cursors with Windows

Heavyweight Toolkit	Lightweight Toolkit
The client associates a cursor with the text field's window, and the X server handles everything without client involvement.	The client tracks all mouse movement in the application. When the mouse enters the area corresponding to the text field, the client sends a cursor-change request. When the mouse leaves, it sends another cursor-change request.

The increased costs of the lightweight toolkit are much additional protocol on the network—mouse events and cursor requests, increased latency, and additional logic in the client, mimicking behavior that is already provided by the X server.

Flashing a Window Border

When the mouse moves into the button area, the button's border lights up. Table 58.7 shows the details.

TABLE 58.7 Heavyweight Versus Lightweight Window Border Flashing

Heavyweight Toolkit	Lightweight Toolkit
The client registers interest in cursor enter- and leave-events for the window containing the button. When those events are received, the client performs the appropriate rendering.	The client tracks all mouse movement in the application. When the mouse enters or leaves the area corresponding to the button, the client performs the appropriate rendering.

The increased costs of the lightweight toolkit are much additional protocol on the network—frequent mouse motion instead of infrequent enter- and leave-events, increased latency, and additional logic in the client, mimicking behavior that is already provided by the X server.

The Bottom Line: Advantages and Disadvantages of Lightweight Toolkits

As the preceding section makes clear, lightweight toolkits earn their name by offloading activity from the windowing system to the network and the application—often at great expense. But lightweight toolkits offer some unique advantages, specifically:

- Startup performance—Complex heavyweight GUIs require heavy client/server interaction and extensive server window allocation at startup; complex lightweight GUIs do not. (As discussed previously, this has become a minor point.)
- Feature flexibility—Lightweight toolkits may implement features not available from the underlying window system. An example is the glass pane found in several Swing components—there is no exact counterpart in the X Window System.
- Feature independence—Lightweight toolkits may implement features not available across all display devices. If, theoretically speaking, the X server offered an extension to support alpha-blending, it would only find support among high-end displays. A client-side "lightweight" implementation of alpha-blending wouldn't care.
- Load balancing—If the client is running on a much more powerful machine than that running the X server, it might better handle the demands of storing and managing the large window hierarchy. (Current practice suggests, however, that this is not a concern for modern X servers running on modern machines.)

Lightweight toolkits suffer the following disadvantages:

- Increased network traffic between client and server compared to heavyweight toolkits.
- Increased latency as certain server-side activities are moved to the client side.
- Lightweight toolkits cannot take advantage of display hardware performance features (as in the alpha-blending example in the previous list).
- Runtime performance can suffer if window, rendering, or buffering operations are less efficient in the client's implementation than in the X server.

The final disadvantage—efficiency of operations—is a culprit in Swing's performance problems. Many operations that could be handled by well-tuned, optimized native code in the X server are instead handled by Java code on the client side: untuned code running in a slow execution environment. Future tuning efforts should improve the Swing story.

Which is ultimately best, lightweight or heavyweight toolkits? It's a moot point: with lightweight toolkits offering features otherwise unavailable from GUIs, they are not about to abandon those features in the interest of runtime performance. In the long run, Swing will benefit—as the X Window System benefited, as Motif benefited, as Microsoft Windows benefited—from the relentless upward march of clockspeeds, memory density, and network bandwidth.

What About Non-X Environments?

This discussion has been highly X-focused, as befits the Linux platform, but what is its relevance to Java in general?

The lightweight concept certainly applies beyond the confines of the X window system. This quote from Sun (which appears in the JDK1.2 documentation bundle, in `docs/guide/awt/designspec/lightweights.html`) sheds some platform-neutral light on Java's notion of lightweight:

> The Lightweight UI Framework is very simple—it boils down to the ability to now directly extend the `java.awt.Component` and `java.awt.Container` classes in order to create components which do not have native opaque windows associated with them.

This proposition, whether applied to X's client/server architecture, Microsoft Windows, or any other environment, means assuming application-side control of windows and application-side duplication of behavior that already exists in the underlying windowing system. Although Swing's performance challenges on X are more extreme than in some other environments, they are not unique to X: The costs discussed in this chapter apply everywhere.

Swing is an excellent toolkit that deserves to succeed. Whether this happens will depend in large part on how effectively it, and Java2D, can be tuned.

Summary

This chapter has discussed lightweight GUI toolkits, with a focus on understanding the performance challenges faced by Swing and comparable toolkits.

CHAPTER 59

AN APPROACH TO IMPROVING GRAPHICAL RENDERING PERFORMANCE

This chapter explores some techniques that I have found useful for improving performance of my AWT-based Swing-based applications under JDK1.2: backing store and event coalescence.

Platforms: JDK1.2

Both techniques discussed in this chapter are well-established routes to improving performance, although Java is not completely supportive of them. The following sections explain why and how to use them.

`Spiral0`: An Introduction

We begin this exploration by introducing a graphics-intensive JDK1.2 application called `Spiral0`.

Synopsis:

`java com.macmillan.nmeyers.Spiral0` *`<width>`* *`<height>`*

`Spiral0` creates a Swing-based `JFrame` window, at the specified size, containing a spiral graphic (see Figure 59.1).

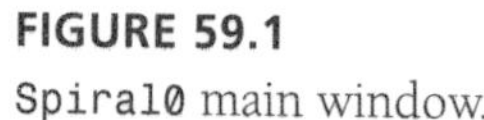

FIGURE 59.1
Spiral0 main window.

The spiral graphic in Figure 59.1 contains two characteristics of particular interest:

- It uses antialiasing, so graphics rendering is expensive.
- It redraws the entire image for every repaint event, as do many real-world applications that lack the capability to refresh just a portion of their rendering area.

An additional characteristic found in many real-world applications, but not in `Spiral0`, is

- The computation required to repaint the window, outside graphical rendering, is expensive.

In other words, `Spiral0` is a simple model for graphical applications that do not want to repaint any more than is absolutely necessary.

`Spiral0` sports another feature to assist in this chapter's activities: every time it repaints, it times the activity and prints out the results.

Using `Spiral0` to Understand Repaint Behavior

After starting `Spiral0`, drag another window over it and watch how it repaints (you will need to have your window manager configured for opaque window moves). In Figure 59.2, a partial screen dump shows the effects of dragging my terminal window over the `Spiral0` window.

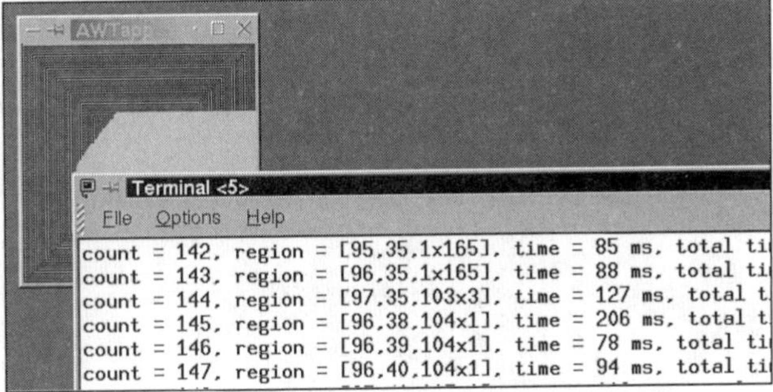
Terminal <5>
File Options Help
count = 142, region = [95,35,1x165], time = 85 ms, total ti
count = 143, region = [96,35,1x165], time = 88 ms, total ti
count = 144, region = [97,35,103x3], time = 127 ms, total t
count = 145, region = [96,38,104x1], time = 206 ms, total t
count = 146, region = [96,39,104x1], time = 78 ms, total ti
count = 147, region = [96,40,104x1], time = 94 ms, total ti

FIGURE 59.2
The effect of dragging an obscuring window over `Spiral0`.

You can see many white areas in Figure 59.2 that have been recently exposed but not yet repainted. The text in the terminal window shows that many repaint events are taking place.

An examination of the timing output shows that the following activities are taking place:

- At startup, the spiral is painted in its entirety several times.
- Whenever areas of the spiral are covered and then exposed, many repaints are generated for small strips of the window (that is, the clipping area in the `Graphics` object passed to `paintComponent()` is a small strip).
- Looking at the repaint times[1], we see that small repaints are faster than full-window repaints. Although the application is redrawing the entire spiral every time, `Graphics2D` is evidently ignoring some of the drawing that occurs outside the clipping area.

Despite the modest internal AWT performance trick observed in the last observation, there is obviously much inefficiency here and far too many repaint requests taking place.

`Spiral0` Source

Listing 59.1 shows the `Spiral0` source.

LISTING 59.1 `Spiral0.java`

```
package com.macmillan.nmeyers;
import java.awt.*;
import java.awt.event.*;
import javax.swing.*;
import java.util.*;

class Spiral0 extends JFrame
{
    Spiral spiral;
    Spiral0(int w, int h)
```

continued on next page

[1]The times reported by this program are useful in a rough way, but be wary of giving them too much significance. It is impossible to accurately time events this brief with the system clock.

continued from previous page

```
    {
        getContentPane().add(spiral = new Spiral(w, h));
        pack();
        setVisible(true);
        addWindowListener(new WindowAdapter() {
            public void windowClosing(WindowEvent ev)
            {
                System.exit(0);
            }
        });
    }
    class Spiral extends JComponent
    {
        int width, height;
        int repaintCount = 0;
        long repaintTime = 0;
        Spiral(int w, int h)
        {
            width = w;
            height = h;
        }
        public Dimension getPreferredSize()
        {
            return new Dimension(width, height);
        }
        public void paintComponent(Graphics g)
        {
            ((Graphics2D)g).setRenderingHint(
                RenderingHints.KEY_ANTIALIASING,
                RenderingHints.VALUE_ANTIALIAS_ON);
            Rectangle bounds = g.getClipBounds();
            g.clearRect(bounds.x, bounds.y, bounds.width, bounds.height);
            ((Graphics2D)g).scale(1.0 / 1.1, 1.0 / 1.1);
            Dimension d = getSize();
            Date date1 = new Date();
            int x1 = 0, x2 = (int)((d.width - 1) * 1.1);
            int y1 = 0, y2 = (int)((d.height - 1) * 1.1);
            while (x1 < x2 && y1 < y2)
            {
                g.drawLine(x1, y1, x1, y2);
                y1 += 2;
                g.drawLine(x1, y2, x2, y2);
                x1 += 2;
                g.drawLine(x2, y2, x2, y1);
                y2 -= 2;
                g.drawLine(x2, y1, x1, y1);
                x2 -= 2;
            }
            Date date2 = new Date();
            repaintCount++;
            long rpTime = date2.getTime() - date1.getTime();
            repaintTime += rpTime;
            System.out.println("count = " + repaintCount +
```

```
64                  ", region = [" + bounds.x + "," +
65                  bounds.y + "," + bounds.width +
66                  "x" + bounds.height +
67                  "], time = " + rpTime +
68                  " ms, total time = " + repaintTime +
69                  "ms");
70          }
71      }
72      public static void main(String[] argv)
73      {
74          int width = 0, height = 0;
75          try
76          {
77              if (argv.length != 2) throw new NumberFormatException();
78              width = Integer.parseInt(argv[0]);
79              height = Integer.parseInt(argv[1]);
80          }
81          catch (NumberFormatException e)
82          {
83              System.err.println("Usage: Spiral0 <width> <height>");
84              System.exit(1);
85          }
86          new Spiral0(width, height);
87      }
88  }
```

The `Spiral0` constructor (lines 10–21) constructs the top-level window by creating and inserting a single instance of the nested class `Spiral0.Spiral`.

`Spiral0.Spiral` is a simple graphical element whose only interesting method is `paintComponent()` (lines 36–70). This method turns on antialiasing (lines 38–40)[2], clears the rectangle being redrawn (lines 41–42), draws the spiral (lines 43–58), and displays some summary statistics on the performance of the repaint.

The `main()` procedure (lines 72–87) parses the command line and creates the main window.

`Spiral1`: Automating `Spiral0`

`Spiral0` illustrated some basic behaviors of AWT repainting. `Spiral1` adds some automation, performing programmatically the manual window-dragging discussed in the section "Using `Spiral0` to Understand Repaint Behavior." `Spiral1` adds an opaque, heavyweight rectangular "puck" on top of the spiral and bounces it around (like a hockey puck) under program control, constantly exposing areas that need to be repainted.

[2] To make the output more interesting, a scaling transformation (line 43) is applied to the spiral. This results in placing the lines of the spiral at varying off-pixel addresses to ensure that the AWT's antialiasing logic is kept busy.

Synopsis:

```
java com.macmillan.nmeyers.Spiral1 <width> <height> <count> <delay>
```

After creating its components, `Spiral1` moves the puck over the spiral `<count>` times, with a specified `<delay>` (in milliseconds) between moves. As it does so, you can see a trailing shadow (see Figure 59.3) of areas that have been exposed and need to be repainted.

FIGURE 59.3
`Spiral1` running.

As the puck (darker rectangle) moves across the surface in Figure 59.3, it exposes areas that are soon repainted. In this image, the puck has moved eight times since the most recent repaint.

Results of `Spiral1`

The output generated by `Spiral1` gives us a view of how much time is spent repainting. When a test is run with a 300x300 spiral and a `<count>` of 200, the first few lines of output

```
count = 1, region = [0,0,296x276], time = 557 ms, total time = 557ms
count = 2, region = [0,0,300x300], time = 568 ms, total time = 1125ms
count = 3, region = [0,0,300x300], time = 635 ms, total time = 1760ms
count = 4, region = [0,0,96x76], time = 147 ms, total time = 1907ms
count = 5, region = [10,10,100x100], time = 156 ms, total time = 2063ms
count = 6, region = [20,20,100x100], time = 193 ms, total time = 2256ms
count = 7, region = [0,0,300x300], time = 565 ms, total time = 2821ms
count = 8, region = [30,30,100x100], time = 159 ms, total time = 2980ms
count = 9, region = [30,30,100x100], time = 195 ms, total time = 3175ms
count = 10, region = [40,40,100x100], time = 157 ms, total time = 3332ms
```

show that the full image was painted four times (due to inefficient Swing/AWT startup behavior), and that partial repaints due to puck movement took about 150–200 ms each. By the time the puck has finished its 200 moves

```
count = 200, region = [60,60,100x100], time = 158 ms, total time = 36544ms
count = 201, region = [50,50,100x100], time = 207 ms, total time = 36751ms
count = 202, region = [40,40,100x100], time = 160 ms, total time = 36911ms
count = 203, region = [30,30,100x100], time = 209 ms, total time = 37120ms
count = 204, region = [20,20,100x100], time = 166 ms, total time = 37286ms
count = 205, region = [10,10,100x100], time = 209 ms, total time = 37495ms
```

the application has spent approximately 37.5 seconds performing repaints.

`Spiral1` Source

`Spiral1` adds the puck component and logic to support moving it around the display. We will highlight the differences rather than showing full code listings. Full source is available on the CD-ROM.

The puck-motion logic is implemented partly in `main()` and partly in a custom layout manager (see Listing 59.2). By placing the logic to move the puck in the layout manager, we ensure that it is executed by the event-handling thread—a requirement (or at least a strong recommendation) when dealing with Swing.

LISTING 59.2 `Spiral1.java` Custom Layout Manager

```
class Spiral1 extends JFrame
{
    Spiral spiral;
    Component puck;
    int puckX = -1, puckY = -1;
    int puckXinc = -1, puckYinc = -1;
    boolean movePuck = false;
    Spiral1(int w, int h)
    {
        getContentPane().setLayout(new LayoutManager() {
            public void addLayoutComponent(String s, Component c)
            {}
            public void layoutContainer(Container c)
            {
                Dimension size = c.getSize();
                spiral.setBounds(0, 0, size.width, size.height);
                Dimension puckSize = new Dimension(size.width / 3,
                                                   size.height / 3);
                if (puckX == -1)
                {
                    puckX = 0;
                    puckY = 0;
                    puckXinc = puckSize.width / 10;
                    puckYinc = puckSize.height / 10;
                }
```

continued on next page

continued from previous page

```
32                  if (movePuck)
33                  {
34                      if (puckX + puckXinc + puckSize.width > size.width ||
35                          puckX + puckXinc < 0) puckXinc = -puckXinc;
36                      if (puckY + puckYinc + puckSize.height > size.height ||
37                          puckY + puckYinc < 0) puckYinc = -puckYinc;
38                      puckX += puckXinc;
39                      puckY += puckYinc;
40                      movePuck = false;
41                  }
42                  puck.setBounds(puckX, puckY, puckSize.width,
➥puckSize.height);
43              }
44              public Dimension minimumLayoutSize(Container c)
45              { return spiral.getMinimumSize(); }
46              public Dimension preferredLayoutSize(Container c)
47              { return spiral.getPreferredSize(); }
48              public void removeLayoutComponent(Component c)
49              {}
50          });
51          getContentPane().add(puck = new Panel());
52          puck.setBackground(Color.red);
53          getContentPane().add(spiral = new Spiral(w, h));
54          pack();
```

The layout procedure (lines 19–43) repositions the puck whenever the `movePuck` flag (set by a timing loop in `main()`) is true. The puck is automatically sized to one-third the size of the spiral (line 23), and it is moved on a diagonal one-tenth its own size (lines 29–30). Lines 34–39 cause the puck to bounce when it hits a wall.

Listing 59.3 shows the changes to `main()`.

LISTING 59.3 `Spiral1.java` Changes to `main()`

```
    public static void main(String[] argv)
    {
        int width = 0, height = 0, count = 0, delayms = 0;
        try
        {
            if (argv.length != 4) throw new NumberFormatException();
            width = Integer.parseInt(argv[0]);
            height = Integer.parseInt(argv[1]);
            count = Integer.parseInt(argv[2]);
            delayms = Integer.parseInt(argv[3]);
        }
        catch (NumberFormatException e)
        {
            System.err.println("Usage: Spiral1 <width> <height> " +
                               "<count> <delay in ms>");
            System.exit(1);
        }
        Spiral1 s = new Spiral1(width, height);
```

```
131             while (count— > 0)
132             {
133                 try { Thread.sleep((long)delayms); }
134                 catch (InterruptedException e)      {}
135                 s.movePuck = true;
136                 s.puck.invalidate();
137                 s.validate();
138             }
139         }
140     }
```

After the logic to handle the new command-line parameters (lines 116–129), `main()` sits in a loop (lines 131–138) and, by setting `movePuck` and calling `invalidate()` and `validate()`, causes the layout manager to be called to move the puck.

`Spiral2`: Adding Backing Store

Backing Store is a common performance technique in graphics. It involves holding the current window contents in a buffer for repainting as needed. Backing store is not to be confused with double-buffering (see Figure 59.4), although the logic is similar.

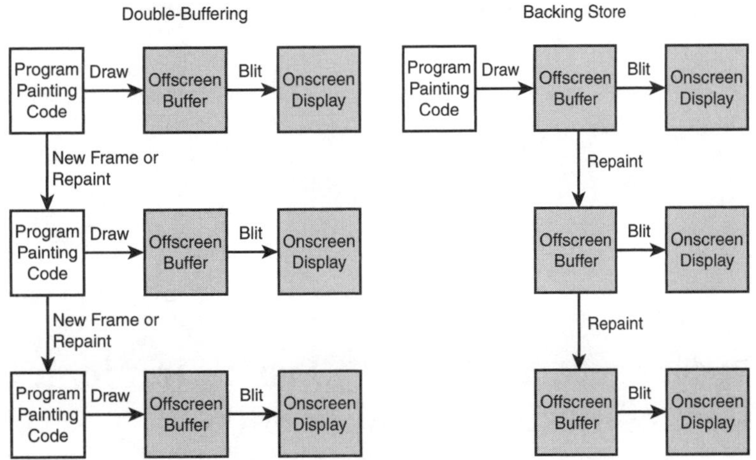

FIGURE 59.4
A comparison of double-buffering and backing store.

The purpose of double-buffering is to hide slow rendering speed—it's a particularly important technique in animation for creating smooth frame-to-frame transitions. With double-buffering, the application does not draw to the display; it draws (perhaps slowly building a scene or image) to an offscreen buffer and then rapidly blits (copies pixel-for-pixel) the image to the display. Whenever the application needs to draw, whether to render a new frame or simply to repaint an exposed area, it employs this two-stage rendering process.

Double-buffering is used in Swing, and it is being employed *every time* `Spiral0` or `Spiral1` repaints any part of its window. So, although drawing the spiral may be a slow process, you do not perceive the slowness; the slow sequence of drawing one antialiased line after another happens offscreen.

By contrast, backing store is designed to avoid involving the application's rendering logic in repainting whenever possible. The application draws to an offscreen buffer (and perhaps concurrently to the screen), and the offscreen buffer is blitted to the screen whenever the image needs to be repainted. The application's rendering logic becomes involved only when needed to change the image.

Backing store can be implemented in the display system: Many X servers allow it to be selectively enabled for individual windows at the request of the application. Or it can be implemented within the application itself. At present, `Graphics2D` and Swing do not provide either option, but we can improve graphics performance by adding our own backing store implementation.

Synopsis:

No significant change from the `Spiral1` invocation:

```
java com.macmillan.nmeyers.Spiral2 <width> <height> <count> <delay>
```

Changes to `Spiral2` Source

The significant change in `Spiral2` is the introduction of a new class, `BackingStore` (see the section "`BackingStore`: A New Class to Implement Backing Store for Lightweight Components"). The changes to the `Spiral2` source are trivial (see Listing 59.4)—the `Spiral2.Spiral` object is now wrapped in a `BackingStore` object.

LISTING 59.4 `Spiral2.java` Significant Changes from `Spiral1.java`

```
class Spiral2 extends JFrame
{
    Component spiral;
    .
    .
    .
        getContentPane().add(spiral = new BackingStore(new Spiral(w, h)));
```

`BackingStore`: A New Class to Implement Backing Store for Lightweight Components

The `BackingStore` class is a container for a single lightweight component, providing a backing store implementation for that component and its descendants.

Theory of `BackingStore` Operation

When backing store is implemented in the display system—for example, enabled for a particular X window—implementation is simple. Exposing part of the window causes the window system to repaint from the offscreen buffer, without even notifying the application of the activity.

Implementing backing store in Java is more challenging. The only hook available for controlling application painting behavior is the `paint()` method, and the backing store logic must ascertain *why* `paint()` is being called. Is it repainting an exposed area of the window, or responding to an application request to repaint? The difference is crucial. If the application requested a repaint, the image has presumably changed, and the app must be allowed to paint its new image.

The design of `BackingStore` is built on two aspects of Swing/AWT behavior:

- Application-requested repainting is handled by the repaint manager (`javax.swing.RepaintManager`), whereas repaint requests caused by exposure events are not. This provides a way to answer the "why are we repainting?" question described previously.
- Lightweight components are painted by painting their parent components—specifically, their `paint()` methods are called by their parents' `paint()` methods. This provides the capability for a parent to intercept and override its child's painting activities.

`BackingStore` maintains an image buffer, exactly the size of the child it contains, and redirects the child to paint into that buffer. When `paint()` is called to repaint exposed areas, `BackingStore` satisfies the request from the buffer. When `paint()` is called by request of the application, `BackingStore` allows the application to repaint the buffer and then blits its contents to the display.

`BackingStore` Source

Listing 59.5 shows the source for the `BackingStore` class.

LISTING 59.5 `BackingStore.java`

```
package com.macmillan.nmeyers;
import javax.swing.*;
import java.awt.*;
import java.awt.event.*;

public class BackingStore extends Container
{
    static boolean repainting = false;
    static boolean installed = false;
    Image bstore = null;
    Component component;
    private class BSRepaintManager extends RepaintManager
    {
        public void paintDirtyRegions()
        {
            repainting = true;
            try { super.paintDirtyRegions(); }
            finally { repainting = false; }
        }
    }
    public BackingStore(Component comp)
    {
        if (!installed)
        {
            installed = true;
            RepaintManager.setCurrentManager(new BSRepaintManager());
```

continued on next page

continued from previous page

```
        }
        component = comp;
        add(component);
        component.addComponentListener(new ComponentAdapter() {
            public void componentResized(ComponentEvent e)
            {
                bstore = null;
            }
        });
        Dimension size = component.getSize();
        setSize(size);
    }
    public Insets getInsets()
    {
        return new Insets(0, 0, 0, 0);
    }
    public Dimension getMinimumSize()
    {
        return component.getMinimumSize();
    }
    public Dimension getMaximumSize()
    {
        return component.getMaximumSize();
    }
    public Dimension getPreferredSize()
    {
        return component.getPreferredSize();
    }
    public void doLayout()
    {
        Dimension size = getSize();
        component.setBounds(0, 0, size.width, size.height);
    }
    public void paint(Graphics g)
    {
        boolean doRepaint = repainting;
        if (bstore == null)
        {
            Dimension size = component.getSize();
            bstore = component.createImage(size.width, size.height);
            doRepaint = true;
        }
        if (doRepaint)
        {
            Graphics g2 = bstore.getGraphics().create();
            g2.setClip(component.getBounds());
            g2.setFont(g.getFont());
            g2.setColor(g.getColor());
            component.paint(g2);
            g2.dispose();
        }
        g.drawImage(bstore, 0, 0, this);
    }
}
```

`BackingStore` is a container that tightly encloses a component for which it provides backing store services.

The core logic is contained in the `paint()` method (lines 60–79), and consists of three steps:

1. If there is currently no backing store bitmap, create one to match the size of the component (lines 63–68).
2. If we know that the application needs to redraw its image—a new bitmap has been created or the repainting flag is set—lines 71–76 create a `java.awt.Graphics` object for the bitmap, copy certain attributes from the original `java.awt.Graphics` object, and call the `paint()` method for the component being managed.
3. Blit the contents of the bitmap to the display (line 78).

The rest of the class contains ancillary logic to support the container and painting behavior:

- The methods in lines 39–59 perform the necessary layout methods to implement the container behavior.
- The `BackingStore.BSRepaintManager` class implements a custom repaint manager whose only purpose is to override the `RepaintDirtyRegions()` method (lines 14–19) to set the repainting flag. This step answers the "why are we repainting?" question.
- The constructor (lines 21–38) installs the custom repaint manager and installs a listener that will discard the current backing store bitmap if the container is resized.

Subtleties

This backing store implementation presents a couple of subtleties:

- As `BackingStore` is currently implemented, painting now passes through two levels of buffering: our backing store buffer and Swing double-buffering. Because of the latter, the `java.awt.Graphics` object passed to `paint()` in line 60 actually points to another offscreen buffer, not to the screen.

If you want to turn off double-buffering, see lines 20–25 of the benchmark in Chapter 57, "Why Is Java Slow?," in the section "Inefficient Graphics" for an example of how to do it. As that benchmark illustrates, however, double-buffering is important for AWT performance and you should use it for every component that is not being managed by `BackingStore`. If you disable double-buffering for the application's main window (as the benchmark does), you can reenable it for individual components by calling their individual `setDoubleBuffered()` methods.

- Notice that all logic dealing with the repaint manager uses static variables (lines 8–9). The repaint manager itself is a global resource, not a per-component resource. These static variables treat it accordingly in the event that more than one instance of `BackingStore` is being used.

Caveats

The design of `BackingStore` is based on certain JDK behaviors that are observed but not documented by Sun. In particular, the relationships between the repaint manager, application-requested repainting, repainting due to exposure events, and calls to `paint()` are not documented.

This logic has been verified to work with JDK1.2 on Linux and Microsoft Windows, and with the JDK1.3 prerelease on Microsoft Windows, but its long-term effectiveness is not certain.

Results of `Spiral2`

The results of adding backing store are spectacular. Running the same test used in the section "Results of `Spiral1`," earlier in this chapter, the application must paint its spiral exactly just twice:

```
count = 1, region = [0,0,292x272], time = 522 ms, total time = 522ms
count = 2, region = [0,0,300x300], time = 591 ms, total time = 1113ms
```

The first paint, at an odd size, is apparently a Swing layout artifact and does not always occur. Beyond the time required to draw the images into the backing store buffer, the blitting of the image during repainting is fast—too fast to measure with the `java.util.Date` class.

Using another measure of application performance—the CPU time measured by the Linux time utility—shows that `Spiral2` requires only 20% of the computing resources required by `Spiral1`.

`Spiral3`: Adding Event Coalescence

An additional optimization is possible: coalescence of repaint events.

As seen in Figure 59.2, the AWT can generate many rapid repaint requests for tiny portions of the screen. These events identify, to pixel accuracy, precisely what areas of the screen need to be repainted. Depending on how an application performs its repainting—in particular, on how expensive it is to repaint—this plethora of micro-paint events might be efficient or might be wildly inefficient.

For repainting from a backing store buffer, the micro-paint events are inefficient. It is much more efficient to coalesce many repaints into a single large repaint.

The AWT provides a facility to support coalescence of events: `Component.coalesceEvents()`. `Spiral3` adds event coalescence to the performance improvements of `Spiral2`.

Synopsis:

The invocation has the same arguments as before:

```
java com.macmillan.nmeyers.Spiral3 <width> <height> <count> <delay>
```

The new code in `Spiral3.java` (see Listing 59.6) does the work of coalescing events.

LISTING 59.6 `Spiral3.java` Changes to Coalesce Events

```
    public AWTEvent coalesceEvents(AWTEvent existingEvent,
                                   AWTEvent newEvent)
    {
        AWTEvent result = super.coalesceEvents(existingEvent, newEvent);
        if (result == null &&
```

```
68              existingEvent.getClass().equals(PaintEvent.class))
69          {
70              Rectangle newRect =
71                  new Rectangle(((PaintEvent)existingEvent).getUpdateRect());
72              newRect.add(((PaintEvent)newEvent).getUpdateRect());
73              result = new
➥PaintEvent(((PaintEvent)existingEvent).getComponent(),
74                                      existingEvent.getID(),
75                                      newRect);
76          }
77          return result;
78      }
```

The new `coalesceEvents()` method first calls the method it is overriding (line 66). If that method does nothing, and if the events being handled are `PaintEvents` (lines 67–68), then the two events are coalesced into a single event (lines 71–75).

The new *update rectangle* (the area to be repainted) for the new event is the smallest rectangle that contains both original update rectangles. Note that this is simple and aggressive coalescence logic: It is possible for two small rectangles to combine into one large one. In the extreme, unusual case, two 1-pixel rectangles at opposite corners of the screen can combine into a single rectangle that fills the screen.

Sun has indicated that the JDK1.3 AWT includes more capable event coalescence logic than currently found in JDK1.2, which might eventually obviate the need for this `coalesceEvents()` implementation.

Summary

This chapter presented some techniques that have, in the author's experience, been useful for improving performance of graphical rendering in Swing-based applications. Until such a time as future AWT tuning or enhancements make them unnecessary, these techniques have shown excellent promise in speeding up Java graphics.

CHAPTER 60

PerfAnal: A FREE PERFORMANCE ANALYSIS TOOL

This chapter presents a personal tool, PerfAnal, that aids in exploring Java application performance.

Platforms: JDK1.2

With the JDK1.2 release, the Java Virtual Machine began paying serious attention to enabling performance analysis tools. The JVM includes a new native interface, the *Java Virtual Machine Profiling Interface* (JVMPI), that allows tool's vendors to create in-process profiling tools.

Figure 60.1 shows the proposed architecture for profiling tools based on JVMPI.

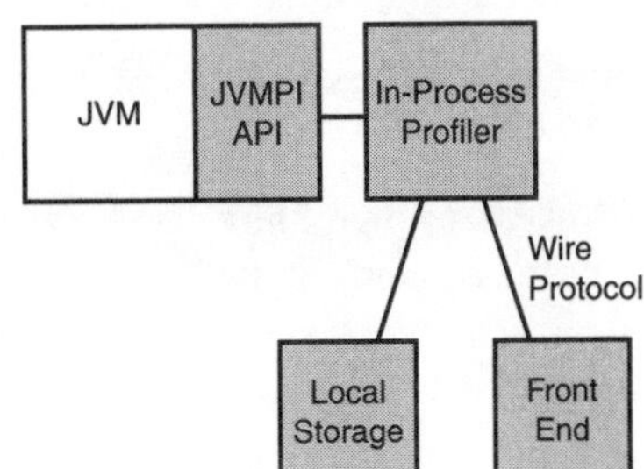

FIGURE 60.1
Sun's proposed architecture for JVMPI-based profiling tools.

The profiling agent (in Figure 60.1) must run in-process with the API, but the connection to the front end is expected to be over a wire protocol to be defined by the individual tools vendor.

Anyone can implement a profiling agent. The API is fully described in the JDK1.2 documentation bundle (in `docs/guide/jvmpi/jvmpi.html`). The hook for starting a profiling agent is in the java launcher invocation:

```
java ... -Xrun<agent>:<agent-args> ...
```

where the agent executable is provided as a shared library named `lib<agent>.so`, and `<agent-args>` are parameters to be parsed by the agent.

Sun's Sample `hprof` Profiler

SDK1.2 includes a sample implementation of a JVMPI-based profiler, `hprof`. It's not sophisticated or particularly friendly, but it demonstrates the sort of data available through JVMPI.

Synopsis:

```
java ... -Xrunhprof:<agent-args> ...
```

Arguments:

Arguments in `<agent-args>` are separated by commas.

- `cpu={samples¦times¦old}`—Collect CPU profiling data for analyzing code performance. The `samples` option uses statistical profiling to collect stack traces showing where code is spending its time; `times` uses instrumented code to report on time spent in individual methods; `old` specifies the format provided by the old JDK1.1 `-prof` option. Default is not to collect CPU profiling data unless this option is used.
- `cutoff=<value>`—Do not report CPU times below `<value>`, which defaults to 0.0001.
- `depth=<size>`—Depth of stack trace to use for `heap=sites` and `cpu=samples` options. Default is 4.
- `doe={y¦n}`—If yes, dump output on exit. Default is yes.
- `format={a¦b}`—Generate profile data in ASCII or binary format. Default is ASCII.
- `file=<file>`—Output profile data to the specified file. Default is `java.hprof` (for binary) or `java.hprof.txt` (for ASCII).
- `heap={dump¦sites¦all}`—Collect heap profiling data for analyzing memory usage and leaks. The `dump` option dumps the contents of the Java heap at program termination; `sites` generates stack traces showing where memory was allocated; `all` does both. If you do not explicitly request heap or CPU analysis options, the default behavior is `heap=all`.
- `lineno={y¦n}`—If yes, include line number information in traces. Note that line numbers are only reported if JIT is disabled. Default is yes.
- `monitor={y¦n}`—If yes, report information on contention for monitors used to synchronize multithreaded code. Default is no.

- net=<*host*>:<*port*>—Send output to a TCP socket listening at the specified port on the specified host. This option is used to send information to a running analysis program instead of saving it to a file.
- thread={y¦n}—If yes, include thread identification with stack traces. Default is no.

Sample hprof Usage

To illustrate the `hprof` profiler, let's use it for statistical profiling of the `Spiral1` program from Chapter 59, "An Approach to Improving Graphical Rendering Performance," in the section "`Spiral1`: Automating `Spiral0`":

```
bash$ java -green -Xrunhprof:cpu=samples,depth=12,file=results.txt,thread=y \
-Djava.compiler= com.macmillan.nmeyers.Spiral1 300 300 200 100
```

The reasons for the `-green` flag and for disabling the JIT are explained in the section "`PerfAnal`: A GUI-Based `hprof` Analyzer" later in this chapter.

After the program has finished moving the puck (the bouncing red rectangle), dismiss it by closing its window. The JVM will dump its profiling information into a file named `results.txt`, which will be approximately 16,000 lines long for this example.

With the options specified in this example, the results file contains some introductory information, followed by three types of interesting output:

- Information on the threads running in the application. For example:

```
THREAD START (obj=81424c0, id = 2, name="Signal dispatcher", group="system")
THREAD START (obj=81426f8, id = 3, name="Reference Handler", group="system")
THREAD START (obj=814b9d0, id = 4, name="Finalizer", group="system")
THREAD START (obj=81caca0, id = 5, name="HPROF CPU profiler", group="system")
THREAD START (obj=81ca9b0, id = 1, name="main", group="main")
THREAD START (obj=82d3f40, id = 6, name="AWT-EventQueue-0", group="main")
THREAD START (obj=82d2b50, id = 7, name="SunToolkit.PostEventQueue-0",
➥group="ma
in")
THREAD START (obj=84d8b28, id = 8, name="AWT-Motif", group="main")
THREAD START (obj=86d7db8, id = 9, name="Screen Updater", group="main")
THREAD END (id = 1)
THREAD START (obj=81ca9c8, id = 10, name="Thread-0", group="main")
```

- Stack traces, collected by statistical sampling, showing where time is being spent. Here is an example:

```
TRACE 330: (thread=6)

sun/java2d/loops/IndexedCompositing.ColorFillAlphaToIndexed(IndexedCompo
siting.java:Native method)

sun/java2d/loops/ColorFillAlphaToIndexed.ColorPaint(IndexedCompositing.j
ava:185)
```

```
sun/java2d/loops/RasterOutputManager.compositeColorLoop(RasterOutputMana
ger.java:1598)
        sun/java2d/pipe/AlphaColorPipe.renderPathTile(AlphaColorPipe.java:79)

sun/java2d/pipe/DuctusShapeRenderer.renderPath(DuctusShapeRenderer.java:
107)
        sun/java2d/pipe/DuctusShapeRenderer.fill(DuctusShapeRenderer.java:55)

sun/java2d/pipe/PixelToShapeConverter.fillRect(PixelToShapeConverter.jav
a:51)
        sun/java2d/SunGraphics2D.fillRect(SunGraphics2D.java:1568)
        sun/java2d/SunGraphics2D.clearRect(SunGraphics2D.java:1584)

sun/awt/image/BufferedImageGraphics2D.clearRect(BufferedImageGraphics2D.
java:1021)
        com/macmillan/nmeyers/Spiral1$Spiral.paintComponent(Spiral1.java:83)
        javax/swing/JComponent.paint(JComponent.java:547)
```

This trace, collected from thread #6 (the AWT event thread), shows a trace that was collected in a native method called `sun.java2d.loops.IndexedCompositing.ColorFillAlphaToIndexed()`. The depth-12 stack trace provides considerable information on how the code got here. For non-native methods, the trace includes information on the source line number (unless JIT is enabled).

- A ranked list of how many samples were collected for each stack trace. Here are the first few lines:

```
CPU SAMPLES BEGIN (total = 5175) Mon Aug 30 16:19:29 1999
rank   self  accum   count trace method
   1  6.98%  6.98%     361   193 sun/awt/motif/MToolkit.run
   2  3.48% 10.45%     180   330 sun/java2d/loops/IndexedCompositing.
ColorFillAl
➥phaToIndexed
   3  2.61% 13.06%     135    83 sun/awt/X11GraphicsEnvironment.initDisplay
   4  2.14% 15.21%     111   342 sun/java2d/loops/IndexedCompositing.
ColorFillAl
➥phaToIndexed
   5  2.14% 17.35%     111   336 sun/dc/pr/PathFiller.writeAlpha8
```

Each entry in the list describes a single stack trace: how many samples were collected for that trace, an identifier to match the trace with the earlier output, and the name of the method where the time was actually spent.

The list indicates that 361 samples (6.98% of total application time) were collected in connection with stack trace #193. In second place, 180 samples (3.48% of total application time) were collected in connection with trace #330—the trace shown previously. Looking down to the fourth entry, we see that more time was spent in that same method—but via a different sequence of calls and a different stack trace.

Between the traces and the list, it is possible to build a detailed understanding of where the application is spending its time. The next section presents a tool that simplifies this task.

Caveats

Statistical profiling is a widely used and highly effective technique for understanding application performance. But it carries some risks, which you must understand to make proper use of the results:

- Statistical profiling is a valuable but imperfect tool. Samples are triggered by a recurring timer, and each sample represents a snapshot of where the program was executing when the timer was triggered. This results in a pretty good picture of where time is being spent, but it is not foolproof.
- For example, a process may be slow due to poor memory locality (a significant risk with Java, see the section "Poor Memory Locality" in Chapter 57, "Why Is Java Slow?"). Such a process may spend significant time in a stalled state, waiting for memory access. When the process is stalled, in-process profiling is also stalled—meaning that no samples are collected during the activity that is taking the most time.
- Profiling is itself disruptive—especially in-process profiling. The normal flow of execution is disrupted to record profiling data, possibly generating results that do not accurately model the behavior of the application without profiling.

Despite the risks, statistical performance profiling is one of the best and most commonly available methods for understanding application performance. And in-process profiling, despite its unique problems, is a portable solution that does not depend on platform-specific profiling capabilities not found in many operating systems.

`PerfAnal`: A GUI-Based `hprof` Analyzer

The 16,000 lines of profiling data generated in the previous section "Sample hprof Usage" provide a good view of the JVMPI capabilities, but the results are difficult to understand and tedious to analyze.

`PerfAnal` is a GUI-based tool of my own, built to analyze the results collected by the `hprof` CPU sampling capabilities. It is not a *live* profiling tool; it analyzes the `hprof` results dumped after a profiled application terminates.

Synopsis:

`java com.macmillan.nmeyers.PerfAnal` *`<profiles>`*

`PerfAnal` analyzes one or more text-format `hprof` profiles generated with the `cpu=samples` option. There are no command-line options for `PerfAnal`, but certain options specified during profiling are important.

Additional `hprof` options (specified as part of the `-Xrunhprof` option during profiling) that are relevant to `PerfAnal`'s behavior are as follows:

- `depth=`*`<size>`*—`PerfAnal` reports where an application is spending its time, and on *whose* behalf an application is spending time—which methods are doing the calling. Collecting deep stack traces (such as depth=12 in the example above) allows `PerfAnal` to provide more detailed analysis.

A side-effect of this option is increased execution time and memory usage—you will almost certainly need to increase memory limits with the java `-Xmx` option when running `PerfAnal`.

- `thread=y`—Capturing thread data in the profile will allow `PerfAnal` to provide per-thread analysis of application performance.

Two java launcher options (specified when the application is profiled) also have important effects on `PerfAnal` results:

- `-green`—Experience with the current JVM suggests that profiling an application running with native threads collects inaccurate profiling results, so you should use the `-green` flag until and unless the problem is corrected. With native threads, each profiling sample evidently comes from some random thread, rather than reliably coming from the thread in which time is being spent.
- `-Djava.compiler=`—Profiling works well with or without JIT. Running without JIT, however, allows you to collect data on specific Java source line numbers where time is being spent. If this is useful, then you should disable JIT. If you need a more accurate representation of where JIT-compiled code spends its time, do not disable JIT.

Using PerfAnal

Here is a sample invocation using the data collected in the section "Sample hprof Usage":

```
java -Xmx64m com.macmillan.nmeyers.PerfAnal results.txt
```

The Four Windows

For each profile file specified on the command line, `PerfAnal` displays a top-level window enclosing four views of the profiling data (see Figure 60.2).

Each subwindow in Figure 60.2 displays a Swing `JTree` showing how much time is spent in various methods. You can double-click to open `JTree` branches to get more detail. Each window slices the data differently, and `PerfAnal` allows you to correlate information between the windows.

The upper-left window (see Figure 60.3) shows which methods consumed the most time, *inclusive* of subroutine calls. The tree is organized by caller; by exploring the tree, you can see how much time was spent in the called methods.

The tree in Figure 60.3 shows methods in order of decreasing execution time—inclusive of subroutine calls. Exploring the tree to identify callees, we see that `javax/swing/JComponent.paint()` spent most of its time in `com/macmillan/nmeyers/Spiral1$Spiral.paintComponent()`, which spent most of its time in `sun/java2d/SunGraphics2D.drawLine()`, and so on.

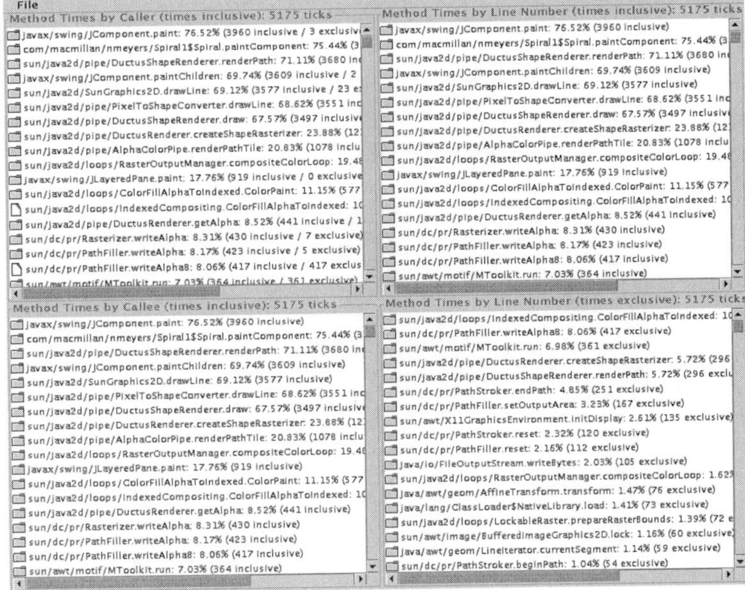

FIGURE 60.2
The `PerfAnal` main window.

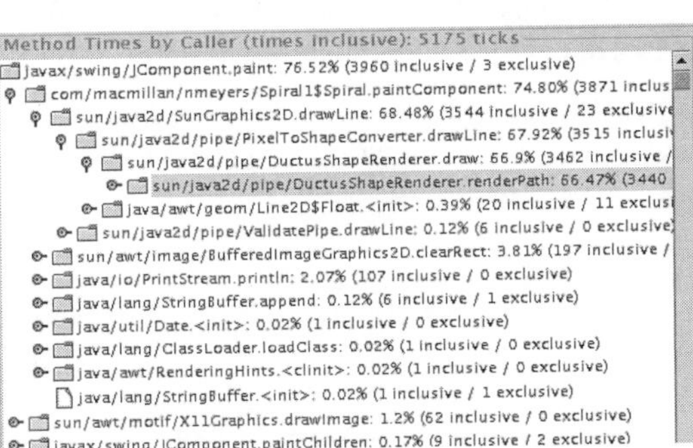

FIGURE 60.3
The upper-left window in `PerfAnal`'s main window.

The lower-left window (see Figure 60.4) displays the same list of methods in the same order, but organized by *callee*. By exploring the tree, you can see on whose behalf the time is being spent.

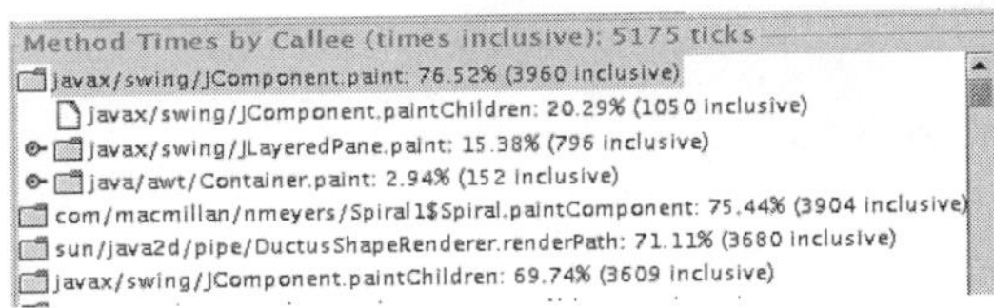

FIGURE 60.4
The lower-left window in `PerfAnal`'s main window.

The tree in Figure 60.4 also shows time spent in various methods, but with information organized by *callee*. You can see three procedures that called `javax/swing/JComponent.paint()`

and can explore further up the call stack. Why don't the numbers add up to 76.52%? Because we only collected 12-deep stack traces. If the missing callers are important to the analysis, we will need to make a profiling run with a higher `depth=` value.

The upper-right window (see Figure 60.5) displays the same list of methods in the same order, but here they are broken down by source line number.

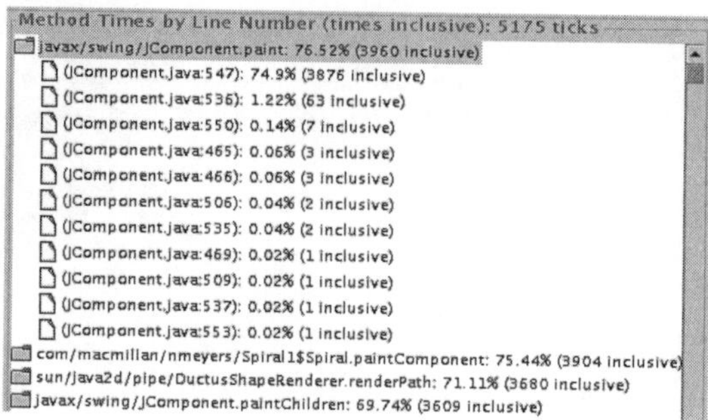

FIGURE 60.5
The upper-right window in `PerfAnal`'s main window.

The tree in Figure 60.5 shows us that the busy `javax/swing/JComponent.paint()` method spent most of its time on line #547, which is obviously (referring back to Figure 60.3) a call to `com/macmillan/nmeyers/Spiral1$Spiral.paintComponent()`.

Finally, the lower-right window (see Figure 60.6) displays the methods—but *in a different order*. This list is *exclusive* of subroutine calls and shows exactly where in the code the application's time is really being spent.

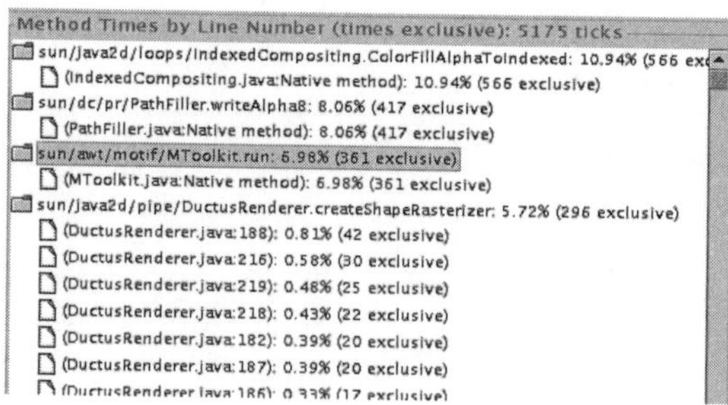

FIGURE 60.6
The lower-right window of `PerfAnal`'s main window.

The tree in Figure 60.6 lists the methods in order of decreasing time, exclusive of subroutine calls. The three busiest methods are native methods; the fourth is a Java method broken down by line number.

Note

All times reported in the analysis windows are in terms of *ticks*—increments of the profiler sampling clock. Because the period of hprof's clock tick is not documented, `PerfAnal` does not attempt to convert ticks into CPU seconds. Nevertheless, the tick times are useful as a relative performance measure within an analysis and between different analyses.

Correlating Information Between the Windows

Each of the four windows provides an interesting slice of the data, but how does that map to performance tuning?

The results begin to get interesting when they are correlated *between* windows. Knowing, for example, that the application is spending 11 percent of its time in a single native rendering method, we can ask why and on whose behalf the time is being spent.

`PerfAnal` provides a facility to correlate the data between windows. We illustrate by exploring the time spent in the native `IndexedCompositing.ColorFillAlphaToIndexed()` method.

Right-clicking on that line (see Figure 60.7) pops up a menu that allows us to `Goto this Method`.

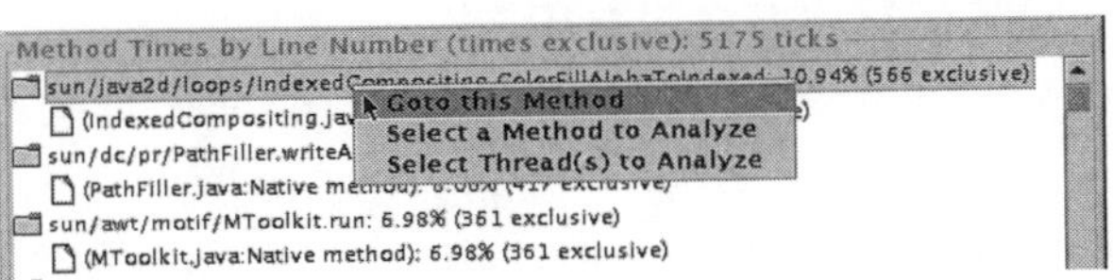

FIGURE 60.7
Right-clicking pops up a menu with utilities for window correlation.

Choosing `Goto this Method` synchronizes all four windows: it selects the corresponding entry in each window. Now, moving to the lower-left window (see Figure 60.8) and exploring the tree from that point exposes more useful detail. Looking up the call stack past the Swing and AWT code (see Figure 60.9) reveals that all the time spent in `IndexedCompositing.ColorFillAlphaToIndexed()` is due to calls from `Spiral1$Spiral.paintComponent()`.

sun/java2d/loops/RasterOutputManager.compositeColorLoop: 19.48% (1008 inclusive)
javax/swing/JLayeredPane.paint: 17.76% (919 inclusive)
sun/java2d/loops/ColorFillAlphaToIndexed.ColorPaint: 11.15% (577 inclusive)
sun/java2d/loops/IndexedCompositing.ColorFillAlphaToIndexed: 10.94% (566 inclusive)
sun/java2d/pipe/DuctusRenderer.getAlpha: 8.52% (441 inclusive)
sun/dc/pr/Rasterizer.writeAlpha: 8.31% (430 inclusive)
sun/dc/pr/PathFiller.writeAlpha: 8.17% (423 inclusive)

FIGURE 60.8
After the last step, the `sun/java2d/loops/IndexedCompositing.ColorFillAlphaToIndexed()` method has been selected in all four windows.

FIGURE 60.9
Exploring up the call stack from `Indexed Compositing.ColorFill AlphaToIndexed()`.

```
sun/java2d/loops/IndexedCompositing.ColorFillAlphaToIndexed: 10.94% (566 inclusive)
  sun/java2d/loops/ColorFillAlphaToIndexed.ColorPaint: 10.94% (566 inclusive)
    sun/java2d/loops/RasterOutputManager.compositeColorLoop: 10.94% (566 inclusive)
      sun/java2d/pipe/AlphaColorPipe.renderPathTile: 10.94% (566 inclusive)
        sun/java2d/pipe/DuctusShapeRenderer.renderPath: 10.94% (566 inclusive)
          sun/java2d/pipe/DuctusShapeRenderer.draw: 7.46% (386 inclusive)
            sun/java2d/pipe/PixelToShapeConverter.drawLine: 7.46% (386 inclusive)
              sun/java2d/SunGraphics2D.drawLine: 7.44% (385 inclusive)
                com/macmillan/nmeyers/Spiral1$Spiral.paintComponent: 7.44% (38
              sun/java2d/pipe/ValidatePipe.drawLine: 0.02% (1 inclusive)
          sun/java2d/pipe/DuctusShapeRenderer.fill: 3.48% (180 inclusive)
            sun/java2d/pipe/PixelToShapeConverter.fillRect: 3.48% (180 inclusive)
              sun/java2d/SunGraphics2D.fillRect: 3.48% (180 inclusive)
                sun/java2d/SunGraphics2D.clearRect: 3.48% (180 inclusive)
                  sun/awt/image/BufferedImageGraphics2D.clearRect: 3.48% (180 i
                    com/macmillan/nmeyers/Spiral1$Spiral.paintComponent: 3.4
sun/java2d/pipe/DuctusRenderer.getAlpha: 8.52% (441 inclusive)
```

This exploration has pointed the finger at the `paintComponent()` code for the spiral. Repeat the process: using `Goto this Method` on that call, we see that this method is (inclusive of subroutine calls) responsible for nearly 75% of execution time. Why is it being exercised so frequently?

Another exploration up the call stack in the lower-left window traces the calls back to the Motif event-handling code: the application is drawing a lot because it is receiving many exposure events![1] One possible solution, as already explored in Chapter 59, "An Approach to Improving Graphical Rendering Performance," is to find a faster way to respond to exposure events.

Other PerfAnal Functionality

The pop-up menu shown previously in Figure 60.7 offers two additional functions:

- `Select a Method to Analyze` allows you to choose any method for further exploration, presented in a dialog as a sorted list (see Figure 60.10).
- `Select Thread(s) to Analyze` allows you to limit the analysis to certain application threads. A pop-up dialog (see Figure 60.11) presents the choices.

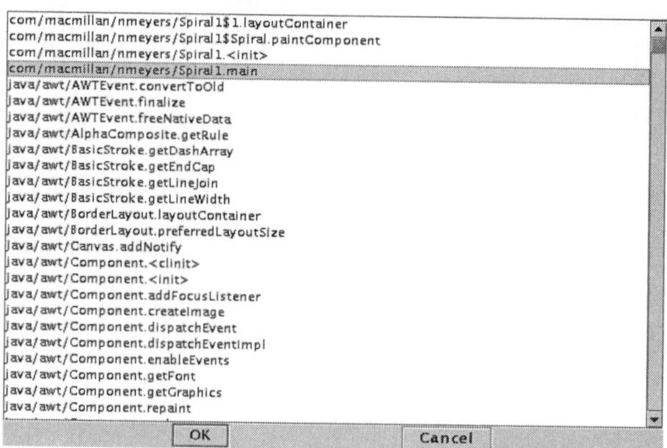

FIGURE 60.10
You can choose any method for further analysis.

[1]You will discover a minor fiction here if you repeat this experiment. Although this sample data was collected with the `depth=12` option, you will need to collect the data with a greater depth value to trace all the way back to Motif event-handling code. Choosing the amount of stack trace information to collect requires compromising between detail and the CPU/memory demands of `PerfAnal` itself.

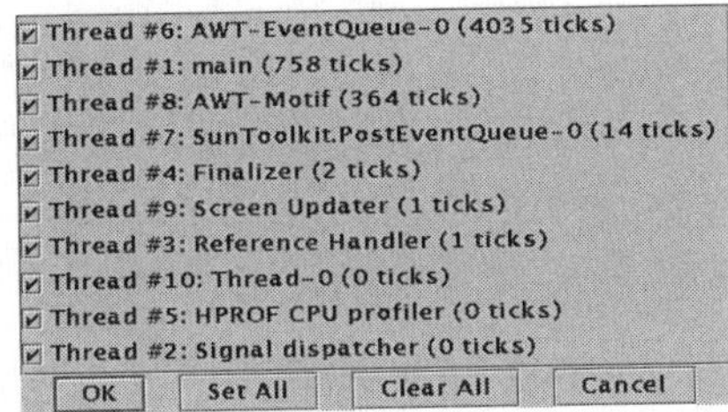

FIGURE 60.11
This dialog allows you to slice the analysis by thread.

Finally, the File menu on the menu bar includes a Save button, which saves all the analysis information from all windows into a text file, using indentation and numbers to represent the tree structure. Here are the first few lines of the text file from this example:

```
Method Times by Caller (times inclusive): 5175 ticks
  1: javax/swing/JComponent.paint: 76.52% (3960 inclusive / 3 exclusive)
    2: com/macmillan/nmeyers/Spiral1$Spiral.paintComponent: 74.80% (3871 inclusive
➥/ 13 exclusive)
      3: sun/java2d/SunGraphics2D.drawLine: 68.48% (3544 inclusive / 23 exclusive)
```

PerfAnal Source

PerfAnal is implemented with 12 top-level classes providing the analysis and GUI capabilities. Complete source is provided on the CD-ROM, and a listing can be found in Appendix B, "Miscellaneous Program Listings."

Summary

This chapter presented the PerfAnal tool, which works in conjunction with the JDK1.2 sample profiling application to provide detailed runtime performance analysis of a Java application. Subsequent chapters will present a tool for heap (memory usage) analysis and a commercial tool that enables live profiling of a running application.

CHAPTER 61

HEAP ANALYSIS TOOL: UNDERSTANDING MEMORY UTILIZATION

This chapter discusses the Sun Heap Analysis Tool, a free tool used to analyze application memory use.

Platforms: JDK1.2

Chapter 60, "`PerfAnal`: A Free Performance Analysis Tool," introduced the JDK1.2 profiling capability and described how it can be used to analyze application CPU usage. The other half of the JVM Profiling Interface is the capability to capture memory usage information and to track memory leaks.

What is a memory leak? In C/C++, it is well recognized as memory you have allocated but later neglected to deallocate. Java, with its garbage collection capabilities, is supposedly immune to memory leaks. But it still suffers from avoidable memory bloat—typically for the following reasons:

- An application may retain references to objects it no longer needs. This reference may be obvious, such as a non-null field in a class or an object. Or it may be subtle—a listener that does not unregister itself or a thread that does not terminate.
- There may be bugs in JNI code that creates, but neglects to remove, references to objects.
- Garbage collection may not run often enough to keep bloat under control.

In any case, memory bloat leads to increased stress on cache and virtual memory, poor locality, and degraded (sometimes drastically) performance. Understanding your application's memory requirements is crucial to understanding its runtime performance.

Collecting Memory Statistics

We discussed general `hprof` usage, including memory-related options, in Chapter 60, "`PerfAnal`: A Free Performance Analysis Tool," in the section "Sun's Sample `hprof` Profiler." The memory profiling options collect three types of data into the profiling output:

- Stack traces, which are identical to the stack traces described in Chapter 60 in the section "Sample `hprof` Usage." These traces, however, are triggered by memory allocation activity rather than by the ticks of a profiling timer.
- A ranked list of allocations, similar to the ranked list described in Chapter 60 in the section "Sample `hprof` Usage," but organized around memory usage. Here is the beginning of the list, as generated by a sample run of `Spiral1` (this program, an illustration of graphical rendering speed, was discussed in Chapter 59, "Graphical Rendering Performance"):

```
SITES BEGIN (ordered by live bytes) Wed Sep  1 11:29:41 1999
          percent          live          alloc'ed  stack class
 rank   self  accum     bytes objs    bytes objs trace name
    1 14.29% 14.29%     90004    1   171704    2  7725 [B
    2  2.60% 16.89%     16388    1    16388    1  1236 [C
    3  2.60% 19.49%     16388    1    16388    1  1245 [C
    4  1.85% 21.34%     11628    3    11628    3   963 [C
    5  1.78% 23.12%     11240  102    11240  102  3260 [C
    6  1.78% 24.91%     11240  102    11240  102  5456 [C
```

  The first entry describes an array of bytes (its Java class signature, shown in the last column, is `[B`) whose allocation was captured in stack trace #7725 (shown elsewhere in the file). Two such objects were allocated during the life of the program, and one was still live when the program terminated.

- One or more dumps of current heap contents. Here is an example entry:

```
OBJ 85c3020 (sz=20, trace=6676, class=java/util/HashMap$Entry@82038a8)
    key          85c3100
    value          85c3130
```

  This entry describes a 20-byte object of class `java.util.HashMap.Entry`, containing references to two other objects. Each of these dump entries also shows the allocated object's handle (`85c3020`, in this case) and the identity of the trace captured when the object was allocated.

  A dump is generated at program termination, but you can also generate dumps while the program is running. At any time during execution, you can generate a current dump by typing Ctrl+\ (control-backslash) to the terminal in which the JVM is running. This allows you to capture baseline traces for purpose of comparison.

As with the CPU performance data, the memory data captured by `hprof` allows you to build a detailed understanding of program resource usage—in this case, you can learn where memory is being used and retained by the application. It, too, is a huge and complex data set, and can benefit from a tool designed to aid in its interpretation. Sun provides such a tool in its Heap Analysis Tool.

The Sun Heap Analysis Tool

Sun distributes, through its developer site (`http://developer.java.sun.com`), an experimental tool called HAT—the *Heap Analysis Tool*—to aid in interpreting memory profiling information. To obtain the tool, visit the developer site and search for "Heap Analysis Tool." The tool is provided as a zip archive: unpack it anywhere.

As of this writing, the tool is in early access and is completely unsupported.

To use the tool, you need to collect `hprof` heap profiling data *in binary format*. A sample invocation to collect the data from a run of `Spiral1` is as follows:

```
bash$ java -Xrunhprof:depth=12,thread=y,format=b,file=results.bin \
com.macmillan.nmeyers.Spiral1 300 300 200 100
```

Running HAT

HAT is provided in a class library, `hat.zip`, in the `bin/` subdirectory of the HAT distribution.

Synopsis:

```
java -cp <installdir>/bin/hat.zip -Xmx100m hat.Main [<options>]
➥<profile>[:<trace#>]
```

The results file collected during profiling is specified in the *<profile>* argument; if it contains more than one heap dump, use the optional *<trace#>* suffix to select which trace to analyze. Example: `results.bin:1`.

Once started, HAT starts up a small Web server. All interaction with HAT is through a browser.

Options:

- `-port=`*<port#>*—Specify port at which to run the Web server. Default is 7000. (If you are running an X font server, the default port number will probably conflict with it.)
- `-baseline=`*<profile>*`[:`*<trace#>*`]`—Specify a heap dump to serve as a baseline. HAT will generate its memory usage statistics by comparing the two dumps. The baseline dump may optionally be in a different file than the one being analyzed.
- `-exclude=`*<excludefile>*—Read a list of fields to exclude from the analysis. The file should contain fully qualified names, one per line, of fields to be excluded from the analysis.

After startup, HAT will analyze the file, output a handful of status messages, and then indicate that the server is ready.

Example:

For the data collected in the sample `Spiral1` invocation in the section "The Sun Heap Analysis Tool," this invocation would run a HAT analysis of the data and report results through port 7005:

```
bash$ java -cp /usr/local/Java/hat/bin/hat.zip -Xmx100m hat.Main -port=7005
➥results.bin
Started HTTP server on port 7005
Reading from results.bin...
Dump file created Wed Sep 01 11:57:35 PDT 1999
Snapshot read, resolving...
Resolving 20025 objects...
Chasing references, expect 40 dots........................................
Eliminating duplicate references........................................
Snapshot resolved.
Server is ready.
```

Interacting with HAT

All interaction with HAT is through a Web browser. Browsing the "home page" at `http://localhost:7005` (using the port number from the previous example) provides a listing of all classes found in the profile. Figure 61.1 shows, for our example, a truncated excerpt of that page.

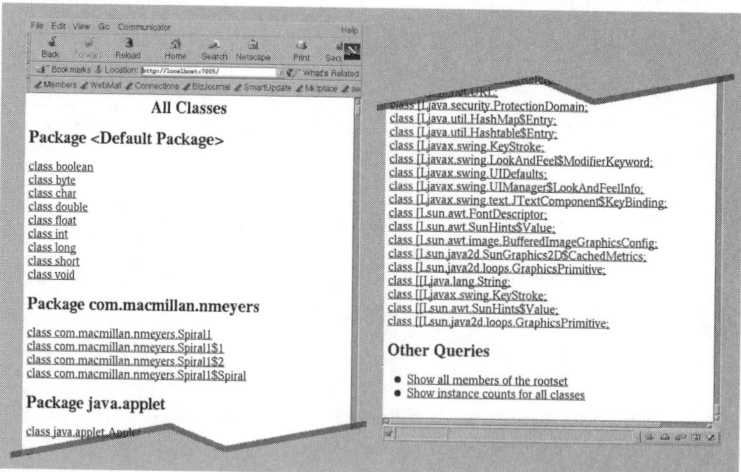

FIGURE 61.1
Excerpts of HAT top-level page showing all classes.

The page shown in Figure 61.1 displays all classes for which allocations were recorded. Following the link for any class leads to a detailed look at the class structure. Figure 61.2 presents a detailed look at the `Spiral1` class; links on this page allow us to study the class and its instances in detail—examining its members, finding all references to and from class instances, and identifying where and by whom all instances were allocated.

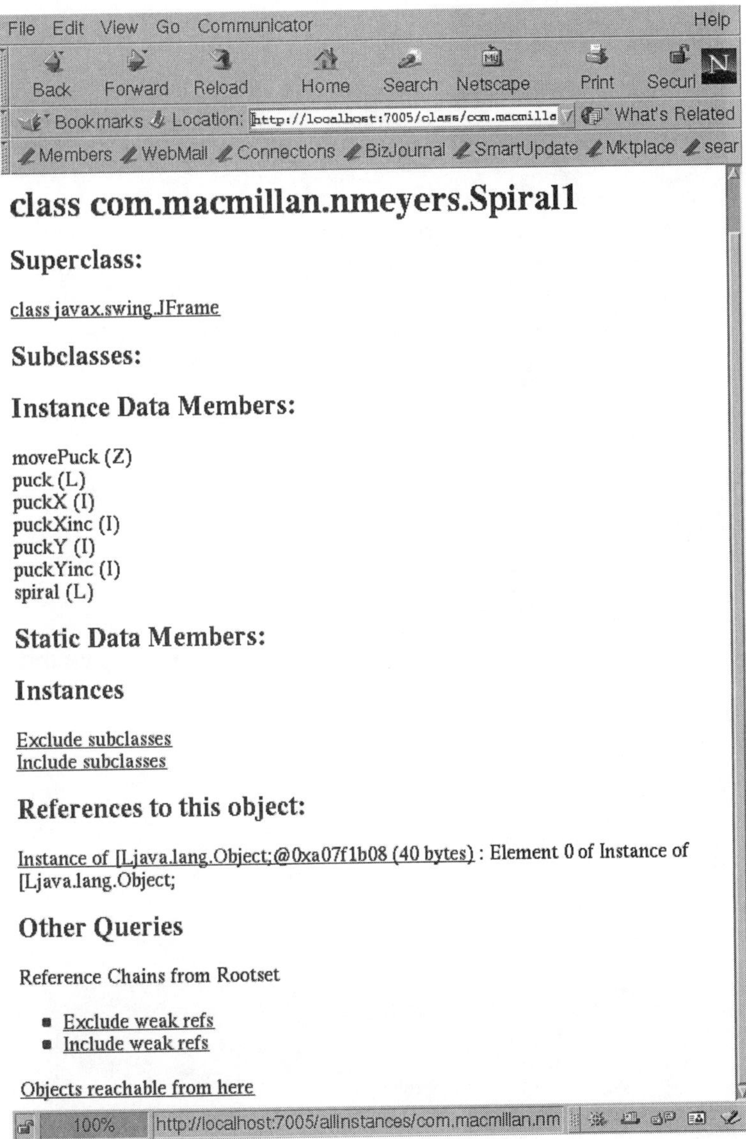

FIGURE 61.2
A detailed look at the structure of the `Spiral1` class.

Many other queries are possible, allowing you to explore objects, allocations, and reference chains. The best documentation on HAT comes from the `README.html` file bundled in the distribution archive.

HAT Weaknesses

HAT provides a powerful tool for exploring the memory allocations and the web of references in a Java application. It is particularly good at slicing the data in many different ways, to help you understand the complex relationships among objects.

Perhaps its biggest shortcoming is that it doesn't answer the simple question of "who is using so much memory?". There is, for example, no query to report that 14% of memory was taken up by just two allocations of byte arrays—as is evident from inspecting the ranked allocation list shown in the section "Collecting Memory Statistics" earlier in this chapter. (Knowing to look for such arrays, further inquiry with HAT reveals that they are members of class `java.awt.image.DataBufferByte`—that is, they are the buffers used for double-buffering.)

So, for the moment, HAT is best used in conjunction with other information—such as a text version of the profile data.

Summary

This chapter looked at HAT, an experimental tool from Sun for analyzing memory statistics generated by JDK1.2's JVM Profiling Interface. By understanding how an application's memory is being used and abused, you can tune your application for improved memory use and run-time performance.

CHAPTER 62

OPTIMIZEIT: LIVE PERFORMANCE ANALYSIS

This chapter explores OptimizeIt, a commercial performance analysis tool available for Linux.

Platforms: JDK1.1/JDK1.2

Sun designed its JVM Profiling Interface (JVMPI) to support the development of third-party profiling tools. The sample `hprof` profiler exploited in Chapters 60, "`PerfAnal`: A Free Performance Analysis Tool," and 61, "Heap Analysis Tool: Understanding Memory Utilization," provides a first glimpse of Java's profiling capabilities, but it misses JVMPI's most exciting potential. It does not perform live profiling of running applications.

OptimizeIt is a commercial tool that addresses this shortcoming. Available for Linux, Solaris, and Windows, OptimizeIt combines the various types of profiling supported by JVMPI—runtime statistical, runtime instrumentation, and heap—into a live GUI that allows detailed analysis of running applications. For applications that must run under JDK1.1, OptimizeIt also supports the limited profiling capabilities provided in that environment.

Obtaining OptimizeIt

You can download, obtain an evaluation license, and purchase OptimizeIt from `http://www.optimizeit.com`. The product is shipped as a gzipped tarball, which you can unpack anywhere.

OptimizeIt ships with its own custom JRE1.1 to run its own classes, but uses your installed JDK to run the applications being analyzed.

Running OptimizeIt

The installation includes a launch script, named OptimizeIt, in the top-level directory.

Synopsis:

```
<install_dir>/OptimizeIt
```

This brings up a configuration dialog (see Figure 62.1) in which you configure the application to be analyzed. For this exploration, we set it up to analyze the `Spiral1` program introduced in Chapter 59, "An Approach to Improving Graphical Rendering Performance."

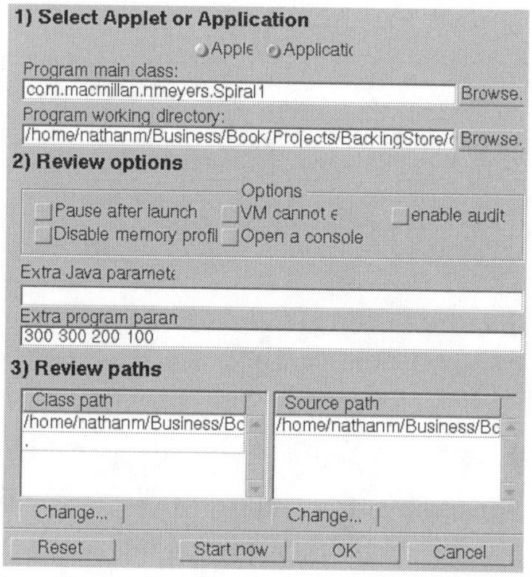

FIGURE 62.1
The OptimizeIt configuration dialog.

After configuration, OptimizeIt presents the main GUI (see Figure 62.2) to control the analysis activity.

The GUI in Figure 62.2 allows you to start, pause, and terminate the application with the buttons on the upper left. The second cluster of buttons allows you to select three analysis modes: virtual memory usage, CPU usage, and heap usage. In this screen shot, the product is performing live heap usage analysis as the application runs.

The following sections explore some of the specific analysis modes available through the main GUI.

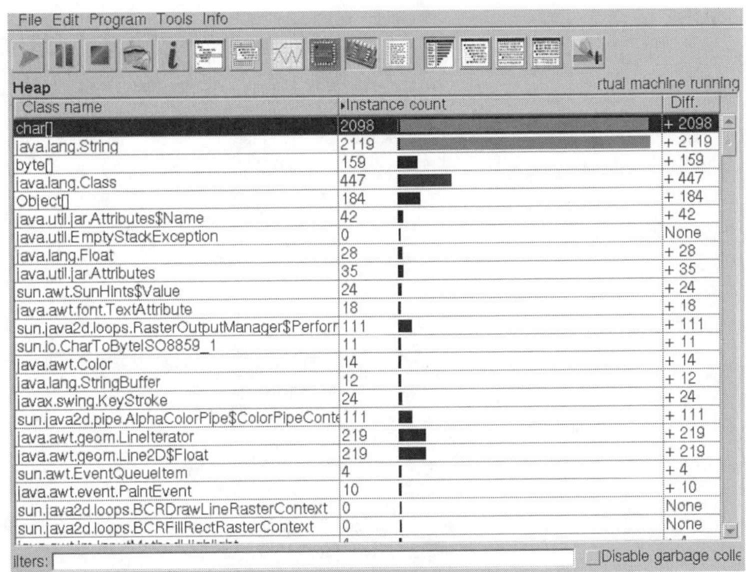

FIGURE 62.2
The OptimizeIt main GUI.

Analyzing Heap Usage

When OptimizeIt is being used to capture heap usage (refer to Figure 62.2), you can examine the details about objects being allocated by the application. To analyze a particular class, select the class (`char[]` is selected in the example) and use the third group of buttons to explore the data in more detail.

You can uses the various analysis modes to explore allocation backtraces (see Figures 62.3 and 62.4) and reference graphs (see Figure 62.5) to understand where memory is being allocated and how it is being used. Another analysis option lets you examine all objects in the JVM (see Figure 62.6).

Text provided after each figure (Figures 62.2–62.6) presents more detail about the analysis being performed.

The tree in the upper window in Figure 62.3 allows you to discover where allocations are taking place. The star icon indicates the location of allocations, whereas the arrow icon points to additional allocations further down the call stack.

The lower window describes which methods are doing the actual allocation: We see that more than 27 percent of the `char` arrays have been allocated by the `StringBuffer` constructor.

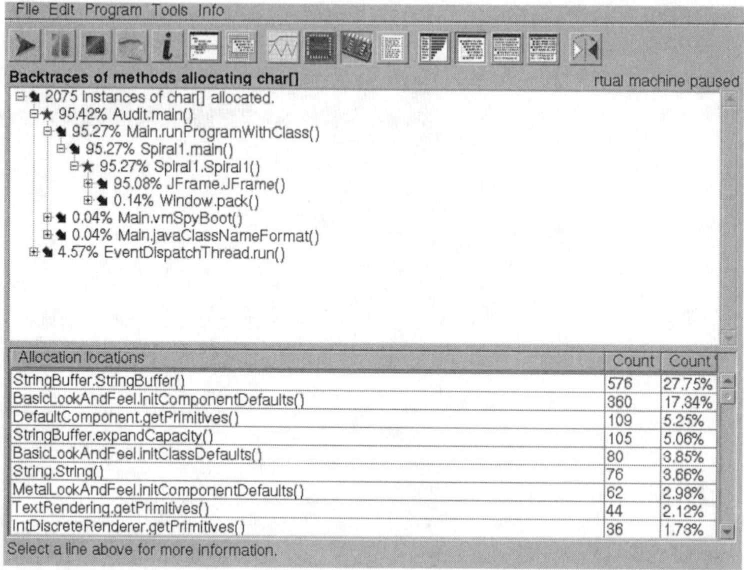

FIGURE 62.3
Examining allocation backtraces.

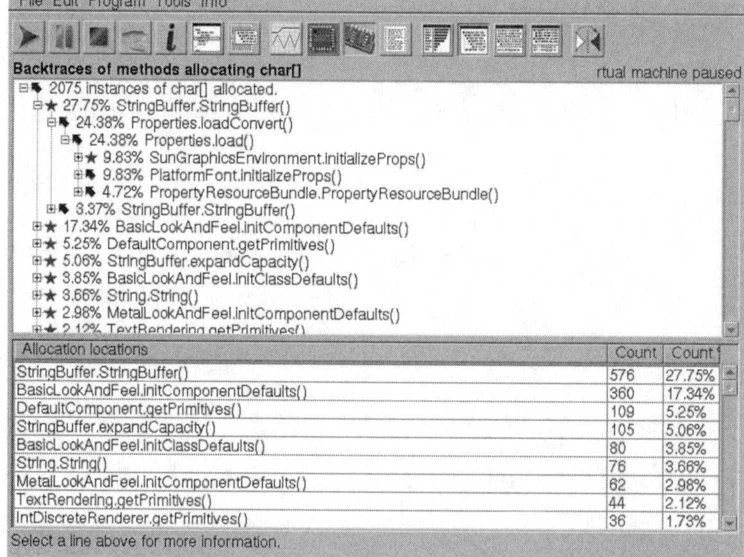

FIGURE 62.4
Examining allocation backtraces up the call stack.

Figure 62.4 reverses the analysis seen in Figure 62.3: You can explore *up* the call stack from the site of allocation traces—ascertaining on whose behalf an allocation was made. This mode is selected with the far-right `Reverse Display` button.

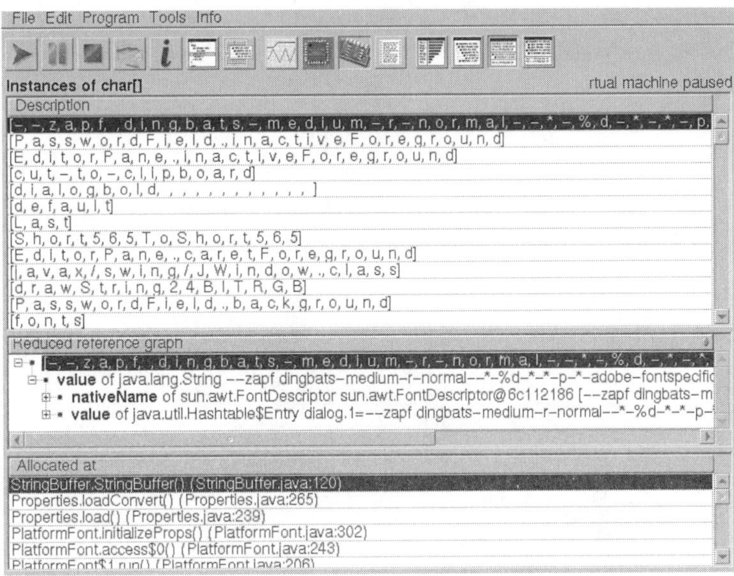

FIGURE 62.5
Examining reference graphs.

You can examine a reference graph—that is, track down who holds references to any object. In Figure 62.5, we begin with a scrolled list (in the upper window) showing the contents of every `char` array.

Selecting one of the arrays—in this case an array containing the X name for the *zapf dingbats* font—provides further analysis in the lower two windows. The middle window contains a reference graph showing that this `char` array is referenced by a `String` object, which is in turn referenced by an AWT font-related class.

The lower window provides a full stack trace that was captured when the array was allocated; this trace is 41 calls deep.

The object graph in Figure 62.6 provides a complete view of all objects in the JVM, organized by class name. When you select an individual object for examination, the lower window provides a stack traceback showing where it was allocated.

Analyzing CPU Usage

Selecting OptimizeIt's Show CPU Profiler button (the 9th button from the left) enables analysis of application CPU use. In this mode, you must ask the tool to record runtime information (see Figure 62.7) and then stop the recording before beginning analysis.

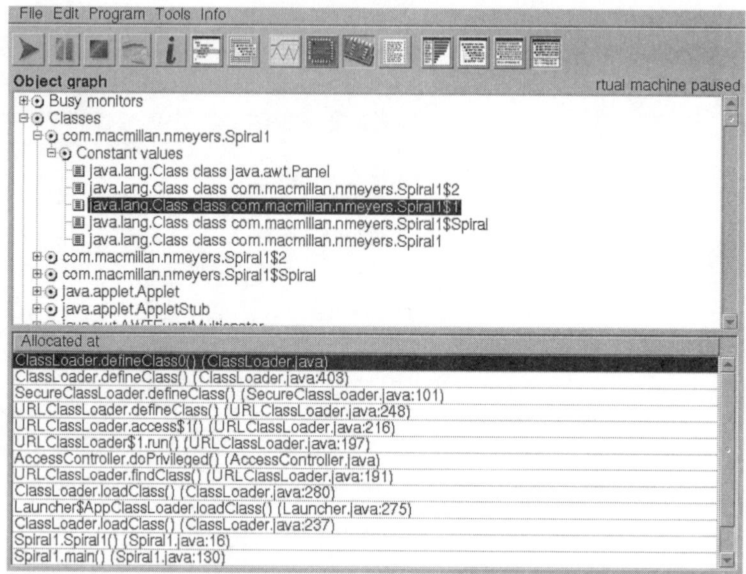

FIGURE 62.6
Examining the object reference graph.

FIGURE 62.7
Profiling CPU activity.

When profiling CPU activity, you can choose to record the data in one of three modes:

- Collect statistically sampled data, using a real-time clock as the sample clock. This captures idle and busy time spent by the program.
- Collect statistically sampled data, using the CPU clock as a sample clock. This is the default choice, and it captures CPU time consumed by the program.
- Collect data from profiler instrumentation in the JVM.

The default mode (CPU clock sampling) is the method used by most profiling tools, and is probably the most useful for discovering application performance problems.

After you end data collection and begin analysis, OptimizeIt presents a pull-down menu (see Figure 62.8) offering you a choice of which thread to analyze.

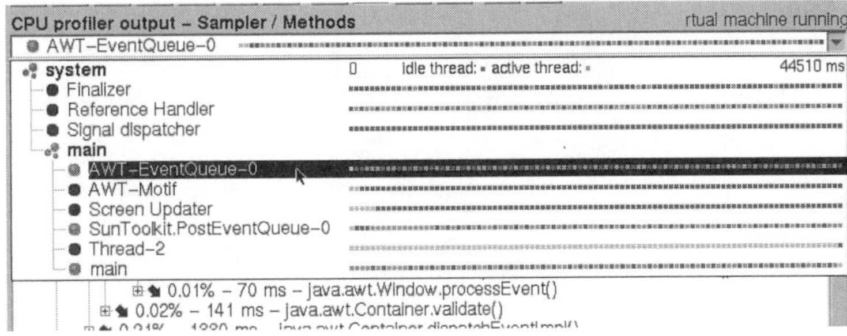

FIGURE 62.8
Selecting a thread for analysis.

The pull-down thread selection menu in Figure 62.8 describes the threads whose CPU activity was captured during profiling. Red and green dots indicate periods of inactivity and activity for each thread, giving you a quick view of where time was spent and how the threads interact.

When analyzing an individual thread, the interface presents traceback and hot spot information (see Figures 62.9 and 62.10) for detailed exploration.

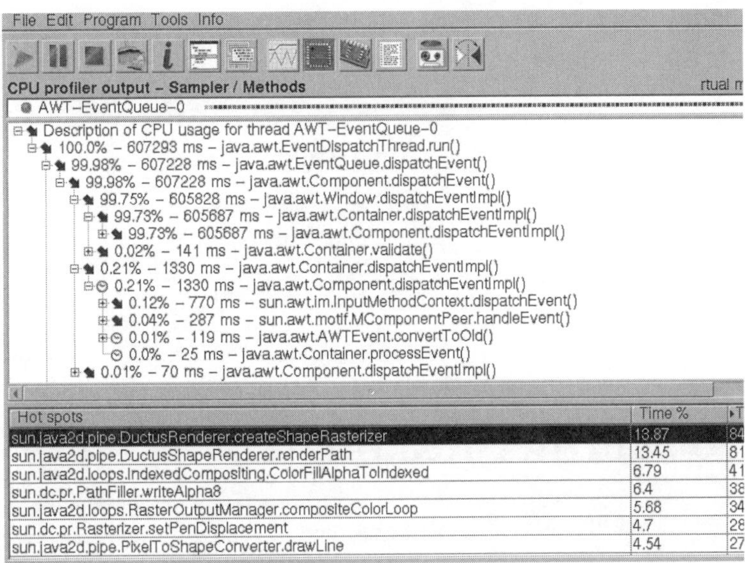

FIGURE 62.9
Analyzing CPU usage.

The upper window in Figure 62.9 allows you to explore down the call stack to see where time is being spent. The lower window displays the top hot spots for this thread.

And, as with the memory usage graph, you can turn the CPU usage graph upside-down (see Figure 62.10) and explore up the call stack from the sites of the hot spots. This allows you to discover on whose behalf CPU time is being spent.

Finally, you can explore the source code associated with hot spots. By selecting an entry in the list of hot spots and activating the source viewer, you are shown a display of source code with the relevant sections highlighted (see Figure 62.11).

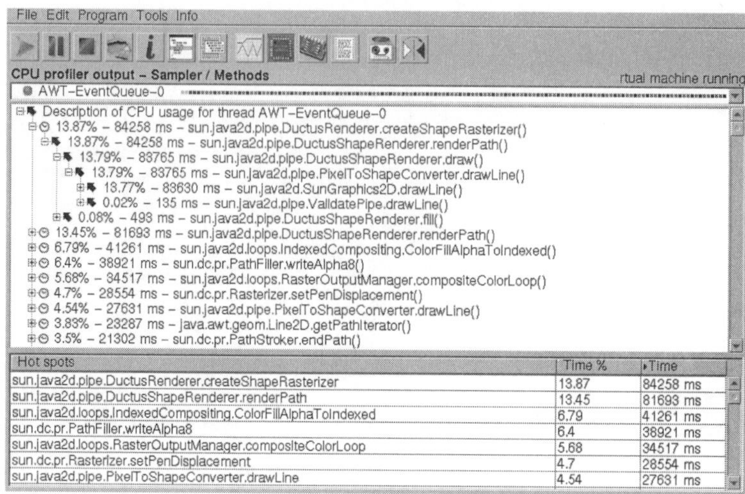

FIGURE 62.10
Analyzing CPU usage up the call stack.

FIGURE 62.11
The source code viewer highlights source code hot spots.

com.macmillan.nmeyers.Spiral1$Spiral – Spiral1.java

```
    int width, height;
int repaintCount = 0;
long repaintTime = 0;
Spiral(int w, int h)
{
    width = w;
    height = h;
}
public Dimension getPreferredSize()
{
    return new Dimension(width, height);
}
public void paintComponent(Graphics g)
{
    ((Graphics2D)g).setRenderingHint(
    RenderingHints.KEY_ANTIALIASING,
    RenderingHints.VALUE_ANTIALIAS_ON);
    Rectangle bounds = g.getClipBounds();
    g.clearRect(bounds.x, bounds.y, bounds.width, bounds.height);
    ((Graphics2D)g).scale(1.0 / 1.1, 1.0 / 1.1);
    Dimension d = getSize();
    Date date1 = new Date();
    int x1 = 0, x2 = (int)((d.width - 1) * 1.1);
```

For Further Reading

OptimizeIt is a commercial product, with extensive documentation and online help. This chapter has presented a few snapshots of some common analysis modes; the included documentation provides a more thorough view of the product's functions and capabilities.

Summary

This chapter described OptimizeIt—a commercial Java performance-tuning tool available for Linux. Its rich set of capabilities is made possible by the JDK1.2 JVM Profiling Interface, and you can expect to see more such tools as JDK1.2 matures.

CHAPTER 63

UNDERSTANDING LINUX KERNEL PERFORMANCE

This chapter discusses techniques for analyzing Java's performance costs in terms of time spent in the Linux kernel.

Platforms: JDK1.1/JDK1.2

The performance tools discussed in Chapters 60, "`PerfAnal`: A Free Performance Analysis Tool," and 62, "OptimizeIt: Live Performance Analysis," focused on one aspect of CPU usage: time spent executing user code. Another important aspect of runtime performance is *system time*—the time spent executing code in the Linux kernel. This time is not recorded in profiles generated by the JVM, but applications enjoy considerable control over how much they stress the kernel.

Consider a simple example. The program in Listing 63.1 generates a specified amount of output using two different output classes. This program takes two command-line parameters, `count1` and `count2`. Lines 13–16 print the letter 'X' `count1` times using the method `java.io.PrintStream.print()`. Lines 18–21 print the letter 'X' `count2` times using the method `java.io.PrintWriter.print()`.

LISTING 63.1 PrintX.java

```
import java.io.*;

public class PrintX
{
    public static void main(String[] argv)
    {
        int count1 = 0, count2 = 0;
        try { count1 = Integer.parseInt(argv[0]);
              count2 = Integer.parseInt(argv[1]); }
        catch (Exception e) { System.out.println(e); System.exit(1); }
        PrintWriter writer =
            new PrintWriter(new OutputStreamWriter(System.out));
        for (int i = 0; i < count1; i++)
        {
            System.out.print('X');
        }
        System.out.flush();
        for (int i = 0; i < count2; i++)
        {
            writer.print('X');
        }
        writer.flush();
    }
}
```

When two different invocations of this program are run side-by-side (sending their output to the bit bucket)

```
bash$ java PrintX 100000 0 >/dev/null
bash$ java PrintX 0 100000 >/dev/null
```

the second invocation runs faster than the first. What's going on?

The GNU `time` Utility

We begin to answer the question by using the GNU **time** utility—a standard component in virtually all Linux distributions. In the unlikely event that **time** is not already installed on your system, it should be available from the installation media. Red Hat users can load it from the **time** RPM.

time provides an easy and useful way to generate a quick analysis of the example program's performance.

Synopsis:

time [<*options*>] <*command...*>

time runs the specified command and reports on the CPU and real time consumed by the process and its children.

Options:

- `-a` or `--append`—Append output to file specified with the `-o` option (below).
- `-f` <*format*> or `--format=`<*format*>—Specify a custom format string for `time` output. The string consists of characters that are output verbatim, and format strings that are replaced with specified values. Possible format string values are

  `%C`: Command string executed

  `%c`: Number of involuntary context switches

  `%D`: Average unshared data size (kB)

  `%E`: Elapsed time (h:mm:ss or m:ss)

  `%F`: Major page faults

  `%I`: File system inputs

  `%K`: Average total size (kB)

  `%k`: Signals delivered

  `%M`: Maximum resident set size (kB)

  `%O`: File system outputs

  `%p`: Average stack size (kB)

  `%P`: Percent of CPU used by command

  `%R`: Minor page faults

  `%r`: Socket messages received

  `%s`: Socket messages sent

  `%S`: System time (seconds)

  `%t`: Average resident set size (kB)

  `%U`: User time (seconds)

  `%W`: Number of swaps

  `%w`: Number of voluntary context switches

  `%X`: Average shared text size (kB)

  `%x`: Exit status

  `%Z`: Page size (bytes)
- `--help`—Generate a usage message.
- `-p` or `--portability`—Generate a standard, "portable" output format.
- `-o` <*file*> or `--output=`<*file*>—Record output in specified file. Default is to send output to `stderr`.

- `-v` or `--verbose`—Generate detailed output, including all the data described for the `--format` option (discussed previously in this list).
- `-V` or `--version`—Print version number.

Using `time` with `PrintX` yields the following results:

```
bash$ time --portability java PrintX 100000 0 >/dev/null
real 8.58
user 8.03
sys 0.38
bash$ time --portability java PrintX 0 100000 >/dev/null
real 3.56
user 3.32
sys 0.13
```

Both invocations printed 100,000 characters, but the first invocation took more than twice as much elapsed time, more than twice as much user-space CPU time, and nearly 3 times as much system (kernel) time.

We could analyze `PrintX` with the tools discussed in the last few chapters and learn which methods are consuming CPU time. But the answer from the Java side is obvious: The application is busy printing! Some relevant information—such as why one kind of printing is slower then another—is beyond the reach of those tools. For that, we need to look at what is happening in the operating system.

The `time` tool provides a good first glimpse at OS activity—the preceding example shows that *something* interesting is going on. But the numbers are rough and include program overhead not directly associated with the application code. We need more detailed tools.

The Linux `strace` Utility

`strace` is a *system call* tracing utility—it traces, in detail, the use of kernel facilities by applications. `strace` is found in most distributions and is usually installed by default. Red Hat users can load it from the `strace` RPM.

Subtleties

What is a system call? The concept is foreign to many Java developers and often a bit bewildering to C/C++ programmers.

As shown in the discussion of UNIX and Linux in Chapter 5, "What Is Linux?" in the section "The Structure of UNIX," there is a clear division of labor between work performed in user space and work performed in kernel space. This division of labor is largely transparent to programmers but is an important activity under the covers.

Consider, for example, what happens when your program writes data to a file on disk:

1. Your user-space code calls a print routine with the data you want to write.
2. User-space code in a library formats the data and appends the formatted bytes to a buffer.
3. When the buffer fills, the library code flushes the buffer by making a *system call* to the kernel, asking it to perform a physical write.

4. Code in the kernel handles the remaining hoary details—shepherding those bytes through the intricacies of the file system, I/O subsystem, device drivers, hardware, and the kernel's other activities, ultimately causing a small recording head to write some bits to a spinning magnetic platter.

Even in native languages such as C++, application programs do not often make explicit system calls; they use the higher-level capabilities provided by libraries (formatted buffered I/O, in this example) and let the libraries make the system calls.

Despite this strong boundary between user and kernel activity, applications have some control over how they use and abuse the kernel, as you see when we use `strace` to analyze our example program.

Synopsis:

`strace [<options>] [<command and args>]`

Run the specified command and arguments, capturing and reporting information on system calls made by the process. The *`<command and args>`* parameter is optional—you do not specify it if you use the `-p` option to analyze an already-running process.

Options:

- `-c`—Generate a summary of system call usage and time. If this option is *not* specified, `strace` generates a voluminous, detailed log of all system calls.
- `-d`—Generate output for debugging of `strace`.
- `-f`—Trace forked processes as they are created.
- `-ff`—Output traces from forked processes into separate files. The filenames are derived from the `-o` option (discussed later in this list) with the process ID appended.
- `-F`—Trace `vforked` processes, if possible.
- `-h`—Display a help message.
- `-i`—Output the user-space instruction pointer value at the time of the system call.
- `-q`—Run quietly.
- `-r`—Print a relative time stamp for each system call—the elapsed time since the previous system call.
- `-t`, `-tt`, or `-ttt`—Print an absolute time stamp for each system call (with varying degrees of detail, depending on which option is used).
- `-T`—Print CPU time consumed by each system call.
- `-V`—Print `strace` version.
- `-v`—Run verbosely: include more detail in the output.
- `-x` or `-xx`—Print non-ASCII strings (`-x`) or all strings (`-xx`) in hex.
- `-a` *`<column>`*—Align system call results data on a specified column.
- `-e` *`<expr>`*—Specify a filter to apply to the data to be printed. This option allows you to apply a number of detailed criteria to selecting the system calls to report. See the `strace` man page for full details.

- `-o` *<file>*—Send results to specified file. Default is `stderr`.
- `-O` *<overhead>*—`strace` has its own heuristics for estimating how much overhead its own activities consume—and subtracting that from the reported results. This option allows you to specify your own value.
- `-p` *<pid>*—Trace an existing process with the specified PID.
- `-s` *<strsize>*—Limit the size of strings printed in the output.
- `-S {time¦calls¦name¦nothing}`—Sort the counts generated by the `-c` option (discussed previously) by the specified value.
- `-u` *<username>*—Run the command under the specified username. You must be the root user to use this option.

Example:

Of the many `strace` options, `-c` is particularly useful. It generates a short summary indicating which kernel functions were called and how much time was spent in those calls. If `-c` is not specified, `strace` generates voluminous output logging *every* system call—which is sometimes useful, but not necessary for our purposes in this chapter. (Also note that many of the `strace` options are not relevant if `-c` is specified.)

Before showing how to apply `strace` to Java, here is an illustration of its use with ordinary programs launched from the command line. The example in Listing 63.2 uses `strace` to run the GNU `ls` command and generate a summary.

LISTING 63.2 Running `strace` on the GNU `ls` Command

```
bash$ strace -c ls /usr/local/Java/jdk1.2
execve("/bin/ls", ["ls", "/usr/local/Java/jdk1.2"], [/* 29 vars */]) = 0

COPYRIGHT  README.PRE-RELEASE  README.linux.src  include      lib
LICENSE    README.html         bin               include-old  src.jar
README     README.linux        demo              jre

% time     seconds  usecs/call     calls    errors syscall
------ ----------- ----------- --------- --------- ----------------
 82.35    0.003779        1260         3           write
  3.66    0.000168          34         5         2 open
  2.09    0.000096          19         5           mmap
  1.57    0.000072          36         2           getdents
  1.50    0.000069          69         1           lstat
  1.44    0.000066          11         6           brk
  1.20    0.000055          28         2           munmap
  1.02    0.000047          47         1           read
  0.94    0.000043          14         3           ioctl
  0.81    0.000037           9         4           fstat
  0.70    0.000032           8         4           close
  0.70    0.000032          32         1           readlink
  0.70    0.000032          32         1           stat
```

```
  0.37    0.000017          17         1           mprotect
  0.33    0.000015           8         2           lseek
  0.17    0.000008           8         1           fcntl
  0.15    0.000007           7         1           time
  0.15    0.000007           7         1           getpid
  0.15    0.000007           7         1           personality
------ ----------- ----------- --------- --------- ----------------
100.00    0.004589                      45         2 total
```

The first line of output shows the system call—`execve()`—that launched the program. This is followed by the output of the program—a listing of the contents of the JDK1.2 directory.

The remaining output is the analysis: `strace`'s report on the use of system calls. Of the .004589 seconds this program spent performing kernel activity, more than 82 percent of it was spent performing writes to the terminal—not a big surprise.

The system calls in the right-hand column may seem cryptic. They are the low-level services provided by the kernel to your application and usually stay hidden behind the capable interfaces supplied by user-space libraries such as `libc` (for C/C++ programmers) and the Java core class libraries.

Using `strace` with Java

As with native applications, using `strace` with Java will give you some visibility into how your Java application is stressing the kernel. The challenge to using `strace` is to run it on the `java` executable, not on the `java` launch script. We do this with a modest trick—using the debugger backdoor built into the `java` launch script.

Synopsis:

```
DEBUG_PROG="strace <options>" java -green ...
```

Setting the `DEBUG_PROG` environment variable causes the `java` launch script to invoke the `java` executable with the specified command. The `-green` flag is needed because `strace` is (at present) confused by native-threaded programs.

Example:

Listings 63.3 and 63.4 show the results of running the example program with `strace`. In Listing 63.4, CPU usage is much lower, particularly for the `read` and `write` system calls.

LISTING 63.3 Running `strace` on the First Invocation of `PrintX`

```
bash$ DEBUG_PROG="strace -c" java -green PrintX 100000 0 >/dev/null
execve("/usr/local/Java/jdk1.2/bin/i386/native_threads/java", ["/usr/local
/Java/jdk1.2/bin/i386/native_threads/java", "Hello", "100000", "0"], [/* 3
3 vars */]) = 0
% time     seconds  usecs/call     calls    errors syscall
------ ----------- ----------- --------- --------- ----------------
 78.70    1.870720          19    100005           write
```

continued on next page

continued from previous page

```
 19.82    0.471126        1098       429           read
  0.47    0.011254         110       102           kill
  0.21    0.005023          27       189           brk
  0.15    0.003659           8       438           _llseek
  0.14    0.003342          47        71        30 open
  0.13    0.003085          23       132           lstat
  0.10    0.002264         162        14        14 SYS_179
  0.07    0.001751          55        32         4 stat
  0.06    0.001404          28        51           mmap
  0.03    0.000796          36        22           mprotect
  0.02    0.000497          16        32           close
  0.02    0.000367           9        43           fstat
  0.01    0.000332          17        19           gettimeofday
  0.01    0.000325          36         9           munmap
  0.01    0.000325          23        14        14 sigreturn
  0.01    0.000180          30         6           readlink
  0.01    0.000145           6        24           SYS_175
  0.00    0.000109           7        15           SYS_174
  0.00    0.000071          71         1           socket
  0.00    0.000064          32         2         1 connect
  0.00    0.000061          61         1           clone
  0.00    0.000045          45         1           pipe
  0.00    0.000029          15         2           uname
  0.00    0.000024           8         3           fcntl
  0.00    0.000020           5         4           getpid
  0.00    0.000018           9         2           lseek
  0.00    0.000014           7         2           getrlimit
  0.00    0.000011           6         2           time
  0.00    0.000011           6         2           setrlimit
  0.00    0.000011           6         2           getdents
  0.00    0.000009           9         1           wait4
  0.00    0.000008           8         1           personality
  0.00    0.000007           7         1           times
  0.00    0.000006           6         1           getuid
------ ----------- ----------- -------- --------- ---------------
100.00    2.377113                101675        63 total
```

LISTING 63.4 Running `strace` on the second invocation of `PrintX`

```
bash$ DEBUG_PROG="strace -c" java -green PrintX 0 100000 >/dev/null
execve("/usr/local/Java/jdk1.2/bin/i386/native_threads/java", ["/usr/local
/Java/jdk1.2/bin/i386/native_threads/java", "Hello", "0", "100000"], [/* 3
3 vars */]) = 0
% time     seconds  usecs/call     calls    errors syscall
------ ----------- ----------- -------- --------- ---------------
 38.68    0.024711          58       429           read
 25.20    0.016099         125       129           kill
  6.86    0.004382          23       189           brk
  5.84    0.003731           9       438           _llseek
  4.66    0.002979          42        71        30 open
  4.32    0.002760          21       132           lstat
  3.11    0.001987         153        13        13 SYS_179
```

```
  2.53    0.001617          51        32         4 stat
  1.99    0.001273          25        51           mmap
  1.46    0.000935          52        18           write
  0.73    0.000464          15        32           close
  0.64    0.000410          19        22           mprotect
  0.63    0.000405          18        23           gettimeofday
  0.60    0.000383          17        23           SYS_175
  0.56    0.000356           8        43           fstat
  0.50    0.000321          36         9           munmap
  0.40    0.000257          86         3           fcntl
  0.27    0.000171          29         6           readlink
  0.17    0.000108           7        15           SYS_174
  0.16    0.000101           8        13        13 sigreturn
  0.10    0.000067          34         2           getdents
  0.10    0.000063          32         2         1 connect
  0.10    0.000061          61         1           clone
  0.09    0.000059          59         1           socket
  0.08    0.000054          54         1           pipe
  0.05    0.000029          15         2           uname
  0.03    0.000019           5         4           getpid
  0.03    0.000018           9         2           lseek
  0.02    0.000014           7         2           getrlimit
  0.02    0.000011           6         2           time
  0.02    0.000011           6         2           setrlimit
  0.01    0.000008           8         1           wait4
  0.01    0.000008           8         1           personality
  0.01    0.000007           7         1           times
  0.01    0.000006           6         1           getuid
------ ----------- ----------- --------- --------- ----------------
100.00    0.063885                  1716        61 total
```

What a difference! The first invocation of the program spent 1.87 seconds performing `writes`—the write system call was invoked 100,000 times. The second invocation only called `write` 18 times and consumed drastically less kernel time. The cause of the performance differences is now obvious: the `java.io.PrintWriter` class is buffering its output, whereas the `java.io.PrintStream` class is not.

This is the sort of detail we can only learn from a trace of kernel activities.

Summary

This chapter examined tools you can use—`time` and `strace`—for understanding how Java applications stress the Linux kernel and for identifying tuning opportunities. The next chapter examines one more performance aspect worth understanding: time spent in native user-space code.

CHAPTER 64

PROFILING USER-SPACE NATIVE CODE

This chapter presents `Profiler`, a native tool that analyzes time spent by Java applications in native code.

Platforms: JDK1.2

The profiling tools discussed in Chapters 60, "`PerfAnal`: A Free Performance Analysis Tool," and 62, "OptimizeIt: Live Performance Analysis," allow you to study how your application is spending its time, but the information they return is oriented around the Java address space. They report time spent on behalf of Java methods, without any indication of why a method may be consuming CPU resources.

Chapter 63, "Understanding Linux Kernel Performance," added a new dimension of information—time spent in the kernel. This chapter discusses another one: time spent in native user-space code.

In a Java application running on Linux, user-space native code is always executing—either running the interpreter or running native code called from the interpreter. And although the earlier tools do capture the time spent in native code, the time is *charged* to an application-level Java method. Something is missing.

Put another way, how is the profiling time reported for any particular Java method really being spent—in the interpreter, JNI code, JIT-compiled code, or some other native library? An answer to this question can help in further understanding application performance.

Profiler: A Native Application Profiler

The Linux and UNIX worlds provide a variety of tools to support application profiling, such as code instrumentation inserted by the compiler, instrumented libraries, sampling-based utilities, and kernel instrumentation.

`Profiler` is a personal tool that leverages one of those existing tools, by bringing an existing `libc` profiling capability to JDK1.2. The information it collects is similar to that from `strace`—a shallow[1] view of where time is being spent, but the view is of the user-space native address space instead of kernel calls. `Profiler` reports time spent in user-space native code and kernel time spent on behalf of user-space native code.

Theory of Profiler Operation

Most of the native code run during Java execution is resident in the JVM's shared library address space. This includes the JVM itself, the JIT, all JNI methods, the C library, all Java support libraries—everything except JIT-compiled code (which can be created and run in data space).

The C library provides a facility, `profil(3)`, to support profiling of native code located in a contiguous chunk of address space. To use `profil(3)`, you must determine a range of addresses to profile, and you must provide an array of counters to collect the profiling data. Figure 64.1 illustrates how the address space is divided among the counters.

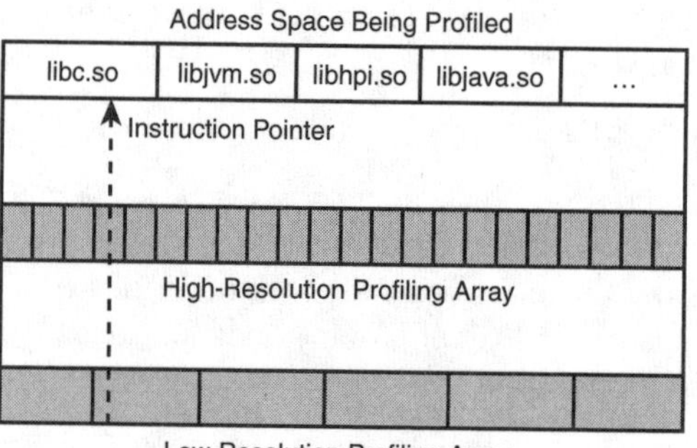

FIGURE 64.1
An illustration of how `profil(3)` uses the profiling array.

Each counter in the profiling array in Figure 64.1 represents activity in some portion of the address space. Every time the profiling timer ticks (every 10ms of CPU time), the value of the instruction pointer is examined and the corresponding array element is incremented. A large array may be used to collect high-resolution data, or a small array to collect low-resolution data.

The information needed to make this profiling facility useful is a mapping between the process's address space and the libraries (and procedures) being executed. That information comes from two sources:

---

[1]A "shallow view" meaning one that lacks the full traceback information that was available with the Java profiles.

- The Linux /proc file system provides this information in a pseudo-file[2] named /proc/<pid>/maps, where <pid> is the process ID. For every shared library used by a process, the file indicates where the library is mapped in the process's address space. Beginning with Linux kernel 2.2, the file also shows the names of the shared libraries—an important feature on which Profiler depends.
- The shared libraries themselves contain symbol tables that allow you to map addresses to the names of individual procedures.

Profiler uses these sources to construct a map of where in native code the application is spending time.

Using Profiler

Profiler is packaged as a shared library that implements the JVM Profiling Interface, similar to hprof (see the section "Sun's Sample hprof Profiler" in Chapter 60). Like hprof, it is used with the JDK1.2 JVM through the -Xrun option.

Synopsis:

```
java -green ... -XrunProfiler[:<options>]
```

The library must be located somewhere the JVM can find it—either in the JDK's central library repository, or in a directory referenced by the LD_LIBRARY_PATH environment variable (as discussed in Chapter 15, "Troubleshooting The Blackdown JSDK/JRE Installation " in the section "Finding JNI Libraries").

The -green option is not mandatory, but not using it can lead to confusing results: the times(2) system call used to report total user time reports incorrect results for native-threaded applications.

Options:

The comma-separated options control Profiler's behavior:

- size=<#bytes>—Specify the size of the profiling array in bytes. A better alternative to this option is scale= (discussed next).
- scale=<#bytes>—Specify the resolution of the profiling array. The smallest possible value, 1, gives you the highest resolution: Every byte of the address space maps to a separate profiling counter (refer to Figure 64.1), and you can precisely identify every procedure where time is being spent. Unfortunately, this also leads to a large profiling array and large memory requirements for Profiler.

2Like everything else in the /proc filesystem, this is not a real file; it is a way to query the kernel for some of its internal data structures. You can learn more about this powerful Linux feature from the proc man page.

The default value is `1024`, meaning that 1024 bytes of address space map to a single counter. This keeps the profiling array relatively small. It will identify which libraries are consuming time, but usually not which procedures. The ***best*** value depends on what you need to learn from profiling: Use a value of `1` to get the best possible list of hot spots; use higher values to keep `Profiler` from using disruptive amounts of memory.

- `expand=<#bytes>` or `expand=<percent>%`—Specify additional space for dynamically loaded libraries.

  `Profiler` determines how much address space to profile to by examining the shared libraries that are loaded after JVM initialization. If any libraries are later dynamically loaded, they will fall outside the address range being profiled. You can specify room for growth—either in bytes or as a percentage of current size—to allow for later shared libraries. The additional space will be profiled by `Profiler`, on the assumption that it will provide useful data.

  An alternate solution to this problem is to preload all shared libraries you need to profile, with the `LD_PRELOAD` environment variable (see the section "Environment Variables Affecting the JSDK/JRE" in Chapter 14).

- `scope=global`—Charge time to globally visible procedures in the shared libraries (default).
- `scope=local`—Charge time to the nearest local label in shared libraries. This is the opposite of the `scope=global` option. When reporting time spent in libraries, it will charge the time to the nearest label at or before the instruction pointer, whether global or local. The nearest label may be a local procedure within the library, or it may be a label inside a procedure. The results are potentially useful, but more likely to be confusing.
- `file=<filename>`—Save profiling results to the specified file. Default is to send results to `stderr`.

Applying Profiler

We apply `Profiler` to the `PrintX` problem we were analyzing with `strace` (see Chapter 63, "Understanding Linux Kernel Performance").

Profiling the Slow Version

First we profile the slow invocation of `PrintX`.

```
bash$ java -green -XrunProfiler:scale=1,file=results.txt PrintX 100000 0 \
>/dev/null
Profiler: profiling over 20467712-byte address range
Profiler: allocating 20467713 profiling elements
```

`Profiler` indicated that it is profiling 20MB worth of shared libraries, creating a suitably large array to capture the high-resolution profiling information requested by the `scale=1` option.

The results begin with a report on overall CPU time:

```
Total time: 8330 ms (7850 ms user, 480 ms system)
Total time profiled: 5280 ms
```

The first line is CPU time reported by the `times(2)` system call; the second is the amount of time captured by the profiler. In this case, the profiler captured only about 63% of the CPU time—the remainder was spent running JIT-compiled code outside the shared library address space. (This difference disappears if JIT is disabled.)

The next section of output is a ranked list of time spent in individual libraries:

```
CPU Use by Library
------------------
/usr/local/Java/jdk1.2/jre/lib/i386/classic/libjvm.so
  Total time: 2020 ms
/usr/local/Java/jdk1.2/jre/lib/i386/green_threads/libhpi.so
  Total time: 1150 ms
  Non-procedure time: 10 ms
/usr/local/Java/jdk1.2/jre/lib/i386/libsunwjit.so
  Total time: 1140 ms
/lib/libc-2.1.1.so
  Total time: 730 ms
/usr/local/Java/jdk1.2/jre/lib/i386/libjava.so
  Total time: 220 ms
/lib/ld-2.1.1.so
  Total time: 10 ms
/usr/lib/libstdc++-2-libc6.1-1-2.9.0.so
  Total time: 10 ms
```

Finally, `Profiler` shows hot spots in the code, broken out by individual library procedure:

```
Hot Spots
---------
/usr/local/Java/jdk1.2/jre/lib/i386/libsunwjit.so:JITGetMethodBlockForPC: 420 ms
/usr/local/Java/jdk1.2/jre/lib/i386/green_threads/libhpi.so:sysMonitorExit: 410 ms
/lib/libc-2.1.1.so:__libc_write: 380 ms
/usr/local/Java/jdk1.2/jre/lib/i386/classic/libjvm.so:monitorEnter2: 270 ms
/usr/local/Java/jdk1.2/jre/lib/i386/classic/libjvm.so:monitorExit2: 260 ms
/usr/local/Java/jdk1.2/jre/lib/i386/classic/libjvm.so:sysInvokeNative: 200 ms
/usr/local/Java/jdk1.2/jre/lib/i386/green_threads/libhpi.so:write: 200 ms
/usr/local/Java/jdk1.2/jre/lib/i386/classic/libjvm.so:JVM_ArrayCopy: 190 ms
/usr/local/Java/jdk1.2/jre/lib/i386/classic/libjvm.so:AddToLoadedClasses: 180 ms
/usr/local/Java/jdk1.2/jre/lib/i386/green_threads/libhpi.so:sysMonitorEnter: 170 ms
/usr/local/Java/jdk1.2/jre/lib/i386/libjava.so:writeBytes: 160 ms
     .
     .
     .
```

Notice how much time is spent in the C library `__libc_write()` procedure and in various JNI- and synchronization-related methods.

Profiling the Fast Version

We try the same test with the fast invocation of `PrintX`:

```
bash$ java -green -XrunProfiler:scale=1,file=results.txt PrintX 0 100000 >/dev/null
Profiler: profiling over 20467712-byte address range
Profiler: allocating 20467713 profiling elements
```

The differences are immediately obvious:

```
Total time: 2630 ms (2610 ms user, 20 ms system)
Total time profiled: 1900 ms
```

We see that less time is spent both in the libraries and in the JIT-compiled code.

The per-library results show us that much less time is spent in all libraries:

```
CPU Use by Library
------------------
/usr/local/Java/jdk1.2/jre/lib/i386/classic/libjvm.so
  Total time: 890 ms
/usr/local/Java/jdk1.2/jre/lib/i386/libsunwjit.so
  Total time: 560 ms
/usr/local/Java/jdk1.2/jre/lib/i386/green_threads/libhpi.so
  Total time: 240 ms
/lib/libc-2.1.1.so
  Total time: 190 ms
/usr/lib/libstdc++-2-libc6.1-1-2.9.0.so
  Total time: 10 ms
/usr/local/Java/jdk1.2/jre/lib/i386/libzip.so
  Total time: 10 ms
```

And the list of hot spots is drastically different:

```
Hot Spots
---------
/usr/local/Java/jdk1.2/jre/lib/i386/classic/libjvm.so:allocObject: 160 ms
/usr/local/Java/jdk1.2/jre/lib/i386/classic/libjvm.so:InitializeRefs: 150 ms
/usr/local/Java/jdk1.2/jre/lib/i386/green_threads/libhpi.so:sysMonitorExit: 100 ms
/usr/local/Java/jdk1.2/jre/lib/i386/classic/libjvm.so:FreeHandleMemory: 90 ms
/usr/local/Java/jdk1.2/jre/lib/i386/classic/libjvm.so:cacheAlloc: 80 ms
/usr/local/Java/jdk1.2/jre/lib/i386/classic/libjvm.so:JVM_ArrayCopy: 80 ms
/usr/local/Java/jdk1.2/jre/lib/i386/classic/libjvm.so:allocArray: 70 ms
/usr/local/Java/jdk1.2/jre/lib/i386/libsunwjit.so:JITGetMethodBlockForPC: 70 ms
/lib/libc-2.1.1.so:memmove: 60 ms
    .
    .
    .
```

The earlier hot spots are gone. The `libc` write call is not being heavily abused, and much of the associated overhead (synchronization, for example) is also gone. The improvement is a direct result of the difference in output buffering behavior: The use of buffering makes `java.io.PrintWriter` much more efficient than `java.io.PrintStream`.

Building Profiler

The source for Profiler is provided on the CD-ROM, and a listing can be found in Appendix B, "Miscellaneous Program Listings."

Building the `Profiler` shared library requires SDK1.2 and a C++ development environment. The necessary commands to build are as follows:

```
g++ -D_REENTRANT -fpic -I$JAVA_HOME/include -I$JAVA_HOME/include/linux \
 -I/usr/include/g++-2 -I/usr/include/g++ -c profiler.C
g++ -shared -o libProfiler.so profiler.o
```

The code makes extensive use of the C++ standard library and depends on headers that are usually found in `/usr/include/g++/` or `/usr/include/g++-2/` (depending on your g++ installation).

Summary

This chapter presented `Profiler`, a tool to assist in understanding how Java JDK1.2 applications use CPU resources in native code. Native profiling of user- and kernel-space CPU usage is a challenging pursuit and not an ideal first line of inquiry as you investigate Java application performance. But they can also provide performance information that is not available through Java profiling and are a useful addition to your development tools arsenal.

PART XIV

JAVA AND LINUX ON SERVERS

One area of increasing success and visibility for both Java and Linux is *servers*—relatively large systems providing file, computation, information, or application services to users on other computers.

What makes a computer a *server*? The word carries less precision than such older terms as *minicomputer* and *mainframe*. A server can be anything from a high-end x86 machine to a heavy-iron IBM box. The common themes among servers—the requirements that distinguish them from laptops and wristwatches—are roughly these:

- System design—Servers have demanding system design requirements. Capacities between components, buses, and interfaces must be well matched, and there must be no bottlenecks in the core hardware and software. (Many home computers flunk this test.)
- Memory—Thrashing is deadly to servers. They need enough physical memory to carry a substantial workload with minimal paging.
- Scalability—As requirements grow, servers can be smoothly scaled up to meet them with the addition of appropriate resources (memory, mass storage, CPUs, and so on).
- Reliability—Servers require highly reliable and fault-tolerant subsystems that can stay alive despite the inevitable problems and failures of computer hardware. Downtime is deadly.

Linux is an increasingly important player in the server market. With server-focused Linux distributions such as TurboLinux and server-focused hardware vendors such as VA Linux Systems, Linux has proven itself a true competitor in the market.

Java's success in the server world is no less dramatic than is Linux's. Technologies such as servlets, Enterprise JavaBeans, and Java Database Connectivity have established Java's power to glue disparate computing resources into a coherent collection of services.

The next several chapters look at the ways in which the two technologies can be brought together in the enterprise and on the Internet.

CHAPTER 65

JAVA ON THE WEB: JAVA SERVLETS AND APACHE JSERV

Apache is the most popular Web server today, running more than half the sites on the Web and easily outselling the combined offerings from Netscape, Microsoft, and all other Web server vendors. It is also, remarkably, a free, open source product.

As the Web evolved from static pages to dynamic content, many technologies grew to support the generation of that content. One of those, Java servlets, brings Java's many application and networking strengths to bear on the problem of generating dynamic Web content.

This chapter looks at Apache and Java Servlets individually and then explains how they can be combined in a Linux environment.

The Apache Web Server

Apache grew out of the pioneering Web development work at the National Center for Supercomputing Applications (NCSA). Along with work by the European Laboratory for Particle Physics (CERN), NCSA's early-1990s design efforts had much to do with development of the methods and protocols that make up today's Web.

Apache History

NCSA's public-domain HTTP Daemon (`httpd`) was the first widely deployed Web server and was, by 1995, the world's most popular. It was also, by 1995, in serious trouble. Its primary developer, Rob McCool, had moved on to other pursuits, and it was kept alive largely through the efforts of tenacious Webmasters whose individual bug-fixing efforts kept them in the Web-serving business.

In early 1995, a new generation of developers outside NCSA decided to pick up the pieces. Brian Behlendorf and Cliff Skolnick set about to organize the salvation of `httpd`. They established a mailing list, a central development site, and incorporated the many floating bug fixes into a single version, which was released in April of that year.

Over the next several months, the code was rearchitected, documented, enhanced, and, after an intense porting and testing effort, released in December as the new Apache Web server.

Apache continues to be maintained by volunteers, under the auspices of the Apache Software Foundation (`http://www.apache.org`), and continues to be enhanced through individual contributions. The Apache project tracks evolving Web standards and keeps current with the protocols as they develop.

Apache is not alone, of course. The Web server market has exploded since Apache's early days, with Microsoft and Netscape leading the pack of some three dozen commercial offerings. But Apache continues to own more than half the market and to prove itself a robust and capable Web server.

Apache's main faults are typical of noncommercial products: It's powerful, but not easy to use. Expert users have no trouble with its interfaces, but many less sophisticated users are better served by the friendly GUI- and Web-based front ends offered by competing products.

Obtaining Apache

Apache is widely available—from the main site (`http://www.apache.org`), from other repositories, and in most Linux distributions. Red Hat users need to install the RPMs for `apache` (for core capabilities) and `apache-devel` (for the capabilities to be described in this chapter).

Java Servlets

Java servlets provide a mechanism for executing Java code on a Web server, in response to requests from clients. They represent a powerful evolution from the early technologies for dynamic Web content generation.

Background: The Common Gateway Interface

Web servers have long supported dynamic generation of content. The original interface for this purpose was the Common Gateway Interface (CGI)—a mechanism that allows Web servers to launch programs instead of simply returning static pages. The resulting Web page is simply the output of the CGI program.

CGI is implemented on Web servers by mapping certain parts of their namespace to programs instead of files. So, for example, a Web server handling a request for a page named `/cgi-bin/foobar.cgi` will probably run a program named `foobar.cgi` rather than send a static page.

A server may need to generate dynamic content for any reason: perhaps to provide up-to-date information (such as current time and temperature), or to respond to data sent by the client (such as a search engine query). To support data sent by clients, the Hypertext Transport Protocol (HTTP) defines several methods a browser can use to send user-supplied information to the server for processing (see Figure 65.1).

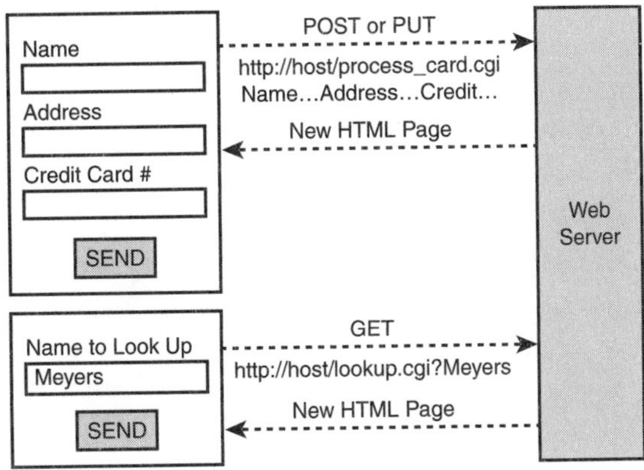

FIGURE 65.1
HTTP support of client input.

Web browsers (on the left side of Figure 65.1) may use the `POST` and `PUT` methods (among others) to upload arbitrary data, or the `GET/QUERY` method, in which the browser appends a client-supplied query to a new page request.

But whether CGI is used to process user input or simply to provide current server-side information, the result is that a program is launched (see Figure 65.2), data is passed to and returned from the program, and a new page is generated from the results.

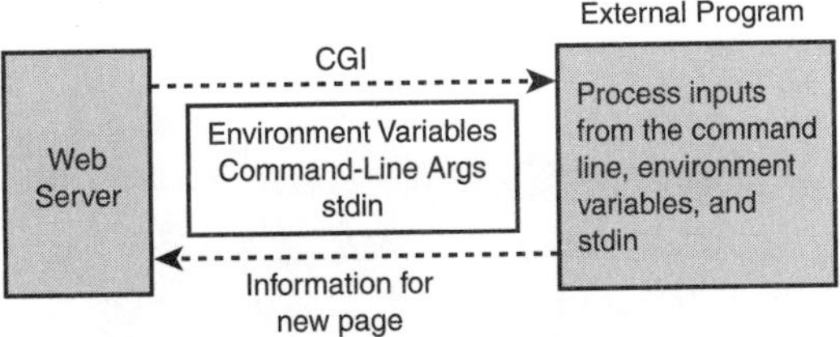

FIGURE 65.2
CGI launches a program to generate a page.

The CGI program terminates after handling one request.

CGI is a simple but capable interface. Because it can launch any arbitrary program, its capabilities are limited only by the imagination of application developers. Most CGI applications are shell or Perl scripts, but any sort of program is possible.

However, CGI also incurs some costs that make it a poor choice for modern, large-scale Web servers:

- Launching a new process for every request is expensive and can add up to a huge drain on busy Web servers.

- Because every request results in execution of a new program, it is difficult and expensive to maintain the state of an interactive session. CGI-based interactive applications, such as e-shopping carts, must respond to every request by running a fresh program that fully restores the session state from disk or DBMS, acts on the request, and then fully saves the new session state.
- There is no well-defined environment in which to develop CGI applications. For example, there are no libraries to support common input processing or output generation tasks.

A number of inventive solutions have appeared to these problems—*servlets* are one of those solutions.

The JSDK Specification

The *Java Servlet Development Kit* (JSDK) is a Sun specification and implementation for Java applications that perform CGI-like functions. The overall architecture is similar to CGI—the servlet takes parameters and input from the client and generates output for the client—but differs in some important implementation details:

- A request is handled by invoking a method on an existing object in a running JVM—a much less expensive approach than launching a new program.
- The life cycle of a servlet is not determined by the life of a single request. Servlets are long-lived, can easily maintain state between requests, and can support interaction among different clients.
- JSDK includes support classes for some common tasks, such as input processing, session management, and cookie management.

Figure 65.3 illustrates the servlet life cycle and relationship to the Web server.

FIGURE 65.3
Servlet life cycle.

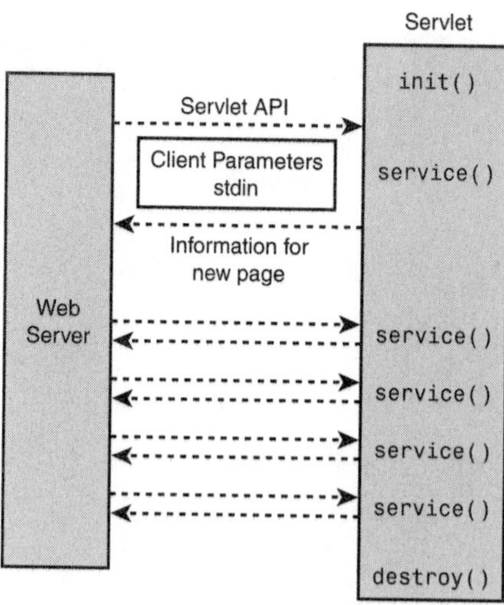

Once created, a servlet instance can handle multiple requests during its lifetime. Service requests may arrive concurrently from multiple threads, each on behalf of a different client—creating an opportunity for interaction between clients *and* a requirement that servlets be coded for proper multithreaded execution.

As of this writing, version 2.2 of the Java Servlet specification is undergoing review. Of the existing versions, 2.0 is widely supported (including by Apache JServ), and 2.1 is available in sample implementation from Sun and in some commercial products.

Sample JSDK Implementations

Sun publishes sample implementations of the JSDK, available from the Java Servlets product page, which you can reach from the main Java site at `http://java.sun.com`. The implementations are entirely in Java and fully usable on Linux. As of this writing, the implementations are published in three forms:

- Java Servlet Development Kit (JSDK) 2.0—A software development kit supporting the Java Servlet 2.0 specification.
- Java Servlet Development Kit (JSDK) 2.1—A software development kit supporting the Java Servlet 2.1 specification.
- JavaServer Web Development Kit (JSWDK) 1.0—A software development kit that subsumes JSDK2.1 and adds JavaServer Pages (JSP), which we will discuss further in Chapter 66, "Java from Web Pages: JSSI and JSP," and Extensible Markup Language (XML).

All three include a primitive servlet runner, intended for testing servlets but not for general use as a Web server. For production servlet deployment, you need support from a production-grade Web server, as discussed in the section "Apache JServ: Adding Java Servlets to Apache" later in this chapter.

The Java Servlet API

The Java Servlet API defines the interface between Web servers and Java servlets, and is one of the smallest and simplest in the Java application universe. Here is a glimpse of the JSDK2.1 classes.

Package `javax.servlet`

The `java.servlet` package defines the basic servlet functions and services, without bindings to any particular Web protocol. Included are classes to support dispatching of requests and management of input and output streams between the servlet and the Web server. Here are the `javax.servlet` public classes and interfaces:

```
public abstract class javax.servlet.GenericServlet extends java.lang.Object
    implements java.io.Serializable
    implements javax.servlet.Servlet
    implements javax.servlet.ServletConfig
```

```
public interface javax.servlet.RequestDispatcher extends java.lang.Object
public interface javax.servlet.Servlet extends java.lang.Object
public interface javax.servlet.ServletConfig extends java.lang.Object
public interface javax.servlet.ServletContext extends java.lang.Object
public class javax.servlet.ServletException extends java.lang.Exception
public abstract class javax.servlet.ServletInputStream extends java.io.InputStream
public abstract class javax.servlet.ServletOutputStream extends
➥java.io.OutputStream
public interface javax.servlet.ServletRequest extends java.lang.Object
public interface javax.servlet.ServletResponse extends java.lang.Object
public interface javax.servlet.SingleThreadModel extends java.lang.Object
public class javax.servlet.UnavailableException extends
➥javax.servlet.ServletException
```

Package `javax.servlet.http`

The `javax.servlet.http` package specializes the `javax.servlet` classes for the HTTP protocol. Its classes include mechanisms for handling each of the HTTP request types, utilities for extracting input and constructing output, authentication hooks, session management, and tools for managing HTTP cookies. Here are the `javax.servlet.http` public classes and interfaces:

```
public class javax.servlet.http.Cookie extends java.lang.Object
    implements java.lang.Cloneable
public abstract class javax.servlet.http.HttpServlet extends
➥javax.servlet.GenericServlet
    implements java.io.Serializable
public interface javax.servlet.http.HttpServletRequest extends java.lang.Object
    implements javax.servlet.ServletRequest
public interface javax.servlet.http.HttpServletResponse extends java.lang.Object
    implements javax.servlet.ServletResponse
public interface javax.servlet.http.HttpSession extends java.lang.Object
public class javax.servlet.http.HttpSessionBindingEvent extends
➥java.util.EventObject
public interface javax.servlet.http.HttpSessionBindingListener extends
➥java.lang.Object
    implements java.util.EventListener
public interface javax.servlet.http.HttpSessionContext extends java.lang.Object
➥(deprecated)
public class javax.servlet.http.HttpUtils extends java.lang.Object
```

Apache JServ: Adding Java Servlets to Apache

Having discussed the basic components of a Java Web solution—a Web server and Java servlets—we pull the pieces together to create a fully functional and free Java Web solution.

The group managing Apache development, the Apache Software Foundation, also oversees the development of several Apache-related projects. One of these, *Apache JServ*, is the Apache servlet add-on.

Apache JServ consists of two pieces, as shown in Figure 65.4: an in-process communications module and a separate, all-Java implementation of a servlet engine.

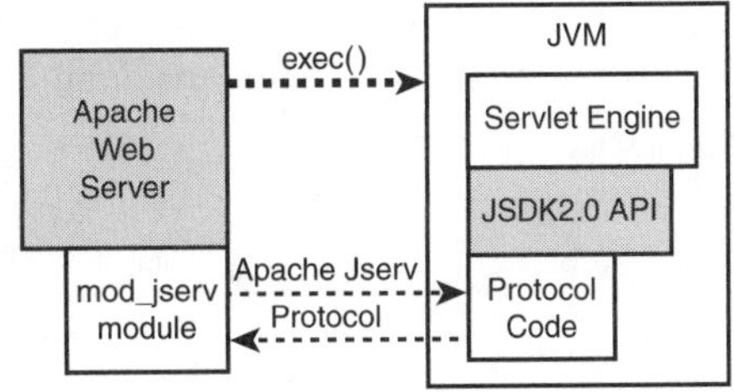

FIGURE 65.4
Apache JServ implements an all-Java servlet engine in a standalone JVM process.

Apache Jserv's components include core engine logic from Apache, the Sun JSDK2.0 sample implementation, and a communications module from Apache. On the Web server side, a native module passes requests, via the Apache JServ protocol, to the engine. The JVM running the servlet engine is launched by Apache at startup.

By running the servlet engine in a separate process, Apache avoids integration complexities between the JVM and the Web server. The only native code in the entire package is in the communications module, `mod_jserv`, used by the Web server. That module can either be compiled into the Web server or introduced as a dynamically loaded plug-in (an optional capability, in Apache versions starting with 1.3, that Apache calls a *Dynamic Shared Object*, or DSO).

Obtaining Apache JServ

Apache JServ is available from `http://www.apache.org/jserv`. Download the gzipped tarball and unpack it into any convenient directory for building.

Building Apache JServ

The details of building Apache and Apache JServ will vary with your configuration. I'll provide some sample instructions, based on a Red Hat 6.0 system.

The Red Hat 6.0 installation media include RPMs for the Apache v1.3 Web server and for development libraries. You will need both of them, `apache` and `apache-devel`, to work with Apache JServ. The RPM installation process will install the Apache components, start up the Web server, and configure your system to restart the Web server at system reboot. After installation, you should find that browsing to your local host

```
http://localhost
```

will give you a welcome screen from the Apache Web server. This installation of Apache was built with support for DSO modules, so you can add Apache JServ without having to rebuild the Web server.

Additional components you need to build Apache JServ are

- SDK1.1 or SDK1.2
- The JSDK2.0 implementation from Sun
- A `gcc` development environment

With these pieces in place, you are ready to build Apache JServ. In the directory where you unpacked the tarball, the following step will configure the build for this environment:

```
bash$ ./configure --with-apache-install=/usr --prefix=<target directory> \
--with-jsdk=<jsdk location>
```

where <target directory> is where you want to install the servlet engine, and <jsdk location> is the location of your installed JSDK2.0 implementation. Example:

```
bash$ ./configure --with-apache-install=/usr --prefix=/opt/apache_jserv \
--with-jsdk=/usr/local/Java/JSDK2.0
```

After configuring, you should be able to build with a single make command:

```
bash$ make
```

Finally, the installation step will place the servlet engine into the target directory and the mod_jserv module into a location (/usr/lib/apache/mod_jserv.so) where Apache can find it:

```
bash$ make install
```

Configuring Apache JServ

Apache JServ creates a powerful and flexible environment for execution of servlets. A full, detailed explanation is beyond the scope of this chapter (the distribution includes 350KB of documentation). But the next section introduces some basic configuration settings and sets up an example servlet project.

A Sample Apache JServ Project

To illustrate setup of Apache JServ, we present an example project. This example is built with Apache Web Server 1.3 and Apache JServ 1.0. If you have dealt with early versions of Apache JServ, note that many configuration instructions changed between pre-release and release. The best source of configuration information is the current documentation from the Apache JServ project.

SimpleServlet: A Project to Report Servlet Parameters

Listing 65.1 shows an example servlet that generates a report about the request that triggered it.

LISTING 65.1 SimpleServlet.java

```
import javax.servlet.*;
import javax.servlet.http.*;
import java.util.*;
import java.io.*;

```

```
6   public class SimpleServlet extends HttpServlet
7   {
8       public void doGet(HttpServletRequest req, HttpServletResponse resp)
9       {
10          // Set up the response writer
11          resp.setContentType("text/html");
12          PrintWriter writer = null;
13          try {
14              writer = resp.getWriter();
15          }
16          catch (IOException e)   { return; }
17
18          // Start output
19          writer.println("<html><title>SimpleServlet Output</title>");
20
21          // Return interesting values
22          writer.println("<H1>Query Parameters</H1>\n");
23          writer.println("Requested URI: " + req.getRequestURI() + "\n");
24          writer.println("<br>Query String: " + req.getQueryString() + "\n");
25          writer.println("<br>Auth Type: " + req.getAuthType() + "\n");
26          writer.println("<br>User Name: " + req.getRemoteUser() + "\n");
27
28          // Find all our headers
29          Enumeration headers = req.getHeaderNames();
30          if (headers != null && headers.hasMoreElements())
31          {
32              writer.println("<H1>Headers</H1>\n");
33              String br = "";
34              while (headers.hasMoreElements())
35              {
36                  String header = (String)headers.nextElement();
37                  writer.println(br + "Header[\"" + header + "\"] = "
38                                 + req.getHeader(header) + "\n");
39                  br = "<br>";
40              }
41          }
42          writer.println("</html>");
43
44          // Close and flush
45          writer.close();
46      }
47      public String getServletInfo()
48      {
49          return "SimpleServlet Example";
50      }
51  }
```

This servlet creates a handler for the HTTP GET request by implementing its own `doGet()` method. After creating the output writer and starting to output HTML (lines 12–19), it queries and generates a report on some request parameters (lines 22–26) and some header strings sent by the browser (lines 30–41).

Configuring Apache

At this point, we have the three components we need to enter the servlet business: the Apache Web server, the Apache JServ servlet engine, and a servlet. We now need three pieces of glue—three configuration files—to assemble them into a solution. The following sections discuss the configuration files needed to turn on our servlet.

Recall that the current installed configuration for the example project is as follows:

- Apache 1.3 has been installed from a Red Hat 6.0 RPM.
- Apache JServ 1.0 was built and installed in the `/opt/apache_jserv` directory.

For deployment of the project, we choose to install servlets under directory `/opt/apache_jserv/servlets`, beginning with a sample project under the `examples/` subdirectory.

Apache JServ Organization

To understand the roles played by configuration files, we take a brief look (see Figure 65.5) at how servlets are organized in an Apache/JServ environment.

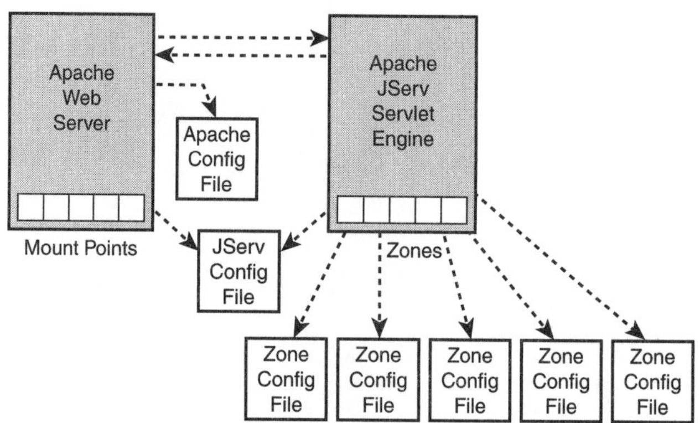

FIGURE 65.5
Architectural overview of servlet organization under Apache.

The environment is configured by three different components:

- The servlet engine organizes servlets into manageable domains called ***zones***, each with its own configuration file (the *Zone Config File* in Figure 65.5) describing the servlets it supplies.
- A configuration file for the servlet engine (the *JServ Config File* in Figure 65.5) handles overall engine setup and identifies the zones being supplied by this engine. This configuration file also contains communication and JVM startup information required by the `mod_jserv` module in Web server.
- A configuration file for the Web server (the *Apache Config File* in Figure 65.5) establishes Apache support for servlets and maps servlet zones to mount points in the Web server namespace.

Apache Configuration File

The first piece of glue needed is for the Apache Web server. It must be configured to recognize requests for servlets and to launch and communicate with the servlet engine. Listing 65.2 shows some lines added to the Apache configuration file (/etc/httpd/conf/httpd.conf, in the Red Hat 6.0 installation). This is a small, bare-bones, low-security example that does not illustrate all available options.

LISTING 65.2 Configuration Directives Added to the Core Apache Configuration File

```
1   # Tell Apache to load the Apache JServ communication module
2   LoadModule jserv_module modules/mod_jserv.so
3
4   # Tell Apache to start the JVM automatically when we need Servlets
5   ApJServManual off
6
7   # Tell Apache JServ where to look for its properties on auto-startup
8   ApJServProperties /opt/apache_jserv/servlets/jserv.properties
9
10  # Default port that Apache JServ is listening to
11  ApJServDefaultPort 8007
12
13  # Disable secret key for Apache JServ access
14  ApJServSecretKey DISABLED
15
16  #  Mount points for the zones Apache will manage
17  ApJServMount /examples /examples
18
19  # Allow localhost to query status under /jserv directory
20  <Location /jserv/>
21    SetHandler jserv-status
22
23    order deny,allow
24    deny from all
25    allow from localhost 127.0.0.1
26  </Location>
```

Line 2 loads the mod_jserv module, which was installed during Apache JServ installation. The module handles configuration of and communication with the servlet engine.

Line 5 enables automatic startup of the servlet engine when servlets are needed.

Line 8 describes a properties file (to be discussed in the next section) for the servlet engine.

Line 11 identifies the default TCP port for communication with the servlet engine.

Line 14 makes this a simple, low-security environment.

Line 17 maps part of the Web server's namespace for use by servlets. Specifically, the /examples mount point will be used to access servlets in a *zone* named "examples." Servlets will be accessed from the Web server under the subdirectory http://<*hostname*>/examples/.

Finally, lines 20–26 allow access to Apache and JServ administrative status to Web browsers running on the local host.

Apache JServ Configuration File

The second piece of glue is a configuration file for the servlet engine. When the engine is launched from the Web server, the Web server tells the servlet engine the location (line 8 in Listing 65.2) of this file. Listing 65.3 shows a bare-bones, low-security Apache JServ configuration file.

LISTING 65.3 `/opt/apache_jserv/servlets/jserv.properties`, Describing the Configuration for the Servlet Engine

```
1   # Specify the wrapper program (JVM) to run for servlets
2   wrapper.bin=/usr/local/Java/jdk1.2/bin/java
3
4   # Entry point for Apache JServ Servlet Engine
5   wrapper.class=org.apache.jserv.JServ
6
7   # Classpath for our JVM
8   wrapper.classpath=/opt/apache_jserv/lib/ApacheJServ.jar
9   wrapper.classpath=/usr/local/Java/JSDK2.0/lib/jsdk.jar
10
11  # Protocol used for signal handling
12  wrapper.protocol=ajpv11
13
14  # Define port for Apache JServ protocol
15  port=8007
16
17  # List of zones managed by this JServ
18  zones=examples
19
20  # Property files for the zones we manage
21  examples.properties=/opt/apache_jserv/servlets/examples/examples.properties
22
23  # Allow only localhost to connect through Apache JServ port
24  security.allowedAddresses=127.0.0.1
25
26  # Enable/disable connection authentication.
27  security.authentication=false
28
29  # Enable/disable the execution of org.apache.jserv.JServ as a servlet.
30  security.selfservlet=true
```

The information in lines 1–12 of this file is for the benefit of the Web server, not the servlet engine. It identifies the *wrapper* (the `java` application launcher), the class path, and the class needed to start the engine.

Line 15 configures the servlet engine to communicate with Apache over TCP port 8007.

Line 18 lists the one zone being served by this engine, `examples`.

Line 21 points to the configuration file for zone `examples`.

Line 24 creates some minimal security: only Apache servers running locally can connect to this engine.

Line 27 turns off other authentication methods on the connection from Apache.

Line 30 allows us access to JServ configuration information from a Web browser.

Zone Configuration File

Finally, the configuration file for the **examples** zone (see Listing 65.4) allows us to configure our servlet for access from Apache.

LISTING 65.4 `/opt/apache_jserv/servlets/examples/examples. properties` File, Configuring the Examples Zone

```
1   # The list of servlet repositories controlled by this servlet zone
2   repositories=/opt/apache_jserv/servlets/examples
3
4   # Define an alias for our servlet
5   servlet.simple.code=SimpleServlet
```

Line 2 identifies the *repositories*—the directories containing servlets for this zone.

Line 5 specifies an alias, **simple**, and the Java class corresponding to that alias. The alias assigns a name by which a particular servlet can be requested—in this case, it points to our example servlet project.

Running the Servlet

With the pieces in place, we need to restart the Apache Web server. In the Red Hat 6.0 environment, this can be done by executing the initialization script as the root user:

```
bash$ /etc/rc.d/init.d/httpd restart
```

Accessing the Servlet from a Browser

The servlet is now available from our Web server, as shown in Figure 65.6.

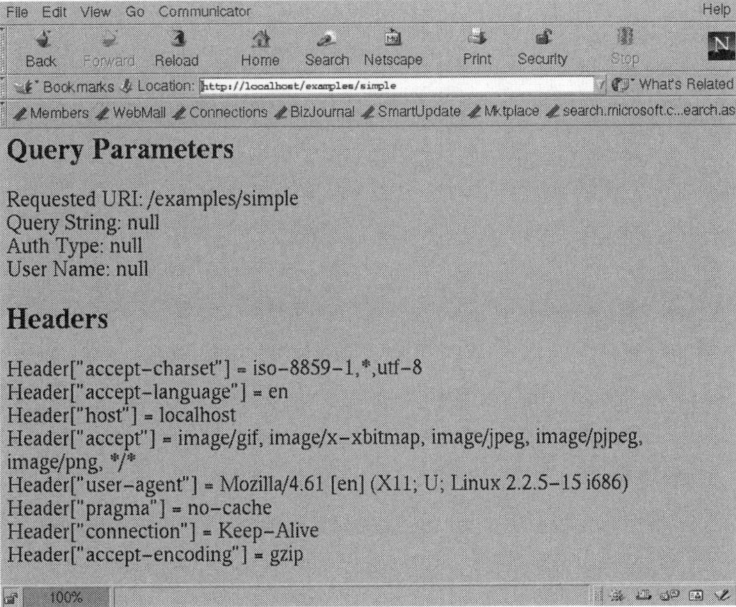

FIGURE 65.6 Browsing to `http://localhost/examples/simple` shows that Apache now supports servlets.

Accessing Apache and Apache JServ Administrative Information

Apache and the servlet engine also provide access to administrative information, through permissions that were set up in the Apache and JServ configuration files. The main status page (see Figure 65.7) allows us to view status on the Web server (see Figure 65.8) and the servlet engine (see Figure 65.9).

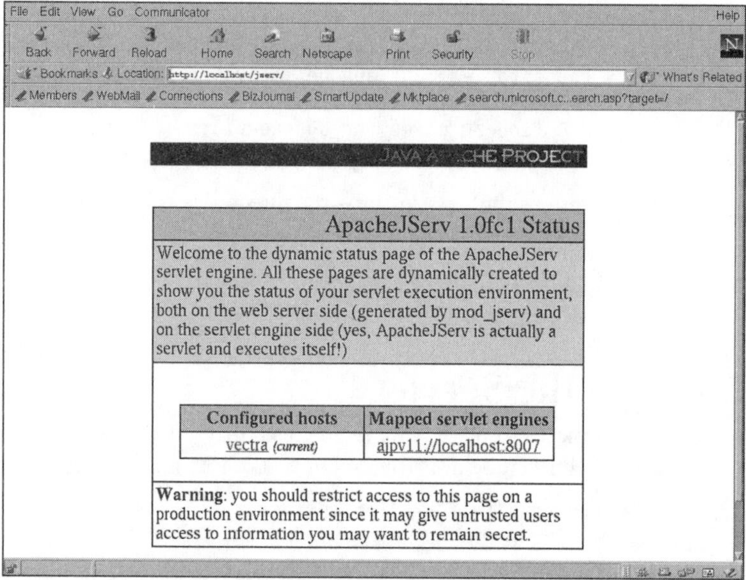

FIGURE 65.7
Browsing to `http://localhost/jserv/` exposes a viewer into Apache and JServ status.

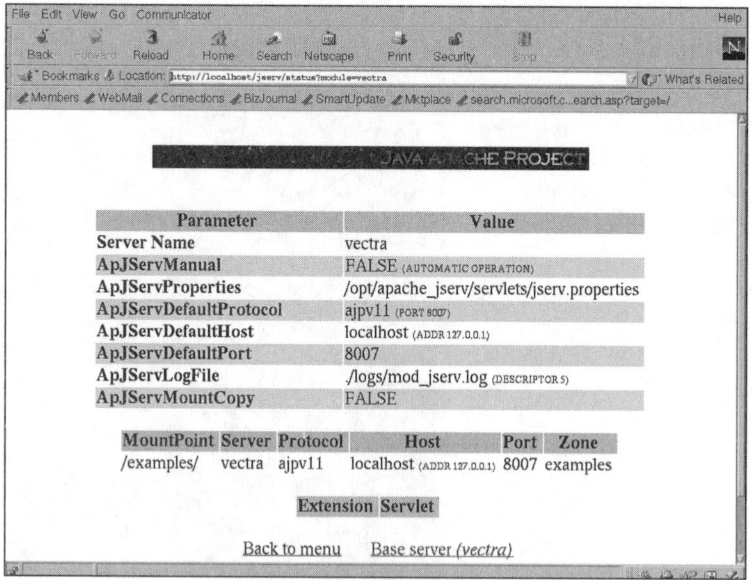

FIGURE 65.8
Information on the Apache side of the Apache/JServ relationship.

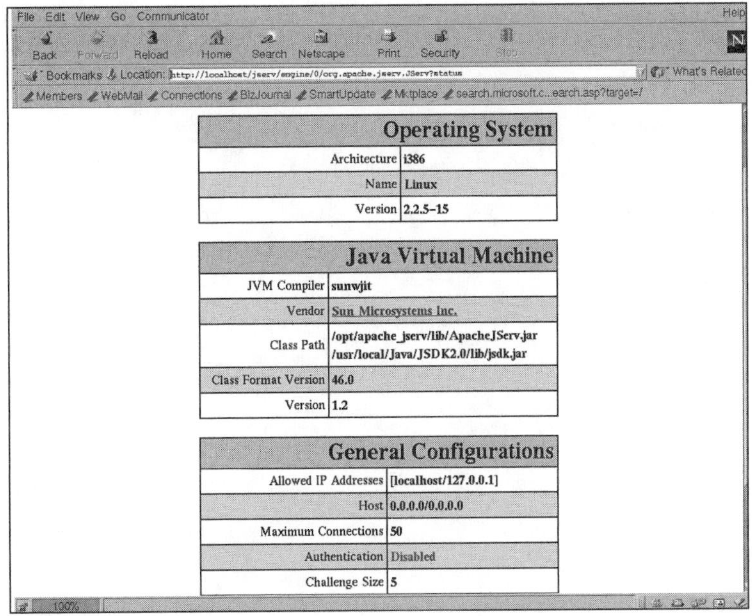

FIGURE 65.9
Information on the JServ side of the Apache/JServ relationship.

For Further Reading

Although Apache's capabilities and configuration requirements may seem overwhelming, they are also well documented. The source distribution includes a `docs/` subdirectory full of detailed documentation. The Java-Apache faq-o-matic (`http://java.apache.org/faq/`) is a repository of wise advice from people who have solved Apache JServ installation and configuration problems.

Apache also enjoys an active community of users and developers. Information on mailing lists can be found at `http://java.apache.org/main/mail.html`.

Summary

This chapter explored the steps to enabling basic servlet support on Linux with the Apache Web server. From here, you can easily enable other interesting technologies, including Java Server-Side Includes, JavaServer Pages, and Three-Tier Application Architectures. We explore these technologies in the next two chapters.

CHAPTER 66

JAVA FROM WEB PAGES: JSSI AND JSP

Having examined servlets, the core technology mixing Java and Web servers, we look at two useful technologies built on top of servlets: ***Java Server-Side Includes*** (JSSI) and ***JavaServer Pages*** (JSP). Although servlets provide a facility by which Java applications can dynamically ***generate*** complete Web pages, JSSI and JSP tackle the problem from the opposite side: running Java from ***within*** static Web pages.

Apache JSSI

JSSI is a Java-flavored extension of traditional ***Server-Side Includes*** (SSI). Traditional SSI is already supported by Apache and many other Web servers.

Traditional SSI

Traditional SSI allows you to embed directives into a static page that are parsed by the Web server and replaced with dynamic content. By common convention, Web pages containing SSI are usually suffixed `.shtml`, and Web servers will not pay attention to SSI commands in pages without that suffix.

SSI provides a rich set of capabilities for server-side parsing and execution. For example, in a .shtml page containing the code

```
<!--#include file="foobar.html" -->
```

the contents of `foobar.html` will be inserted into the page at the site of the directive. SSI commands can do much more, including run programs, to generate dynamic content. Detailed instructions on using and configuring SSI with the Apache Web server are included in FAQs from Apache (`http://www.apache.org/`).

Java SSI

JSSI is the Java-flavored version of traditonal SSI—it allows you to run servlets from within Web pages. By allowing you to embed Java programs in a page, JSSI does for servlets on the server side exactly what browsers do for applets on the client side. Under Apache, JSSI files are conventionally suffixed `.jhtml`, and they embed servlets in the page with the `<SERVLET>` tag (which closely resembles the `<APPLET>` tag supported by browsers). For example:

```
<SERVLET CODE=FooBar.class>
</SERVLET>
```

As with applets, servlets allow parameters to be included in the HTML and read by the servlet code. Parameters are specified with `<PARAM>` tags between the `<SERVLET>` and `</SERVLET>` tags:

```
<SERVLET CODE=FooBar.class>
<PARAM NAME="arg1" VALUE="foo">
</SERVLET>
```

When the tag is encountered, the servlet is run and its output substituted into the Web page.

Subtleties

Sun Microsystems is also in the Web server business and has, not surprisingly, integrated Java SSI more closely with traditional SSI than has Apache. On Sun's Web servers, `.shtml` usually represents a Web page that can use both conventional SSI tags and `<SERVLET>` tags.

By contrast, the Apache JSSI implementation discussed in this chapter provides partial support for conventional SSI in a `.jhtml` page. Future plans include improved support for mixing the two SSI technologies.

To further confuse the situation, Sun's Web server (along with other products on the market) uses `.jhtml` to designate something completely different: *page-compiled* Java—Java source embedded in Web pages, similar to the JSP technology discussed later in this chapter.

The bottom line is that the relationship between a Web page suffix and the server-side technology it exploits is not a standard mapping. It's more a matter of convention for a particular Web server product and, ultimately, configuration decisions made by a Webmaster.

Obtaining Apache JSSI

Apache JSSI is available from the project site at `http://java.apache.org/jservssi/`. You can obtain a gzipped tarball or zipfile and unpack it anywhere. The distribution includes source and a compiled jarfile in the `src/java/` subdirectory. The example in this section is built on JSSI release 1.1.2.

Requirements

Apache JSSI requires JDK1.1 or JDK1.2 and a servlet engine, such as Apache JServ. It may also run with other servlet engines.

Configuring Apache JSSI

With the Apache JServ pieces already in place, adding JSSI is straightforward. JSSI is a servlet; you need to configure it to be run from the Apache JServ engine when it is needed.

First, you must add the Apache JSSI jarfile as a repository to be managed by one of your Apache JServ zones. Returning to the `examples` zone used for the sample project in Chapter 65, "Java on the Web: Java Servlets and Apache JServ," we update the zone properties file by adding a new repository pointing to the JSSI installation. For this example (see Listing 66.1), Apache JSSI was unpacked into the directory `/usr/local/Java/ApacheJSSI-1.1.2`.

LISTING 66.1 Updated `/opt/apache_jserv/servlets/examples/ examples.properties`

```
# The list of servlet repositories controlled by this servlet zone
repositories=/opt/apache_jserv/servlets/examples
repositories=/usr/local/Java/ApacheJSSI-1.1.2/src/java/ApacheJSSI.jar

# Define an alias for our servlet
servlet.simple.code=SimpleServlet
```

This addition to `examples.properties` has two effects:

- It adds the JSSI code as a servlet, available in the `examples` zone.
- It allows JSSI to run other servlets found in the `examples` zone.

The other necessary change is to configure Apache to recognize `.jhtml` files and invoke the JSSI servlet to process them. The following one-line addition is needed in the main configuration file (`/etc/httpd/conf/httpd.conf` in our example installation):

```
ApJServAction .jhtml /examples/org.apache.servlet.ssi.SSI
```

After making this change, restart the Apache Web server. In our example Red Hat 6.0 installation, this command will do the job:

```
bash$ /etc/rc.d/init.d/httpd restart
```

Using Apache JSSI

After the configuration changes described previously, the Apache Web server should handle `.jhtml` pages. Listing 66.2 contains a small Web page to test the results.

LISTING 66.2 `testjhtml.html` Draws a Table, with the `<SERVLET>` Tag in the Second Row

```
<HTML>
<HEAD>
<TITLE>Apache JHTML Test</TITLE>
</HEAD>
<BODY>
<table border="1" cols="1">
<tr>
  <td>
<center><b>Here are the results of running the servlet</b></center>
  </td>
</tr>
<tr>
  <td>
<SERVLET name=SimpleServlet>
SERVLET DID NOT WORK
</SERVLET>
  </td>
<tr>
</table>
</BODY>
</HTML>
```

Figure 66.1 shows the results of browsing the page.

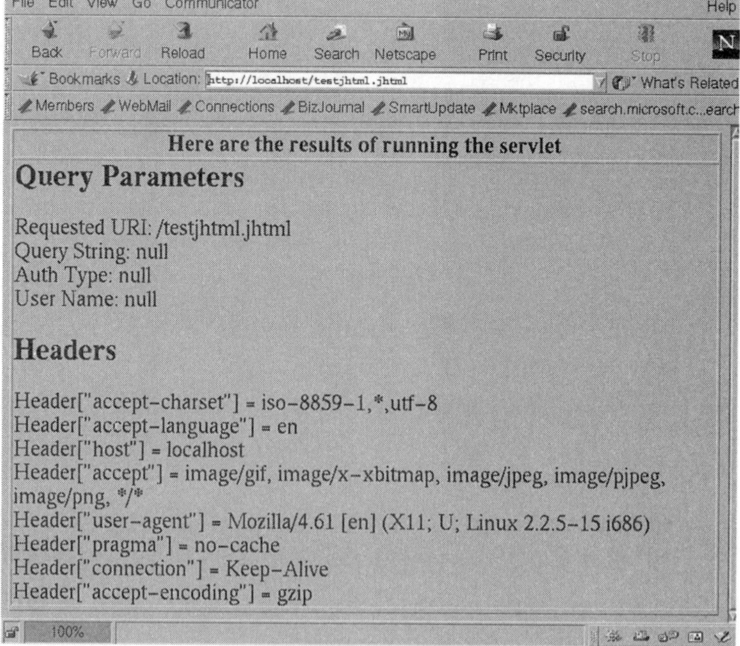

FIGURE 66.1
Browsing the page defined in Listing 66.2 shows the results of the `<SERVLET>` tag embedded in a table.

JavaServer Pages

The Apache JServ technology discussed in Chapter 65 brought Java to the Web browser. JSSI brought servlets into the Web page. *JavaServer Pages* (JSP) take things one step further: They bring Java source code directly into HTML Web pages.

JSP is Sun's answer to Microsoft's *Active Server Pages* (ASP), in which scripts embedded in Web pages are processed by Microsoft's *Internet Information Server*. The scripting languages supported by ASP are *VBScript* (a dialect of Visual Basic) and *JScript* (a descendant of the JavaScript language used in browsers). JSP scripts, by contrast, are written in Java and enjoy more portability than do ASP scripts.

The Sun JSP1.0 specification is complete, and JSP1.1 is in review. In a (highly simplified) nutshell, JSP defines HTML tags for embedding Java source in a Web page and provides a class library to support the requirements of dynamic content generation. By convention, Web pages employing JSP have the suffix `.jsp`.

Subtleties

A JSP Web page looks similar to a static Web page—mostly HTML, but with special tags enclosing Java source code. In reality, the page is a stylized Java source file defining a servlet. When the page is processed by the Web server, it is filtered into true Java source (all literal HTML on the page is transformed into *print* statements), compiled, and run as a servlet.

Because a JSP page is Java source, it must respect the requirements of the language. A single line of bad Java will break the entire page, not just the affected line. The page must, after filtering by the JSP logic, look like a valid source for a servlet implementation. In other words, it's not difficult to write a bad JSP page.

JSP imposes an additional requirement for printing: You should not use the normal `java.io` classes for output. To print from Java in a JSP page, enclose the expression to be printed within the special tags <%= and %>. JSP provides its own output methods to avoid synchronization problems with output buffers managed by the `java.io` classes.

There are three current JSP projects worth watching:

- The Sun *JavaServer Web Development Kit* (JSWDK) is a development kit combining (as of version 1.0) the reference implementations of JSDK2.1 and JSP1.0.
- The Apache Jakarta project (`http://jakarta.apache.org`) is targeted at building an implementation of JSDK2.1 and JSP1.0 for use with the Apache Web server.
- GNUJSP is a free, cleanroom implementation of the JSP specification, built on JSDK2.0 capabilities and usable with Apache JServ and many other servlet engines. As of this writing, it is rapidly approaching compliance with the JSP1.0 spec.

There are also commercial products—Allaire's JRun, among others—that bring JSP to the Apache Web server. For our purposes in this chapter, we will focus on using GNUJSP.

Obtaining GNUJSP

The GNUJSP home page at `http://www.klomp.org/gnujsp/` provides project information, status, and downloads for GNUJSP. Downloads are available as gzipped tarballs and zipfiles. They include source and a jarfile and can be unpacked anywhere. The example in this section is built on the 0.9.10 release.

Requirements

GNUJSP requires JDK1.1 or JDK1.2, a Java compiler, and a servlet engine, such as Apache JServ. It is also known to run with many other servlet engines.

Configuring GNUJSP

JSP requires more plumbing than JSSI—interpreting a JSP page involves a Web server, a servlet engine, and a Java compiler to handle the embedded code.

Revisiting the existing installation for the `examples` zone, we must create a directory in which GNUJSP can hold its compiled classes and give it access modes that will allow read/write access to Apache and GNUJSP:

```
bash$ mkdir /opt/apache_jserv/servlets/examples/jspstore
bash$ chmod a+rw /opt/apache_jserv/servlets/examples/jspstore
```

The zone configuration file requires some new entries. Listing 66.3 shows the addition (in bold italic) of a new repository pointing to the JSP installation and an initialization argument for the JSP servlet. For purposes of this example, GNUJSP is installed in the `/usr/local/Java/gnujsp-0.9.10` directory.

When GNUJSP needs to compile, its default behavior is to launch the `javac` (Sun's Java compiler) `main` class—which it expects to find in the class path. But configuration is flexible; you can add options to this file (described in the GNUJSP documentation) to use alternate compilers.

LISTING 66.3 Updated `/opt/apache_jserv/servlets/examples/ examples.properties`

```
# The list of servlet repositories controlled by this servlet zone
repositories=/opt/apache_jserv/servlets/examples
repositories=/usr/local/Java/ApacheJSSI-1.1.2/src/java/ApacheJSSI.jar
repositories=/usr/local/Java/gnujsp-0.9.10/lib/gnujsp.jar

# Define an alias for our servlet
servlet.simple.code=SimpleServlet

# Define an alias for the GNUJSP
servlet.gnujsp.code=org.gjt.jsp.JSPServlet
servlet.gnujsp.initArgs=repository=/opt/apache_jserv/servlets/
➥examples/jspstore
```

The initialization file for the servlet engine also requires some new information. Listing 66.4 shows one addition (in bold italic) to the class path for the servlet engine. The new entry adds the class library supplying the `javac` compiler `main` class. If we were running under SDK1.1, that compiler would be found in `classes.zip` in the standard class path.

LISTING 66.4 /opt/apache_jserv/servlets/jserv.properties

```
# Specify the wrapper program (JVM) to run for servlets
wrapper.bin=/usr/local/Java/jdk1.2/bin/java

# Entry point for Apache JServ Servlet Engine
wrapper.class=org.apache.jserv.JServ

# Classpath for our JVM
wrapper.classpath=/opt/apache_jserv/lib/ApacheJServ.jar
wrapper.classpath=/usr/local/Java/JSDK2.0/lib/jsdk.jar
wrapper.classpath=/usr/local/Java/jdk1.2/lib/tools.jar

# Protocol used for signal handling
wrapper.protocol=ajpv11

# Define port for Apache JServ protocol
port=8007

# List of zones managed by this JServ
zones=examples

# Property files for the zones we manage
examples.properties=/opt/apache_jserv/servlets/examples/examples.properties

# Allow only localhost to connect through Apache JServ port
security.allowedAddresses=127.0.0.1

# Enable/disable connection authentication.
security.authentication=false

# Enable/disable the execution of org.apache.jserv.JServ as a servlet.
security.selfservlet=true
```

We need one final piece of plumbing—instructions to the Apache Web server on what to do when it encounters `.jsp` files. Add this line to the Apache configuration file (`/etc/httpd/conf/httpd.conf` in our example installation):

```
ApJServAction .jsp /examples/gnujsp
```

Everything is now in place to support JSP. Restart the Web server to activate the changes:

```
bash$ /etc/rc.d/init.d/httpd restart
```

Using GNUJSP

To test GNUJSP, we combine elements from the previous Apache JServ (see Listing 65.1) and Apache JSSI (see Listing 66.2) examples: an HTML page containing a table, with dynamic Java output in the second row of the table. This time, the output is generated by source code—adapted from Listing 65.1—embedded directly in the Web page.

Listing 66.5 shows the new Web page source. Java code appears in `<% ... %>` tags. Note the freely interspersed HTML and Java, even inside a loop (lines 32–40). Note also that the code does not use the `java.io` classes for output; it places objects to be printed inside `<%= ... %>` tags.

LISTING 66.5 `testjsp.jsp`, Adapted from the Previous `SimpleServlet.java` Example

```
1   <HTML>
2   <HEAD>
3   <TITLE>GNUJSP Test</TITLE>
4       <%@ import="javax.servlet.http.*,java.util.*" %>
5   </HEAD>
6   <BODY>
7   <table border="1" cols="1"
8   <tr>
9     <td>
10  <center><b>Here are the results of running the JSP code</b></center>
11    </td>
12  </tr>
13  <tr>
14    <td>
15      <H1>Query Parameters</H1>
16      Requested URI:
17      <%= request.getRequestURI() %>
18      <br>Query String:
19      <%= request.getQueryString() %>
20      <br>Auth Type:
21      <%= request.getAuthType() %>
22      <br>User Name:
23      <%= request.getRemoteUser() %>
24      <%
25          Enumeration headers = request.getHeaderNames();
26          if (headers != null && headers.hasMoreElements())
27          {
28      %>
29      <H1>Headers</H1>
30      <%
31              String br = "";
32              while(headers.hasMoreElements())
33              {
34                  String header = (String)headers.nextElement();
35      %>
36      <%= br %>
37      Header["<%= header %>"] = "<%= request.getHeader(header) %>"
38      <%
39                  br = "<br>";
40              }
41          }
42      %>
43    </td>
44  </tr>
45  </table>
```

```
</BODY>
</HTML>
```

Figure 66.2 shows the results of browsing the `.jsp` page. Except for the formatting of null strings by the JSP print methods, the results are identical to the earlier `.jhtml` example in Figure 66.1.

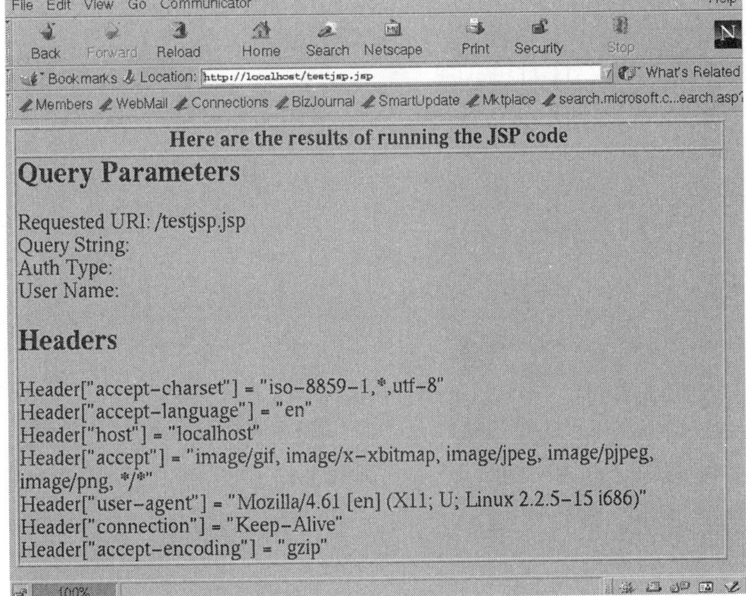

FIGURE 66.2
Browsing the `.jsp` page.

Summary

This chapter has built on Java servlets to bring two new server capabilities to a Web server running on Linux: Java SSI and JavaServer pages. With the Apache JServ configuration described in Chapter 65, installation of these new features involves minimal changes.

CHAPTER 67

JAVA, LINUX, AND THREE-TIERED ARCHITECTURES

One role for Java that has led to outstanding success is that of enterprise application integration—wiring together the resources of an enterprise into a coherent set of services. Java has found an important role in the middle tier of three-tiered application architectures.

The Three Tiers

What is a three-tiered architecture? No two sources will give you the same answer to that question—it's nearly impossible to find a description that does not include a vendor's name firmly affixed to one of the layers. But, after extensive research, I am able to provide a precise and accurate abstraction of all existing and future three-tiered architectures (see Figure 67.1).

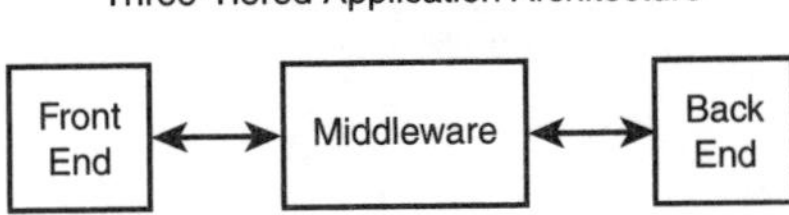

FIGURE 67.1
A vendor-neutral three-tiered application architecture.

The front end is the client, which, in modern environments, is often a Web browser.

The back end is a collection of computational and information resources used in an enterprise: database management systems (DBMS), accounting, inventory, order fulfillment, transaction processing, personnel, and so on.

The middleware acts as an agency between the back-end services and the client, and is where much of the action is happening in Java today. Many of the technologies in the Java 2 Enterprise Edition are focused on this layer, for example:

- Enterprise JavaBeans (EJB)—A middleware framework for delivery of services
- Java Database Connectivity—Access from the middle tier to DBMS
- Java Naming and Directory Interface—Access from the middle tier to directory services
- Java Servlets and JSP—Support for middle-tier applications running under Web servers
- Java Messaging—Support for reliable data exchange
- Java Transactions—Transaction support for middle-tier components
- CORBA and RMI—Support for distributed objects in the enterprise

Middleware is about ***delivering services***. Its role is to decouple the creation and maintenance of those services from the very different problem of providing them to users[1]. At its simplest, middleware acts as a gateway to the back end. For more complex requirements, middleware can integrate or aggregate services, act as an agent on behalf of the back end (for example, by caching database entries in the middle layer), act as an agent on behalf of clients (for example, by performing batch processing for a user), and so on.

The available selection of middleware products in today's market is impressive, overwhelming, and complicated by the usual technology battles—EJB versus Microsoft's Windows ***Distributed interNet Applications*** (DNA), for example—and the present immaturity of the technologies.

Linux in the Middle

As a competitive server platform, Linux can comfortably fill the middle tier in three-tier architectures.

Given the performance demands of enterprise environments, you may find that currently available JDKs fall short—but this story is still being written. The IBM JDK (see Chapter 25, "The IBM JSDK Port") shows good promise in industry benchmarks, and the TowerJ platform (see

[1]In many descriptions of three-tier architectures, the middle tier is described as the repository of business logic or business rules governing the use of back-end resources—somehow suggesting a unique role for middleware applications. In reality, the middle tier can fulfill this role, and often does, but it cannot own this role. A great deal of business logic resides irrevocably in the back end. The broader concept of delivering services seems a more accurate description of middleware's role.

Chapter 32, "TowerJ: A Server-Side Hybrid Java Environment") is proving to be a world-beater. The Volano reports (`http://www.volano.com/report.html`), which benchmark server environments, show that Linux more than holds its own as a server platform for Java applications.

For the final project in this book, we create our own middle-tier Java application. The simplest, and probably most common, realization of the three-tier architecture on the Web is the use of the Apache Web server to access a back-end database. For this, you need Apache, servlets, and a Database Management System.

DBMS for Linux

There is no shortage of choice when you are in the market for a Linux Database Management System (DBMS). Most commercial vendors, from small niche players to big names such as Oracle, Sybase, Informix, IBM, and Computer Associates, have Linux DBMS offerings. Many commercial vendors offer free personal-use licenses, and you can also choose from such professional-grade free products as PostgreSQL and MySQL.

Moving beyond the mainstream world of relational databases, the market includes several object databases for Linux. And, beyond native-code implementations, Java-based DBMSes are available.

A good starting point in the search for Linux DBMS offerings is the Linux Center project (`http://www.portalux.com/applications/databases`).

For an example project, we will use the MySQL DBMS—a popular product that supports the ***Structured Query Language*** (SQL) standard for programmatic interaction with databases. MySQL is governed by liberal licensing terms that keep it free for most personal and commercial applications on non-Microsoft Windows boxes.

Installing MySQL and a JDBC Driver

MySQL is available from the main Web site, `http://www.mysql.com`. Source and binary versions are provided as compressed tarballs and as RPMs. They can be installed using the techniques discussed in Chapter 8, "Installing Additional Linux Software." You should install both server and client components.

Depending on the installation environment, you may need to start the database server yourself. The necessary instructions are included in the distributions. In the Red Hat 6.0 environment, installation from the Red Hat client and server RPMs (provided at the MySQL download site) handle all the details—just run `rpm` to install MySQL, and the database is up and running when it finishes.

The one additional component you need to use MySQL from Java is a JDBC driver. This is the glue between Java's database I/O abstractions and the actual database, and is unique to a particular database technology. You can obtain MySQL JDBC drivers from `http://www.worldserver.com/mm.mysql/`. Download a current release and unpack it anywhere; the distribution includes a jarfile you can add to your class path.

Setting Up the Database

MySQL includes an excellent tutorial—installing from the Red Hat distribution places it at `/usr/doc/MySQL-<release number>/manual.html`. One of the first tools to learn is `mysql`, the text-based interactive database front end. We use `mysql` to set up our database.

For this example, we use the `test` database provided with the MySQL installation (see Listing 67.1). After indicating that we want to work with that database (the `USE` command) and checking its current contents (the `SHOW TABLES` command shows it to be empty), we create a database table, `phonelist`, with five named fields. This table will be used by our example servlet to implement a telephone book application.

LISTING 67.1 Setting Up the Example Database

```
bash$ mysql
Welcome to the MySQL monitor.  Commands end with ; or \g.
Your MySQL connection id is 4 to server version: 3.22.25

Type 'help' for help.

mysql> USE test
Database changed
mysql> SHOW TABLES;
Empty set (0.00 sec)

mysql> CREATE TABLE phonelist (lastname varchar(20),
    -> firstname varchar(20),
    -> countrycode varchar(5),
    -> areacode varchar(5),
    -> number varchar(15));
Query OK, 0 rows affected (0.23 sec)

mysql> QUIT
Bye
bash$
```

Creating a Middle-Tier Application

With an initialized DBMS, a JDBC driver, and an Apache Web server with servlet support, we have all the needed equipment for an Apache-based middle-tier application. We will create a Web-based telephone book, with the capability to query for existing telephone listings and to store new listings. The tools used in this example are the existing servlets set up from Chapter 65, "Java on the Web: Java Servlets and Apache JServ," MySQL release 3.22.25, and release 1.2b of the the MySQL JDBC driver.

The telephone book will be implemented by a servlet named `PhoneBook`. Figure 67.2 shows `PhoneBook`'s GUI design: a five-element form with buttons to support saving and querying entries. When data is queried, results will be returned in a table below the form.

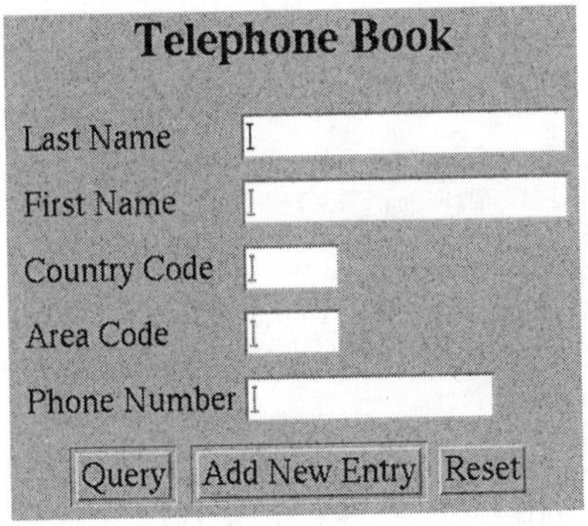

FIGURE 67.2
GUI design for the `PhoneBook` servlet.

Listing 67.2 shows the complete servlet implementation of the application.

LISTING 67.2 `PhoneBook.java`

```
import javax.servlet.*;
import javax.servlet.http.*;
import java.util.*;
import java.io.*;
import java.sql.*;

public class PhoneBook extends HttpServlet
{
    Connection connection = null;
    public void init(ServletConfig config) throws ServletException
    {
        // Servlet initialization
        super.init(config);
        try
        {
            // Load the MySQL JDBC driver
            Class.forName("org.gjt.mm.mysql.Driver");
        }
        catch (ClassNotFoundException e)
        { throw new ServletException(e.toString()); }
    }
    private void doOutput1(PrintWriter writer)
    {
        writer.println(
        "<HTML>\n" +
        "<HEAD>\n" +
        "<TITLE>Phone Book</TITLE>" +
        "</HEAD>\n" +
        "<BODY>\n" +
        "<CENTER>\n" +
        "<H1>Telephone Book</H1>\n" +
        "<FORM ACTION=\"PhoneBook\" METHOD=\"POST\">" +
```

continued on next page

continued from previous page

```
                "<TABLE>\n" +
                "<TR>\n" +
                "  <TD>Last Name</TD>\n" +
                "  <TD><INPUT TYPE=\"TEXT\" SIZE=20 NAME=\"LastName\">
                  ➥</TD>" +
                "</TR><TR>\n" +
                "  <TD>First Name</TD>\n" +
                "  <TD><INPUT TYPE=\"TEXT\" SIZE=20 NAME=\"FirstName\">
                  ➥</TD>" +
                "</TR><TR>\n" +
                "  <TD>Country Code</TD>\n" +
                "  <TD><INPUT TYPE=\"TEXT\" SIZE=5 NAME=\"CountryCode\">
                  ➥</TD>" +
                "</TR><TR>\n" +
                "  <TD>Area Code</TD>\n" +
                "  <TD><INPUT TYPE=\"TEXT\" SIZE=5 NAME=\"AreaCode\">
                  ➥</TD>" +
                "</TR><TR>\n" +
                "  <TD>Phone Number</TD>\n" +
                "  <TD><INPUT TYPE=\"TEXT\" SIZE=15 NAME=\"PhoneNum\">
                  ➥</TD>" +
                "</TR>\n" +
                "</TABLE>" +
                "<INPUT TYPE=\"Submit\" NAME=\"Query\" VALUE=\"Query\">\n" +
                "<INPUT TYPE=\"Submit\" NAME=\"Add\" VALUE=\"Add New
                  ➥Entry\">\n" +
                "<INPUT TYPE=\"Reset\" VALUE=\"Reset\">\n" +
                "</FORM><BR>"
                                );
    }
    private void doOutput2(PrintWriter writer)
    {
        writer.println("</BODY></HTML>");
    }
    public void doGet(HttpServletRequest req, HttpServletResponse
            ➥resp)
    {
        // Get action puts up the query form.
        resp.setContentType("text/html");
        PrintWriter writer = null;
        try {
            writer = resp.getWriter();
        }
        catch (IOException e)   { return; }
        doOutput1(writer);
        doOutput2(writer);
        writer.close();
    }
    public synchronized void doPost(HttpServletRequest req,
                                    HttpServletResponse resp)
    {
        // Post action puts up the query form and responds to the
          ➥post
```

```
        resp.setContentType("text/html");
        PrintWriter writer = null;
        try {
            writer = resp.getWriter();
        }
        catch (IOException e)   { return; }

        // Output the form
        doOutput1(writer);

        // Open or reopen the connection if needed
        try
        {
            // Open a connection to the server - no login or
          ➥password.
            // The form of the URL (first parameter) is dictated
          ➥by the
            // MySQL jdbc driver. Default MySQL TCP port is 3306
            if (connection == null || connection.isClosed())
                connection = DriverManager.getConnection(
                    "jdbc:mysql://localhost:3306/test", "", "");
        }
        catch (SQLException e)
        {
            writer.println("Error: Cannot open database
          ➥connection\n");
            doOutput2(writer);
            writer.close();
            return;
        }

        // Open input from the POST data
        ServletInputStream instream = null;
        Hashtable postData = null;
        try
        {
            // Build a hashtable of the posted data
            postData = HttpUtils.parsePostData(
                req.getContentLength(), req.getInputStream());
        }
        catch (IOException e)
        {
            writer.println("Error: Cannot read post data\n");
        }
        if (postData.containsKey("Add"))
        {
            // User requested to add a new entry... make sure
            // at least last name is non-empty
            if (((String[])postData.get("LastName"))[0].length()
          ➥== 0)
                writer.println("Error: No last name specified for
          ➥Add");
```

continued on next page

continued from previous page

```
            else try
            {
                // Construct and execute an SQL statement to
           ➥insert
                Statement stmt = connection.createStatement();
                stmt.executeUpdate(
                    "INSERT INTO phonelist VALUES (" +
                    "'" +
                    ((String[])postData.get("LastName"))[0] +
                    "','" +
                    ((String[])postData.get("FirstName"))[0] +
                    "','" +
                    ((String[])postData.get("CountryCode"))[0] +
                    "','" +
                    ((String[])postData.get("AreaCode"))[0] +
                    "','" +
                    ((String[])postData.get("PhoneNum"))[0] +
                    "');");
                writer.println("New entry added for " +
                    ((String[])postData.get("LastName"))[0]);
            }
            catch (SQLException e)
            {
                writer.println("Error: " + e.toString());
            }
            catch (NullPointerException e)
            {
                // This will trigger if a form field is missing
           ➥from
                // the post.
                writer.println("Error: " + e.toString());
            }
        }
        else
        {
            // User requested a query...
            ResultSet results = null;
            try
            {
                // Construct an SQL query string. First figure out
                // the qualifiers based on form input
                StringBuffer queryQualifiers = new StringBuffer();
                appendQueryQualifiers(queryQualifiers, "lastname",
                    (postData.get("LastName")));
                appendQueryQualifiers(queryQualifiers,
           ➥"firstname",
                    (postData.get("FirstName")));
                appendQueryQualifiers(queryQualifiers,
           ➥"countrycode",
                    (postData.get("CountryCode")));
                appendQueryQualifiers(queryQualifiers, "areacode",
                    (postData.get("AreaCode")));
```

```
                appendQueryQualifiers(queryQualifiers, "number",
                    (postData.get("PhoneNum")));

                Statement stmt = connection.createStatement();
                results = stmt.executeQuery(
                    "SELECT * FROM phonelist" +
                    queryQualifiers +
                    ";"
                );

                if (results == null)
                    writer.println("Null result from query");
                else
                {
                    // Print headers
                    writer.println(
"<TABLE BORDER=\"2\">\n" +
"<TR>\n" +
"  <TD><CENTER><B>Last Name</B></CENTER></TD>\n" +
"  <TD><CENTER><B>First Name</B></CENTER></TD>\n" +
"  <TD><CENTER><B>Country Code</B></CENTER></TD>\n" +
"  <TD><CENTER><B>Area Code</B></CENTER></TD>\n" +
"  <TD><CENTER><B>Phone Number</B></CENTER></TD>\n" +
"</TR>");

                    while (results.next())
                    {
                        writer.println(
"<TR>" +
"  <TD>" + results.getString(1) + "</TD>\n" +
"  <TD>" + results.getString(2) + "</TD>\n" +
"  <TD>" + results.getString(3) + "</TD>\n" +
"  <TD>" + results.getString(4) + "</TD>\n" +
"  <TD>" + results.getString(5) + "</TD>\n" +
"</TR>");
                    }
                    writer.println("</TABLE>");
                }
            }
            catch (SQLException e)
            {
                writer.println("Error: " + e.toString());
            }
        }
        doOutput2(writer);
        writer.close();
    }
    // appendQueryQualifiers: A utility to assist in constructing
    // the query string
    private void appendQueryQualifiers(StringBuffer qualifiers,
                                       String dbfield,
                                       Object formdata)
```

continued on next page

continued from previous page

```
225         {
226             if (formdata == null) return;
227             String forminfo = ((String[])formdata)[0];
228             // Was anything specified for this form field?
229             if (forminfo.length() > 0)
230             {
231                 // Yes
232                 if (qualifiers.length() == 0)
233                     qualifiers.append(" WHERE");
234                 else
235                     qualifiers.append(" AND");
236                 qualifiers.append(" " + dbfield + " = \"" +
237                                   forminfo + "\"");
238             }
239         }
240         public String getServletInfo()
241         {
242             return "PhoneBook";
243         }
244     }
```

The `init()` method (lines 10–21) is executed once when the servlet is first loaded. Its only job is to ensure that the JDBC driver for MySQL databases has been loaded.

The two HTTP requests supported by `PhoneBook` are `GET` (`doGet()`, lines 61–73) and `POST` (`doPost()`, lines 74–219). The `doGet()` method, called when the page is browsed, does nothing more than display the form, calling `doOutput1()` and `doOutput2()` to generate the HTML.

The `doPost()` method is called when the form is used to query or add to the database. After outputting the HTML form by calling `doOutput1()`, it handles the request, outputs the results, and finally outputs the end-of-page HTML tags by calling `doOutput2()`.

The database activity begins in lines 94–96, with the opening of a connection (or reopening of one that was automatically closed). Lines 107–114 parse the `POST` data that was sent with the request, placing the results in a `java.util.Hashtable`. The hash table will contain an entry for every field of the HTML form, plus one indicating which button was pressed (`Query` or `Add New Entry`). The `Hashtable.get()` calls used to retrieve entries from the hash table (lines 165–174 and elsewhere) return a `String[]`, from which the form data is extracted.

Lines 123–154 process the `Add New Entry` request. After a trivial error check (checking that a Last Name was specified), it constructs an SQL statement of the form

```
INSERT INTO phonelist VALUES ('<lastname>', '<firstname>', '<countrycode>',
 '<areacode>', '<phonenumber>');
```

where the actual values are derived from the form data. After processing the request (129–141), the servlet displays a success message and concludes its activities (lines 217–218).

Lines 159–215 process the `Query` request. The database query is created and the query performed in lines 162–181, by an SQL statement of the form

```
SELECT * FROM phonelist [WHERE lastname="<lastname>" AND ...]
```

with optional qualifiers based on data extracted from the HTML form. If all form fields are empty, the query will retrieve all records from the table.

If the query returns a non-null `results` array, the servlet outputs the table headers (lines 188–196) and steps through the `results` array row by row, generating HTML table rows (lines 198–208).

Configuring and Running PhoneBook

Our existing Apache JServ configuration requires two additions:

- The servlet must be installed in a repository, such as the `examples/` directory used in previous chapters.
- The JDBC driver must be added to the JVM class path. This can be accomplished with this addition to the Apache JServ configuration file, `/opt/apache_jserv/servlets/jserv. properties`:

  ```
  wrapper.classpath=/usr/local/Java/mm.mysql.jdbc-1.2b/mysql_comp.jar
  ```

After restarting Apache to update the JServ class path, the `PhoneBook` servlet is available in the `examples/` servlets zone. In Figure 67.3, the form is filled out with information to be added to the directory.

FIGURE 67.3
Browsing to the servlet displays the form.

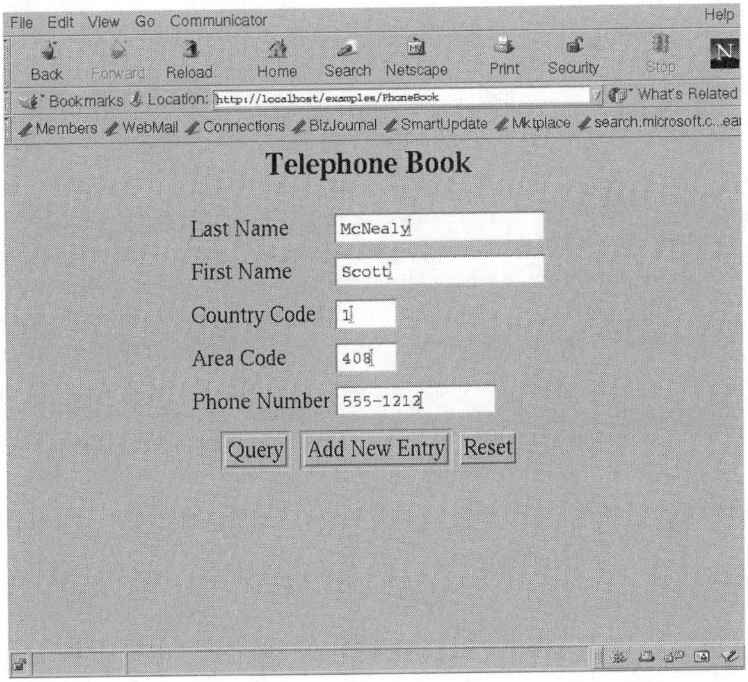

Information is added to tye directory by filling in the fields of the form (see Figure 67.3) and pressing the `Add New Entry` key.

The directory can be searched by filling in any of the fields—or leaving all fields blank to return all entries. Figure 67.4 shows the results of pressing `Query` with a value of `408` in the `Area Code` field.

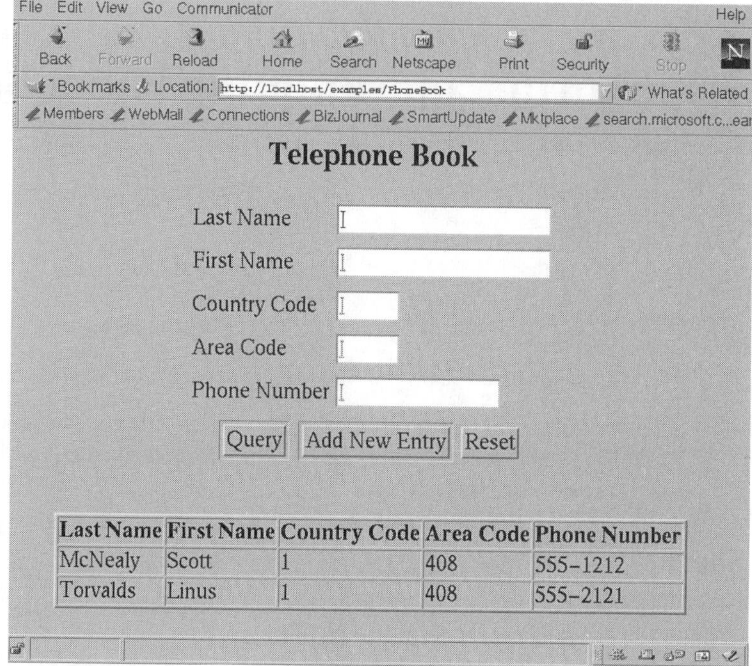

FIGURE 67.4
The results of a query are displayed in a table below the form.

Summary

Three-tier application architectures are a hotbed of activity in Java and an area in which Linux is a strong offering. This chapter presented a simple example—browser access to a back-end database—of the middleware application area. As the Java 2 Enterprise Edition matures, expect that Linux platforms will become increasingly significant in such enterprise applications.

PART XV

APPENDIXES

APPENDIX A

INDEX OF TOOLS AND PROGRAMS

This appendix provides a quick reference to the examples and projects provided in this book. The programs listed here fall into three categories:

- Functional tools that perform a useful task
- Benchmarks
- Example projects that are large enough to mention

Functional Tools

Many tools listed here are personal tools I use in my own development work. Source listings are provided in the book, and source and compiled versions are available on the CD-ROM.

DumpClass

Platform: Versions for JDK1.1 and JDK1.2

Discussion: Chapter 47, "DumpClass: A Tool for Querying Class Structure"

Listing: Appendix B

A utility to dump a list of class members, `DumpClass` includes information about ancestor classes organized into convenient groupings. This is a personal tool I use when I want a listing of class members more comprehensive than that provided by the SDK `javap` utility.

An alternate version, `DumpClass11`, is provided on the CD-ROM. `DumpClass11` works under JDK1.1 but uses class-loading mechanisms that make it slightly less robust than `DumpClass`.

JMakeDepend

Platform: Versions for JDK1.1 and JDK1.2

Discussion: Chapter 48, "JMakeDepend: A Project Build Management Utility"

Listing: Appendix B

This is a personal tool I use for development projects to allow the use of GNU `make` with Java. Several aspects of Java development violate standard `make` assumptions; this tool works around the problems.

An alternate version, `JMakeDepend11`, is provided on the CD-ROM. Because `JMakeDepend` depends on some classes (the Sun Collections classes) whose package name changed between JDK1.1 and JDK1.2, this version supports JDK1.1.

PerfAnal

Platform: JDK1.2

Discussion: Chapter 60, "`PerfAnal`: A Free Performance Analysis Tool"

Listing: Appendix B

This is a personal tool I use to analyze performance data collected by the JDK1.2 sample profiler. When applied to output from Sun's `hprof` profiler (a standard JDK1.2 component), `PerfAnal` allows a detailed exploration of where and why an application is spending its time.

Profiler

Platform: JDK1.2

Discussion: Chapter 64, "Profiling User-Space Native Code"

Listing: Appendix B

This is a personal tool that provides visibility into where, in the native code address space, an application is spending time. `Profiler` allows you to identify which core activities—JVM execution, JIT, JNI methods, C library activity, and so on—are consuming CPU time.

See also the discussion of `strace` in Chapter 63, "Understanding Linux Kernel Performance." This Linux utility will help you understand how a Java application uses kernel resources.

ShowFonts11

Platform: JDK1.1/JDK1.2

Discussion: Chapter 14, "Configuring the Linux JSDK/JRE Environment," in the section "Adding, Changing, and Configuring Fonts in JDK1.1" and Appendix B

Listing: Appendix B

This tool generates a GUI-based listing of available fonts.

ShowFonts12

Platform: JDK1.2

Discussion: Chapter 14, "Configuring the Linux JSDK/JRE Environment," in the section "Adding, Changing, and Configuring Fonts in JDK1.2" and Appendix B

Listing: Appendix B

This tool generates a GUI-based listing of available fonts, using a JDK1.2 method that returns much more information than the JDK1.1 method used in `ShowFonts11`.

`SlideShow`

Platform: JDK1.2

Discussion: Chapter 3, "A Look at the Java Core Classes," in the section "Package `java.awt.image`" and Appendix B

Listing: Appendix B

This utility demonstrates some JDK1.2 graphical capabilities by implementing an image viewer with image enhancements capabilities. I wrote **`SlideShow`** while preparing for a talk in which I needed to show some image files. It allows you to step through a list of image files, effectively functioning as a slide projector.

`WaterFall`

Platform: JDK1.2

Discussion: Chapter 3, "A Look at the Java Core Classes," in the section "Package `java.awt`" and Appendix B

Listing: Appendix B

This utility demonstrates some JDK1.2 font-rendering capabilities by creating a typographic *waterfall chart* showing a font in a range of sizes. Versions of the chart are created with and without new JDK1.2 rendering capabilities (antialiasing and fractional font metrics) to show their effect on font appearance.

`XClipboard`

Platform: JDK1.1/JDK1.2

Discussion: Chapter 56, "X Window System Tips and Tricks," in the section "XClipboard: A JNI-Based Cut-and-Paste Tool"

Listing: Appendix B

This JNI-based class library provides access to X Window System inter-client data transfer capabilities that are not exposed through the `java.awt.datatransfer` classes. Among other things, it allows you to use the X ***primary selection*** mechanism that, in many X clients, is accessed from the middle mouse button (but that the Java AWT does not support).

`xwinwrap`

Platform: JDK1.1/JDK1.2/Any X Application

Discussion: Chapter 56, "X Window System Tips and Tricks," in the section "xwinwrap: Controlling Colormap and Visual Usage"

Listing: Appendix B

This shared library allows you to run an X client (such as a Java AWT-based program) with a custom colormap and a nondefault visual. It can be used to solve colormap crowding problems, or to run a Java application with a visual it likes better than the X server's default visual.

Benchmarks

This section describes two performance measurement tools I have found useful for understanding Java application performance on Linux.

`FontPerf`

Platform: JDK1.1/JDK1.2

Discussion and Listing: Chapter 57, "Why Is Java Slow?," in the section "Inefficient Graphics"

This benchmark measures the performance of text rendering and is useful for understanding text slowdowns between JDK1.1 and JDK1.2.

`Memstress`

Platform: Linux

Discussion: Chapter 57, "Why Is Java Slow?," in the section "Poor Memory Locality" and Appendix B

Listing: Appendix B

This native benchmark measures the effect of poor memory locality on memory access speeds.

Example Projects

Among the code examples in this book, the three projects mentioned here provide some useful functionality you can apply to your own projects.

Backing Store

Platform: JDK1.2

Discussion and Listing: Chapter 59, "An Approach to Improving Graphical Rendering Performance"

This project explores techniques you can use to improve graphical rendering performance, including a backing store implementation that can drastically reduce the repainting workload of an application for which repaints are expensive.

`FileStatus`

Platform: JDK1.1/JDK1.2

Discussion and Listing: Chapter 55, "JNI: Mixing Java and Native Code on Linux"

This project describes a JNI-based component that accesses native platform capabilities—ownership and permissions information about files—that are not supported from Java.

PhoneBook

Platform: JDK1.1/JDK1.2

Discussion and Listing: Chapter 67, "Java, Linux, and Three-Tiered Architectures"

This project illustrates three-tier application architectures with a Java servlet implementing database access.

APPENDIX B

MISCELLANEOUS PROGRAM LISTINGS

The 67 chapters of this book include a number of small Java examples that were illustrated with code listings in the chapter. This appendix provides the listings for 11 larger projects and examples not listed in the individual chapters.

All sources here are also available on the book's CD-ROM. The two versions do not exactly match—the electronic versions include open source copyright notices and other comments not reproduced here.

For programs whose instructions were not provided in the chapters, this appendix includes usage instructions.

`DumpClass`: Print Detailed Class Structure Information

This utility, described in Chapter 47, "DumpClass: A Tool for Querying Class Structure," prints out detailed information about class structure.

Platform: JDK1.1/JDK1.2 (two different versions)

Separate versions, `DumpClass` and `DumpClass11` are provided for JDK1.2 and JDK1.1 (respectively). Although nearly identical, the versions differ in two small details:

- The Sun Container classes, on which `DumpClass` depends, were an extension in JDK1.1 and part of the core classes in JDK1.2. The package name changed between the two releases, requiring different versions of the program.
- The JDK1.2 version uses a class-loading method that was unavailable in JDK1.1, and is more robust than the JDK1.1 counterpart.

Both versions are provided on the CD-ROM. Listing B.1 shows the source listing for the JDK1.2 version.

LISTING B.1 `DumpClass.java`

```
package com.macmillan.nmeyers;
import java.lang.*;
```

continued on next page

continued from previous page

```
import java.lang.reflect.*;
import java.util.*;
import java.awt.*;

class DumpClass
{
    static class ClassMember implements Comparable
    {
        Member member = null;
        ClassMember(Member m)    { member = m; }
        public String toString()
        { return member.toString(); }
        public String getName()
        {
            String result = member.getName();
            int pos = result.lastIndexOf('.');
            if (pos != -1) result = result.substring(pos + 1);
            return result;
        }
        // Implementation of compareTo: create an ordering between
        // ClassMember representations of members.
        public int compareTo(Object m)
        {
            if (!member.getClass().equals(((ClassMember)m).member.
➥getClass()))
            {
                return member.getClass().toString().compareTo(
                        ((ClassMember)m).member.getClass().toString());
            }
            if (member.getClass().equals(Constructor.class))
            {
                final Constructor constructor1 = (Constructor)member;
                final Constructor constructor2 =
                    (Constructor)((ClassMember)m).member;
                int result = constructor1.getName().compareTo(
                                constructor2.getName());
                if (result != 0) return result;
                Class[] parm1 = constructor1.getParameterTypes();
                Class[] parm2 = constructor2.getParameterTypes();
                for (int i = 0; i < parm1.length && i < parm2.length;
➥i++)
                {
                    result = parm1[i].toString().compareTo(parm2[i].
➥toString());
                    if (result != 0) return result;
                }
                return parm1.length - parm2.length;
            }
            if (member.getClass().equals(Method.class))
            {
                final Method method1 = (Method)member;
                final Method method2 = (Method)((ClassMember)m).member;
```

```
                int result = method1.getName().compareTo(
                                 method2.getName());
                if (result != 0) return result;
                Class[] parm1 = method1.getParameterTypes();
                Class[] parm2 = method2.getParameterTypes();
                for (int i = 0; i < parm1.length && i < parm2.length;
➥i++)
                {
                    result = parm1[i].toString().compareTo(parm2[i].
➥toString());
                    if (result != 0) return result;
                }
                return parm1.length - parm2.length;
            }
            if (member.getClass().equals(Field.class))
                return member.getName().compareTo(
                    ((ClassMember)m).member.getName());
            return member.toString().compareTo(
                ((ClassMember)m).member.toString());
        }
    }
    // Our own implementation of a set, with some filtering on the
➥add()
    // operation
    static class MemberSet extends TreeSet
    {
        boolean showProtected = true;
        boolean showPackage = false;
        boolean showPrivate = false;
        boolean showInaccessible = false;
        String clsName = null;
        String packageName = null;
        MemberSet(Class cls, boolean f1, boolean f2, boolean f3,
➥boolean f4)
        {
            showProtected = f1;
            showPackage = f2;
            showPrivate = f3;
            showInaccessible = f4;
            clsName = cls.getName();
            int ppos = clsName.lastIndexOf(".");
            packageName = (ppos >= 0) ? clsName.substring(0, ppos) :
➥"";
        }
        public boolean add(Class cls, ClassMember element)
        {
            int modifier = element.member.getModifiers();
            // Root out inaccessible members
            if (!showInaccessible)
            {
```

continued on next page

continued from previous page

```
                String cName = cls.getName();
                int ppos = clsName.lastIndexOf(".");
                String pName = (ppos >= 0) ? clsName.substring(0, ppos)
➥: "";
                // Private ancestor members
                if (Modifier.isPrivate(modifier) &&
                    !cName.equals(clsName) ||
                // Ancestor constructors
                    element.member.getClass().equals(Constructor.class)
➥&&
                    !cName.equals(clsName) ||
                // Package-visible ancestors from different packages
                    !Modifier.isPublic(modifier) &&
                    !Modifier.isProtected(modifier) &&
                    !pName.equals(packageName))
                    return false;
            }
            // This logic assumes relationships between permission
            // levels that will always be true (e.g. showPrivate->show
➥all).
            if (Modifier.isPublic(modifier) ||
                showPrivate ||
                Modifier.isProtected(modifier) && showProtected ||
                !Modifier.isPrivate(modifier) && showPackage)
                return super.add(element);
            else return false;
        }
    }
    // We don't need to link classes: provide a classloader that skips
    // that step.
    static class MyClassLoader extends ClassLoader
    {
        public Class loadClass(String c) throws ClassNotFoundException
        { return super.loadClass(c, false); }
    }
    static void usageMsg()
    {
        System.err.println("Usage: DumpClass [options] <classes>");
        System.err.println("\nOptions:");
        System.err.println("  -public");
        System.err.println("  -protected        (default)");
        System.err.println("  -package");
        System.err.println("  -private");
        System.err.println("  -suppress:{name,interfaces," +
                           "hierarchy,headings,keys,all}");
        System.err.println("  -noancestors");
        System.err.println("  -inaccessible");
        System.exit(1);
    }
    public static void main(String[] argv)
    {
        int argn;
```

```
        boolean showProtected = true;
        boolean showPackage = false;
        boolean showPrivate = false;
        boolean showName = true;
        boolean showInterfaces = true;
        boolean showHierarchy = true;
        boolean showHeadings = true;
        boolean showKeys = true;
        boolean showAncestorMembers = true;
        boolean showInaccessible = false;
        for (argn = 0;
             argn < argv.length && argv[argn].startsWith("-");
             argn++)
        {
            if (argv[argn].equals("-public"))
                showProtected = showPackage = showPrivate = false;
            else if (argv[argn].equals("-protected"))
            {
                showProtected = true;
                showPackage = showPrivate = false;
            }
            else if (argv[argn].equals("-package"))
            {
                showProtected = showPackage = true;
                showPrivate = false;
            }
            else if (argv[argn].equals("-private"))
                showProtected = showPackage = showPrivate = true;
            else if (argv[argn].equals("-noancestors"))
                showAncestorMembers = false;
            else if (argv[argn].equals("-inaccessible"))
                showInaccessible = true;
            else if (argv[argn].startsWith("-suppress:"))
            {
                String args = argv[argn].substring(10);
                while (args.length() > 0)
                {
                    int comma = args.indexOf(',');
                    String arg;
                    if (comma > 0)
                    {
                        arg = args.substring(0, comma);
                        args = args.substring(comma + 1);
                    }
                    else
                    {
                        arg = args;
                        args = "";
                    }
                    if (arg.equals("name") || arg.equals("all"))
                        showName = false;
```

continued on next page

continued from previous page

```
                    if (arg.equals("interfaces") || arg.equals("all"))
                        showInterfaces = false;
                    if (arg.equals("hierarchy") || arg.equals("all"))
                        showHierarchy = false;
                    if (arg.equals("headings") || arg.equals("all"))
                        showHeadings = false;
                    if (arg.equals("keys") || arg.equals("all"))
                        showKeys = false;
                }
            }
            else
            {
                usageMsg();
            }
        }

        MyClassLoader loader = new MyClassLoader();
        // For each class requested
        for (boolean firstClass = true;
             argn < argv.length;
             firstClass = false, argn++)
        {
            Class cls;
            // Load the class
            try
            { cls = loader.loadClass(argv[argn]); }
            catch (ClassNotFoundException e)
            { System.err.println("Class " + argv[argn] + " not found");
              continue; }

            // Build a set of members
            MemberSet memberSet =
                new MemberSet(cls, showProtected, showPackage,
➥showPrivate,
                              showInaccessible);

            // Step up the class hierarchy until we run out. The indent
            // controls indentation of classes in the hierarchy chart,
➥and
            // is also used to ascertain when we're operating on the
            // requested class or an ancestor.
            for (String indent = "";; indent += "  ")
            {
                if (showName)
                {
                    if (indent.equals(""))
                    {
                        // Do some processing specific to the requested
➥class
                        if (!firstClass) System.out.println("");
                        int modifiers = cls.getModifiers();
                        String modString =
➥Modifier.toString(modifiers);
```

```
                // Filter out weirdness in handling of "interface"
                // modifier
                int pos = modString.indexOf(" interface");
                if (pos >= 0)
                    modString = modString.substring(0, pos) +
                                modString.substring(pos + 10);
                if (modString.length() > 0)
                    System.out.print(modString + " ");
            }
            if (showHierarchy || indent.equals(""))
                System.out.print(indent + cls);
            // For the requested class, but not superclasses, list
            // the supported interfaces
            if (indent.equals("") && showInterfaces)
            {
                Class[] interfaces;
                interfaces = cls.getInterfaces();
                if (interfaces != null && interfaces.length > 0)
                {
                    System.out.print(" implements " +
                                     interfaces[0].getName());
                    for (int j = 1; j < interfaces.length; j++)
                        System.out.print(", " +
                                     interfaces[j].getName());
                }
            }
            if (showHierarchy || indent.equals(""))
                System.out.println("");
        }

        if (showAncestorMembers || indent.equals(""))
        {
            // Build a list of methods for this class
            Method[] methods;
            try
            { methods = cls.getDeclaredMethods(); }
            catch (SecurityException e)
            { System.err.println("Security exception calling " +
                                 "getDeclaredMethods() for " +
                                 argv[argn]);
              break; }
            for (int j = 0; j < methods.length; j++)
                memberSet.add(cls, new ClassMember(methods[j]));

            // Build a list of constructors for this class
            Constructor[] constructors;
```

continued on next page

continued from previous page

```
                    try
                    { constructors = cls.getDeclaredConstructors(); }
                    catch (SecurityException e)
                    { System.err.println("Security exception
➥calling " +
                                             "getDeclaredConstructors()
➥for " +
                                                argv[argn]);
                        break; }
                    for (int j = 0; j < constructors.length; j++)
                        memberSet.add(cls,
                                         new
➥ClassMember(constructors[j]));

                    // Build a list of fields for this class
                    Field[] fields;
                    try
                    { fields = cls.getDeclaredFields(); }
                    catch (SecurityException e)
                    { System.err.println("Security exception
➥calling " +
                                                "getDeclaredFields() for " +
                                                argv[argn]);
                      break; }
                    for (int j = 0; j < fields.length; j++)
                        memberSet.add(cls, new ClassMember(fields[j]));
                }

                // We're done when we run out of classes to analyze
                if (cls.equals(Object.class)) break;
                cls = cls.getSuperclass();
                if (cls == null) break;
            }

            // Output results
            Class currentMemberType = null;
            for (Iterator j = memberSet.iterator(); j.hasNext();)
            {
                ClassMember mm = (ClassMember)j.next();
                if (showHeadings &&
                    !mm.member.getClass().equals(currentMemberType))
                {
                    currentMemberType = mm.member.getClass();
                    if (currentMemberType == Constructor.class)
                        System.out.println("\nConstructors\n");
                    else if (currentMemberType == Field.class)
                        System.out.println("\nFields\n");
                    else
                        System.out.println("\nMethods\n");
                }
                if (showKeys) System.out.print(mm.getName() + ": ");
                System.out.println(mm.toString());
```

```
340                 }
341             }
342             System.exit(0);
343         }
344     }
```

`DumpClass` uses the Reflection API to study classes. Because certain capabilities found in `javap`—identifying the source file and identifying inner classes—can only be achieved by reading the class file (not through the Reflection API), `DumpClass` does not provide those capabilities. (We presented a project that *does* read class files in Chapter 48, "JMakeDepend: A Project Build Management Utility.")

Most of the heavy lifting in `DumpClass` is performed by two classes:

- `DumpClass.ClassMember` (lines 9–70), a wrapper for `java.lang.reflect.Member` objects that implements an ordering relation.
- `DumpClass.MemberSet` (lines 73–121), a specialized `TreeSet` used to filter and organize the collected information.

A customized class loader is introduced in lines 124–128, which loads classes but does not link them. Although linking is necessary when a class is to be instantiated, it's not necessary for our purposes and can trigger errors (for example, missing native library) that `DumpClass` does not care about. This trick only works under JDK1.2; we must load classes using `Class.forName()` under JDK1.1.

After initializing (lines 156–211) and instantiating the custom class loader (line 213), `DumpClass` loops through the command-line arguments (lines 214–217) for processing.

For each class requested, `DumpClass` loads the class (line 222), allocates a `DumpClass.MemberSet` (line 228), and populates it with information obtained through reflection (lines 236–320). It then processes the parent class, ascending the inheritance hierarchy until it runs out of classes.

Lines 324–340 step through the `DumpClass.MemberSet`, dumping class information to `stdout`. The behavior of `java.util.TreeSet` ensures that the information is sorted and that overridden ancestor class members are not shown.

`JMakeDepend`: Generate Dependency Information for GNU make

This utility, presented in Chapter 48, "JMakeDepend: A Project Build Management Utility," can be used in conjunction with GNU `make` to manage Java projects.

Platform: JDK1.1/JDK1.2 (two different versions)

GNU `make` offers powerful logic for managing dependencies between sources and objects, but Java's unique requirements make it difficult to use this logic. `JMakeDepend` works around the `make` limitations, enabling `make`'s use in Java environments.

`JMakeDepend` consists of two top-level classes:

- `JMakeDepend` is the core utility.
- `ClassFileContents` reads class files, providing information needed for `JMakeDepend` to do its job. Much as we would like to use the Reflection API to study class files, it cannot tell us everything `JMakeDepend` needs to know. In particular, Reflection will not report the source name from which a class was compiled, and it will not return information about what external classes are referenced.

Two versions of `JMakeDepend` are provided on the CD-ROM:

- `JMakeDepend`: Usable under JDK1.2.
- `JMakeDepend11`: A JDK1.1-only version that depends on the Sun Container class library. The package name of these classes changed when they were integrated into the JDK1.2 core.

Listing B.2 provides the `ClassFileContents` source, and Listing B.3 provides the `JMakeDepend` source.

LISTING B.2 `ClassFileContents.java`

```
package com.macmillan.nmeyers;
import java.io.*;

public class ClassFileContents
{
    // Class file layout from Java spec
    int magic;
    short minor_version;
    short major_version;
    int constant_pool_count;
    cp_info constant_pool[];
    final static byte CONSTANT_Utf8 = 1;
    final static byte CONSTANT_Integer = 3;
    final static byte CONSTANT_Float = 4;
    final static byte CONSTANT_Long = 5;
    final static byte CONSTANT_Double = 6;
    final static byte CONSTANT_Class = 7;
    final static byte CONSTANT_String = 8;
    final static byte CONSTANT_Fieldref = 9;
    final static byte CONSTANT_Methodref = 10;
    final static byte CONSTANT_InterfaceMethodref = 11;
    final static byte CONSTANT_NameAndType = 12;
    public class cp_info
    {
        byte tag;
    }
    // Reader for next cp_info entry
    cp_info read_cp_info(DataInputStream is) throws IOException
    {
```

```
        byte tag = is.readByte();
        switch (tag)
        {
            case CONSTANT_Utf8:
                return new CONSTANT_Utf8_info(tag, is);
            case CONSTANT_Integer:
                return new CONSTANT_Integer_info(tag, is);
            case CONSTANT_Float:
                return new CONSTANT_Float_info(tag, is);
            case CONSTANT_Long:
                return new CONSTANT_Long_info(tag, is);
            case CONSTANT_Double:
                return new CONSTANT_Double_info(tag, is);
            case CONSTANT_Class:
                return new CONSTANT_Class_info(tag, is);
            case CONSTANT_String:
                return new CONSTANT_String_info(tag, is);
            case CONSTANT_Fieldref:
                return new CONSTANT_Fieldref_info(tag, is);
            case CONSTANT_Methodref:
                return new CONSTANT_Methodref_info(tag, is);
            case CONSTANT_InterfaceMethodref:
                return new CONSTANT_InterfaceMethodref_info(tag, is);
            case CONSTANT_NameAndType:
                return new CONSTANT_NameAndType_info(tag, is);
        }
        throw new IOException("Unrecognized tag " + tag);
    }
    // Subclasses of cp_info for Java types
    public class CONSTANT_Class_info extends cp_info
    {
        int name_index;
        CONSTANT_Class_info(byte t, DataInputStream is)
            throws IOException
        {
            tag = t;
            name_index = is.readUnsignedShort();
        }
        public String toString()
        {
            return "[Class:name_index:" + nameIndex(name_index) + ']';
        }
    }
    public class CONSTANT_Fieldref_info extends cp_info
    {
        int class_index;
        int name_and_type_index;
        CONSTANT_Fieldref_info(byte t, DataInputStream is)
            throws IOException
        {
            tag = t;
            class_index = is.readUnsignedShort();
```

continued on next page

continued from previous page

```
            name_and_type_index = is.readUnsignedShort();
        }
        public String toString()
        {
            return "[Fieldref:class_index:" + class_index +
                   ",name_and_type_index:" + name_and_type_index + ']';
        }
    }
    public class CONSTANT_Methodref_info extends cp_info
    {
        int class_index;
        int name_and_type_index;
        CONSTANT_Methodref_info(byte t, DataInputStream is)
            throws IOException
        {
            tag = t;
            class_index = is.readUnsignedShort();
            name_and_type_index = is.readUnsignedShort();
        }
        public String toString()
        {
            return "[Methodref:class_index:" + class_index +
                   ",name_and_type_index:" + name_and_type_index + ']';
        }
    }
    public class CONSTANT_InterfaceMethodref_info extends cp_info
    {
        int class_index;
        int name_and_type_index;
        CONSTANT_InterfaceMethodref_info(byte t, DataInputStream is)
            throws IOException
        {
            tag = t;
            class_index = is.readUnsignedShort();
            name_and_type_index = is.readUnsignedShort();
        }
        public String toString()
        {
            return "[InterfaceMethodref:class_index:" + class_index +
                   ",name_and_type_index:" + name_and_type_index + ']';
        }
    }
    public class CONSTANT_String_info extends cp_info
    {
        int string_index;
        CONSTANT_String_info(byte t, DataInputStream is)
            throws IOException
        {
            tag = t;
            string_index = is.readUnsignedShort();
        }
        public String toString()
```

```
        {
            return "[String:string_index:" + string_index + ']';
        }
    }
    public class CONSTANT_Integer_info extends cp_info
    {
        int bytes;
        CONSTANT_Integer_info(byte t, DataInputStream is)
            throws IOException
        {
            tag = t;
            bytes = is.readInt();
        }
        public String toString()
        {
            return "[Integer:bytes:" + bytes + ']';
        }
    }
    public class CONSTANT_Float_info extends cp_info
    {
        float value;
        CONSTANT_Float_info(byte t, DataInputStream is)
            throws IOException
        {
            tag = t;
            value = is.readFloat();
        }
        public String toString()
        {
            return "[Float:value:" + value + ']';
        }
    }
    public class CONSTANT_Long_info extends cp_info
    {
        long value;
        CONSTANT_Long_info(byte t, DataInputStream is)
            throws IOException
        {
            tag = t;
            value = is.readLong();
        }
        public String toString()
        {
            return "[Long:value:" + value + ']';
        }
    }
    public class CONSTANT_Double_info extends cp_info
    {
        double value;
        CONSTANT_Double_info(byte t, DataInputStream is)
            throws IOException
        {
```

continued on next page

continued from previous page

```
            tag = tag;
            value = is.readDouble();
        }
        public String toString()
        {
            return "[Double:value:" + value + ']';
        }
    }
    public class CONSTANT_NameAndType_info extends cp_info
    {
        int name_index;
        int descriptor_index;
        CONSTANT_NameAndType_info(byte t, DataInputStream is)
            throws IOException
        {
            tag = t;
            name_index = is.readUnsignedShort();
            descriptor_index = is.readUnsignedShort();
        }
        public String toString()
        {
            return "[NameAndType:name_index:" + nameIndex(name_index) +
                   ",descriptor_index:" + descriptor_index + ']';
        }
    }
    public class CONSTANT_Utf8_info extends cp_info
    {
        int length;
        byte bytes[];
        CONSTANT_Utf8_info(byte t, DataInputStream is)
            throws IOException
        {
            tag = t;
            length = is.readUnsignedShort();
            bytes = new byte[length];
            for (int i = 0; i < length; i++)
                bytes[i] = is.readByte();
        }
        public String getString()
        {
            String stringInfo = null;
            try { stringInfo = new String(bytes, "UTF8"); }
            catch (UnsupportedEncodingException e)  {}
            return stringInfo;
        }
        public String toString()
        {
            return "[UTF8String:length:" + length + ",bytes:" +
                   getString() + ']';
        }
    }
```

```
        short access_flags;
        final short ACC_PUBLIC=0x0001;
        final short ACC_FINAL=0x0010;
        final short ACC_SUPER=0x0020;
        final short ACC_INTERFACE=0x0200;
        final short ACC_ABSTRACT=0x0400;

        int this_class;
        int super_class;
        int interfaces_count;
        int interfaces[];
        int fields_count;
        field_info fields[];
        public class field_info
        {
            short access_flags;
            final short ACC_PUBLIC = 0x0001;
            final short ACC_PRIVATE = 0x0002;
            final short ACC_PROTECTED = 0x0004;
            final short ACC_STATIC = 0x0008;
            final short ACC_FINAL = 0x0010;
            final short ACC_VOLATILE = 0x0040;
            final short ACC_TRANSIENT = 0x0080;
            int name_index;
            int descriptor_index;
            int attributes_count;
            attribute_info attributes[];
            field_info(DataInputStream is) throws IOException
            {
                access_flags = is.readShort();
                name_index = is.readUnsignedShort();
                descriptor_index = is.readUnsignedShort();
                attributes_count = is.readUnsignedShort();
                attributes = new attribute_info[attributes_count];
                for (int i = 0; i < attributes_count; i++)
                    attributes[i] = new attribute_info(is);
            }
            public String toString()
            {
                String result =  "[access_flags:" + hex(access_flags) +
                                 ",name_index:" + nameIndex(name_index) +
                                 ",descriptor_index:" + descriptor_index +
                                 ",attributes_count:" + attributes_count +
                                 ",attributes:[";
                for (int i = 0; i < attributes_count; i++)
                {
                    if (i > 0) result += ',';
                    result += attributes[i].toString();
                }
                result += "]]";
                return result;
```

continued on next page

continued from previous page

```
        }
    }
    int methods_count;
    method_info methods[];
    public class method_info
    {
        short access_flags;
        final short ACC_PUBLIC = 0x0001;
        final short ACC_PRIVATE = 0x0002;
        final short ACC_PROTECTED = 0x0004;
        final short ACC_STATIC = 0x0008;
        final short ACC_FINAL = 0x0010;
        final short ACC_SYNCHRONIZED = 0x0020;
        final short ACC_NATIVE = 0x0100;
        final short ACC_ABSTRACT = 0x0400;
        int name_index;
        int descriptor_index;
        int attributes_count;
        attribute_info attributes[];
        method_info(DataInputStream is) throws IOException
        {
            access_flags = is.readShort();
            name_index = is.readUnsignedShort();
            descriptor_index = is.readUnsignedShort();
            attributes_count = is.readUnsignedShort();
            attributes = new attribute_info[attributes_count];
            for (int i = 0; i < attributes_count; i++)
                attributes[i] = new attribute_info(is);
        }
        public String toString()
        {
            String result =  "[access_flags:" + hex(access_flags) +
                             ",name_index:" + nameIndex(name_index) +
                             ",descriptor_index:" + descriptor_index +
                             ",attributes_count:" + attributes_count +
                             ",attributes:[";
            for (int i = 0; i < attributes_count; i++)
            {
                if (i > 0) result += ',';
                result += attributes[i].toString();
            }
            result += "]]";
            return result;
        }
    }
    int attributes_count;
    attribute_info attributes[];
    public class attribute_info
    {
        int attribute_name_index;
        int attribute_length;
```

```
        byte info[];
        attribute_info(DataInputStream is) throws IOException
        {
            attribute_name_index = is.readUnsignedShort();
            attribute_length = is.readInt();
            info = new byte[attribute_length];
            for (int i = 0; i < attribute_length; i++)
                info[i] = is.readByte();
        }
        public String toString()
        {
            String result = "[attribute_name_index:" +
                            nameIndex(attribute_name_index) +
                            ",attribute_length:" + attribute_length +
                            ",info:0x";
            for (int i = 0; i < attribute_length; i++)
                result += hex(info[i]);
            return result + ']';
        }
    }
    static public class Exceptions_attribute
    {
        int attribute_name_index;
        int attribute_length;
        int number_of_exceptions;
        int exception_index_table[];
        Exceptions_attribute(attribute_info info) throws IOException
        {
            attribute_name_index = info.attribute_name_index;
            attribute_length = info.attribute_length;
            DataInputStream is =
                new DataInputStream(
                    new ByteArrayInputStream(info.info));
            number_of_exceptions = is.readUnsignedShort();
            exception_index_table = new int[number_of_exceptions];
            for (int i = 0; i < number_of_exceptions; i++)
                exception_index_table[i] = is.readUnsignedShort();
            is.close();
        }
    }

    public ClassFileContents(InputStream is) throws IOException
    {
        DataInputStream inputStream = new DataInputStream(is);
        magic = inputStream.readInt();
        if (magic != 0xcafebabe) throw new IOException(
➥"Not a class file");
        minor_version = inputStream.readShort();
        major_version = inputStream.readShort();
        constant_pool_count = inputStream.readUnsignedShort();
        constant_pool = new cp_info[constant_pool_count];
```

continued on next page

continued from previous page

```
            constant_pool[0] = null;
            for (int i = 1; i < constant_pool_count; i++)
            {
                constant_pool[i] = read_cp_info(inputStream);
                // Kluge around strange classfile representation of
                // longs and doubles in the constant pool. The spec
                // indicates that this representation was not, in
                // retrospect, a good idea.
                if (constant_pool[i].getClass().equals(
                        CONSTANT_Long_info.class) ||
                    constant_pool[i].getClass().equals(
                        CONSTANT_Double_info.class))
                    constant_pool[++i] = null;
            }
            access_flags = inputStream.readShort();
            this_class = inputStream.readUnsignedShort();
            super_class = inputStream.readUnsignedShort();
            interfaces_count = inputStream.readUnsignedShort();
            interfaces = new int[interfaces_count];
            for (int i = 0; i < interfaces_count; i++)
            {
                interfaces[i] = inputStream.readUnsignedShort();
            }
            fields_count = inputStream.readUnsignedShort();
            fields = new field_info[fields_count];
            for (int i = 0; i < fields_count; i++)
            {
                fields[i] = new field_info(inputStream);
            }
            methods_count = inputStream.readUnsignedShort();
            methods = new method_info[methods_count];
            for (int i = 0; i < methods_count; i++)
            {
                methods[i] = new method_info(inputStream);
            }
            attributes_count = inputStream.readUnsignedShort();
            attributes = new attribute_info[attributes_count];
            for (int i = 0; i < attributes_count; i++)
            {
                attributes[i] = new attribute_info(inputStream);
            }
        }
        // Build a huge and generally unusable String representation of
        // ClassFileContents.
        public String toString()
        {
            String result = "[";
            result += "magic:0x" + hex(magic);
            result += ",minor_version:0x" + hex(minor_version);
            result += ",major_version:0x" + hex(major_version);
            result += ",constant_pool_count:" + constant_pool_count;
            result += ",constant_pool:[";
```

```
        for (int i = 0; i < constant_pool_count; i++)
        {
            result += (i > 0 ? "," : "") + constant_pool[i];
        }
        result += "],access_flags:0x" + hex(access_flags);
        result += ",this_class:" +
                  constant_pool[((CONSTANT_Class_info)
                               constant_pool[this_class]).name_index];
        result += ",super_class:" +
                  constant_pool[((CONSTANT_Class_info)
                              constant_pool[super_class]).name_index];
        result += ",interfaces_count:" + interfaces_count;
        result += ",interfaces:[";
        for (int i = 0; i < interfaces_count; i++)
        {
            result += (i > 0 ? "," : "");
            result += constant_pool[interfaces[i]].toString();
        }
        result += "],fields_count:" + fields_count;
        result += ",fields:[";
        for (int i = 0; i < fields_count; i++)
        {
            result += (i > 0 ? "," : "");
            result += fields[i].toString();
        }
        result += "],methods_count:" + methods_count;
        result += ",methods:[";
        for (int i = 0; i < methods_count; i++)
        {
            result += (i > 0 ? "," : "");
            result += methods[i].toString();
        }
        result += "],attributes_count = " + attributes_count;
        result += ",attributes:[";
        for (int i = 0; i < attributes_count; i++)
        {
            result += (i > 0 ? "," : "");
            result += attributes[i].toString();
        }
        result += "]]";
        return result;
    }
    // Utilities
    public static String hex(byte n)
    {
        final char[] hexdigits = { '0','1','2','3','4','5','6','7',
                                   '8','9','a','b','c','d','e','f' };
        return "" + hexdigits[(n >> 4) & 0xf] + hexdigits[n & 0xf];
    }
    public static String hex(short n)
    {
        return hex((byte)((n >> 8) & 0xff)) +
```

continued on next page

continued from previous page

```
                hex((byte)((n) & 0xff));
    }
    public static String hex(int n)
    {
        return hex((short)((n >> 16) & 0xffff)) +
                hex((short)((n) & 0xffff));
    }
    String nameIndex(int n)
    {
        String result = "" + n;
        if (constant_pool.length > n &&
            constant_pool[n].getClass().equals(
                CONSTANT_Utf8_info.class))
        {
            result += "(" +
                ((CONSTANT_Utf8_info)constant_pool[n]).getString()
                + ")";
        }
        return result;
    }
    // Utility to decompile Java method signatures
    public static String decompile(String descriptor)
    {
        String result = "", term;
        int arrayCount = 0;
        boolean lastKeyWord = false;
        while (descriptor.length() > 0)
        {
            int increment = 1;
            boolean keyWord = true;
            switch (descriptor.charAt(0))
            {
                case 'B': term = "byte"; break;
                case 'C': term = "char"; break;
                case 'D': term = "double"; break;
                case 'F': term = "float"; break;
                case 'I': term = "int"; break;
                case 'J': term = "long"; break;
                case 'S': term = "short"; break;
                case 'V': term = "void"; break;
                case 'Z': term = "boolean"; break;
                case 'L':
                    int endLoc = descriptor.indexOf(';');
                    term = descriptor.substring(1, endLoc);
                    increment = endLoc + 1;
                    break;
                case '[':
                    term = "";
                    arrayCount++;
                    break;
                default:
                    term = descriptor.substring(0, 1);
```

```
546                     keyWord = false;
547                     break;
548                 }
549                 descriptor = descriptor.substring(increment);
550                 if (term.length() > 0)
551                 {
552                     if (lastKeyWord && keyWord) result += ", ";
553                     result += term;
554                     for (int i = 0; i < arrayCount; i++)
555                         result += "[]";
556                     arrayCount = 0;
557                     lastKeyWord = keyWord;
558                 }
559             }
560             return result;
561     }
562 
563     // Give this class a main() method... mainly for testing.
564     public static void main(String[] argv)
565     {
566         for (int i = 0; i < argv.length; i++)
567         {
568             ClassFileContents cf = null;
569             FileInputStream is;
570             try
571             {
572                 is = new FileInputStream(argv[i]);
573                 cf = new ClassFileContents(is);
574             }
575             catch (FileNotFoundException e)
576             { System.err.println(argv[i] + ": " + e); }
577             catch (IOException e)
578             { System.err.println(argv[i] + ": " + e); }
579             System.out.println("\n" + argv[i] + "\n\n" + cf);
580         }
581     }
582 }
```

This class defines Java structures for various class file structures (lines 58–379), and reads the class file (lines 381–431). It also defines a `toString()` function to generate an unwieldy and useless string representation of a class file, and a useful `decompile()` utility (lines 515–561) to demangle method signatures.

When reading the class file, the constructor steps through and interprets the contents according to the file format documented by Sun (`http://java.sun.com/docs/books/vmspec/2nd-edition/html/ClassFile.doc.html`). After reading a few scalar values found at the beginning of the file (lines 384–390), it reads the constant pool (lines 391–403), a few more scalar values, followed by the interfaces, fields, methods, and attributes (lines 409–430).

The end result, an instance of `ClassFileContents`, is used by the `JMakeDepend` class shown in the next listing.

`JMakeDepend` (see Listing B.3 for the JDK1.2 version) does the real work, tracking down class references and building a dependency a list for use by GNU `make`. The code is written in Generic Java, and depends on the compiler discussed in Chapter 38, "Generic Java Compilers", in the section "GJ: The Generic Java Compiler."

LISTING B.3 `JMakeDepend.java`

```
package com.macmillan.nmeyers;
import java.io.*;
import java.util.*;

class JMakeDepend
{
    static class Dependencies
    {
        String clsfile;
        String srcfile;
        String clsname;
        HashSet<String> providers;
        HashSet<String> visited;
        Dependencies(String c, String s, String o)
        {
            clsfile = c;
            srcfile = s;
            clsname = o;
            providers = new HashSet<String>();
            visited = new HashSet<String>();
            providers.add(o);
            visited.add(o);
        }
        boolean add(String s)
        {
            boolean result = providers.add(s);
            if (result && visited.size() > 1)
            {
                visited.clear();
                visited.add(clsname);
            }
            return result;
        }
        boolean add(Collection<String> s)
        {
            boolean result = providers.addAll(s);
            if (result && visited.size() > 1)
            {
                visited.clear();
                visited.add(clsname);
            }
            return result;
        }
        public void parseAndAddClasses(String s)
        {
```

```
            int idx = 0;
            while ((idx = s.indexOf('L', idx)) != -1)
            {
                int idx2 = s.indexOf(';', idx);
                if (idx2 == -1) break;
                add(s.substring(idx + 1, idx2));
                idx = idx2;
            }
        }
        public int hashCode()
        {
            return clsname.hashCode();
        }
    }
    static int convb(byte[] b)
    {
        int result = 0;
        for (int i = 0; i < b.length; i++)
        {
            int b2 = b[i];
            if (b2 < 0) b2 += 0x100;
            result = (result << 8) + b2;
        }
        return result;
    }
    private static String ddollar(String s)
    {
        String result = "";
        int idx1 = 0, idx2;
        while ((idx2 = s.indexOf('$', idx1)) != -1)
        {
            result += s.substring(idx1, idx2) + "$$";
            idx1 = idx2 + 1;
        }
        result += s.substring(idx1);
        return result;
    }
    public static void processClassFile(
        String filename,
        HashMap<String, Dependencies> dependencies)
    {
        // Read classfile
        ClassFileContents cf = null;
        FileInputStream is;
        try
        {
            is = new FileInputStream(filename);
            cf = new ClassFileContents(is);
        }
        catch (FileNotFoundException e)
        {
```

continued on next page

continued from previous page

```
        System.err.println(filename + ": " + e);
        return;
    }
    catch (IOException e)
    {
        System.err.println(filename + ": " + e);
        return;
    }

    // Note the name of the class file
    String clsfile = filename;

    // Compute the name of the class
    String clsname = ((ClassFileContents.CONSTANT_Utf8_info)
        cf.constant_pool[
            ((ClassFileContents.CONSTANT_Class_info)
                cf.constant_pool[cf.this_class]).name_index]).
                    getString();

    // Compute the name of the source
    String srcfile = null;
    for (int j = 0; j < cf.attributes_count; j++)
    {
        String attrname =
            ((ClassFileContents.CONSTANT_Utf8_info)
                cf.constant_pool[
                    cf.attributes[j].attribute_name_index]).
                        getString();
        if (attrname.equals("SourceFile") &&
            cf.attributes[j].attribute_length == 2)
        {
            int sourceNameIndex = convb(cf.attributes[j].info);
            srcfile = ((ClassFileContents.CONSTANT_Utf8_info)
                cf.constant_pool[sourceNameIndex]).getString();
            break;
        }
    }
    if (srcfile == null)
    {
        System.err.println(clsfile + ": No source name found");
        return;
    }

    // We can add a dependency record
    Dependencies depend = new Dependencies(clsfile, srcfile, clsname);
    if (dependencies.containsKey(clsname))
    {
        System.err.println(clsfile + ": Class " + clsname +
                           " already loaded");
    }
    dependencies.put(clsname, depend);
```

```

        // Now find all classes we depend on...

        // ...the superclass...
        String superclass = ((ClassFileContents.CONSTANT_Utf8_info)
            cf.constant_pool[
                ((ClassFileContents.CONSTANT_Class_info)
                    cf.constant_pool[cf.super_class]).name_index]).
                        getString();
        depend.add(superclass);

        // ...the interfaces...
        for (int j = 0; j < cf.interfaces_count; j++)
        {

            String interfaceName = ((ClassFileContents.
                CONSTANT_Utf8_info)cf.constant_pool[
                    ((ClassFileContents.CONSTANT_Class_info)
                        cf.constant_pool[cf.interfaces[j]]).
➥name_index]).
                            getString();
            depend.add(interfaceName);
        }
        // ...the fields...
        for (int j = 0; j < cf.fields_count; j++)
        {
            String fieldDescriptor = ((ClassFileContents.
                CONSTANT_Utf8_info)cf.constant_pool[
                    cf.fields[j].descriptor_index]).
                        getString();
            depend.parseAndAddClasses(fieldDescriptor);
        }

        // ...and the methods
        for (int j = 0; j < cf.methods_count; j++)
        {
            String methodDescriptor = ((ClassFileContents.
                CONSTANT_Utf8_info)cf.constant_pool[
                    cf.methods[j].descriptor_index]).
                        getString();
            depend.parseAndAddClasses(methodDescriptor);
        }

        // Finally, since the previous step has missed all of
        // the locals, step through the constant pool and
        // log all of the classes found there
        for (int j = 0; j < cf.constant_pool_count; j++)
        {
            if (cf.constant_pool[j] != null &&
                cf.constant_pool[j].getClass().equals(
                    ClassFileContents.CONSTANT_Class_info.class))
            {
```

continued on next page

continued from previous page

```
                String className = ((ClassFileContents.
                    CONSTANT_Utf8_info)cf.constant_pool[
                        ((ClassFileContents.CONSTANT_Class_info)
                            cf.constant_pool[j]).name_index]).
                                getString();
                depend.add(className);
            }
        }
    }
    private static void usage()
    {
        System.err.println("Usage: JMakeDepend [-noinner] " +
                           "[<classfiles>]");
        System.err.println("\nClass file names read from stdin if
➥no " +
                           "<classfiles> specified");
        System.exit(1);
    }
    public static void main(String[] argv)
    {
        HashMap<String, Dependencies> dependencies =
            new HashMap<String, Dependencies>();
        boolean hideInnerClasses = false;

        int firstarg = 0;
        while (firstarg < argv.length && argv[firstarg].startsWith
➥("-"))
        {
            if (argv[firstarg].equals("-noinner"))
                hideInnerClasses = true;
            else usage();
            firstarg++;
        }

        // Process cmdline args if any
        for (int i = firstarg; i < argv.length; i++)
            processClassFile(argv[i], dependencies);

        // If none, accept filenames from stdin, one per line
        if (firstarg == argv.length)
        {
            BufferedReader reader = new BufferedReader(
                new InputStreamReader(System.in));
            String line;
            try
            {
                while ((line = reader.readLine()) != null)
                    processClassFile(line, dependencies);
            }
            catch (IOException e)
            {
                System.err.println(e);
```

```
            }
        }

        // Now for the O(N^2) part: identify higher-order
➥dependencies.
        for (boolean done = false; !done;)
        {
            done = true;
            // Step through our current dependency records
            for (Iterator<Dependencies> i = dependencies.values().
➥iterator();
                 i.hasNext();)
            {
                Dependencies dep = i.next();
                // Step through each class in this record
                {
                    // Make a copy of the classes in the record to
➥avoid
                    // fast-fail on the iterator
                    HashSet<String> temp = new HashSet<String>(dep.
➥providers);
                    for (Iterator<String> j = temp.iterator(); j.
➥hasNext();)
                    {
                        String key = j.next();
                        if (!dep.visited.add(key)) continue;
                        // Is there a dependency record for this
➥object?
                        Dependencies dep2 = dependencies.get(key);
                        if (dep2 == null) continue;
                        // Yes... transfer its dependencies to dep's
                        // record
                        if (dep.add(dep2.providers)) done = false;
                    }
                }
            }
        }

        // If we're hiding inner classes, merge their dependencies
➥into
        // outer-class dependency list
        if (hideInnerClasses)
        {
            HashMap<String, Dependencies> outerClasses =
                new HashMap<String, Dependencies>();
            // Step through our objects, compiling a list of outer
➥classes
            for (Iterator<Dependencies> i = dependencies.values().
➥iterator();
                 i.hasNext();)
            {
                // Next entry
```

continued on next page

continued from previous page

```
                Dependencies dep = i.next();
                // Is it an inner class? If not, add to our outerClasses map
                // keyed by source filename
                if (dep.clsname.indexOf("$") == -1)
                    outerClasses.put(dep.srcfile, dep);
            }
            // Step through a copy of our set of objects (to avoid
            // iterator fast-fail) and weed out inner classes.
            ArrayList<Dependencies> list =
                new ArrayList<Dependencies>(dependencies.values());
            for (Iterator<Dependencies> i = list.iterator(); i.hasNext();)
            {
                // Next entry
                Dependencies dep = i.next();
                // Is it an inner class?
                if (dep.clsname.indexOf("$") != -1)
                {
                    // Yes. Look for the enclosing class based on the
                    // source name.
                    Dependencies outer = outerClasses.get(dep.srcfile);
                    if (outer != null)
                    {
                        // Found it! Transfer the dependencies
                        // (this step is probably redundant)
                        outer.add(dep.providers);
                        // And remove ourself from the master map
                        dependencies.remove(dep.clsname);
                    }
                }
            }
        }

        // Print out dependencies
        HashSet<String> allSources = new HashSet<String>();
        HashSet<String> allTargets = new HashSet<String>();
        for (Iterator<Dependencies> i = dependencies.values().iterator();
             i.hasNext();)
        {
            Dependencies dep = i.next();
            allSources.add(dep.srcfile);
            allTargets.add(dep.clsfile);
            // Print out the source dependency
            System.out.print(ddollar(dep.clsfile) + ": " +
                             ddollar(dep.srcfile));

            // Collect the secondary sourcefile dependencies
            HashSet<String> otherSources = new HashSet<String>();
            for (Iterator<String> j = dep.providers.iterator(); j.hasNext();)
```

```
340                 {
341                     String key = j.next();
342                     if (key.equals(dep.clsname)) continue;
343                     Dependencies dep2 = dependencies.get(key);
344                     if (dep2 == null ¦¦ dep.srcfile.equals(dep2.srcfile))
345                         continue;
346                     otherSources.add(dep2.srcfile);
347                 }
348                 // Print them out
349                 for (Iterator<String> iterator = otherSources.iterator();
350                      iterator.hasNext();)
351                     System.out.print(" " + ddollar(iterator.next()));
352 
353                 // Print the command
354                 System.out.println("\n\techo $< $? >>.rawtargets\n");
355             }
356 
357             System.out.print("JSOURCES =");
358             for (Iterator<String> i = allSources.iterator(); i.hasNext();)
359                 System.out.print(" " + ddollar(i.next()));
360             System.out.print("\n\nJOBJECTS =");
361             for (Iterator<String> i = allTargets.iterator(); i.hasNext();)
362                 System.out.print(" " + ddollar(i.next()));
363             System.out.println("\n\n.rawtargets:\t$(JOBJECTS)");
364             System.out.println("\n.targets:");
365             System.out.println("\trm -f .rawtargets");
366             System.out.println("\t$(MAKE) .rawtargets");
367             System.out.println("\t[ -f .rawtargets ] && tr -s ' ' '
➥\\012' " +
368                                "<.rawtargets ¦ sort -u > .targets ¦¦
➥true");
369             System.out.println("\trm -f .rawtargets");
370             System.exit(0);
371         }
372     }
```

The `main()` procedure steps through the class files (lines 222–250), calling `processClassFile()` (lines 83–207) to handle each one.

For each class file, `processClassFile()` extracts the classname (lines 109–114), the source name (lines 117–138), the classnames of the superclass (lines 152–157), all interfaces (lines 160–169), all fields (lines 171–178), and all methods and method arguments (lines 181–188). Finally, the constant pool is scanned (lines 193–206) for any other referenced classes—for example, from local variables.

Back to `main()`. All classes found are recorded in a master map (`dependencies`, line 218), with information on the originating class file and source file, if available. After all class files have been processed, lines 253–279 iterate on the collected data, propagating dependencies to all dependent classes. If we are hiding inner classes, lines 283–322 remove them and propagate their dependencies to the enclosing class. Finally, lines 325–369 generate the output.

memstress: Measure Effect of Locality on Performance

Chapter 57, "Why Is Java Slow?," discussed the importance of memory locality on application performance. We presented a plot showing how drastically performance can be impacted by poor locality. This small C program generated the data in the plot.

Platform: UNIX/Linux

The invocation allows you to specify the size of the memory block to be tested. Choosing a size significantly larger than your CPU cache will show the dramatic results of stressing the cache. Choosing a size larger than your physical memory will cause heavy paging activity.

Synopsis:

`memstress <#bits of address space> <#repetitions>`

Running `memstress` allocates 2^n bytes of memory, where *n* is the number of address bits specified in the first argument. It then loops through the memory block with various ***stride*** values (see Figure B.1) to test the effect of locality on performance. For each stride value, it touches every address in the block once and then repeats the operation the specified number of times.

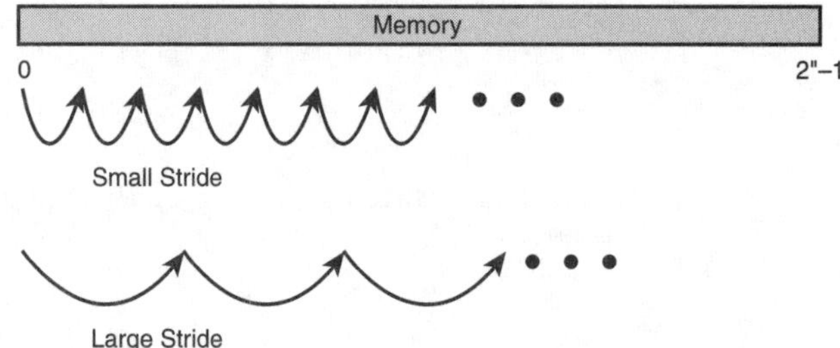

FIGURE B.1
Stride values affect the order in which memory is touched.

Depending on such variables as the amount of available RAM, the amount of available memory cache, and the details of how caching and paging work, performance will greatly vary with different stride values. The stride values used for the test are 1, 3, 7, 15, ..., where each value is a power of 2 minus 1. Here is some output from a run with the command `memstress 24 5`:

```
Memory size = 16777216 bytes (1 << 24)
Number of repetitions = 5

      Stride    Time
      ------    ----
           1    2.120818 sec (39553643.924126 bytes/sec)
           3    2.876940 sec (29158091.583309 bytes/sec)
           7    3.957169 sec (21198508.327656 bytes/sec)
          15    6.000262 sec (13980402.855712 bytes/sec)
          31    12.428373 sec (6749562.472913 bytes/sec)
          63    12.871100 sec (6517397.891404 bytes/sec)
```

```
     127    12.991733 sec (6456881.464543 bytes/sec)
     255    13.246348 sec (6332770.360562 bytes/sec)
     511    13.743164 sec (6103840.425677 bytes/sec)
    1023    14.633202 sec (5732585.390412 bytes/sec)
    2047    11.654724 sec (7197603.306624 bytes/sec)
    4095    5.299311 sec (15829620.114795 bytes/sec)
    8191    9.262438 sec (9056587.477280 bytes/sec)
   16383    15.920155 sec (5269174.829023 bytes/sec)
   32767    16.717737 sec (5017789.190002 bytes/sec)
   65535    16.570820 sec (5062276.942240 bytes/sec)
  131071    16.280092 sec (5152678.498378 bytes/sec)
  262143    16.227264 sec (5169453.088332 bytes/sec)
  524287    15.561468 sec (5390627.670866 bytes/sec)
 1048575    11.181644 sec (7502124.016816 bytes/sec)
 2097151    7.901720 sec (10616179.768454 bytes/sec)
 4194303    3.817173 sec (21975970.174622 bytes/sec)
 8388607    2.623275 sec (31977615.766360 bytes/sec)
16777215    2.116233 sec (39639340.281042 bytes/sec)
```

The results are dramatic—a nearly 8x difference between best-case and worst-case locality. For this test, the memory size fits well within the available memory on the workstation; tests that result in paging show much more extreme differences.

Listing B.4 contains the `memstress` source.

LISTING B.4 `memstress.c`

```
#include <stdio.h>
#include <stdlib.h>
#include <string.h>
#include <unistd.h>
#include <sys/time.h>

int main(int argc, char **argv)
{
    int nbits, repetitions;
    size_t stride, memsize, memsizemask;
    char *memory;
    if (argc != 3)
    {
        fprintf(stderr, "Usage: %s <#bits of address space> <#repetitions>\n",
                argv[0]);
        exit(1);
    }

    nbits = atoi(argv[1]);
    repetitions = atoi(argv[2]);

    /* Allocate our memory */
    memsize = (size_t)1 << nbits;
```

continued on next page

continued from previous page

```
24        memsizemask = memsize - 1;
25        memory = (char *)malloc(memsize);
26        if (!memory)
27        {
28            fprintf(stderr, "Insufficient memory to allocate %ld bytes\n",
29                    (long)memsize);
30            exit(1);
31        }
32
33        /* Touch the memory before we start */
34        memset(memory, 255, memsize);
35
36        /* Start our output */
37        printf("Memory size = %ld bytes (1 << %d)\n", (long)memsize,
➥nbits);
38        printf("Number of repetitions = %d\n", repetitions);
39        printf("\n      Stride    Time\n");
40        printf("        ------    ----\n");
41
42        /* Stress the memory, with different stride values */
43        for (stride = 1; stride < memsize; stride = stride * 2 + 1)
44        {
45            struct timeval time1, time2;
46            struct timezone tz;
47            double delta, rate;
48            register size_t offset = 0;
49            register long count;
50            volatile register char *mem = memory, chr;
51            gettimeofday(&time1, &tz);
52            printf("%12ld    ", stride);
53            fflush(stdout);
54            /* Start accessing memory */
55            for (count = (long)memsize * (long)repetitions;
56                 count--;
57                 offset = (offset + stride) & memsizemask)
58            {
59                chr = mem[offset];
60            }
61            gettimeofday(&time2, &tz);
62            delta = time2.tv_sec + time2.tv_usec / 1.0e6 -
63                    time1.tv_sec - time1.tv_usec / 1.0e6;
64            rate = (double)memsize * repetitions / delta;
65            printf("%lf sec (%lf bytes/sec)\n", delta, rate);
66        }
67
68        exit(0);
69    }
```

The outer loop (lines 43–66) steps through the various stride values, timing the results for each value. The inner loop (lines 55–60) uses a memory pointer declared volatile, to ensure that memory accesses are not optimized away. The choices of stride values make the calculation required to correctly step through the memory (line 57) simple.

PerfAnal: Analyze Application CPU Usage

Chapter 60, "PerfAnal: A Free Performance Analysis Tool," presented a tool that could be used in conjunction with JDK1.2's sample profiler to study the CPU usage of an application.

Platform: JDK1.2

`PerfAnal` consists of 12 top-level classes, shown in Listings B.5–B.16. We include with each listing a brief description of the class' role.

`CalleeInclusive` (see Listing B.5) encapsulates the by-callee information in the analysis. Given the collection of per-procedure information and tracebacks passed to the constructor (line 12), the tracebacks are analyzed and their data massaged into the tree presented in the lower-left window of the main GUI.

LISTING B.5 CalleeInclusive.java.

```
 1   package com.macmillan.nmeyers;
 2   import java.util.*;
 3   import javax.swing.tree.*;
 4   import java.text.*;
 5
 6   // This class encapsulates a tree, consisting of
➥DefaultMutableTreeNodes,
 7   // of performance data by procedure, broken down by caller,
➥inclusive of
 8   // called procedures.
 9   class CalleeInclusive extends PerfTree.PerfTreeNode implements
➥Comparable
10   {
11       HashMap kidInfo = new HashMap();
12       CalleeInclusive(HashMap procedures, int totalCount)
13       {
14           super(new ProcCountInfo(new Procedure("")));
15           ((ProcCountInfo)getUserObject()).count = totalCount;
16           // Build a list of procedures, sorted by usage
17           Iterator iterator = procedures.values().iterator();
18           while (iterator.hasNext())
19           {
20               ProcCountInfo info = new
➥ProcCountInfo((Procedure)iterator. next());
21               add(info);
22           }
23           if (children == null) return;
24           // Step through the procedures, and populate the tree with
25           // descendant information
26           for (iterator = children.iterator(); iterator.hasNext();)
27           {
28               CalleeInclusive child = (CalleeInclusive)iterator.next();
```

continued on next page

continued from previous page

```
                Procedure.TraceInfo prevTraceInfo = null;
                // Step through all of the tracebacks relevant to this proc
                for (Iterator traceIterator =
                    ((ProcCountInfo)child.getUserObject()).
                        procedure.myTraces.iterator();
                    traceIterator.hasNext();)
                {
                    Procedure.TraceInfo traceInfo =
                        (Procedure.TraceInfo)traceIterator.next();
                    // We want only the last instance of a particular
                    // traceback for this Procedure... it will have the
                    // deepest caller stack. Earlier instances are
➥recursion
                    // and muddle the results.
                    if (prevTraceInfo != null &&
                        !prevTraceInfo.traceBack.equals(traceInfo.
➥traceBack))
                        child.addDescendants(prevTraceInfo.traceBack,
                                             prevTraceInfo.depth + 1);
                    prevTraceInfo = traceInfo;
                }
                if (prevTraceInfo != null)
                    child.addDescendants(prevTraceInfo.traceBack,
                                         prevTraceInfo.depth + 1);
            }
            // Propagate the timing information
            processNodes();
        }
        TreePath findThisProc(String procName)
        {
            // Linear search for child with given name
            Iterator iterator = children.iterator();
            while (iterator.hasNext())
            {
                CalleeInclusive child = (CalleeInclusive)iterator.next();
                ProcCountInfo pci = (ProcCountInfo)child.getUserObject();
                if (pci.procedure.procName.equals(procName))
                    return new TreePath(child.getPath());
            }
            return null;
        }
        private CalleeInclusive(ProcCountInfo pci)
        {
            super(pci);
        }
        private CalleeInclusive add(ProcCountInfo pci)
        {
            CalleeInclusive pi = new CalleeInclusive(pci);
            kidInfo.put(pci.procedure.procName,
                       new KidInfo(pci.procedure.procName, pi));
            add(pi);
            return pi;
```

```
        }

    // processNodes() traverses the tree, doing assorted important
➥processing:
    //
    // Null out the kidInfo pointer to free up memory we no longer need
    // Propagate our profile times upward
    // Sort the children into descending time order

        private void processNodes()
        {
            // Clean out some memory we no longer need
            kidInfo = null;
            // Initialize our count with time spent in this method
            ProcCountInfo pci = (ProcCountInfo)getUserObject();
            if (getLevel() > 0) pci.count = pci.myCount;
            // Recursively handle the children, and add their time to ours
            if (children != null)
            {
                ListIterator iterator = children.listIterator();
                while (iterator.hasNext())
                {
                  CalleeInclusive pi = (CalleeInclusive)iterator.next();
                  ProcCountInfo childPci = (ProcCountInfo)pi.
➥getUserObject();
                    pi.processNodes();
                    if (getLevel() > 0) pci.count += childPci.count;
                }
                Collections.sort(children);
            }
        }
        private void addDescendants(TraceBack traceBack, int depth)
        {
            if (traceBack.thread != null && !traceBack.thread.enabled)
                return;
            if (depth < traceBack.entries.size())
            {
                String procName =
                    ((TraceBack.TraceBackEntry)traceBack.
                        entries.get(depth)).procName;
                KidInfo ki = (KidInfo)kidInfo.get(procName);
                CalleeInclusive ci;
                if (ki == null)
                    ci = add(new ProcCountInfo(new Procedure(procName)));
                else
                    ci = ki.kid;
                ci.addDescendants(traceBack, depth + 1);
            }
            else
                ((ProcCountInfo)getUserObject()).myCount += traceBack.
➥traceCount;
```

continued on next page

continued from previous page

```
        }
        public int compareTo(Object o)
        {
            return ((ProcCountInfo)getUserObject()).compareTo(
                ((PerfTree.PerfTreeNode)o).getUserObject());
        }
        public String toString()
        {
            ProcCountInfo rootPci = (ProcCountInfo)
                ((PerfTree.PerfTreeNode)getRoot()).getUserObject();
            if (getLevel() == 0)
                return "Method Times by Callee (times inclusive): " +
                       rootPci.count + " ticks";
            ProcCountInfo pci = (ProcCountInfo)getUserObject();
            return pci.toString(rootPci.count);
        }
        public String getProcName()
        {
            return ((ProcCountInfo)getUserObject()).procedure.procName;
        }
        static class ProcCountInfo implements Comparable
        {
            Procedure procedure;
            int count = 0;
            int myCount = 0;
            static DecimalFormat format = new DecimalFormat("##0.##%");
            ProcCountInfo(Procedure p)
            {
                procedure = p;
            }
            public String toString(int totalCount)
            {
                return procedure.procName + ": " +
                       format.format((double)count / (double)totalCount) +
                       " (" + count + " inclusive)";
            }
            public int compareTo(Object o)
            {
                return ((ProcCountInfo)o).count - count;
            }
            public boolean equals(Object o)
            {
                return count == ((ProcCountInfo)o).count;
            }
        }
        static class KidInfo implements Comparable
        {
            String kidName;
            CalleeInclusive kid;
            KidInfo(String kn, CalleeInclusive k)
            {
                kidName = kn;
```

```
            kid = k;
        }
        public int compareTo(Object o)
        {
            return kidName.compareTo(((KidInfo)o).kidName);
        }
    }
}
```

CallerInclusive (see Listing B.6) is similar to `CalleeInclusive` but organizes the tree around callers instead of called procedures.

LISTING B.6 `CallerInclusive.java.`

```
package com.macmillan.nmeyers;
import java.util.*;
import javax.swing.tree.*;
import java.text.*;

// This class encapsulates a tree, consisting of
➥DefaultMutableTreeNodes,
// of performance data by procedure, broken down by callee, inclusive
➥of
// called procedures.
class CallerInclusive extends PerfTree.PerfTreeNode implements
➥Comparable
{
    HashMap kidInfo = new HashMap();
    CallerInclusive(HashMap procedures, int totalCount)
    {
        super(new ProcCountInfo(new Procedure("")));
        ((ProcCountInfo)getUserObject()).count = totalCount;
        // Build a list of procedures, sorted by usage
        Iterator iterator = procedures.values().iterator();
        while (iterator.hasNext())
        {
            ProcCountInfo info = new
➥ProcCountInfo((Procedure)iterator. next());
            add(info);
        }
        if (children == null) return;
        // Step through the procedures, and populate the tree with
        // descendant information
        for (iterator = children.iterator(); iterator.hasNext();)
        {
            CallerInclusive child = (CallerInclusive)iterator.next();
            Procedure.TraceInfo prevTraceInfo = null;
            // Step through all of the tracebacks relevant to this
➥proc
            for (Iterator traceIterator =
```

continued on next page

continued from previous page

```
                ((ProcCountInfo)child.getUserObject()).
                    procedure.myTraces.iterator();
                traceIterator.hasNext();)
            {
                Procedure.TraceInfo traceInfo =
                    (Procedure.TraceInfo)traceIterator.next();
                // We want only the first instance of a particular
                // traceback for this Procedure... it will have the
                // deepest callee stack. Later instances are recursion
                // and muddle the results.
                if (prevTraceInfo != null &&
                   prevTraceInfo.traceBack.equals(traceInfo.traceBack))
                    continue;
                prevTraceInfo = traceInfo;
                child.addDescendants(traceInfo.traceBack,
                                     traceInfo.depth - 1);
            }
        }
        // Propagate the timing information
        processNodes();
    }
    TreePath findThisProc(String procName)
    {
        // Linear search for child with given name
        Iterator iterator = children.iterator();
        while (iterator.hasNext())
        {
            CallerInclusive child = (CallerInclusive)iterator.next();
            ProcCountInfo pci = (ProcCountInfo)child.getUserObject();
            if (pci.procedure.procName.equals(procName))
                return new TreePath(child.getPath());
        }
        return null;
    }
    private CallerInclusive(ProcCountInfo pci)
    {
        super(pci);
    }
    private CallerInclusive add(ProcCountInfo pci)
    {
        CallerInclusive pi = new CallerInclusive(pci);
        kidInfo.put(pci.procedure.procName,
                    new KidInfo(pci.procedure.procName, pi));
        add(pi);
        return pi;
    }

// processNodes() traverses the tree, doing assorted important
➥processing:
//
// Null out the kidInfo pointer to free up memory we no longer need
// Propagate our profile times upward
```

```
// Sort the children into descending time order

    private void processNodes()
    {
        // Clean out some memory we no longer need
        kidInfo = null;
        // Initialize our count with time spent in this method
        ProcCountInfo pci = (ProcCountInfo)getUserObject();
        if (getLevel() > 0) pci.count = pci.myCount;
        // Recursively handle the children, and add their time to ours
        if (children != null)
        {
            ListIterator iterator = children.listIterator();
            while (iterator.hasNext())
            {
                CallerInclusive pi = (CallerInclusive)iterator.next();
                ProcCountInfo childPci = (ProcCountInfo)pi.
➥getUserObject();
                pi.processNodes();
                if (getLevel() > 0) pci.count += childPci.count;
            }
            Collections.sort(children);
        }
    }
    private void addDescendants(TraceBack traceBack, int depth)
    {
        if (traceBack.thread != null && !traceBack.thread.enabled)
            return;
        if (depth >= 0)
        {
            String procName =
                ((TraceBack.TraceBackEntry)traceBack.
                    entries.get(depth)).procName;
            KidInfo ki = (KidInfo)kidInfo.get(procName);
            CallerInclusive ci;
            if (ki == null)
                ci = add(new ProcCountInfo(new Procedure(procName)));
            else
                ci = ki.kid;
            ci.addDescendants(traceBack, depth - 1);
        }
        else
            ((ProcCountInfo)getUserObject()).myCount += traceBack.
➥traceCount;
    }
    public int compareTo(Object o)
    {
        return ((ProcCountInfo)getUserObject()).compareTo(
            ((PerfTree.PerfTreeNode)o).getUserObject());
    }
    public String toString()
```

continued on next page

continued from previous page

```
        {
            ProcCountInfo rootPci = (ProcCountInfo)
                ((PerfTree.PerfTreeNode)getRoot()).getUserObject();
            if (getLevel() == 0)
                return "Method Times by Caller (times inclusive): " +
                       rootPci.count + " ticks";
            ProcCountInfo pci = (ProcCountInfo)getUserObject();
            return pci.toString(rootPci.count);
        }
        public String getProcName()
        {
            return ((ProcCountInfo)getUserObject()).procedure.procName;
        }
        static class ProcCountInfo implements Comparable
        {
            Procedure procedure;
            int count = 0;
            int myCount = 0;
            static DecimalFormat format = new DecimalFormat("##0.##%");
            ProcCountInfo(Procedure p)
            {
                procedure = p;
            }
            public String toString(int totalCount)
            {
                return procedure.procName + ": " +
                       format.format((double)count / (double)totalCount) +
                       " (" + count + " inclusive / " + myCount + " exclusive)";
            }
            public int compareTo(Object o)
            {
                return ((ProcCountInfo)o).count - count;
            }
            public boolean equals(Object o)
            {
                return count == ((ProcCountInfo)o).count;
            }
        }
        static class KidInfo implements Comparable
        {
            String kidName;
            CallerInclusive kid;
            KidInfo(String kn, CallerInclusive k)
            {
                kidName = kn;
                kid = k;
            }
            public int compareTo(Object o)
            {
                return kidName.compareTo(((KidInfo)o).kidName);
            }
        }
    }
```

`LineExclusive` (see Listing B.7) encapsulates the tree presented in the lower-right window of the main GUI, providing per-line-number performance information, exclusive of subroutine calls.

LISTING B.7 `LineExclusive.java`

```
package com.macmillan.nmeyers;
import java.util.*;
import javax.swing.tree.*;
import java.text.*;

// This class encapsulates a tree, consisting of
➥DefaultMutableTreeNodes,
// of performance data by procedure, broken down by line number,
➥exclusive
// of called procedures.
class LineExclusive extends PerfTree.PerfTreeNode implements
➥Comparable
{
    LineExclusive(HashMap procedures, int totalCount)
    {
        super(new ProcCountInfo("", totalCount));
        // Build a list of procedures, sorted by usage
        Iterator iterator = procedures.values().iterator();
        while (iterator.hasNext())
        {
            Procedure procedure = (Procedure)iterator.next();
            ProcCountInfo thisProcInfo =
                new ProcCountInfo(procedure.procName, 0);
            LineExclusive li = new LineExclusive(thisProcInfo);
            add(li);
            Iterator lines = procedure.lines.iterator();
            ProcCountInfo prev = null;
            while (lines.hasNext())
            {
                Procedure.Line line = (Procedure.Line)lines.next();
                if (line.thread != null && !line.thread.enabled)
➥continue;
                thisProcInfo.count += line.countExclusive;
                if (prev != null &&
➥prev.procName.equals(line.lineInfo))
                    prev.count += line.countExclusive;
                else li.add(new LineExclusive(prev =
                    new ProcCountInfo(line.lineInfo, line.
➥countExclusive)));
            }
            if (li.children != null) Collections.sort(li.children);
        }
        if (children != null) Collections.sort(children);
    }
```

continued on next page

continued from previous page

```
    TreePath findThisProc(String procName)
    {
        // Linear search for child with given name
        Iterator iterator = children.iterator();
        while (iterator.hasNext())
        {
            LineExclusive child = (LineExclusive)iterator.next();
            ProcCountInfo pci = (ProcCountInfo)child.getUserObject();
            if (pci.procName.equals(procName))
                return new TreePath(child.getPath());
        }
        return null;
    }
    private LineExclusive(ProcCountInfo pci)
    {
        super(pci);
    }
    public int compareTo(Object o)
    {
        return ((ProcCountInfo)getUserObject()).compareTo(
            ((PerfTree.PerfTreeNode)o).getUserObject());
    }
    public String toString()
    {
        ProcCountInfo rootPci = (ProcCountInfo)
            ((PerfTree.PerfTreeNode)getRoot()).getUserObject();
        if (getLevel() == 0)
            return "Method Times by Line Number (times exclusive): " +
                     rootPci.count + " ticks";
        ProcCountInfo pci = (ProcCountInfo)getUserObject();
        return pci.toString(rootPci.count);
    }
    public String getProcName()
    {
        if (getLevel() > 1)
            return ((PerfTree.PerfTreeNode)getParent()).getProcName();
        return ((ProcCountInfo)getUserObject()).procName;
    }
    static class ProcCountInfo implements Comparable
    {
        String procName;
        int count;
        static DecimalFormat format = new DecimalFormat("##0.##%");
        ProcCountInfo(String p, int c)
        {
            procName = p;
            count = c;
        }
        public String toString(int totalCount)
        {
            return procName + ": " +
                     format.format((double)count / (double)totalCount) +
```

```
                    " (" + count + " exclusive)";
        }
        public int compareTo(Object o)
        {
            return ((ProcCountInfo)o).count - count;
        }
        public boolean equals(Object o)
        {
            return count == ((ProcCountInfo)o).count;
        }
    }
}
```

`LineInclusive` (see Listing B.8) is structured almost identically to `LineExclusive`, but adds time spent in subroutine calls to the per-line performance information.

LISTING B.8 LineInclusive.java

```
package com.macmillan.nmeyers;
import java.util.*;
import javax.swing.tree.*;
import java.text.*;

// This class encapsulates a tree, consisting of DefaultMutableTreeNodes,
// of performance data by procedure, broken down by line number, inclusive
// of called procedures.
class LineInclusive extends PerfTree.PerfTreeNode implements Comparable
{
    LineInclusive(HashMap procedures, int totalCount)
    {
        super(new ProcCountInfo("", totalCount));
        // Build a list of procedures, sorted by usage
        Iterator iterator = procedures.values().iterator();
        while (iterator.hasNext())
        {
            Procedure procedure = (Procedure)iterator.next();
            ProcCountInfo thisProcInfo =
                new ProcCountInfo(procedure.procName, 0);
            LineInclusive li = new LineInclusive(thisProcInfo);
            add(li);
            Iterator lines = procedure.lines.iterator();
            ProcCountInfo prev = null;
            while (lines.hasNext())
            {
                Procedure.Line line = (Procedure.Line)lines.next();
                if (line.thread != null && !line.thread.enabled) continue;
                thisProcInfo.count += line.countInclusive;
```

continued on next page

continued from previous page

```
                if (prev != null &&
➥prev.procName.equals(line.lineInfo))
                    prev.count += line.countInclusive;
                else li.add(new LineInclusive(prev =
                    new ProcCountInfo(line.lineInfo, line.
➥countInclusive)));
            }
            if (li.children != null) Collections.sort(li.children);
        }
        if (children != null) Collections.sort(children);
    }
    TreePath findThisProc(String procName)
    {
        // Linear search for child with given name
        Iterator iterator = children.iterator();
        while (iterator.hasNext())
        {
            LineInclusive child = (LineInclusive)iterator.next();
            ProcCountInfo pci = (ProcCountInfo)child.getUserObject();
            if (pci.procName.equals(procName))
                return new TreePath(child.getPath());
        }
        return null;
    }
    private LineInclusive(ProcCountInfo pci)
    {
        super(pci);
    }
    public int compareTo(Object o)
    {
        return ((ProcCountInfo)getUserObject()).compareTo(
            ((PerfTree.PerfTreeNode)o).getUserObject());
    }
    public String toString()
    {
        ProcCountInfo rootPci = (ProcCountInfo)
            ((PerfTree.PerfTreeNode)getRoot()).getUserObject();
        if (getLevel() == 0)
            return "Method Times by Line Number (times inclusive): " +
                   rootPci.count + " ticks";
        ProcCountInfo pci = (ProcCountInfo)getUserObject();
        return pci.toString(rootPci.count);
    }
    public String getProcName()
    {
        if (getLevel() > 1)
            return ((PerfTree.PerfTreeNode)getParent()).getProcName();
        return ((ProcCountInfo)getUserObject()).procName;
    }
    static class ProcCountInfo implements Comparable
    {
        String procName;
```

```
        int count;
        static DecimalFormat format = new DecimalFormat("##0.##%");
        ProcCountInfo(String p, int c)
        {
            procName = p;
            count = c;
        }
        public String toString(int totalCount)
        {
            return procName + ": " +
                   format.format((double)count / (double)totalCount) +
                   " (" + count + " inclusive)";
        }
        public int compareTo(Object o)
        {
            return ((ProcCountInfo)o).count - count;
        }
        public boolean equals(Object o)
        {
            return count == ((ProcCountInfo)o).count;
        }
    }
}
```

`PerfAnal` (see Listing B.9) implements the top-level interface. The constructor (lines 24-131) builds the main GUI and drives parsing of the analysis file. Other methods in this class implement the callbacks for various pull-down and pop-up menu selections.

LISTING B.9 `PerfAnal.java`

```
 1  package com.macmillan.nmeyers;
 2  import java.io.*;
 3  import java.util.*;
 4  import javax.swing.*;
 5  import java.awt.*;
 6  import java.awt.event.*;
 7
 8  class PerfAnal extends JFrame implements PerfTree.FindMethod,
 9                                           SaveDialog.DoSave,
10                                           SelectThreads.ChooseThread
11  {
12      HashMap traceBacks = new HashMap(); // For holding TraceBack
➥objects
13      HashMap procedures = new HashMap(); // For holding Procedure
➥objects
14      HashMap threads = new HashMap();    // For holding ThreadInfo
➥objects
15      CallerInclusive callerInclusive;
16      CalleeInclusive calleeInclusive;
17      LineInclusive lineInclusive;
18      LineExclusive lineExclusive;
```

continued on next page

continued from previous page

```
    PerfTree tree1, tree2, tree3, tree4;
    SelectMethod selectMethod;
    SelectThreads selectThreads;
    int totalCount = 0;
    static int frameCount = 0;
    PerfAnal(String fileName, Reader reader)
    {
        super("Performance Analysis: " + fileName);
        // Build our one little menu
        JMenuBar menuBar = new JMenuBar();
        setJMenuBar(menuBar);
        JMenu fileMenu = new JMenu("File");
        menuBar.add(fileMenu);
        // Button to save analysis data to a file
        JMenuItem menuItem = new JMenuItem("Save...");
        fileMenu.add(menuItem);
        menuItem.addActionListener(new ActionListener() {
            public void actionPerformed(ActionEvent e)
            {
                new SaveDialog(PerfAnal.this, PerfAnal.this);
            }
        });
        fileMenu.add(new JSeparator());
        // Button to quit
        menuItem = new JMenuItem("Exit");
        menuItem.addActionListener(new ActionListener() {
            public void actionPerformed(ActionEvent e)
            {
                System.exit(0);
            }
        });
        fileMenu.add(menuItem);
        getContentPane().setLayout(new GridLayout(2, 2));
        // Start parsing input file. Look for lines that mark the start
        // of a stack trace or info on a thread
        LineNumberReader lineReader = null;
        if (reader != null) try
        {
            lineReader = new LineNumberReader(reader);
            String line;
            while ((line = lineReader.readLine()) != null)
            {
                // Check for start of the next section
                if (line.startsWith("CPU SAMPLES BEGIN")) break;
                if (line.startsWith("THREAD START") &&
                    line.indexOf("name=") != -1)
                {
                    ThreadInfo info = ThreadInfo.parse(line);
                    if (info != null)
                        threads.put(new Integer(info.threadNumber),
                                    info);
                }
```

```
                if (line.startsWith("TRACE ") && line.indexOf(':') != -1)
                {
                    // This looks like a real traceback.
                    TraceBack traceBack = TraceBack.parse(line, lineReader,
                                                          threads);
                    if (traceBack == null)
                        throw new IOException("Cannot parse stack trace");
                    traceBacks.put(new Integer(traceBack.traceNumber),
                                   traceBack);
                }
            }
            // We're to the second section — the CPU sample counts.
            // Waste the next line, which is a header.
            lineReader.readLine();
            // Now start parsing these entries, building our list of
            // procedure references and counts as we go.
            while ((line = lineReader.readLine()) != null)
            {
                // Check for end of this section
                if (line.startsWith("CPU SAMPLES END")) break;
                totalCount += Procedure.parse(line, procedures, traceBacks);
            }
        }
        catch (IOException e)
        {
            displayError("Line " + lineReader.getLineNumber() + ": " +
                         e, this);
        }
        // Create our method selection dialog
        selectMethod = new SelectMethod(this, this, procedures);
        // Create our thread selection dialog
        selectThreads = new SelectThreads(this, this, threads);
        // Create trees for our inclusive procedure call counts
        callerInclusive = new CallerInclusive(procedures, totalCount);
        lineInclusive = new LineInclusive(procedures, totalCount);
        calleeInclusive = new CalleeInclusive(procedures, totalCount);
        lineExclusive = new LineExclusive(procedures, totalCount);
        // Ready to roll
        getContentPane().add(tree1 = new PerfTree(callerInclusive, this, this));
        getContentPane().add(tree2 = new PerfTree(lineInclusive, this, this));
        getContentPane().add(tree3 = new PerfTree(calleeInclusive, this, this));
        getContentPane().add(tree4 = new PerfTree(lineExclusive, this, this));
        pack();
```

continued on next page

continued from previous page

```
        // Try to keep this from getting too big
        Dimension screenSize = Toolkit.getDefaultToolkit().
➥getScreenSize();
        Dimension mySize = getSize();
        if (mySize.width > 3 * screenSize.width / 4)
            mySize.width = 3 * screenSize.width / 4;
        if (mySize.height > 3 * screenSize.height / 4)
            mySize.height = 3 * screenSize.height / 4;
        setSize(mySize);
        setVisible(true);
        incFrameCount();
        addWindowListener(new WindowAdapter() {
            public void windowClosing(WindowEvent ev)
            {
                dispose();
                decFrameCount();
            }
        });
    }
    public void findMethod(String s)
    {
        if (s == null)
            selectMethod.setVisible(true);
        else
        {
            tree1.selectThisProc(s);
            tree2.selectThisProc(s);
            tree3.selectThisProc(s);
            tree4.selectThisProc(s);
        }
    }
    public void chooseThread()
    {
        selectThreads.setVisible(true);
    }
    public void recomputeTotals()
    {
        super.setEnabled(false);
        super.setCursor(Cursor.getPredefinedCursor(Cursor.WAIT_CURSOR));
        callerInclusive = new CallerInclusive(procedures, totalCount);
        lineInclusive = new LineInclusive(procedures, totalCount);
        calleeInclusive = new CalleeInclusive(procedures, totalCount);
        lineExclusive = new LineExclusive(procedures, totalCount);
        tree1.initializeRoot(callerInclusive);
        tree2.initializeRoot(lineInclusive);
        tree3.initializeRoot(calleeInclusive);
        tree4.initializeRoot(lineExclusive);
        invalidate();
        validate();
        super.setCursor(Cursor.getDefaultCursor());
        super.setEnabled(true);
    }
```

```
    public void doSave(File file)
    {
        PrintWriter writer = null;
        try
        {
            writer = new PrintWriter(new BufferedWriter(new
➥FileWriter(file)));
            tree1.saveData(writer);
            writer.println("");
            tree2.saveData(writer);
            writer.println("");
            tree3.saveData(writer);
            writer.println("");
            tree4.saveData(writer);
        }
        catch (IOException e)
        {
            displayError(e.toString(), this);
        }
        finally
        {
            if (writer != null) writer.close();
        }
    }
    static void displayError(String s, final JFrame parent)
    {
        final Window dialog =
            (parent == null ?
            (Window)(new JFrame("Error")) :
            (Window)(new JDialog(parent, "Error", true)));
        ((RootPaneContainer)dialog).getContentPane().
            add(new JLabel(s), BorderLayout.CENTER);
        JButton OKButton = new JButton("OK");
        ((RootPaneContainer)dialog).getContentPane().
            add(OKButton, BorderLayout.SOUTH);
        ((RootPaneContainer)dialog).getRootPane().setDefaultButton(
➥OKButton);
        OKButton.addActionListener(new ActionListener() {
            public void actionPerformed(ActionEvent e)
            {
                dialog.dispose();
                if (parent == null) decFrameCount();
            }
        });
        dialog.addWindowListener(new WindowAdapter() {
            public void windowClosing(WindowEvent ev)
            {
                dialog.dispose();
                if (parent == null) decFrameCount();
            }
```

continued on next page

continued from previous page

```
        });
        dialog.pack();
        dialog.setVisible(true);
        if (parent == null) incFrameCount();
    }
    static void incFrameCount()
    {
        frameCount++;
    }
    static void decFrameCount()
    {
        if (—frameCount == 0) System.exit(0);
    }

    static public void main(String argv[])
    {
        if (argv.length == 0)
            new PerfAnal("stdin",
                new InputStreamReader(System.in));
        else
        {
            for (int i = 0; i < argv.length; i++)
            try {
                new PerfAnal(argv[i],
                    new FileReader(argv[i]));
            }
            catch (FileNotFoundException e)
            {
                displayError(e.toString(), null);
            }
        }
    }
}
```

`PerfTree` (see Listing B.10) implements the GUI portion of the individual analysis trees and defines the basic `PerfTree.PerfTreeNode` class that is specialized for each of the four analysis trees.

LISTING B.10 `PerfTree.java`

```
package com.macmillan.nmeyers;
import java.awt.event.*;
import javax.swing.*;
import javax.swing.tree.*;
import java.io.*;
import java.util.*;

class PerfTree extends JScrollPane
{
    JTree tree = null;
    JPopupMenu popupMenu = null;
```

```
    FindMethod findMethod;
    SelectThreads.ChooseThread chooseThread;
    PerfTreeNode root;
    MouseListener mouseListener = null;
    PerfTree(PerfTreeNode n, FindMethod fm, SelectThreads.ChooseThread ct)
    {
        setBorder(BorderFactory.createTitledBorder(n.toString()));
        root = n;
        findMethod = fm;
        chooseThread = ct;
        initializeRoot(n);
    }
    void initializeRoot(PerfTreeNode n)
    {
        if (tree != null)
        {
            tree.removeMouseListener(mouseListener);
        }
        tree = new JTree(root = n);
        tree.setLargeModel(true);
        tree.setRootVisible(false);

        if (popupMenu == null)
        {
            popupMenu = new JPopupMenu();
            popupMenu.add(
                new AbstractAction("Goto this Method") {
                    public void actionPerformed(ActionEvent e)
                    {
                        PerfTreeNode node =
                            (PerfTreeNode)tree.getSelectionPath().
                                getLastPathComponent();
                        findMethod.findMethod(node.getProcName());
                    }
                });
            popupMenu.add(
                new AbstractAction("Select a Method to Analyze") {
                    public void actionPerformed(ActionEvent e)
                    {
                        findMethod.findMethod(null);
                    }
                });
            popupMenu.add(
                new AbstractAction("Select Thread(s) to Analyze") {
                    public void actionPerformed(ActionEvent e)
                    {
                        chooseThread.chooseThread();
                    }
                });
        }
        popupMenu.setInvoker(tree);
```

continued on next page

continued from previous page

```

            if (mouseListener == null)
                mouseListener = new MouseAdapter() {
                    public void mousePressed(MouseEvent e)
                    {
                        if (e.isPopupTrigger())
                        {
                            int x = e.getX();
                            int y = e.getY();
                            int row = tree.getRowForLocation(x, y);
                            if (row != -1)
                            {
                                tree.setSelectionRow(row);
                                popupMenu.show(tree, x, y);
                            }
                        }
                    }
                    public void mouseReleased(MouseEvent e)
                    {
                        if (e.isPopupTrigger())
                        {
                            int x = e.getX();
                            int y = e.getY();
                            int row = tree.getRowForLocation(x, y);
                            if (row != -1)
                            {
                                tree.setSelectionRow(row);
                                popupMenu.show(tree, x, y);
                            }
                        }
                    }
                };
            tree.addMouseListener(mouseListener);

            setViewportView(tree);
        }
        void selectThisProc(String procName)
        {
            if (procName == null) return;
            TreePath path = root.findThisProc(procName);
            if (path != null)
            {
                tree.setSelectionPath(path);
                tree.scrollPathToVisible(path);
            }
        }
        void saveData(PrintWriter writer)
        {
            root.saveData(writer);
        }
        abstract static class PerfTreeNode extends DefaultMutableTreeNode
        {
```

```
        PerfTreeNode(Object o) { super(o); }
        abstract String getProcName();
        abstract TreePath findThisProc(String procName);
        void saveData(PrintWriter writer)
        {
            int level = getLevel();
            for (int i = 0; i < level; i++) writer.print("  ");
            if (level > 0) writer.print("" + level + ": ");
            writer.println(toString());
            if (children != null)
            {
                Iterator iterator = children.iterator();
                while (iterator.hasNext())
                    ((PerfTreeNode)iterator.next()).saveData(writer);
            }
        }
    }
    interface FindMethod
    {
        void findMethod(String method);
    }
}
```

`Procedure` (see Listing B.11) encapsulates per-procedure information parsed from the analysis file.

LISTING B.11 `Procedure.java`

```
package com.macmillan.nmeyers;
import java.util.*;

// This class holds profile information for individual methods.
// Because the traces do not include full signature information, we
// cannot distinguish among multiple versions of a method.
class Procedure implements Comparable
{
    public String procName;
    public int countInclusive = 0;
    public int countExclusive = 0;
// "lines" keeps track of profile info for individual lines of source.
    TreeSet lines = new TreeSet();
// "mytraces" keeps track of which stack traces reference us
    LinkedList myTraces = new LinkedList();
    Procedure(String str)
    {
        procName = str;
    }
// Allocate a new Procedure object and add to the map, or return
➥existing one
// from the map
    public static Procedure factory(String str, HashMap map)
```

continued on next page

continued from previous page

```
    {
        Procedure result = (Procedure)map.get(str);
        if (result != null) return result;
        result = new Procedure(str);
        map.put(str, result);
        return result;
    }
// Parse the trace information from the CPU sample counts, update
// the caller's procedures tree and our own tree of line number data
    public static int parse(String str,
                            HashMap procedures,
                            HashMap traceBacks)
    {
        StringTokenizer tokenizer = new StringTokenizer(str);
        // Parse the sample data. Ignore rank, self, and accum fields.
        tokenizer.nextToken();
        tokenizer.nextToken();
        tokenizer.nextToken();
        // Read the count and trace fields
        int count = Integer.parseInt(tokenizer.nextToken());
        Integer traceNum = new Integer(tokenizer.nextToken());
        TraceBack tb = (TraceBack)traceBacks.get(traceNum);
        // Update the count in the traceback
        tb.traceCount = count;
        if (tb.thread != null) tb.thread.count += count;
        // For each entry in the callback, update appropriate Procedure
        // and Line counts, and add this traceback to the Procedure
        // traceback chain.
        if (tb != null && !tb.entries.isEmpty())
        {
            int depth = 0;
            Iterator iterator = tb.entries.iterator();
            // Keep track of procedures and lines we've recorded from
            // this traceback, in an attempt to reduce confusion caused
            // by recursion.
            TreeSet procsRecorded = new TreeSet();
            TreeSet linesRecorded = new TreeSet();
            while (iterator.hasNext())
            {
                TraceBack.TraceBackEntry traceBackEntry =
                    (TraceBack.TraceBackEntry)iterator.next();
                // Find (or create) an entry for this procedure
                Procedure procedure =
                    Procedure.factory(traceBackEntry.procName,
➥procedures);
                // Find (or create) an entry for this line
                Line line =
                    Line.factory(traceBackEntry.procLineNum,
                                 procedure.lines,
                                 tb.thread);
                // Update inclusive counts, avoiding repeats from
➥recursion
```

```
                    // in an attempt to make inclusive counts somewhat
➥useful.
                    if (procsRecorded.add(procedure))
                        procedure.countInclusive += count;
                    if (linesRecorded.add(procedure))
                        line.countInclusive += count;
                    // Update exclusive counts if we're at top of stack
                    if (depth == 0)
                    {
                        procedure.countExclusive += count;
                        line.countExclusive += count;
                    }
                    // Add this stack trace to our collection
                    procedure.myTraces.add(new TraceInfo(tb, depth));
                    depth++;
                }
            }
            return count;
        }
        public int compareTo(Object o)
        {
            return procName.compareTo(((Procedure)o).procName);
        }
        public boolean equals(Object o)
        {
            return procName.equals(((Procedure)o).procName);
        }
        static class TraceInfo
        {
            public TraceBack traceBack;
            public int depth;
            TraceInfo(TraceBack tb, int d)
            {
                traceBack = tb;
                depth = d;
            }
            public String toString()
            {
                return "[traceBack=" + traceBack + ",depth=" + depth +
➥']';
            }
        }
    // This class holds profile information for a particular line number
    // of a procedure.
        static class Line implements Comparable
        {
            public String lineInfo;
            public int countInclusive = 0;
            public int countExclusive = 0;
            public ThreadInfo thread = null;
            private Line(String str, ThreadInfo thr)
            {
```

continued on next page

```
                lineInfo = str;
                thread = thr;
            }
    // Allocate a new Line object and add to the set, or return existing one
    // from the set
            public static Line factory(String str, TreeSet set, ThreadInfo thr)
            {
                Line result = new Line(str, thr);
                if (set.add(result)) return result;
                else return (Line)set.tailSet(result).first();
            }
            public int compareTo(Object o)
            {
                int result = lineInfo.compareTo(((Line)o).lineInfo);
                if (result == 0 && thread != null)
                    result = thread.compareTo(((Line)o).thread);
                return result;
            }
            public boolean equals(Object o)
            {
                return lineInfo.equals(((Line)o).lineInfo) &&
                       (thread == null ||
                        thread.equals(((Line)o).thread));
            }
            public String toString()
            {
                return "[lineInfo=" + lineInfo +
                       ",countInclusive=" + countInclusive +
                       ",countExclusive=" + countExclusive +
                       ",thread=" + thread + ']';
            }
        }
        public String toString()
        {
            return procName;
        }
    }
```

`SaveDialog.java` (see Listing B.12) is a simple file-saving dialog.

LISTING B.12 `SaveDialog.java`

```
package com.macmillan.nmeyers;
import javax.swing.*;
import java.awt.*;
import java.awt.event.*;
import java.io.*;

class SaveDialog extends JDialog
{
    JFrame parent;
```

```
    DoSave doSave;
    File file;
    SaveDialog(JFrame frame, DoSave ds)
    {
        super(frame, "Save Analysis Data to a File", true);
        parent = frame;
        doSave = ds;
        JFileChooser fileChooser = new JFileChooser() {
            public void approveSelection()
            {
                file = getSelectedFile();
                dispose();
                if (file.exists()) new ApproveSaveFile(parent);
                else doSave.doSave(file);
            }
            public void cancelSelection()
            {
                dispose();
            }
        };
        fileChooser.setDialogType(JFileChooser.SAVE_DIALOG);
        getContentPane().add(fileChooser);
        pack();
        setVisible(true);
    }
    interface DoSave
    {
        void doSave(File f);
    }
    class ApproveSaveFile extends JDialog
    {
        ApproveSaveFile(JFrame p)
        {
            super(p, "Overwrite File?", true);
            getContentPane().add(new JLabel("Overwrite file " + file +
➥"?"),
                                 BorderLayout.CENTER);
            Box box = Box.createHorizontalBox();
            getContentPane().add(box, BorderLayout.SOUTH);
            box.add(Box.createGlue());
            JButton button = new JButton("OK");
            button.addActionListener(new ActionListener() {
                public void actionPerformed(ActionEvent e)
                {
                    dispose();
                    doSave.doSave(file);
                }
            });
            box.add(button);
            box.add(Box.createGlue());
            button = new JButton("Cancel");
            button.addActionListener(new ActionListener() {
```

continued on next page

continued from previous page

```
                public void actionPerformed(ActionEvent e)
                {
                    dispose();
                }
            });
            box.add(button);
            getRootPane().setDefaultButton(button);
            box.add(Box.createGlue());
            pack();
            setDefaultCloseOperation(WindowConstants.DISPOSE_ON_CLOSE);
            setVisible(true);
        }
    }
}
```

`SelectMethod` (see Listing B.13) implements the dialog allowing the user to select a method for analysis by name. It displays all available classes in a list, allowing the user to select one for analysis in the four analysis windows.

LISTING B.13 `SelectMethod.java`

```
package com.macmillan.nmeyers;
import java.awt.*;
import java.awt.event.*;
import javax.swing.*;
import java.util.*;

class SelectMethod extends JDialog
{
    JList list;
    PerfTree.FindMethod findMethod;
    SelectMethod(JFrame owner, PerfTree.FindMethod fm,
                 HashMap procedures)
    {
        super(owner, "Select a Method to Analyze", true);
        // For performance reasons, we keep procedures in a hashmap
➥instead
        // of treemap, and sort when we need to
        Object[] procs = procedures.values().toArray();
        Arrays.sort(procs);
        list = new JList(procs);
        list.addMouseListener(new MouseAdapter() {
            public void mouseClicked(MouseEvent e) {
                if (e.getClickCount() == 2)
                {
                    setVisible(false);
                    Object result = list.getSelectedValue();
                    if (result != null)
                        findMethod.findMethod(result.toString());
                }
            }
```

```
        });
        findMethod = fm;
        getContentPane().add(new JScrollPane(list), BorderLayout.
➥CENTER);
        Box box = Box.createHorizontalBox();
        getContentPane().add(box, BorderLayout.SOUTH);
        box.add(Box.createGlue());
        JButton button = new JButton("OK");
        button.addActionListener(new ActionListener() {
            public void actionPerformed(ActionEvent e)
            {
                setVisible(false);
                Object result = list.getSelectedValue();
                if (result != null)
                    findMethod.findMethod(result.toString());
            }
        });
        box.add(button);
        getRootPane().setDefaultButton(button);
        box.add(Box.createGlue());
        button = new JButton("Cancel");
        button.addActionListener(new ActionListener() {
            public void actionPerformed(ActionEvent e)
            {
                setVisible(false);
            }
        });
        box.add(button);
        box.add(Box.createGlue());
        pack();
    }
}
```

`SelectThreads` (see Listing B.14) implements the thread selection dialog. It presents a list of threads, each with its own check box, that can be selected for analysis.

LISTING B.14 `SelectThreads.java`

```
package com.macmillan.nmeyers;
import javax.swing.*;
import java.util.*;
import java.awt.*;
import java.awt.event.*;

class SelectThreads extends JDialog
{
    Box box1;
    ChooseThread chooseThread;
    SelectThreads(JFrame owner, ChooseThread ct, HashMap threads)
    {
        super(owner, "Select Thread(s) to Analyze", true);
```

continued on next page

continued from previous page

```
        chooseThread = ct;
        ArrayList list = new ArrayList(threads.values());
        Collections.sort(list, new Comparator() {
            public int compare(Object o1, Object o2)
            {
                return ((ThreadInfo)o2).count - ((ThreadInfo)o1).count;
            }
            public boolean Equals(Object o)
            {
                return false;
            }
        });
        box1 = Box.createVerticalBox();
        getContentPane().add(new JScrollPane(box1), BorderLayout.
➥CENTER);
        for (Iterator i = list.iterator(); i.hasNext();)
        {
            ThreadCheckBox checkBox = new ThreadCheckBox((ThreadInfo)i.
➥next());
            box1.add(checkBox);
        }
        Box box2 = Box.createHorizontalBox();
        getContentPane().add(box2, BorderLayout.SOUTH);
        box2.add(Box.createGlue());
        JButton button = new JButton("OK");
        button.addActionListener(new ActionListener() {
            public void actionPerformed(ActionEvent e)
            {
                setVisible(false);
                Object[] boxes = box1.getComponents();
                for (int i = 0; i < boxes.length; i++)
                    ((ThreadCheckBox)boxes[i]).thread.enabled =
                        ((ThreadCheckBox)boxes[i]).isSelected();
                chooseThread.recomputeTotals();
            }
        });
        box2.add(button);
        getRootPane().setDefaultButton(button);
        box2.add(Box.createGlue());
        button = new JButton("Set All");
        button.addActionListener(new ActionListener() {
            public void actionPerformed(ActionEvent e)
            {
                Object[] boxes = box1.getComponents();
                for (int i = 0; i < boxes.length; i++)
                    ((ThreadCheckBox)boxes[i]).setSelected(true);
            }
        });
        box2.add(button);
```

```
        box2.add(Box.createGlue());
        button = new JButton("Clear All");
        button.addActionListener(new ActionListener() {
            public void actionPerformed(ActionEvent e)
            {
                Object[] boxes = box1.getComponents();
                for (int i = 0; i < boxes.length; i++)
                    ((ThreadCheckBox)boxes[i]).setSelected(false);
            }
        });
        box2.add(button);
        box2.add(Box.createGlue());
        button = new JButton("Cancel");
        button.addActionListener(new ActionListener() {
            public void actionPerformed(ActionEvent e)
            {
                setVisible(false);
            }
        });
        box2.add(button);
        box2.add(Box.createGlue());
        pack();
    }
    static class ThreadCheckBox extends JCheckBox
    {
        ThreadInfo thread;
        ThreadCheckBox(ThreadInfo thr)
        {
            super(thr.toString());
            thread = thr;
        }
    }
    public interface ChooseThread
    {
        public void chooseThread();
        public void recomputeTotals();
    }
    public void setVisible(boolean vis)
    {
        if (vis)
        {
            Object[] boxes = box1.getComponents();
            for (int i = 0; i < boxes.length; i++)
                ((ThreadCheckBox)boxes[i]).
                    setSelected(((ThreadCheckBox)boxes[i]).thread.
➥enabled);
        }
        super.setVisible(vis);
    }
}
```

`ThreadInfo.` (see Listing B.15) encapsulates the per-thread information parsed out of the analysis file.

LISTING B.15 ThreadInfo.java

```
package com.macmillan.nmeyers;
import java.util.*;

// This class holds info on threads.
class ThreadInfo implements Comparable
{
    public String threadName;
    public int threadNumber;
    public int count = 0;
    public boolean enabled = true;
    ThreadInfo(String str, int n)
    {
        threadName = str;
        threadNumber = n;
    }
    static ThreadInfo parse(String str)
    {
        int idx = str.indexOf("id = ");
        if (idx == -1) return null;
        int comma = str.indexOf(',', idx);
        if (comma == -1) return null;
        int threadNumber = Integer.parseInt(str.substring(idx + 5,
➥comma));
        int quote1 = str.indexOf("\"");
        if (quote1 == -1) return null;
        int quote2 = str.indexOf("\"", ++quote1);
        if (quote2 == -1) return null;
        String threadName = str.substring(quote1, quote2);
        return new ThreadInfo(threadName, threadNumber);
    }
    public int compareTo(Object o)
    {
        return threadNumber - ((ThreadInfo)o).threadNumber;
    }
    public boolean equals(Object o)
    {
        return threadNumber == ((ThreadInfo)o).threadNumber;
    }
    public String toString()
    {
        return "Thread #" + threadNumber + ": " + threadName +
                " (" + count + " ticks)";
    }
}
```

`TraceBack` (see Listing B.16) encapsulates the information for each traceback parsed out of the analysis file.

LISTING B.16 TraceBack.java

```
package com.macmillan.nmeyers;
import java.util.*;
```

```
import java.io.*;

// This class holds the data parsed from a stack trace in the
// profiler output. For each trace, we store the trace number
// (which is also the sort key), the trace count, and an array
// of entries corresponding to the traceback.
class TraceBack
{
    public int traceNumber;
    public int traceCount = 0;
    public LinkedList entries = new LinkedList();
    public ThreadInfo thread = null;
    TraceBack(int t, ThreadInfo th)
    {
        traceNumber = t;
        thread = th;
    }
// A TraceBack class factory that parses the traceback data from
// the input file.
    public static TraceBack parse(String currentLine,
                                  BufferedReader reader,
                                  HashMap threads)
        throws IOException
    {
        // Current line is of the form "TRACE <number>:"
        StringTokenizer tokenizer = new StringTokenizer(currentLine);
        int traceNumber = 0;
        ThreadInfo thread = null;
        try
        {
            // Extract the trace number...
            if (!tokenizer.nextToken().equals("TRACE")) return null;
            String numberToken = tokenizer.nextToken(" \t\n\r\f:");
            // ... and parse it
            traceNumber = Integer.parseInt(numberToken);
            try
            {
                if (tokenizer.nextToken("=").indexOf("thread") != -1);
                Integer threadNum = new Integer(tokenizer.nextToken(
➥"=)"));
                thread = (ThreadInfo)threads.get(threadNum);
            }
            catch (NoSuchElementException e) {}
            catch (NumberFormatException e) {}
        }
        catch (NoSuchElementException e) { return null; }
        catch (NumberFormatException e) { return null; }
        // So far so good. Allocate an instance.
        TraceBack result = new TraceBack(traceNumber, thread);
        // Start parsing lines. We'll do this by calling the
➥TraceBackEntry
```

continued on next page

continued from previous page

```
        // factory.
        TraceBackEntry traceBackEntry;
        while ((traceBackEntry = TraceBackEntry.parse(reader)) != null)
            result.entries.add(traceBackEntry);
        return result;
    }
    public boolean equals(Object o)
    {
        return traceNumber == ((TraceBack)o).traceNumber;
    }
// This class represents individual entries in the stack traceback
➥data.
// Encapsulates info on the procedure name and the line number.
    public static class TraceBackEntry
    {
        public String procName;
        public String procLineNum;
        private TraceBackEntry(String pN, String pLN)
        {
            procName = pN;
            procLineNum = pLN;
        }
// Parse a traceback entry from the input file.
        public static TraceBackEntry parse(BufferedReader reader)
            throws IOException
        {
            // The lines we care about begin with a tab
            reader.mark(1);
            if (reader.read() != '\t')
            {
                reader.reset();
                return null;
            }
            // Get the line and look for the start of the line number
➥info
            String procName = reader.readLine();
            int pos = procName.indexOf('(');
            if (pos == -1) return null;
            String procLineNum = procName.substring(pos);
            procName = procName.substring(0, pos);
            // We've got all of the info. Build a TraceBackEntry.
            return new TraceBackEntry(procName, procLineNum);
        }
        public String toString()
        {
            return "[" + procName + procLineNum + "]";
        }
    }
    public String toString()
    {
        return "[traceNumber=" + traceNumber +
               ",traceCount=" + traceCount +
```

```
                        ",entries=" + entries;
        }
    }
```

Profiler: Analyze CPU Time Spent in Native Code

Chapter 64, "Profiling User-Space Native Code," presented a tool to analyze time spent by a Java application in native code, including native methods, JVM, and JIT-compiled code.

Platform: JDK1.2

`Profiler` is a native shared library that interfaces with JDK1.2 through the JVM Profiling Interface. Listing B.17 contains the C++ source file.

LISTING B.17 `Profiler.C`

```
#include <jvmpi.h>
#include <iostream.h>
#include <strstream.h>
#include <fstream.h>
#include <pfstream.h>
#include <stdlib.h>
#include <unistd.h>
#include <string.h>
#include <sys/times.h>
#include <sys/utsname.h>
#include <vector>
#include <string>
#include <algorithm>

// Our main profiler class, which sets up, starts, and stops the
➥profiler.
// Everything in this class is static... the static functions are
➥usable
// with the C interfaces required by JVMPI.

class profiler
{
public:
    static JVMPI_Interface *jvmpi_interface;
    static unsigned long size, user_scale, scale, expand;
    static unsigned long low_address;
    static unsigned long high_address;
    static unsigned long address_range;
    static unsigned long array_size;
    static int expand_is_percent, global;
    static string filename;
```

continued on next page

continued from previous page

```
        static jint JVM_OnLoad(JavaVM *jvm, char *options);
        static void NotifyEvent(JVMPI_Event *event);
        static jint usage();
        static ostream *outfile;
        static struct tms initial_times;
    };

    // This class encapsulates data on hot spots
    class hotspot
    {
    public:
        string label;
        unsigned int count;
        hotspot() : label(""), count(0)     {}
        hotspot(string s, unsigned int c) :
            label(s), count(c)      {}
        hotspot& operator=(const hotspot &src)
        {
            label = src.label;
            count = src.count;
            return *this;
        }
        friend int operator==(const hotspot &lhs, const hotspot &rhs)
        {
            return lhs.label == rhs.label;
        }
        static int compare(const hotspot &lhs, const hotspot &rhs)
        {
            return lhs.count > rhs.count;
        }
        hotspot& operator+=(const hotspot &hs)
        {
            count += hs.count;
            return *this;
        }
    };

    // This class encapsulates a line of data from the /proc/<pid>/maps file
    // describing the address range covered by a mapped shared library
    class shared_library
    {
        shared_library() : lib_total_time(0),
                           lib_no_procedure_time(0),
                           nm_pipe(0),
                           current_addr(0),
                           next_addr(0),
                           current_proc(""),
                           next_proc("")    {}
    public:
        unsigned long range_start, range_end;
        unsigned long lib_total_time;
```

```
    unsigned long lib_no_procedure_time;
    string filename;
    static shared_library *factory(string &);
    istream *nm_pipe;
    string current_proc, next_proc;
    unsigned long current_addr, next_addr;
    static int compare(shared_library *a,
                       shared_library *b)
    {
        return a->range_start < b->range_start;
    }
    static int compare2(shared_library *a,
                        shared_library *b)
    {
        return a->lib_total_time > b->lib_total_time;
    }
    void charge_time(unsigned long, unsigned long, unsigned int, int);
    vector<hotspot> hotspots;
    void cleanup()
    {
        if (nm_pipe) delete nm_pipe;
        nm_pipe = 0;
    }
    ~shared_library()   { cleanup(); }
};

// This class encapsulates data read from the /proc/<pid>/maps file
class memory_map
{
public:
    vector<shared_library *> libraries;
    memory_map();
    ~memory_map();
};

// External entry point to match JVMPI's requirements - calls a static
// class function to handle initialization.
extern "C"
jint JNICALL JVM_OnLoad(JavaVM *jvm, char *options, void *)
{
    return profiler::JVM_OnLoad(jvm, options);
}

JVMPI_Interface *profiler::jvmpi_interface;
unsigned long profiler::size = 0;
unsigned long profiler::user_scale = 1024;
unsigned long profiler::scale;
unsigned long profiler::expand = 0;
unsigned long profiler::low_address;
unsigned long profiler::high_address;
unsigned long profiler::address_range;
unsigned long profiler::array_size;
```

continued on next page

continued from previous page

```
ostream *profiler::outfile;
struct tms profiler::initial_times;
int profiler::expand_is_percent = 0;
int profiler::global = 1;
string profiler::filename = "";
u_short *profile_buffer = 0;

// Handle initialization: load the JVMPI pointer, parse args, set up
// profiling.
jint profiler::JVM_OnLoad(JavaVM *jvm, char *options)
{
    // Get our JVM interface pointer
    if (jvm->GetEnv((void **)&jvmpi_interface, JVMPI_VERSION_1) < 0)
        return JNI_ERR;

    // Set up pointer to our NotifyEvent function
    jvmpi_interface->NotifyEvent = NotifyEvent;

    // Initialize output file
    outfile = &cerr;

    // Legal options:
    //   size=<#bytes>  Allocate #bytes for the profile array
    //   scale=<scale>  Map <scale> bytes per profile array entry
    //   expand=<#bytes>  Allow for <#bytes> growth of shared lib space
    //   expand=<percent>%  Allow for <percent> grown of shared lib space
    //   scope=local    Report local & global addresses
    //   scope=global   Report global addresses (default)
    //   help
    while (options && *options)
    {
        char *p2;
        if (!strncmp(options, "file=", 5))
        {
            options += 5;
            p2 = strchr(options, ',');
            int len = p2 ? p2 - options : strlen(options);
            if (!len) return usage();
            filename = options;
            filename.erase(len);
            options = p2 ? p2 : options + len;
        }
        else if (!strncmp(options, "size=", 5))
        {
            options += 5;
            size = strtol(options, &p2, 0);
            if (p2 == options) return usage();
            options = p2;
        }
        else if (!strncmp(options, "scale=", 6))
```

```
        {
            options += 6;
            user_scale = strtol(options, &p2, 0);
            if (user_scale < 1) user_scale = 1;
            if (p2 == options) return usage();
            options = p2;
        }
        else if (!strncmp(options, "expand=", 7))
        {
            options += 7;
            expand = strtol(options, &p2, 0);
            if (p2 == options) return usage();
            options = p2;
            if ((expand_is_percent = (*options == '%'))) options++;
        }
        else if (!strncmp(options, "scope=local", 11))
        {
            options += 11;
            global = 0;
        }
        else if (!strncmp(options, "scope=global", 12))
        {
            options += 12;
            global = 1;
        }
        else return usage();
        if (*options && *options++ != ',') return usage();
    }

    if (filename.length())
    {
        outfile = new ofstream(filename.c_str());
        if (outfile->fail())
        {
            cerr << "Cannot open " << filename << " for output\n";
            return JNI_ERR;
        }
    }

    // Indicate that we want only the init-done and shutdown events
    jvmpi_interface->EnableEvent(JVMPI_EVENT_JVM_INIT_DONE, 0);
    jvmpi_interface->EnableEvent(JVMPI_EVENT_JVM_SHUT_DOWN, 0);
}

jint profiler::usage()
{
    cerr << "Profiler usage: -XrunProfiler:[<option>=<value>,
➥...]\n\n"
         << "Option Name and Value    Description\n"
         << "---------------------    -----------\n"
         << "size=<#bytes>            Allocate #bytes for profile
➥array\n"
```

continued on next page

continued from previous page

```
                << "scale=<#bytes>          Alternative to #bytes; map
➥#bytes\n"
                << "                        per profile array entry\n"
                << "expand=<#bytes>         Allow for #byte expansion in
➥shared\n"
                << "                        libs\n"
                << "expand=<percent>%       Allow for <percent>% expansion
➥in\n"
                << "                        shared libs\n"
                << "scope=global            Report time against global
➥procedures\n"
                << "                        (default)\n"
                << "scope=local             Report time against local
➥labels\n"
                << "file=<filename>         Save output to specified
➥file\n\n";
        return JNI_ERR;
    }

    // Memory map constructor. Read the contents of the /proc/<pid>/maps
    // file and build a map of shared library regions.
    memory_map::memory_map()
    {
        // Figure out the name of the memory map file
        char namebuf[NAME_MAX + 1];
        ostrstream(namebuf, sizeof(namebuf)) << "/proc/" << getpid()
                                             << "/maps" << '\0';
        // Open the mapfile
        ifstream mapfile(namebuf);
        // Start reading...
        string line;
        while (!getline(mapfile, line).fail())
        {
            // See if we can build a shared_library entry from it
            shared_library *range =
                shared_library::factory(line);
            // Got one... add it to our vector
            if (range) libraries.push_back(range);
        }
        // Sort our vector, although it's probably already in order
        sort(libraries.begin(), libraries.end(), shared_library::compare);
    }

    // Memory map destructor: free our entries.
    memory_map::~memory_map()
    {
        vector<shared_library *>::iterator first = libraries.begin();
        vector<shared_library *>::iterator last = libraries.end();
        while (first != last) delete(*first++);
    }

    // NotifyEvent: Here is where we get the events that start and stop
```

```
// profiling
void profiler::NotifyEvent(JVMPI_Event *event)
{
    // Create a map of shared libraries. We do this twice, once at
    // startup to figure out how large an area to profile, and again
    // at shutdown to map the addresses profiled to the shared
    // libraries.
    memory_map map;
    if (event->event_type == JVMPI_EVENT_JVM_INIT_DONE)
    {
        // Sanity check
        if (map.libraries.empty())
        {
            cerr << "Profiler: Could not identify shared libs to profile\n";
            // Figure out our Linux release; complain if <2.2.
            struct utsname utsbuf;
            uname(&utsbuf);
            int major, minor;
            char ch;
            if ((istrstream(utsbuf.release) >> major
                                            >> ch
                                            >> minor).fail() ||
                major < 2 || major == 2 && minor < 2)
                cerr << "Profiler requires Linux version >= 2.2\n";
            jvmpi_interface->ProfilerExit(1);
        }
        // We're starting up. Figure out where shared libs start and end
        low_address = map.libraries.front()->range_start;
        high_address = map.libraries.back()->range_end;
        // Another sanity check
        if (high_address <= low_address)
        {
            cerr << "Profiler: Could not identify address range to profile\n";
            jvmpi_interface->ProfilerExit(1);
        }
        // Compute the size of the address range to profile
        address_range = high_address - low_address;
        // If a fudge factor was specified, apply it
        if (expand > 0)
        {
            address_range += expand_is_percent ?
                             address_range * expand / 100:
                             expand;
        }
        // Announce the address range of the shared libs we're profiling
        cerr << "Profiler: profiling over " << address_range
             << "-byte address range\n";
        // Compute the dimension of the array we need
```

continued on next page

continued from previous page

```
        array_size = (size > 0) ?
                         size / sizeof(u_short) :
                         address_range / (user_scale) + 1;
        // Announce it
        cerr << "Profiler: allocating " << array_size
             << " profiling elements\n";
        // Allocate the array
        profile_buffer = new u_short[array_size];
        if (!profile_buffer)
        {
            // Bomb if necessary
            cerr << "Profiler: failed to allocate profile buffer\n";
            jvmpi_interface->ProfilerExit(1);
        }
        cerr << '\n';
        // Clear the counters
        memset(profile_buffer, 0, array_size * sizeof(u_short));
        // Compute the scale value profil() needs
        scale = (unsigned long)
            ((unsigned long long)array_size * 131072 / address_range);
        if (scale < 1) scale = 1;
        // Record current user time
        times(&initial_times);
        // Turn on profiling
        profil(profile_buffer, array_size * sizeof(u_short),
                low_address, (u_int)scale);
    }
    else if (event->event_type == JVMPI_EVENT_JVM_SHUT_DOWN)
    {
        // Shutdown... we're done profiling
        profil(0, 0, 0, 0);
        struct tms curr_times;
        times(&curr_times);
        // Step through the profile addresses and the library addresses
        // in parallel, looking for libraries and functions to charge.
        // Depending on how much address space is covered by a profiling
        // element, a count might be chargeable to a single procedure,
        // to a single library, or to the entire application. Record
        // each case appropriately.
        vector<shared_library *>::iterator first = map.libraries.begin();
        vector<shared_library *>::iterator last = map.libraries.end();
        unsigned long app_total_time = 0;
        unsigned long app_no_library_time = 0;
        for (int i = 0; i < array_size; i++)
        {
            // Do we have a hit in the profile buffer?
            if (profile_buffer[i])
            {
                // Yes.
                app_total_time += profile_buffer[i];
```

```
                // See where it falls in the libraries.
                unsigned long addr1 =
                    (unsigned long)
                        ((unsigned long long)i * 131072 / scale) +
                        low_address;
                unsigned long addr2 =
                    (unsigned long)
                        ((unsigned long long)(i+1) * 131072 / scale) +
                        low_address;
                while (first != last && addr1 > (*first)->range_end)
                {
                    // Move on to the next library, performing cleanup
                    // for the current one
                    (*first++)->cleanup();
                }
                // If first != last, we've found the library where this
                // profile range starts. Does it also end in this library?
                if (first != last && addr2 <= (*first)->range_end)
                {
                    // Yes. Charge time to this library.
                    (*first)->charge_time(addr1, addr2,
                        (unsigned int)profile_buffer[i], global);
                }
                else app_no_library_time += profile_buffer[i];
            }
        }
        // Report results
        *outfile << "Total time: "
                 << (curr_times.tms_utime + curr_times.tms_stime -
                     initial_times.tms_utime - initial_times.tms_stime) *
                    1000 / CLK_TCK
                 << " ms ("
                 << (curr_times.tms_utime - initial_times.tms_utime) *
                    1000 / CLK_TCK
                 << " ms user, "
                 << (curr_times.tms_stime - initial_times.tms_stime) *
                    1000 / CLK_TCK
                 << " ms system)\n";
        *outfile << "Total time profiled: " << app_total_time * 10
                 << " ms\n";
        if (app_no_library_time)
            *outfile << "Non-library time profiled: "
                     << app_no_library_time * 10 << " ms\n";
        *outfile << "\nObserved total time > profiled time "
                 << "can be due to:\n"
                 << " + JIT-compiled code not running in the shared "
                 << "library address space\n"
                 << " + Unprofiled dynamically loaded shared libraries "
```

continued on next page

continued from previous page

```
                << "(use expand= option)\n"
                << "Observed total time < profiled time "
                << "can be due to:\n"
                << " + Native-threaded apps can confuse the times(2) "
                << "system call\n";
        if (app_no_library_time)
        {
            *outfile << "Non-library time profiled can be due to:\n"
                     << " + Dynamically loaded shared libraries (use "
                     << "expand= option)\n";
            if (user_scale > 1)
                *outfile << " + Profile data that cannot be resolved to "
                         << "a single library\n"
                         << "      (use smaller scale= option, "
                         << "current value = " << user_scale
                         << ")\n";
        }
        *outfile << "\nCPU Use by Library"
                 << "\n----------\n";
        first = map.libraries.begin();
        last = map.libraries.end();
        sort(first, last, shared_library::compare2);
        vector<hotspot> global_hotspot_list;
        int found_non_procedure_time = 0;
        while (first != last)
        {
            // Any hits for this library?
            if ((*first)->lib_total_time)
            {
                // Yes. Report them
                *outfile << (*first)->filename << "\n"
                         << "  Total time: "
                         << (*first)->lib_total_time * 10
                         << " ms\n";
                if ((*first)->lib_no_procedure_time)
                {
                    *outfile << "  Non-procedure time: "
                             << (*first)->lib_no_procedure_time * 10
                             << " ms\n";
                    found_non_procedure_time = 1;
                }
                // Any hotspots recorded for this library?
                if (!(*first)->hotspots.empty())
                {
                    // Add them to the global list
                    global_hotspot_list.insert(
                        global_hotspot_list.end(),
                        (*first)->hotspots.begin(),
                        (*first)->hotspots.end());
                }
            }
```

```
            // Move on to the next library
            first++;
        }
        if (found_non_procedure_time && user_scale > 1)
        {
            *outfile << "\nNon-procedure time can be due to:\n"
                     << " + Profile data that cannot be resolved
➥to a "
                     << "single procedure\n"
                     << "      (use smaller scale= option, "
                     << "current value = " << user_scale
                     << ")\n";
        }
        if (!global_hotspot_list.empty())
        {
            *outfile << "\nHot Spots\n—————-\n";
            if (found_non_procedure_time && user_scale > 1)
                *outfile << "Hot spot information is reported for "
                         << "profiling data that can\nbe resolved to "
                         << "individual library procedures. The most "
                         << "accurate\nresults will generated by
➥using "
                         << "small values for the scale=\noption "
                         << "(current value = " << user_scale
                         << ")\n\n";
            sort(global_hotspot_list.begin(),
                 global_hotspot_list.end(),
                 hotspot::compare);
            for (vector<hotspot>::iterator hsit =
                     global_hotspot_list.begin();
                 hsit != global_hotspot_list.end();
                 hsit++)
            {
                *outfile << hsit->label
                         << ": " << hsit->count * 10
                         << " ms\n";
            }
        }
    }
}

void shared_library::charge_time(unsigned long addr1,
                                 unsigned long addr2,
                                 unsigned int ticks,
                                 int global)
{
    // Charge the tick count to the total time
    lib_total_time += ticks;
    // Have we started reading nm data from the shared library?
    if (!nm_pipe)
    {
        // No. Give it a try. Put together a command string to gather
```

continued on next page

continued from previous page

```
        // the data and massage it appropriately
        string cmdline = "|nm —portability ";
        cmdline += filename;
        cmdline += " | grep ";
        if (!global) cmdline += "-i ";
        cmdline += "' T ' | sort +2 2>/dev/null";
        nm_pipe = new ipfstream(cmdline.c_str());
    }
    string line, tempbuf;
    // Read library addresses until we find nearest label <= IP
    while (!current_addr || addr1 >= next_addr)
    {
        current_proc = next_proc;
        current_addr = next_addr;
        // Can we read more?
        if (getline(*nm_pipe, line).fail())
        {
            // No. fix final address range.
            next_addr = range_end;
        }
        else
        {
            // Yes. Read next address
            istrstream(line.c_str()) >> hex >> next_proc >> tempbuf
                                     >> next_addr;
            next_proc = filename + ":" + next_proc;
            next_addr += range_start;
        }
    }
    // While the next label is at same address, skip ahead
    while (current_addr == next_addr &&
           !getline(*nm_pipe, line).fail())
    {
        istrstream(line.c_str()) >> hex >> next_proc >> tempbuf
                                 >> next_addr;
        next_proc = filename + ":" + next_proc;
        next_addr += range_start;
    }
    if (addr1 >= current_addr && addr2 <= next_addr)
    {
        // We have a hit on the current procedure. Find it in the
        // hotspot array or append it
        hotspot newspot(current_proc, ticks);
        if (!hotspots.empty() && hotspots.back() == newspot)
            hotspots.back() += newspot;
        else hotspots.push_back(newspot);
    }
    else
    {
        // The address range did not fit within the boundaries of one
        // procedure. Don't credit it to a particular procedure.
        lib_no_procedure_time += ticks;
```

```
578         }
579     }
580
581     // shared_library::factory - build an element from an input line
582     // read from /proc/<pid>/maps, if it is relevant. A relevant line
583     // will be in the address range used by shared libraries, have
584     // the executable bit set, and show a filename - the latter is
585     // a Linux 2.2 feature.
586     shared_library *shared_library::factory(string &line)
587     {
588         shared_library *result = 0;
589         long range_start, range_end;
590         string tempbuf, permissions, filename;
591         char dash;
592         // Extract the fields we care about
593         if (!(istrstream(line.c_str()) >> hex >> range_start >> dash
594                                        >> range_end >> permissions >> tempbuf
595                                        >> tempbuf >> tempbuf >> filename).fail()
596             && range_start >= 0x40000000
597             && range_end < 0x80000000
598             && permissions.substr(2, 1) == "x")
599         {
600             result = new shared_library;
601             result->range_start = range_start;
602             result->range_end = range_end;
603             result->filename = filename;
604         }
605         return result;
606     }
```

JVMPI-based profilers are called, when first loaded, at a fixed entry point (lines 118–122), to perform load-time configuration.

Initialization is handled in lines 142–225 and consists of parsing the options, setting up the output file, and registering the profiling events we care about (lines 223–224).

`Profiler` is next called after the JVM completes its initialization, executing lines 286–353 to start the process of profiling. First, a map is built of all currently loaded shared libraries (line 286—the `memory_map` class is described later). Based on the address space covered by the map, and on option values, `Profiler` creates the profiling array (line 334), computes the parameters required for the `profil(2)` call (lines 345–346), and starts the profiler (lines 351–352).

`Profiler` is next called at JVM shutdown to execute lines 286 and 356–511. After building a new map of shared libraries (line 286), `Profiler` steps through the profiling array (lines 370–402) looking for nonzero profiling counts and charges the time to various libraries and procedures within the libraries. It then collects and reports the global results (lines 404–441), the per-library results (lines 442–487), and the hot spots (lines 488–511).

The two workhorse classes in `Profiler` are `memory_map` and `shared_library`.

The memory_map class tracks the use of the address space. At class construction, it reads the contents of /proc/<pid>/maps and builds a vector of shared_library records.

The shared_library class (definition in lines 69–105) encapsulates the information on individual shared libraries. Its factory() method (lines 586–606) generates a new instance based on a line of data parsed from the /proc/<pid>/maps file. Its charge_time() method (lines 511–557) processes profiling data that needs to be charged to the library. It includes logic to read the library's symbol table and correlate profiling addresses with procedures in the library (lines 515–579). The charge_time() method also builds the table of hot spots (lines 568–571) for procedures within a particular library.

ShowFonts11: Display Available Fonts

ShowFonts11 was used in Chapter 14, "Configuring the Linux JSDK/JRE Environment," in the section "Adding, Changing, and Configuring Fonts in JDK1.1," to generate a GUI-based catalog of fonts installed in a JDK1.1 environment.

Platform: JDK1.1/JDK1.2

ShowFonts11 can be used to view specific fonts by name or all fonts. Note that the method used for querying available fonts may not find all fonts in a JDK1.1 environment, and is likely to miss most fonts in a JDK1.2 environment. The ShowFonts12 utility (discussed in the next section) uses a JDK1.2 query that provides much better information about available fonts.

Synopsis:

```
java com.macmillan.nmeyers.ShowFonts11 [<familynames> ...]
```

The optional font family names should specify only family name (serif, courier, and so on), not style or point size information. If no family names are specified, ShowFonts11 obtains a list of available font families from Toolkit.getFontList().

Listing B.18 contains the ShowFonts11 source. Each font name is placed in its own java.awt.Label, which is displayed in the corresponding font. Labels are laid out in a two-wide grid in the main window. ShowFonts11 has entry points defined that make it usable as both an application and an applet.

LISTING B.18 ShowFonts11.java

```
package com.macmillan.nmeyers;
import java.applet.*;
import java.awt.*;
import java.awt.event.*;

public class ShowFonts11 extends Applet
{
    public ShowFonts11()
    {
        initialize(null);
```

```
    }
    public ShowFonts11(String[] altfonts)
    {
        if (altfonts.length == 0) altfonts = null;
        initialize(altfonts);
    }
    public void initialize(String[] altfonts)
    {
        // Build a scrolled pane containing a collection of labels
        // showing all of the available fonts
        String[] fonts = altfonts;
        if (altfonts == null)
            fonts = Toolkit.getDefaultToolkit().getFontList();
        ScrollPane pane = new ScrollPane();
        setLayout(new GridLayout(1, 1));
        add(pane);
        // We'll put our labels in a panel with a gridlayout
        Panel panel = new Panel();
        panel.setLayout(new GridLayout(0, 2));
        pane.add(panel);
        // Start creating and adding labels with 16-point fonts
        for (int i = 0; i < fonts.length; i++)
        {
            String fontname = fonts[i] + "-plain-16";
            Label label = new Label(fontname);
            label.setFont(Font.decode(fontname));
            label.setForeground(Color.black);
            label.setBackground(Color.white);
            panel.add(label);
            fontname = fonts[i] + "-bold-16";
            label = new Label(fontname);
            label.setFont(Font.decode(fontname));
            label.setForeground(Color.black);
            label.setBackground(Color.white);
            panel.add(label);
            fontname = fonts[i] + "-italic-16";
            label = new Label(fontname);
            label.setFont(Font.decode(fontname));
            label.setForeground(Color.black);
            label.setBackground(Color.white);
            panel.add(label);
            fontname = fonts[i] + "-bolditalic-16";
            label = new Label(fontname);
            label.setFont(Font.decode(fontname));
            label.setForeground(Color.black);
            label.setBackground(Color.white);
            panel.add(label);
        }
    }
    public static void main(String[] argv)
    {
```

continued on next page

continued from previous page

```
            Frame frame = new Frame();
            ShowFonts11 api = new ShowFonts11(argv);
            frame.add(api);
            frame.pack();
            frame.setVisible(true);

            frame.addWindowListener(new WindowAdapter() {
                public void windowClosing(WindowEvent ev)
                {
                    System.exit(0);
                }
            });
        }
    }
```

ShowFonts12: Display Available JDK1.2 Fonts

`ShowFonts12` was used in Chapter 14, "Configuring the Linux JSDK/JRE Environment," in the section "Adding, Changing, and Configuring Fonts in JDK1.2" to generate a GUI-based catalog of fonts installed in a JDK1.2 environment.

Platform: JDK1.2

The `ShowFonts12` design is similar to `ShowFonts11` discussed in the previous section, but it uses several JDK1.2 additions:

- The `GraphicsEnvironment.getAvailableFontFamilyNames()` method is used to catalog the available fonts. This returns substantially more information than the JDK1.1 `Toolkit.getFontList()` method.
- Some `Graphics2D` rendering techniques—antialiasing and fractional font metrics—are used to show how they affect font appearance.
- The GUI is built on Swing.

Synopsis:

`java com.macmillan.nmeyers.ShowFonts11 [<familynames> ...]`

Listing B.19 contains the source. Except for its use of JDK1.2-isms, the design is similar to that for `ShowFonts11`. This application adds an inner class, `ShowFonts12.FontLabel`, that handles creating and customizing the labels.

LISTING B.19 `ShowFonts12.java`

```
package com.macmillan.nmeyers;
import javax.swing.*;
import java.awt.*;
import java.awt.event.*;
```

```

public class ShowFonts12 extends JApplet
{
    public ShowFonts12(String[] argv)
    {
        if (argv != null && argv.length == 0) argv = null;
        initialize(argv);
    }
    public ShowFonts12()
    {
        initialize(null);
    }
    private static class FontLabel extends JLabel
    {
        FontLabel(String fontname)
        {
            super(fontname);
            setFont(Font.decode(fontname));
            setForeground(Color.black);
        }
        public void paintComponent(Graphics g)
        {
            ((Graphics2D)g).addRenderingHints(new RenderingHints(
                RenderingHints.KEY_TEXT_ANTIALIASING,
                RenderingHints.VALUE_TEXT_ANTIALIAS_ON));
            ((Graphics2D)g).addRenderingHints(new RenderingHints(
                RenderingHints.KEY_FRACTIONALMETRICS,
                RenderingHints.VALUE_FRACTIONALMETRICS_ON));
            super.paintComponent(g);
        }
    }
    public void initialize(String[] families)
    {
        // Build a scrolled pane containing a collection of labels
        // showing all of the available fonts
        Box box = Box.createVerticalBox();
        // Build a panel with a 2-wide gridlayout to hold our styled labels
        JPanel panel = new JPanel(new GridLayout(0, 2));
        panel.setBackground(Color.white);
        box.add(panel);
        getContentPane().add(new JScrollPane(box));
        // Get our list of font families. Even if user has specified families
        // to display, this step seems necessary to make them available.
        String[] availableFamilies =
            GraphicsEnvironment.getLocalGraphicsEnvironment().
                getAvailableFontFamilyNames();
        if (families == null) families = availableFamilies;
        // Start creating and adding labels with 16-point fonts
        for (int i = 0; i < families.length; i++)
```

continued on next page

continued from previous page

```
        {
            panel.add(new FontLabel(families[i] + "-plain-16"));
            panel.add(new FontLabel(families[i] + "-bold-16"));
            panel.add(new FontLabel(families[i] + "-italic-16"));
            panel.add(new FontLabel(families[i] + "-bolditalic-16"));
        }
    }
    public static void main(String[] argv)
    {
        JFrame frame = new JFrame();
        ShowFonts12 api = new ShowFonts12(argv);
        frame.getContentPane().add(api);
        frame.pack();
        frame.setVisible(true);

        frame.addWindowListener(new WindowAdapter() {
            public void windowClosing(WindowEvent ev)
            {
                System.exit(0);
            }
        });
    }
}
```

`SlideShow`: A Graphical Image File Viewer

`SlideShow` is an illustration of the JDK1.2 image processing capabilities, and was used in Chapter 3, "A Look at the Java Core Classes," in the section "Package `java.awt.image`" to illustrate the use of the image processing classes.

Platform: JDK1.2

`SlideShow` is a viewer for one or more graphical image files, with navigation buttons and image controls.

Synopsis:

`java com.macmillan.nmeyers.SlideShow [<width> <height>]`

`SlideShow` reads a list of image filenames from `stdin` and displays them in a window of the specified size (default 100x100).

The main SlideShow GUI (see Figure B.2) contains an image viewing area, buttons to navigate through the collection of images, and buttons to control the appearance of the image.

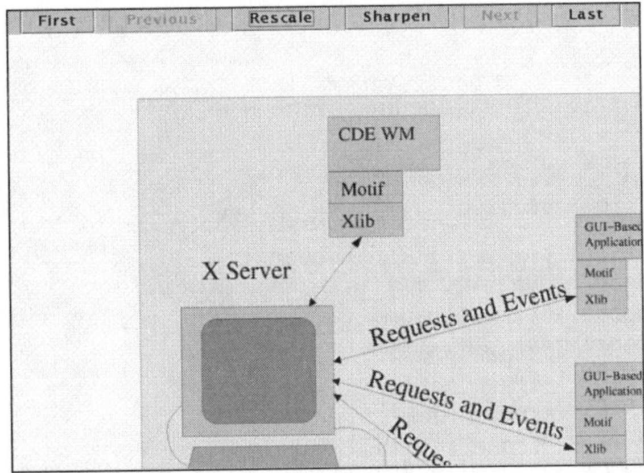

FIGURE B.2
The SlideShow GUI, with an image from an earlier chapter.

The Rescale button causes `SlideShow` to rescale its image up or down to fit in the viewing area (see Figure B.3).

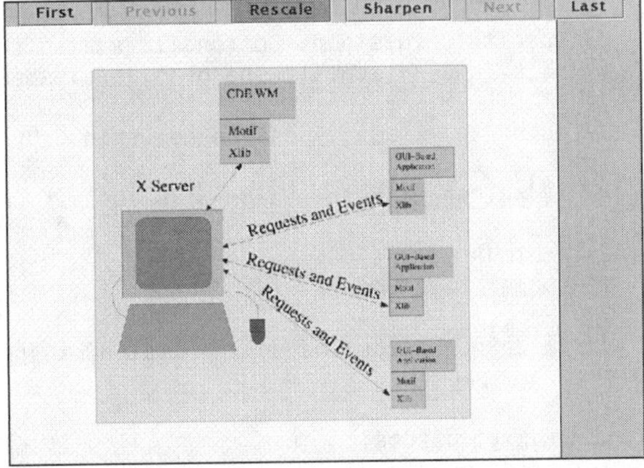

FIGURE B.3
The image has been rescaled to fit in the viewing area.

The Sharpen button applies a sharpening filter to the image (see Figure B.4).

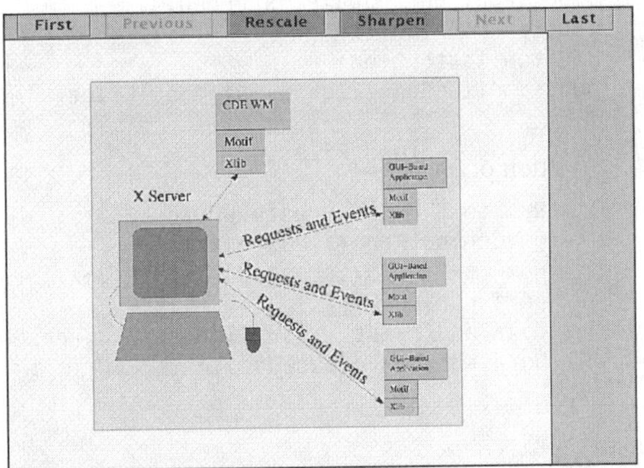

FIGURE B.4
The rescaled image has been algorithmically sharpened.

Both the rescaling and sharpening capabilities are standard features in the JDK1.2 AWT image pipeline.

Listing B.20 contains the `SlideShow` source.

LISTING B.20 SlideShow.java

```
package com.macmillan.nmeyers;
import java.awt.*;
import java.awt.geom.*;
import java.awt.image.*;
import java.util.*;
import java.io.*;
import javax.swing.*;
import java.awt.event.*;

public class SlideShow extends JFrame
{
    //
    // SlideShow: View a collection of graphical images (gif, jpeg, etc.)
    // specified in stdin. Optionally scales the images to the window
    // size, and optionally sharpens the images.
    //
    // Supported image types are determined by the Java environment itself;
    // if we can read the image with Toolkit.createImage, we can view it.
    //
    // Usage: SlideShow [ width height ]
    //
    // SlideShow reads the entire list of images from stdin before beginning.
    //
    LinkedList slides;
    int slideIndex = 0;
    Slide slide;
    JButton firstButton;
    JButton leftButton;
    JToggleButton rescale, sharpen;
    JButton rightButton;
    JButton lastButton;
    public SlideShow(LinkedList inputFiles, int width, int height)
    {
        slides = inputFiles;

        Box box1 = Box.createVerticalBox();
        getContentPane().add(box1);
        Box box2 = Box.createHorizontalBox();
        box1.add(box2);
        box1.add(slide = new Slide(width, height));
        box2.add(Box.createHorizontalGlue());
```

```
        firstButton = new JButton("First");
        firstButton.addActionListener(new ActionListener() {
            public void actionPerformed(ActionEvent e)
            {
                if (slideIndex > 0)
                {
                    slideIndex = 0;
                    slide.showSlide((String)slides.get(0));
                    leftButton.setEnabled(slideIndex > 0);
                    rightButton.setEnabled(slideIndex < slides.size()
➥- 1);
                }
            }
        });
        box2.add(firstButton);
        box2.add(Box.createHorizontalGlue());
        leftButton = new JButton("Previous");
        leftButton.addActionListener(new ActionListener() {
            public void actionPerformed(ActionEvent e)
            {
                if (slideIndex > 0)
                {
                    slide.showSlide((String)slides.get(--slideIndex));
                    leftButton.setEnabled(slideIndex > 0);
                    rightButton.setEnabled(slideIndex < slides.size()
➥- 1);
                }
            }
        });
        box2.add(leftButton);
        box2.add(Box.createHorizontalGlue());
        rescale = new JToggleButton("Rescale");
        rescale.addActionListener(new ActionListener() {
            public void actionPerformed(ActionEvent e)
            {
                slide.reshowSlide();
            }
        });
        box2.add(rescale);
        box2.add(Box.createHorizontalGlue());
        sharpen = new JToggleButton("Sharpen");
        sharpen.addActionListener(new ActionListener() {
            public void actionPerformed(ActionEvent e)
            {
                slide.reshowSlide();
            }
        });
        box2.add(sharpen);
        box2.add(Box.createHorizontalGlue());
        rightButton = new JButton("Next");
        rightButton.addActionListener(new ActionListener() {
            public void actionPerformed(ActionEvent e)
```

continued on next page

continued from previous page

```
                {
                    if (slideIndex < slides.size() - 1)
                    {
                        slide.showSlide((String)slides.get(++slideIndex));
                        leftButton.setEnabled(slideIndex > 0);
                        rightButton.setEnabled(slideIndex < slides.size()
➥- 1);
                    }
                }
            });
            box2.add(rightButton);
            box2.add(Box.createHorizontalGlue());
            lastButton = new JButton("Last");
            lastButton.addActionListener(new ActionListener() {
                public void actionPerformed(ActionEvent e)
                {
                    if (slideIndex < slides.size() - 1)
                    {
                        slideIndex = slides.size() - 1;
                        slide.showSlide((String)slides.get(slideIndex));
                        leftButton.setEnabled(slideIndex > 0);
                        rightButton.setEnabled(slideIndex < slides.size()
➥- 1);
                    }
                }
            });
            box2.add(lastButton);
            box2.add(Box.createHorizontalGlue());
            if (slides.size() > 0) slide.showSlide((String)slides.get(0));
            else
            {
                firstButton.setEnabled(false);
                lastButton.setEnabled(false);
            }
            leftButton.setEnabled(false);
            rightButton.setEnabled(slides.size() > 1);
        }
        public class Slide extends JComponent implements ImageObserver
        {
            int width, height;
            Image slide = null, transformedSlide;
            int imageWidth, imageHeight;
            boolean abort = false;
            public Slide(int w, int h)
            {
                width = w;
                height = h;
                addComponentListener(new ComponentAdapter() {
                    public void componentResized(ComponentEvent e)
                    {
                        Dimension d = getSize();
                        width = d.width;
```

```
            height = d.height;
            reshowSlide();
        }
    });
}
private Dimension getSlideDimension()
{
    abort = false;
    imageWidth = slide.getWidth(this);
    imageHeight = slide.getHeight(this);
    while (!abort && (imageWidth == -1 ¦¦ imageHeight == -1))
    {
        // Dimensions not available yet. Wait for other thread
➥to
        // finish loading the image
        synchronized(this)
        {
            try { wait(); }
            catch (InterruptedException e)      {}
            imageWidth = slide.getWidth(this);
            imageHeight = slide.getHeight(this);
        }
    }
    return new Dimension(imageWidth, imageHeight);
}
public boolean imageUpdate(Image img, int infoflags, int x,
➥int y,
                            int wid, int ht)
{
    // We hang out here waiting for the width and height to
    // become available
    if ((infoflags & (ImageObserver.ABORT ¦ ImageObserver.
➥ERROR)) != 0)
        abort= true;
    boolean result = super.imageUpdate(img, infoflags, x, y,
                                        wid, ht);
    synchronized(this) { notifyAll(); }
    return result;
}
public Dimension getPreferredSize()
{
    return new Dimension(width, height);
}
public void showSlide(String filename)
{
    setTitle(filename);
    // Read our original image
    slide = Toolkit.getDefaultToolkit().createImage(filename);
    reshowSlide();
}
public void reshowSlide()
{
```

continued on next page

continued from previous page

```
            if (slide == null) return;
            transformedSlide = slide;
            // If we want to rescale, set up the filter
            if (rescale.isSelected())
            {
                // Find our current image size
                Dimension dim = getSlideDimension();
                if (dim == null) return;
                double xscale = (double)width / (double)dim.width;
                double yscale = (double)height / (double)dim.height;
                double xyscale = Math.min(xscale, yscale);
                // Set hints for maximum quality
                RenderingHints hints =
                    new RenderingHints(
                        RenderingHints.KEY_ANTIALIASING,
                        RenderingHints.VALUE_ANTIALIAS_ON);
                hints.add(
                    new RenderingHints(
                        RenderingHints.KEY_COLOR_RENDERING,
                        RenderingHints.VALUE_COLOR_RENDER_QUALITY));
                ImageFilter rescaleFilter =
                    new BufferedImageFilter(
                        new AffineTransformOp(
                            AffineTransform.getScaleInstance(xyscale,
➥xyscale),
                            hints));
                transformedSlide = Toolkit.getDefaultToolkit().
➥createImage(
                            new FilteredImageSource(
                                transformedSlide.getSource(),
➥rescaleFilter));
            }
            // If we want to sharpen, set up the filter
            if (sharpen.isSelected())
            {
                float ctr = 2, offc = -.125f;
                ImageFilter sharpenFilter =
                    new BufferedImageFilter(
                        new ConvolveOp(
                            new Kernel(3, 3, new float[]
                                            { offc, offc, offc,
                                              offc, ctr , offc,
                                              offc, offc, offc })));
                transformedSlide = Toolkit.getDefaultToolkit().
➥createImage(
                            new FilteredImageSource(
                                transformedSlide.getSource(),
➥sharpenFilter));
            }
            repaint();
        }
        public void paintComponent(Graphics g)
```

```
        {
            g.drawImage(transformedSlide, 0, 0, this);
        }
    }
    static public void main(String[] argv)
    {
        int width = 100, height = 100;
        // Handle the args
        if (argv.length == 2)
        {
            try
            {
                width = Integer.parseInt(argv[0]);
                height = Integer.parseInt(argv[1]);
            }
            catch (NumberFormatException e)
            {
                usage();
            }
        }
        else if (argv.length != 0) usage();

        // Build our list of input files
        LinkedList inputFiles = new LinkedList();
        BufferedReader reader =
            new BufferedReader(
                new InputStreamReader(System.in));
        // Read words until we can't... could use StreamTokenizer here,
        // but its defaults are too strange for this.
        try
        {
            for (;;)
            {
                // Skip whitespace
                int ch;
                while ((ch = reader.read()) != -1 &&
                       Character.isWhitespace((char)ch));
                if (ch == -1) break;
                StringBuffer buffer = new StringBuffer();
                // Read a filename
                buffer.append((char)ch);
                while ((ch = reader.read()) != -1 &&
                       !Character.isWhitespace((char)ch))
                    buffer.append((char)ch);
                // Add to the list
                inputFiles.add(buffer.toString());
                if (ch == -1) break;
            }
        }
        catch (IOException e)   {}
```

continued on next page

continued from previous page

```
288             SlideShow slideShow = new SlideShow(inputFiles, width,
➥height);
289             slideShow.addWindowListener(new WindowAdapter() {
290                 public void windowClosing(WindowEvent ev)
291                 {
292                     System.exit(0);
293                 }
294             });
295             slideShow.pack();
296             slideShow.setVisible(true);
297         }
298         static public void usage()
299         {
300             System.err.println("Usage: SlideShow [<width> <height>]");
301             System.exit(1);
302         }
303     }
```

The `main()` procedure (lines 241–302) builds a list of files to display and instantiates the `SlideShow` object.

The `SlideShow` constructor (lines 32–126) builds the GUI, installs handlers for the buttons, and creates an instance of the nested `SlideShow.Slide` class.

The `SlideShow.Slide` class implements the core functionality. The standard model for image loading and rendering in the AWT uses an asynchronous mechanism: a `Toolkit.createImage()` call initiates loading, and a callback mechanism is used to return results.

The loading of the original image is triggered on line 186. If the image requires any rescaling, it is piped through another stage (lines 194–219). If sharpening is required, it is piped through yet another stage (lines 221–234). Any coordination between application logic and the asynchronous loading of the image is handled through the `ImageObserver` interface and its `imageUpdate()` callback B.20 `SlideShow.java`(lines 166–177).

`WaterFall`: Show Cascading Typeface Examples

`WaterFall` was used in Chapter 3, "A Look at the Java Core Classes," in the section "Package java.awt," to illustrate the effect of JDK1.2 font rendering capabilities on the appearance of rendered characters.

Platform: JDK1.2

In the typography business, a *waterfall* chart is a tool for examining a typeface in a range of sizes. This program draws two waterfall charts in separate GUI windows, with and without antialiasing and fractional font metrics enabled, to illustrate their effects on appearance of text.

Synopsis:

```
java com.macmillan.nmeyers.WaterFall <family> <style> <minsize> \
<maxsize> <increment>
```

`WaterFall` will display the charts in two separate windows. The JDK1.2 AWT has two different paths for obtaining fonts (discussed in Chapter 14 in the section "Adding, Changing, and Configuring Fonts in JDK1.2"). If the font is realized by the AWT's built-in font rasterizers, the two windows will have visibly different results. If, instead, the font is obtained from the X server, the AWT cannot use its advanced rendering techniques and the two windows will look identical.

Arguments:

- *`<family>`*—The family name of the font: either a standard Java logical name, or an actual font family name. You can use the `ShowFonts12` utility to obtain a list of available fonts.
- *`<style>`*—The font style, either `plain`, `bold`, `italic`, or `bold-italic`.
- *`<minsize>`*—The smallest font size, in points, to be displayed.
- *`<maxsize>`*—The largest font size, in points, to be displayed.
- *`<increment>`*—The size increment. The window will show a range of sizes from *`<minsize>`* to *`<maxsize>`*, incrementing by *`<increment>`* points between samples.

Example:

```
java com.macmillan.nmeyers.WaterFall sansserif plain 20 40 1
```

Listing B.21 contains the `WaterFall` source.

LISTING B.21 WaterFall.java

```
package com.macmillan.nmeyers;
import java.awt.*;
import java.awt.event.*;
import javax.swing.*;

class WaterFall extends JFrame
{
    String fontname, style;
    String testString = "ABCDEFGHIJKLMNOPQRSTUVWXYZ";
    int size1, size2, sizeInc;
    static int frameCount = 0;
    RenderingHints renderingHints;
    WaterFall(String fn, String st, int s1, int s2, int si,
            RenderingHints hints)
    {
        fontname = fn;
        style = st;
        size1 = s1;
```

continued on next page

continued from previous page

```
        size2 = s2;
        sizeInc = si;
        renderingHints = hints;
        getContentPane().add(new WaterFallComponent());
        pack();
        setVisible(true);
        incFrameCount();
        addWindowListener(new WindowAdapter() {
            public void windowClosing(WindowEvent ev)
            {
                dispose();
                decFrameCount();
            }
        });
    }
    static void incFrameCount()
    {
        frameCount++;
    }
    static void decFrameCount()
    {
        if (—frameCount == 0) System.exit(0);
    }
    private class WaterFallComponent extends JComponent
    {
        WaterFallComponent()
        {
            setBackground(Color.white);
            setForeground(Color.black);
        }
        public void paintComponent(Graphics g)
        {
            final Graphics2D g2 = (Graphics2D)g;
            int offset = 0;
            Rectangle bounds = g2.getClipBounds();
            g2.setColor(getBackground());
            g2.fillRect(bounds.x, bounds.y, bounds.width, bounds.
➥height);
            g2.setColor(getForeground());
            if (renderingHints != null) g2.addRenderingHints(
➥renderingHints);
            if (size1 > 0 && sizeInc > 0)
            {
                for (int i = size1; i <= size2; i += sizeInc)
                {
                    Font font = Font.decode(fontname + "-" + style +
➥"-" + i);
                    g2.setFont(font);
                    FontMetrics metrics = g2.getFontMetrics();
                    offset += metrics.getAscent();
                    g2.drawString(testString, 0, offset);
                    offset += metrics.getDescent();
```

```
                }
            }
        }
        public Dimension getPreferredSize()
        {
            Graphics g = getGraphics();
            FontMetrics m1 = g.getFontMetrics(
                Font.decode(fontname + "-" + style + "-" + size1));
            FontMetrics m2 = g.getFontMetrics(
                Font.decode(fontname + "-" + style + "-" + size2));
            int totalAscentPlusDescent =
                (m1.getAscent() + m1.getDescent() +
                 m2.getAscent() + m2.getDescent()) *
                 ((size2 - size1) / sizeInc + 1) / 2;
            int width = m2.stringWidth(testString);
            return new Dimension(width, totalAscentPlusDescent);
        }
    }
    public static void main(String[] argv)
    {
        String fontname = "";
        String style = "";
        int size1 = 0, size2 = 0, sizeInc = 0;
        if (argv.length != 5)
        {
            System.err.println("Usage: WaterFall <font> <style>
➥<min_size> " +
                               "<max_size> <increment>");
            System.exit(1);
        }
        try
        {
            fontname = argv[0];
            style = argv[1];
            size1 = Integer.parseInt(argv[2]);
            size2 = Integer.parseInt(argv[3]);
            sizeInc = Integer.parseInt(argv[4]);
        }
        catch (NumberFormatException e)
        {
            System.err.println("Usage: WaterFall <font> <min_size> " +
                               "<max_size> <increment>");
            System.exit(1);
        }

        GraphicsEnvironment.getLocalGraphicsEnvironment().
            getAvailableFontFamilyNames();
        new WaterFall(fontname, style, size1, size2, sizeInc, null);

        RenderingHints renderingHints = new RenderingHints(
            RenderingHints.KEY_TEXT_ANTIALIASING,
```

continued on next page

continued from previous page

```
118                 RenderingHints.VALUE_TEXT_ANTIALIAS_ON);
119             renderingHints.put(RenderingHints.KEY_FRACTIONALMETRICS,
120                                 RenderingHints.VALUE_FRACTIONALMETRICS_ON);
121
122             new WaterFall(fontname, style, size1, size2, sizeInc,
➥renderingHints);
123         }
124     }
```

The `main()` method parses command-line arguments (lines 99–103) and creates two instances of `WaterFall`, one with no rendering hints (line 114), and one with rendering hints requesting antialiasing and fractional font metrics (lines 116–122). The call to `GraphicsEnvironment.getAvailableFontFamilyNames()` ensures that the AWT can find all installed fonts.

The two interesting methods in `WaterFall` are `paintComponent()` (lines 49–70), which steps through the font sizes and draws the text, and `getPreferredSize()` (lines 71–84), which examines the font metrics to determine a window size that should just contain the text being drawn.

`XClipboard`: Access the X Primary Selection Buffer

`XClipboard` was presented in Chapter 56, "X Window System Tips and Tricks," in the section "XClipboard: A JNI-Based Cut-and-Paste Tool," as an example of accessing native X Window System capabilities not supported by Java.

Platforms: JDK1.1/JDK1.2

`XClipboard` consists of a Java front end and a JNI-based native back end that does most of the real work. Listing B.22 shows the front end, and Listing B.23 the back end.

LISTING B.22 `XClipboard.java`

```
package com.macmillan.nmeyers;

public class XClipboard
{
    // Static constructor: get our library
    static {
        System.loadLibrary("XClipboard");
    }
    public XClipboard()
    {
        SecurityManager security = System.getSecurityManager();
        if (security != null) security.checkSystemClipboardAccess();
        privateXData = openXConnection();
```

```
    }

    protected void finalize()
    {
        closeXConnection(privateXData);
    }

    // Public methods for buffer access

    public byte[] readCutBuffer0()
    {
        return readCutBuffer0(privateXData);
    }

    protected synchronized native Object
        readSelection(byte[] dp, byte[] selection, byte[] target);

    public String readPrimarySelectionString()
    {
        byte[] result = (byte[])readSelection(privateXData,
                new String("PRIMARY").getBytes(),
                new String("STRING").getBytes());
        return (result == null) ? null : new String(result);
    }

    public String readSecondarySelectionString()
    {
        byte[] result = (byte[])readSelection(privateXData,
                new String("SECONDARY").getBytes(),
                new String("STRING").getBytes());
        return (result == null) ? null : new String(result);
    }

    public String readClipboardSelectionString()
    {
        byte[] result = (byte[])readSelection(privateXData,
                new String("CLIPBOARD").getBytes(),
                new String("STRING").getBytes());
        return (result == null) ? null : new String(result);
    }

    public static void main(String[] argv)
    {
        XClipboard xc = new XClipboard();
        String selection = xc.readPrimarySelectionString();
        if (selection != null)
            System.out.println("Primary Selection (length = " +
                               selection.length() + "): " + selection);
        selection = xc.readSecondarySelectionString();
        if (selection != null)
            System.out.println("Secondary Selection (length = " +
                               selection.length() + "): " + selection);
```

continued on next page

continued from previous page

```
66             selection = xc.readClipboardSelectionString();
67             if (selection != null)
68                 System.out.println("Clipboard Selection (length = " +
69                                 selection.length() + "): " + selection);
70             selection = new String(xc.readCutBuffer0());
71             if (selection != null)
72                 System.out.println("CutBuffer0 (length = " +
73                                 selection.length() + "): " + selection);
74         }
75 
76         // Private native methods to do the grunt work
77         private synchronized native byte[] readCutBuffer0(byte[] dp);
78         private synchronized native byte[] openXConnection();
79         private synchronized native long closeXConnection(byte[] dp);
80         protected byte[] privateXData;
81     }
```

The constructor (lines 11–13) checks the Java security methods for permission to access the Clipboard and then calls the native `openXConnection()` method to create the needed X resources. The method returns a string of bytes, containing structures allocated and used by the native code, that will be stored in the object. These bytes are passed to the native code in subsequent native calls.

Lines 23–26 provide a method to read `CutBuffer0`, an ancient cut/paste method used only by ancient X clients.

Lines 28–29 describe the core native method, `readSelection()`, that powers this class. We'll see it in more detail in the native listing, shown in Listing B.23. Identical native technology is used to read the primary selection (lines 31–37), the secondary selection (lines 39–45), and the Clipboard (lines 47–53). Reading the Clipboard duplicates, in a modest way, capabilities found in `java.awt.datatransfer.Clipboard`. The other capabilities are unique to this class.

Lines 55–74 contain a `main()` method that tests this class by reading and dumping current clipboard and selection values. Normally, you would use this class by calling its various read methods; `main()` provides a trivial test you can run (just execute the class) without additional programming.

LISTING B.23 `XClipboard.c`

```
#include "com_macmillan_nmeyers_XClipboard.h"
#include "X11/Xlib.h"
#include <string.h>

/* Native component to XClipboard class */

/* We will store some platform-specific values - the Display* pointer
   and a Window ID - in a byte array. The following functions handle
   the conversions back and forth to native values. */
jbyteArray bytes_to_byte_array(JNIEnv *env, void *bytes, int nbytes)
```

```
{
    jbyteArray ptr_bytes = (*env)->NewByteArray(env, nbytes);
    jboolean is_copy;
    jbyte *ptr_bytes_elts =
        (*env)->GetByteArrayElements(env, ptr_bytes, &is_copy);
    memcpy(ptr_bytes_elts, bytes, nbytes);
    (*env)->ReleaseByteArrayElements(env, ptr_bytes, ptr_bytes_elts,
➥0);
    return ptr_bytes;
}

void byte_array_to_bytes(JNIEnv *env, jbyteArray ptr_bytes, void
➥*bytes,
                         int nbytes)
{
    jboolean is_copy;
    jbyte *ptr_bytes_elts =
        (*env)->GetByteArrayElements(env, ptr_bytes, &is_copy);
    memcpy(bytes, ptr_bytes_elts, nbytes);
    (*env)->ReleaseByteArrayElements(env, ptr_bytes, ptr_bytes_elts,
➥0);
}

typedef struct
{
    Display *display;
    Window window;
} platform_data;

/* Open the connection at object construction. A pity the JVM won't
   share its connection with us. */
jbyteArray JNICALL
➥Java_com_macmillan_nmeyers_XClipboard_openXConnection
    (JNIEnv *env, jobject obj)
{
    platform_data platform;
    platform.display = XOpenDisplay(0);
    platform.window = XCreateWindow(platform.display,
                                    DefaultRootWindow(platform.display),
                                    0, 0, 1, 1, 0, CopyFromParent,
                                    CopyFromParent, CopyFromParent,
                                    0, 0);
    return bytes_to_byte_array(env, &platform, sizeof(platform));
}

/* Close the connection at object finalization */
jlong JNICALL Java_com_macmillan_nmeyers_XClipboard_closeXConnection
    (JNIEnv *env, jobject obj,
                                                   jbyteArray pdata)
{
    platform_data platform;
    byte_array_to_bytes(env, pdata, &platform, sizeof(platform));
```

continued on next page

continued from previous page

```
    XCloseDisplay(platform.display);
}

/* Read cutbuffer0, in the unlikely event anyone cares about it */
jbyteArray JNICALL
➥Java_com_macmillan_nmeyers_XClipboard_readCutBuffer0
    (JNIEnv *env, jobject obj, jbyteArray pdata)
{
    int nbytes;
    platform_data platform;
    char *result;
    jbyteArray result_array;
    jboolean is_copy;
    jbyte *result_array_elts;

    byte_array_to_bytes(env, pdata, &platform, sizeof(platform));
    result = XFetchBytes(platform.display, &nbytes);
    result_array = (*env)->NewByteArray(env, (jsize)nbytes);
    result_array_elts =
        (*env)->GetByteArrayElements(env, result_array, &is_copy);
    memcpy(result_array_elts, result, nbytes);
    (*env)->ReleaseByteArrayElements(env, result_array,
➥result_array_elts, 0);
    return result_array;
}

jobject JNICALL Java_com_macmillan_nmeyers_XClipboard_readSelection
  (JNIEnv *env, jobject obj, jbyteArray pdata, jbyteArray jselection,
   jbyteArray jtarget)
{
    platform_data platform;
    Atom selection, target;
    jbyte *bptr;
    jboolean is_copy;
    XSelectionEvent *sel_event;
    XEvent event;
    Atom return_type;
    long offset, length;
    int return_format, return_result;
    unsigned long return_nitems;
    unsigned long return_bytes_remaining;
    unsigned char *return_data;
    jobject result_array;
    void *result_bytes;

    /* Recover our platform data */
    byte_array_to_bytes(env, pdata, &platform, sizeof(platform));
    /* Get atom for the selection */
    bptr = (*env)->GetByteArrayElements(env, jselection, &is_copy);
    selection = XInternAtom(platform.display, (char *)bptr, True);
    (*env)->ReleaseByteArrayElements(env, jselection, bptr, 0);
    if (selection == None) return 0;
```

```
    /* Get atom for the target */
    bptr = (*env)->GetByteArrayElements(env, jtarget, &is_copy);
    target = XInternAtom(platform.display, (char *)bptr, True);
    (*env)->ReleaseByteArrayElements(env, jtarget, bptr, 0);
    if (target == None) return 0;
    /* Convert the selection to the designated target type; we'll use
       the selection name as the target property name. */
    XConvertSelection(platform.display, selection, target, selection,
                      platform.window, CurrentTime);
    /* Wait for the selection to happen */
    for (;;)
    {
        XNextEvent(platform.display, &event);
        if (event.type == SelectionNotify &&
            (sel_event = (XSelectionEvent *)&event)->selection ==
➥selection)
            break;
    }
    if (sel_event->property == None) return 0;
    /* We have a hit! How big? */
    return_result =
        XGetWindowProperty(platform.display, platform.window,
                           sel_event->property, 0L, 0L, False,
                           AnyPropertyType, &return_type,
                           &return_format, &return_nitems,
                           &return_bytes_remaining, &return_data);
    if (return_result != Success) return 0;
    XFree(return_data);
    /* Allocate a result */
    switch (return_format)
    {
        case 8:
            result_array =
                (*env)->NewByteArray(env, (jsize)
➥return_bytes_remaining);
            result_bytes =
                (*env)->GetByteArrayElements(env, result_array,
➥&is_copy);
            break;
        case 16:
            result_array =
                (*env)->NewShortArray(env, (jsize)
➥return_bytes_remaining / 2);
            result_bytes =
                (*env)->GetShortArrayElements(env, result_array,
➥&is_copy);
            break;
        case 32:
            result_array =
                (*env)->NewIntArray(env, (jsize)
➥return_bytes_remaining / 4);
            result_bytes =
```

continued on next page

continued from previous page

```
155                 (*env)->GetIntArrayElements(env, result_array,
➥&is_copy);
156             break;
157         }
158         /* Grab the bits */
159         offset = 0;
160         length = 1024;
161         while (return_bytes_remaining)
162         {
163             return_result =
164                 XGetWindowProperty(platform.display, platform.window,
165                                    sel_event->property, offset, length,
➥True,
166                                    AnyPropertyType, &return_type,
167                                    &return_format, &return_nitems,
168                                    &return_bytes_remaining, &return_data);
169             if (return_result != Success) break;
170             memcpy((char *)result_bytes + offset * 4,
171                    return_data,
172                    return_nitems * return_format / 8);
173             offset += return_nitems * return_format / 32;
174             XFree(return_data);
175         }
176         /* Release the result */
177         switch (return_format)
178         {
179             case 8:
180                 (*env)->ReleaseByteArrayElements(env, result_array,
181                                                  (jbyte *)result_bytes, 0);
182                 break;
183             case 16:
184                 (*env)->ReleaseShortArrayElements(env, result_array,
185                                                  (jshort *)result_bytes, 0);
186                 break;
187             case 32:
188                 (*env)->ReleaseIntArrayElements(env, result_array,
189                                                  (jint *)result_bytes, 0);
190                 break;
191         }
192         return result_array;
193     }
```

The startup procedure, `openXConnection()` in lines 39–50, opens a connection to the X server and creates an unmapped window that will be needed to implement the various read functions. This creates some data—an X `Display` pointer and a `Window` ID—that must be kept for the life of the object. That data is packed into a byte array and stored on the Java side. Lines 10–35 contain utility code and structures to manage this data.

`closeXConnection()`, lines 53–60, is responsible for disposing of resources when the class is finalized.

`readCutBuffer0()`, lines 63–81, supports an obsolete cut/paste method used only by ancient X clients.

`readSelection()`, lines 83–193, is the core technology in this class. It requests the current selection value (lines 105–117) and then reads events from the X server (119–125) until it detects a result. If a selection is available, it computes the size of the result (lines 128–133) and allocates a result-type-dependent **`byte`**, **`short`**, or **`int`** Java array to hold the result (lines 137–157). It then reads data chunks into the new array (loop, lines 161–175), hands the arrays back to Java memory management (lines 177–191), and returns.

`xwinwrap`: Select Non-Default X Visuals and Colormaps

`xwinwrap` was presented in Chapter 56, "X Window System Tips and Tricks," in the section "xwinwrap: Controlling Colormap and Visual Usage," as a way to access non-default X Window System visuals and colormaps no available from Java.

Platforms: Linux

`xwinwrap` is a native shared library, loaded with the `LD_PRELOAD` mechanism of the Linux dynamic loader. There are no Java-related calls, and it is usable with any X client.

Listing B.24 shows the `xwinwrap` source file:

LISTING B.24 `xwinwrap.c`

```
#include <X11/X.h>
#include <X11/Xlib.h>
#include <X11/Xutil.h>
#include <dlfcn.h>
#include <stdio.h>
#include <stdlib.h>

#define deffunc(X) typeof(X) static *p_ ## X = 0;
#define findfunc(X) p_ ## X = dlsym(handle, #X);
#define callfunc(X) (*p_ ## X)

deffunc(XAllocColor)
deffunc(XCreateColormap)
deffunc(XCreateGC)
deffunc(XCreateWindow)
deffunc(XFree)
deffunc(XGetVisualInfo)
deffunc(XGetWindowAttributes)
deffunc(XOpenDisplay)

static void *handle = 0;
```

continued on next page

continued from previous page

```

/* Initialization: Load the X11R6 library and find the
➥XCreateWindow()
   entry point. */
void _init()
{
    handle = dlopen("libX11.so.6", RTLD_GLOBAL | RTLD_LAZY);
    if (handle)
    {
        /* Find the entry points we'll be needing */
        findfunc(XAllocColor)
        findfunc(XCreateColormap)
        findfunc(XCreateGC)
        findfunc(XCreateWindow)
        findfunc(XFree)
        findfunc(XGetVisualInfo)
        findfunc(XGetWindowAttributes)
        findfunc(XOpenDisplay)
    }
    else abort();
}

Display *XOpenDisplay(const char* displayName)
{
    int screenNo;
    VisualID user_visual_id = 0;
    char *env_value;
    /* Open the display */
    Display *display = callfunc(XOpenDisplay)(displayName);
    /* Get our environment data */
    if (env_value = getenv("XWINWRAP_VISUALID"))
        user_visual_id = strtoul(env_value, 0, 0);
    /* Step through the display's screens */
    for (screenNo = 0; screenNo < ScreenCount(display);
➥screenNo++)
    {
        Screen *screen = ScreenOfDisplay(display, screenNo);
        XVisualInfo *info, template;
        Visual *visual = 0;
        Window bogusWin;
        Colormap colormap;
        XColor color;
        XSetWindowAttributes attributes;
        unsigned long white_pixel, black_pixel;
        GC gc;
        int count = 0;
        int new_depth;
        /* Look for desired visual */
        if (!user_visual_id)
            user_visual_id = DefaultVisualOfScreen(screen)->
➥visualid;
        template.screen = screenNo;
```

```
        info = callfunc(XGetVisualInfo)(display,
                                        VisualScreenMask,
                                        &template,
                                        &count);
        if (info)
        {
            int visNo;
            for (visNo = 0; visNo < count; visNo++)
            {
                if (info[visNo].visualid == user_visual_id)
                {
                    visual = info[visNo].visual;
                    new_depth = info[visNo].depth;
                    break;
                }
            }
        }
        if (!visual)
        {
            fprintf(stderr,
                    "XWINWRAP: Requested visual ID 0x%lx is "
                    "not available on screen #%d\n",
                    (long)user_visual_id, screenNo);
            if (info)
            {
                static char *visual_classes[] = {
                    "StaticGray",
                    "GrayScale",
                    "StaticColor",
                    "PseudoColor",
                    "TrueColor",
                    "DirectColor",
                };
                int visNo;
                fprintf(stderr, "Available visuals:\n");
                for (visNo = 0; visNo < count; visNo++)
                    fprintf(stderr, "  0x%lx: depth %d %s\n",
                            info[visNo].visualid,
                            info[visNo].depth,
                            visual_classes[info[visNo].class]);
            }
            continue;
        }
        /* Create a colormap for the screen */
        colormap = callfunc(XCreateColormap)(display,
                                             RootWindowOfScreen(
➥screen),
                                             visual, AllocNone);
        /* Create a bogus window */
        attributes.colormap = colormap;
        bogusWin = callfunc(XCreateWindow)(display,
```

continued on next page

continued from previous page

```
                                                RootWindowOfScreen(screen),
                                                0, 0, 1, 1, 0, new_depth,
                                                InputOutput, visual, CWColormap,
                                                &attributes);
            /* Create a GC for the bogus window */
            gc = callfunc(XCreateGC)(display, bogusWin, 0, 0);
            /* Get the two basic pixels */
            color.red = color.green = color.blue = 0x0;
            callfunc(XAllocColor)(display, colormap, &color);
            black_pixel = color.pixel;
            color.red = color.green = color.blue = 0xffff;
            callfunc(XAllocColor)(display, colormap, &color);
            white_pixel = color.pixel;

            /* Here's where most of the magic happens. We've created
               a colormap, visual, and default GC that conform to the
               user's requests. Now we violate the opacity of the
               Screen structure and drop these in as defaults. Do
               not try this at home! */

            /* Replace the depth... */
            screen->root_depth = new_depth;
            /* Replace the root visual... */
            screen->root_visual = visual;
            /* Replace the default GC... */
            screen->default_gc = gc;
            /* Replace the default colormap... */
            screen->cmap = colormap;
            /* And replace the two standard pixels */
            screen->white_pixel = white_pixel;
            screen->black_pixel = black_pixel;
            /* We're done violating the screen structure. */
        }
        return display;
    }

    /* XCreateWindow: This is the hijacked version executed by the application.
       We look for creation of top-level windows, and apply the user preferences
       to the arguments we're passing through. */
    Window XCreateWindow(Display *display,
                         Window parent,
                         int x,
                         int y,
                         unsigned int width,
                         unsigned int height,
                         unsigned int border_width,
                         int depth,
                         unsigned int class,
```

```
169                          Visual *visual,
170                          unsigned long valuemask,
171                          XSetWindowAttributes* attributes)
172   {
173       Screen *screen;
174       XWindowAttributes win_attributes;
175       XSetWindowAttributes tempbuf;
176       callfunc(XGetWindowAttributes)(display, parent, &win_
➥attributes);
177       /* We now have a Screen* */
178       screen = win_attributes.screen;
179       /* Is parent the root window */
180       if (parent == RootWindowOfScreen(screen))
181       {
182           /* We need one other piece of magic. In case the
➥application has
183              its own ideas about depth, visual, and colormap, we
➥enforce
184              the user's preferences here. */
185           depth = DefaultDepthOfScreen(screen);
186           visual = DefaultVisualOfScreen(screen);
187           valuemask |= CWColormap;
188           if (!attributes) attributes = &tempbuf;
189           attributes->colormap = DefaultColormapOfScreen(screen);
190       }
191       return callfunc(XCreateWindow)(display, parent, x, y, width,
➥height,
192                          border_width, depth, class, visual,
193                          valuemask, attributes);
194   }
```

The `_init()` procedure, lines 25–41, is executed when the library is first loaded. It loads the X library and collects pointers to various Xlib entry points needed later.

`XOpenDisplay()`, lines 43–155, intercepts calls to the Xlib procedure of that same name. It opens the display (line 49) and then loops through all the screens (line 54), performing the following steps:

1. Look for the requested visual (lines 68–87) and complain (lines 88–113) if that visual is not found.
2. Create a private colormap with the requested visual (lines 115–117).
3. Create a new default Graphics Context (lines 120-126).
4. Allocate a black pixel and a white pixel in the new colormap (lines 128–133).
5. Replace various fields in the Screen structure with the new default values (lines 141–151).

`XCreateWindow()`, lines 160–194, intercepts calls to the Xlib procedure of that same name. It ascertains whether this is a top-level window (lines 176–180). If so, it substitutes various non-default parameter values (lines 185–189). It then calls the real Xlib `XcreateWindow()` function from line 191.

APPENDIX C

IMPORTANT INFORMATION RESOURCES

The Web is so crowded with Java and Linux resources that any list is destined to be woefully incomplete. This is my own "favorite hits" page—a list of resources I rely on for help during development work.

You can find an online version of this list at the book's home page, `http://www.javalinux.net`.

Linux Support

- The Linux Online Home Page (`http://www.linux.org`) is a popular first-line resource for Linux support. The site includes an excellent collection of How-To and Mini-How-To documents with advice on hundreds of Linux configuration and administration issues.
- Metalab, at the University of North Carolina, formerly known as SunSITE, is home to huge Linux software repositories. The home page is `http://metalab.unc.edu` and includes a search service for Linux software. Metalab's FTP repository, at `ftp://metalab.unc.edu/pub/Linux`, offers access to extensive collections of Linux software and distributions.
- RPMFind (`http://rpmfind.net/linux/RPM/`) offers a large index of RPMs published for Red Hat, SuSE, Caldera, and other RPM-enabled Linux platforms.
- FirstLinux (`http://www.firstlinux.com`) publishes the Linux Guide, a Linux-focused online dictionary and documentation repository.
- The Linux Software Encyclopedia (`http://stommel.tamu.edu/~baum/linuxlist/linuxlist/`) provides a huge list of descriptions and pointers to projects throughout the Linux world.
- Linux.com (`http://www.linux.com`), sponsored by VA Linux Systems, focuses on current events in the Linux community and hosts a repository of support articles.
- Linux Links (`http://www.linuxlinks.com`) is a well-organized repository of links to all matters Linux.
- The Linux Center (`http://www.portalux.com/`) provides extensive, well-organized collections of links to articles about Linux tools.

- FreshMeat (`http://www.freshmeat.net`) is a large application repository focused on open source software (OSS). The FreshMeat home page is probably the Web's most important announcement site for new OSS releases.
- Cygnus Solutions (`http://www.cygnus.com`) is the publisher of the GNU compiler suite and the site of some of the best available online documentation for `gcc` and related tools.
- And, of course, the distribution vendors discussed in Chapter 8, "Installing Additional Linux Software," all provide product support and knowledge bases on their own Web sites.

Java Support

- The Blackdown site (`http://www.blackdown.org`) is the home of the Blackdown JDK port for Linux. In addition to information about the port, the site contains extensive links to sites of interest for Java/Linux developers.
- Sun's main Java site (`http://java.sun.com`) is the source for all distributions from Sun, including many Java-only packages that are usable on Linux. The site also boasts a wealth of documentation and some excellent tutorials on all areas of Java development.
- Sun's Java Developer Connection (`http://developer.java.sun.com/`) focuses on Sun development tools and on the development of Java itself. Using the site requires you to become a member (no charge) and includes access to the Java Bug Parade, described in more detail in the next section.
- Netscape's DevEdge Online (`http://devedge.netscape.com/`) supports all aspects of Netscape Navigator technology. This includes Java, JavaScript, HTML, and other technologies important to the Web. Technologies of particular interest are the Open Java Interface (discussed in Chapter 11, "Choosing an Environment: 1.1 or 1.2?" in the section "Option 2: Netscape Open Java Interface"), the Plug-in SDK (if you need to develop Netscape plug-ins), and tools for signing objects (to create trusted applets).
- The Microsoft Developers Network (`http://msdn.microsoft.com`) is the launch point for information about Microsoft technologies. Technologies of particular interest include Java/ActiveX integration (discussed in Chapter 51, "Crossing Platform Component Models: Bringing Java to ActiveX") and tools for signing objects (to create trusted applets and ActiveX controls).
- IBM's AlphaWorks Site (`http://alphaworks.ibm.com`) hosts some of the most interesting Java development activity on the planet. IBM provides early access here to many of its leading-edge Java development efforts. Even if you cannot use any of IBM's technologies, this site provides insight into some truly exciting Java work.
- JavaLobby (`http://www.javalobby.org/`) devotes itself to representing the interests of Java software developers. The site provides current Java news unslanted by Sun or its competitors and many links to Java technologies and information.

Java Bug Parade

Behind its explosive growth, Java is still a young technology. One of the best inside views of the state of the art is the Java Bug Parade, which is part of Sun's Developer Connection site. After you have become a member (`http://developer.java.sun.com/`), you can access the Bug Parade at `http://developer.java.sun.com/developer/bugParade`. When you encounter a bug in the Blackdown Linux port, this is the first place to look for known problems.

The main Bug Parade page is a query form: specify a category and some keywords to search for bugs. The information on a particular bug report includes details about the bugs and an opportunity for user input. You can add information, read input from other users, and even *vote* on bugs. Sun uses the information to create prioritized lists of defects and enhancement requests.

Sun's record of responsiveness to the Bug Parade is mixed; some high-priority defects have been known to hang around for a long time. But it's also a remarkable phenomenon. Few commercial products dare put their defect reports on public display for public discussion. It's an example worth noting.

APPENDIX D

TOOLS NOT COVERED

Having devoted roughly 40 chapters to development tools, this book has managed to scratch the surface. Java development tools are a hot and volatile market, and any list is destined for quick obsolescence. A good source of current information is the Blackdown site (`http://www.blackdown.org`), whose pages include links to Java development tools usable on Linux.

This appendix lists some development tools *not* covered in the chapters—with due apologies for any omissions.

You can find an online version of this list at the book's home page, `http://www.javalinux.net`.

IDEs

Many Java IDEs are, like Inprise JBuilder, implemented in Java. Here are some of JBuilder's competition:

- NetComputing's AnyJ (`http://www.netcomputing.de/`) includes a free license for Linux users.
- NetBeans Developer was acquired by Sun Microsystems (`http://java.sun.com`) in late 1999. Sun has indicated that it plans to distribute versions for low-end (at no charge) and high-end (at enterprise-level prices) developers.
- Data Representations' Simplicity for Java (`http://www.datarepresentations.com/`) boasts a "Code Sourcerer" for rapid project setup.
- Omnicore's CodeGuide (`http://www.omnicore.com`) boasts incrementation compilation technology to assist in quick error detection.
- BulletProof's JDesignerPro (`http://www.bulletproof.com/`) is targeted at development of database-enabled Java applications.
- Elixir Technology's ElixirIDE (`http://www.elixirtech.com/`) includes a free Lite version.
- Penumbra Software's SuperMojo (`http://www.penumbrasoftware.com/`) boasts a separate enterprise solution pack for three-tier application architectures.

- SoftwareBuero's WipeOut (`http://www.softwarebuero.de/wipeout-eng.html`) supports Java, C++, Eiffel, and Fortran development by providing an IDE interface to existing tools.
- IST's VisaJ (`http://www.ist.co.uk/visaj`) is being promoted by SGI for the Linux platform.
- FreeBuilder (`http://www.freebuilder.org`) is an open source IDE being built with volunteer effort.
- SCubed's JIG (`http://www.scubed.cc/`) boasts ease of navigation through complex class hierarchies.
- Viosoft's Arriba! (`http://www.viosoft.com`) includes integration with Viosoft's own VioRunner debugger.

The list of available Java IDEs implemented natively on the Linux platform is small, but growing. Here are some current offerings:

- IBM VisualAge (`http://www.software.ibm.com/ad/vajava/`) ships in three versions at various price points (the lowest being free). The Linux version is in prerelease as of this writing.
- Cygnus Solutions Code Fusion (`http://www.cygnus.com`) mates an IDE with the native code compilation capabilities of `gcj` (discussed in Chapter 31, "`gcj`: A Compiled Java Solution").
- Code Crusader (`http://www.cco.caltech.edu/~jafl/jcc/`) is an open source, multi-language IDE. Distributions are also available from standard code repositories such as Metalab.

GUI Builders

- Tek-Tools JForge (`http://www.tek-tools.com/jforge/`) is focused on graphical construction of GUI JavaBeans.
- Scriptics' SpecTcl (`http://www.scriptics.com/products/spectcl`) is a Tcl-based GUI builder that grew out of Sun's brief relationship with Tcl inventor John Ousterhout.
- IST's XDesigner (`http://www.ist.co.uk/xd/`) is a native application that supports several target toolkits, including Java.
- Softera's SoftModeler (`http://www.softera.com/products.htm`) includes reverse-engineering tools to work from existing class files.
- Lava (`http://www.hnet.demon.co.uk/products/lava/index.html`) is a free, Java-based GUI builder.

Debuggers

- MetaMata's Debug (`http://www.metamata.com/products/debug_top.html`) includes remote debugging capabilities for multiplatform distributed debugging.
- Viosoft's VioRunner (`http://www.viosoft.com`) boasts multiplatform, distributed debugging.

UML Tools

All tools listed here are implemented in Java and should be usable on Linux.

- Tendril Software's StructureBuilder (`http://www.tendril.com`) offers full UML modeling and automatic code generation.
- Elixir Technology's ElixirCASE (`http://www.elixirtech.com/`) includes a free Lite version.
- Object Domain System's ObjectDomain (`http://www.objectdomain.com/domain`) is a UML-based modeler and code generator.
- Object International's TogetherJ (`http://www.togetherj.com/`) offers a free "whiteboard edition" and a full enterprise version.

Packagers

Here is some of the competition to InstallShield (see Chapter 52, "InstallShield: Creating Self-Installing Java Applications"):

- Zero-G's InstallAnywhere (`http://www.zerog.com/`) is a full-featured packager, whose offerings include a free, lightweight version.
- AlphaWorks' InstallToolkit for Java (`http://alphaworks.ibm.com/tech/install-toolkit`) is an IBM research project into Java packaging technologies.

Obfuscators/Optimizers

Here is some of the competition to DashO-Pro (see Chapter 53, "DashO: Optimizing Applications for Delivery").

- 4thPass's SourceGuard (`http://www.4thpass.com/`) offers versions from low-end to enterprise-level.
- AlphaWorks' JAX (`http://alphaworks.ibm.com/tech/JAX`) is an IBM research project into optimization and obfuscation of Java applications.
- Force5's JCloak (`http://www.force5.com/JCloak/ProductJCloak.html`) is focused on obfuscating applets.

- Eastridge Technology's JShrink (`http://www.e-t.com/jshrink.html`) offers obfuscation and size reduction.
- Condensity (`http://www.condensity.com/index.html`) offers multiplatform obfuscation and size reduction.
- RetroLogic's RetroGuard (`http://retrologic.com/`) is an open source obfuscator.
- Zelix's KlassMaster (`http://www.zelix.com/klassmaster/`) includes obfuscation and decompilation capabilities.

Decompilers

- WingSoft's WingDis (`http://www.wingsoft.com/wingdis.shtml`) is a non-GUI decompiler that can integrate with WingSoft's WingEditor for optional GUI capabilities.
- Ahpah's SourceAgain (`http://www.ahpah.com/`) includes GUI and non-GUI versions for various platforms, including Linux.
- SourceTec's Decompiler (`http://www.srctec.com/decompiler.htm`) is a shareware decompiler.
- ClassCracker (`http://www.pcug.org.au/~mayon/`) is a GUI-based decompiler product.

INDEX

Symbols

A

B

C

D

E

F

G

H

I

J

M

N

O

P

Q

R

S

T

U

V

W

X-Y

Z

WHAT'S ON THE DISCS

The companion CD-ROM contains all the source code from the book, GNU gcc/gpp, gnu make, and ddd.

Installation

1. Insert the CD-ROM in your CD-ROM drive.
2. Mount the CD-ROM onto your filesystem. Typically, this is done by typing:
   mount –tiso9660 /dev/cdrom /cdrom

Note

The mount point must exist before you mount the CD-ROM. If you have trouble mounting the CD-ROM, please consult the man page for the mount command or contact your system administrator.

3. Please view the file README.1ST in the root directory of the CD-ROM for detailed installation instructions.

Java Execution Environment on Linux

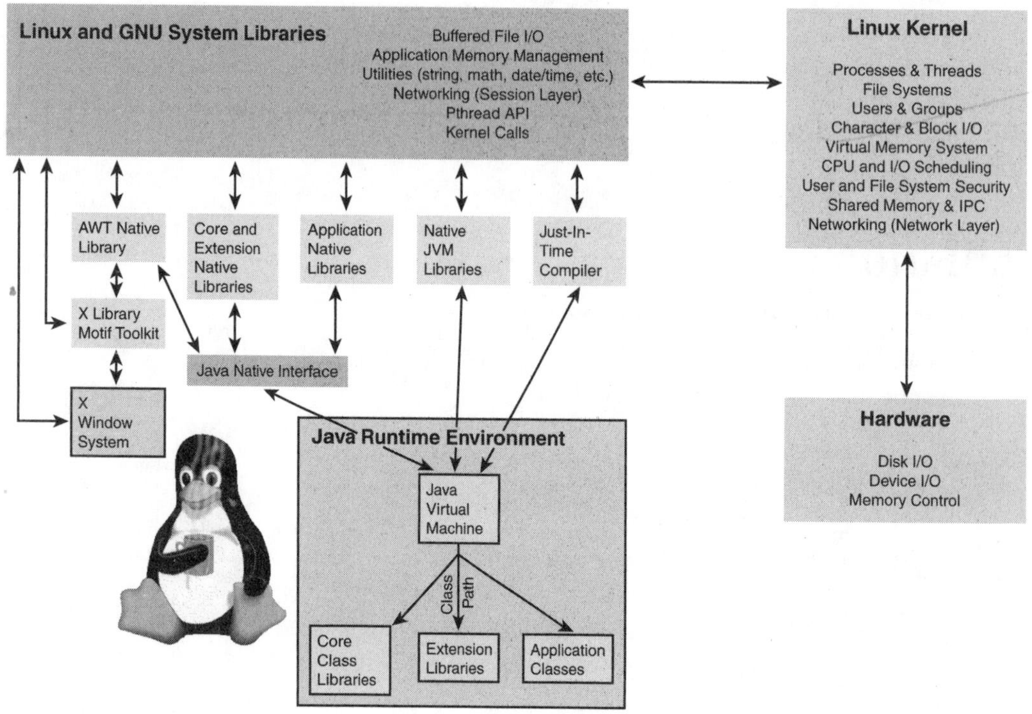

Tux the Penguin's image by Larry Ewing: modifications by Nathan Meyers. All work performed with The GIMP.